WORLD WAR II SNIPERS

"He lay in the deep grass, his head down-hill. His helmet had rolled down almost to the path. His face, chest and the grass around him were covered with blood and bluish clots which I presumed to be brains. He had probably been killed by a sniper for there was a bullet hole near the center of his forehead."[1]

Pvt. Harry M Caudill
Fifth (U.S.) Army, Italy

C CASEMATE | ILLUSTRATED | SPECIAL

WORLD WAR II SNIPERS

THE MEN, THEIR GUNS, THEIR STORIES

GARY YEE

Note about names and places

Transliteration of Cyrillic is always difficult and has been made more so over the years as different interpretations have appeared in print. Thus, the man whose name has appeared in many English language books as Vasily Zaitsev is shown as Vassili on his *Notes of a Russian Sniper*. We have left the original versions in any quotations but otherwise have modified accordingly.

German wartime transliteration included j where English speakers would have used y—thus *Jugoslawien* for Yugoslavian—and, anyway, many of the central European place names changed with the boundary alterations at the end of the war meaning that old cities changed name such as Königsberg to Kaliningrad or Bromberg reverted to its Polish name of Bydgoszcz. Wherever possible we have used or included the modern place names.

Military units

All units in the Allied sections are American unless noted otherwise. Infantry regiments are generally subdivided into battalions. The first number indicates the battalion and the second number indicates the regiment. Thus 1/15 would indicate 1st Battalion, 15th Regiment. Sometimes when the British Army amalgamated regiments, both regimental numbers were retained so as to maintain their heritage—such as the 16th/5th Lancers, amalgamating 16th, The Queen's Lancers, with the 5th Royal Irish Lancers. However, most British nomenclature links battalion number with the regimental name, so 2nd Ox and Bucks = 2nd Battalion, Oxfordshire and Buckinghamshire Light Infantry Regiment.

CISS0013

Published in the United States of America and Great Britain in 2022 by
CASEMATE PUBLISHERS
1950 Lawrence Road, Havertown, PA 19083, USA
and
The Old Music Hall, 106–108 Cowley Road, Oxford OX4 1JE, UK

Copyright © 2022 Gary Yee

Hardback Edition: ISBN 978-1-63624-098-5
Digital Edition: ISBN 978-1-63624-099-2

A CIP record for this book is available from the British Library

Design by Eleanor Forty-Robbins
Printed and bound in Malta by Melita Press Ltd

For a complete list of Casemate titles, please contact:
CASEMATE PUBLISHERS (US)
Telephone (610) 853-9131
Fax (610) 853-9146
Email: casemate@casematepublishers.com
www.casematepublishers.com

CASEMATE PUBLISHERS (UK)
Telephone (01865) 241249
Email: casemate-uk@casematepublishers.co.uk
www.casematepublishers.co.uk

To those who served, may peace be their companion.

Contents

| Preface

"A single shot punctuated the silence. A sniper. An officer passed the word; 'Tell Osborne to come up here.' He was asking for Pfc. Floyd Osborne, 18, an Indian youth from Fort Hall, Idaho, an expert scout. The officer waited, 'Where's Osborne?' he whispered hoarsely. The message came up to him passed from man to man. 'That was Osborne the sniper got. Right between the eyes.'"[2]

S/Sgt. Gerald A. Waindell

While in high school in the mid-1970s, my introduction to sniping came from William Craig's *Enemy at the Gates*. In his classic account of the Battle of Stalingrad, Craig devoted an entire chapter to the duel fought between Vassili Zaitsev and a German super-sniper. Zaitsev's memoir had been in circulation in the Soviet Union and Craig must have acquired it. It was not available in English until later and shortly afterward, a novelized version (David Robbins's *War of the Rats*) and a major motion picture based on Zaitsev's duel were produced. To my young mind, Craig's book was nothing more than an interesting read. Little did I suspect that, decades later, I would find myself voraciously reading any nonfiction book on sniping.

Later in the 1980s when I became a deputy sheriff, my buddy Doug Chin and I applied for the FBI sniping school and were accepted. Doug and I never attended since our department decided that the risk of an employee injury and temporary loss of personnel exceeded the cost of having trained snipers. Still, the interest remained and Peter Senich's works on sniping became a reading mainstay. Later, long out of print classics such as Herbert McBride's *A Rifleman Went to War* and Hesketh-Prichard's *Sniping in France* were reprinted. American interest in sniping remained a niche market until Charles Henderson's book on Carlos Hathcock, *Marine Sniper*, exploded on the scene and captured the public's imagination. Henderson's book had a significant impact in two ways. First, it made sniping acceptable to the general public and inspired servicemen to emulate Carlos Hathcock. Second, it threw into the limelight the men who had often operated in anonymity. The public appetite demanded more sniping literature and this fueled more snipers to pen their memoirs or for descendants to publish their father's stories.

Thus an explosion of books—such as the *Death From Afar* series from the Chandler brothers and memoirs by current snipers—became popular. Finally, fresh scholarly research from authors like

Martin Pegler expanded the knowledge of sniping. I absorbed it all solely for entertainment purposes. Perhaps the most influential book in my life's path was Capt. Clifford Shore's *With British Snipers to the Reich*. Shore not only covered sniping but also mentioned the Royal Americans.[3] This plunged me into researching blackpowder-era marksmanship that, after nine years, yielded my first book on the blackpowder sharpshooter.

Despite being drawn into the muzzle-loader era, my original interest in sniping remained, and I continued to collect sniping literature along with a few sniper rifles. With three books already to my credit, I was asked to prepare a work on sniping—closing the circle as I had started with sniping, transitioned for a decade into sharpshooting, and now return to sniping.

As source material, besides sniping books or memoirs, I've relied on accounts by ordinary infantrymen of all nationalities. Experience has taught me that people write about things they find interesting. What may not be found worthy for recording in a postwar unit history may sometimes be found in a soldier's memoirs. Unit histories can vary in quality: some are hardly better than a high school yearbook; others take a more journalistic approach and are invaluable for understanding the circumstances in which a particular soldier found himself.

The internet became a major research tool. In soldiers' postwar memoirs, it is not unknown for them to be unaware of their location. Sometimes they even forget the date. Contemporary newspaper articles withheld such critical information in the interest of national security, often making it difficult to put a soldier's account into context. Units and locations were passed off as "somewhere in the Pacific" or "somewhere in France." To identify the actual location, one first needs to identify the unit and then use the unit history and a rough date to approximate the location of the incident. How to identify the unit? The website findagrave.com was helpful. Additionally, the internet has interviews with veterans. While time-consuming to go through, these often provided insights that had not been put to paper and were otherwise unrecorded.

The internet does have its limitations. Film producers who make historical films rely on file footage with scant attention to accuracy—they are more concerned with telling the story. This arose when I tried to determine the colors of the parachutes used by the *Fallschirmjäger* on Crete. Were they white or camouflaged, or were both used? I don't place any reliance on historical films and tend to shy away from them—even contemporary documentaries are subject to a film editor's indiscretions.

When it was first proposed I write a book on snipers and sniping, I recognized a limitation. Numerous German and Russian accounts have been published, but the Western Allies are more sparsely covered, and Japanese accounts are nonexistent. The high mortality rate among the Japanese infantrymen means that there is no known memoir of a surviving sniper. For the British, the Ministry of Defence told snipers to keep mum lest they become victims of postwar retaliation. Most Americans shelved their bad memories and got on with their lives. If any bias appears, it reflects the lack of memoirs or journals that have been published.

The reader should be warned that this book was not written for historians, and is not designed to impart an understanding of the war, its campaigns, or battles. Rather, it is intended for sniping enthusiasts, for the rifleman, and the shooting community generally. It is narrowly focused on snipers and sniping, and any information on a battle or campaign is merely to convey to the reader the circumstances under which an incident occurred.

It is highly doubtful that this work will be definitive. Rather it is a starting point for others to build upon over the time as more archives are opened and diaries, letters, memoirs, or journals are shared by descendants of the soldiers who fought in the war.

Over a decade ago Rocky Chandler (deceased) read my first book, encouraged me to write about sniping, and passed the torch to me. His friend, retired British sniper Sgt. Harry Furness, was also impressed. I hope they aren't disappointed.

Gary Yee
Colorado

| Acknowledgments

The author gratefully acknowledges in no particular order the assistance of: Trinidad State College staff including Greg Boyce, Ryan Newport, Calvin Smith, and last but not least Raven Paiz, whose photoshopping skills made many older pictures available; Jacob and Sabina Chingizovna Dent for their research assistance in procuring, translating, and providing insights into the Russian culture; my former classmate at Trinidad Rob Schaefer and his wife Alexandra; Nina Endelman and the Gendelman family for sharing information and images of their father, 99th Infantry Division sniper Max Gendelman; 106th Infantry Division sniper Herb Sheaner; Soviet sniper Yulia Zhukova; S/Sgt. David Kong, his son Stephen, and nephew Gary; British sniper Sgt. Harry Furness; Dr. Al Nofi; Sacramento State University, Prof. Robert Humphrey for answering questions about the 99th Infantry Division; California Polytechnic State University Professor Phillip R. Rosenkrantz, whose suggestion led to a flood of information; Steve Norton for sharing his research, articles, images, and expertise on the Marine Corps sniper rifles; noted author and British firearms expert Ian Skennerton for his insights and images; British sniper researcher Nigel Greenway; Lt. Col. Tom McKinnley; K98k website forum members and Mauser K98k sniper rifle experts and collectors Dave Roberts, Mark Darnell, A. Lundberg, Brian Glenwright, Jarrith Kiel, Jim Tomkiewicz, J. Terrill Biedenham, and Georg Oberaigner, all of whom enthusiastically shared their insights and images; Bruce Canfield; Springfield Armory National Historic Monument Ranger Alexander McKenzie; former National Firearms Museum Curator Doug Wicklund; National Infantry Museum and Soldier Center Arms Curator Christopher Goodrow; Virginia Military Institute Museum Director Col. Keith E. Gibson; Julia Chervinksi, Natalia Smotrov, and the Bavatnik Archive Foundation; David Golus; www.paratrooper.be webmaster Has Wouter; British Para Data Manager Ben Hill; Mosin-Nagant expert and author Aleander Yuschenko; MilSurp webmaster Doug Peel; M. Sherrick McCray; Andreas Hartinger; Kai-Petri Hänninen; Jean Otto of Livermore, CA; Stephan Horak of Griffin & Howe; noted author and sniping authority Martin Pegler, who expressed confidence that I could address the topic; Albert De Guzman for translating Tagalog; and my readers June Norman and Elias Santiago. I'd also like to thank my agent, Ted Savas of Savas Beatie Publishing for his help, Casemates Publisher Ruth Sheppard and Felicity Goldsack, and packager Simon Forty for making a good book better. There are others known to me only by their internet monikers and declined recognition. For anyone overlooked, please accept my apologies for my oversight.

| Introduction

"Lepore grabbed a guy from the water who'd been hit in the chest. He could walk; we ushered him toward the big rock below the machine gun nest on the left.

"'What can we do for him?' screamed Lepore.

"Before I could come up with something, my medic and friend fell against me. His helmet spun to the ground, a foot away. A sniper's bullet had gone straight through, killing him instantly."[1]

S/Sgt. Ray Lambert
16th Infantry Regiment, 1st Infantry Division
Normandy, June 6, 1944

Staff Sergeant and medic Ray Lepore landed on Omaha Beach from the same landing craft as Lambert. Now Lepore's lifeless body lay beside him. Whether the fatal bullet had been fired by a German sniper hidden in a trench overlooking the beach or by an ordinary infantryman will never be known.

A similarly ambiguous sniping attempt took place the same day on Sword Beach with the British 1st Special Service Brigade led by Brig. Lord Lovat. His piper, Bill Millin, was leading the commandos with Lovat trailing a few paces behind. As they passed a row of poplars, Millin spotted a German in one. The German fired. Millin stopped his playing while Lovat dropped to a knee. Several commandos charged forward, firing their guns angrily in response. They were joined by Lovat whose rifle also chimed in. The German rapidly descended and sought cover in a cornfield. The commandos killed him there, dragged his body back and dumped it unceremoniously onto the road.[2] If he was indeed a sniper, he was a novice. While German snipers were trained to use trees, this one had chosen his nest too close to the road and was, therefore, visible to his intended victims.[3]

Whether a soldier was killed by a sniper, a regular infantryman, or even a wayward bullet is impossible to determine. In the confusion of a battlefield, to discern or attribute a shot to any particular individual is near impossible. Not every long-distance shot was fired by a sniper and stray bullets can be deadly, too—the adage that even a blind squirrel occasionally finds a nut comes to mind. "Thunderbird" (Co. I, 180th Infantry Regiment, 45th Division) Pvt. Stan Richardson qualified as "Expert" with the M1 rifle. In Germany, his training was put to the test.

"As I watched, I could see a German soldier running toward the town. He wasn't much of a target at 500 yards but I felt I had to at least shoot in his direction. I took aim, gave him a little 'Kentucky windage,' (estimating where he'd be by the time my bullet got there) and fired. I couldn't believe my eyes when I saw him fall."[4]

Pvt. Richardson was no sniper, just an ordinary rifleman who was skilled with his rifle.

The U.S. Army's prewar definition of sniper was: "An expert rifle shot detailed to pick off enemy leaders or individuals who expose themselves."[5] Let us refine the definition to be a skilled military marksman who shoots from a position of concealment and is skilled at camouflage and stalking. He may or may not be equipped with an optically equipped rifle. To exclude those who fought without optically equipped rifles would bar the Australians who served as snipers but, lacking optics, were issued with target-sight, heavy-barreled SMLEs. Even worse, it would mean omitting the famous Finnish sniper Simo Häyhä, who disliked scoped rifles as they required more exposure to use. The majority of snipers were trained but there were talented individuals in many armies who were experienced hunters and applied fieldcraft learned during the chase. The "one-shot Sam" who was lucky once doesn't count.

Snipers were few and far between in every army, and it is almost impossible to determine whether a solider or officer fell victim to a sniper's bullet. It certainly sounds more appealing to accredit the death of a noble and brave soldier at the moment of victory to a skulking enemy sniper as opposed to a lowly rifleman who just got lucky. Either way, the end results are the same. Someone died and a friend was lost. For survivors there was a lingering fear of an unseen enemy that ran concurrently with anger at the loss of a respected individual. Two excellent examples of this are shown by the deaths of two brave soldiers who were awarded the Victoria Cross posthumously: Sgt. Aubrey Cosens of the Queen's Own Rifles of Canada and Naik Yeshwant Ghadge of 3rd Battalion, 5th Mahratta Light Infantry.

In the Upper Tiber Valley, Italy, on July 10, 1944, Ghadge, his company commander dead, stormed a machine-gun nest. When he reached it he discovered he was out of ammunition and had no alternative but to club the remaining enemy gunners to death. After this, "A sniper brought him down with a mortal wound, and he died across the bodies of his enemies."[6] A similar story played out during the battle of the Rhineland when Cosens, his platoon commander dead, single-handedly cleared enemy strongpoints in three buildings, killing 20 men in the process. At the moment of victory "he was slain by an enemy sniper."[7] (In neither case is there any confirmation the shots were fired by snipers.)

Another problem hampering research is that many Americans or other soldiers attributed small-arms fire to snipers. Thus it came to pass that German soldiers hiding in trees, haystacks, ruins, or ditches and armed with machine guns or submachine guns were called snipers by Allied soldiers in Europe. Even the U.S. War Department's *Intelligence Bulletin* applied the term incorrectly.[8] The same may be said of Japanese soldiers whose marksmanship was only average. Even the Japanese themselves were guilty of referring to regular soldiers as snipers.[9] The only soldier this researcher has found to correctly distinguish between a sniper and the normal enemy infantry was 101st Airborne paratrooper Donald R. Burgett. Perhaps with the benefit of hindsight when he penned his postwar memoirs, Burgett wrote:

"It's strange how many GIs hit by rifle bullets later said they had been hit by a sniper. A sniper is a highly trained individual who is usually left behind when an outfit has to withdraw from an area. He is an expert on camouflage and concealment and is an excellent shot. He usually picks a spot from which he can watch and cover such things as water pumps, holes, gateways, narrow approaches and roadways, and hardly ever fires if there is more than one person. He is not there to commit suicide, but rather to kill a lone enemy whenever he can do it without getting spotted or caught. He usually has an escape route picked out ahead of time in case things get too hot. We had had several

men killed or wounded by plain ordinary enemy CLs. [sic] A sniper hardly ever just wounds a man. With a scope and a steady place to shoot from, he nearly always kills with the first shot."[10]

If the soldiers were careless, so were the journalists who accompanied them to the front. One short and partially correct sentence offering a definition was often reprinted in many newspapers of the era. "The word 'sniper' dates back to the Revolutionary War and means one who shoots from cover as when shooting snipe."[11] It is very possible that this was the definition as understood by the majority of the media. Perhaps the most glaring exaggeration or attribution is the death of American journalist Ernie Pyle to a Japanese sniper. While tragic—Ernie was a hero to all GIs who met him or followed his news column—it was a machine gunner who slew him, not a sniper as the papers claimed. Another incorrect media usage saw the German heavy cruiser *Deutschland* dubbed a "German Pocket Battleship Sniper."

The term sniper was creatively used by newspapers and generally carried a negative connotation. One furniture ad urged Americans not to be snipers by speaking "carelessly, unwisely and intolerantly" against Jews, Catholics, Protestants, and in so doing, do Hitler's work for him.[12] Another described "snipers" as desperate smokers who picked up discarded cigarette butts in an attempt to satiate their addiction to nicotine.[13] Used politically, "sniping" was an insult that inferred dirty dealings or tactics.[14] Australian cabbies in Sydney called private motorists who operated clandestinely as taxis "snipers," because they "sniped" fares that should go to legitimate drivers.[15] By contrast to these negative non-military uses of the term, the American 90th Infantry Division had a daily mimeographed newssheet called "The Sniper," but this was not read by the general public.[16]

In light of the loose application of "sniper" by all soldiers, we could question whether the famous American "sniper killer," T/Sgt. Frank Kwiatek, actually slew 19 enemy snipers as reported in a well-read *Yank* magazine article.[17] Sgt. Kwiatek's veracity is not in question, but whether or not the men he killed were snipers or ordinary *Landser* (the colloquial German word for infantrymen) fighting from concealment. The same may be said of New Zealand Sgt. Alfred Clive Hulme, VC, who

Naik (Cpl.) Yeshwant Ghadge, 10th Indian Division who was awarded a posthumous VC in Italy. *GF Collection.*

T/Sgt. Frank Kwiatek was captured on December 17, 1944, and listed MIA the next day. He was liberated from a PoW camp on April 13, 1945. He was awarded the Silver Star and Purple Heart with Oak Leaf Cluster. *Used by permission of Peter Kwiatek.*

was credited with killing 33 snipers on Crete. That he killed some snipers is not in question. He was armed with a scoped German rifle he had captured; but the German sniper effort at the time of Operation *Merkur* (Mercury) was not as widespread as it became after the invasion of the Soviet Union, and 33 kills suggests a very loose definition of sniper was applied. Similarly, Soviet Sniper Lyudmila Pavlichenko claimed to have fought against an entire German sniping platoon at a time when no such thing existed. Fighting from concealment or behind shelter was something virtually all armies instructed their infantry to do. This is not meant to demean any of these soldiers or their

Sniping became widespread during World War I. Seen here are Austrian snipers of the Hapsburg Empire. *Image courtesy the Blavatnik Archive Foundation (http://www.blavatnikarchive.org).*

Tiroler Kaiserjäger-Scharfschützen mit Fernrohrgewehren.

Mit Genehmigung der Illustrirten Zeitung, Leipzig.

Д 351

accomplishments and contribution to the final Allied victory. After all, the lessons of the Great War taught the follies of crossing over open ground and that cover is your friend.

Sharpshooting and snipers have a long history but they came of age internationally in World War I. The Germans started the conflict with a clear lead over the other countries, but by 1916 British sniping had caught up. By the end of the war the boot was on the other foot. Martin Pegler notes that between New Year and March 1918 British 38th Division's snipers were responsible for 387 confirmed kills. Other countries on both sides—the Turks for example at Gallipoli, the Australians and Canadians, and the Americans after they entered combat in 1917—proved fast learners and soon became adept at sniping in the trenches. The one country's army that didn't was Russia's—but they wouldn't make the same mistake in the run-up to World War II, and during the war their snipers racked up impressive "kill" statistics.

Invariably when sniping in World War II is discussed, the conversation turns to statistics and the bragging rights of which nation fielded the best or most effective sniper. Every nation had a different standard for confirming "kills" and most generally required eyewitnesses before credit was given to the sniper. How strictly this was enforced is subject to conjecture and whether there was a kill or not is difficult to ascertain. One cannot necessarily collect the identity disk, dogtag, or papers from a fallen foe without grave hazard to oneself. It's not worth the risk just to know. What may appear to be a kill may be only a wounding event. Take for example this observation by *Großdeutschland* mortarman *Gefreiter* Hans Heinz Rehfeldt:

> "A few metres away from me a small group of infantry was standing surveying the village with binoculars. A sniper bullet hit one of the party who threw up his arms and collapsed. They carried the casualty down into the gully, unbuttoned his greatcoat and field blouse and searched for the wound: there was no blood, he was only gasping for breath. Ah! The bullet had hit his Infantry Assault Badge and had been deflected. The wound to the skin was relatively minor."[18]

The Soviet sniper had scored a solid hit and any observer would have been convinced of a kill. Credit for a kill would be awarded but as Rehfeldt pointed out, the soldier was very much alive and had not entered Valhalla. Would the Soviet sniper or his observer be dishonest in their report of a kill? Absolutely not. However, it is a simple mistake which proves near impossible for the sniper or observer

Camouflaged M1903 Springfield sniper rifle with a Warner & Swazey telescopic sight, France, May 1918. Two models of W&S sights were used in WW1: the 1908 and 1913. Over 2,000 of the 1908 were procured, although not all were fitted to Springfields. Its many problems were reduced with the development of the Model 1913—but not by much. Over 5,700 of the latter were delivered, although only some 1,500 were used during the war. *U.S. National Archives (hereafter NARA).*

to think otherwise. Even the German soldiers who initially examined him thought he was wounded.

There are several examples arising in the Pacific Theater where the soldier or marine was hit in the eye but survived. A sniper made a successful headshot and his spotter (if any) would see the target go down and think it was another kill. In the case of Lt. Brunham L. Peters, he survived but lost his left eye.[19] Another was Pfc. Lloyd David Gunnels who, while serving on outpost duty, was credited with shooting 17 Japanese before being shot in the right eye (newspapers later bloated that number to 75 and as high as 100). Gunnels did go down but survived and was discharged after he recovered—although he lost an eye. He passed away on December 24, 1964.[20]

A similar situation arises in the midst of combat with onrushing waves of the foe being held back by a thin line of infantrymen. As some snipers candidly asserted, who knows whose bullet accounted for a victim? Was it the sniper's, a machine gunner's, another infantryman, or shrapnel from artillery or a grenade? In the heat of battle it is often impossible to discern. Yet it is suspected that some snipers may have padded their score and if not them, in the case of a propagandist, the propaganda officer, writer, or newspaper man. Soviet Sniper Roza Shanina discusses scoring:

"Let me explain. When we have to defend, I sometimes shoot at a lot of targets, but it's hard to tell if it's a kill or not. Logically back at school I always hit training targets accurately, and I hit a standing Fritz more often than I miss. And in most cases, I

Not all head shots are fatal. Lieutenant Tom Heaton's life was spared when a bullet failed to penetrate his helmet. He is seen here holding the flattened bullet he kept as a souvenir from Bougainville. *Author's collection.*

shoot at stationary targets or slowly moving soldiers, for those who run are hard to hit, you'd only scare them. Sometimes I don't have them scored at all, sometimes the score is very rough, sometimes it's undue, but I have no falsely killed Fritzes to my account. If one time I have a kill scored for no reason, the other time a real kill is not scored, and sometimes the score is just made blindly."[21]

Vassili Zaitsev would not count a kill unless he was 100% certain that his target was dead. He complained about observers who credited kills by counting the number of shots fired. Zaitsev also noted that the observer's viewpoint of the battlefield would be different from that of the sniper's but that did not deter them from crediting a kill. Even worse were observers who accepted the sniper's word without witnessing or verifying it. Instead of marking it

down as a probable or denying a claim, they added to the tally.[22]

Hunters know the only way to be sure of a kill is to see the corpse—often not possible in wartime. They allied fieldcraft with shooting ability: if you are after a pelt, you don't want to spoil it with a misplaced shot. One Australian kangaroo hunter turned sniper killed 47 Japanese on Timor but only claimed 25, saying: "you can't count a 'roo unless you saw him drop and know exactly where to skin him."[23]

Another issue is a soldier who is wounded by the sniper. The victim falls from sight, but is taken by his comrades to the hospital. He may die in an hour, a few days, or in the case of one Australian, months later in an army hospital.[24] The sniper's bullet may have been the proximate cause of the victim's death, but not the immediate cause.

There's another caveat when it comes to kill scores and scoring: propaganda. Within the Soviet Union snipers were feted as heroes. Writers like Vasily Grossman and others glorified the success of their snipers and both postcards and postage stamps were issued honoring them. Germany mimicked the Soviets, adopting special sniper badges to recognize their success (but as Allerberger noted, smart snipers never wore anything to distinguish themselves from the common *Landser*). In contrast, the United Kingdom kept mum about theirs and there was a feeling that they were "unsporting." Australia was proud of her snipers and not only released images of them, but also published their names in the papers. The United States praised its own snipers with some good morale-boosting publicity, but most news articles condemned enemy snipers who were always dastardly men who shot heroic American soldiers or marines. There was also some public exposure to sniping during the War Bond drives. The army organized *Here's Your Infantry* traveling exhibits to promote the war effort. Included in the display were the weapons of the infantryman including the M1 Garand, cartridges (presumably dummies), cleaning equipment, rifle grenades, the M1 Carbine, .45 caliber submachine guns, the BAR, light and heavy machine guns, bazookas and their rockets, as well as 60mm and 81mm mortars and their communication equipment were also displayed. Finally, a sniper observation post with snipers in camouflaged uniform were present to test the public's power of observation and to engage the visitors in conversation. Under supervision, the public was allowed to handle (unloaded) small arms.[25]

It wasn't just the figures of the totalitarian regimes that were inaccurate: the Western Allies were often also wrong when it came to statistics—one look at the newspaper tallies of aircraft losses in the Battle of Britain shows that. The reasons were often for

propaganda purposes, but this massaging of the figures by western propagandists can't compare with those of the propaganda machines of Joseph Goebbels or of Stalin's Soviet regime. Indeed, there is math and then there is Soviet math. Zara Witkins, an American engineer working in the Soviet Union, once calculated the marchers in the May 1, 1932, May Day parade in Moscow to be at 300,000. A communist official corrected him and stated it was a million. Initially taken aback, Witkin recovered and explained his math and asserted that math is independent of social order. The communist official denounced this as counter-revolutionary mathematics and explained:

> "Truth. You do not understand truth as we do. With you, it is only a bourgeois concept. With us, it has a different meaning. 300,000 means nothing. When we go before the world and we say a million workers marched in Red Square today, that means something. People understand the meaning of a million. That is the truth from our point of view."[26]

Soviet math was applied to production figures, harvest figures, and in victorious military claims.

Thus the assertion that a platoon outside of Moscow killed 1,900 Germans in one month, or another sniper platoon led by Lt. Motrichenko killed 2,100 Germans in one month alone and that 10 Siberian ace snipers killed 1,062 Germans in May 1943 cannot be taken seriously. The most outrageous assertion is that a 30-strong sniper platoon had pledged itself that each man kill 300 Germans by the anniversary of Russian Revolution on November 7 and that it met its pledge with a tally of 9,000 Germans![27] More modest but still implausible is the claim that a Soviet Baltic Fleet sniper unit killed 2,388 Germans of which 225 were killed in three days.[28] Propaganda was refined to a high art but loses plausibility when assertions become too grandiose. For example the claim that "there are about 250 snipers to each battalion, although the battalions led by Gusez and Tyashev consist entirely of snipers."[29] No training program could produce that number of competent snipers and no pool of talent is that great lest it deprive other units of snipers. Last, there is the claim that "the best shot in the war" by an unidentified sniper killed German *Generalfeldmarschall* Paul von Kleist in 1942 near the Terek River in the Caucasus. Besides not being killed (von Kleist died in Soviet captivity in 1954), von Kleist was not promoted to field marshal until 1943.[30]

World War II sniper rifles

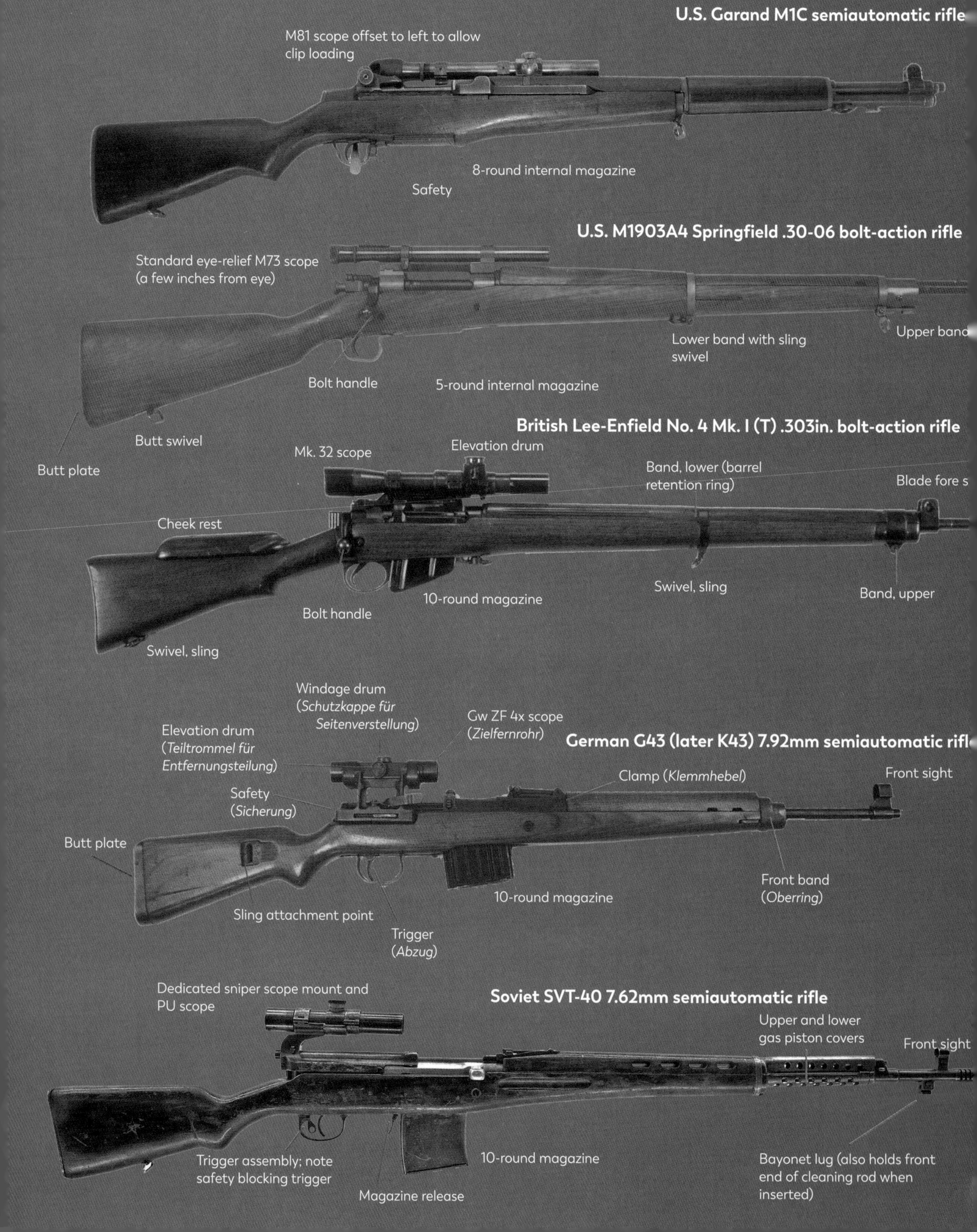

U.S. Garand M1C semiautomatic rifle

M81 scope offset to left to allow clip loading

8-round internal magazine

Safety

U.S. M1903A4 Springfield .30-06 bolt-action rifle

Standard eye-relief M73 scope (a few inches from eye)

Lower band with sling swivel

Upper band

Bolt handle

5-round internal magazine

Butt swivel

Butt plate

British Lee-Enfield No. 4 Mk. I (T) .303in. bolt-action rifle

Mk. 32 scope

Elevation drum

Band, lower (barrel retention ring)

Blade fore s

Cheek rest

Band, upper

10-round magazine

Swivel, sling

Bolt handle

Swivel, sling

German G43 (later K43) 7.92mm semiautomatic rifl

Windage drum (*Schutzkappe für Seitenverstellung*)

Gw ZF 4x scope (*Zielfernrohr*)

Elevation drum (*Teiltrommel für Entfernungsteilung*)

Clamp (*Klemmhebel*)

Front sight

Safety (*Sicherung*)

Butt plate

Front band (*Oberring*)

Sling attachment point

10-round magazine

Trigger (*Abzug*)

Soviet SVT-40 7.62mm semiautomatic rifle

Dedicated sniper scope mount and PU scope

Upper and lower gas piston covers

Front sight

Trigger assembly; note safety blocking trigger

Magazine release

10-round magazine

Bayonet lug (also holds front end of cleaning rod when inserted)

Finnish M/39-43 7.92mm bolt-action rifle

Ajack 4x M43 scope with Finnish Depot 1 mount

Pistol grip (cf M91/30 below)

5-round clip-loaded magazine

Stock take down disk (*Platte*) used for disassembling and reassembling the bolt

Long eye-relief ZF41 scope (note distance down rifle)

German K98k 7.92mm bolt-action rifle

Receiver (*Hülse*)

Bolt shroud with safety (*Sicherung*)

Front sight (*Korn*) and front sight cover (*Kornschutz*)

tt plate
olbenkappe)

Sling (*Riemen*)

Sling swivel (on reverse) (*Riemenbügel*)

Cleaning rod

5-round internal magazine (*Magazin*)

Sling cutout (*Durchbruch für den Riemen Kolben*)

Bolt handle (*Kammerstengel*)

High-turret mounted Dialytan 4x scope

German K98k 7.92mm bolt-action rifle

PE scope

Soviet Mosin-Nagant M91/30 7.92mm bolt-action rifle

Straight stock (cf M/39-43 above)

5-round clip-loaded magazine

Japanese Type 99 7.92mm bolt-action rifle

4x 7 adjustable scope

Folding monopod beneath the stock

5-round clip-loaded internal magazine

15

Were the Soviets snipers good? Yes. Were they supermen? No. As humans, they made human mistakes and paid for it like any other soldier. Could they have accumulated tallies greater than 500? Very possibly—especially if one accepts that in the short time Simo Häyhä fought, he attained his score of 259 confirmed and possible cumulative of 542. If this is true, then why not some of the Soviets claims? Many Soviet snipers fought for a longer time than Häyhä, and unless pulled from the front to become instructors or transferred to another duty, fought on until they were killed, seriously incapacitated or, if lucky, the war ended.[31]

German sniper scores seem to have been more carefully credited, particularly after the *Scharfschützenabzeichen* (Sharpshooters' badge—the Germans didn't use the term "sniper") came in and each kill required confirmation by an NCO or more senior rank. This information was kept in a specially provided notebook. There were strict rules that meant only kills under certain circumstances could be included.

While the Germans and Russians kept score, most Western Allies did not—or at least did not publicize it with the same enthusiasm. Part of the reason was the view that sniping was "unsporting." Take General Lord Horne's comment in his foreword to Maj. H. Hesketh-Prichard's *Sniping in France*: "Perhaps as a nation we failed in imagination. Possibly Germany was more quick to initiate new methods of warfare or to adapt her existing methods to meet prevailing conditions. Certainly we were slow to adopt, indeed, our souls abhorred, anything unsportsmanlike."

However, times change. Newspaper men in the American media promoted sniping to buoy morale and make fighting appear easy. Later in the war the American newspaper men exercised greater restraint. The war was going well and there was no need to pad the books. By contrast, the British media was reticent from the start and was less likely to report on British snipers. Hence their scores are known only to the records of the Ministry of Defence, the officers of the battalion, and the snipers themselves. This doesn't necessarily make the figures any more accurate, but the fact that they were not used directly for propaganda lends credibility. For example, how accurate is a report from British units in Burma that says the snipers from two brigades (48 in total) killed 296 Japanese in a two-week period, for the loss of two men?[32]

Sniping received favorable media coverage in Australia and the Australian sniper effort was promoted by newspaper articles such as those by a World War I sniper, Ion Idriess. In one he wrote:

"the most dangerous individual soldier is the sniper—the 'lone wolf' who is feared more than the tank, more than the aeroplane. In all our mechanized armies, in the titanic movement of massed troops, he is the one man who is independent of them all. He wages his own deadly war regardless of air fleets, panzer divisions, armies; and he does it with a rifle."[33]

A June 14, 1941, article had drawings illustrating sniping techniques which, unfortunately, reflected sniping in World War I. One columnist advocated beards for snipers:

"Why is the face conspicuous? Because it is a shaven face? Imagine one of these soldiers trying to act as a sniper, trying to lie hidden, trying to 'see without being seen.' He might make quite a serviceable camouflage for his body with a few branches, and for his helmet with some leaves; but he could not find it easy to conceal his white, shaven face, and his presence would probably be betrayed by it. That is why in the last war the sniper wore a complete robe if possible, or, failing that, a hood—at all cost to hide his white face. The fact that a sniper was ordered to shave, thus making his face as conspicuous as possible, and then ordered to wear a hood to hide that conspicuous shaven face, was one of the mysteries left unsolved at the end of the last war."[34]

Not all reporting was honest and the most preposterous was a "story" by Patty McKee Wright who told of an Australian who, after being wounded, captured a Japanese sniper and made him carry his captor back to Australian lines.[35]

June 7, 1941, article published by *The Australasian* newspaper that provided information on what were, in reality, World War I sniping techniques that were fine for trench warfare on the Western Front but less suitable in jungle or desert warfare where most Australian units ended up fighting. *Author's collection.*

This work proposes to study sniping in World War II and to share the lessons learned from it. The scope of the work is so vast that space limitation makes it prohibitive to discuss each campaign or theater in detail, and only a cursory overview can be included to put into context the situation where the sniping incident occurred and in an apolitical and neutral manner. Not that there weren't good guys or bad guys—there were but it serves no purpose for this work to moralize. Please be aware that any preponderance of information from one belligerent is only a reflection of the material found and not a preference for one side over another. In that sense, it doesn't matter who the teacher (sniper) was and for which side they fought. It is the lesson passed down that is relevant. To this end, no effort has been made to justify or glorify one side and demonize another. I accept that war in and of itself is a horrible waste of lives and resources and Confederate Lt. Gen. Robert E. Lee put it best when he said: "It is well that war is so terrible, or we would grow too fond of it."

The story of World War II sniping can be conveniently told in three parts.

Part I covers the selection and training of snipers. While there are generalities, each nation approached sniping and sniper training uniquely with some being better than others.

Actual incidents of sniping are related in Part II which is subdivided geographically into the West (Africa, the Mediterranean, and northwestern

Europe), the Eastern Front (the war between Germany and the Soviet Union, including the fighting in and against Finland), and the war against Japan—India, Burma, China, southeast Asia, and the Pacific.

The final section, Part III, covers the technology of the era looking at sniper rifles and scopes.

Please note that the notes on pp. 322–33 refer directly to the magazine articles and books in the bibliography using the author's surname and date of publication to identify them.

This study was both hampered and helped by time. Most World War II veterans passed away before this work was initiated in 2019. On top of this, snipers suffered high casualties. It's been said that Fifth (U.S.) Army's snipers suffered up to 80 percent losses. Slightly better was the 24th Marine Regiment after Iwo Jima, nine of whose 24 snipers survived—37.5 percent.[36]

Finally, there needs to be a disclaimer. During the war derogatory slurs were used by soldiers and journalists alike. Wartime newspapers and propagandists did their best to dehumanize and ridicule the opposition. Comments like "In a very real sense, the Japanese sniper can be said to be in his natural habitat" reflect this.[37] These are not reflective of my own beliefs but since this book relies heavily on contemporary accounts, I have decided to leave the slurs intact and trust that the reader is sensible enough to appreciate history without the whitewashing or sanitizing that characterizes today's politically correct world. War respects no "safe space."

Part I Selection and Training
| 1 Prewar and Early War Years

"A sniper is the hardest thing in the world to fight. You can't see him, you can't see smoke from his gun. All you can do is listen to the bullets whistles and hope and pray."[1]

S/Sgt. O. L. Brotherton
36th Infantry Division

Britain & the Commonwealth

World War I saw sniping develop into a much-practiced skill. Trench warfare fostered this development as British Major H. Hesketh-Prichard discussed in his seminal *Sniping in France*. The Germans were the leaders in the early war:

"I had been there before, in the previous March, and had seen the immense advantages which had accrued to the Germans through their superiority in trench warfare sniping.

"It is difficult now to give the exact figures of our losses. Suffice it to say that in early 1915 we lost eighteen men in a single battalion in a single day to enemy snipers. Now if each battalion in the line killed by sniping a single German in the day, the numbers would mount up. If any one cares to do a mathematical sum, and to work out the number of battalions we had in the line, they will be surprised at the figures, and when they multiply these figures by thirty and look at the month's losses, they will find that in a war of attrition the sniper on this count alone justifies his existence and wipes out large numbers of the enemy.

"But it is not only by the casualties that one can judge the value of sniping. If your trench is dominated by enemy snipers, life in it is really a very hard thing, and moral must inevitably suffer. In many parts of the line all through France and Belgium the enemy, who were organized at a much earlier period than we, certainly did dominate us. Each regiment and most soldiers who have been to France will remember some particular spot where they will say the German sniping was more deadly than elsewhere, but the truth of the matter is that in the middle of 1915 we were undergoing almost everywhere a severe gruelling, to say the least of it."[2]

However, when peace came, the lessons so hard-learned in the trenches were quickly forgotten. Whether it was the hope that such warfare was over forever or simply the same reactionary retrenchment that saw the slowing of the development of the tank, most countries downgraded or dispensed with their sniping arm. Indeed, the British and Commonwealth countries went as far as disposing of most of their sniper rifles, including their best design, the American-built Enfield P14, a good number of which had been manufactured—as had suitable scopes which were sold on the open market. As late as 1936 one Australian gunsmith/importer was advertising a three-power scoped surplus rifle for £4 10s 0d.[3]

This is not to say that marksmanship and sniping skills were completely forgotten. In Britain, the Corps of Small Arms and Machine Gun Schools (SA&MGS) had been set up in 1923, amalgamating the Small Arms (the Hythe School of Musketry on the Kent coast) and Machine Gun (Netheravon, Wiltshire) schools. However, although British infantry units continued to employ snipers, training was expected to take place within units, sometimes using instructors from the corps. The SA&MGS would be expanded to staff a wing at Bisley—the National Rifle Association (NRA) Wing—during World War II. Bisley is a name with worldwide connotations as it has been the NRA center since 1890, supported the setting up of civilian gun clubs in the UK after the Second Boer War, and was handed over to military control in 1939. As we shall see in the next chapter, the sniping courses at Bisley would be put to good use. Additionally, in 1940 after the setting up of the Local Defence Force (later the Home Guard) Bisley acted as a training location.

The British Royal Marines (RM) Small Arms School in Browndown, Gosport, Hampshire, also opened in 1923. This had been a range used by the RM from the early 1850s but was expanded substantially in 1923 and further in 1937. It was established "for the

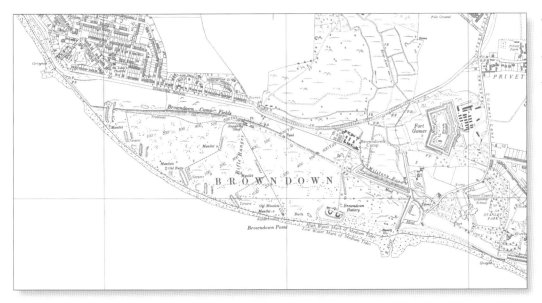

instruction of NCOs and others who would return to their units as instructors."[4]

The British Army's Military *Training Pamphlet No. 3 Notes on the Tactical Handling of the New (1938) Battalion*, identifies two "stalker-snipers" per section, who should be given training in fieldcraft, sniping, and the use of telescopic sights. The notes emphasized working in pairs and the tasks of observation and reporting as well as sniping to restrict the enemy's attempts to do the same. There was a December 1938 amendment that said: "Two men per section will be given a fuller [rifle] course, and from these eight men will be selected and trained to act as battalion snipers in defence, using the eight sniper rifles on charge of battalions."[5]

At the outbreak of the war most sniper selection and training was being handled by the infantry units themselves. The British *Army Training Memoranda* (ATM) in 1940 identify:

"Battalion snipers will be trained by and work under the orders of the intelligence officer. As their name implies, they will be trained as expert scouts, observers, and snipers, and will also be grounded in intelligence duties."[6]

"Snipers and Infantry Training Centres Proper facilities for the training of snipers do not exist at Infantry Training Centres. This form of training is therefore deleted from the syllabus."[7]

The first British sniping manual, *Notes on the Training of Snipers, Military Training Pamphlet No. 44* of October 2, 1940, emphasizes early on that:

"In order to check and co-ordinate intelligence reports and to prevent successful enemy

observation, all infantry units have an intelligence section within which are incorporated eight snipers … the battalion intelligence officer will be responsible to the commanding officer for observation, sniping and intelligence, and therefore for training the intelligence section and the snipers. The eight snipers who form part of this battalion intelligence section will work under his orders. Each rifle company in the battalion should supply two snipers and be responsible for replacing its own in the event of casualties. A reserve, therefore, must be maintained and earmarked.

"One sniper will be an N.C.O., who will be appointed to assist the intelligence officer. He should have attended a course at an army school."[8]

ATM No. 37 of December 1940 confirms the role of the intelligence officer in training, but also identifies his role in battle to post snipers. This was reiterated in *Military Training Pamphlet No. 14 (India): Infantry Section Leading 1941*:

"14.iv. The Intelligence Section consisting of one Officer, one Sergeant/Havildar and six O.Rs., is included in the battalion headquarters (see Section 56). There is no special establishment for the eight battalion snipers who work under the Intelligence Officer.

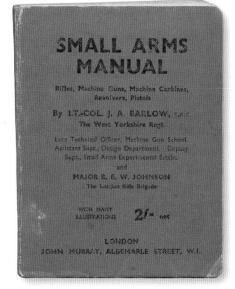

They are provided at the expense of the infantry companies."

There was a further alteration to the infantry battalion organization in May 1942 when ATM No. 43 outlined that:

"Every infantry battalion must have a proper sniping organization in order that the battlefield may be dominated from first contact. The following steps will therefore be taken:

i. The training of snipers in a battalion, previously the responsibility of the intelligence officer, will in future be carried out by the battalion weapon training officer.

ii. Each company will select two known good shots for training as company snipers. These men should be allotted the telescopic sights at present authorised for a battalion.

"In addition to company snipers, one man in each section will be trained as the section sniper. Section snipers will be equipped with the P.14 rifle. This will also be issued to company snipers until telescopic sights are available. Local commanders will arrange to redistribute P.14 rifles accordingly.

"Units should aim at training a 100 per cent reserve of snipers."[9]

As we have seen, the SA&MGS established a school at Bisley Camp, Brookwood: the NRA Bisley Snipers' Wing. It trained sniper personnel with a staff of six officers and 13 NCOs. The number of students is identified as 30 officers and 70 NCOs every fortnight.[10] The War Diary of the 2nd Battalion, Welsh Guards, lists attendance at the initial courses:

"October 15
2/Lieutenant P. J. McCall and 6 Other Ranks to 1st Snipers' Course, BISLEY
November 3
2/Lieutenant P. J. McCall and 6 Other Ranks from 1st Snipers' Course, BISLEY
November 5
2/Lieutenant P. T. Petley and 6 Other Ranks to 2nd Snipers' Course, BISLEY"[11]

The Hythe School of Musketry was bombed out and forced to move to Bisley.[12] (Hythe reopened later in the war.) A small school was set up in Scotland with the limited purpose of instructing ghillies on the use of the scoped rifle. The course was three weeks in

duration and included advanced map reading, finer points of marksmanship, field sketching, advanced compass work, camouflage, and the construction of hides. Before Dunkirk, a small school was also established temporarily in France.

A sniper wing was established as part of the Advanced Handling and Fieldcraft School. It provided four to six courses of six weeks' duration. It later moved to Bisley under the Small Arms School as the weather conditions in North Wales were unsuitable for such training. The chief instructor was Major The Hon. F. A. H. Wills, Lovat Scouts, assisted by Major Owen Underhill, O.B.E., KSLI, one of the pioneers of sniping during World War I.

Sniper training by the Royal Marines was handled at the Snipers' School at Penally near Tenby in Pembrokeshire, South Wales. In 1942 the RM Division's infantry battalions were reorganized as commandos and from July 1943 sniper training moved to the south coast of England and became the RM Snipers Wing at the RM Small Arms School at Browndown, Hampshire. Snipers would play an important operational role in commando raids such as that on Dieppe (see pp. 78–9).

In Australia, it was proposed as early as December 1939 by Lt. Col. J. C. W. Baillon of the 2nd Australian Division that with each battalion there should be eight snipers equipped with scoped rifles. His suggestion was not acted on and for the first two years of the war Australian battalions did not have a formal sniper establishment. If some did, it was on an ad hoc basis and because the battalion commander had World War I experience which gave him an understanding of snipers' usefulness. For example, Lt. Col. Kenneth Eather, CO of 2/1st Battalion's, 16th Infantry Brigade, had two to three marksman in each company. 2/30th Battalion Lt. Col. Frederick "Black Jack" Galleghan had several marksmen equipped with scoped P14 rifles.

Not all marksmen's rifles were scoped and some marksmen carried the SMLE Mk. III (H). These were heavy-barreled SMLEs equipped with commercial rear aperture sights. Besides the rear aperture, a large H was stamped into the stock near the cocking piece. By late 1941, sniping was introduced into the curriculum at the Australian Army's Small Arms School at Randwick, NSW. Rather than train individual snipers, it trained officers and NCOs as sniper instructors and taught them use and care of the sniper rifle, setting up ranges and observation exercises. Graduates then returned to their battalion to instruct eligible marksmen. At the same time, Australia established an eight-man sniper section consisting of a sergeant, one corporal, two lance corporals, and four privates in each battalion—a move preceding the British

No. 19 SNIPERS COURSE, R.M.S.A.S., 22.7.44 - 5.8.44.

Army by over a year. From one newspaper article, we learn that two men were drawn from each company and in case of casualties, a reserve "was always in training."[13] Ideally, they were under the command of the battalion intelligence officer who was supposed to direct them. In November 1942 the sniper section strength was increased to 12 men who were now attached to headquarters company. So great was the need for snipers that in 1944 it became one sniper per section or 32 per battalion.[14] High casualties and lack of equipment meant this lofty goal was never attained.

United States

As far as the American military goes, we learn from an April 8, 1941, memo from the Marine Corps Director of the Division of Plans and Policies to the Marine Corps Commandant that the peacetime U.S. Army had no sniping program. In part the memo read:

> "No special training program for snipers is contemplated by the Army and no steps are being made to procure special equipment. Training of snipers and their employment is covered briefly in *FM7–5*, §288, in which this responsibility is placed on the company commander."[15]

Sniping had a very low priority. The U.S. Army of July 1, 1939, had fewer than 130,000 men although it was getting bigger as the world prepared for war. By the fall of 1939 it reached 227,000 men including those overseas. By the summer of 1941, including the regulars, reserves, and National Guard, it had swollen to 1,500,000 and was still growing.[16] The rapid expansion meant there was no time early in the war to design and implement a sniper training program. Army Replacement Training Centers had only five weeks to give all newly inducted soldiers basic training and then eight weeks for their specialty training (lengthened to nine weeks on June 11, 1943). Of that five weeks, 16 hours were supposed to cover field fortification and camouflage, and a minimum of eight hours on elementary map reading.[17] Four hours of scouting, observation and messenger were added in 1943. However, from December 9, 1943, to November 4, 1944, scouting was no longer listed in the skills taught and may have been incorporated into the 40 hours devoted to patrolling.[18]

By 1944 there had been improvements. American doctrine by then held that snipers could either operate individually as a mobile sniper or stationary in pairs in prepared positions. *FM21–75 Scouting, Patrolling, and Sniping* included 13 pages on the subject, including §165a:

> "The mobile sniper acts alone, moves about frequently, and covers a large but not necessarily fixed area. He may be used to infiltrate enemy

RM sniper training

The sniper course at RMSAS Gosport was two weeks long. Marine Dennis Cooper (seen in the back row, far left of photo 5, opposite, above) told his son, Peter, that:

"It was a two-week course run by Lt. Col. Nevill Armstrong who was 72 at the time my father was there. I have a copy of his book, *Fieldcraft, Sniping and Intelligence*, written in 1942. Evidently, it was mainly Royal Marine Commandos on the course with some Army Commandos and one or two from the regular army. Most of the men were selected for the course but volunteers were interviewed and if they seemed suitable were sent."

1. No. 4 Commando in sniper training in Aberdovey. Two Rifle No. 3 Mk. I* (T)s may be seen in this iamge. Capt. Murdoch McDougal is seated in the back row, third from the right. *Image from the collection of Capt. Murdoch McDougal Family. Commando Veterans Archive https://www. commandoveterans.org/.*

2. A pair from No. 4 Commando training with their Rifle No. 3 Mk. I* (T)s at Aberdovey Sniper Training. *Image from the collection of Capt. Murdoch McDougal Family. Commando Veterans Archive https://www. commandoveterans.org/.*

3. Men from No. 4 Commando attending Aberdovey. The snipers, who are using No. 3 Mk. I* (T)s, are thought to be Bill Johnson and Guardsman J. Spearman. Medical Orderly LCpl. Cunningham is seen in the background. *Image from the collection of Capt. Murdoch McDougal Family. Commando Veterans Archive https://www. commandoveterans.org/.*

4. Fred Peachy of No. 2 Commando posing with his Rifle No. 3 Mk. I* (T) at Inverailort Castle, south of Lochailort, Scotland. Inverailort Castle was requisition by the War Office in May 1940 for use as the Special Training Centre where irregular forces (what would become the Commandos) were trained. *Image from the Mark Brammel Collection. Commando Veterans Archive https://www. commandoveterans.org/.*

5. No. 38 Snipers Course, RMSAS, June 23–July 7, 1945. Dennis Cooper back row, far left; Lt. Col. Armstrong front row, second left. *Image from the Dennis Cooper Collection. Commando Veterans Archive https://www. commandoveterans.org/.*

6. No. 1 Snipers' Refresher Course for the Royal Marines. A week-long course, a No. 4 Mk. I (T) is in the left foreground and a No. 3 Mk. I* (T) in the right. Scout-scopes are seen mounted on tripods and were part of the sniper's tool kit. 42 RM Commando Philip Bennett is seen standing in the last row, third from the left.
Image courtesy the Chris Bennett collection. Commando Veterans Archive https://www.commandoveterans.org/.

The role of the sniper

Dated October 1, 1940, *Infantry Field Manual 7–5, Organization and Tactics of Infantry: The Rifle Battalion*'s §288 shows a mere eight paragraphs describing the role of the sniper.

Snipers were to work with observers, with the latter observing the shot. Snipers were to be coordinated within a company to ensure coverage of the entire front. Besides being camouflaged (hands, face, equipment) they were to fire from camouflaged posts and were cautioned not to project the muzzle beyond the loophole and to prevent dust from being kicked up and betraying their location. Smoking was prohibited and anything that could shine was to be kept hidden.

In positional warfare, most targets were visible at early dawn or dusk. The sniper was to be mindful of the sun and how it could be used to his advantage and also against him. In anticipation of trench warfare, the

WAR DEPARTMENT

INFANTRY FIELD MANUAL

*

ORGANIZATION AND TACTICS OF INFANTRY THE RIFLE BATTALION

manual advocated night firing up to 200 yards by pre-aiming rifles at known loopholes, dugout entrances, and machine guns.

Finally, it had one counter-sniping instruction: "locate the direction from which hostile sniping comes." To do this, suspected sniper fire should be reported to the sniper for investigation.[19]

lines and seek out and destroy appropriate targets along enemy routes of supply and communication. It is essential that the mobile sniper hit his target with the first round fired. If the sniper is forced to fire several times, he discloses his position and also gives the enemy opportunity to escape. Therefore, although the mobile sniper must be an expert shot at all ranges, he must be trained to stalk his target until he is close enough to insure that it will be eliminated with his first shot."[20]

Kliment Voroshilov had a checkered career. In 1939–40 he commanded Soviet troops in Finland during the disastrous Winter War, but in 1953–60 he was Chairman of the Presidium of the Supreme Soviet—one of the top dogs in the USSR. As People's Commissar for Defense of the USSR his name was given to the Voroshilov Marksman award. *Author's collection.*

Training programs of various qualities were set up both domestically and in England.

Soviet Union

Elsewhere the totalitarian regimes—fascist and communist—were in the process of militarizing their countries, and ensured that marksmanship was a skill to be taught to the masses through official gun clubs. The Soviets created the *Osoaviakhim* in 1927, a paramilitary organization with marksmanship an important factor. Lt. Gen. G. E. Morozoff wrote in the *Moscow News* that the Soviets were largely influenced by British Maj. H. Hesketh-Prichard's book, *Sniping in France*. Gen. Morozoff asserted that when the Red Army was formed, snipers were placed on a special footing and taught the principles outlined in Prichard's book.[21] As early as 1933 the Soviets issued a sniper training manual, *Sniper: Methods for Training Snipers* by V. Vostruknov and M. Kavardin and excerpts from it were secured by the American military attaché, Maj. W. E. Shipp, in Riga, Latvia which he forwarded to Washington.[22]

Outside the *Osoaviakhim*, all school-aged Soviet children were instructed in rifle marksmanship at school. Soviet children attended school from ages seven to 16/17; or 10 years. After the eighth grade a child could matriculate to a trade school in lieu of finishing the ninth and tenth grade. The youngest this writer found was a marksmanship medal awarded to 14-year-old seventh-grader Roza Shanina.[23] Schools were issued the TOZ-8 single-shot bolt-action .22

long rifle. Marksmanship was also promoted through competition within the school, between schools, in the city, and inter-cities. Additionally, medals were awarded to the champions and could be worn on both civilian attire and uniform. However, not all sniper-trained *Osoaviakhim* became snipers and while Mikhail Zamarin worked briefly as a sniper instructor within *Osoaviakhim*, his war included being an artilleryman and later commander of a Guards infantry regiment.[24]

Italy

Here, it was the *Unione Italiana Tiro al Segno* (Italian Target Shooting Union), a nationwide society that had its roots in the 19th century, that aimed to improve the nation's marksmanship. The Italian snipers this produced helped contribute significantly during World War I. In the early 1930s, Mussolini's regime passed laws that changed the structure and aims of the organization, culminating in a law of 1935 that placed it under the Voluntary Militia for National Security which was tasked with the training of those in pre-military and post-military education, as well as those who required a license to carry a firearm. Municipal and Provincial Shooting Societies were replaced by a national body and shooting ranges were set up at the expense of the state. As with the Soviet *Osoaviakhim*, there were *tiratore scelto*—sharpshooter (rather than

Mikhail Zamarin (on the right) was an *Osoaviakhim* sniper instructor who, after attending the artillery school in Kharkov, became an anti-tank gun battery commander in the 169th Infantry Division. When Romania was forced to cede Bessarabia to the Soviet Union, Zamarin was among the Soviet Army contingent that reclaimed it. Later, as a senior lieutenant, he became a battalion commander and as major, a regimental commander. *Image courtesy The Blavatnik Archive Foundation. (http://www.blavatnikarchive.org).*

Osoaviakhim

The Voroshilov Marksman award was introduced in 1932. It was named after Marshal Kliment Voroshilov who was a Stalin loyalist, a member of the Politburo, and the People's Commissar for Military and Naval Affairs—a role he held until 1934. During his tenure, in 1927 he help create the *Osoaviakhim* (Volunteer Society for the Cooperation with the Army, Aviation, and Navy) that promoted marksmanship. Through winning shooting competitions, a youth could earn the prestigious Voroshilov Marksman badge such as the one seen here. Numerous snipers earned the Voroshilov Marksman award as civilians. *GF collection.*

Anticipating its civil defense needs in a war, the prewar Soviet Union created the *Osoaviakhim* in 1927. Open to any Soviet citizen aged 14 or older, and regardless of gender, the *Osoaviakhim*— the "Society for the Support of Defence, Aviation and Chemical Engineering"— was a paramilitary organization designed to teach preparedness. It could include simple use of the gas mask, marching, physical fitness, sports, scouting, sentry duties, messenger, infantry attack and defense, defense against tanks, first aid, military history, and aviation.[25] Marksmanship and sniping was one of the skills promoted.

At the Baranovksy Training Ground in summer 1932, People's Commissar Kliment E. Voroshilov witnessed a shooter empty his revolver at a target. Inspecting the target, Voroshilov observed that it was untouched. The embarrassed shooter muttered as an excuse that the revolver was bad. Taking the revolver, Voroshilov reloaded it and fired at the target, getting a high score of 59. Having proven the gun's accuracy, Voroshilov returned it to the man and admonished, "There are no bad weapons, there are bad shooters." The next day, a newspaper published a photo of Voroshilov's target with the words, "Learn to shoot like Voroshilov!" The patriotic slogan caught on and in 1932 the Central Council of the *Osoaviakhim* approved the "Voroshilov Marksman" award and two years later in 1934 the "Young Voroshilov Marksman." By 1936 over 20,000 Soviets were awarded the first-class Voroshilov Marksman badge, and 1,000 the second class. The next year over 6,600 small-bore ranges were established in factories or workplaces across the Soviet Union for people to practice their marksmanship.[26]

During the prewar era, Lyudmila Pavlichenko was working at an arsenal when she began participating in *Osoaviakhim* recreational activities. With aspirations of flight, Pavlichenko tried gliding but airsickness put her off it. Fortunately for her, the factory also had its own shooting range and instructor. One day, Pavlichenko and marksmanship instructor Fyodor Kushchenko were ejected from a Young Communist League meeting. Both were stunned and Kushchenko suggested they practice shooting to calm themselves. Skeptical, she asked if it was helpful and was told that

sport shooting is for calm people. They went to the range where he pulled a Tula-made single-shot, TOZ-8 bolt-action rifle and instructed her on how to use it. He then gave her bullets and had her fire four shots. He brought the target back and complimented her on it. Afterward, Pavlichenko attended shooting sessions every Saturday which included studying the bolt-action mechanism, field stripping it including the bolt, care, and maintenance. Classes included ballistics, influence of wind, spin of the bullet, and drop. The history of firearms was also included as well as some insights into the manufacturing process.

Naturally, there was shooting from standing, lying, from a rest, kneeling, and aiming with the aid of the sling. Non-firearms training included general physical fitness including running, vaulting, and push-ups. She earned the coveted Voroshilov Marksman badge, Second Degree. Land navigation and grenade throwing were included in her *Osoaviakhim* training.[27] She was not a sniper yet and her training only made her a skilled sharpshooter with some insights into military skills. Pavlichenko was accepted into university when her old instructor, Fyodor Kushchenko suggested she attend the *Osoaviakhim* sniper school at the Kiev University. The prerequisite was possession of a Voroshilov Marksman badge, Second Degree. Additionally, she had to supply references from both her former employer and the university, as well as a resume.

She was accepted and at the university her training included two sessions a week for a total of five hours. The sniper students were given special uniforms that emphasized the seriousness of their training, as well as passes that granted them access to the training areas. Other training included politics, four hours of drill, 60 hours on tactics, 30 hours on military engineering, 20 hours in hand-to-hand fighting as well as 220 hours of firearms training.

Besides promoting marksmanship, the *Osoaviakhim* curriculum included sniper tactics as described by Lt. Col. M. Kriventsov:

"The principal task of the sniper is the destruction of the most important targets he can find, and by that I mean: enemy officers, observers, scouts, liaison officers, enemy snipers, crews manning enemy machine guns, anti-tank riflemen, trench mortars, and motorcycle skirmishers. Their job is to blind the enemy armored-car and tank

drivers by firing at their visors and bringing down low-flying and diving enemy aircraft.

"As a rule, snipers get their assignments in offensive actions from their platoon or company commanders; they work in twos or threes, going into the front and flanks under cover of the company but before the rifle sections open fire. When the platoon fire begins, snipers try to destroy the enemy machine guns and trench mortar crews, spotting and destroying targets that might be dangerous to the advance of their army and firing on the enemy's main line of resistance."[28]

A final exam was administered and those who received an "excellent" grade were registered in a special list for city/district enlistment offices and had to attend regular refresher courses as well as competitions. Pavlichenko believes that the prewar training produced 1,500 experts who could attain first-shot hits.[29] Other graduates from the *Osoaviakhim* include Vladimir Pchelintsev, Joseph Pilyushin, and Nina Petrova.

Vladimir Pchelintsev was born in 1919 in Tambov and lost his father at age one to the Revolution. His stepfather was an NKVD officer and young Vladimir grew up in Moscow, Yaroslavl, Petrozavodsky, and finally Leningrad, which had a sniping school by 1934. As a 16-year-old, in 1935 he earned the Voroshilov Marksman badge and in 1937 headed his school in the national championships and won first place, winning a TOZ-8 .22-caliber rimfire long rifle. As a college student, he also attended the *Osoaviakhim* sniping program and completed it before the war erupted.[30]

Another graduate of the Leningrad school, Nina Petrova earned her spot there for being a champion shot in the Transportation Companies'

Unions. Upon completion, she was retained as an instructor there. The school was known to have produced 102 Voroshilov badge winners in 1936. Petrova taught women shooters until June 22, 1941 when the war broke out.[31] Being over 40 years old, she was rejected as a volunteer but joined the medical battalion of the 4th Division of the Citizens' Militia of Leningrad. A shortage of regular soldiers forced the Soviets to commit the militia alongside the army. Private Petrova became a sniper instructor in the 1st Rifle Battalion, 86th Taratutskaya Infantry Division. She quickly rose to sergeant major (*starshina*) in command of the snipers. Besides training new snipers, she also fought as a sniper.

sniper)—badges, although there was no specific military sniper training.

Unlike World War I where the Italian Army used scoped rifles, this does not appear to have been the practice in the Western Desert or in the Soviet Union. Rifles that met certain accuracy standards at the factor were stamped with a *Trio a Segno Nazionale* marking (two crossed rifles superimposed over a bullseye target) for the best marksmen. Lt. Eugeno Corti used a scoped SVT-40 in his ad hoc role as a *cecchino* (Italian for sniper/marksman).[32]

Finland

Finnish marksmanship training before the war wasn't given to army personnel but had been part of the training of the *Suojeluskunta* (Finnish Civil Guard). There were few sniper rifles available, but the training was good, as is shown by the exploits of the most famous guardsman, Simo Häyhä.

As the Continuation War against the Soviet Union coagulated into trench warfare, so sniper and anti-sniper training became more important. In October 1942, the Finnish nine-man rifle squad was organized with one sniper, although lack of training and suitable weapons gave the well-trained Soviets the edge.

In spring 1943, the first ad hoc sniper training courses were organized at regimental level—18-men strong. In the autumn, a more standardized program was set up at battalion level. It was a two-stage course with 14 men in the first part of it, which lasted nearly a month, and the best of these going on to the next stage working in pairs or larger teams. However, there were never sufficient scoped rifles—even with captured weapons—to give every trained man a weapon.

Germany

The Nazis, slightly surprisingly remembering the German skills in World War I, didn't initially have sniper schools or train snipers. Their sharpshooters, however, started their lessons in marksmanship from an early age. The Hitler Youth (HJ—*Hitlerjugend*) organization was, in effect, a military school for all 14–18-year-old youths under the regime. There were three levels of shooting awards: proficient (*Schützen*), sharpshooters (*Scharfschützen*), and champions (*Meisterschützen*). Before youths joined the HJ there was the DJ—the boys section (*Deutsches Jungvolk in der Hitlerjugend*) for those aged 10 to 14—and they, too, had a shooting badge.

Both the Germans and the Soviets

practiced sniper tactics and skills during the Spanish Civil War—and tested the weapons that would be used in 1939–45. The German Condor Legion and Franco's Nationalists made use of scoped Mausers and, latterly, K98ks; the Republicans, Mosin-Nagants.[33] The developments included the improvement to the Soviet PE scope leading to the PEM. George Orwell was famously wounded by a "Fascist sniper," on May 20, 1937, near Huesca:

"It was at the corner of the parapet, at five o'clock in the morning. This was always a dangerous time, because we had the dawn at our backs, and if you stuck your head above the parapet it was clearly outlined against the sky. ... Suddenly, in the very middle of saying something, I felt—it is very hard to describe what I felt, though I remember it with the utmost vividness ... The next moment my knees crumpled up and I was falling ... I heard a Spaniard behind me say that the bullet had gone clean through my neck.

"The meaninglessness of it! To be bumped off, not even in battle, but in this stale corner of the trenches, thanks to a moment's carelessness! I thought, too, of the man who had shot me—wondered what he was like, whether he was a Spaniard or a foreigner, whether he knew he had got me, and so forth. I could not feel any resentment against him. I reflected that as he was a Fascist I would have killed him if I could, but that if he had been taken prisoner and brought before me at this moment I would merely have congratulated him on his good shooting."[34]

Japan

The Japanese, similarly, saw a significant military involvement in education, particularly drill and bayonet training, although rifle shooting and weapons training was also taught. From the 1920s, the government ensured all junior and senior high school boys had two hours a week of military training. Training rifles—often made from older military models or parts of them—were produced until the late 1930s. Not all these rifles could be fired and of those that did, some fired wooden bullets. Almost all of these training rifles could carry bayonets. The emphasis of Japanese training may not have been on accuracy, but—as with every army—marksmanship was important and there were shooting drill badges. The result was patchy, ranging from those who found Japanese sniping to be excellent and the many, such as Col. Russell P. Reeder at Guadalcanal (see p. 255), who didn't. Again, the distinction between trained sniper and infantryman shooting from a tree isn't always clear when it comes to the Pacific War.

Sepp Dietrich and a young Hitler Youth marksman. *Narodowe Archiwum Cyfrowe.*

28

Marksmanship awards

In anticipation of war, armies worldwide promoted marksmanship and recognized a soldier's achievements with decorations worn on the uniform that instilled a certain pride to the individual.

In the U.S. Army and Marine Corps, the awards were, from highest to lowest, expert (wreathed cross with target in center), sharpshooter (eight-pointed cross), and marksman target (irreverently called by marines the "pizza box" or "Red Baron" after the frozen pizza—or also the "toilet bowl"). There were also different ratings for the weapons including rifle, pistol, carbine, etc.

Similarly, the Waffen-SS had four classes which from included *Meister-schützen* (master shooter), *Scharfschützen* (sharpshooter), *I. Schiessklasse* (First Class Shooter) and *II. Schiessklasse* (Second Class Shoooter). In lieu of badges, both the Heer (German Army) and Luftwaffe awarded silver cords that were worn from the right epaulet and attached to the top tunic button. The German marksmanship cord tradition exists today and may be traced back to Scharnhorst of the Napoleonic era.

Japanese military marksmanship recognition badges trace back to March 15, 1874, when the first regulations were drafted. No award was worn and that waited for 1882 when a cloth chevron was authorized to be worn on the elbow. In 1888 the cherry blossom petal badge with crossed rifles made its debut. Initially it was awarded in four grades:

Gold with silver highlights
Silver with gold highlights
Copper brown with gold highlights
Copper brown with silver highlights

1. Cherry blossom petal badge with crossed rifles—third level, copper brown with gold highlights.

2. German army marksman lanyards had been instituted on June 29, 1936, to replace the sleeve stripes used by the Weimar Republic. Luftwaffe lanyards were instituted on September 30, 1936, to enlisted men or NCOs who passed marksmanship standards. The award was the *Schützenschnur*, a braided lanyard worn on the right shoulder. The three grades were: lanyard; lanyard + artillery shells; lanyard + acorns. The army stopped awarding them on February 14, 1941, but Luftwaffe men kept wearing them throughout the war. *Richard Charlton Taylor.*

3. L–R: U. S. Army Expert, Sharpshooter, and Marksman badges. *U.S. Army.*

4. L–R: USMC Expert, Sharpshooter, and Marksman badges. *Husnock and McChizzle/WikiCommons.*

5. The Waffen-SS had four classes of badge:
a. II class; **b.** I class;
c. *Scharfschützen* class;
d. *Meisterschützen* class.

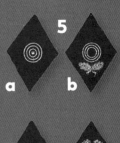

RIFLE

RIFLE EXPERT

RIFLE SHARPSHOOTER

RIFLE MARKSMAN

2ND AWARD

a

b

c

d

1. Hitler Youth *Schießauszeichnung für Scharfschützen*—shooting award for sharpshooters.

2. RKKA sniper's badge. Note СНАЙЛЕР or sniper and Cyrillic rendering of RKKA.

3. The "Excellent" awards were instituted from May 21, 1942. The word СНАЙЛЕР or sniper appears above the hammer and sickle.

4. British snipers would have worn this badge during the war, the S appearing above the crossed rifles postwar.

The Hitler Youth recorded shooting scores in the *Schießbuch. GF Collection.*

Before World War II, there were four categories:

1. NCO to encourage marksmanship in the NCO ranks.
2. Enlisted Men's Special Rifle Shooting badge was worn by enlisted men in recognition of their second year of being awarded a marksmanship award. Initially awarded on the basis of two men per company, the award had silver rifles, petals, and stamen and issued on a 1:5 ratio to every five first-year Special Marksmen and second year Special Marksmen.
3. Enlisted men's Type 1 second-year badge was grey and awarded to 1/20 of the men in the company who did not qualify for the Special.
4. Enlisted men's Type 2 badge was brown and awarded to 1/18th of the men who had not earned the Type 1 badge. Originally cupronickel, shortage of this metal in November 1941 resulted in aluminium being substituted.

The award was worn by enlisted men on the left breast and between the third and fourth buttonhole. This was probably done to create space for war medals.[35]

Youth marksmanship badges or awards

Starting in 1936, the head of the Hitler Youth, Balder von Schirach, instituted sharpshooting awards for HJ and DJ boys. The basic level badge was worked up to through three classes (*Anfänger*/ beginners; *Ausbildungs*/training; *Sonder*/special). Once reaching *Sonderklasse* they could shoot for the badge. The weapon used was a 5.56mm (.22 caliber) *Deutsches Sport Modell* fired from 50m. To win the award the competitor had to hit a target divided into 11 rings and a bullseye, worth from 1 (outer) to 12 (bull) points firing five shots from each of three positions: prone (rifle supported on a sandbag: 45 points), prone (unsupported:

40 points), and kneeling (unsupported: 30 points). The *Shießbuch* (shooting book) recorded the qualifications and the badge was worn on the right breast pocket below the *Leistungsabzeichen* (proficiency badge). In 1938 the *Scharfschütze* badge was introduced (it included standing and rapid fire); in 1939 the DJ badge (shot at 8m using Mars Junior, Haenel Junior or Diana Junior air rifles; also in three classes); and in 1941 the *Meisterschütze* (included pistol shooting). To end 1943, the following awards had been made:

Basic	273,545
Scharfschütze	31,904
Meisterschütze	852
DJ	580,872

Preceding Germany, the USSR promoted marksmanship in and among schools through competition and top shooters were given the Voroshilov Marksman award, the visible sign of which was a badge (see p. 26). While definitely not in the same category as the *Hitlerjugend* or Russian *Komsomol*, the American Boy Scouts had marksmanship merit badges but participation was entirely voluntary. Sir Baden Powell's original book, *Scouting For Boys*, encouraged shooting and the British Boy Scout first issued a marksmanship merit badge in 1910. The scout must score 60 points out of possible 100, firing 20 rounds (in any position) at NRA Standard Target, 200 or 100 yards open range or 200 yards target reduced for miniature rifle to 15 or 25 yards; (Scoring: bull 5; inner 4; mapgie 3; outer 2); and judge distances on uknown ground; (five trials up to 300 yards, fire between 300 and 600 yards); average error on ten trials not to be more than 25 per cent.

Sniper badges

In 1938, the Workers' and Peasants' Red Army— *Rabo-che-Krest'ya-nskaya Kra-snaya Armiya*—the Red Army or RKKA instituted a badge for those who had completed a sniping course. The Soviet Union

3

initiated awards for its accomplished snipers on May 21, 1942, when it created its Excellent Sniper award. That was only one of several "Excellent" awards and others included artillery, tanker, machine gunner, mortar, submariner, torpedo man, railway worker, mine specialist, medic, scout, signaler, driver, cook, etc. The brass badges were 43mm tall, 35.4mm wide and besides the crossed rifles, had "sniper" emblazoned over the hammer and sickle that was common to other Excellent awards.

The British Army stared the war with a wool cloth sleeve patch with crossed rifles that was worn by both musketry instructors and those at Small Arms Schools, skill at arms competition winners (various forms with star/crown/wreath but not used in wartime),

4

and marksmen. From 1944, the crossed rifles was worn by musketry/weapons training instructors and marksmen. The sniper badge—the crossed rifles with an "S" between them—didn't come in until postwar (introduced November 10, 1945). Harry Furness received his in 1946 (see p. 34). Such insignia wouldn't have been worn in battle.

Late to the game in recognizing snipers, on August 20, 1944, the German sharpshooter badge was available in three grades: third class with no cord (20 kills), second class with silver cord (40 kills), and first class (60 kills) with gold cord. The kills were counted from September 1, 1944, and did not include close quarter combat kills (there was another award for that). Each kill had to be witnessed and recorded. Snipers who earned this award could wear it on their lower right sleeve and above any specialty insignia (e.g., *Gebirgsjäger Edelweiß* badge). This award system was further refined to include other intermediary and advanced awards:

10 kills Iron Cross, Second Class plus seven days' leave and mention in divisional orders.
30 kills Fourteen days' leave, mention in corps orders.
50 kills Iron Cross, First class, 20 days' leave and mention in army orders.
75 kills German Cross in Gold.

Wearing medals and badges

Snipers didn't advertise their profession on the battlefield. No photographic evidence has ever been found showing any German sniper wearing the *Scharfschützenabzeichen* in the field.[36] Russian orders and medals were usually worn only on parade uniforms. Russian medals were the property of the state not the recipient, and duplicates weren't issued if the originals were lost. At other times, the ribbons took their place, although in the field even these were dispensed with. The same is true of the other belligerents.

5

5. German award for snipers. Trimmed in gold, this is the first class award for 60 kills. The second class was trimmed in silver and awarded for 40 kills. The third class had no trim and was awarded for 20 kills. Created on August 20, 1944, the kills had to be witnessed and reported to the unit. Smart snipers like Sepp Allerberger who did not want to be distinguished from the common *Landser* did not sew them on their uniform. *GF Collection.*

6. This postcard shot of Senior (or staff) sergeant A. I. Zhuravlev ("Courageous sniper, killed 50 'Fritzes'. Awarded the 'For courage' medal") shows him wearing his medal (over left pocket) and Excellent Sniper badge (over his right pocket). *Image courtesy The Blavatnik Archive Foundation.* (http://www.blavatnikarchive.org).

| 2 Selection

"The art of the hunter coupled with the wiles of the poacher and the skill of the target expert armed with the best aids that science can produce."[1]

Maj. Nevill A. D. Armstrong

Britain & the Commonwealth

"The sniper will be selected for his character, physique, intelligence and education," says *Notes on the Training of Snipers, Military Training Pamphlet No. 44* of October 2, 1940. "He must have good sight and hearing, must be self-confident and full of initiative. He must be able to move skilfully, making use of any sort of ground. He must not use his weapon except to achieve his object, and must have a quick eye for estimating distances. He must be continually on the watch for movement for any curious or unnatural objects, and be able to keep them under observation once seen."

Dunkirk may have saved many of its men, but the fall of France cost the British Army much of its heavy equipment and caused a rifle crisis only slightly eased by Lend-Lease. Most of the weapons provided by the Americans—mainly .30 Eddystone M1917s and '03 Springfields—went to the Home Guard and there was some news reporting that England was training its army to be sharpshooters.[2] While overall this was inaccurate, a letter from British MP Duncan Sandys to Winston Churchill dated August 8, 1940, mentions the mission of auxiliary units of the Home Guard as being:

> "small bodies of men especially selected and trained, whose role it will be to act offensively on the flanks and in the rear of enemy troops who may obtain a foothold in this country. Their action will particularly be directed against tanks and lorries in laager, ammunition dumps, small enemy posts and stragglers. Their activities will also include sniping."[3]

The Germans were very concerned that their invasion force could be harassed by snipers or *franc-tireurs* as experienced in Norway and issued a warning that the German Army was prepared "to impose sharply the international war usage [interpreted by the British as execution] of non-uniformed Britons shooting at German forces."[4] In response, King George VI appointed himself as "Head Sniper" to which the German replied disparagingly in *Nachtausgabe*: "This is the first time

in the history of civilized mankind that any head of a state has associated himself with a gang whose avowed purpose is insidious murder—the murder of German soldiers."[5] While Home Guard snipers were largely fictional due to the initial shortage of small arms, specifically rifles, with which the Home Guard could be equipped, it demonstrates the effectiveness of British propaganda against the Germans.

By 1942, the RAF's denial of air superiority to the Luftwaffe over England's skies meant that the threat of invasion had passed. The British Army was granted a breather to rebuild and reorganize and formalize its sniping establishment. During this period, a sniper establishment of eight snipers per battalion was approved. Similarly, the Royal Marines started its sniper school in November 1942 and it was headed by a "67-year-old man who conducted the Canadian Sniper School in the last war." This was Maj. Nevill Alex Drummond Armstrong who was born in 1874, was a sniper instructor during World War I and author of *Fieldcraft, Sniping and Intelligence*.[6] Since most of the fighting had now shifted to the Mediterranean and in particular North Africa, sniper training was initiated by the Middle East Weapons Training School at Bir Salem near Jaffa in Palestine. Another was possibly at Helwan or Alexandria, Egypt[7] as a November 5, 1940, newspaper article reported.[8] It is said to have included a ten-week long curriculum where snipers were taught marksmanship, fieldcraft, stalking, patience, target selection including artillery spotters, leaders, and people (crew served weapons, communications) and especially enemy snipers. Other skills taught there included map reading, unarmed combat, mines and booby traps, and artillery spotting.[9] Finally, a little sniping was taught at the mountain warfare school in Lebanon. All these schools anticipated the need for snipers in the liberation of Europe.

Llanberis in North Wales operated a school from September 1943 to March 1944. There was another school at Amberley, England, and it is known that in December 1942 the Canadian snipers of the Stormont, Dundas and Glengarry Highlanders (3rd Canadian

Fieldcraft, Sniping and Intelligence

This is the classic early war appreciation of sniping by Maj. Nevill A. D. Armstrong, a Canadian officer who served on the Western Front in World War I, becoming the Commandant of the Canadian Corps School of Sniping 1917–18. At the start of World War II, he became an instructor in the Sniping Wing of the SA&MGS at Hythe and Bisley before taking over as commandant of the RM Sniping School at Browndown, and being promoted to lieutenant colonel. While its overtones are of the Great War, it was an important document that covered all aspects of sniping, fieldcraft, and intelligence and was used by the British Army and Home Guard. His views on sniper selection:

"In order to be of any benefit to a battalion and to warrant the special and careful training given to them, men to act as specialists should be carefully selected by their officers or N.C.Os., and in no case should they be detailed (by numbers, so to speak) to attend a specialist course, or any other course for that matter.

"Men must be highly trained to become expert observers, and no time should be wasted in an effort to train illiterate or unsuitable men.

"The Adjutant of every battalion should apply for a syllabus of the training being carried on at all important schools where men of his battalion may be sent. This applies in a marked degree to specialist schools.

"Company Commanders dislike parting with really good and efficient men even temporarily, and in the past have detailed men to attend schools because they may be undisciplined and a general nuisance to the company, have bad eyesight, be deaf or lazy, and for many other causes. This practice is unfair to the men and to those detailed to train them, and the battalion which repeatedly sends a poor type of man to important schools very quickly earns a bad name for itself, as men of other units are apt to judge the discipline and smartness of the whole battalion from the character of the man it sends to schools. And the judgement has generally proved to be correct."

"Important Qualifications

1. Good eyesight—if possible, quick sight; some men are born with this, others acquire it. In any event, observers, scouts and snipers must try to develop this quality. The eyes should always be restless when in the field. Try to develop animal sight, or from flank to flank.
2. Should not be colour blind or deaf.
3. Should be keen and intelligent.
4. Persistent, patient and plucky.
5. It is doubtful if men of an excitable nature will make good observers; probably give their position away very soon.
6. Must be truthful.

"Generally, try to select men who have led an out-of-door life, preferably in the woods, such as—Game hunters, Trappers, Prospectors, Surveyors, Lumberjacks, Poachers, etc."[10]

Fieldcraft, Sniping and Intelligence was Maj. Nevill Armstrong's classic 1942 treatise. *GF Collection.*

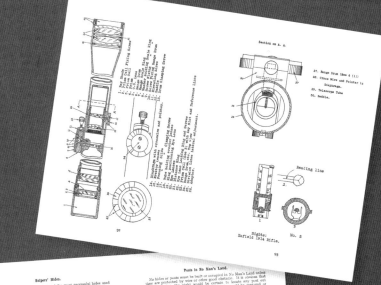

Harry Furness' tips

- "Concentrate on the reticle not on the target."[11]
- "The heavier your rifle barrel the more solid you can hold (especially in a cross wind). A heavy rifle barrel is more tiring to carry, but when you are tired you will shoot a heavy gun better than a light gun because your barrel will not wave in the breeze."[12]
- "When forward of your own troops, never be tempted to make use of a captured enemy sniper rifle. Each make of weapon has its own distinctive sound bite, and friendly troops behind you hearing an enemy rifle out front are likely to bring heavy fire onto your position."[13]
- "The Sniper who takes a great load of ammunition with him won't return. He will shoot too much and they will get him."[14]
- "Few snipers keep their gun books accurately. If a Sniper's gun book records two thousand rounds fired, recognize that the actual number is probably four thousand. Keep that in mind when you hear reports of 7.62 barrels being shot out in 2,000 rounds or less."[15]

With his knack for shooting, Sgt. Furness was invited to become a sniper and attended numerous schools prior to engaging in combat. He became Britain's most successful wartime sniper. Below is his postwar sniper badge. *Images courtesy AFPU (above) and Harry Furness (below).*

Division) attended it. After D-Day, the 21st Army Group established a sniping school near Courcelles, Belgium. It became operational in August 1944 and later moved to Zon.[16] From a newspaper article we learn that the 3rd (British) Infantry Division's sniper school was led by Lt. Jim Fetterly, late of the Royal Winnipeg Rifles and on loan to the East Yorkshire Regt. Lt. Fetterly remarked:

> "A few of the men were getting a bit fed-up because since D+10 days, they hadn't fired a shot at the Germans so we started this school of sniping in order to get a crack at the enemy. The course of instruction lasts for a week and includes instruction, not only in sniping but in fieldcraft."

Fetterly was no stranger to sports and had been shooting since he had reached the lofty height of four feet tall. He added, "You've got to be pretty wise to move about in the open to deal with the German snipers. Set a sniper to catch a sniper."[17]

We are fortunate to know the training history of one British sniper, Harry Furness. One advantage that helped Furness through his training was his prewar background as a stage hand (theater technician) where he helped build sets and scenery. This taught him the importance of shape and shadows. As a volunteer in the Manchester Army Cadets, he learned to shoot a P14 (an American-produced version of the Enfield rifle in .303 caliber and outwardly similar to the American M1917) before joining the army at age 17. As an excellent shot, Harry Furness enlisted in the 6th Green Howards and was asked to volunteer for sniper training. There was incentive in the form of an extra sixpence daily. His initial training was an eight-day course taught at the Bisley Sniper Wing. This was followed by a two-week intensive course at Llanberis in north Wales under Maj. O. Underhill. Underhill previously served in World War I as a sniper instructor under the tutelage of Maj. Hesketh Vernon Hesketh-Prichard. Later, Furness attended an extreme long-range sniping course at Hythe. One part of the course was adapted from an anti-tank training technique. Basically, it was shooting at a tow-tugged target at a thousand yards' distance.[18]

Not every soldier who initially attended the sniper training represented the cream of the crop like Furness. On the contrary, some officers sent their worst and most undesirable men; if nothing else to be rid of them—if only for a few days! They were quickly identified and universally RTU'd (returned to unit).[19] Rifleman Alex Bowlby and his mate Dick Saddler were summoned by their major, Dunkerly, and asked if they would like to be company snipers (D Coy., 3rd Battalion, Rifle Brigade). Both accepted even though Bowlby noted that his observation skills were not on a par with Saddler's. On one patrol, Saddler had spotted a camouflaged German working on a camouflaged wire. Despite his best effort, Bowlby failed to see him. Saddler was eventually given some stalking exercises but it does not appear that he attended a formal school, nor was he issued a No. 4 Mk. I (T) sniper rifle.[20] Indeed, later when a German who was taking pot-shots at their positions was located, a platoon was sent out to flank him.[21]

One man who attended and took sniping seriously was Cpl. Arthur Hare. Born in 1910 in the Cambridgeshire village of Steeple Morden, Hare hunted birds with a slingshot and later, after having saved the money, a Daisy BB gun, and finally with a

Early war image showing Canadian sniper training with WW I Ross rifle equipped with Warner & Swazey prismatic scope—a type withdrawn from service in 1944. Note that the rifle isn't cocked. *Library and Archives of Canada (hereafter LAC).*

double-barreled shotgun that had only one hammer. He enlisted into the army in 1932 and remained for seven years serving in India before returning to the United Kingdom. His hunting experience paid off in India when in 1934 he won the battalion shooting match and the pool for being the best shot in his battalion. He was discharged for only four weeks before being recalled in 1939. Hare fought in Greece, Crete, Palestine, Burma, and finally North Africa where he fought at Tobruk as a machine gunner. He didn't become a sniper until after the Normandy landings.[22]

Hare's sniper section was, according to the British practice, a battalion asset and the men answered only to the colonel commanding. Administratively, the regimental sergeant major had some say, but was relatively powerless to do anything to them. Other men in the section included 33-year-old Pte. William Packham of Bognor Regis, a town in West Sussex, LCpl. Smith, Pte. Brook, and three other men.

The Canadian Army taught its men rudimentary camouflage and sniper training after the British model. Under the instruction of Capt. D. B. Buell of the Royal Canadian Regiment, numerous units were taught camouflage techniques. Buell also visited the British scouting and sniping schools.[23] In Britain, Lt. Al Stewart of Toronto headed a sniping school that trained students from the Ontario Regiment.[24] In 1942 Farley Mowat, a subaltern, found himself commanding the Hastings and Prince Edward Regiment's (aka the "Hasty Ps") 20-strong scout and sniper section because of his inexperience and youthful peach-fuzz appearance. Quite frankly, it was

felt he could do less harm there than by commanding an infantry platoon. Mowat was never trained for intelligence work and was later given an infantry platoon.[25] By 1944 the British practice of raising dedicated scout platoons and attaching it to HQ company was universally adopted.[26]

Lt. A. Stewart was head of a sniping school in Britain where he instructed students from an Ontario regiment. *Author's collection.*

As in other armies, officers were loath to part with good men and it was not unknown for them to send the least good soldiers for sniper training.[27] Selection initially favored experienced hunters but it was found that city dwellers could also be trained. Remorse, reluctance, and sympathy were driven out of the men during their training. It was a job that needed to be done. Regardless of their background, they had to be marksmen endowed with a fighting spirit like that exhibited by "Hasty Ps" sniper Pte. "Slim" Sanford. Sanford was among the trapped men being decimated near San Maria di Scacciano. When a German officer entreated, "Surrender you English gentlemen—you are surrounded and will only die," Sanford's response was neither heroically memorable like the laconic Leonidas at Thermopylae nor crude like the Imperial Guard at Waterloo. It was pure Canadian backwoods defiance on all points. "We ain't English. We ain't gentlemen—and Goddamned if we'll surrender!"[28]

United States

In America, there had been little consideration given to sniper selection in the early 1940s, but by 1944 a U.S. Army publication recommended:

> "When selecting men to be trained as snipers, special care must be taken to obtain individuals capable of acting on their own. This means steady nerves, physical strength and agility, patience and judgment. Above all they must possess good eyesight and be natural marksmen."[29]

It is apparent that the army had recognized by then that the key to sniper effectiveness was personnel selection. Naturally, this began by selecting men who were already excellent shots. Second, the candidate or aspirant must have the fieldcraft or be able to be trained in fieldcraft. With respects to the former, Native Americans with some traditional upbringing enjoyed a huge advantage.[30] *FM21–75* of 1944 said:

> "Within each platoon, several men will be given sniper training. These men will be selected from among the most proficient marksmen in the unit and will be given training in scouting and camouflage and in the use of the sniper's rifle."[31]

With the inconsistencies in U.S. Army doctrine, it should not come as any surprise that the distribution of sniper rifles was equally inconsistent. When the Army Specialized Training Program was closed down, former civil engineering student Earle Slyder found himself as an infantryman who had to choose between carrying a BAR or a sniper rifle. "I looked at that 25-pound BAR and looked at the eight-round sniper rifle and I volunteered for sniper training."[32] Similarly Thor Ronningen was selected to attend sniper school. "There wasn't any particular reason I was selected. It seems they only chose two or three men from the company to attend the course."[33]

Easily the most unusual soldier to possess a M1903A4 sniper rifle was 384th Artillery Battalion (155mm howitzers) artilleryman Jim Kendall. Their guns being long range, the artillerymen should never have to resort to using small arms to defend themselves, but as with other artillerymen in his battery, Kendall wanted something to protect himself with. Kendall found his and carried it until a lieutenant ordered everyone to surrender unauthorized weapons.[34] One did not have to be a trained sniper to be issued a sniper rifle and one could be a trained sniper but not be issued a sniper rifle. Pvt. Ted Gunny of the 99th Infantry Division was issued the sniper rifle because he had shot expert at boot camp. Expert rifleman Pvt. Charles Davis, Co. L, 415th Regiment, 104th Infantry Division (the Timberwolves), became a sniper after he saw a scoped Springfield rifle (M1903A4 with a Weaver scope) and asked for it. He did not have experience with scoped rifles, not much opportunity to sight it in properly, and most significantly, received no training.[35] Without any sniper training, Pvt. John Bistrica of Co. C, 16th Infantry Regiment, 1st Infantry Division remembered momentarily having a sniper rifle: "A lieutenant, who was a 90-day wonder, called me to his CP, gave me a sniper's rifle, told me to find a tree and start picking off Germans." Luckily his captain intervened. "Bistrica, where are you going with that weapon?" I told him. Briggs said, "Give me that rifle and go back to the lieutenant and get your M-l and tell him I want to see him."[36]

When the previous sniper was promoted, Fifth (U.S.) Army Pfc. Richard E. Tucker who had served as the spotter received the rifle. He told the reporter:

> "I wasn't always a sniper, Sir, I was a sniper's observer. Then my sniper became a noncom. You can't be a sniper and a noncom, so I got his rifle. I've been sniping for four months now and it's the best job in the army. You're sort of on your own."

Pfc. Tucker is correct in that NCOs were generally not allowed to be snipers. They were supposed to be leaders and serving as snipers meant they weren't performing their duties as small unit leaders. There were exceptions and this doctrine was not rigidly enforced. NCOs could and did carry sniper rifles. When Sgt. Arthur Duebner arrived as a replacement in the 82d Airborne, weapons were scarce and the only available was an M1903A4. Sgt. Joe Curtis, 84th Infantry Division, carried both the radio and the M1903A4 sniper rifle.[37] Sgt. William E. Jones, Co. I, 8th Infantry Regiment, was the best shot in his company and was entrusted to be their sniper and given the M1903A4. Having shot expert at boot camp, when Sgt. Daniel Inouye joined the 442d in Italy, his captain liked him and observed that he had no bad habits, and issued him the sniper rifle.[38] After capturing Hill 192 on the road to Saint-Lô, 2Lt. Tom Quigley's 2d Platoon (E Co, 2d Battalion, 43d Infantry Regiment, 2d Infantry Division) saw Germans at 1,000yd distance. Seizing the opportunity, he ordered a sniper rifle from storage and entrusted it to a career army man, 1st Sgt. Clarence L. Umberger. He then instructed Sgt. Umberger that he would spot while Umberger shot. Per Lt. Quigley, "He knocked down nine Germans going across that road."[39] Umberger was no sniper but being a regular in the prewar army, was very well schooled in rifle marksmanship.

Platoon Sgt. Robert K. Palassou of Co. L, 363d Infantry Regiment, 91st Infantry Division had his sniper rifle taken from him when he was transferred out of the platoon. His lieutenant announced, "I want to change some assignments in the platoon. I want the best man possible as the platoon first scout." He then designated Palassou and ordered him to surrender the sniper rifle lest it should be captured and to arm himself with a M1 Thompson instead.

"I knew for sure he wanted me eliminated because I had embarrassed him earlier in the patrol action. He told me I was to carry a Thompson and wanted to take away my sniper rifle. I got off my helmet, jacked a shell out of the rifle and said, 'Lieutenant, if you want this rifle take it.'"

Palassou was ordered to report to the captain, who transferred him out of the platoon (for the safety of the lieutenant) and Palassou exchanged his sniper rifle for a M1.[40]

Similarly when Pfc. Edward J. Foley, Co. G, 143d Infantry Regiment, 36th Infantry Division, decided the chances for his survival as a sniper would be short as it attracted too much fire against him, he exchanged his sniper rifle for an M1 Garand. Additionally, he discarded the helmet camouflage to appear like any other infantryman in his platoon. Another trained sniper who exchanged his sniper rifle for the M1 was Thor Ronningen who, after his first battle, disliked its slow rate of fire.[41] It appears that one could not be compelled to use a sniper rifle in the U.S. Army.

There were cases where sniper rifles were placed in the right hands like the one entrusted to Pfc. James McGill of the 34th Infantry Division in Italy. At Monte Cassino with one shot he eliminated a German machine gunner who was pinning down his platoon.[42] Sgt. Elbert L. Day of Salt Lake City served as a sniper with the 143d Infantry Regiment, 36th Infantry Division until January 1945 when he was shot in the forehead in the fighting around Weyersheim, France. Left for dead, he miraculously survived and after several surgeries, recovered and had to relearn to walk and talk again.[43] Another expert shot who was given an M1903A4 sniper rifle was Pvt. Herb Sheaner of the 106th Infantry Division. His captain, Keilmeyer,

Sgt. Inouye in Italy. Daniel Inouye went on to serve as Senator for Hawaii from 1963 until his death in 2012. *Image courtesy Daniel K. Inouye Institute.*

Pfc. Edward J. Foley, Co. G, 143d Infantry Regiment, 36th Infantry Division, is seen cleaning his sniper rifle near Velletri, Lazio, Italy on May 29, 1944. Snipers in all armies were instructed to keep their rifle meticulously clean. Foley realized that sniping brought too much return fire upon him and swapped his rifle for a regular M1 Garand. He also discarded the helmet camouflage cover so as not to distinguish himself from his fellow soldiers. *U.S. Army.*

selected Sheaner as the company runner and sniper because he was the best shot available.

"I was the only sniper in company 'G', 422d Regt., 106th Infantry Division … As far as I know the Company Commander appointed me as sniper because I attained the score 'expert' rifleman on the rifle range the summer when so many other privates were shipped out as replacements. I too would have been a replacement if not for my scoring expert on the rifle range. One other company 'G' man had a higher score than me and he was a sergeant squad leader and was not eligible or selected to be the company sniper."[44]

Prior to boot camp, Pvt. Max Gendelman had never fired a gun his life but this didn't prevent him from qualifying expert. While his unit was in England preparing for the invasion of Normandy, he was pulled aside by an officer. Gendelman wrote:

"I wondered now what had I done. He introduced himself, ordered me at ease, and said my name had been given to him as being a good candidate for further training as a sniper. The training course was six weeks long and given there in England. Since I had a Marksman Medal for being an expert in marksmanship, I was considered a good candidate.

"I asked, 'Even if our unit is called for D-Day, does that mean I would still finish the course?' 'Absolutely,' he said. 'We have a great need for snipers.'

"I thought this would allow me to miss D-Day, and who knows, maybe the war would be over by then. With that in mind, and with the prospect of enjoying some extra time in London, I said,

Right: A happy Max Gendelman poses for the camera after returning to the United States. While a PoW, Gendelman was befriended by a Luftwaffe lieutenant. Along with the German lieutenant, he and another GI escaped to American lines. The lieutenant told any sentry that he was escorting the PoWs. Once they reached American lines, it became Gendelman and the other GI's responsibility to get their German escort into captivity safely. Elements of his uniform are obviously missing in this Signal Corps photo. *Nina Endelman.*

'Sir, count me in. I'll be glad to be trained as a sniper.'"[45]

After completing his training, Gendelman was posted to the 394th Infantry Regiment, 99th Division.

While the 82d Airborne's Sgt. Dubner was issued a sniper rifle, 101st Airborne's Darrell "Shifty" Powers of the famous Co. E "Band of Brothers" never saw one:

"I never used a scope. None of us did. I wouldn't say we even had a real sniper in our outfit. McClung, Sergeant Taylor, and me were about the three best shots in the company, but we always just aimed our rifles at whatever we needed to, then hit what we needed to hit."[46]

Powers served in 2/506th PIR and was unaware that first scout Robert J. Emary of Co. I, 3/506th PIR, was armed with a M1903A4 sniper rifle and even jumped into Holland with it.[47] The 551st PIB was also issued sniper rifles and Sgt. Douglas Dillard used one while attached to the Seventh Army.[48] It may have been an officers' prerogative that allowed Lt. James Megellas of Co. H, 3/504th PIR to jump into Holland with not only his M1 Thompson SMG but also with a sniper rifle. Weighing 180lb, he was carrying two-thirds of his own body weight or 120lb gear when he jumped! Having survived Market Garden and the Battle of the Bulge, Lt. Magellas was still using a sniper rifle when he was fighting in Germany too.[49]

Soviet Union

Noted Soviet sniper, Senior Guard Lt. Vladmir Pchelintsev felt that neither hunters nor top-shot athletes made successful snipers. They had shooting skills that were the foundation necessary for a candidate to become a sniper.[50] A successful sniper must be able to stalk his prey, have patience, keen eyesight, and endurance and be able to outthink his opponent. On the Sevastopol (then Sebastopol) front, Sgt. Lyudmila Pavlichenko was instructed to train snipers. She was given ten candidates for five days. She immediately began weeding out those who were overconfident, temperamental, or impatient. She also kicked out anyone who could not take orders from a woman. Pavilchenko's experience and ability to outshoot her students gave her credibility as an instructor and as there was a war to be won, she did not suffer fools gladly.[51] Ideally, snipers were drawn from among hunters, competitive shooters, new recruits who were excellent shots, and from volunteers thought to be qualified or trainable. Sometimes an officer would take note of a soldier's marksmanship and recommend he become a sniper.[52]

Being literate, Muscovite Jr. Lt. Alexander Mikhailovich Gak attended the M.V. Frunze Military Academy after enlisting. Prewar he belonged to the Karl Liebknecht Pedagogical Institute's history department and in his non-working hours either edited their newspaper or perfected his shooting skill at the institute's firing range. After being trained, he joined the 38th Rifle Division's 115th Rifle Regiment. A few days after his 19th birthday (September 1), and because he had asked for it, the sergeant major gave him a new sniper rifle which Gak immediately cleaned and sighted in.[53]

Germany

On October 21, 1943, the Russians attacked the German 3d *Gebirgsjäger* Division's defenses at the Nikopol bridgehead. Most of the attacking Soviets were mowed down but two survived to jump into a trench where they were faced by six *Jäger* who had exhausted their ammunition. A classic trench fight ensued. The first Russian was cleaved with an entrenching tool but the surviving Russian parried or eluded the thrusts against him and slew one *Jäger* after another. Finally, the Russian was about to overpower the last surviving *Jäger* when he entered a sniper's crosshair. *Gefreiter* Josef "Sepp" Allerberger (note the German army did not use the British term "sniper" and instead used sharpshooter—*Scharfschütze*) fired, ending the contest. Of the incident, Allerberger recalled that the sniper should not only be an excellent shot, but have the self-discipline to wait for the moment that the shot may be taken. This was not a skill easily taught and Allerberger had not yet attended a sniper school.

Germany's reliance on quick and modernized warfare (dubbed *Blitzkrieg* by the Western media) meant sniping did not immediately have a role in German war plans. While the Allied *Intelligence Bulletin* frequently covered Japanese snipers and sniping tactics, nothing is mentioned about the Germans in the early war years because sniping was not widespread among the German Army and there was no formal German training program to support it. The first notice by Western Allies was in the July 15, 1943 *Tactical And Technical Trends* published by the American War Department's Military Intelligence Service. Besides including excerpts that could have been lifted directly from the German manual, there was a comment, "This is evidence of increased German interest in sniping on a large scale. It is known that the Germans have been much impressed by the Russian sniping methods." It was prophetic in stating that a special sniper badge was considered.[54] The bulletin was released two months after the first German sniper manual issued by the

The Zf41 long eye-relief scope mounted on a Kar98k didn't produce a quality sniper rifle but was designed to assist marksmen. However, it saw major use during the war, made by three main manufacturers: Berliner-Lübecker and two Mauserwerke at Borsigwalde and Oberndorf. *Bundesarchiv Bild 101I-455-0013-15.*

Oberkommando des Heeres (Army High Command) on May 15, 1943.

The manual covered selection of personnel:

"Only the best shooters are to be used for sniper training. The telescopic rifle belongs in their hands regardless of their rank. A high degree of hunter-like behavior, patience, perseverance and cunning are required of the sniper. Cold-blooded consideration, skilful use of the terrain and all camouflage possibilities as well as excellent powers of observation must distinguish him both in stalking the enemy position as well as in attacking the enemy.

"The will to get the enemy in his sights under all circumstances, to hit and destroy him, must be particularly strong in the sniper.

"Being a sniper is an honor."[55]

Earlier in the war *Obergefreiter* W. Rohde was a machine gunner in the 228th *Jäger* Regiment, 101st *Jäger* Division. He fought in the Caucasus and on the Taman Peninsula, and was wounded by a shell fragment in February 1944. Hospitalized, after a partial recovery (he lacked full use of his hand), he was placed on light duty but grew bored and volunteered for sniping school.

"In the summer of 1944, a sniper training session was held, for which I volunteered. For me it was a welcome change from the boring service in the garrison. The roughly 25 participants were mostly members of the recovery company plus a few recruits who had shown especially good shooting achievement. We [each] received a new Carbine 98k and Telescopic Sight 41."

"Every day was divided between theoretical instruction, in which we were taught special features of sniping, and practice on the shooting range or the nearby troop training center. Great emphasis was placed on range estimation— otherwise one did not hit anything. It soon transpired that only half of the soldiers had the prerequisites for the course. Some shot too badly (perhaps even on purpose), the others proved to be too stupid for the theory or made themselves too obvious in the field.

"My shooting performance was again very good. The concentrated aiming pleased me, and I also felt very good in the field. We were also shown an instructional film.

"After two weeks the course ended and we were issued training certificates for our pay books. They stated that one had taken part in a sniper course and with what success. In my case, great success. Then I had to go to the troop doctor, who certified me as capable of war service again. Thus I was 'k.v.' [*kriegsverwendungsfähig*— fit for war service] and, with most of the others and other replacements, could go back to the front."[56]

In spite of being warned by their sergeant against serving as sharpshooters because "when the Russians attack, the sharpshooters are the first ones they go after because the sharpshooters keep killing their commissars," 7th Panzer Division *Pionier* (combat engineer) Helmut Jung and his friend Hans Meier—

along with 36 other men from the division—were accepted as volunteers. They received their training at a camp in either Poland or the Ukraine.

When he joined the 144th *Gebirgsjäger* Regiment, Sepp Allerberger was initially a machine gunner. Wounded by a splinter in the left hand, he was sent to the rear for medical attention and spent two weeks recuperating. As an apprentice carpenter, he was assigned to the regimental armorer and began repairing damaged Mauser stocks. Among the stockpile of weapons Allerberger found a Mosin 91/30 sniper rifle. The armorer let him practice with it and he soon became proficient. Impressed by Allerberger's shooting skills, the regimental armorer told him to take it with him.

Rejoining his company, his company commander issued him a pair of 8x binoculars and instructed, "Whatever else you do, remember to keep your arse down, particularly as a sniper. Now fall out and get Ivan annoyed." In his first trip to the line, his comrades complained that they were subjected to fire from an unseen sniper. How Allerberger killed him will be covered later.

Photographic evidence supports the fact that the Luftwaffe's *Fallschirmjäger* acquired sniper rifles in time for Operation Mercury (*Merkur*), the invasion of Crete. Perhaps experience from the capture of Belgium's Fort Eben Emael raised an awareness that snipers were useful if for nothing else than to eliminate pillbox defenders.

It is unknown how the Luftwaffe selected sniper candidates from among its *Fallschirmjäger*. *Oberjäger* Paul was selected in March 1944 by his commanding officer, *Leutnant* Winterstein of the IV/ *Fallschirmjäger Aufklärungs-Abteilung* 12 on the condition that he either attend *Oberjäger* school or sharpshooter school. Paul wrote:

"I choose the second possibility. So off I went to land combat school … After advanced instruction in sharpshooting, I became an *Oberjäger* then started training sharpshooters in *Fallschirm-Aufklärungs-Abteilung* 12 [Airborne Reconnaissance Unit 12]. We received new weapons fitted with sights. We trained at night and during the day and the terrain in Champagne was ideal for training with its hedges, trees and hills."

It was very likely that during the course of his instruction Paul was shown the Luftwaffe prepared training film on sniping.[57] The reader should be cautioned that this singular example cannot be indicative of the practice by the Luftwaffe.

Finland

During the Winter War (1939–40), the Finnish Army relied on marksmen, outdoorsmen, and target shooters who were already in uniform to serve as snipers and to counter-snipe Soviet snipers. The huge successes of the Finnish snipers—such as Suko Kolkka and Simo Häyhä—made the Soviets rethink their sniper tactics. They would teach their snipers to be more aware of camouflage and fieldcraft, and to be more self-reliant. Under the mostly static trench warfare that characterized the later Continuation War (1941–44) the Finns were outclassed by the Soviet snipers. Initial Finnish responses were defensive in nature including: careful movement and use of cover, camouflage, deeper trenches with overhead struts that compelled men to stoop, snow suits, warning signs in trenches, and for officers not to be distinguished from their men, and better use of artillery against snipers. Finnish snipers, if available and not training or practicing, were not to be used for other duties.[58]

Side-mounted PEM-scoped M/91-30 rifle in the hands of a Finnish marksman. Even with captured weapons the Finns had insufficient rifles to arm all their snipers. *Finnish Armed Forces Photograph (hereafter SA-kuva).*

In October 1942 the Finnish Army ordered that each squad designate a soldier as its squad sniper. Purely administrative, neither training nor equipment accompanied the order. Finland lacked both optically equipped rifles and a training program to develop snipers. In the winter of 1942–43, training was given on a regimental level on an un-standardized basis and varied from a mere two days to two weeks. Tardily, in September 1943 Finland issued its first sniper training manual, which consisted of instructions on how to adjust eye relief on a scope, how to use the sights and make adjustments for varying distances, distance estimation, and leading a walking and running target. Thirty pages long, 18 of them were a translation of Soviet notes issued to its snipers in Finland.[59] Later, on October 27, 1943, orders went out for all battalions to form nine-man sniper teams. The initial qualification was that the candidate had to place all ten bullets into the target (size not specified) at 300m (330yd). Those selected could then attend a sniper school.

The biggest problem was not the shortage of qualified men but of equipment. Small numbers of scopes were obtained from Germany and Sweden, but the Soviet Union was also a supplier, with captured weapons being turned against its former users. The captured weapons were highly prized and were not necessarily turned over to the regiment for distribution to trained snipers.[60]

Japan

Japanese jungle-fighting tactics including tree platforms for snipers, two-man foxholes, and infiltration—learned, according to one article, from studying the Burmese War of 1824. Lengthy study of that war prepared them for the jungle warfare they were to wage throughout the Pacific.[61] Depending on the terrain, the Japanese were known to dig tunnels leading to fighting holes, hospitals, and living quarters.[62]

Sniper selection was merit-based and made by the platoon leader who generally picked the best marksman from among them: 80 percent of those selected were a superior private, the equivalent to an American corporal. Being selected was not considered a special honor but as just another aspect of training. Believing that short men had an easier time concealing themselves and were smaller targets, the Japanese preferred short men over tall men. Candidates were not disqualified from becoming a sniper if they wore glasses.[63]

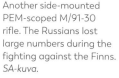

Another side-mounted PEM-scoped M/91-30 rifle. The Russians lost large numbers during the fighting against the Finns. *SA-kuva.*

3 Training

"We study *Man Tracking* so that we will know what someone following us will be looking for. *Man Tracking* knowledge will help us to stay undiscovered and assist us in getting away. Being able to track an enemy could be valuable but is secondary to our own safety."[1]

Sgt. Harry Furness

UK & the Commonwealth

The first British sniping manual, *Notes on the Training of Snipers, Military Training Pamphlet No. 44* of October 2, 1940, had its roots in the British World War I experience and many surviving sniping instructors from that period would resume their former roles.

"Most of the World War I veterans were still alive and much of their knowledge could be salvaged. We were fortunate that many soldiers who had served as trench Snipers in the first World War were still not old and provided a cadre of instructors for our training centers. Their experience was especially important to the re-establishment of our Sniper Schools."[2]

The manual summed up the sniper's role pithily: "The primary object of a sniper is *to kill*"[3] and "The sniper's first task is to assist in gaining moral ascendancy by killing any enemy who exposes himself."[4] While it did not anticipate *Blitzkrieg*, it did suggest: "Snipers may be usefully employed to deny enemy tank reconnaissance by ensuring that any attempt on the part of the tank crews to open up will be immediately dealt with."[5]

The update provided by *ATM* No. 43 in May 1942 said about training:

"Emphasis must be laid on the value in mobile warfare of snipers who are highly skilled in fieldcraft, camouflage, and marksmanship. Normally, company snipers will work in pairs, and should be given latitude to move wherever they wish on the axis of advance. They should be trained to deploy and get into action automatically and rapidly the moment contact is gained. Any information they obtain will be handed to the nearest troops for re-transmission. Their main task will be to locate and kill enemy commanders, reconnaissance parties, and snipers. By intelligent fieldcraft they should never have to shoot at a range of more than 300 to 400 yards, and it should be a point of honour never to miss once they have

pressed the trigger. In certain circumstances, the snipers of reserve companies may work in conjunction with those of forward companies.

"The section sniper must be trained to assist—often without orders—the advance of his section by locating and killing the enemy in any strongpoint that is holding up his section."[6]

The rapidity of *Blitzkrieg* and mobile warfare meant that much of the static warfare techniques of World War I were obsolete—although they would come into play when defences coagulated as they so often

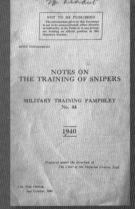

Notes on the Training of Snipers

"1. This pamphlet is intended as a guide to all commanders in the training and employment of snipers. It indicates the scope of the instruction in sniping, observing and fieldcraft given at the Small Arms School Sniper Wing. It is not intended, however, to give the impression that sniping must be confined only to specially trained men with special weapons. It is the duty of every man to be skilled in the use of his rifle and in fieldcraft.

2. The object of all such training is to assist in securing and maintaining the initiative on the whole battlefront. To achieve this it is necessary:

    i. To anticipate enemy movement by observation properly related to intelligence.

    ii. To deny enemy intelligence by sniping his observers, harassing his patrols and forestalling his raids.

    iii. To establish a complete moral and physical domination of no man's land if static warfare develops.

3. The Small Arms School Sniper Wing trains officers and N.C.Os. to be regimental instructors, but there is only time to give an outline of what to teach and how to teach it and to lay down the general principles. Originality, inventiveness and adaptability are essential to success."[7]

Harry Furness sniper techniques

• "It happens at times that military units on active service, who are in the line against enemy forces, may find periods when hostile activities are quiet, and Officers and NCO's find they can move around in reasonable safety for they have the knowledge they are protected by their own Sniper Shield. Under these circumstances it is a gross error of misjudgment for a senior Officer to withdraw his Snipers to make them available along with the rest of his men for various duties and fatigues. Never at any time in line conditions should Snipers be relegated to other duties, it can only lead to disastrous consequences from enemy Snipers who would see their opportunity to move in for the kill. It is only the direct knowledge that the enemy will realize we will have Snipers deployed at all times that the threat to our battlefield leaders can be lessened. It is vital that this message is included in the training of all Officer Cadets."[8]

• "When you observe an enemy patrol that you intend to engage, forget the point man and leave the officer or NCO in command for your second shot. Kill the radioman first, otherwise he will call artillery in on your position.

• "First the radioman, second the officer, then move your position as quietly as possible. Maybe later you will get another shot at the leaderless patrol from your *pre-chosen* alternate position."[9]

Opposite: *FM5-15 (1940)* includes a section on sniper's posts which should be "located and used by specially detailed men ... within 400 yards of the enemy." Sniper post requirements are concealment from enemy observation, good view and field of fire, and—where possible—a loophole for rifleman and observer. This shows "a portable sniper's post which can be shifted readily from one location to another in a night." *U.S. Army.*

did on the Eastern Front, and in Normandy and the Netherlands in 1944–45. Dummies, to a limited extent, were still useful and Harry Furness observed:

"A useful technique that might trap an inexperienced Sniper was to place your decoys closer to your own lines than your hide. In that way an enemy might be induced to crawl too close because he was concentrating on the dummy. … A poor decoy is far worse than no decoy. Everyone seemed to realize that, and the quality of the decoys we received was of a high standard. Snipers are astute fighting men, and if they spotted a decoy they ignored it and were inclined to search diligently for the concealed Sniper they knew must be nearby."

In his battalion, Furness said they ignored using a "dead soldier" decoy lest some poor medic expose himself in rushing to give it medical assistance. For moving dummies, the snipers in Furness's battalion did not manipulate them but trained other soldiers to do it for them. The dummy operators "remained concealed and protected as they worked the dummies, and our Snipers were posted well away and prepared to instantly respond to any exposure the dummies initiated."[10] There are many stories about German and Russian use of dummies during the war.

While sniper techniques were updated to reflect motorized warfare during the war, it wasn't until 1944 when the War Office issued *Army Training Instruction No. 9: The Organization, Training, and Employment of Snipers* which provided uniformity within the UK ground forces. Sniper candidates should have perfect eyesight so they could locate concealed foes, patience, observation, good physique, confidence, initiative, intelligence, aptitude for fieldcraft, and be good shots.

To qualify for sniper school, they had to shoot 6 inches or better at 100yd. Once trained they had to be capable of making headshots at up to 350yd and body shots at 500yd with regularity. The manual recommended usage in pairs:

• Two snipers per company or eight per battalion (British battalions were four companies strong).

• So that they would be best used, the snipers should be under the command of an officer who had attended sniping school himself.

• Snipers to work in pairs so that one did the spotting and noted the bullet's impact. This also afforded protection for the sniper. Anticipating losses, a "learner" with prospects should be attached to each official sniper.

The manual's tactical recommendations were:

• When accompanying an advance guard, snipers should select positions that offered the ability to observe the enemy. If the enemy could not be detected, they should be able to stalk their way forward to engage them or give verbal instructions to the company commander. Alternatively, the manual suggested the use of tracers to designate a target.

• When supporting a tank attack, snipers were to locate and engage anti-tank gun crews. If possible, snipers were to infiltrate the enemy and either attack their flank or attack from their rear. Night attacks were a different matter and snipers were to be held in reserve.

• In the defense, the snipers' first task was to engage the enemy's snipers. Second, they were to engage at up to 800yd distance to harass the enemy. If the enemy were beyond their range, they were to work with forward observers to direct artillery onto the enemy. In defending a reverse slope, snipers were to provide a covering screen on the high ground. From it they could kill key enemy personnel and disorganize an attack.

• Should a unit be compelled to withdraw, snipers along with machine guns and mortars were to inflict injury disproportionate to their numbers. They were expected to shift their firing positions so as to mislead the enemy as to their strength.

• Wooded terrain presented its own problems with its limited viewing range. Trees were to be seldom used. However, by contrast, city or town fighting offered numerous opportunities and snipers were encouraged to take advantage of roofs, chimneys, windows, and piles of rubble.

• During periods of static warfare, snipers were encouraged to build several hides at night that would allow them to observe the enemy undetected. Hides offered certain comforts to the occupants so limited movement was allowed. Access to the hide should never be during daylight hours when the snipers could be observed. Loopholes were constructed like a castle's embrasure: narrow in the front and wide in the rear. This offered the greatest field of fire with the minimum of exposure. Dummy loopholes and other distractions were built to deceive the enemy as to the hide's location.[11]

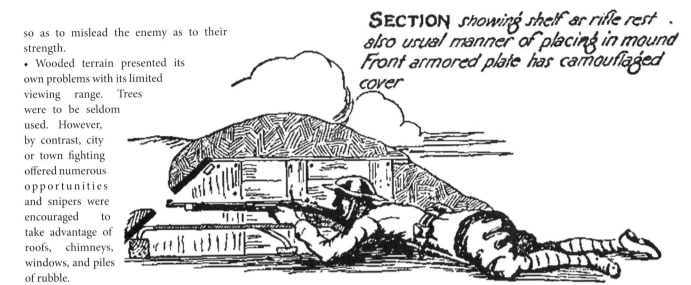

SECTION *showing shelf as rifle rest. also usual manner of placing in mound Front armored plate has camouflaged cover*

Besides shooting instructions and directions on adjusting the scope, the 1944 manual also had identification tips for German ranks and specialties. It was obviously Europe-oriented and did not contain the same for the Japanese Army or Naval Landing Forces.

Much of the sniper training, of course, was centered on the weapon—maintenance, sighting, the telescopic sights, and shooting. Describing the training at Perth Barracks—probably the Queen's Barracks in Perth, Scotland—Bill McMillan of 1st Battalion, Black Watch, remembered:

The sniper's duties

From *Job Analysis (Field): The Infantry* of April 1945.
"1. Choose concealed and usually elevated positions to dominate the chosen target e.g. crossroads, supply point, bridge or any special strategic enemy position. He will make frequent use of alternative positions, so that the enemy never knows where the next shot will come from. He will study the enemies' routine, and is provided with binoculars, watch and compass to help him do this.

"In certain types of country he may stick up 'dummies' to draw the enemy fire and so reveal their positions, so that he can 'pot' them from his own position away from the dummies.

"2. Snipe the enemy by intermittent bulls' eye shooting, so that no-man's-land is dominated and no German can move in the open without being shot. In a more active role such as street fighting he will take cover in houses or on roof tops, but in all cases practising the art of concealment.

"In the attack the sniper is *not* in the assaulting sections;

he kills in his own way, using his own methods, usually from the flanks.

"He must be very patient, have complete self-confidence and be alert, agile and quick to realise that any position he holds will soon get too hot for safety. His position may involuntarily be given away by a damp atmosphere which causes rifle-smoke to hang about and so betray the position. If the muzzle of the rifle is over a patch of sand or loose dry soil this may be disturbed by blast on firing and so betray the sniper's location. At all times, therefore, he is planning ahead for his next move. He must know how to use ground with both eyes and body. Men of 18–19 are usually found too keen and impatient—it is the 24–26 men who prove better at the job.

"In short he must be skilled at being a maximum nuisance to the enemy with the minimum exposure of himself.

"Snipers often work in pairs, but there is also great scope for the man who likes to be independent. There is no rigidity about dress or equipment. 'The poacher does not go on parade.'"

Rifle accuracy

The heart of a rifle's accuracy is the barrel, and careful selection of the barrel (or barreled action) is important in producing the sniper rifle. Even with a perfect bore, the crown must be concentric so that the gases are equal around the bullet's base as it exits the muzzle. Even if one has a good barrel, other factors affect the rifle's performance. For World War II rifles, wood stocks needed to be sealed against the weather. Humidity, moisture, and temperature can affect wood and can cause it to swell or bend. This changes the pressure on the gun parts and in particular the barrel. The harmonics are changed and this lack of consistency means the point of impact will vary. Resin-impregnated plywood stocks were more weather-resistant but plywood was used by the Germans as an expedient measure and not with accuracy in mind.

The wood especially affected the Tokarev SVT-40 and its effective range as a sniper weapon was only about 400m. Also working against the SVT-40 was the fact it was a semiautomatic. This meant more moving parts and looser tolerances to ensure that the weapon would work when dirty. Additionally, it is harder to keep a multitude of moving parts performing consistently than on a period bolt-action rifle. This means the harmonics of the barrel will vary as the bullet travels down the bore. The Germans learned the same lesson about semiautomatics with the Gewehr 43 and, especially, the FG42 *Fallschirmjägergewehr*. Neither could be made to shoot as accurately as the bolt-action K98k.

Ammunition is another factor. Sepp Allerberger was told to get accuracy-testing cartridges which were more accurate than standard ammunition. Similarly, American GIs found that the black-tipped armor-piercing 30-06 was superior to the normal M2 ball. It was up to the sniper to find which worked best in their rifle and then secure a supply.

"I shot five bullseyes on the target with .22 ammo, which at that time was good shooting. Much later I was taught about camouflage etc., even to see how near I could get to some sheep without being detected [stalking]. Later again with .303 ammo on the range, I scored a two-inch group from two hundred yards. The officer in charge pulled me back to three hundred yards and you may not believe me, but I got four shots on the bull, for my last shot I received a flag, which meant I missed the target completely. How I could have missed the target I thought, but on closer examination at the butts it was changed to five bulls and another two-inch group, two shots almost on the same mark. Much later with a stalker at hand we went shooting deer around the Domoch area with telescopic sights, you couldn't miss!"[12]

As we have seen, one of the British responses to the fall of France was the creation of the Local Defence Volunteers, who became the Home Guard. Initially short of weapons, American Lend-Lease equipment saw some 800,000 weapons being donated by American sportsmen. Training of the large numbers of volunteers was difficult. Marksmanship was practiced at Territorial Army ranges. Other skills were leaned at schools such as the one at at Osterley Park set up by Republican veteran of the Spanish Civil War, Tom Wintringham.

Britain was not unique in raising Home Guard units. Australia raised three battalions. Patterned after the British model with each headquarters company having a scout and sniper section, they took training seriously. The *Adelaide Advertiser* of July 26, 1941, promoted the mystique around sniping by its alluring description of bravery, observation powers, necessary marksmanship, camouflage, and instilling of fear. "Nothing is so demoralizing to an enemy to know a man is as good as dead …"[13]

The Scout-Sniper platoon of HQ Coy., 1st Battalion of the Home Guard met at Walkerville sandpits for instruction on the selection and construction of observation posts.[14] On the following week WO Cowles instructed the Second Battalion scout-snipers on long distance observation.[15] On May 16, Co. A, First Battalion Home Guard snipers were trained in fieldcraft in the Orange Golf Club.[16] The Second Battalion had instruction on a hide construction in June.[17] Around July 10, 1943 Cowles conducted a battalion sniper class for the Second Battalion.[18] This was followed up range practice at the Adelaide range.[19] Another follow-up range session class was held afterward on August 1.[20] Headquarters Company of the 3rd Battalion in Fremantle had Cowles instructing its sniper section on August 8, 1943, in camouflage and concealment.[21] The Australians even promoted shooting through its Volunteer Defence Corps and one newspaper announcement read: "Next Friday night at 1930 hours, sniper scouts will shoot on the miniature range. … Sniper scouts will carry out range practice, and for the remainder training will be as per syllabus."[22]

New Zealand Home Guard units receive some training in camouflage and marksmanship and were called sniper platoons or companies, with one company being controlled and equipped with .303 caliber rifles furnished by the Auckland Rifle Association.[23]

Some New Zealand army units that formed when war began became part of the 2NZEF that travelled to Britain to prepare to fight off the anticipated German invasion. One of these units was the 22nd (Wellington) Battalion, 2NZEF. It formed at Trentham Camp, Wellington in November 1939, with Lt. Col. Leslie Andrew (a World War I Victoria Cross winner) in charge. From the start the units had snipers, but their training would have to wait until they reached Britain.

Until then, marksmanship was an important part of the training. The War Diary details the mustering and training that took place before the long trip to England, where:

"On November 8, 1939 officers selected for the 22 (Wgtn) Bn reported to the District School of Instruction at Trentham. For one month officers carried out intensive training mainly as a refresher course …

"On December 9, 1939 the N.C.O.'s selected for the Bn. reported to the same school to undergo training …

"On January 12, 1940 the troops marched into Camp … a real effort was made to sort out specialists for H.Q. Coy. and Bn. H.Q.

"Trentham Camp 15. Jan A programme of training commenced today. The early training concentrated on elementary drill, musketry (rifle and L.M.G.), fieldcraft, anti-gas training, bayonet-training and P.T. Specialized training was to be postponed as far as possible until arrival overseas.

"Trentham Camp 5 Feb … Steady progress was being made with training, and more advanced work was proceeded with … Range practice was now a large part of each week's programme.

"Trentham Camp 8 Apr It was decided to zero all rifles and this was carried out in the course of normal range work."

Between May 2 and June 18 the battalion traveled to Britain, landing in Greenock, Scotland, before moving by train to Mytchett Camp in Surrey. The diary reported: "Mytchett 10 July More work on Pirbright Range – Bren and rifle. Also special work with Sniper Section."

Its responsibilities were "countering any action by enemy parachutists or other airborne troops" but after six months in Britain, between early January and early April 1941, the battalion was transported to Greece via Egypt. On April 16 they fought a major engagement with the advancing Germans, stopping them in their tracks at the Mount Olympus passes where the rifle training paid off: "All through the afternoon a D Company sniper, Barney Wicksteed, had prevented enemy pioneers from working on the smashed bridge in front of B Company."

Stranded in a static warfare mode in Italy in March 1944, Lt. Col. Ronald "Ronnie" Waterman, DSC, of the West Nova Scotia Regiment, 1st Canadian Division, Eighth (BR) Army, ordered Capt. Don Rice to select from each platoon men whom he believed were the most qualified as candidates for a scout-sniper platoon.

Smoking

When Medical Orderly LCpl. Marusya Mitrofanova asked Nikolaev to teach her how to snipe, he asked her if she smoked. When she admitted she did he told her that he would not take her unless she stopped. The last thing he wanted was for her to have the smoker's cough that would betray their presence.[24] German sniper Bruno Sutkus would not smoke and British sniper Harry Furness warned that smoking would kill a sniper.[25] British regulations prohibited smoking and snipers who smoked had to indulge very early in the morning before the smoke became visible. One German sniper's habit of smoking divulged his location to Cpl. Arthur Hare and Pvt. William Packham. However, they had to wait until the next day to shoot him.[26]

Capt. Rice selected 40 men who underwent two weeks of training some three miles away on the Arielli front opposite the Gustav Line. They were instructed on use of the telescope, map-reading, and interpreting aerial photos, compass, sketching, distance estimation, stalking, silent dispatch of sentries using the knife and camouflage, memory development, and on reporting their observations. Since cigarette or other smoke could betray their presence, they were also told not to smoke on duty. Of the 40 men, 23 qualified for the scout-sniper platoon. They were issued the No. 4 Mk. I (T) rifle, binoculars, and for reconnaissance work where firepower was needed, the M1A1 Thompson submachine gun. The men also acquired scissors telescopes (nicknamed "donkey ears"—artillery spotter scopes) from the Germans which they used for observation and for looking around corners.

The platoon was under the command of Capt. Rice who was responsible for scouting and patrolling for the regiment. Rice would plan their mission and send pairs or even three men who would depart in the darkness of the night, remain in the field all day, and return only when darkness returned. It was not uncommon for their missions to last 12 hours. Upon returning they were debriefed by Capt. Rice and the battalion intelligence officer for the intelligence they gathered. Capturing prisoners was not unknown, and one scout-sniper, Oren Foster, recalled, "Our job was to go into No Man's Land at night and capture prisoners for interrogation. A very risky business. Throughout the war fear was our constant companion." Fear heightened their senses and while it helped keep them alive, the strain must have been tremendous.[27] Oren Foster was legendary to the West Novas. He was awarded the British Empire Medal for saving four men in England in January 1942, the citation reading: "when an assault boat capsized in a swift tidal river, he, although unable to swim,

Training films

Toward the end of World War I some training films were produced, but it was World War II that saw extensive use of film by the military. Some of these were simply propaganda movies, such as the First Motion Picture Unit's *Winning Your Wings* (starring Lt. James Stewart) or the many American films produced by the Office of War Information, many with Disney animations. However, others were specifically designed for training purposes

Sniping may not have been shown as often as some subjects, but it was certainly covered. *Kill or Be Killed*, for example, was a 1942 training/ propaganda film directed by Leonard Lye for the British Ministry of Information. In it, a British sergeant duels with a German sniper before using the latter's corpse to tempt a German patrol into his kill zone. Emphasizing natural camouflage, patience, and fieldcraft, it brought home to the viewer many important elements of sniping.

The U.S. Signal Corps produced similar films for American soldiers. Indeed, one *training* film—*Baptism of Fire*—was nominated for Best Documentary at the 16th Academy Awards in 1944. (It lost out to *Desert Victory*, a British *documentary*.) In 1943's T.F. 21 1020 *How to get killed in one easy lesson*, part of the "Fighting Men" series, two Japanese snipers discuss how ten American soldiers were easy meat through poor fieldcraft. Dr Seuss, using his real name—Theodor Geisel—helped Chuck Jones (*Looney Tunes*) produce animated cartoon training films using humor and the character Private Snafu.

The Germans also produced similar films. The Luftwaffe *Scharfschütze in der Geländeausbildung* (Sharpshooters' field training) looked at camouflage and deception; *Scharfschütze im Einsatz: Die unsichtbare Waffe* (Sharpshooters in action: The unseen weapon) showed a sharpshooter stalking a Russian light machine-gunner and then, while fighting on the defensive against the British, a German sharpshooter shot an unwary officer and used a string to move bushes to distract enemy snipers and cover his retreat. Finally, it showed the use of props— heads and dummies—to attract attention.

A still from the film *Kill or Be Killed*. British Official.

launched a reconnaissance boat and in constant danger of overturning he was successful in rescuing four drowning men." He received his medal from HRH King George VI at Buckingham Palace.

The Canadians were early arrivals in Britain, the first troops arrived in 1940 and were soon manning the Channel coast defenses. As Col. Stacey outlines in the official history, during 1941 the Canadian Training School began work in earnest. On May 1, 1941, it took over Havannah Barracks, Bordon in Hampshire and soon, was training drivers, infantry commanders, anti-gas instructors, etc. By September all the wings were functioning and No. 3 (Weapons) Wing was training in the 3-inch mortar and platoons weapons. This was expanded later to include courses for machine gunners and snipers.

United States

Not all men were fortunate enough to receive sniper training in the United States. Pvt. George N. Burr (42d Infantry Division; later, the 79th) did. After completing boot camp, he attended training at Camp Phillips, KS.[28] If there was little or no training for snipers in 1940, there was certainly none for officers on how to use them. When the U.S. Army began swelling its ranks, the OTC officer aspirants did not receive any instruction on sniping or how to use snipers in their platoon or company. It is highly unlikely if any 1940–42 infantry officer would understand any of the instructions in *FM7–5* §288. One sniper observed, "I had one lieutenant who acted like I was his personal hit man. If some Kraut had the audacity to shoot at him, he'd say, 'Slyder, get that guy!'"[29] While no evidence has been found so far showing that infantry officers received any training, the Quartermaster OTC School at Camp Lee, VA treated its officer candidates to a demonstration by sniper suit-clad Cpl. Kenneth E. Gibbons.[30] It was not until February 1944 when *FM21-75* was issued that there were any guidelines.

After the Army Specialized Training Program was closed, Pvt. Earle Slyder was given an accelerated six to eight week basic infantry training program before volunteering for sniper training (Camp Maxey, TX) instead of becoming a BAR man.

"In the sniper course, they taught us the basics on what to do and what not to do. The first thing they did was teach us how to creep, crawl and sneak around without getting spotted. We were issued 1903A4s with a four-power Weaver scope. Once we had them zeroed, we were told if under any circumstance we missed a target at 100 yards, we were out. Every day, the nine of us in the battalion

Equipment and skill development
(from *FM21–75*)

"Specially designed rifles with telescopic sights are used in fixed sniping posts or where long-range firing is contemplated. ... When the telescopic sight is used at varying ranges or against fleeting targets it is necessary to 'hold-off' in order to hit the target. For ranges varying from 0 to 600 yards it is recommended that the sight be zeroed at 400 yards. The distance that it is necessary to 'hold-off' at various ranges is shown. ... The following steps in sniper training will serve as a guide in the development of skill and proficiency:

(1) Advanced training in rifle marksmanship.
(2) Elimination based on shot groups fired at 300 and 600 yards.
(3) Additional practice in range estimation under all conditions of visibility.
(4) Training in identifying and locating sound to include those of weapons.
(5) Training in selection of firing positions.
(6) Training in observation and visual searching of areas under varying conditions of visibility.
(7) Use of concealment and camouflage.
(8) Firing at field targets at unknown distances with iron sights.
(9) Nomenclature and care of telescopic sight.
(10) Zeroing telescopic sight at 400 yards.
(11) Study of trajectory, drift, effects of wind and light.
(12) Known-distance firing with telescopic sight to determine hold-off.
(13) Firing at unknown ranges, using telescopic sight.
   (a) Fairly obvious targets.
   (b) Concealed targets.
(14) Training in selection of and movement by concealed routes.
(15) Final examination over terrain not previously used."[31]

WAR DEPARTMENT BASIC FIELD MANUAL
FM 21-75

SCOUTING,
PATROLLING,
AND SNIPING

WAR DEPARTMENT • 6 FEBRUARY 1944

United States Government Printing Office
Washington : 1944

Scouting, Patrolling, and Sniping was published in 1944 and had a significantly enhanced section on sniping. *GF Collection.*

Hold-off distances from *Scouting, Patrolling, and Sniping* included sniper aiming suggestions.

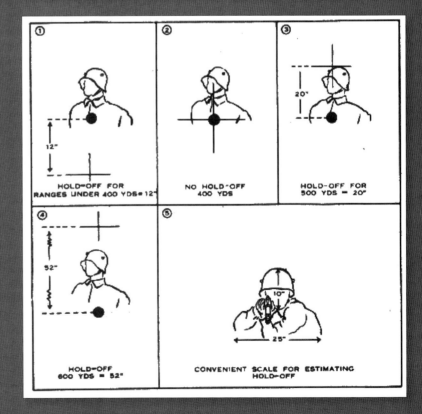

were issued a big wooden crate of ammo. The order was to go to the range and shoot all day long ... We trained on the regular known distance range out to 500 yards. On the unknown distance range we estimated the furthest target was at 800 yards. Most of us could hit the bull four out of five times at 500 yards. When we qualified on the unknown distance range, they had the targets set up like machine gun nests. There were three silhouette target groups and they gave us five rounds for each. We had to have one hole in each silhouette. The targets were scattered all over at different ranges. We had to estimate the range and windage and fire at them. The targets would drop when you hit them. They didn't care where you hit them as long as you hit them. Your score would be based on how many bullets you had left over after you hit all the targets."[32]

Also attending sniper school at Camp Maxey from 99th Infantry Division was Thor Ronnigen, who was from Co. I, 395th Infantry Regiment.

"Most of the sniper training was very similar to the marksmanship training we had done, shooting on the known distance range. We did some range estimation and fired out to 400 or 500 yards, which in most cases was pretty ridiculous. They very perfunctorily covered stalking and hiding during the course. The majority of the course was basic marksmanship."[33]

Sniper being trained under Col. Sidney Hinds. Unlike most regimental commanders, competitive shooter Hinds took a keen interest in marksmanship and emphasized it within his regiment. *Author's collection.*

One thing Slyder and Ronnigen may have been taught at Camp Maxey was from *The Infantry Journal* that read:

"(I) Don't leave the scope on the rifle during landing operations. Wrap it in pliofilm tobacco pouch or a rubber substitute, and carry it inside your jacket. You won't need it in the initial phase anyway." [34]

An unidentified stateside sniping school instructed its students on boresighting as a preliminary step in sighting in their rifles.[35] This entailed resting the rifle on sandbags, removing the bolt on a bolt-action rifle, peering down the bore and centering the target at 25yd distance with respects to the bore. The telescopic sight was then checked against the target and adjusted until the crosshair or reticle was on the target. The theory was that if the bore was sighted on the target and then the sights adjusted, at least the first shots would appear on the paper at that distance. Further adjustments could then be made at greater distances (100yd, 200yd, etc.). Regarding an in-country school,

"The instructors were sincere, and the students earnest. These men had all learned that war is a pretty grim business. On exercises, the enemy was represented by school troops completely outfitted in captured German uniforms and equipment. The students had already learned to think of the foe as a German, and this realism heightened the realism of the exercise.

"Marksmanship was the objective of the sniper's course. Each student shot his own '03 rifle. In addition to mastering the technique of his weapon, he learned all the other things a sniper should know. The rifle range was laid out so that both down hill and up hill targets could be shot from the same firing point."[36]

When he was transferred from the ASTP to the 26th Infantry Division, Jim Haar shot expert and was given five or six days of sniper training. Haar commented:

"Not that we were going to be assigned into a particular sniper unit, but simply to receive some extra training. It wasn't a long course, just five or six days. We did some additional marksmanship training and then some training on hiding, estimating ranges and movement, things like that."[37]

Sniper training in the U.S. Army during World War II was decentralized and depended on the discretion of the division, regiment, or battalion commander.

96th Infantry Division's executive officer, Brig. Gen. Claudius Easley, was a competitive shooter in the late 1920s and 1930s and emphasized training and sniping in that division.[38] Another enthusiast was 2d Armored Division's 41st Armored Infantry Regiment commander, Col. Sidney Hinds. Hinds' background included being a competitive shooter before the war—he had represented the United States in the 1924 Olympics. The battlefield application was demonstrated when Hinds used a scoped Springfield M1903A4 to hit a crawling German in his hindquarters at 900yd. It comes as no surprise that Hinds emphasized marksmanship within his regiment. He described his training program:

"The purpose of the rifle program is simple. We simply want every soldier to have enough confidence in his M1 to know that with it, used correctly, he can hold off any reasonable number of Jerries coming his way. The best way to do this is a combination of three things: He must learn to shoot on a target range—not the front lines. He must understand that the basic fundamentals (position, squeezing, and aiming) are just as effective on the front lines as they are on the range at Benning. The 'bolo' [miss or failure] there is the casualty here. The next thing is to develop confidence in the weapon by showing the soldier both the capabilities of his weapon and its limitation."[39]

In the Panamanian jungle, under the directions of Chief of the Panama Mobile Forces Maj. Gen. Robert M. Lewis, the soldiers assigned to protect the Panama Canal were trained in jungle warfare and in camouflage by Capt. Cresson H. Kearny. Kearny's prewar experience included being an explorer in South American jungles. They were also trained in jujutsu and in machete fighting, the latter being very useful considering the nature of jungle warfare.[40]

In America, various efforts were made to develop camouflage clothing for snipers. 84th Division engineer Pfc. Joseph Arasimewicz designed "baggy, pajama-like uniforms dyed with various shades of red, browns and greens to match the seasonal foliage the sniper picks to hide in."[41] In Fort Ord, CA, Maj. William Mohr's engineer battalion included a lithograph artist, an art director for a theater, and a former background artist for Disney Studios. The soldiers visited the Pacific Grove Natural History Museum to study nature's methods of camouflage and afterward designed a camouflage uniform which they humorously called a "zoot suit." It enabled the wearer to hide, to the untrained eye, in plain sight.[42]

Army and Navy V-12 students (equivalent to the Army Specialized Training Program where recruits were sent to college)—including snipers—were given camouflage instruction at Cornell University's test garden near Varna, NY.[43] Public awareness of the need for camouflage was so great that lest a white handkerchief draw sniper fire, Alma Gutterson, a 77-year-old woman from Pasadena, CA, made dozens of khaki handkerchiefs for soldiers on guard duty.[44]

William E. Jones of Co. I, 8th Infantry Regiment, 4th Infantry Division was the highest scoring enlisted man in his company and was volunteered to become a sniper. Unlike Fulcher, he received no sniper training and had to apply the fieldcraft he had acquired in Tennessee as a child during the Great Depression hunting rabbits, squirrels, or possums for his family table. Pfc. Joseph Motil of Co. L, 3d Battalion, 22d Infantry, 4th Infantry Division, claims to have received sniper training at Camp Gordon after basic. He admitted to pulling the bullets of eight M2 30-06 cartridges and adding powder to them. The kick, he said, felt like it broke his arm but he mentions that he used one to kill a German "sniper" with his M1 Garand.[45] As any cartridge reloader knows, adding powder changes the ballistics of the cartridge. Second, unless tested, the point of impact with the increased pressure and velocity would be unknown. If Motil's training was anything like that of Theodore Finkbeiner (discussed below), it was trigger time with little other instruction. One 415th Infantry Regiment private, Charles Davis, received no training before receiving his sniper rifle. This meant he had to learn in the field:

"It was just about at this point a German stepped from a side door of the house to my right front. He was tall and erect and looked as if he were dressed and groomed for a parade or review. The range was less than one hundred yards. He was standing still and appeared to be looking around and trying to decide just where to move next. The shot from my '03 ended his indecision. But that's all it did; it was a clean miss! He leaped like an antelope into the doorway and disappeared before I could eject the empty case … But I missed other good shots that day and also later.

"Analyzing my misses is not an easy job. It must be remembered that conditions vary greatly, especially between target ranges and actual combat. I don't mean to say that range practice is worthless. Everything is the same in the course of firing the rifle except position and of course the natural strain of knowing that someone is also shooting at you. Since I was a very careful man, this knowledge of the fact that someone was also

Distance estimation

No bullet travels in a straight line. As it exits the bore, it rises in an arc before descending. Overestimating the target's distance makes the shooter aim higher with the bullet's arc carrying it over the target's head. Underestimating makes the shooter aim lower, making the bullet's arc drop the bullet beneath the point of aim. The sniper must know the ballistics of his cartridge, be able to estimate the distance to the target, adjust his sights (or hold) accordingly, account for the wind and, if the target is moving, its speed. Bernhard Averbeck, 195th *Panzerjäger* Battalion, 95th Infantry Division, was in reserve and sitting on a brick wall resting near the Voshnya tributary to the Tim River when he was fired at and survived a near miss. The Russian who fired at him either misjudged the distance, held too low, or was inexperienced and had what Americans call "buck fever." Averbeck recalled the incident:

"We continued fighting for another four to five days until reaching our designated destination, we stopped.

"Enemy snipers haunted the front line. Russian sharpshooters carried a fully automatic ten-shot rifle with a scope. They were good with their rifles and we learned from them what we could and couldn't do. Usually one mistake was all that was allowed; appropriate behavior became second nature.

"I was relaxing on a brick wall, enjoying the rays of a sun that contained promise of a warm summer. The 'PHHHT' sound that threw up red brick dust sent me tumbling for cover. The sniper's bullet had passed between my legs and buried itself in the bricks. My white winter trousers had made a fine target. A little higher and the rifleman could have ended my thought of ever raising a family and higher still he could have ended my thoughts altogether."[46]

In the U.S. Army, distance estimation was sometimes taught by sound. The trainee would see the flash and then count the seconds before he heard the sound. From it, he could approximate the distance.[47] Scout George F. Schneider described his method taught to him in school:

"On a training mission in the woods, we were fired upon (with blanks) by a machine gun that was visible at an unknown distance. Our assignment was to estimate the distance. Estimates ranged from lows of 50 feet to highs of a couple of hundred. While we were estimating the distance, our lieutenant sent someone out to pace the distance. I remembered that in high school, my science teacher, Mr. Haight, had shown us a trick to estimate distance to an object. I applied his simple mathematical maneuver using only my finger and eyes. Holding my arm stretched out in front of me, I lifted my finger and visually placed it on the tree. Alternatively, I blinked my eyes and announced that the distance was 145 feet. I endured laughter and howls from my comrades until the scout returned to announce, that, according to his pace, the distance to the machine gun was 145 feet. Their taunting hoots immediately turned into exclamations of incredulity, and I was urged to explain my seemingly magical technique to the platoon. First, I had to find an object adjacent to the machine gun. That object needed to be a known dimension. In this instance, I choose a particular species of tree because all of these trees in this area were about the same size in trunk diameter and height. I zeroed my fingertip in on one tree adjacent to the machine gun. As my vision shifted from right eye to left, my finger moved left to right across the tree trunk. Knowing the diameter of the tree, I was able to extrapolate the distance my finger was moving. I then multiplied that number by 10 and arrived at a distance of 145 feet. The distance you see your finger move gives you a good estimate if there is a reference material of a known dimension such as bricks on a wall or a vehicle. The multiplication by 10 is general and dependent on the length of your arm and the interpupillary distance between your eyeballs."[48]

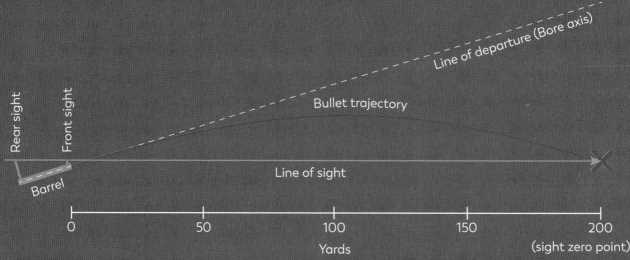

52

trying to hit me, did not add anymore butterflies to my stomach or 'bring the lump up' anymore than if I were on the firing line in an important rifle or pistol match.

"Perhaps my misses were due to an incorrect sight picture. I had had very little experience with rifle scopes. As I found out later, the point of impact was low and to the left. One of the wounded Germans had been shot through the right hand."

"A man that I had fired at several times was hit in the right side of the head. Another German got hit when he cut sharply to the left as he was running away from me. We can add to this the fact that all my shots were in the standing position, most of the time half bent over in order to shoot through the small attic window and holes in the roof. The blowing curtains added to the hazy picture."[49]

A lot of his mistakes could have been prevented if Davis had been trained.

During the war expedient ranges were set up near the front for men to sight in their rifles. This measure was necessary because of the high volume of casualties among riflemen that required replacements. Men needed to sight in the rifle before going into battle. At Anzio, a 200-yard range was set up for any new replacement to sight in his rifle. Lt. John B. Meyers explained to war correspondent Kenneth Dixon:

"When a sniper gets a new rifle he knows what the zeroing point is supposed to be and what it has to be and what it is are two different thing when it comes time to use it. As you might guess, the sniper doesn't get much chance to test a new rifle when he's busy with his day's work—it has to be right the first time. So this range is a God-send to him. He brings his rifle down here, gives it a good going over and tests its sights, and when he leaves he knows exactly what its zeroing point is."

As a 45th Infantry Division sniper got up to leave, Meyers pointed him out, "There goes one sniper now. Next time he uses that gun it won't be in practice."[50]

We are fortunate to know what Sgt. Theodore Finkbeiner of the 504th PIR, 82d Airborne, did at sniper school. Finkbeiner qualified by scoring expert in boot camp and he—along with another trooper who had also scored expert—was sent from Camp Walthers, TX where they had received their basic training to Fort Bragg, NC for sniper training.

"I think it was two of them from each company … They took us out there and issued us a sniper rifle, an 03A3 with a star gauge barrel, a star gauge[51] about one in a thousand with good rifling in it and a little four-power Weaver scope that people wouldn't even want to own now. After they took us out there, they turned us loose. We'd go by and pick up the ammunition we wanted and everybody in the battalion and go to the rifle range and shoot the guns. We'd go down the pits ourselves and hold up targets and move them [he meant scoring them] and just shoot, shoot at anything we wanted to shoot at. Just shoot the guns and learn how to shoot the gun. And that's what we did for days on end. We got back in with the regular training."

When asked if there was any specialized training for snipers Finkbeiner responded, "That was it." He added:

"When we got to North Africa, why, in training over there we'd go out there and take a spotter with us, put a GI can up on the side of the hill, and shoot at extreme ranges up to about 1100–1200 yards and they'd spot where we hit (five hundred yards was about the most we've ever shot in the States, most of it was 300), and learn how to judge long range distance with a rifle like that."[52]

Apparently Fort Bragg's sniper training concentrated on little else than shooting practice with no instruction on cover, concealment, stalking, tactics, observation, scouting, sketching, map reading, compass, navigation, or other things taught by other armies. This is confirmed by Pfc. John M. Khoury, L Co., 399th Infantry, 100th Infantry Division, who adds that they were instructed on the use and care of the scope as well as practicing on stationary and pop-up targets.[53] Like Finkbeiner, after finishing sniper school Khoury did not take the scoped Springfield he trained with overseas. On top of this, despite being trained as a sniper, Finkbeiner neither fought as a sniper in Africa nor Sicily and was not issued a sniper rifle until he reached Naples.

Unlike Finkbeiner, Robert Flagg of the 103d Infantry Division not only trained with his scoped M1903A4 rifle but took the same rifle overseas with him.

"I really did love that rifle because, I guess, I spent so much time with it in the States. As a first scout-sniper, I got to spend extra time on the rifle range while the rest of the company was doing something like closer order drill or policing the area. I fired away at targets up to 500yd. Over and over, picking up superior scores."[54]

Last, an article promoting war bonds in Beatrice, NE, enticed the public to attend to see the display of infantry weapons including a sniper rifle and demonstration of infantry tactics. There were other sniping schools including those at Fort Benning, GA,[55] Camp Phillips, KS,[56] Fort Lewis, WA,[57] and Camp Mackall, NC.[58] Unfortunately, the curriculum at these schools is unknown.

U.S. Marine Corps

In 1940, Col. Julian C. Smith recommended for consideration to the commandant the Lyman Alaskan, Noske (2.5–4 power) and Weaver 330 and 440 (also 2.5–4 power) telescopic sights. No action was taken until July 19, 1942, when the Division of Plans and Policies wrote to the commandant:

> "It is believed that sniper training should be initiated in the Marine Corps in the near future; that a suitable course be tentatively adopted for this purpose; and that after adoption of such course, sniper schools should be established …"

It also pointed out that the snipers' course developed by Maj. Van Orden was available on file at the Weapons School at Quantico, VA and that an outline of a British snipers' course was available too. In June 1941 the Marine Corps had a sniper-observer-scout class with 31 officers and men. It was a one-time stopgap measure until the formal schools were established.[59] Not long after its completion, the commandant ordered that sniping schools be established on both the east and west coasts.

Unwilling to wait for the corps to provide snipers and sniper training, by March 1942 2d Marine Division under Maj. Gen. Charles F. B. Price had numerous schools that offered specialized training including machine gun, intelligence, bayonet, anti-tank, and chemical defense, as well as a scout-sniper

When stateside schools could not train enough marine-snipers quickly enough, field schools were established overseas to train more scout-snipers. Seen here is GySgt. Emmett Orr instructing Pvt. Joseph Cooney on a M1903 rifle equipped with either a Winchester A5 or Lyman 5A telescope. *Author's collection*.

school.[60] Similarly, 1st Marine Division had Col. William Whaling organize and conduct a scout-sniper school on Guadalcanal. Whaling drew two marines from each company.

In December 1942, the Marine Corps opened its east coast school at Camp Lejeune near New River, NC under Capt. Walter R. Walsh, a former FBI Agent and a Distinguished Marksman. (Postwar, in 1952 Col. Walsh won the National Rifle Matches at Camp Perry.) The school had 20 students per class for its three-week course,[61] although Everett Hampton remembers it lasting four weeks when he attended in fall 1942. "They taught us sniper techniques and we did additional rifle marksmanship. We did a lot of firing at long range; most of our shooting was done at 300 and 500 yards. It wasn't difficult to hit targets at those ranges with the 03."[62]

Shortly after the east coast school opened, the west coast school under 1Lt. Claude N. Harris opened at Green's Farm, Camp Elliot, near San Diego, CA. Lt. Harris held a distinguished marksman badge and was a mustang—an enlisted man who was commissioned—who shot competitively, was on seven championship USMC rifle teams, and won the 1935 National Rifle Championship. He fought in Haiti and in Nicaragua and was serving in the Pacific when he was recalled to start the school. The west coast school accepted 15 expert riflemen from each replacement battalion. Del Schultz, who graduated first in his sniping school class, said they began with 30 candidates of whom only 18–20 graduated.[63]

Harris's sniping course was five weeks long and the top five graduates were sent to the Marine Raiders for an additional three weeks of training. (The raiders were a short-lived special forces unit similar to the British commandos: the 1st Battalion was activated on February 16, 1942; the second three days later. Both were deactivated on February 1, 1944.) Rifle instruction included shooting up to 1,000yd at moving and disappearing targets (closer range).[64] These expert riflemen were trained in reconnaissance, and course material included camouflage, concealment and construction of hides and spider traps, map and compass reading, aerial photographic reading, range estimation, sketching including drawing maps from memory, use of the telescopic sight, scouting and patrolling, night operations, etc. Because they were also trained as scouts, they were given extensive hand-to-hand combat training which incorporated elements of jujutsu, Tae Kwon Do, judo, karate, and kung fu. Additionally, they were given Japanese language training. Upon graduation, the men were distributed three per company as specialists and were not attached to any platoon. By 1944, Harris's course seems to have been lengthened to six weeks in duration.[65]

Among the marines in the first class of the west coast school was Del Schultz who enlisted into the corps at age 17. Like other marines, Schultz underwent marksmanship training and was anxious to learn the results.

"I waited to hear how I fared in the first phase, but heard nothing. Finally a guy approached me one day and said, 'You have to reshoot,' so I did. Once again I heard nothing. Then the same guy requested that I shoot the course again, but I would have an NCO by my side. Silence. This is when I started getting a little scared. When I received a third invite, this scared the hell out of me. At that time, I already knew I was skilled— my rifle practically grew out of my finger. I craved to be an expert rifleman. Finally, on the designated day, I reported to the range where a large set of bleachers was set up for an audience. Twenty to thirty brass lined up to watch me. I didn't know what the hell was going on, but I knew I had to perform here and now. I did my best that afternoon, showing my skill. No one really stated how well I did. One officer simply said, 'My God, we have an Annie Oakley with a gun,' and they placed me directly in the sniper pool. After Basic, I attended the very first Scout/Sniper School the Marines offered."[66]

Unlike the army, the USMC consistently gave their scout-snipers extensive training and Schultz recalled:

"As a scout, we were trained to move forward with our combat units while as a sniper we learned how to retreat … Through rigorous training, officers pounded into us that we could not wait or rely on someone else. We must plan an escape route on our own. Relying on one's own intelligence and will had to be balanced by orders from higher up."

In the field, Schultz applied his training as a scout.

"I relied on my eyesight, my hearing, and my senses to alert me to the possible danger ahead. I learned how to operate by placing myself in the enemy's shoes. I thought about how they would defend themselves. I moved ahead slowly, as deliberate as possible and listened as intently to the silence ahead of me."[67]

Understandably, because of the trauma associated with recalling bad memories, Schultz only shared few insights into his activity.

"I traveled light with no extra ammo, just a rifle I carried at all times. I slept with my rifle. One needed intelligence and endurance. Once you got in, you stayed in. We were not the down and dirty front line operations, like the Army. We were trained as scouts, spending a lot of time observing the enemy through field glasses, then eventually, we moved in and did the job that was required of us."[68]

Sgt. Lawrence W. Kirby was born in Brookline, MA. After graduating from high school, he waited until he was 18 before enlisting into the Marine Corps in the summer of 1942. Sent to boot camp at Parris Island, SC he qualified as expert with the M1903 rifle. Afterward he was sent to Camp Lejeune, NC for advanced infantry training and shot expert with the M1 Garand. Additionally, he learned how to use all small arms available to the corps including Thompson and Reising SMGs, rifle grenade, both air and water-cooled .30cal and .50cal machine guns, as well as bangalore torpedoes. Kirby also attended communication school where he learned radio operations and field repairs, as well as telephone switchboard and wires. Sent to Camp Pendleton, CA for scout-school, he learned camouflage. The graduation test was to stand still along a path and the officer-in-charge as well as the sergeant instructors would walk down the path and attempt to locate the student. Anyone discovered did not graduate. Training also included vehicle operations (jeep, 2$\frac{1}{2}$ton truck, the amphibious Weasel, M4 Sherman and anything a marine may have to operate). As a sniper, he trained on the Unertl-equipped M1903 rifle

Originally captioned to describe a Marine sniper in New Britain who said that late in the war the Marine Corps acquired some M1903A4 sniper rifles, Pvt. Daniel Barrineau's brother remembers him saying that in reality he was handed the rifle and asked to pose with it. After honoring the photographer's request, the rifle was taken from him, never to be seen again. Photo was taken on Pavuvu (Russell Islands), May 13, 1944. *USMC.*

and was taught ballistics.[69] Post-graduation he joined the 2/9 Marines, 3d Marine Division, where he served as a scout and was never called upon to serve as a sniper. As a scout he'd depart before sunrise, study the enemy position, and return with the intelligence.

While the location is uncertain, we also know that Lt. George P. Hunt, USMC, managed a sniper school "somewhere in the South Pacific." Assisted by Gunny Emmet Orr—along with other marines from Brooklyn and the Colorado Rocky Mountains—he instructed the men in "expert marksmanship, scouting, demolition, jujutsu, study of aerial photography, compass, map reading, infiltration, camouflage, concealment and were trained to go into the field with only a rifle, ammunition, K-rations, maps and compass." As part of their training, men would spend days in the jungle on their own too. Besides using the rifle, they were also refreshed in using the shotgun, pistol, and Tommy guns on moving targets, silhouettes, and hidden targets. Lt. Hunt added: "We teach the men instinctive patrolling. They work in teams, training together, learning to anticipate each other's moves instinctively. There's no guess work. They operate like a well-coordinate basketball team."[70]

Pfc. Robert P. Magnan of 7th Marine Regiment, 1st Marine Division fought at Guadalcanal. Here, he was sent on scouting missions behind Japanese lines. He had no prior training but developed his fieldcraft from boyhood where he stalked the woods for small game with a BB gun and later a .22 long rifle. After Guadalcanal, the 7th Marines were sent to Australia to recuperate and train for the next battle. Magnan was approached by his lieutenant about attending the newly started scout-sniper training there. Magnan began training on July 14 but had to withdraw several times because of malaria. He finished his sniper training on August 11. After graduating fourth in his class, he received further training in jungle warfare in New Guinea.[71]

On January 11, 1944, when 6th Marine Regiment (2d Marine Division) was in Hawaii preparing for the invasion of Saipan, Col. James Riseley ordered mustang officer 1Lt. Frank Tachovsky to raise a 40-strong scout-sniper platoon that would be a regimental asset. Tachovsky recruited not only Tarawa combat-experienced marines who had qualified as expert on the range, he also wanted proven men. Specifically, he wanted brawlers. "If a guy's spent any officer hours [slang for brig time] for brawling that shows he's been in trouble and can handle himself. The guy that fights that wins is thrown the brig, the other guy goes to the infirmary. The guy in the brig is the kind of guy we want."[72]

Once the men were selected, they were trained at Parker Ranch on Waimea, HI. Training included explosives, navigation by compass, map reading including plotting, map sketching, aerial photograph interpretation, estimating enemy strength, camouflage, surveillance, hand signals, stalking, hand-to-hand combat (judo, jujutsu, Biddle method of fighting), patience, and target practice. Not all initial candidates completed the training and replacements were called for. From May 19 their final training would be with the rest of the regiment and included descending cargo nets into landing crafts and practice landings. Their training was considered complete and on May 30 they boarded the USS *Bolivar* bound for Saipan.

Nicknamed the "Black Raiders" or "Forty Thieves" by other marines, they were issued eight M1903A1 Springfields equipped with eight power Unertl scopes (four other similarly scoped rifles remained with the regiment). Breaking with corps tradition, the mission took priority and a wounded or injured man who couldn't keep up was left to fend for himself.

In contrast to the U.S. Army's inconsistent methodology in training snipers, the Marine Corps' selection and training placed its snipers on par with their counterparts in the British Commonwealth, the Soviet Union, and Germany. Marine Corps doctrine, though, seems to have favored using scout-snipers primarily as scouts for intelligence gathering and only secondarily as snipers.

Soviet Union

"The Russian soldier was and is an individual fighter, a factor that must not be underestimated and indeed, the Russian sniper has for a long time been a very real factor which has influenced the training of our own infantry." So said *Hauptmann* Borsdorf in the *Hamburger Fremdenblatt*, in May 1944.[73] To meet the demand for snipers, on March 20, 1942, what became the Central Sniper Instructor School was opened in Veshnyaki, a *raion* (administrative district) of Moscow. This was in response to the Soviet goal of having three snipers per platoon and nine snipers per company or 87 in each infantry regiment.[74] Like all ambitious plans, this was never attained but it certainly produced more snipers and sniper instructors than any other belligerent.

Schools at infantry training centers or formal sniper schools

Muscovite Evgeni Bessonov had just graduated from high school on June 17, 1941. Four days later Germany invaded the Soviet Union and he found himself drafted into the army. Being bright, he was sent to a six-month officer school instead of the normal two-year military academy most officer candidates attended. His training was based on the 1936 *Infantry Field Manual* which covered the duties and tasks of anyone from a private to a captain and included all small arms, 37mm to 82mm mortars, and political instruction. Upon graduation in May 1942, he was retained as a training officer at the academy and received further training in the anti-tank rifle. In July 1942, Jr. Lt. Bessonov was sent to the 365th Reserve Rifle Regiment of the 46th Reserve Rifle Brigade. Since Bessonov was an excellent shot, he became a leader (and trainer) in the battalion's sniper company. Instruction included studying of the Mosin-Nagant rifle, marksmanship, entrenchment, camouflage, and grenade throwing. Sniper training was extended beyond that of an ordinary infantryman, after which the men were sent as replacements. Besides training men, he also trained women. Bessonov would not depart for the front until mid-1943 and we shall meet him again later.[75]

Under direction of Stalin, 400 Communists and *Komsomol* members were to be trained as sniper instructors. Among them was Leonid Naftulovich Solodar.

> "The sniper movement had already started at the time and had produced several Heroes of the Soviet Union who played their role in the war effort. We were sent to Moscow after the Germans had been pushed back. I remember very well that Moscow was gray. That was in April 1942. I finished my training at the central sniper classes of the Soviet Union. After I graduated, I was assigned to train new snipers despite my ethnicity [Solodar was Jewish]."

It would be a long time before he would see any fighting and he remained in Moscow instructing sniper candidates.[76]

After passing his medical examination, collective farm worker and former wagon driver turned medical technician student Nadol'ko Nikolai Dmitrievich was sent directly on the nine-month-long course at the 14th Sniper School of the Central Asian Military District which he attended from November 1943 to August 1944. Housed in a dugout lit only by oil lamps, the underfed students were roused from their sleep at 0500 hours, were given a brief period of political indoctrination, the news, and then a lot of shooting practice. Dmitrievich remembered:

> "At the shooting-ground we had different fire exercises, mostly at small-sized targets. A 'head' appeared from a blindage embrasure for a short while—you should strike it in several seconds.

And, God forbid, our platoon had failed the exercises—on our way back we would have to carry out plenty of commands 'Air!', 'Tanks on the right', 'Tanks on the left!'"

These prompted the students to dive headfirst into the snow and not stir until the command was given to emerge. He described their marksmanship training: "Initially the exercises were easy. The size of a target—full-length, half-length, and running targets. Then they complicated the exercises gradually. The most difficult thing was to fire at a 'head' target that suddenly appeared for several seconds at a distance about 300–400 meters." They were also instructed in basic infantry tactics, bayonet fighting, camouflage,

Rifle training for Red Army cadets near Moscow. Note that the first five are armed with scoped SVT-40s and the remainder with the M91/30 bolt-action rifle. *albumwar2.com.*

patience, and to bear any condition including heat, cold, thirst, hunger, and to refrain from coughing.[77]

Mark Epshtein experienced the siege of Leningrad as a teenager. When he was old enough to be drafted (August 1942), he was sent to the 78th Infantry Reserves Company, a sniper unit.

"We were trained there for about two months or so. The conditions were similar to the front. We rose at 6am, wearing only our breeches, no shirt, and our lace-up shoes, which we nicknamed 'He loves me, He loves me not' because of how long it took to wrap them around. We had three minutes to get lined-up. So we had our dugouts in the ground and we would make a dash for the lake. We had to bathe in the lake, undress quickly. Obviously there was nothing to dry ourselves with, so we ran back to the dugout.

"There were plank beds in the dugouts. I can't say that it was cold to sleep. As for people getting sick … I don't remember any of that happening during the war. The immune systems were unbelievably tough. No one would get sick. No illnesses, no runny noses, no coughs; at least, I didn't have any nor did my fellow Red Army buddies. What did our training consist of? We walked. We laid down on those parapets. We were given rifles with an optic long-range view/ scope … So, at a distance of say, 300 or 200m, there were these dug out holes in the ground. There were Red Army men sitting inside them— guys who were guilty of something, who had disobeyed the commander's orders. They were ordered by an officer to lift these targets out— target dummies: head, torso, full body-sizes, etc. They brought them out and lined them up and we were expected to shoot them. We were each ordered to fire at a certain time and then we'd shoot. Unfortunately, a tragedy happened. My neighbor cannot be held accountable for it but it turned out that one of the Red Army guys stuck himself out instead of the target by accident. Right at that moment he was ordered to shoot. The long-range view/scope [of the rifle] would magnify the target dummy or target board [depending on which target was being used] by four. Well, that Red Army soldier died. We felt terrible after witnessing the death of someone who was no different from us. I think that we were trained for no more than two months. After that, we had combat training, which was very arduous. We dealt with tanks, with artillery, other forms of ammunition, mortar shells, etc. We were preparing to attack the enemy by going through very fierce, alarming, and nerve-wracking training for a few days [ordered by the commanding officers]."[78]

Front-line field schools

At Leningrad, Pchelintsev suggested establishing front-line schools and each battalion had every platoon select one man to attend. After classroom work, the sniper candidates completed their internship at the front. Including the internship, Pchelintsev's school ran for 15 days after which the students returned to their units as snipers.[79] These students went on not only to become accomplished snipers, but also instructed their comrades on marksmanship and sniping. The Red Army's demand for snipers resulted in field schools being improvised with duration and quality of instruction varying from school to school.

During a lull in the German assault on Leningrad, the 154th NKVD Regiment, 21st NKVD Rifle Division, conducted an informal 15-day sniping

Military preparedness included marksmanship training that was taught to school age children and promoted through interschool and regional competitions. The winner was awarded the Voroshilov Marksman badge that could be worn on civilian clothes and on their military uniform. These are but four of the many Voroshilov marksmen who fought in various capacities during WW II.
1. Lev Dratver, volunteered for the army despite being only 17 and fought at Odessa, Stalingrad, and on into Hungary and Czechoslovakia.
2. Savely Dukhovniy, photographed a few days before leaving for the front in July 1941, also fought through to Czechoslovakia in spite of being wounded six times.

school as proposed by 5th Company commander Lt. Vasily Butorin. Butorin was an experienced soldier who had fought in the Winter War against Finland. He was aware of sniping in World War I and the Russian Civil War. Since the regiment had unused sniper rifles in its regimental stores, Butorin thought it was wasteful if the rifles were not put to use. Commissar Ivan Agashin approved and even suggested a few candidates for the school and included men from the reconnaissance unit as well as an experienced hunter.[80]

Butorin placed Yevgeni Nikolaev in charge of the squad. Nikolaev had attended the Tambov Railway Technical School for two years, during which time he developed a keen interest in shooting. He was among the four selected from the school team to join the city team. He had completed many classes and qualified for the Voroshilov Marksman award.

According to Nikolaev, their academy was in a gully near Sheremetyev Park. The first exercise was target practice to test their marksmanship. They progressed onto camouflage and selection of sniping positions. Physical fitness was not ignored and included running, strengthening exercises, jumping, as well as grenade throwing and sambo wrestling. At the end of the day, weapons would be cleaned and oiled followed by lectures on the weapon with particular attention to the telescopic sight. Other lessons included observation and development of memory.

The observation lesson included spreading objects out on the ground. The student was then asked to leave and return in two–three minutes after which he was asked what was missing or moved. Sometimes this observation was done on the spot. Nikolaev had the advantage of having worked as a theatrical artist but even with this background he was not perfect. Sniper survival, Nikolaev was taught, depended on the ability

to observe and then deduce from those observations. Snipers who were deficient in those things would not have a long career. He was instructed that besides being an accurate shooter, a sniper had to discern important targets and put a bullet into them.

The students mastered those skills, and to do it they started with paper targets and objects of ever-diminishing size. Empty bottles were shot through their bottoms. If the sniper was good, the bullet would pass through the neck and exit the bottom without damaging the rest of the bottle. Matchboxes were suspended on a string and the sniper-trainee taught to cut the string without damaging the matchbox. Moving targets were also used as well as rapid shooting—from 10 to 12 shots a minute. (This could only be done with an unscoped rifle since PE or PEM-scoped M91/30s could not be loaded by clip. The Finns solved this problem with their version of the scoped M91/30 by inventing a curved stripper clip that allowed for rapid loading.)

When their training was completed, the snipers were paired off for their examination on the front line. It was not dark yet and Nikolaev's partner became bored and suggested leaving. Nikolaev told him it was too light, inferring that they themselves could be sniped if they moved and it was better to wait. Then he spotted three Germans, the last two hauling huge heavy sacks which Nikolaev suspected contained potatoes. He decided to take them on. After adjusting for wind and movement, he fired at the last German and dropped him. Quickly reloading, he shot the last man again. The first soldier turned around, waved his arms as if urging his comrade to rise. This gave Nikolaev time to reload and drop him too. With this successful stalk, they were now snipers.[81]

Field school candidates included women, and one woman who attended was 20-year-old Latvian

3. Matvey Milyavsky was drafted in January 1943 and was assigned to the 6th Airborne Brigade. As a paratrooper, he made 111 parachute jumps. He took part in crossing the Svir River (near Lodeinoye Pole) and fought at the Sandomierz Bridgehead, in Hungary, and in Austria. **4.** Boris Tsalik was deployed to the Seventeenth Aviation Army as the commander of platoon communications in 1941. As part of the Third Ukrainian Front, he advanced through Ukraine, Romania, Bulgaria, Hungary, Yugoslavia, and Austria, and celebrated victory day in Vienna. *Images courtesy the Blavatnik Archive Foundation (http://www. blavatnikarchive.org).*

Lyudmila Pavlichenko is probably the best-known Soviet sniper in the West. Her story seems to be a mixtures of fact and conjecture. For a more detailed discussion see pp. 196–7. *Courtesy the Central Museum of the Armed Forces, Moscow via Stavka.*

Monica Meikshane. She was serving as a medical orderly who decided that instead of being a healer, she would be a killer. What brought about her change of heart? The village serving as her field hospital was attacked at night. Meikshane was fortunate enough to escape and after she returned, she found all the patients were either burnt to death or, like the medical personnel, shot. She announced to her friends, "I have had enough of this. I want to shoot at least one German myself. Who is coming with me? I am going to volunteer as a sniper."

Meikshane and two other women were trained in marksmanship by Commander Voropayez. "Press the butt firmly into your shoulder. Grasp the trigger with the second joint of the index finger. Squeeze evenly and lightly, at the same time holding your breath." Because of her short stature, the rifle did not fit her and she had poor cheek weld. Her first two shots resulted in the scope hitting and bruising her face. As a remedy, the armorer removed about an inch of wood from the stock, making it fit her better. It helped and by the end of her training, she fired a three-shot group the size of a matchbox at 400yd.

Teamed up with a middle-aged private who was to serve both as an observer and mentor, they left the trench early in that autumn morning and crawled toward the German trench and hid themselves at a spot where they could observe it. Despite waiting all day, no opportunity presented itself and they returned in the evening. Her jubilant friends were luckier and between them they had killed three Germans. The next day Meikshane and her observer crawled into a disabled tank and when there was enough daylight, saw a dead German. "Watch carefully. They will be

certain to try to drag that one back," suggested her observer. Meikshane adjusted her sights and after shouldering the rifle, trained it on the dead man. Her patience was rewarded when a German crawled over the parapet to his fallen comrade. When the German reached him, he made the mistake of raising his head. Meikshane fired and dropped him. In her excitement, she exclaimed, "I got him! I've shot a German!" She also raised herself and bumped her head on the tank hatch. Placing his hand on her shoulder, her observer advised, "Quiet girl, you'll have to shoot a lot more of those damned murderers and people are always excited after their first shot."

Her observer's words were prophetic and she shot another German that day along with two more the next day. Within a few days, she and her friends had a cumulative score of 12 kills.[82]

Another female sniper known only as "Catherine" who hailed from the village of Dimi (near Leningrad) was outraged by the atrocities committed against peasants. She begged to be allowed to enlist. "You must let me serve in the army. Don't send me away. I want to make the Germans pay for what they did to our people." When asked what skills she had, she blurted out: "I can work as a laundress." Thus began her service as a laundress at a field hospital. Later, like Monica Meikshane, she begged to be taught to shoot. Someone taught her and she became a killer. When asked how she felt about killing, Catherine replied: "They're not human beings. They murder children, they kill girls. I hate them. Now they run amok in the villages." Pointing at a German she had shot she said, "There he lies! It serves him right! We didn't invite him; why did he come? Let him lie in the earth. That is the proper place for Nazis. One Fascist less. Tomorrow I'll shoot another, and that will mean two less."

A composite letter from the female snipers including Catherine to the women of Moscow read:

"Dear girls of Moscow, the volunteer sniper girls send warm greetings from the front to you. A short while ago, like you, we were far away from the front, but the thought of how we could best help our country gave us no peace. Now we are soldiers. War is no easy matter but we have learned to fight against odds with our chins up. The day when we go hunting with our sniper rifles is a day of rejoicing with us. To get to the advance lines of defense we have to overcome many obstacles, under an incessant hail of artillery and machine-gun fire, often in mud and water up to the waist as we creep to our positions. The cold wind goes to the marrow of our bones but we won't feel anything but hatred for the enemy. With our eyes on the telescope sights we examine the enemy's defenses. You can imagine what a grand feeling it gives us to shoot down one of the dark figures. One certainly needs a lot of will-power and nerve to spend several hours in the snow in order to sight a Hitlerite."

Catherine, the peasant girl turned sniper, was credited with shooting 22 Germans.[83]

Central Women's School of Sniper Training

While Lyudmila Pavlichenko is easily the most famous female Soviet sniper of the war, she was not unique. There were many other women who broke from the traditional female roles and became warriors. Under the Soviet Constitution, women enjoyed equal rights and obligations to society as the men did. However, this did not extend to women serving as soldiers. As early as a month into the war, patriotic Soviet women who were refused admission into the armed forces served as guerrillas if they lived in occupied areas. It wasn't long before women began entering the ranks in auxiliary roles (nurses, medics, communication specialists, clerks, typists).[84] This soon extended to fighting roles for Soviet women which included artillerists, antiaircraft gunners, tankers, and bomber or fighter pilots.

Perhaps the most unique thing the Soviet Union did for sniper development was its creation of the Central Women's School of Sniper Training which served 1943–45.[85] Set up to train female snipers, it was a boot camp that specialized in training snipers. Its first class graduated in June 1943. Cadets were members of the Young Communist League between 18 and 22 years of age, and candidates were selected on the basis of keen eyesight and prior shooting experience.[86] They were subjected to further screening and if not accepted, sent off for training in other specialties. Those who remained were organized in groups of 10 or 11 by height and then as trainees, were given boys' haircuts. The tallest were in the first platoon and the shortest in the last. It is speculated that the reasoning was probably foxhole size that would work for each pair as well as clothing issuance. Paired off, much like the *comrades d'bataille*, they trained together, sat next to each other during class, and slept next to each other on bunk beds. The Soviets wanted them to rely on each other. At the front, for example, if they had only two greatcoats, in the absence of a blanket one could be placed on the ground and the other shared as a blanket.

Reveille was at 0600 hours and they were marched a mile to the river to wash. At the canteen, they had to learn to eat fast if they wanted to finish their meal. Returning to the barracks, they were taught theory

which included ballistics and their equipment. Besides range practice, there was also plenty of drill. There was no shortage of marching during which they all had to sing. Failure to sing resulted in punishment ("Down! Crawl!"). Yulia Zhukova said there were no textbooks to read or study so classes were taught by lecture and field training. She was shown no instructional films when she attended. Sometimes an experienced sniper like Vladimir Pchelintsev visited the school to share his Leningrad sniping experience. Other classes included different types of foxholes, camouflage, night ambush (and patience), navigating the terrain, stalking, observation and memory development (especially of the landscape and details), hand-to-hand combat, and grenade throwing. During target practice, they first dug and camouflaged their foxholes before shooting at targets that were full-sized, waist upward, chest upward, running, and fixed. They used the standing, kneeling, supported, and unsupported, firing on the move and while stationary. After all the shooting was done, they had to practice their crawling to recover their spent cases.[87]

Among the instructor cadre were graduates from the first class of cadets (now promoted to sergeant) or male officers who had been injured and reassigned from front line duty. They were harsh but only because they had seen the horrors of combat and wanted to prepare them for it. When the class graduated after three or six months (when first opened the school lasted three months and by the end, up to seven), the instructor sergeants were promoted to officers and accompanied them to the front. Most of the newly minted officers softened since they were no longer at the school. One who didn't, Sgt. Shatrova, continued to find fault in

Female sniper trainees from the Central Women's School of Sniper Training. Note some of the scoped rifles have protective covers over their scopes. *Courtesy the Central Museum of the Armed Forces, Moscow via Stavka.*

Anastasia Mikhailovna Stepanova was called up in September 1941. At first a nurse, by January 1943 she was a sniper in the 1076th Infantry Regiment (314th Infantry Division, Volkhov Front), and on the 15th of that month she was awarded the For Courage medal which she's wearing her above her left pocket; an Excellent Sniper badge can be seen over her right pocket. Later, in June 1943, she was awarded the Order of the Red Star. *Courtesy the Central Museum of the Armed Forces, Moscow via Stavka.*

them. She died at the front and those who knew her suspected she was killed by her own platoon.[88]

Since the program was very demanding, naturally there were failures. Dropouts were reassigned to other duties (many women served as signalers, nurses, or clerks). Two women actually deserted but were caught and sent to a penal company. One shot herself in the foot. Her classmates in the platoon suspected she did it because she was afraid of being on guard duty alone in the dark and too ashamed to admit it (especially if they came from *Komsomol*, the Young Communist League).[89]

Their final exit exam was not a written test but a practical one. Each student was given a different task and then told to execute it. Zhukova was instructed to destroy an enemy machine gun nest. She began running and heard "Enemy machine gun fire!" Immediately she dropped and crawled sideways toward cover. From it she began scanning the land in front of her. She scanned the left and right, observing it for anything that looked out of place. Failing to find anything, she continued scanning methodically from left to right and right to left. Time passed and she feared failing. She finally spotted the machine gun's barrel. It was barely discernable to her. After much deliberation, she carefully aimed and struck the target behind it. Zhukova passed with an "excellent" grade and was promoted to sergeant.

School began to wind down. Her class had a day of rest, a graduation ceremony followed by an evening banquet that included wine. Before departing they were issued padded jackets and trousers, warm underwear, new foot wrappings, mittens with a finger for the trigger finger, and even white American socks. They marched out—559 strong—with the school's unfurled banner leading, the brass band playing patriotic music, to the well wishes of Soviet citizens as they made their way to the railroad station for their journey to the front.[90]

Initially there was some reluctance at the front to accept female snipers. Sgt. Bella Epstein recalls:

"When we arrived at the 2d Belorussian Front, they wanted to have us stay at division headquarters. Meaning: you're women, why go to the front line? 'No,' we said, 'we're snipers, send us where we're supposed to go.' Then they said, 'We'll send you to a regiment where there's a good commander, he takes care of girls.' There were all sorts of commanders. So we were told. The colonel met us with these words: 'Lookout, girls, you've come to fight, so fight, but don't get up on to anything else. There are

men around, and no women. Devil knows how else I can explain things to you. It's war, girls.' He understood that we were still very young things."[91]

When the war broke out, 17-year-old Nina Alexeyevna Lobkovskaya attempted to enlist. Rejected as too young, she stayed in school and like Pavlichenko, became active in the *Osoaviakhim* and earned the Voroshilov Marksman award. Because of her skill, she was sent to the Central Women's School of Sniper Training. She describes her school training:

"As soon as I started studying I realized that the mere desire to fight the enemy was not enough. You had to have skill, too. Women are said to be more patient than most men and, therefore, make good snipers. But we discovered that being a sniper is a difficult art and we mastered it only after months of daily lectures and training. We would go to the firing range at dawn and return after dark, tired and dirty. In winter it was not easy to crawl with a heavy rifle through the snow and try to hit the target when your fingers froze on the trigger. It was equally tough performing long marches with a full pack on your back."[92]

Lobkovskaya was in the first class to graduate from the Central Women's School of Sniper Training. In June 1943, she—along with 50 other female snipers—was initially assigned to Third Shock Army of the Kalinin Front during the battle of the Ptakhinskaya Heights which ended on July 6. She and her partner, Leningrader Vera Artamonova, went to 21st Guards Rifle Division, and on the first foray onto the battlefield decided to use a destroyed Russian tank as their lair. She goes on:

"[W]e could see the German trenches rather well, but it was almost impossible to shoot from inside the tank. Out of nowhere, we were under artillery fire. Shells were exploding right next to us. The tank was shaking from the explosions of the shells hitting us from all sides. We were scared stiff and sure that it was the end of us. Then the artillery fire stopped just as suddenly as it had started. When our soldiers saw just where we had taken up our positions, they really gave us an earful. They told us that we should avoid taking up such a highly visible observation post which the enemy often uses as a reference point. After that misadventure, the command attached an experienced soldier, a *frontovik*, to each sniper pair. We got a soldier named Chernykh."

Self-taught snipers

Not all Soviet snipers were school-trained: many of the most notable were self-taught.

Sgt. Fyodor Maveyevic Ohiopkov was a Yakut farmer and hunter in the 234th Rifle Regiment with 429 kills.

Capt. Ivan Mikhailovich Sidorenko, a dropout who was drafted, had 500 kills.

Senior Warrant Officer (later Captain) Vassili Grigoryevich Zaitsev, a shepherd and hunter before enlisting into the navy, was no stranger to shooting. As a youth he was instructed by his grandfather on tracking, camping in the cold frost without a tent, how to shoot, and most importantly, how to hunt. Zaitsev became a sniper when a commissar witnessed him killing a three-man German machine gun crew in rapid succession. Visibly impressed, the commissar ordered that Zaitsev be given a sniper rifle.[93] A sniper instructed him on how to use a scoped rifle and another gave him a three-day orientation. The rest he figured out himself.

Dmitri Chudinov, an assistant machine gunner, became a sniper almost by accident. After his gunner was killed, he flattened himself when the gun was overrun by a German tank. Now isolated and behind the Germans lines, he grabbed his rifle, made his way to a shell hole, and began shooting the Germans who were closest to him. Then he became more discrete and began aiming for the officers. His tally in that one battle was 40 which was impressive enough for him to be made a sniper.[94]

Cpl. Maria Ianovna Morozova grew up in the village of Diakovskoe, now part of Moscow. Maria was 17 when war broke out. She and her friends enlisted and were given some basic training which she described:

> "They taught us to shoot a combat rifle, to throw hand grenades. At first ... I'll confess, I was afraid to hold a rifle, it was unpleasant I couldn't imagine that I'd go and kill somebody, I just wanted to go to the front. We had forty people in our group. Four girls from our village, so we were all friends. Five from our neighbors'; in short—some from each village. All of them girls."[95]

Capt. Ivan Mikhailovich Sidorenko, a Hero of the Soviet Union from June 4, 1944, was self-taught but trained snipers as well as achieving over 500 kills. In this 1941 photo his M91/30 is equipped with a top-mounted PE 4x scope. His helmet is a wider SSh36. *albumwar2.com.*

Joseph Pilyushin was another successful sniper turned instructor who fought on the Leningrad front. Born in 1903, he had previously served in the Red Army in 1926 and was discharged and placed into the reserves. He worked as a welder in the arsenal in Leningrad and through its *Osoaviakhim* training acquired marksmanship. It is unknown whether he earned the Voroshilov Marksman award. When the war broke out, Pilyushin joined a workers' battalion which was amalgamated into the 105th Separate Rifle Regiment. It was later absorbed into the 14th Red Banner Regiment, 21st NKVD Division—the very same unit Nikolaev served in.[96] Blinded in his dominant eye, Pilyushin had to retrain himself to shoot with his left eye and hand. It was shortly afterward that he was instructed to form the regimental sniping school. His knowledge as a sniper was considered invaluable and the regiment badly wanted it passed on to other soldiers. Pilyushin then met with the chief of staff, Major Ragozin, who told him that as the only sniper specialist in the regiment, he had to pass his knowledge onto newer men. Pilyushin was given 15 days. He protested about the shortness but was brushed off and told that finishing school would be in the trenches. Pilyushin adds at that point that the regiment maintained a sniping school for new snipers.[97]

As their mentor, he taught them about the Germans and even accompanied them behind German lines.

Soviet training: Elevation

Whether uphill or downhill, shooting from a different elevation is a tricky skill. A lot of practice was needed to master something helped today by laser and multiplying by cosine to get the actual distance. Zaitsev encountered the issue of different elevation or angled shooting when one of his trainees raised the subject during their evening debriefing. Pvt. Lomako confessed that he had shot at three different Germans at the same distance and missed each time. His curiosity piqued, Zaitsev accompanied Lomako to his hide which was 10yd up in a chimney. When a German was sighted, Zaitsev fired and missed. The German did not quicken his pace and walked on unconcerned. Reloading, he adjusted his sight and fired again and missed. That German also disappeared from view. Zaitsev adjusted his sight before firing again and when the third German appeared, Zaitsev fired and dropped him. Thus he concluded that for angled shooting downhill, raise the sight. During that day's debriefing, he instructed his students that when shooting downhill, to adjust the sight lower and when shooting uphill, to raise the sight.[98] If this sounds contradictory, remember that no one at that time had cosine indicators and knew the math to adjust the sights accordingly.

Later on Mamayez Hill, Zaitsev and another sniper spotted a machine gun that was downhill from them. Zaitsev instructed his partner to adjust his sight for 400 while he would set his sight at 350. They fired simultaneously and the machine gunner dropped. Later they spotted a German hauling pails of water, Zaitsev told his comrade to ignore him and to let him be. He also instructed that distance estimation was difficult for downhill shooting, to add ten percent to the distance.[99] While we know today this is not correct, he was on the right track. He also cautioned about heat mirage and that it made targets appear closer than they were. Perhaps Zaitsev's best advice for shooting at targets that are at a different elevation was to fire a test shot to know for certain.

Sgt. Evdokia Motina, 21st Guards Rifle Division. Her medals from left to right are: Excellent Sniper Badge, Guards badge, Order of the Red Banner (above left pocket). *Courtesy the Central Museum of the Armed Forces, Moscow via Stavka.*

Klavdia Kalugina was just 15 when the war started. She immediately went to work in a munitions factory where she joined the *Komsomol*, which required her to complete her secondary education. When the Central Women's School of Sniper Training opened, at age 17 she was the youngest to join. Initially they had to build the school, so she chopped wood, carried water, and help construct the target range. Her shooting was dismal until her squad leader, Marusia Chikhvintseva, took her under her wing and personally coached her.

They fired up to 1,200m but most of the time in it was 200–300m. Instruction included firing in crosswinds and moving targets. She learned to fire only once from any position and learned patience. If a shot could not be made, it was not to be taken. As a sniper, she carried two grenades. One was for the Germans and the other for herself.

After graduating, they were sent as a 12-person squad to the front where they initially became part of the 1156th Rifle Regiment, 344th Rifle Division, Thirty-third Army. They were issued white camouflage coveralls and wrapped bandages around their rifles. The snow required the Germans to clear their trenches and many Germans were exposed. However, Kalugina and squad leader Chikhvintseva could not bring themselves to shoot. When they returned to their squad dug out, they learned of the success of the other snipers and reproached themselves for their hesitation. The next day she killed a German machine gunner who was clearing his embrasure. After that everyone only cleared their embrasures at night.

Aware that there were Soviet snipers present, the Germans summoned one of their own. Since snipers weren't that effective at night, the women watched the German lines in the day and some men were posted at night. One ominous day, her partner Marusia Chikhvintseva had a sense of foreboding and told her commander, "I don't want to, I can't go today," and asked to be excused from standing post. She was ordered to go anyway and the pair began their watch with Kalugina standing the first watch. Kalugina's eyes grew tired and Chikhvintseva offered to relieve her. "Let me take the watch now," said Marusia. Kalugina remembered, "She got up, it was a sunny day, and she apparently moved the lens. As soon as she got up, there was a shot, and she fell. Oh how I cried … She was my best friend."

When they reached the Dnieper, the Germans had prepared some defensive works from which they dominated the terrain. Regiment commander Leonid Verdiukov ordered, "Eliminate them." Kalugina said, "There were maybe twelve of us, we aimed, and of course, we eliminated them." While fighting on the Dnieper, her longest kill was about a kilometer's distance against a machine gunner and an opposing sniper.

While her unit remained a regimental asset, there were times when the entire platoon of 36 women were all sent to the 52nd Regiment. Then they were split again into squads to serve among the 52nd, 54th and 56th Regiment.

Like other female snipers, they were sometimes called upon to serve as medics and recover the injured. They did this twice—once before crossing the Dnieper and once afterward.

They fought their way into Poland and up to the Baltic Sea where she participated in the capture of Königsberg (today's Kaliningrad).[100]

Germany

Allerberger was largely self-taught and accomplished before he finally received formal training at the sniper school at Judenburg in the Seetal Alps starting on June 5, 1944. The school lasted for 27 days:

> "In the last few months of 1943 at the larger military depots, firing ranges were introduced for sniper training. The course lasted four weeks. Those taking part were recruited from recent conscripts but also included veterans from the front who had been identified by their company commanders as good prospects."[101]

Allerberger's class had 60 students who were divided into five equal groups of a dozen students each. The instructors were all veterans; many of whom had been injured and rendered unfit for front line service.

While at school Allerberger was shown the 1935 Soviet film, *Choice of and Constructing Positions.* One portion of the film showed men climbing trees with the subtitle, "Treetops with plenty of leaf are an outstanding position! The rifleman cannot be seen, but has a good view of the landscape and an outstanding field of fire!" With the German tradition of hunting from tree stands, many took it to heart with fatal consequences for them once detected. The German sniper training manual even shows the use of a shelter-half as a climbing sling to ascend a tree. §8 of the manual of May 15, 1943, reads "In grain fields, bushes, trees, trenches, and holes and in the roof hatches of houses he must find a well-camouflaged position." It is possible Allerberger may also have seen a Russian infantry training film where the Russians were "taught to camouflage themselves and their equipment so that they would be almost invisible and blend into the country side."[102] Another captured Russian film shown to snipers "showed how the Russians were trained to look for those officer insignias, how to pick off officers and leave the soldiers leaderless."[103]

Not all recruits without combat experience were as unlucky as Allerberger, and the most gifted one was Tyrolean Matthäus Hetzenauer. Unlike Allerberger and Rohde who were experienced soldiers before attending sniping school, Germany's soon-to-be top-scoring sniper Matthäus Hetzenauer also attended sniper school at the Seetal Alps Training Depot immediately after finishing his basic training as a *Gebirgsjäger.* Having been a prewar hunter and an excellent shot probably qualified him for inclusion. Hetzenauer probably attended from March 27 to July 16, 1944, and after completing his training, he was transferred to VII Company, 379th Battalion, 144th Mountain Rifle Regiment.

At the Seetal school trainees were broken into groups of 20. Those who wore glasses were rejected because their glasses could become fogged or reflected glare and thereby divulge their location. Theory was limited to only one hour a day and afterward the trainees spent the remainder of their time in the field. Since Seetal was at high elevation, wind was always present and so they learned to adjust for it. They were expected to locate a camouflaged target, camouflage themselves and approach it, make a hide, shoot their target, and then withdraw undetected. Students were expected to make head shots at up to 400yd. The longest range available was 800yd.

The first day of class was on range estimation. As part of their training, the men were paired up and worked

Germany's highest-scoring sniper, Matthäus Hetzenauer. He served in the 144th *Gebirgsjäger* Regiment, 3d *Gebirgsjäger* Division and is credited with 345 confirmed kills. Note the turret-mounted scope on the K98k. *Jaroslav Alexandr Dvořák/ WikiCommons (CC BY-SA 4.0).*

German sniper training establishments[104]

Scharfschützen-Ausbildungskompanie (Nr.) Sharpshooter training company (No.)	Wehrkreis Military district	Truppenübungsplatz Military training area
101	I	Stablack
102	II	Groß-Born (today's Borne Sulinowo, Poland)
103	III	Wanderen
104	IV	Zeithain
105	V	Böttingen bei Münsingen
106	VI	Sennelager
107	VII	Hohenfels
108	VIII	Lamsdorf
109	IX	Wildflecken/Röhn
110	X	Munsterlager
111	XI	Bergen/Celle
112	XII	Heidelberg
113	XIII	Grafenwöhr/Ost
Military Shooting School	XVII	Bruck an der Leitha
118	XVIII	Seetal Alps (near Judenburg, Austria)
120	XX	Obergruppe
(121?)	XXI	Altwarp/Uckermark
Denmark Military District		Oksböl
Training Staff I	III	Döberitz
154th Field Training Division	Protectorate	Deutsch-Brod (today Havlíčkův Brod, Czech Rep.)
Sniper Inspectorate-Shooting School	XVII	Döllersheim

Sniper School

Replacement Brig (Mot) *Großdeutschland*	III	Cottbus
Replacement Brig (Mot) *Feldherrnhalle*	XX	Danzig-Langfuhr (today Wrzeszcz)
233d Reserve Panzer Division		Denmark
Panzer troop	III	Küstrin
Panzer troop	VI	Coesfeld
Panzer troop	IX	Erfurt
Panzer troop	XIII	Bamberg
Panzer troop	XVII	Vienna
Panzer troop	XXI/II	Kalisch (today Kalisz)

Care of weapons and equipment was stressed to snipers of all armies. The soldier on the right has a turret-mounted K98k. Note the chain pull-through bore-cleaner in his left hand. These two are cleaning their equipment in Romania. The pull-through was contained in the K98k cleaning kit (*Reinigungsgerät*) which included oil, brushes, cotton, and a take-down tool (not illustrated). *Richard Charlton Taylor.*

in teams of two. If anyone failed any examination along the way, they were returned immediately to their unit. Jung had trouble with distance estimation but a corporal took him under his wing and used a 19th-century technique of making the estimation, writing it down, and then pacing it off. Over time, he became adept at this crucial skill. After a week, the men were tested in new ground they had not seen before. Any estimate off by ten percent meant failure.

On the second week, those who remained were issued Mauser K98ks with 4x Zeiss scopes as well as 100 rounds of ammunition with which they could sight in their scopes. Once they were sighted, they were tested for marksmanship and half of the surviving class was washed out. Training continued for those who remained and consisted of more distance estimation, learning how a sniper or team of snipers fought, and night shooting.

Part of the training for the sniper recruits at Munsterlager included hatred for the enemy. Their instructor led with, "Every shot must kill a Jewish Bolshevik," to which the recruits replied, "Every shot!" The NCOs then shouted, "Kill the British swine!" and were answered with, "Every shot must kill!" While dehumanizing the enemy made it easier to kill him, one wonders if it could not be taught by other means or if the time spent could have been put to better use.[105]

The first German sniper manual—*Anleitung für die Ausbildung und den Einsatz von Scharfschützen* (Instructions for the training and use of snipers)—of May 15, 1943 (see also p. 70) covered mundane things that today's shooters take for granted, such as: use and care of the telescopic sight as well as correct eye picture, use of terrain, use of binoculars for observation, spotting, and distance estimation up to 500yd with certainty; the causes of underestimation (sun at sniper's back, across water, snow, plains, bright background, and surfaces) or overestimation (cloud, fog, rain, twilight, target has sun in the background, woods, dark background/surfaces, etc.). It suggested the sniper go to an oblique position to make the estimate.[106] Master of terrain and camouflage, the sniper was to avoid "careless movements" that could attract the enemy's observation. Snipers were not to shoot from windows but from within the room where the muzzle blast and smoke was less visible.[107] Shooting exercises included all types of weather including night conditions where moonlight helped the sniper. The sniper was instructed to prioritize the most dangerous opponents—snipers and observers were to be removed first followed by "sensitive" targets that included commanders, messengers, and ammunition carriers.[108] The manual encouraged the snipers to work with observers.

Drafted on July 22, 1943, Bruno Sutkus impressed his training company commander and the battalion commander with his shooting skill. Sutkus was no stranger to firearms before entering the army. Having been a member of the *Sturmabteilung* (he had transferred to it from the mandatory Hitler Youth when he turned 18), he received his first firearms instruction there and was given a .22 rifle and ammunition to encourage his skill. He used it on the farm to shoot sparrows and later crows. As the sparrows became leery of him and took flight when he appeared, Sutkus learned to stalk. Sutkus's stay at the infantry school was cut short when he was sent on a five-month course to the sniping school in Vilnius, Lithuania.

"We were shown (a) captured Russian film from which we gained an idea of the things a sniper had to master, especially fieldcraft, concealment, marksmanship (of course) and range estimation. Over these five months we learnt to absorb all the minute details a sniper had to bear in mind in order to spot the enemy hidden in the natural environment and to avoid being picked out himself. The instructors were good. In the countryside they taught us how to recognize a target, pass information, estimate range and shoot at moving targets. I developed great accuracy in the latter. I realized that in those five months I had to absorb what I could in order to survive in the field. At the end of the course all those who qualified received the most modern sniper's rifle with telescopic sights, binoculars and a camouflage jacket [*Tarnjacke*]."[109]

Hunting sparrows and crows as a youth and sniping school were not Sutkus's only experience with fieldcraft. Much of it was rooted in his childhood smuggling activity. Since Sutkus grew up on the border between East Prussia and Lithuania, he learned to avoid the border guards on both sides. He would smuggle things of great demand and scarcity—such as lighters, flints, and pumice stone—into Lithuania and return to East Prussia with hams, sausage, butter, fowl, etc. "[O]ne had to keep a good lookout near where the border guards were stationed or might be hiding under camouflage. I loved nature and had learnt how to observe it. This made it easy for me to spot the border guards."[110] After graduating, Sutkus returned to his training battalion which was then absorbed into the 196th Grenadier Regiment, 68th Infantry Division.

Waffen-SS snipers

As early as 1939 the Waffen-SS began placing emphasis on sniping, and in 1940 an effort was made to acquire captured Polish sniper rifles. Early experience in fighting in Russia only added impetus to the need for snipers. In an incident observed by Henk Kistemaker, a company from 5th SS Panzer Division *Wiking* (Viking) passed Dniepropetrovsk (today's Dnipro), could not advance, and asked for a sniper. This is evidence that even though no formal SS sniper schools were open at that time, men with skill and knowledge were available and could be called upon to snipe. The German sniper who was dispatched was likely pressed into service because of the circumstances. Kistemaker recalled:

"They say the only way to get a sniper is with another sniper, so we radioed command to ask for a German sniper. They sent us a guy and we explained to him the situation, and where we thought the sniper could possibly be located. The German sniper heard all our stories about where and when the shots were fired, and in which spot our men had been killed or wounded. He nodded after hearing all this information, like he had a good mental picture of the whole situation, and left for the forest. We watched him entering the forest and soon he was gone.

"We waited two days, and still he hadn't appeared. In the meantime, we lost another comrade and another one was badly wounded. Could the German sniper have become a victim of that Russian sniper too?

"Then, on the morning of the third day, our sniper came out of the forest. He walked slowly. We didn't see any signs of success from his body language. Maybe he couldn't find him, and the Russian guy was just too good? When he was within range we shouted: 'And? Did you kill the son of a bitch?' He nodded, but still no sign of triumph, so we started to wonder what was wrong with him. Surely he must be feeling proud?

"Now he was back in our lines and he jumped into the trench. 'Yes,' he said, 'I got your sniper, but it wasn't what I expected it to be.'

"'Why? What?' we all started to ask him. 'It was a young woman,' he said." [111]

Unfortunately Kistemaker did not describe the German's sniper rifle. Additionally, it is likely that the dead Russian sniper's rifle was pressed into service too.

As an independent organization that considered itself superior to the army, the SS adopted its own sniping manual in 1944 after the army had theirs. The selection process for the SS sniper included: completion of regular training, a good and calm shooter, quick intelligence, excellent vision, ability to fight alone, and trained in the use of telescopic sights. It advocated that snipers be paired up, with both men having telescopic-sighted rifles and one man having binoculars for spotting or observing.

Training at an SS sniper school was two weeks long (100 hours) and included observation (including locating small, camouflaged targets), distance estimation, target selection, camouflage, use of terrain, use of telescopic

An SS sniper armed with a Zf41-scoped K98k engaging the Soviets near Rshev. *NARA.*

sights, movement (no hasty movement), tactics and tactical exercises, shooting up to 650yd, moving targets, two-person sniper teams, and use of artificial light, twilight, and moonlight. When in the open, the manual encouraged snipers to use well-camouflaged dugouts with small apertures to fire from. When fighting from a trench, only a small loophole that was oblique to the enemy was to be used. As in the army manual, buildings or ruins could be used and bricks removed to create loopholes. Regarding explosive bullets, the manual only cited examples used by the Russians and noted that because the bullet exploded, it made it difficult to judge the direction from which it was fired.

Tactics-wise the SS considered their snipers too valuable to be included in an infantry assault.[112] Instead, the sniper(s) were to provide covering fire for an attack. Tracer ammunition was used only during training and not to be used in the field by the sniper.[113] Initially, SS snipers could be used individually but in face of increasing reliance by the Soviets on sniping, doctrine now mandated that snipers operated in pairs or at least with an observer.[114]

A valuable inclusion in the SS manual that was not found in the 1943 army manual is an excerpt on sniping from the Soviet "Collection of Tactical Examples from the Experience of the Patriotic Wars," which covers much of the material discussed earlier in this work.[115]

In late 1944 Germany was hard-pressed with the Red Army pushing in the east and southeast and the Americans, British, Canadians, and French edging the Germans out of France and the Low Countries. On August 20, 1944 to promote sniping, a reward program that featured cloth patches (*Scharfschützenabzeichen*) depicting an eagle with oak leaves and an acorn was adopted, with high scorers to be recognized by *Reichsführer*-SS Himmler and given an opportunity to hunt on his estate. The patch was to be sewn on the right sleeve. Third class was awarded for 20 kills; second class, with a silver cord around the border, for 40 kills; a gold cord around the border denoted 60 kills—all dating from September 1, 1944. Close-quarter kills were not counted and every kill had to be witnessed and reported to the unit which would keep tally.

Germany was also scraping the bottom of the barrel and drafted older, middle-aged men, many of whom had fought for the Kaiser in World War I. Germany also began training teens 16 to 17 years of age into service and some received a very brief sniper course.[116] Sepp Allerberger remembered seeing an SS platoon of youth armed with scoped rifles headed for the front. He didn't think they would last long. German policy in 1944 was to conscript teens and by 1945 even children, including girls, were told to fight for the Führer with those refusing being hung. Company B, First Battalion, Second Infantry Regiment of the American Fifth Infantry Division once captured an 11-year-old boy who was armed with a scoped rifle, wore a camouflage cape and had papers attesting to his age.[117]

SS-Sturmbrigade Dirlewanger was best known for its brutality and war crimes. The unit was originally composed of convicts and poachers who were already skilled in elusiveness or hunting. This is one of its snipers. *GF collection.*

Anleitung für die Ausbildung und den Einsatz von Scharfschützen*

*Instructions for the training and use of snipers.

Contents

A. Purpose and role of the sniper

B. Sharpshooter Training
1. The sharpshooter
2. The shooting instructor
3. Lessons
   a) Aiming
   b) Target error
   c) Hold points [This references where to look through the scope and placement of the scope's reticle on the target. It must be horizontal and not canted since a canted scope can cause the point of impact to deviate.]
4. Aim and firing-position exercises
5. Visual exercises and identification of targets
6. Target address
7. Estimating distances
8. Camouflage and use of spades
9. Stalking exercises
10. The sharp shot
   a) Target practice for sharpshooters [For both replacement and field army.]
   b) Objectives

C. Use of the sharpshooter
1. Attack
2. Defense
   a) Working with an observer
   b) In front of the HKL
[*Hauptkampflinie*—main combat line]
   c) In forest positions

D. Treatment and care of the telescopic sight and telescopic rifle

Appendices
1: Examples of the use of the sharpshooter
2: Target practice for the reserve army
3: Target practice for the field army
4: Table for lead dimensions
5: Description of the riflescope 41
6: Description of the 4x riflescope (commercially available)

"Attack and Defense

1. Attack
In the attack, the sharpshooter can be given the following tasks:
• Particularly dangerous targets that hinder progress
• Monitoring the actions of the group or a patrol
• Taking over the flank protection

When attacking, the sharpshooter positions himself a little to the side of the group in order to be able to shoot unhindered.

"As a rule, the sharpshooter must choose the most dangerous targets … commanders of tanks, etc."

2. Defense
In defense, the sharpshooter must dominate enemy trenches with his fire. No careless movement of the enemy must escape him. For this reason the sharpshooter is to be given freedom of movement in the selection of his position in the section of group, platoon, and often also the company. The sharpshooter can, therefore, depending on location and terrain, be in the front line or further back, e.g. take position at a commanding height or in a tree.

"In order not to give himself away, the sharpshooter should generally not fire more than three to six shots from a position and often take alternating positions.

"Continuous observation of the enemy by sharpshooters must be ensured.

"If the enemy behaves too cautiously as a result of sharpshooter activity, it is advisable to stop shooting for one or more days in order to induce the enemy to make careless movements again. On bright and sunny days, with snowfall in winter, the opponent tends to be careless about food and drink, so that a good sharpshooter will always find targets."[118]

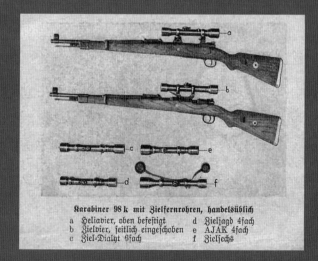

Above: One of the pages from the training manual covers commercially available scopes and mounts.
a) Turret-mounted Kahles Heliavier 4x
b) Early short-rail mounted Zeiss Zielvier 4x
c) Hensoldt Ziel-Dialyt 6x
d) Hensoldt Ziel-Jagd 4x
e) Ajack 4x 90
f) Zeiss Zielsechs 6x with lens protectors

Japan

Fifty rounds of ball ammunition were issued a day for range practice. Occasionally, flat-nosed, reduced-charge ammunition was issued for the 50yd range. The morning was spent with each man being personally supervised by the officer during firing practice. Scopes were used for 300–600yd shooting. Under 300yd the men used iron sights. Both eyes were to remain open during practice.[119]

Their four-week-long training included advanced infantry training and sometimes scout training. Training was conducted on a regimental or battalion level. Lessons included range estimation from 200 to 600yd. Officers would place objects at varying distances and the men would estimate the distance. Strangely, the men were not required to estimate distance of objects over water. For objects over 600yd, the men were instructed to sight in on a closer object which could readily be ranged, and then to estimate the difference between that object and the target itself.

Naturally, camouflage—especially of the upper half of the body—was important. Helmet and body nets were standard issue. Foliage could be added to the netting to enhance the camouflage. Some Japanese found the nets to be cumbersome as they could be snagged in vines or shrubs. Those who disliked nets cut off branches or twigs to insert into their clothing. Where the background was not verdant, the sniper had to improvise by using "dry branches and leaves and dry bark to blend with the color of the background."[120] Camouflage was also used when snipers were expected to gather intelligence. On an information gathering mission, they were not expected to shoot but to observe and report their observations back to their commander.[121]

No training was given in muffling sounds from operating the bolt or the ejection of the spent cartridge case. It was up to the individual to move his bolt as slowly as possible to minimize the noise that could betray his position.[122]

Live fire exercises were conducted under all weather conditions with open sights and later a scoped rifle. Per captured documents, the sniper's mission included:

• Kill or capture hostile personnel, especially leaders and snipers.
• Neutralize or destroy hostile installations that might obstruct a unit's mission.
• Destroy heavy equipment and its personnel.
• Deal with targets of opportunity.[123]

"In many respect snipers caused the Marines more trouble than any other single factor."[124] In removing

leaders, the Japanese figured out American tactics and knew that the first two soldiers in the squad were the scout and then assistant scout. The squad leader would generally be the third or fourth person in line and was the preferred target. Japanese also looked for men who talked. Order givers equaled leaders. Some officers made themselves conspicuous by wearing their insignia in combat. In the Philippines (1944–45), one GI complained:

"In our company we have had 10 different officers. Not one is an officer who originally started the campaign with us. We have had four different C.O.'s. We have had five noncoms commissioned; out of these five, only one is left in the lines. In the whole company now we have two officers.

Graphic instruction from *Scouting, Patrolling, and Sniping* (see p. 49) to ensure dead enemy soldiers really were dead. Scouts, wrote Leon C. Sandifer, were to "'advance boldly and aggressively' directly at the suspected enemy positions. Under this concept, the real purpose of the scout was to draw fire. The scout got killed, but the patrol escaped." The Japanese soon got wise to the U.S. patrol tactics and aimed for the officer in preference to the scout.[125]
GF Collection.

"The Japs have a knack for getting the leader. He's zeroed in just as soon as the patrol is spotted, because of the aforementioned reasons."[126]

Japanese doctrine also asserted that, "In defensive combat, positions will be constructed to employ the principle of sudden fire at opportune moments. Sudden fire and sniping will be especially stressed at close range."[127] Hindsight tells us that sniping at close range does not take full advantage of the longer distance a scoped rifle can engage from (and the sniper's escape). According to one prisoner, there was a sniper in every LMG squad. However, not all snipers were equipped with scoped rifles. If killed or disabled, the eleventh man, the assistant machine gunner who was an ammunition carrier, was generally trained to replace the sniper.

Initially, the Japanese were not defensively oriented. If a superior force attacked, the squad and the sniper were to lay down a heavy fire. It is noteworthy that the sniper was not instructed to aim and that volume of fire took precedence over accuracy. The purpose was to alert other Japanese units that a superior force was being engaged. The defending squad was to withdraw but not directly toward the parent unit. Presumably this would be to allow the parent or larger unit to

flank the enemy. If the superior force flanked them, the sniper was expected to deal with it until the unit could respond. This implies that the discretion to retreat was not an option. As Japan found itself more on the defensive, it was compelled to adopt defensive tactics including pillboxes, interlocking fields of fire, and snipers to protect pillboxes and machine guns. In Burma, the British found that Japanese snipers were sometimes protected by a rifleman who was posted in a camouflaged position to his rear.[128]

As with other belligerents, sometimes Japanese snipers covered the withdrawal and watched road blocks, obstacles, the flanks of defensive areas or pillboxes, and lines of communications. Sometimes they allowed their victims to pass before shooting them in the back. This would compel the entire unit to halt and search for him. After some experience, the Allied assault troops would continue toward their objective and leave small mop-up patrols to deal with the sniper.[129]

Snipers were urged to take prisoners whenever possible. If a sniper were to engage a unit, unit leaders and then heavy weapons personnel were to be engaged first as their removal could reduce unit morale and make it easier to take prisoners. Leaders were identified by those carrying sidearms or giving commands. Another prime target of the Japanese snipers were Allied snipers. They were a threat to the machine gun and the gunners.

The sniper was expected to remain within voice command of his leader. If this was unfeasible, then hand signals were used. Often though, the squad leader left the sniper to his own device.[130] They were also known to resort to bird calls, whistles, and tapping on logs to communicate.[131]

At Attu, sniper posts and observation posts were located according to the terrain. "They had no paths leading to them, and were well camouflaged with grass and, in some instances, turf and moss … The Japanese sniper or sentry apparently approached his post from a different direction each time he reported." This avoided creating a well-trodden path that was discernible. Additionally, the relief parties did not approach the post and only the individual soldier did.[132] Individual soldiers at Attu were provided with hooded, camouflaged 9ft × 6ft capes that blended well with the tundra. Made of rain-resistant tar paper they were held together with string.[133]

American wartime movies and cartoons ridiculed the Japanese with stereotypes characterized by buckteeth and coke-bottle glasses. They, along with wartime newspapers, made it seem easy to defeat the Japanese as they were not formidable opponents. As pure wartime propaganda designed to encourage enlistment and buoy morale, some naïve Americans believed it wholeheartedly, and after being on field maneuvers one marine complained, "Well, I'll tell ya, I'm sick and tired of all this training. I want to get over and slap me a Jap." His sergeant who was wounded at Guadalcanal exploded:

"Hold on, sonny! Let me tell you a thing or two about the Japanese soldier! Number one, he is not the caricature you see in newspapers with bombsight glasses and buck teeth. The average Japanese soldier has five or more years of combat experience. Their army doesn't have a 'boot division' like ours … Japs are the world's best snipers, expert at the art of camouflage, and get by on a diet of fish heads and rice. They will never surrender and will commit hari-kari rather than be taken prisoner. Heck, they don't have corpsmen; if they are wounded, they are considered damaged goods. So, sonny, mull all over that, and don't ever let me hear you complain about your training again."[134]

Very little survived in the way of Japanese accounts, but a fragment of one Japanese sniper's diary luckily survived and reads:

"We were instructed that our jobs was to hold up the American advance, and to kill as many as possible before we were killed. Dying in the service of the Emperor was an honourable thing … but we should not take unnecessary risks for the longer we stopped the enemy, the greater the achievement."[135]

The Japanese went to enormous pains to prepare their positions with perfect camouflage and concealment. One battalion commander commented that he had four marines killed "by a wounded sniper who had three holes in him. He was lying in thick bush 15 yards away from my CP. He was camouflaged and passed over for dead. You have to kill to put them out."[136]

When appropriate, as during the fighting on the Solomons Islands, the Japanese wore fiber cloaks that blended perfectly with coconut-tree trunks.[137] Marine Cpl. Burke West of Arvin, CA complained, "Even though you know there's a sniper in a tree, and you have field glasses, you still can't see him."[138] Covered-in pits had been prepared for mortars and machine guns. Pits were dug beneath fallen trees with only a small hole left in the tree branch for the barrel of the gun. Snipers were hidden in trees … Rarely were Japanese seen.[139] One Japanese helmet was so cleverly camouflaged that it was described as "a terrific $95 hot house creation of a millinery shop."[140]

Many Japanese climbed trees and, after tying themselves to it, camouflaged themselves with palm fronds. They knew that trees offered little protection, but by tying themselves they wouldn't fall if hit and would leave their enemy wondering if they had missed, thus compelling them to expend more ammunition to remove all doubt. Sometimes after penetrating Allied lines and climbing a tree, the Japanese soldier would wait for a few days before firing.[141] Another trick was to remove the bark around certain trees. This would provide a convenient range marker to help them with their hold. Other times they dug rifle pits which they covered with a lid camouflaged with local vegetation. After firing, they could drop the lid and remain invisible to their enemy. Most times the Japanese sniper worked alone but when brigaded together at the regimental level they worked as teams to deny crossings or roads to the enemy.[142]

To counter the Japanese infiltration and the sniper, Australian troops were given the following instructions which they shared with American intelligence:

"3. *Japanese infiltrate through our lines. They expect and intend that we fall back.*

Countermeasure: Don't fall back. Hold your line. If you fall back there will be no opportunity to reorganize your line. The Japanese may be in behind us, but we are also in behind them. When they fail to demoralize us, they don't know what to do next.

"4. *Japs place snipers and machine guns in trees and cover, and leave them there while we pass.*

Countermeasure: Do the same, only better, and don't fall back or be demoralized by sniping. Keep a lookout to observe the enemy. He won't fire until he is on your flank or rear."[143]

Stalker-snipers

For the British and Australians, once a sniper was discovered, the recommended method of disposing of him was with "stalker-snipers" who would crawl long distances to kill their quarry. Dry creek beds and gullies were useful for this and at confluences between gullies or creek beds, the stalker-snipers could discuss their meetings under cover.[144]

Part II Wartime Sniping

| 4 Western Europe, North Africa, and Italy

"The Boys can't lift their heads out of the trenches all day without a sniper firing."[1]

Lt. Thomas Beckwith
Morris, IL

Lt. Beckwith and his men, pinned down in Italy, were not the first Allied soldiers to draw the unwelcome attention of a sniper, and sniping in the ETO predates the invasion of Italy. While snipers had a minor role in North Africa, they had a phantom-like affect on the soldiers who fought there. In this chapter, we will learn of the sniping from 1939 to 1944 and around the Mediterranean from Africa to Italy.

Sniping played its part from the start of the war. During the invasion of Poland in Bydgoszcz (Bromberg in German) on September 3–4, 1939, German infiltrators and local paramilitary snipers shot at and killed a number of retreating Polish troops. In the gun battle and Polish reprisals that ensued, a number of Germans were killed. These, in turn, led to even more horrific Nazi massacres when the area was in German hands. *Generalmajor* Otto von Knobelsdorff, chief operations officer to *Generalleutnant* Georg Brandt of the German 3d Border Guards (*Grenzschutz-Abschnittkommando 3*), "noted in the unit's war diary on September 4 that fighting with Polish snipers in Katowice was so intense,"[2] although, like the Germans, the Poles did not have "snipers" as such but sharpshooters.

On April 9, 1940, the German attacks on western Europe began with the invasion of Denmark and Norway. At Grantanger north of Narvik, the Germans met heavy resistance and most of the 150 killed were attributed to Norwegian snipers. In response to Norwegian resistance in Oslo, particularly snipers, the Germans responded by threatening death for any sniper caught.[3] The Norwegian king attributed his and his parliament's escape from Norway in part to the fighting at Elverum where the German advance was stifled by a small garrison supplemented by members of a local gun club. It was called, "a kind of Lexington" in reference to the Rebel stand against British forces at

the outbreak of the American Revolution,[4] although it's difficult to equate the Redcoats in 1775 to the Nazi invaders of 1940!

The British deployed snipers with its units in Norway and also did so in France. In 1940, during the Phoney War period, a German infantryman (dubbed "George" and described as a German sniper) would regularly appear in the open at 900 yards to do his morning exercises. Efforts to snipe him failed—which doesn't say much for the British snipers (if they were snipers) who tried to get him or for their equipment.[5]

Sitzkrieg became *Blitzkrieg* on May 10, 1940, when Germany unleashed its attack on the west. The 154th Regiment of the 58th Infantry Division (German XXIII Army Corps) entered Luxembourg and then France, flanking the Maginot Line. Upon crossing the border, they ran into resistance from a French colonial division, possibly the 82e African Infantry Division. Electrician's apprentice now *Gefreiter* William Lubbecke hailed from a farming family from the small village of Püggen (then in the Gau Magdeburg-Anhalt) and had been assigned to the communications platoon of a heavy weapons company. He remembered:

"Once our regiment reached the front, I learned how bitter the initial fighting had been. Advancing into action, our division had confronted ferocious resistance from a French-Algerian division from North Africa. In what proved the 58th's toughest combat of the campaign, these Algerian troops were firing down at our infantry from concealed positions up in the trees. To make progress, our infantry had to deploy snipers and spray machine-gun fire into the trees. In some cases, they even used flamethrowers to burn the Algerians out."[6]

After pushing back the French-Algerians, they began turning south. Between Beaumont-en-Argonne and Dun-sur-Meuse the regiment ran into French snipers.

> "Upon my arrival at a church in a small town a little further south, I heard that two French snipers perched high in the steeple had picked off a number of our troops a few hours earlier. Following the capture of the two French soldiers, many of our troops wanted retribution for the deaths they had caused among our men. As punishment, an officer in our regiment ordered that the snipers be forced to spend a couple of hours kneeling on the concrete steps in front of the church's altar before being led back to one of our prisoner-of-war camps."[7]

That punishment was rather merciful: certainly, many of the French colonial troops who surrendered or were captured were tortured and massacred by the Germans.

As the Allies were pushed back by the German advance, Edgar Rabbets was a British sniper with the 5th Battalion, Northamptonshire Regiment, who had been in France since the start of the year. A country boy and an excellent shot with exemplary fieldcraft, he was called into action in Belgium when a German sniper was dominating a town square from a position in a roof. Rabbets did what so many snipers would do during the course of the war. First, he questioned the eyewitness, a British officer who had had a narrow escape. Having identified the likely location of the enemy sniper, he then found himself a position in a nearby house and observed the area, noting that slates had been removed in two places: that of the sniper and probably that of his observer.

Fortunately, the sniper exposed himself and was an easy kill. When that happened, the observer fired towards Rabbets whose position, deep inside the room, couldn't be seen. The German missed but the British sniper's response didn't. "That," Rabbets said, "was his lot."

On another occasion Rabbets saw a German MP waiting at a crossroads. Why would he do that? To direct oncoming troops, reasoned the sniper, and carefully closed the distance to confirm his suspicions.

> "He gave himself away by continually looking up the road to where he expected the unit to come from, and because there was only one direction to our lines, I knew roughly where they were going to. I shot him and then bundled him out of the way so that when the enemy got to the crossroads they wouldn't know where they were going. Then I went back to my unit to give them this intelligence."[8]

The campaign in France ended in capitulation six weeks later. Some 330,000 British and French troops escaped from the beaches of Dunkirk and other French ports, but the British left behind 11,000 dead and some 40,000 captured and most of their heavy weapons. The experiences of the soldiers were reflected in the publication on October 2, 1940, of *Military Training Pamphlet* No. 44 which advised:

> "in the recent fighting both in Norway and in France … snipers proved to be indispensable, and by their use of ground, endurance and expert shooting, were able to put large numbers of enemy weapons out of action by operating on the flanks of the attacking troops. They also succeeded, on several occasions, in putting enemy batteries out of action by shooting down the gun crews."[9]

With the northern coast of Europe in enemy hands, military action moved south to the Mediterranean and north Africa.

Operation Exporter

(Syria-Lebanon campaign, June 8–July 12, 1941)
To prevent the Germans from establishing bases in Syria and Lebanon (then part of Vichy Syria) from where they could attack Egypt, the British Army—18,000 Australians, 9,000 British, 2,000 Indians, and 5,500 Free French—invaded on June 8, 1941. The Australian column that was advancing on Damascus was delayed an entire day by sniping. In one case (June 11), a 25pdr field gun was brought up and at 1,000yd distance, silenced a sniper.[10]

In the fighting around Merdjayoun in Lebanon (June 19–24, 1941) the 2/33rd Battalion of the Australian 25th Brigade from Palestine engaged a French Senegalese sniper. Hidden on a rocky ridge near Merdjayoun, he "caused a lot of casualties" and "every attempt to locate and dislodge him had failed." A Queensland kangaroo hunter volunteered to find him. Camouflaging himself with grass, he hid in a corn field and waited for hours. Frustrated, the Queenslander exposed himself and was rewarded with a bullet to the shoulder. After plugging his wound, he continued waiting. Finally, "A bush on the hillside moved slightly as the sniper tried to see what had become of his victim. The kangaroo shooter's rifle spoke once, and the body of a Senegalese rifleman rolled out from under the brush." The loss of blood caused the Queenslander to faint and his mates found him and got him medical care.[11] Certainly his wounding could have been prevented if he had a spotter. In another incident south of Damour, one Senegalese sniper stubbornly defended his post until he was surrounded. Only after he was injured did he finally surrender.[12]

Henry Gonnell, a reporter for United Press who had worked in Spain during the civil war and who went on to file the first report from the D-Day beaches, discussed the French sniping techniques against the British and its Commonwealth allies in Syria:

"they are using the sniper tactics the Germans taught the French Foreign Legion to use against the Australians in Syria in June, 1941. They put their snipers in diamond formation, mostly up trees. They allow our men to come forward along the lanes and then when they flop to avoid surprise volleys from camouflaged machine-

guns—squads, the snipers pot them one by one— if one sniper misses, generally one of his mates doesn't."[13]

As the Australians reached Beirut the French sued for an armistice (Armistice of Saint Jean d'Arc) which went into effect on July 12 and the campaign concluded. Success had stopped any chance of the Germans mounting a campaign from Syria, but manpower for the operation came at the expense of the British Eighth Army. This contributed to the failure of Operation Battleaxe to clear eastern Cyrenaica and lift the siege of Tobruk.

Crete
(May 20–June 1, 1941)
Under the code name Operation Mercury (*Merkur*), *Fallschirmjäger* of German 7th Airborne Division were dropped on the island on May 20, 1941. They were later reinforced by *Gebirgsjäger* of 5th Mountain

Map showing the German assault on Crete. *U.S. Military Academy.*

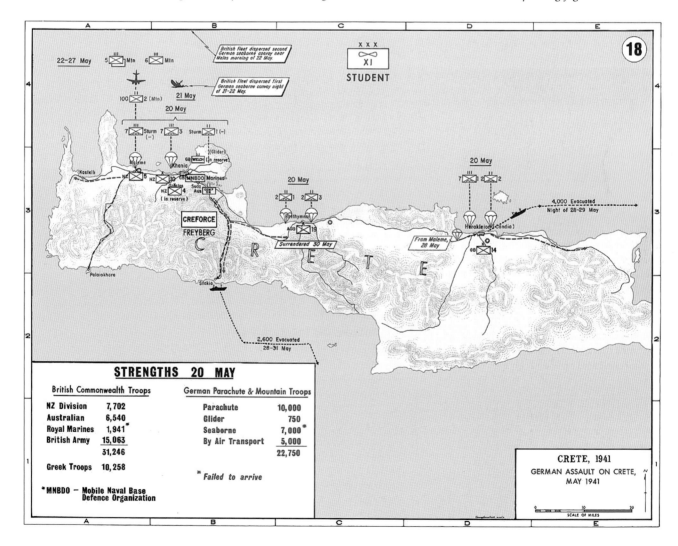

Division. After heavy fighting they overwhelmed the British Commonwealth and Greek defenders of the island, although at a high cost—Hitler refused to allow large airborne operations after this.

Distinguishing himself as a counter-sniper on Crete, Sgt. Alfred Clive Hulme was running the Field Punishment Centre of the 23rd (Canterbury-Otago) Battalion, 5th Brigade, 2nd Division, 2NZEF, when the Germans arrived.[14] Hulme was raised on a farm in New Zealand and learned stalking as a child from having to round up cows. Some cows were particularly obstinate and would flee at his approach. To make his chore easier, he learned to stalk quietly without breaking any sticks and so catch the cow by surprise and prevent it from running off.

When the German *Fallschirmjäger* began to descend into the gullies near the Maleme airfield, he organized his men and they attacked the Germans with grenades. Trapped, more than 120 dead Germans were counted. When he returned to his battalion, he found he had no duties and so took it upon himself to stalk Germans.

He "had acquired two items from parachutists he had shot which gave him some protection on his stalking patrols and may possibly have misled the Germans. These were a camouflage suit or blouse which he wore over his battle-dress tunic and a camouflage hat, which could be worn either rolled up like a balaclava or down in a hood, with eye-slits, over the face."[15] He had also captured a Mauser sniper rifle from a weapons container dropped for the *Fallschirmjäger* (unlike American and British practice, the German paratroopers did not jump with their rifles or machine guns and they had to retrieve them from parachuted drop containers).[16] Hulme stalked Germans not only from the British lines but also from within the German lines. Knowing they liked high vantage points, he stalked the hills and often got within pistol distance to kill them. Then he had to evade detection and had to crawl backward downhill to safety. Hulme also killed nine Germans with a bayonet and five with his sheath knife. Other times he used the Mauser. His thirst for German blood redoubled when he learned his brother, Cpl. "Blondie" Hulme of 19th Battalion, had died of wounds on May 26, 1941.

"At one stage I found myself actually advancing with the Jerries towards our own boys. Several of them were camouflaged and so was I, so they took me for one of them. I lay alongside them as they fired and put my sights up to 700 yards so that my shots would go high and I wouldn't hit my own cobbers. A German spoke to me. I knew no German and couldn't answer him, so I crawled over and knifed him."

New Zealand's Sergeant Clive Hulme used a captured German sniper rifle to kill numerous Germans. *Unknown author, natlib.govt.nz/ records/23110916, Public Domain/WikiCommons.*

Hulme once deliberately revealed himself to draw German fire:

"I walked up and down on the edge of a ridge to draw their fire while others watched, but they refused to be drawn. And then I happened to spot, in the glow of the setting sun, a glint of glass in an olive tree about 100 yards away. A Jerry was straddling a branch up against the trunk and the glint of glass had come from his gas mask, which he had worn all day, so that the white of his face could not be seen. We charged the olive grove at dusk and got the issue."[17]

Hulme was injured when he fired at a German sniper. Because he forgot to adjust his sights for a lower elevation, the shot went high, the German sniper heard it, swung around and shot him. Injured in the shoulder, he was ordered to the rear. Hulme would not go until he organized stragglers into groups. Having killed numerous snipers—the official citation says 33—most of whom he had stalked and killed from the rear along with numerous other deeds, Hulme was awarded the Victoria Cross. Hulme was declared medically unfit and retired as a warrant officer in 1943.

Another hunter of snipers was "Tiny" Pyke, a musician from Auckland. After two Australians were killed by an unseen sniper, Tiny and two others set off to flank him at night. They departed and sometime later Tiny and his two comrades also parted company. The two returned and nothing was heard of Tiny. Two days later he returned to camp and had on him a P08

Luger. His only comment was, "There's one ***** who won't do anymore sniping."[18]

Finally, LAC Donald F. Cooper traded shot for shot with the Germans. Cooper wrote home stating:

> "But the enemy couldn't shoot for bean. The nearest only cut my helmet strap. What a place Crete was! And it sure was a game while it lasted. Now they're trying to make me out that I'm a blinking hero. You know, mentioned in dispatches. Well, I did bump off a sniper at 800 yards. I enjoyed the fight."

After being evacuated from Crete, Cooper transferred to the RAF.[19]

Dieppe
(August 19, 1942)

The raid on Dieppe was planned and executed by Combined Operations Headquarters to temporarily seize and hold a major port for a few hours just to prove that it could be done, gather intelligence, and indirectly, to boost morale. The bulk of the force was supplied by 2nd Canadian Division (5,000 men), along with British commandos (c. 1,100), 50 U.S. Rangers (of these, six were killed, seven wounded, and four captured), and 15 French commandos: they were well served by snipers. Cameron Highlander Pte. Alexander Huppe served as one. After landing on Pourville Beach to the west of Dieppe, the German fire directed at him did not disturb his aim and his return fire was deadlier to the enemy. As he went inland, he hid behind trees or anything else that could conceal him and picked off Germans. His Military Medal citation mentioned that he:

> "carried out his duties through the entire operation with outstanding courage and total disregard for his own safety. He several times disposed of enemy snipers who were hindering his advance. In the fighting around the La Scie river this sniper was exposed to heavy enemy fire, nevertheless, was exceedingly accurate and prevented the Germans from making a flank attack which would have caused the loss of a piece of ground that was vital to our troops."

One officer remarked, "Huppe was like a kid on the midway shooting up targets with a .22." Huppe modestly remarked, "All the Germans we could see we bumped off with pleasure."[20]

Another Canadian who distinguished himself was Cpl. Joseph Arthur Gregory of the South Saskatchewan Regiment. As a scout-sniper attached to battalion HQ, he went out alone four times to stalk and silence Germans soldiers who were sniping at them. Each time he was successful in his mission but on one he lost an eye. In recognition of his bravery, he was awarded the Distinguished Service Medal. Gregory was no youngster either. Born on December 14, 1900, he was a sniper with the 1st Canadian Mounted Rifles during the Great War too.[21]

Embedded with the South Saskatchewan Regiment was correspondent Wallace Rayburn of the *Montreal Standard*.

"In one Dieppe street as we advanced, I noticed a young French boy who must have read about cowboys and Indians. As German snipers peppered the streets incessantly, the boy dodged in and out among the buildings. He was wearing a blue beret. Hiding behind the edge of a building, he put his beret on a stick, held it out around the building edge, then, when he assured himself that the coast was clear, he put his beret on his head and dashed across the street.

"These snipers were constant trouble despite the excellent house clearing done by the Canadians. I encountered Sergeant Howard Graham of Swift Current, Saskatchewan. The jacket of his battle dress was bulging with incendiaries. I asked where he was going. He replied: 'There's a sniper along that road who is picking our boys off. I am going to smoke him out. I'll go along the road setting each house afire until I get him or he'll get me. He will come running outdoors and I will pick that bastard off with a Sten gun.'

"There was a determined set to Graham's jaw as he said, 'So long boys,' and set off down the road. I didn't see Graham until several hours later, when we were making for the beach. He recognized me, saying. 'Oh by the way, newspaperman, I got that bloody sniper all right.'"[22]

Another Cameron Highlander sniper who landed at Pourville, Pte. William Hopkin was awarded the Military Medal for his actions when the withdrawal was taking place. His citation reads:

"Private Hopkin passed up his own chance to escape when some boats arrived by deliberately drawing the enemy's fire from the hillside in order that some of his comrades struggling in the water might reach the boats. With only a couple of logs

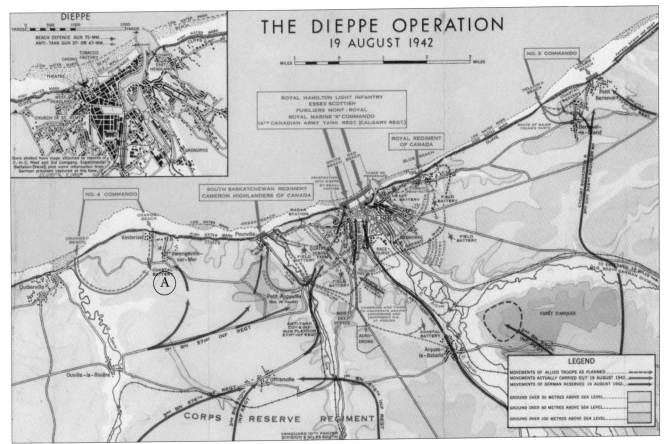

THE DIEPPE OPERATION
19 AUGUST 1942

British & Commonwealth rifles

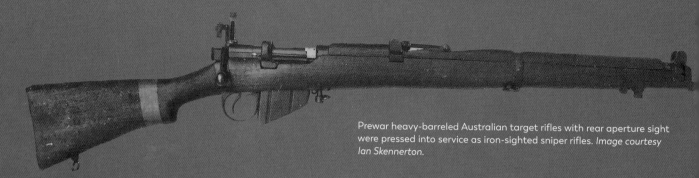

Prewar heavy-barreled Australian target rifles with rear aperture sight were pressed into service as iron-sighted sniper rifles. *Image courtesy Ian Skennerton.*

Rifle No. 3 Mk. I* (T) with Pattern 18 scope
Caliber: .303in. (7.696mm)
Weight: 10lb 9 oz (4.791kg)
Weight w/scope: 11lb 5oz (5.131kg)
Length: 46.4in. (1.168m)
Barrel: 26 in. (66.04cm)
Magazine: 5-round

Rifle No. 3 Mk. I* (T)A
Caliber: .303in. (7.696mm)
Weight: 11lb 5 oz (5.131kg)
Weight w/scope: 12lb 9oz (5.698kg)
Length: 46.4in. (1.179m)
Barrel: 26in. (66.04cm)

Rifle No. 1 Mk. III* HT with Pattern 1918 (Aldis)
Caliber: .303in. (7.696mm)
Weight: 10lb 10oz (4.819kg)
Weight w/scope: 11lb 9.5oz (5.259kg)
Length: 44.5in (1.13m)
Barrel: 25.2in (65.01cm)
Magazine: 10-round detachable box

Rifle No. 4 Mk. I (T)[23] with No. 32 Mk. I scope
Caliber: .303in (7.696mm)
Weight: 11lb 10 oz (5.273kg)
Weight w/scope: 13lb 15 oz (6.322kg)
Length: 44.5in. (1.13m)
Barrel: 25.2in. (64.01cm)
Magazine: 10-round box, detachable

Postwar sniper Sgt. Maj. Mark Spicer tells that British snipers used regular ball ammunition and set their zero at 275yd. At that distance, the sniper aimed for the middle of the head. Such a zero would allow the sniper to hit a man from 25yd to 300yd at anywhere between the top of the head and the chest. For greater distance the sniper would either hold over and if necessary, adjust the elevation knob on the scope.[24]

The No. 4 Mk. I (T) was the standard British sniping rifle during World War II. The scope was originally intended for the Bren gun the 3x No. 32 scope tube was steel and had cast base and rings. *Greene Media Ltd.*

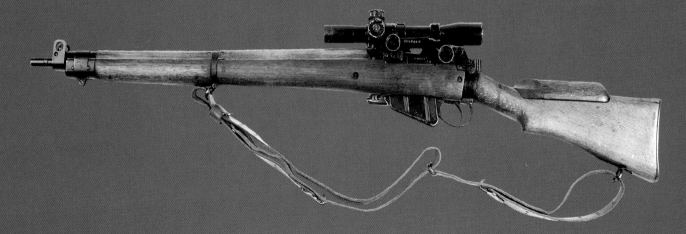

A Canadian sniper with a No. 3 Mk. I (T)—P14—during an assault landing course. LAC.

Canadian sniper with No. 3 Mk. I (T) equipped with a WW I Warner & Swazey prismatic sight near Orsogna, Italy. In the foreground a Bren gun. January 29, 1944. LAC.

for protection, he engaged the enemy so effectively that they rained mortar, machine gun and rifle fire at him which previously had been directed at the men in the water. He had several narrow escapes, but undaunted, kept up his fire until the grease was running out of the seams of his rifle and the bolt was so overheated it would not close. Private Hopkin, who was one of the finest shots in the battalion, was later taken prisoner."

Another of the Rangers was 26-year-old Ranger Sgt. Ken G. Kenyon who enlisted in 1940 and whose previous civilian occupation was as a grocery store clerk in Millbank, SD. He too landed at Pourville on Green Beach and was credited as the first American infantryman to shoot a German—although that is also credited to Cpl. Koons (see below). According to his mother, Kenyon's hunting experience as a youth included a lot of rabbits and gophers.[25]

The only completely successful part of the operation was Operation Cauldron on the west flank. Lt. Col. The Lord Lovat's No. 4 Commando landed on

The first American soldier to fire a shot in anger on the continent of Europe, Franklin "Zip" Koons was awarded the Military Medal for his part in Operation Jubilee. *NARA.*

Orange Beaches and destroyed a German strongpoint at Varengeville the main target being the 813d Army Coastal Artillery Battery's six 150mm guns. The force included four American Rangers, two of whom were part of the 20-strong sniper team—Sgt. Alex J. Szima and Cpl. Franklin M. "Zip" Koons—who became a national hero for being the first American soldier to fire a shot in anger on the continent of Europe, and is also credited with the first kill. Koons, who later saw service in North Africa, Italy, and northwest Europe, was supplying supporting fire for the men attacking the coastal guns. "I found a good spot for sniping," Koons recalled. "It was over a manger, and I fired through a slit in a brick wall."[26] When he spotted a German, he aimed, fired, and brought him down. After their mission was accomplished, Koons volunteered to be in the rearguard to protect his buddies and fellow soldiers. His actions won him the British Military Medal, the U.S. Silver Star, and the Canadian Dieppe Medal. He ended the war having moved through the ranks from private to first lieutenant.

All the men—British and American—were due to wear British uniforms, faces and hands were to be camouflaged brown, while those of snipers were to be green. However, as Szima relates, the Rangers decided to wear American uniforms:

"after hearing a speech on the 18 August, on board ship prior to leaving, in which Mountbatten ended by exclaiming. 'Tomorrow we deal the Hun a bloody blow ... we expect over 60 per cent casualties, and to those of you that will die tomorrow, may God have mercy on your souls.'"[27]

Finally, another sniper received a Military Medal that day at Dieppe: LCpl. Richard Mann, of C Troop, 4 Commando. The medal citation for Mann, from the Royal Berkshire Regiment, reads:

"L/Cpl. Mann was a picked Sniper who crawled forward over open ground with a telescopic sighted rifle and with his hands and face painted green. He worked his way to the edge of the enemy wire and although fully exposed, succeeded in killing a great number of the enemy gun crews. His sniping was so accurate that it became impossible to service the battery guns."

The success of the commandos and the snipers unfortunately did not reflect the overall outcome of the mission. The raid was a disaster for many reasons and while the difficult lessons learned from the experience may have, in part, informed the successful invasion on D-Day—if for no other reason than that it made the

Germans overconfident—it doesn't take away from the fact that there were heavy losses, especially for the Canadians who suffered at least 916 killed and 2,450 wounded, with many of the latter captured.

Western Desert

(1940–43)

Mussolini sought to build a new Roman empire and ordered his Tenth Army to invade Egypt. If the Suez Canal was captured, the British route to India and the Pacific would be far longer and require ships to sail via the Cape of Good Hope. Additionally, from Egypt the oilfields of Persia could be threatened and the Axis could attack the Soviet Union from the Caucasus. Holding Egypt was important to stop Axis expansion, to protect the oilfields, and to provide an alternate route by which the Soviet Union could receive Lend-Lease aid.

In an early action, the Free French Camel Corps from Chad crossed the Sahara and headed north for the Italian airbase at Murzuk, Libya. Their arrival caused the Italians to withdraw to the fort, leaving the airfield and its planes unprotected. The Free French destroyed everything before withdrawing in the evening. It was not without casualties and the French commander, Lt. Col. Durnana is alleged to have been killed by an Italian sniper.[28] In fact, there were no specifically trained Italian snipers—there were

marksmen, *tiratore scelto* (selected shooters), who had access to better rifles and ammunition although there were no Italian scopes made.

The Italian offensive from Libya into Egypt was thrown back by the British. It appeared that Libya would be lost and to shore up his Italian ally, Hitler dispatched *Generalleutnant* Erwin Rommel with a small force that became the Afrika Korps. Ordered to remain on the defensive, Rommel began the first of his smashing offensives that drove the British out of Libya. North Africa would become a seesaw of the Germans/Italians chasing the British and the British chasing them in turn until Montgomery took command.

Sniping in Africa presented its own problems. First, the dust raised whenever a rifle was fired betrayed the sniper's location. That would invite mortar or artillery fire. Second, the haze in the desert helped to obscure the target. Third, there was no support for the sniper's paraphernalia in the desert. No armorer had parts or equipment to keep the rifle in good condition. The lack of support was critical as the Canadian balsam that joined the ocular lens sets melted, ran, and obscured the view.[29] Capt. Shore also pointed out that the uniform clothing, especially short-sleeved shirts, was impractical when crawling over the hot desert rocks. Then there was the sparsity of cover. All this meant that snipers were not used in great numbers by either side—although all units had them. The problems did not prevent the British Commonwealth from operating several training schools in anticipation of liberating Europe. Accounts of Commonwealth snipers in North Africa are difficult to find but we do know that the Australians employed snipers. A German report by Maj. Ernst-Otto Ballerstedt, 2d Battalion, 115th Motorized Infantry Regiment (he later commanded the 104th and, later still, the 160th *Panzergrenadier* Regiments in North Africa) complained about the Australian snipers in the Western Desert including the excellence of Australian marksmanship:

"The Australian is unquestionably superior to the German soldier: in the use of individual weapons, especially as snipers; in the use of ground camouflage; in his gift of observation … In every means of taking us by surprise. Enemy snipers have astounding results. They shoot at anything they recognize. Several N.C.O.s of the battalion have been shot through the head with the first shot while making observations in the front line. Protruding sights in gun directors have been shot off, observation slits and loopholes have been fired on, and hit, as soon as they were seen to be in use … The enemy shoots very accurately with

Mann volunteered for the commandoes from the Royal Berkshire Regiment, joining C Troop, No. 4 Commando. Firing from a tree and ground positions he kept the German battery crew away from their guns and unable to fire on the assault. Lord Lovat—who had picked him for the role—recommended him for a medal. *Commando Veterans Archive (Carole Mann) https://www. commandoveterans.org/.*

The International Match of 1943

Matches are useful to promote marksmanship under safe conditions. Most unusually, in the middle of the war, in 1943 a five-day international match was held between allies near the pyramids (actually at the Egyptian Army Small Arms Training School at Almaza northeast of Cairo). It was first suggested by the British military mission liaison to the school, WO2 (his regular rank was sergeant major) Paddy Rochford of 3rd Battalion, Coldstream Guards, to the school commandant, Col. Seif el-Yasin Khalifa. Rochford was responsible for bringing the school up to World War II standards—prior to his appointment it had been using Boer War methodology. Targets were set at 200, 300 and 500 yards. While no scoped firearms were used, the Americans used Springfields (the earlier '03 with leaf sights), the South Africans used Enfields that were equipped with vernier sights.[30] Other participants included New Zealand, King Farouk's Royal Bodyguard as well as the Egyptian Army, the British Army, and the winning team, the Swiss.[31] The Swiss placed first with the Americans and Royal Bodyguard tying for second. The British Army performed poorly as its best soldiers were at the front fighting.

The winning team. *Courtesy the Boseley Collection/ http://www.22battalion.org.nz/index.php.*

his high angle infantry weapons. He usually uses these in conjunction with a sniper—or MG."[32]

Near Tobruk, when one Gurkha grew weary of being shot at by a German, he armed himself only with his kukri and disappeared into the darkness. He returned one hour later with a matching pair of ears.[33]

Inside Tobruk, the Australian garrison was annoyed by a German sniper. Sapper Sydney Parsell of 1st Field Company Engineers was among them and remembered: "We were holding that post despite its dangerous position. Some of that sniper's bullets came particularly close and it shouldn't have been a laughing matter." With no sniper of their own to neutralize the German, one Australian resorted to taunting him instead. Each time the German fired, the Australian raised his rifle butt first and waved it back

and forth to indicate a miss. Apparently it angered or unnerved the German. Sgt. Parsell continued, "I don't know if the German signals are the same as ours, but the sniper completely lost his block. After each he sent in a vicious burst of fire, and his aim got wilder and wilder. Ultimately he was right off the target."[34]

Airpower, command of the sea lanes, and the arrival of General Bernard Montgomery to take command allowed the British Eighth Army to build up sufficient strength to drive Rommel and Panzer Army Afrika—renamed the German-Italian Panzer Army during the retreat—from Libya and into Tunisia. Additionally, the British would soon be joined by the Americans in Africa, making the Axis presence even more untenable.

Operation Torch
(November 8, 1942)

America's entry into the ETO began with ground forces staging through England before departing for Africa and the NATOUSA, North African Theater of Operations, U.S. Army. Operation Torch saw Allied ground forces landing in Morocco (Western Task Force under Maj. Gen. George S. Patton) and Algeria (Central Task Force under Maj. Gen. Lloyd Fredendall). If the Allies thought the Vichy French would welcome them with open arms as liberators, they were mistaken. True to the armistice with the Germans to protect the sovereignty of Vichy French soil, the French fought the Allies. The landing at Safi (south of Casablanca) began with two APD (high speed transport) destroyers dashing in and disgorging soldiers into landing craft. It was not without casualties and one correspondent recalled:

> "Master Sergeant Frank Heints of Covington, La., was standing on the beach when a sniper's bullet plowed through the head of his buddy. A major standing nearby told me to go get the sniper," Heints recounted. "I rounded up half a dozen men and we started off when the major shouted, 'Hell, wait a minute. I am going along.' He did and we got the sniper too."[35]

In another incident, a French sniper was in a tree and shooting at the Americans. According to William H. Hull, his sergeant opened on the tree with a tommy-gun and removed the threat.[36] Casablanca was captured on November 11. Even then some franc-tireur fought on and former Pennsylvania Governor Lt. Cdr. George H. Earle was walking in Casablanca when a bullet struck near his foot.[37]

Of the three-pronged invasion, the easiest was that of the Eastern Task Force (Lt. Gen. Kenneth

Anderson) that landed in Algeria. Embedded with the American troops was journalist Ernie Pyle who reported the death of an American at the hand of an unseen assailant.

"They started back in their jeep to a command post several miles to the rear. Captain Gale was sitting beside the driver. Sergeant Harrington was in the back seat. The top was down, and the windshield folded flat and covered—for a windshield can create a glare that makes a perfect target for snipers. It's funny the things a man learns in war. For instance, the soldiers were issued sunglasses before coming ashore, but they had to abandon them because the glasses caught the sun and made nice targets.

"The three drove on along the highway, among vineyards, under a warm African sun. Everything was quiet. The Algerian phase of the war seemed about over.

"Suddenly the driver, for no apparent reason, fell over his steering wheel, and the jeep swerved. Blood splashed down over his uniform. He never uttered a sound. Unheard and unseen, a sniper's bullet had taken him just over the right eye. He died instantly.

"Harrington reached over the body and grabbed the wheel. Captain Gale got his foot around the dead driver's leg and shoved the throttle to the floor. Two more shots zipped past but missed. The jeep roared on down the road and out of danger, with one man steering and another man at the throttle."[38]

The 1st Infantry Division (nicknamed the Big Red One) landed on November 8 in Algeria as part of the American landing force. BAR man Pvt. Demetrius Lypka of G Co., 2d Battalion, 16th Infantry Regiment was among them. They advanced westward toward Oran and on the next day, Lypka encountered a *franc-tireur*. The name comes from patriotic French civilians of the Franco-Prussian War (1870–71) who took up arms, fought as irregulars and sniped at the invading German army.

"That morning we continued our advance. There was a little artillery fire now, and not very accurate. As we approached the town called Fleurus-Le Grand, we began to run into a lot of sniper fire. One of the snipers picked me as his target. I dove for the ditch along the roadside. It didn't afford much protection, as it was very shallow. As I got up to get a better view of where the firing was coming from, he fired again.

Somewhere in Italy this American soldier—Pvt. Charles Cooper—is equipped with the M1C Garand sniper rifle. His ammunition pouches appear to be empty. *NARA.*

Fortunately, he wasn't a good marksman and he missed again. He jumped up from behind some shrubs with his hands in surrender. He was a French civilian. He demanded that we release him at once so he could return to his home. I don't know what his eventual fate was, but he wasn't released at that point."[39]

Fleurus-Le Grand was captured after its light resistance was brushed aside.

UP Correspondent Phil Ault landed with the troops on Arzew beach, 25 miles east of Oran. Fighting their way there, they found themselves at the city's outskirts two days later.

"After dawn on Tuesday I hitched a ride on an infantry truck going forward and was told that the infantry's overnight march had put it 2½ miles from the center of Oran, despite fire from batteries on a height overlooking their right flank. At 9:15 a. m. I boarded a jeep for a dash to advance headquarters. The officers aboard were armed with tommy guns, pistols and hand grenades ready for instant heaving. The jeep dropped me off at headquarters and continued on its way. Ten minutes later the driver was killed by a roadside sniper."[40]

Entering Oran was not without resistance and Sgt. Charles Embso recalled that:

"a sniper shot from a window at a tank about four tanks ahead of mine. He wounded a Frenchman who was just handing a tangerine up to the man in the turret. Instantly the gunner in the next tank raised his 37-mm and blew the sniper right out the window. Almost at the same moment a tank-destroyer fired with its heavy gun and practically blasted the corner of the building."[41]

Oran surrendered a little past noon and Pvt. Lypka and the Big Red One occupied it peacefully.

While at Oklahoma A&M (Agriculture and Mechanical), Lt. Charles Scheffel enrolled in ROTC and after graduation was commissioned as a reserve lieutenant. He was assigned to the 39th Infantry Regiment, 9th Infantry Division and landed in Algiers with the Big Red One. After Algiers was secured, the 9th and other American units advanced in Tunisia to envelop the Afrika Korps and other Axis units being chased there by the British Eighth Army. Scheffel's battalion was now advancing towards Bizerte in Tunisia.

"Late one afternoon the company crossed a rock crest and dug into a defensive position on the forward slope that overlooked a wide, barren valley. We had outrun our supply lines and had orders to hold at the edge of some evergreen woods.

"After we settled in, I walked along the ridge to visit another platoon leader, a friend I'd known since Algeria. We sat in the shade off by ourselves, looking out over the plain. Almost a mile away a road cut diagonally across in front of us. It led to Mateur, which was still in German hands. I glanced across the plain and saw what looked like a truck moving toward us along the road, kicking up dust. 'That can't be ours,' I said.

I took a closer look with my field glasses and saw that it was towing something. The truck pulled off the road and stopped on the far side of a small bridge. Men got out and bustled around the rear of the truck. 'Germans,' I said. 'They're pulling an artillery piece.'

"I picked up my rifle and fumbled with the rear sight. To shoot that far, I would have to raise it. Aiming over the front sight through the raised rear sight would bring the barrel up so that the round would arc in a rainbow trajectory toward the distant target.

"Firing a rifle at long range is generally not effective and can disclose the soldier's position, bring enemy fire down on him. It's a matter of self-preservation. Nevertheless, I raised the rear sight until it looked about right.

"The tow truck started turning around to go back down the road. 'Let's see if these sights are any good.' I lay in a prone position, drew a bead, held my breath, and squeezed off a round. 'He's down!' yelled my friend.

"Incredibly, at more than half a mile, I had hit one of the Germans. The rest ran to catch the truck as it drove away, leaving the gun sitting there. Those soldiers were obviously support troops, not infantrymen; my silent kill had scared them off. They never heard the crack of the bullet because it hit the guy, and I know they didn't hear the muzzle thump, not that far away. If they did, it would have sounded like somebody stepping on a stick."[42]

Driving the Axis north from Libya, the British Eighth Army included 21-year-old Coldstream Guards Capt. The Lord Leveson, who was also a nephew of then British Queen Elizabeth (mother of Queen Elizabeth II). Accompanied by Drill Sgt. Kent, they belonged to a reconnaissance party approaching Medjez-el-Bab when they spotted a seven-man German patrol on a hillside that was 600–870yd away. Capt. Leveson's first shot winged a German but Kent told him his distance was spot on. He managed to shoot four Germans before the other three disappeared beneath the crest.[43]

At war's outbreak, Bill Cheall enlisted in a territorial battalion of the Green Howards. Territorial battalions were supposed to remain at home as a defense force but the need for men was so pressing in 1940 that they were sent without any rifle instruction to France as a labor battalion for the British Expeditionary Force. Besides a lot of digging, they had some makeshift weapons instruction and the battalion received its sole Bren gun. Despite orders to discard equipment, they took it with them when they evacuated at Dunkirk. Still a soldier with the 6th Green Howards, Cheall's battalion belonged to the 69th Brigade which, along with the 51st Highland and 4th Indian Divisions, were to attack at Wadi Akarit in Tunisia.

It began on April 6 and they moved out at 0400 hours. Pvt. Cheall describes their attack.

"We were now attacking as platoons and sections, and our section, led by Lance Corporal Coughlan, bending low to the ground, moved to the right and we had to tread warily because we were very often overlooked. We must have advanced about two hundred yards, not realizing that we were being observed from a concealed trench. All of a sudden machine-gun fire came from our right and we dropped flat. We all knew roughly where the fire came from, and quite unexpectedly Coughlan did a silly thing without any command he stood up to move forward, instead of giving us instructions to fire while he observed. He was no sooner on his feet than a single shot rang out and Coughlan, who was next to me on my right, dropped dead in an instant."

Being senior private, an enraged Cheall grabbed Coughlan's submachine gun and shouted, "Come on lads, kill the bastards, send them to hell, but keep firing and don't forget your grenades."[44]

They didn't take a single Italian prisoner and at the end of the battle on April 7, the entire Italian 80th Infantry Division, *La Spezia*, was either killed or captured by the East Yorkshires and Green Howards.

Further north, where the American were fighting, Cpl. Dixon belonged to a tank destroyer unit. When a lone German sniper held up an American advance, a volunteer was called for to dispatch the sniper. Dixon responded, ran out, and was taken under fire by the sniper immediately. Hiding behind a bush, Dixon began scanning the terrain. Finally, he saw a dark spot in a white bush some distance away and suspected it was the sniper. He fired and missed him with his first shot, but adjusted his aim and nailed him on the second attempt.[45]

More dramatic was the experience of Ranger sniper Cpl. Robert M. Bevan. His accomplishment was to silence a German machine-gun nest at 1,350yd.

"As a sniper I picked targets that were out of range for the riflemen, so I started working on this machine-gun nest. I was using our sniper rifle—a plain old '03 with telescopic sights. I ranged in with tracers and then put two shots right into the position. The gun was quiet for a couple of minutes … then a crazy thing happen. Somebody threw a dirty towel over the gun and then the crew came out and sat down."[46]

The machine gunners were probably already demoralized to allow themselves to be defeated from a distance to a single sniper!

Like the 22nd Battalion (see pp. 46–7), 2NZEF's 23rd (Canterbury-Otago) Battalion, was formed just after the war started on November 8, 1939. It, too, fought in Greece, Crete, Libya, Egypt, El Alamein, and on into Tunisia. On April 19–20, 1943, the 5th New Zealand Brigade attacked and took the 650ft Takrouna summit in Tunisia. The brigade withstood one counterattack, was driven off by a second, and finally retook the hill. A few men of the 23rd Battalion took part in the battle but the bulk of the unit was further forward at Cherachir where Lt. Fred Marett reported, "A German sniper must have been close because for two hours his odd shots played havoc. A C Coy. man on the Bren was definitely a marked man. He spent an hour getting into position, looked up once, and was shot clean through the head."[47]

On May 7, 1943, during the fight for eastern Bizerte, concealed riflemen attempted to delay the Allies. Correspondent John Lardner was among the British forces that entered the port city.

Sniper with the 505th PIR, 82d Airborne Division, photographed in North Africa. NRA correspondent William F. Shadel spoke with many front-line soldiers for their views on the U.S. Army sniper rifle.

"Opinion seems to weigh heavily against the sniper equipment we are using here. The sniper gun is the '03A4, with the 330 Weaver scope. A few snipers respect the delicacy with which a scope should be handled, get along all right with it. The larger numbers, however, complain that the scope fogs up under weather encountered here, and that ordinary handling under battle conditions results in scope damage. Some officers consider the scope mount satisfactory, but they criticize the scope itself. Others object to the necessity of loading one cartridge at a time, due to the fact that the scope prevents clip loading. They say targets often demand quick repeated shots. The commonest physical damage to scopes is the breakage of crosshairs. Post reticles have stood up better under battle conditions."[48] *U.S. Army.*

"Your correspondent walked out onto the dusty terrace and found the business of war going on as usual. Rifle fire on the eastern side of town kept snapping intermittently. 'They're snipers,' said a French Commando, 'They have unpleasant natures, these people. We will have to kill them all.'

"'We're off to a good start,' said a British lieutenant of antiaircraft. 'One sniper on a tower was popping at my men a little while ago. I turned our big gun on him full blast and the air was full of pieces of sniper.'"[49]

Thankfully, the disjointed German command in Africa prevented Rommel and the Axis from using the advantage of Napoleon's favorite strategy of the central

Lessons from the Sicilian campaign

Use of Snipers and Dealing with Enemy Snipers

"Snipers were freely used by both Allied and Axis forces. The terrain and the nature of the campaign made effective sniping a valuable asset to all infantry units. Commanders recommended a higher degree of sniper training for units not yet in action, and pointed out that the capable sniper must be more than a crack marksman with a special rifle. The elements of patience, study of enemy habits, and ability to operate and move with almost perfect concealment were all stressed. Frequent change of position after firing was also a point that was emphasized.

"Enemy snipers firing from concealed delaying positions and from mountains were a major nuisance. Units learned to deal with them in a number of ways, the most effective of which was the use of specially trained squads of 'sniper killers.' These groups would locate the hostile snipers, and part would engage the sniper's attention and fire while the remainder would work around to the flanks and eliminate him. German snipers in civilian clothes were especially annoying in Sicily, since our troops had strict orders not to molest civilians. In the passage of towns, it became difficult to distinguish local civilians from German snipers in disguise."[50]

position whereby one concentrates on destroying the weaker of two enemies forces before turning against the stronger. On May 13, 1943, with over 230,000 Germans and Italians captured, Africa was free of the Axis. Absent from the victors was Bill Cheall and the 6th Green Howards. They had already been sent back to Egypt to train for their next campaign: Sicily.

Sicily

(July 9–August 17, 1943)

Following the capture of Axis forces in Africa, the next major assault was Operation Husky, an airborne and amphibious assault against Sicily which had to be captured before Italy itself could be invaded. The British Eighth Army landed on the southeast coast of Sicily and the Seventh (U.S.) Army's II Corps—consisting of 1st, 3d, and 45th Infantry Divisions—on the central southern coast. British 1st Airborne Division was dropped near Syracuse and the 82d U.S. Airborne around Gela.

The 2/505th PIR was dropped from 350 to 400ft instead of the planned 500–600ft. While 24 paratroopers suffered broken ankles or legs, the unplanned benefit of the low drop was that they were not overly dispersed—although they weren't where they expected to be. Unfortunately, they found themselves among an Italian pillbox complex which they had to capture before they could safely move out. The battalion commander, Maj. Mark Alexander, was able to assemble about 475 men with whom he could accomplish this task. The pillboxes were captured by the morning and they marched off toward the coast to join the Americans who were landing by sea. As darkness approached, they were just northwest of the coastal village of Marina di Ragusa. While settling in, they were subjected to machine gun and sniper fire from the north. Alexander summoned one of his officers, Lt. Arthur Miller. "Art, do you know Morse code?" When Miller responded affirmatively, Alexander ordered, "Well, do you see the outline of that British cruiser out there just offshore?"

"Affirmative."

"Then get a flashlight and signal that cruiser in Morse that there's a bunch of Krauts or Eyties out to our front and ask if they can plaster them with some big stuff."

Lt. Miller scrounged up a flashlight from one of the troopers and began signaling the cruiser. Skeptical troopers looked on while others continued to shelter themselves. Then they waited. The silence of the night air was pierced only by the staccato of the machine guns and rifle fire. Suddenly, the cruiser lit up with bright flashes followed by the boom of its guns. The slope where fire was coming from erupted in flames and smoke. The harassment fire ended. Turning to Miller, Alexander instructed, "Flash our British friends a message that they were right on target, and be damned sure to thank them."[51] American soldiers were probably not trained in warship recognition and it is likely that it was an American cruiser (either USS *Savannah* or her sister USS *Boise*) that lent its six-inch guns in support. Regardless of the ship's nationality, it proved that the 100lb shells thrown by a cruiser's bigger guns works wonder in silencing snipers and machine guns.

Landing south of Gela and joining up with Maj. Alexander's battalion was the 1st Infantry Division which relieved the 82d as they pushed inward. No stranger to combat, 2Lt. Stewart H. Patton had fought in Africa, and was leading a platoon when he landed in Sicily. Despite the darkness, he kept drawing enemy fire. "I couldn't figure out how he could find me," Patton said, "until one of my men came up and yanked off the tape. We'd put that tape there to find each other during the darkness around the beachhead. Those bullets were really close." Like Capt. Charles Scheffel, Patton also believed in "Crack! Thump" to locate a foe. "By the crack of the rifle and the thump of the bullet when it lands, pretty soon you find out exactly where the enemy is firing from."[52]

Now a combat veteran, 1st Division's Pvt. Demetrius Lypka joined in the hard fighting that drove the Italians and Germans north towards Messina. Lypka was ordered to take a few men and to scout a hill to the left of his platoon's position. His orders were to fire a flare if the hill was occupied and if not, to remain there for the night. Accompanied by Jimmy Diaoczok from heavy weapons company (Co. H) who tagged along as an observer for the mortar section of that company, they worked their way uphill. Trucks using the road to support the company had been harassed by anti-tank gunfire and Diaoczok wanted to see if he could spot it. After daybreak, Diaoczok spotted something that appeared unnatural. Lypka also saw something glistening in the sunlight but was unable to identify its nature. Diaoczok called down mortar fire that tore away the camouflage netting and exposed the gun, causing its crew to flee. Their mission successful, they returned safely to the company but Lypka wasn't quite out of danger. He would have a close brush with death which he describes:

"[W]hen daylight came, we would get sniper fire from our rear or flanks. This was very unnerving since it was difficult to find where the snipers were hidden. They usually had well-camouflaged positions and sometimes were left behind on purpose to harass us. We should have to send out a squad or two in order to find them and put

them out of business. I had just returned from a patrol early one morning to where our company was located, and sat down at the foot of a small ledge, leaning my rifle against it. Just as I did this, I felt something graze against my lip, and at the same time, heard a loud crack where my rifle was. Looking in that direction, I found my rifle stock smashed. It had been hit by a sniper's bullet, which was meant for me. We found this sniper shortly and shot him. Very few snipers were taken prisoner."[53]

During the Allied effort to capture Sicily, Lt. Gen. Omar Bradley, who had just been promoted for the capture of Tunisia, was in his command car along with two enlisted men. Correspondent Ernie Pyle describes Gen. Bradley's response.

"General Bradley seldom gets nervous, and he is never excited. Once here in Sicily, a sniper took a pot shot at him as he was riding in a command car, whereupon the general and two enlisted men, armed only with carbines, got out of the car and started looking for the sniper. The sniper beat it, and they couldn't find him."[54]

It wasn't the best thing for a general to do.

Near Messina, when two Germans in the same tree shot at the GIs, the Americans responded quickly as Sgt. Michael Bozovich remembered: "We shot one German sniper hiding in a tree through the arm after killing his buddy." Less fortunate was a British unit that was harassed by an Italian *franc-tireur* who fired all night at them. At dawn the unit did a house-to-house search for the sniper. He eluded them by discarding his boots, rifle, and kit before changing into civilian clothes.[55]

Besides the British, the Canadians also fought in Sicily and snipers and scouts of the Seaforth Highlanders of Canada mounted themselves on horses to give themselves a mobility that their carriers couldn't. Led by Sgt. George McKee, they patrolled ahead of their battalion in the drive from Leonfonte to Aderno. When they encountered resistance, they selected (and counted) officers as their targets.[56]

Despite German reinforcements sent to Sicily, the Allies captured the island on August 17. The stage was now set to invade the Italian mainland. After Sicily fell, British 51st Highland Division produced an unofficial report *Intelligence from Alamein to Messina*, which mentioned sniping in the desert:

"Although training states that snipers should be under control of the IO the occasion has never yet arisen when snipers have been posted forward of the rifle companies. In the desert the distance between the opposing forces was usually about 2,000yd, and the German and Italian policy of holding rear slopes in daytime leaving only the odd machine gunners on watch has not left much scope for sniping. In Sicily the reverse slope principle seemed again to hold good and although company snipers were on duty not more than 500yd from enemy positions, they seldom had chance for a shot. Possibly the most effective snipers would be, like their German counterparts, Bren gunners firing from tripods."[57]

Italy (September 9, 1943)

Not since AD535, when Byzantine general Flavius Belisarius liberated Italy from the Goths, has the country been invaded from the south. Yet this is exactly what the Allies attempted in early September 1943 when they followed their victory in Sicily by landing at Salerno, and in Calabria and Taranto. The mountainous terrain of Italy was vastly different from the deserts of North Africa and the Allies found fighting up the Italian peninsula much more difficult than anticipated.

Landing on September 9 at Salerno with their battalion HQ after the beach had been secured, 36th (U.S.) Infantry and other Fifth (U.S.) Army divisions were hard-pressed for a week before breaking out and forcing the Germans back. John Fulcher and five other snipers from his battalion penetrated into German lines and paired off, each pair taking a hilltop position at different bends on the same road. Fulcher and his partner were the furthest when they spotted a company of Germans with their officer at the head, marching down the road. Their uniforms were crisp, suggesting they were fresh to the front. Fulcher and his partner exchanged glances. A nod and they agreed to shoot. Fulcher thought:

"Let's take them. They're green. Even if they organized an assault, we could be gone off the ridge before they got halfway across the field to us. ...

"My hands remained as steady as when I shot my second deer. As cool as it could be, I cross-haired the officer and shot him through the belly. He looked momentarily surprised. He plopped down on his butt in the middle of the road. The report of the shot reached him as he fell over onto his back. He was dead by the time I brought my rifle down out of recoil and picked him up again in my scope. His legs were drumming on the road, but he was dead. His body didn't know it yet."[58]

The company was stunned and only broke out of it when Fulcher's partner shot another German. Then they scattered to the safety of a ditch or shell craters. Fulcher and his partner refrained from shooting lest their position be located. Gradually, one officer appeared, scanned the area, berated the men who scrambled from hiding and fell back into formation. They then resumed their march and disappeared around the bend. Two more shots rang out. Fulcher and his partner knew that the second pair had also scored. The demoralization effect must have been tremendous to the Germans. Soon after the event, Fulcher was promoted to sergeant when their squad leader was killed.

Serving as an artillery observer, 27-year-old infantry Lt. Hilston Thomas Kilcollins was at his observation post when he almost became a fatality. "The telephone rang and I turned my head to answer it just as a bullet whizzed past. It nicked the bridge of my nose. If the phone hadn't rung it would have got me between the eyes." Knowing the direction the bullet was fired from, Hilston, a former high school mathematics instructor and avid hunter, borrowed a rifle and tracked down the German.[59]

With the battle of Salerno in the balance, in the face of a powerful German counterattack, Fifth (U.S.) Army commander Lt. Gen. Mark Clark made a personal request to 82d Airborne Division's CG, Matthew Ridgway, for assistance. The 504th PIR stepped up to the plate, air-dropping into the beachhead and the counterattack was held and then broken. As the 504th advanced, they crossed a pontoon bridge that spanned the Volturno River while chasing the retreating Germans. As one man, Carlton, walked along a bend in the trail, a submachine gun fired by the rearguard killed him. The men were incensed but could not find the killer who outpaced them. As evening fell, they settled on a hilltop that overlooked a valley. In the morning, they found themselves peering down the valley at a German armored division. Pvt. Ross Carter remembered the action of one of his buddies.

"Big Casey woke up the next morning, cleaned his rifle, and climbed a bushy tree for a look over the country. About eight hundred yards to the rear and off the trail, he spotted a Mark V tank [PzKpfw V Panther]. He put his hands up to his eyes, simulating binoculars, and we handed him up a pair. He saw a soldier climb up on the tank and begin to eat something out of a can. Casey looked down at us with his pale eyes gleaming and asked if he could shoot him. Toland went to the captain, who radioed the little colonel [the lieutenant colonel], who went to his 81st mortar crew and climbed a tree to have a look. He sent word that Casey could fire one shot when the mortar got ready to fire at the tank. We all began to dig like hell, for when you shoot at tanks they usually shoot back. Casey dusted off his rifle again, set the sights, checked the windage, got a comfortable position in the tree, and waited for the word. When it came, Casey's pale eyes squinted confidently down the barrel. He fired. The Krauthead dropped his chow, grabbed his chest, and fell off the tank to the ground. Casey skinned down the tree, and as he ran a patch with bore-cleaner through his rifle he remarked, 'That was for Carlton.'"[60]

Another 504th paratrooper, Pvt. Theodore Finkbeiner trained as a sniper at Fort Bragg. He was armed with an M1 Garand when he jumped into Italy. He had extensive target practice with the M1903A4 sniper rifle at Bragg and even in Africa, but was never issued one for combat. While his training didn't include fieldcraft, his childhood hunting experience with a .22 long rifle came in handy. Between Salerno and Naples he found a sporterized German rifle "with a big scope" but ordnance wanted it and it was the last he saw or heard of it.[61] His best shot of the war was with an M1 rifle at 1,100–1,200yd against a German dispatch rider.

"He was coming around the mountain and we were across the valley and he was on a motorcycle, a dispatch rider and I guess that's what they called him, but I shot and killed him. But the motorcycle and him come off the hill when I hit him and of course he went down. Of course, we went over and got him and he was all torn to heck. He had a folder or dispatch papers of some kind and we turned them over. I never saw or heard of that either."

Word got around and Finkbeiner earned a reputation for himself.

"It don't take much and you get a reputation like that in the army and shoot, it's good and bad. Anytime they got people from the other side they'd call and want me to come over to that side and help them. Which I did. I liked doing it. I was good at it. We had practice shots and knew about how much it would drop from what we practiced in North Africa; but we had a scope then."[62]

Afterwards Finkbeiner and the 504th were sent to Anzio.

Pte. F. J. McPhee of the Canadian Seaforth Highlanders providing cover near Foiano, Italy, October 6, 1943. He was previously wounded on July 20, 1943, near Leonfante (Mt. Etna) and killed in action on December 26, 1943. LAC.

Snipers were often used as part of scouting and intelligence-gathering operations. An example of this took place on the night of November 26–27, 1943, on the Sangro River as 2NZEF readied for its first action in the Italian campaign, part of an assault on the Gustav Line. 2Lt Geoff De Their of 23rd Battalion, 5th Brigade, took a patrol of ten men "from the assault pioneer platoon whose men were organised and trained as snipers and infantry sappers, to reconnoitre suitable crossings of the river. De Thier and his men were responsible for stretching ropes across the Sangro to prevent any men from being swept downstream by the current." On the 28th two brigades crossed the river and soon armor was crossing on Bailey bridges.[63]

On December 20, 1943, near Ortona, Canadian Pte. A. Keen escorted a file composed of an Iron Cross decorated German Spieß (sergeant major) and 12 infantrymen back as prisoners. Keen's sniper fire had killed so many of their comrades that, totally demoralized, the survivors opted to surrender rather than die themselves.[64]

Associated Press Correspondent Relman Morin did not look favorably upon German snipers when he wrote: "The snipers aren't so bad. They lie in houses, usually on the second floor, and occasionally kill somebody, soldier or civilian. It seems to make no difference to the snipers which it is. How they choose their victims is a great mystery."[65] Apparently the shooters were not snipers per se, but men left behind with orders to delay the Allied advance. No sensible sniper would shoot non-military targets (unless they were acting as scouts for the enemy) and risk

The fighting in Anzio was often at very close range and house-to-house. *Battlefield Historian.*

the possibility of divulging their location or inviting retaliation. It is well known that if the infantry couldn't deal with a sniper, tanks or artillery was the next step. A good example of the latter was in the earlier Sicilian campaign where an American 155mm fired on a house to silence its occupants.

In not so polite terms, snipers were sometimes asked by their own infantry to leave. Once a sniper's presence was known, artillery fire would be called down upon his suspected position and the local troops the sniper was supporting would also suffer from the bombardment. Such was the case when a company had complained about receiving sniper fire and Harold Baldwin and his partner were dispatched to address it.

> "[W]e went upstairs and knocked out two bricks from the corner of the wall, you always kept away from the windows. Anyway, we had a good morning and scored quite a few hits and the enemy stopped being as brave as they had been. About 2:00 AM we were subject to the biggest load of shell fire and mortar fire. I had known the Germans had eight barreled mortars and they were very clever with them. [In fact, the Nebelwerfer had five (NbW 42) or six (NbW 41) barrels.] We were all lying downstairs and hoping for the best. I was lying alongside the fireplace and there was a figure of the Madonna on the mantelpiece and the blast came in through the window and blew it in half. We managed to get back to H.Q. and were detailed to go again. When we got there they would not let us in because as snipers we would draw a lot of fire down and the farmhouse may have had a direct hit."[66]

Between January and May 1944, the Allied advance up the Italian peninsula was stopped cold by the Gustav Line, the lynchpin of which was Monte Cassino. While the town of Cassino itself was captured, the monastery that overlooked it was to become the subject of intense fighting. A New Zealand brigade suffered heavily in its attempt to take the heights. A major explained how one German sniper inflicted 34 casualties. "We just can't find the bloke in this rubble. We can't even run a tank over the spot where the fire comes from and think we've surely silenced him, but he shows up again a few minutes later."[67]

On March 19, 1944, 23rd Battalion, New Zealand 5th Brigade, was involved in an attack on Cassino. The trouble was that the Germans were well hidden behind cover and could pick off the New Zealanders seemingly at will. Pte. Bill Stirling, a wireless operator, was at the back of his unit when he saw a German in a doorway. Stirling fired at him with his revolver but missed. Next, he took the rifle from a wounded man and fired into the doorway. He followed this by using the squad's Bren, shooting off a magazine. Nothing. Stirling realized that the German sniper was just biding his time so he, too, waited. Sure enough, just as his unit moved off, "the German appeared, ready to take another shot. Stirling took a more careful shot with his revolver— 'a lucky shot,' he recorded later—and the German fell forward. Much elated, Stirling ran forward to join the others, shouting in some excitement: 'I got the bastard! I got the bastard!'"[68]

While breaking through the Liri Valley, I Canadian Corps of British Eighth Army came across some stubborn German resistance. Al Lust was a welterweight champion before entering service. On May 23, a few days before the breakthrough, he received a blow to the jaw that would invalid him out of service. They were fighting for over half an hour when Lt. Crabtree was hit by a bullet behind the ear which exited right below his eye. Crabtree went down and Lust rushed to his aid. "Get down lower Al or that sniper will get you!" shouted one of his comrades. Too late. Lust was struck in the jaw and the bullet exited the back of his neck. "I guess the same sniper that got Lt. Crabtree got me too." Lust fortunately survived and spent four months in the hospitals before returning to Canada where he was invalided out with an honorable discharge.[69] Three days later, on May 26, II Polish and I Canadian Corps broke through and the Gustav Line collapsed.

Canadian snipers—like their predecessors in World War I—demonstrated that their skill was not forgotten in World War II. In May 1944, sniper Sgt. L. Kraemer of Princess Patricia's Canadian Light Infantry, earned the Military Medal for rescuing a wounded soldier at

Ponte Corvo near the Hitler Line. While he declined speaking about his deeds as a sniper, an admiring Pte. J. P. Hora cheerfully shared his observations: "I saw him knock off eight or nine Jerries from a window in the upper story of a farm house which had been cleared because of danger from enemy artillery. He stayed there despite the danger and knocked them down like flies."[70]

Another notable Canadian, LCpl. M. Pelletier on October 27, 1944, was credited with 27 kills. Pte. R. J. Forsythe had grown up hunting in British Columbia. Originally he was a scout but, fascinated by sniping, transferred over. He modestly claimed only a couple of kills but others in the sniper sections had each gotten a dozen. Sgt. Tom Evenden had 19 to his credit.[71] Another was former Mountie, Maj. Tom Lowe. When one of his men was shot, Lowe became obsessed with getting his killer. Knowing the general area from where the sniper shot, he lay in wait and after two hours was rewarded when the German gave his position away by moving and the Mountie got his man.[72]

While Florence was declared an open city, the Germans who withdrew fired at any exposed Canadians. They killed a sniper of the Hastings and Prince Edwards Regiment and it enraged his mates for revenge.

"In one day the Regiment snipers bagged seven of the enemy in retaliation for one of their own who had been killed by long range rifle fire. Occupying houses separated by only narrow water, the troops of both sides became adept at shooting without being shot at."

Even Bren gunners joined in and rigged up their guns to be fired with a string. Pre-aimed, the Bren gunners used a mirror to watch the sights and pulled a string only after an unwary German appeared.[73]

Seeking to break the deadlock by landing behind the German defensive lines, the Allies launched an amphibious assault on Anzio, 40 miles south of Rome. Pushing inland proved difficult and the initiative passed to the Germans who contained the bridgehead, pouring in new units to oppose it. Among the British who landed was Lt. L. F. Edwards of the 1st Infantry Division. Edwards dragged a telephone line behind him and served as a forward observer. He directed artillery on a big house that was used by the Germans as an observation post. He then "tried to get back to his original position, but was pinned by a German sniper and forced to lie there until noon with no chance of getting back in time for lunch." Not to be denied his lunch, Edwards picked up the phone and ordered it. The lunch was attached to the telephone line which Edwards pulled to him hand over hand. "Later in the afternoon when it began to rain, and when Edwards saw the sniper remove the telescopic sight from his

Born in Edmonton, Alberta, in 1910, Lowe (at back on right) joined the RCMP in 1929. He took his discharge in 1940 and was appointed second lieutenant in the Edmonton Fusiliers and then a captain in the Cape Breton Highlanders in 1941. He attained the rank of acting major while overseas and was discharged in 1945, rejoining the force. He retired in 1950 and died in 1972. *Photo courtesy Ric Hall. RCMP Veterans Vancouver, BC and rcmpgraves.com Superintendent Healy.*

rifle and begin to wipe them off, he made a break for it and won."[74]

At Anzio, American Ranger Sgt. Reese E. Carter was serving as a sniper with an M1903A4 sniper rifle. He was shooting from beneath a bush at German road traffic. When he awoke, he found himself in a hospital. Having fired too often from the same location, the Germans identified his hide and dropped a mortar shell on him. While the shell did not explode, it destroyed part of his liver. Luckily he survived.[75]

The breakout would not occur until June 2 when, in the wake of the fall of the Gustav Line, the German defense collapsed. Fearing another Stalingrad, Hitler approved Kesselring's abandonment of Rome without a fight. While advancing on Rome, the Americans of the 34th Infantry Division found that the tunnels dug for ancient Roman aqueducts had been converted into barracks by the Germans. Each had to be cleared and when it came to the turn of Sgt. Ralph Schaps, 135th Infantry Regiment, he took a new man with him. While clearing a tunnel they saw Walther P38 pistols, as well as a few sniper rifles, and Nazi flags. Schaps cautioned the new man against touching anything as they were probably booby-trapped. The Germans had hastily abandoned the tunnel and upon reaching the exit, they found 25 Germans who readily surrendered.[76]

Rome was captured on June 5 but the event was immediately overshadowed by events in Normandy. More significantly, Mark Clark had missed the opportunity to encircle and destroy beaten Germans and they escaped to a new pre-prepared defensive line.

By now 504th PIR paratrooper Finkbeiner was a staff sergeant and squad leader. Adept at scouting because of his hunting experience, he was frequently called upon to scout for the rest of the platoon. Wounded, while still recovering at Anzio, he was asked to return to combat before being completely healed. Being the platoon sergeant now, he felt obligated to serve with his men and returned, finally being issued with his own sniper rifle.[77] Having been in near-continuous action from Salerno (September 11, 1943) to Anzio (March 23, 1944), Finkbeiner and the 504th rejoined the 82d too late for D-Day but they did jump in Operation Market Garden. Afterward, he was sent on leave and upon returning, was stuck at a replacement depot and never fought again. Postwar he returned to Monroe, LA and spent 37 years as a firefighter before retiring.[78]

The failure to trap the German army meant that it was able to retreat back in stages through the Trasimene and Arno lines to the Gothic Line, a significant hurdle. The Lamone River was part of it,

American infantry patrol and its sniper clearing a town somewhere in Italy. *U.S. Army.*

Entering towns[79]

"When conditions made the envelopment of a town or city impracticable, the system used was for one company to move straight into town on a designated phase line, then immediately break open the doors, put lookouts on adjacent roofs, and send patrols along side streets to the edge of town. ... Tanks followed each company to take care of snipers and armored cars.

"Towns here in the Naples area, and throughout Italy, consist of all-stone buildings with thick walls, heavy doors ... Numerous large churches with high domes or steeples provided snipers and enemy observers with excellent observation for several hundred yards down principal streets and side streets.

"It was found necessary to place stationary observers on buildings for sniper protection. ... It is advisable, in addition to patrols down side streets, to send patrols promptly to investigate church steeples and tall buildings overlooking the route of march, as these were frequently found to be occupied by snipers."

Sniper Cpl. J. Fortain of Royal Canadian 22e Regiment near Rimini, Italy. He finished with 31 kills. The rifle appears to be a standard No. 4 Mk. I (T) Lee-Enfield sniper rifle with a No. 32 scope and M1907 sling. Canadian snipers overseas in WWII were issued sniper rifles from British stores. Most Canadian-made sniper rifles went into this British pool of rifles. This man appears to have survived the war as he is not listed in the Commonwealth War Graves Commission. LAC.

running from the Province of Florence, past Faenza, reaching the sea north of Ravenna. A patrol had crossed during the night but one man failed to return. In the morning, he was seen lying wounded on the German side. The entire battalion sniper section was called out and they engaged in a six-hour duel against the Germans before completely dominating them. Only then did a two-man patrol cross in a boat to recover the wounded man and return him to safety. Three days later when the German defenses were breached, four fresh graves with the date of the engagement were found.

In another incident along the Lamone, rifle fire was exchanged with the Germans. Then the Germans propped some helmets on sticks and began walking along the river bank, exposing the helmets in hope of drawing sniper fire. The British snipers waited at the river bends where they could enfilade the Germans. Enfilade them they did, and after a few casualties the game was stopped.[80]

To ensure that the armor would be able to cross the Lamone, two companies of 23rd Battalion, 5th Brigade, 2NZEF, sent patrols out on December 12, 1944, to check:

"concerning the 'going' for tanks and proposed lines of approach to enemy houses. Not on patrol but as a sniper in a forward observation

post in C Company's area, Private Bruning did good work until he was wounded. He was able to claim one 'certainty' and one 'possible', but his good shooting had also discouraged German observers of C Company positions. By noon on December 13, 80 New Zealand tanks had crossed."[81]

As the war crept up the Italian boot, the "Hasty Ps" (Canadian Hastings and Prince Edward Regiment) became more proficient. Intelligence Officer Farley Mowat recognized this in the regimental history:

"Sniping was encouraged as a major occupation and the results were posted daily for all ranks to see. The battalion snipers, always excellent, now begin to surpass themselves, and ordinary riflemen enthusiastically joined in to show their individual prowess. One Bren-gun team sniped six enemy in a single morning and the unit's pride in this achievement was immense."[82]

The shortage of snipers resulted in Princess Louise Dragoon Guards Trooper and PIAT (anti-tank) man Louis Winters becoming a sniper when the regiment approached Ravenna. With some coaching from his section mates, he became quite the marksman.[83]

The West Nova Scotia Regiment snipers

The Canadian regiment's scout-snipers were paired off as observers and manned forward observation posts (OPs). As they were relieved every six hours by another pair, the approach must have been camouflaged and via a trench system. The OPs were equipped with telephones allowing them to report troop movement and artillery flashes. Their knowledge of the compass and distance estimation assisted them in calling down counter-battery fire on the enemy artillery or Jabos (fighter bombers).

When on sniping missions they operated in pairs, although it was not unknown to send out a single sniper. Reconaissance photos, intelligence from other patrols, and observations from the OPs were studied prior to the mission. The sniper(s) would depart in darkness to the selected location, dig a slit trench, and camouflage it. Besides water, his rations included bully beef and biscuits (hard tack). As they knew shooting could betray their location, they waited for days before taking that that one perfect shot. One such sniper was Harry "Snake Eyes" Gates, who laid in wait for three days and observed one German who routinely left his safety in the early morning to attend to the call of nature. Snake Eyes Gates waited for the German to complete his task and pull his pants up before shooting him.

Once, when the Scotias were being heavily mortared with great accuracy, scout-sniper Oren Foster was summoned to locate the spotter. Advancing forward stealthily, Foster hid himself. Patiently waiting, he noticed slight movement in a haystack. He then stalked his way there and captured the spotter, whom he compelled to carry his wireless set back to Canadian lines.

Rifle fire from a cave on the right flank of the West Nova Scotia was impairing its patrols and Capt. Rice's men were called upon to resolve it. After studying the cave, the scout-snipers decided upon a somewhat unorthodox method to seal the cave's occupants. They took three PIAT anti-tank weapons with them and from 250 yards, over twice the normal range of 115 yards, fired six volleys (18 rounds in total) which collapsed the cave entrance, killing or sealing in the occupants.[84]

Newfoundlander Charlie Fleet came to the platoon as a replacement. Appearing like a swashbuckler, Fleet often tucked a six-shot revolver in his belt and a personally owned knife. If available, he armed himself with a German MP40 submachine gun with 32-round magazines. Often he badgered Oren Foster to go on patrol with him. When Foster asked why, Fleet responded that he thought Foster was his personal good luck charm. After the pair crept up to German lines, Fleet amused himself by stirring the Germans up with a hand grenade. Foster noted of Fleet, "Charley was a strong man and threw Mills bombs like baseballs! One time we were out and Charley had thrown his grenades and I was scared silly as the German machine gun opened up, then all went quiet and I started to sweat. Next thing I hear is Charley snoring!" Charlie Fleet also patrolled with others, including Doucette; once, they were so well camouflaged that a German patrol walked through their post without even realizing it!

Oren Foster had his own share of adventures without Charlie Fleet, too. Accurate mortar fire led Capt. Rice to believe there was an observer in an olive grove. Tasked with neutralizing him, Foster stalked up to the German who reached for his gun until he noticed that Foster had him dead in his sights. Wisely, the German surrendered and was escorted to the West Nova Scotias' lines. As a veteran of the Eastern Front, the German was grateful to have been spared by Foster and showed it by talking freely when interrogated. Later in 1944, when a German machine gun was firing from the second story of an Italian farmhouse and causing problems, Foster flanked the house and came across the Italian farmer whose house it was. The Italian pointed out the stairwell and Foster went up, opened the door and ordered the German to surrender at gunpoint. Foster wanted to capture the weapon, too, and ordered the German to pick it up. The German protested in English. "I can't. I don't feel well." Replying curtly, Foster said, "Pick it up or you'll feel a lot worse." Submitting to the Canadian's infallible logic, the German carried his machine gun back to Canadian lines.

Progress north improved and in 1945 the West Nova Scotia Regiment reached the towns of Sagnacavallo (January 21) and Bagnacavallo (January 26). Besides killing Germans, the scout-snipers also began shooting dogs they believed were German *Diensthunde* (German for service dogs) who carried messages, detected explosives, and perhaps most importantly, barked warnings whenever a Canadian approached.

Cap badge of the West Nova Scotia Regt. *GF Collection.*

5 Liberation of Northwestern Europe

"I broke out a D-ration hard chocolate candy bar I had in my field pack and gave it to him. In a ditch beside the road, I closed my eyes again, warmed by burning buildings all around me. It was 0200 and I had been awake, except for a few catnaps here and there, since leaving Holland the day before.

"I think it was about an hour later when I woke up and found the other GI still in the ditch with me, asleep. I looked around but could see no one else anywhere. I got the disturbing feeling the town had been abandoned. I shook the man beside me to whom I had given the ration and asked where everyone was, and then I saw the dented helmet and the bullet hole in it. My ditch companion was dead, meaning there was a sniper somewhere in the inferno surrounding us."[1]

Pfc. Roscoe C. Blunt
84th Infantry Division

Normandy (June 6–August 30, 1944)

On June 6, 1944, Operation Overlord saw Allied armies landing in Normandy, France—a major step toward the liberation of Western Europe. Normandy is characterized by its hedgerows, the walls of which were dirt parapets upon which grew scrubs and trees. Planted centuries ago to mark boundaries between irregularly shaped plots of land, they made excellent terrain for defensive operations. Tanks could climb over them, but in so doing exposed their soft underbellies to German anti-tank guns or deadly infantry-launched, hand-held *Panzerfaust* hollow-charge weapons. Infantry attempting to cross into the field were met with rifle and machine-gun fire as well as mortar barrages. Snipers could engage unwary infantrymen from concealment and withdraw safely to another fighting post. While the Americans had been aware of the hedgerows—indeed, the narrow lanes of Devon and Dorset where they had trained were similar—little specific training was given to fight in them as it was not anticipated that the Allies would remain in Normandy for long. Events would prove otherwise.

From east to west, the initial landing would include: the British 3rd Infantry Division and the 27th Armoured Brigade at Sword Beach; the 3rd Canadian Infantry Division along with the 2nd Canadian Armoured Brigade at Juno Beach; the British 15th Division and the British 8th Armoured Brigade had Gold Beach; the U.S. V Corps at Omaha; and at Utah Beach the U.S. VII Corps. The British and Canadians

planned to capture Bayeux and Caen; the Americans' objectives were to capture Carentan and Isigny before cutting the Cotentin Peninsula, taking the port of Cherbourg and advancing to Saint-Lô.

To protect the invasion flanks, three airborne divisions would land: British 6th in the east—this including the 1st Canadian Parachute Battalion—and U.S. 82d and 101st in the west. The British airborne

Prime Minister Winston Churchill attends a review on March 24, 1944, of the U.S. Army's 2d Armored and 9th Infantry Divisions at Tidworth. Eisenhower and Bradley are to the Prime Minister's right. Maj. Gen. Hugh Gaffey is to Churchill's left. D-Day is only weeks away. The photo has been retouched to give a better view of the PM's face by moving the scope slightly forward and to the left side of the rifle. *U.S. Army Signal Corps.*

The accuracy of the landing of the three gliders whose passengers assaulted the bridge at Bénouville is emphasized by these photographs. The second of the gliders to land carried Maj. John Howard and sniper Pte. Denis Edwards. *Battlefield Historian.*

only two of their number, captured the bridge. Two of the second set of three gliders landed near the Orne bridge and took it. Howard was able to radio back the codewords "Ham and Jam," meaning both bridges were under his control. Now the paras had to hold them until the 1st Special Service Brigade (commandos) arrived against concerted German attacks from land, down the canal, and from the air.

Riding in the same glider as Maj. Howard was one of his snipers, Pte. Denis Edwards, who was equipped with a Lee-Enfield No. 4. Edwards only received his scoped No. 4(T) much later on July 25.[2]

When daylight came, the Ox and Bucks found themselves subjected to intense sniper fire as described by Pte. Edwards:

"Generally the night was quieter than we expected but with the dawn came Germans in droves and from all directions. Under cover of darkness their snipers had climbed into tall trees and buildings and from daylight onwards began firing their high-powered rifles with deadly accuracy. My first indication was the distant 'crack' as they fired and, almost instantaneously, one of our lads would crash to the ground. They were fantastic marksmen and seldom let off a shot without hitting what they were aiming at. We quickly learned to respect these highly skilled Germans who were well concealed several hundred yards away, yet could pick off a man who only had the top of his head above ground level."[3]

The same was true for the 1st Canadian Parachute Battalion that had landed as part of 6th Airborne. Having fulfilled its initial tasks—blowing bridges

assault was spearheaded by a daring *coup de main* operation to take and hold two bridges at Bénouville—over the Canal de Caen and the River Orne—along with an attack on the Merville Battery and blowing other bridges over the rivers Dives and Divette.

Riding three Horsa gliders, Maj. John Howard's Coy. D (with two platoons of Coy. B), 2nd Battalion, Oxfordshire and Buckinghamshire Light Infantry (Ox and Bucks), landed within a short distance of their first objective, Bénouville Bridge (today's Pegasus Bridge) on the Caen Canal. They caught the Germans by surprise and after a brief fight in which they lost

ASSAULT PARTY GLIDERS
PEGASUS BR. 6 JUN '44

to ensure the flank of the invasion was safe from armored attack—it took up a defensive postion around an important crossroads, Le Mesnil between Bréville and the Bois de Bavent, just south of another dramatic battle involving the Canadian paras, around the Château Saint-Côme.

> "As soon as the first paratroopers of the Battalion's HQ Company reached Le Mesnil that morning, they immediately came under accurate and deadly fire. In a very short time, the marksmanship of the German snipers resulted in several casualties including one officer … 'I was the fifth to take over as Company Sergeant-Major,' recalled John Kemp. 'It was mostly snipers picking them off.'"[4]

One of the immediate effects was that the paratroopers removed all insignia. Another was to stop using tracer rounds: they gave the firer's position away too easily to snipers. They then had to combat the hidden enemy which they did by aggressive patrolling, day and night. They may not have killed many snipers, but they forced the Germans to take up positions further away from the Canadian positions. The battalion's own snipers were busy: "Throughout the attack, Privates R. A. Geddes and W. Noval, armed with a Bren gun and a sniper's rifle, accounted for approximately twenty-five Germans killed."[5] The incessant sniping had another effect: anger. Seeing friends and colleagues fall victim to snipers made the Canadians very angry and ensured that "an increasing toll of revenge" was taken on any German sniper unfortunate enough to be cornered.[6]

* * * * *

Pinned on Juno Beach, Johnny Paicheck was in Canada's 3rd Infantry Division. He was already soaking wet—his landing craft had been gutted by one of Rommel's underwater obstacles. Now, along with his comrades, he lay there at the embankment while the German machine guns on the ridge ahead of them chattered away. John Finocchio was hit when he tried to crawl to higher ground. Phil Salter was hit when he moved. Paicheck remained still since anyone trying to move beyond the embankment drew angry tracers from two machine guns that held them in a crossfire. Apart from mortar fire, he was relatively safe—until some German climbed a tree and began to methodically pick them off. He took his time to avoid being spotted and only the cry from his victim announced that he had fired again. Paicheck waited until the machine guns paused. Then he started

to crawl slowly to the left of where the sniper was. He only stopped when he reached some tall grass beneath a cluster of three or four trees. Paicheck waited for more daylight. When it came, he began to carefully scan each tree. The German by now had stopped firing. An uneasiness overcame Paicheck, as if he sensed the German was sighting in on him. He remained still until it passed. Suddenly Paicheck realized that something was odd with a tree to the right. There was a fork in the tree and the object in the fork didn't belong there. It was a German boot. Aiming carefully, Paicheck fired once and the sniper tumbled out. When the German attempted to crawl away, Paicheck fired again, nailing him for good. The Canadian advance resumed.[7]

When the 6th Green Howards landed on Gold Beach, Cpl. Harry Furness was among them. Furness excelled in fieldcraft and shooting and was trained at Bisley, Hythe, and Llanberis. Attached to Company HQ of the Hallamshire Battalion of the York & Lancaster Regiment, he was temporarily attached to the Green Howards to help bring the latter up to full strength. At Normandy on D-Day, his LCA grounded on a sandbank and he and his equipment were drenched from wading to the beach. Cpl. Furness's first shot of the war was only to test his rifle to see if it worked.

> "On D-Day I only fired my rifle three times, the first shot into the sand as I came ashore to see

Maj. Howard at Chateau Saint-Côme with the snipers of D Coy.., Ox and Bucks. L–R Waite, Musty, Clarke, Howard, Bright, O'Donnell, Edwards. (The other sniper, Cpl. Wally Parr, wasn't in the photographed as he had been wounded.) Info from *pegasusarchive. org. Battlefield Historian.*

Treatment of captured snipers

Originally part of the Seventh (U.S.) Army that liberated Southern France, the 14th Armored Division was later transferred to Third (U.S.) Army. In April 1944 its 94th Cavalry Reconnaissance Squadron along with Tpr. Hugh West was already in Germany and sometimes stood guard while the engineers cleared the roads. His unit would roar down the road with machine guns blazing at every suspected sniper location. When snipers were located, they were distracted and while distracted, flanked. West observed, "No one liked snipers. We didn't even like our own snipers."[8]

If snipers were universally despised, the chances that their surrender would be accepted were slim. Sniper Harry Furness recalled that the average lifespan of a sniper was only three weeks. He observed that many sniper pairs went out never to return. Postwar when the British PoWs were released and returned to their units, the missing snipers were not among them.[9] Whether snipers were taken prisoners or executed depended on several things. Pvt. Michael Bilder said:

In the pursuit across France, Germans serving as rearguard sometimes exchanged their uniform for civilian clothing. Footwear was more difficult and this out-of-uniform German was probably caught because of his boots. It is unknown if he survived or was shot as a spy. *Author's collection.*

"In pitched battles snipers slowed our advance, forcing us to be especially careful when moving up. Often during firefights someone who seemed to be very well protected by cover and out of the line of fire would suddenly get hit and collapse from a shot that seemingly came out of nowhere. We knew immediately that the shot had come from a sniper. As we advanced toward an objective that appeared quiet, sometimes a single shot rang out and took down one of our men. Everyone dove for cover, and the inevitable question, 'Anybody see where that came from?' resonated throughout the ranks.

"As I mentioned previously, an enemy sniper kept hitting our guys in the back of their ankles, blowing out their Achilles' tendons and crippling them for life. The screams of agony these men let out as they were hit made our hair stand on end and our blood boil. What's more, the pain of these wounded men was so excruciating that they couldn't stop screaming. The natural tendency was to run out and help whoever was hit, but this is exactly what the sniper wanted. It was a tactic intended to produce new victims.

"We spotted the sniper and sprayed fire in his general directions, which sent him scurrying down out of his tree. He jumped down in front of us, threw up his hands, and yelled, 'Kamerad!' The GI closest to him hesitated for a moment then said, 'Comrade my ass,' and shot him with a burst from his BAR. I wouldn't have done it, but on the other hand I didn't suffer any angst over it."[10]

The sentiment of the BAR man would confirm Trooper West's view and a Checkerboard (99th Division) soldier said: "[A] sniper is kind of like somebody slipping up behind your back and taking you out without a chance to defend yourself."[11] Thus the gunning down of a sniper was no isolated incident either. A strikingly similar account was given by H/317th Infantry Regiment's Lt. Andy Adkins.

"Lt. Mike Damkowitch ran into snipers and a Kraut killed one of his sergeants. The German ran out of ammunition and came out with his hands up. He took about two steps and had enough lead in him to make him weigh a ton. That was the dirtiest thing a Kraut could do: kill your men until he ran out of ammunition and then come out with a grin like it was all in fun and try to give himself up."[12]

Neither Lt. Mike Damkowitch and his men nor Michael Bilder's buddy had to worry about repercussions either, as their army group commander Lt. Gen. Omar Bradley would turn a blind eye. Bradley's aide de camp, Maj. Chester B. Hansen, remarked that Bradley said, "[H]e will not take any action against anyone that decides to treat snipers a little more roughly than they are being treated a present. A sniper cannot sit around and shoot and then capture when you close in on him. That's not the way to play the game."[13] If Brad didn't want to hear of it, his subordinate Patton was even more tolerant.

Snipers faced an uncertain future when captured. These were taken by 3d (U.S.) Infantry Division on January 24, 1944, in the Acciarella area in Italy. The original caption highlights the fact that one sniper wears a Red Cross armband although he had been found with a rifle that had been fired. *NARA.*

He was willing to quietly shelve the entire Biscari Massacre affair by having the parties involved report, "that the dead men were snipers or had been attempting to escape or something."[14] Patton supposedly also told his men, "When you are sniped at, especially from the rear, the snipers must be destroyed."[15]

In another incident in Frankfurt, Michael Bilder himself came under fire. It was dusk when he was approaching a fork in the street. Hugging the wall, a bullet smashed into the concrete just above his head. Bilder sprinted to a doorway as another bullet splattered just above him. Incensed, Bilder wanted revenge. Having seen the flash of the second shot, he flanked his opponent, entered the building from the rear, and stealthily approached the lair. Peering around the corner, he spotted his assailant looking out the window in search of prey. With his Tommy gun selector set on semiautomatic (single shot), Bilder steadied himself against the door frame and fired one shot, dropping his target. With Tommy gun still in hand and pointing at the German, Bilder approached and turned him over. All hatred and bloodlust evaporated immediately when Bilder realized he just had shot a child. In conversing with his opponent, Bilder learned he was a 16-year-old Polish draftee who had been told that the Americans would not take him prisoner. Bilder applied first aid, assured him that he would recover and then summoned a medic to tend to the wound. Afterward the medic had the prisoner transported to a field hospital.[16]

The "stay behind" was certainly no sniper. In 1944 the OKH issued commandments for snipers, one of which read, "Fight fanatically!" Concurrently, another instruction (not one of the Ten Commandments) instructed the sniper to consider, "The line of retreat."[17] That youth was left there to die.

To become eligible to attend sniping school, Sepp Allerberger was demoted by his captain to sniper prospect. Snipers were already in short supply so no active sniper could attend. Before departing for sniping school, Allerberger returned his PU scope-equipped Mosin-Nagant sniper rifle to the regimental armorer who in turn issued it to a young *Jäger.* The armorer explained the notches to the replacement and told him to do his duty with honor. Allerberger then emptied his pockets of the explosive ammunition and handed it to his replacement with the advice to be good to the armorer who could then keep an eye out for more. After training, Sepp Allerberger returned to his unit and asked about his replacement. The armorer replied him that he had failed to return one day and several days after his disappearance was found by a patrol. His body had been horribly mutilated with over a thousand cuts along with dismemberment. Thereafter, Allerberger discarded the habit of carving notches and removed any evidence that suggested he was a sniper.[18]

In another incident, Allerberger relates the horrible fate of one captured sniper. The battalion received a new sniper who accompanied a patrol that was ambushed by a larger partisan unit. He became separated and the patrol saw him surrender and led away. A stronger patrol was immediately organized to rescue

A worried *Panzergrenadier* from the Hermann Göring Division captured on the Gustav Line. *Battlefield Historian.*

Valentina Binĕvská strikes a pose with her SVT-40. A sniper with the 1st Czechoslovak Independent Battalion along with Maria Ljalková, her first fighting was at Sokolov in 1943 during which she suffered badly from hypothermia. After she recovered, she trained as a nurse for the 2d Czechoslovak Parachute Brigade and took part in the Slovak National Uprising, fighting as a guerrilla after the uprising was suppressed. Captured by the Gestapo in February 1945, she escaped and ended the war as a sergeant. Postwar she stayed in the army until the 1950s, becoming an officer. She died in 1992 with a chestful of Russian and Czech medals and awards. *Courtesy the Central Museum of the Armed Forces, Moscow via Stavka.*

him and defeat the partisans. They successfully drove the partisans back and destroyed them to a man. Afterward, they found their sniper inside the saw mill. His limbs had been sawn off and his torso sawn half-way up to his navel.[19] The lesson was not lost on Allerberger who kept a submachine gun at hand so if he was captured, he would surrender with it instead of the sniper rifle. He explained that to be caught with a sniper rifle was suicidal.[2] While not equipped with a scoped rifle, *Obergrenadier* Helmut Altner was behind Russian lines in Berlin and feared being mistaken for a sniper.[21]

Valentina Binêvská was a female Czech resistance fighter and sniper who not only survived captivity, but also escaped.[22] It is likely her captors were unaware of her role as a sniper. In another case two American "snipers" were captured as described by Karl Krauss.

"Sometimes we came under fire from the GI snipers, but they were often not good shots, and their hidings [places] were usually very easy to find. They were not trained well I think, and once we captured two. They had good rifles with small telescopes but they did not know much of camouflage and they fired too many shots from their hiding place, so we found them. We kept their rifles and sent the men back to the rear as prisoners. I do not think they were real snipers."[23]

Perhaps the most infamous incident where "snipers" were executed was the Biscari Airfield Massacre in Sicily on July 14, 1943. Among the units involved in invading Sicily was the green and untested 45th Infantry Division. It had been fighting for three days when its 180th Regiment was ordered to capture the Biscari Airfield. One platoon of 36 soldiers suffered a dozen casualties, including medics who had rushed out to aid the fallen. The airfield was finally captured and the victorious American captors, thinking the prisoners were snipers, organized a firing squad and executed 35 Italians and two Germans.

Some snipers survived the war because they disappeared. Sepp Allerberger destroyed his sniper rifle and carried a submachine gun which he discarded when captured by the Americans. Helmut Jung became separated from his unit and was caught by the Red Army. Under interrogation, he admitted to having been trained as a sniper but lied when asked if he actually fought as a sniper. He explained there was a shortage of scoped rifles in the *Wehrmacht* which the interrogator knew was true. Jung later escaped and rejoined the *Wehrmacht* and surrendered in the west.

Being able to make the transition from sniper to ordinary combatant and then to a prisoner of war depended on whether the sniper could dispose of his sniper rifle in time; the degree of his opponents' bloodlust, which was fueled by the casualties inflicted prior to the capture (as at Biscari); whether prisoners were needed by intelligence; and the degree of command and control exercised by the officer. Pvt. Roscoe Blunt of U.S. 84th Division dryly observed, "that snipers were seldom taken alive unless they were needed by G-2 for information."[24]

While the Japanese proclivity to kill prisoners is well known, and the German treatment of Soviet PoWs saw 57 percent die as prisoners, no World War II belligerent can claim clean hands whether the captor was Soviet, American, or British. Human nature transcends nationality and is the same regardless of it. *C'est la guerre.*

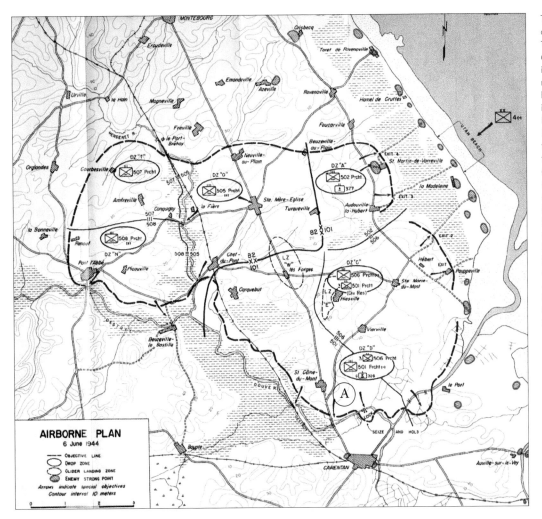

AIRBORNE PLAN
6 June 1944

OBJECTIVE LINE
DROP ZONE
GLIDER LANDING ZONE
ENEMY STRONG POINT
Arrows indicate special objectives
Contour interval 10 meters

if the seawater affected it, and during the day two more shots, each time dropping NCO's who were both moving targets. I used 'Kentucky Windage' to aim off and I know my eyes were wet through with water when I 'fired in anger' for the first time."[25]

After being wounded in a mortar barrage, he was reposted to the Hallamshire Battalion, 146th Brigade, 49th Division. Furness would become one of Britain's most successful snipers of World War II.

Two American airborne divisions, the 101st and 82d, landed in Normandy behind Utah Beach by parachute and glider. One of their missions was to secure the causeways to the beach and stop German troops moving to defend against the landings. Maj. Larry Legere was the 501st PIR's assistant operations officer to Lt. Col. Raymond Millener. He led what men he could gather for the attack on Pouppeville, a village about three miles to the south of Utah. Legere went a few paces down a road when a shot rang out

and he collapsed. A medic, T/5 Edwin Holh, whose Red Cross armband clearly identified his role, ran up to him, bent over to minister to his wounds, and fell over him dead. Holh was killed by a bullet to his chest. Although Maj. Legere's wound was huge and gaping, he survived to be evacuated. Radioman George Koskimaki examined a dead German and learned that they had pink-colored hollow wooden bullets—training bullets that were deadly at close range.[26] Similarly, back at Utah Beach 1/116th Infantry (29th Division) Sgt. Dean Friedline was hit by a wooden bullet that shattered the explosive block he was carrying in his vest. While it shattered, the block didn't detonate.[27]

The 506th PIR, 101st Division, was tasked to seize two causeways that led to Utah Beach. The drop had scattered the regiment but the paratroopers united with others regardless of their parent unit. An assortment of 506th, 502d, and even 82d Airborne made their way to the causeway and came under sniper fire from a church tower. 506th T/5 Bill

Snipers from the sky

As has already been discussed, German *Fallschirmjäger* initially didn't jump with their personal weapons and had to retrive them from a canister.

For "Overlord," 101st Airborne paratroopers with the M1 Garand disassembled their weapons into its three major components (barreled action, stock, trigger group), placed the parts into the Griswold storage bag, and reassembled it on the ground. (On later jumps the rifle was left assembled.) The same could not be done for the longer M1903A4 where the soldier needed a screwdriver to separate the action from the stock. While riggers could sew an extension for the Griswold Bag to accommodate the M1903A4, the extent of this ad hoc measure is unknown. Paratrooper rifle grenadier Cpl. Spencer F. Wurst of the 82d Airborne describes the issues with jumping with the Springfield:

"The '03 rifle also presented me with the very immediate problem of how to get out of the plane. We jumped with our M1s field stripped into the three main pieces. We carried the dismounted rifle in a well-padded jump case, worn across our fronts, which permitted us to jump without hampering us. But I had to jump with my '03 in one piece. If I held it cross-wise, I wouldn't be able to get out the door, so I had to mount it intact almost parallel to my body. The mind boggles at what could happen when landing with a rifle sticking up in one long piece."[28]

Taken at face value, Wurst's technique could expose the scope to damage or injure the trooper. Because of the scope's fragility, it is likely that any 82d or 101st Airborne paratrooper jumped with it diagonally in front of the body and beneath the reserve chute and with the bolt side away to prevent injury on landing. With the rifle carried diagonally, the jump would not be impeded and both the paratrooper's body and reserve parachute provided some protection for the scope. Some substantiation is provided by 82d Airborne's CG James Gavin:

German rifles and heavy weapons were mainly dropped in containers. These had wheels and a handle that allowed them to be pulled. *Narodowe Archiwum Cyfrowe.*

"After Sicily all the survivors wanted to jump with the rifle right on their person and ready to use. We therefore put the rifle underneath the reserve parachute against the trooper's body and moved it into a vertical position to get out of the door. The muzzle was near his face and the butt of the rifle between his knees. Once the parachute opened and vertical descent began, he maneuvered the rifle into a horizontal position so it did not interfere with the landing."[29]

Similarly, *Band of Brothers* marksman Darryl "Shifty" Powers learned to jump with his M1 beneath the harness and with his arms wrapped about the rifle.[30]

The British and Canadian Airborne troops had a sniper complement as part of the intelligence/scout units, attached to battalion HQ. Originally, this was only an intelligence sergeant. In 1942, HQ Coy. had an intelligence section of a sergeant and ten men. By 1944 the section was led by an intelligence officer (a subaltern), with under him a sergeant and seven men; from this date its armament included eight sniper rifles. Each of the three sections of the Rifle Coy. platoon was also allotted a sniper rifle.

Because British and Canadian paratroopers used a leg bag to take their weapons, the snipers had two options. They could remove the scope (this did not affect the zeroing) and protect it with padding in a pocket or similar. Once they landed refitting took less than 30 seconds. Alternatively, they could leave the scope on the rifle and protect it by wrapping netting around it. The leg bag meant that the rifle usually hit the ground butt first, and a simple bore-sighting technique—when time or the situation permitted—could ensure the zero hadn't been lost.

Lt. (later Major General) Peter Downward completed his parachute course in August 1944 and went to 13th (Lancashire) Para Battalion, fighting in the Ardennes where he was part of the 6th Airborne counterattack that included the hard-fought battle of Bure (January 3–5, 1945). After the battle the unit was taken out of the line having suffered heavy casualties. Back in England, at Larkhill, Downward,

"was told by Peter Luard I was to take over the Scout Platoon (Snipers) and I was to give them as much practice as I could in the way of field firing night work. I took my new command down to Cranbourne Chase. I had something like 26 snipers, 2 radio operators and 2 dog handlers [The para dogs sniffed out mines and enemy positions. One of them, Bing, received the Dicken Medal, the UK's highest honor for animals.] ... My Platoon Sergeant was Sergeant Birkbeck, a gamekeeper, a good shot and an expert in field craft, camouflage and wildfire.

"We set up in a farm and occupied a barn; there was a village nearby with a good pub, which of course became our evening drinking spot. The snipers worked in pairs and would keep a constant watch through their telescopic sights and record time and place of movement. Only if Sgt Birkbeck or I appeared in the 'killing area' would they fire their blanks. If we spotted them first, it was a 'no kill'."[31]

13th Para went on to take part in Operation Varsity, the northern Rhine crossing, and fought to Wismar on the Baltic, which they reached just before the Soviets.

USAAF Station AAF-469—RAF Ramsbury—June 5, 1944, as Lt. Col. Robert L. Wolverton, commander of the 3/506th PIR, 101st Airborne, and his battalion prepare to board the C-47 that will take them to Normandy. *NARA*.

105

First Nations' snipers

"Hasty P" Pte. W. J. Brant was a descendant of the famous Indian Chief Thayendanegen or Joseph Brant, and enlisted in the "Hasty Ps" on September 2, 1939. He was with them when they evacuated France and served as a scout-sniper in that regiment. When the "Hasty Ps" were sent to Sicily, he was on a reconnaissance party when he crept up and killed his first German. He was wounded twice in Italy, the last time being May 18, 1944, and was discharged in December 1944.[32]

Another Canadian Indian sniper, 32-year-old Cree Raymond Prince had nine kills to his credit in Normandy but only counted those who fell from the first shot. "Sometimes I miss with the first shot and get him with the second or third; but that's no good." His ninth kill that he counted was a German for whom he waited from 0900 hours until 1600 hours. The German was hidden in a wheatfield 350 yards away when Prince fetched his man. Prince advised, "If you just sit tight long enough, Jerry will always show his chest. That's the time to shoot, not before."[33]

Cap badge of the "Hasty Ps." *GF Collection.*

Maslowski was among the troopers and had landed in water. (The Germans had flooded much of the hinterland.) The immersion ruined his SCR-300 radio as well as rendering his firearm inoperable. He picked up a German K98k and joined the column. They came under fire and ended it with superior firepower. "We came to a town after four of us had joined the larger body of troops and were firing at enemy snipers in the church bell tower with a bazooka." After silencing the snipers, Maslowski was reunited with his company. [34]

Also jumping with the 506th was Donald R. Burgett. It is said that the Germans fought for their

Vaterland (or *der Führer*), the British for King and Country, the Soviets for Mother Russia, and the Americans for souvenirs. Trooper Burgett of Detroit was drafted fresh out of high school and was no exception. In Normandy he came across some German rifles:

"Looting was a favorite pastime, even among the troopers. It was while I was busy at this occupation that I came across several sniper rifles. They were equipped with scopes and flash hiders. The mechanisms worked like glass. They were beautiful weapons and I longed to send one home for deer hunting after the war. This was impossible, so I took them one by one and smashed them against the tree so no one else could use them against us."[35]

The only German rifle that had both scope and a flash suppressor was the German *Fallschirmjägergewehr* FG42.

Lost and unable to find anyone from his stick, S/Sgt. Bob Webb of the 3/506th landed in the River Douve near La Barquette. He got out on the south side. He was close to the lock keeper's house and hearing German voices, made for the barn. Inside he found Cpl. Ben Hiner and five other men from his battalion hiding in the loft. They decided to make their way to the canal, steal a boat, and cross it. Leading the others, Webb left the barn and stealthily moved toward some trees by the edge of the canal near Saint-Hilaire. Their machine gunner set up his gun to provide covering fire if they needed it. He never fired a shot and slumped over from a bullet that was placed perfectly between the eyes. The shot had come from the second story of a house on the other side of the canal. Cpl. Hiner spotted a blonde female in the window and for some unknown reason thought that she was the shooter. Hiner recalled, "I don't know what she was doing there, but she saw me and waved. The next thing I knew shots were being fired. I realized it was this blonde and fired back with my M1. We didn't stick around to see what happened but I think I may have killed her."[36] It is more plausible that the blonde acted as decoy for a German soldier but whether she was or wasn't, Webb and Hiner along with the four other men decided not to cross the canal. They eluded the Germans, crossed the river onto the north bank further down, and united with other troopers at Pénème.

American paratroopers found a dubious way to entice the Germans to divulge their location. Flight Officer (glider) Richard F. Brown, described it. "Another reason they liked seeing us glidermen was that they like our flak suits. When the gliders come in the paratroopers go for those vests. They wear them when they're looking for snipers—snipe-hunting, they call it."

Flight Officer Primo Ceravolo provided further insight. "One paratrooper I saw had on three flak suits. The paratroopers work in teams of three or four. One man meets the fire to draw it out, while the others cover him and pick off the snipers when their gun flashes. Well, this guy with the three flak suits just walked out into the field and drew fire, and his buddies kept picking off the snipers. You could see the German fire coming at him, but he kept going."[37]

Donald Burgett recalled one trooper who did this:

"Phillips said, 'That was some stunt that Jackson pulled the other day, wasn't it?' 'I don't know,' I replied. 'What was it?' 'Well, there was a sniper somewhere in the hedges near town and no one could locate him. He killed a couple of troopers when they were alone. Jackson put on a couple of flak vests, one over the other, that he had gotten off several dead pilots in the field. Then he walked into the center of the field where the sniper was supposed to be and made out like he was looking for something on the ground while Wisniewski hid in a hedge to shoot the Kraut when he opened up at Jackson. The first shot caught Jackson just to the left of the breast bone, spinning him around.' 'Why didn't you shoot?' he asked Whiskey. 'I didn't see him,' Whiskey replied. Jackson and Wisnsiewski were close friends and Jackson, along with the rest of us, called him 'Whiskey' for short. The second shot hit Jackson squarely in the chest, knocking the wind out of him. 'I see him,' Jackson called, and he fired a shot that caught the sniper in the head, killing him instantly."[38]

The 82d Airborne was due to land west of the 101st. 508th PIR Trooper Dwayne T. Burns was among one isolated group of 82d paratroopers who were trapped on three sides by the Germans. With water behind them, retreat was not an option. Slowly, they were picked off either by artillery or by an unseen German in a tree. Like other paratroopers, they resorted to the expediency of donning flak armor, in this case three layers, and exposing themselves to entice Germans to shoot. The waiting troopers promptly shot down the German. Then another trooper would don the armor and make his mad dash. After the Germans suffered four consecutive casualties, they caught on to the trooper's tactics and desisted from playing tree sniper.[39] It's unlikely that these Germans

were proper snipers—flak jackets didn't cover heads: see Bob Slaughter's story below.

On D+4 (June 10), Co. F, 2/505th was attempting to cross a railway embankment when they came under machine-gun fire. Pfc. Wurst was among the troopers who were pinned down. Luckily for Co. F, it had a sniper and Wurst describes their sniper's response:

"Watro was out a little further than the rest of us, having gone across a short field. He motioned to us that he was going to change his position to see if he could locate the machine gun. He disappeared from sight, and then we heard shooting off in his direction. Twenty minutes or a half hour later, he crawled back into view with a big grin on his face. He held up three fingers. He'd gotten a German MG crew with his scoped rifle."[40]

Pfc. Thomas L. Watro was with the 505th PIR from its inception. Serving as a squad sniper was quite unusual considering snipers were generally platoon assets. Watro sometimes served at times as second scout.

S/Sgt. Bob Slaughter landed on Utah Beach. Before finishing high school and over his parents' objection, Slaughter enlisted in the National Guard in Roanoke, VA. Becoming a guardsman gave him a chance to earn money and each drill paid a dollar. Slaughter belonged to Co. D, 1st Battalion, 116th Infantry Regiment. By the time of Pearl Harbor, Slaughter had risen to corporal. As the army expanded, he became a sergeant and section leader. The 116th Infantry belonged to the 29th Infantry Division (the Blue and Gray Division) and sailed for England aboard the *Queen Mary*. They witnessed the horrific collision at sea when *Queen Mary* sliced escorting cruiser HMS *Curacao* in half—337 men died. Now on D-Day Slaughter's platoon was part of the second wave on Utah Beach where they received their baptism of fire. Initially floundering

You'd need to be seriously optimistic to use this sort of flak jacket as the primary defense against snipers. *NARA.*

The FG42 was the Luftwaffe's gas-operated selective-fire 20-round magazine-fed 8mm Mauser rifle. The first version is on top and the second below. Their semiautomatic nature meant that, although scoped, they were not as accurate as the more rigid manual bolt-action rifle when used as sniper weapons. In Normandy, Donald Burgett came across rifles like these and smashed them against a tree to deny the enemy their use of them. *Objects are in the collection of the Museum of the Brazilian Army.*

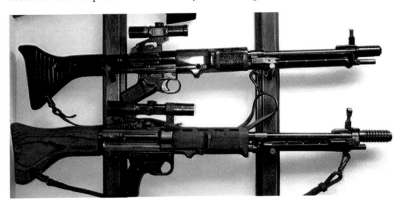

Near Cherbourg, France, 2d Infantry Division T/Sgt. Meredith J. Roger was unscathed from a shot that struck his helmet. *NARA.*

in the water, he was among the first in his landing craft to reach the sea wall. After sustaining more casualties, they reached the hill that overlooked the beach and dug in in anticipation of the German counterattack. His company had already sustained 72 casualties and it was only the first day of the liberation of Europe. On the second day, they began moving inland. This was when they realized that while they had trained extensively for boat clearing and mine clearing, they were not trained for hedgerow fighting. It was also Slaughter's introduction to the German sniper:

"The dreaded German sniper was almost as highly respected as the 88. Sharpshooters give no warning, taking careful aim with sniper-scoped Mausers. The receiving end would hear the sharp crack and instantaneous whine of the bullet. If you heard the report of the bullet leaving the muzzle, it wasn't for you."

By the second day Slaughter's company had liberated Vierville and were pushing beyond it when they received small arms fire and artillery. Their advance was halted but a resourceful lieutenant "grabbed some 'volunteers' and went after the obstruction. After a few BAR bursts, the sharpshooter-artillery spotter was brought to military justice. Cleverly hidden by camouflage in a fixed artillery observation post in a tree, that lone shooter was responsible for delaying our progress for over an hour, and lost us several good men."[41]

On June 8, 116th Infantry Regiment and S/Sgt. Bob Slaughter were advancing on Maisy, some eight miles west along the coast. The village had been softened up generously by the U.S. Navy and apart from isolated German riflemen and mortar fire, they captured it and went into divisional reserve. Slaughter was becoming seasoned and witnessed a high turnover as replacements filled the gaps vacated by the fallen. He observed:

"German snipers nearly always aimed for the head if it was visible and in range. Most infantrymen never removed their helmets except when they shaved … The 8mm bullet could easily pass through the helmet, through the head, and out on the other side with enough energy to do more damage. I saw men get hit between the

eyes or just above the ears, which killed them instantly. If the bullet missed the helmet, the entry hole was usually neat and showed only a small trickle of blood. But after the steel-jacket bullet hit the helmet or skull, the bullet flattened, causing the exit wound to shatter the other side of the head away."[42]

After helping hard-pressed Rangers at Maisy, the 116th pressed on towards Couvains. S/Sgt. Slaughter remembered the death of another sergeant: "A *Wehrmacht* sniper put an 8mm bullet between Sergeant Romeo B. Bily's eyes and killed him instantly." Artillery was brought down on Couvains' church belfry and when that failed, covering fire that allowed the engineers to place TNT at the belfry's base. The ensuing explosion brought it down and ended all sniping as well as artillery spotting from it.[43]

While the 116th and the 29th Division were expanding their beachhead, Pfc. Wurst's company (82d Airborne) was advancing (on June 16) towards Saint-Sauveur-le-Vicomte. They had advanced so fast that an airstrike intended for the Germans fell on them instead with resulting casualties. This was despite the orange marker panels and smoke the 505th put out for identification. After the planes departed, they came under small-arms fire. Again their sniper moved out and Wurst remembered:

"We got held up by sniper fire and light small arms fire coming from the houses in town. Tommy Watro moved off some distance from our position to stalk some of the enemy snipers and riflemen. He came back a little while later with another one of his big grins on his face and held up a couple of fingers to signify he had gotten the Germans who were firing at us. He later swore they were five hundred to six hundred yards out. I don't dismiss his claim. All men armed with the M1 used to fire courses at two hundred to three hundred yards without a scope and got good scores. Watro, using an M1903 rifle with a scope could do much better."[44]

German sniping was nothing new and the Allies had experienced it in both Sicily and Italy. But it was in Normandy that sniping was applied more energetically than elsewhere. The American GIs' experience with snipers in Normandy was no different to their British and Canadian counterparts. American reporter Ernie Pyle wrote:

"In past campaigns our soldiers would talk about the occasional snipers with contempt and disgust. But in France sniping became more important, and taking precautions against it was something we had to learn and learn fast. One officer friend of mine said, 'Individual soldiers have become sniper-wise before, but now we're sniper-conscious as whole units.'[45]

The 4th (U.S.) Infantry Division unit also landed on Utah Beach. In the confusion after the landing, Co. B's Pfc. Johnny Prislupski became separated from his unit, had a slight abdominal rupture, and was told to find the field hospital. On the fifth day after the landing, a sniper shot his gas mask. He was in a foxhole with an 82d Airborne trooper when they were fired at. The paratrooper said, "Let's go get that *** ** * *****." Prislupski and the paratrooper were nearly nailed but the sniper made the mistake of ejecting his spent cartridge down on them. Prislupski remembered:

"The paratrooper made me crawl along the hedgerow—knew all about it and wasn't scared, but I was scared to death. The paratrooper got him, and the rifle dropped down … the sniper was snuggled to a limb there, tied up in a tent for camouflage. This guy cut him out of the tree. We knocked out three more snipers along the hedgerows."

Their adventures didn't end there. They knocked out a machine gun, killing its three-man crew with a grenade. When a German light tank approached, Prislupski loaded the paratrooper's bazooka and scored a hit on the tank. They also knocked out an 88mm gun with grenades. On the eighth day they were hunting for snipers when a machine gun injured the paratrooper. Prislupski carried his buddy to the medics and both were evacuated to England.[46]

Wading ashore with the 4th Division was Sgt. William E. Jones of Item Company, 8th Infantry Regiment. In the fighting at Normandy, Jones heard a single shot followed by the cry, "Medic! Medic!" He wiggled forward on his belly into a gully where he met a red-haired sergeant. Two men were already down and the sniper had to be removed. Jones scanned the open field that stopped at a hedgerow. Beyond it rose a hill upon which sat an old farmhouse. He studied it and then returned to the trees in the hedgerow. The redheaded sergeant brought his attention to a tree on the right.

"I detected a large dark knot high in the top of the tree. I studied it for a second and was about to slide on past, thinking it was a deformity in the tree, when it moved. I watched it intently, finally concluding that I must have seen a bird, although most of the birds had left. I scoped slowly down on the hedgerow, hoping the sniper would reveal himself.

"When nothing else stirred, I returned to the knot for the lack of anything more probable. The more I looked at it, the more it resembled a man hugged tight to the tree trunk. The redheaded sergeant cleared his throat.

"'It's either him,' I replied, 'or a knot in a tree.'

"'Shoot it and see what happens.'

"'I'll wait.'

"I didn't want the sniper spotting me first if that really was a knot. I studied the length of the hedgerows again before returning to the tree. Several minutes passed. The sergeant fidgeted.

"'I want him to break first.'

"The next time the knot moved, I knew it was not a bird.

"'Okay, I have him!' I said triumphantly

"A slight breeze drifted across the field from left to right, stirring with its breath a few pale spears of grass. I clicked in a degree of windage and clicked one up on elevation. The workings were smooth. I kept them that way. The good sun provided me a sharp picture through the scope, although the foliage concealed most of what I at first mistook to be a 'knot.'

"The sucker had shot at least two of our boys. With that in mind and nothing else, I drew in a deep breath filled with the smell of the rich soil on which I lay, let half of it slowly escape, and then gently stroked the trigger. The rifle recoiled.

"When I brought it back down, I saw the tree shaking violently. The 'knot' seemed to be throbbing and pulsating. I quickly bolted in another round and put my crosshairs back on target. Sometimes you had to hit a squirrel two or three times when it was high in the reaches of some sycamore or cottonwood and all you could get the first time was a piece of him.

"I squeezed off another round. The German turned and lost his perch just like a squirrel does and bounced off the limbs down through the tree until his body hit the ground."[47]

Sgt. William Jones ceased being a sniper when his cherished rifle was destroyed by mortar fire. It was never replaced.

Earlier, in Italy, American sniper John Fulcher suggested to his partner, "Krauts don't watch Roy Rogers … Let's give him a target and see if he shows himself."[48] While Fulcher and his partner located and

German use of trees

Snipers Capt. Clifford Shore and Sgt. Harry Furness were both highly skeptical of professional snipers using trees. They point out that once detected, there was little chance for escape. It was only after the war when he examined German manuals Shore learned that the Germans did use trees. Furthermore, both German army and SS manuals mention using trees.[49] T/5 Paul T. Bradecky was in combat for a few days and was being relieved when he was shot in the foot. "He [the sniper] was in one big tree and one of my buddies knocked him out, but he was tied to the tree. One of our boys had to go up and cut him loose after he was hit."[50] Likely the majority of Germans in Normandy who fired from trees were not snipers. The Germans often constructed platforms from which, if they so desired or needed to, artillery observers could fight. Their primary mission, though, was to call down artillery fire for the unit(s) they were supporting or on targets of opportunity. It was not unknown for their observation platforms to have ladders for accessibility. Some even had camouflaged foxholes near the ladder. On the Destrés farm at La Croix, half a mile from Saint-Côme-du-Mont, the Germans built wood platforms in the trees to dominate any advance from the marsh.[51] This area they commanded would be a landing zone for the 101st Airborne.

Around the town of La Haye-du-Puits, about 30 young German soldiers were found tied to trees from which they shot at Americans. Capt. Francis K. Kelley reported, "They fire at us all day long, but they usually miss. If they do hit anybody it's usually the leg or foot. It gets to be pretty damn annoying." In lieu of the regular *S Patronen* spitzer bullet (from *Spitzgeschoss*, pointed projectile), those Germans were using wooden training bullets which are strictly short range. It is doubtful if any of the Germans involved were actual snipers but rather ordinary soldiers ordered to fight from tree posts. "They're pretty smart and plenty dangerous," one airman added, "they wait until there's an artillery barrage and then they pop at you. That way you can't hear their fire and locate them." One was wounded and captured and treated by the American medics.[52]

Noted German sniper Bruno Sutkus fired from a tree and learned the vulnerability of it. He was rewarded with a mortaring that wounded him.[53] After recovering from his wound, he was in another tree and spotted two Russian officers. After shooting both, he hurriedly descended to avoid the return fire. He continued climbing trees and on July 7, 1944, killed a Russian at 600m. The Russian soldier he shot may have been bait because immediately after making the shot "all hell broke loose and nine Russians who had spotted my perch began a long period of firing at me using MGs and SMGs." He stayed and, "at 2015 hrs shot a machine gunner."[54]

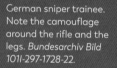

German sniper trainee. Note the camouflage around the rifle and the legs. *Bundesarchiv Bild 101I-297-1728-22.*

killed the sniper, Fulcher's statement was inaccurate. As children, many German soldiers attended the cinema and the American "Cowboy and Indians" genre was popular with them. They recognized cowboy actors like Tom Mix, Buck Jones, John Wayne, among many others, even Roy Rogers. *Gefreiter* Günther Horst Beetz's combat engineer unit was rushed via bicycle to Normandy where they were engaged in the hedgerow fighting. Beetz's comrade, Werner, "did the old 'helmet trick' and this time it worked." It enticed an American to shoot and for someone else to spot him.[55]

Summarizing the sniping to which Americans were exposed, war correspondent Ernie Pyle wrote:

"Snipers killed as many Americans as they could, and then when their food and ammunition ran out they surrendered. Our men felt that wasn't quite ethical. The average American soldier had little feeling against the German soldier who fought an open fight and lost. But his feelings about the sneaking snipers can't very well be put in print. He was learning how to kill the snipers before the time came for them to surrender."

As for American tank crews, Pyle added: "They hated snipers worse than anything else. That is because visibility is pretty poor in a tank and the commander usually rides with his turret cover open and his head sticking out. Unseen snipers were always shooting at them."[56]

The linkup between the American forces that landed at Utah and Omaha beaches was essential and to accomplish this, Carentan needed to be wrestled from the defending German 6th *Fallschirmjäger* Regiment. After completing its initial mission, 101st Airborne was now tasked with capturing the town and on June 10 began its assault. Several times they were held up by concealed Germans and it fell upon Darryl "Shifty" Powers of E Co. 2/506th PIR to help. William "Wild Bill" Guamere wrote:

"Shifty Powers picked off a couple snipers. When there was a sniper, you sent Shifty in to take him out. Shifty was a damn good soldier in 3d Platoon. He was from the mountains of West Virginia, born and raised with a gun in his hand, not like us city slickers. He was like an Indian, lived off the ground, was very observant, was in tune with nature. He could pick out movement a mile away."[57]

The attacks were successful and 101st Airborne dug in awaiting the German counterattack. When it came, Pvt. Bill Galbraith from 2d Pl., I Co., 3/506th PIR, witnessed

the destruction of two light M5 Stuart tanks by a StuG III. As the Germans gathered (probably for a push), Galbraith killed one with his rifle—a captured German weapon. "I could see another group of Germans gathering and fired my sniper rifle, hitting one of them. I tried to squeeze off another shot but the trigger wouldn't work. In all the excitement I'd forgotten that the rifle was bolt action and I hadn't reloaded." It wasn't long after that when Pfc. Sam Porter of Co. H was hit and Galbraith dragged him down to the safety of the gully. He left his rifle on one side while he got help to carry Porter. When he went to retrieve his rifle, it had gone—someone must have taken it. That someone was a lieutenant from another outfit. Much later at 2300 hours as the 506th began withdrawing to Carentan as the divisional reserve, someone spotted the rifle. "'Galbraith, there's a guy with your rifle.' They spotted a lieutenant from another platoon and sure enough he had my gun. 'Excuse me, that's my gun, sir,' I said. 'Well, it's mine now son.'" Galbraith spoke with Capt. Shettle who told him, "If you see the gun again, let me know and I'll make sure you get it back."[58]

* * * * *

The Allied breakout from Normandy had stalled amid Normandy's bocage. In the west, the Americans had to fight an attritional battle in the hedgerows heading to Saint-Lô. The Germans had recovered from their initial surprise and, while the landings and airborne operations were successful, German reinforcements stiffened the defenders' resolve—in particular the arrival of the panzers. However, the Allies always kept the initiative—the reason for Montgomery's continued armored attacks—and this forced the Germans to introduce their divisions piecemeal. They were never able to mount a successful counterattack, although the armored battles took a terrible toll on British and Canadian tanks.

So did the German snipers. The fear of sniper fire caused half of the officers of the 6th Bn., Duke of Wellington's Regiment, 49th (West Riding) Division, XXX Corps, as well as the non-commissioned officers, to forego wearing their rank. Similarly, the newly arrived officers to U.S. 328th Infantry Regiment were advised never to appear like an officer (forego insignia, remove helmet markings, and distinctive clothing).[59] The practice of removing insignia became so pervasive within the First (U.S.) Army that its commander, Lt. Gen. Courtney Hodges, issued an order reminding the officers that they must wear their rank insignia.[60]

Attached to Montgomery's staff as an aide, Capt. Carol Mather (of the Welsh Guards and SAS) recalled the hazards posed by Germans left behind in

Psychological aspects of sniping

"A comrade had set himself down on its trunk to bolster himself with his march rations and to smoke a pipe. And no doubt sitting like that he had been hit by the bullet of a Russian sniper. Death must have come over him very suddenly. Even in death he had his pipe in his hand, his stiffened hands clutching it tightly, the breadbag lying open in his lap. He leaned in a sitting position with his back on the trunk and the ruptured wide open eyes seemed to be astonished at the suddenness with which his life had been taken from him. You could hardly make out the tiny bullet hole."[61]

So recorded *Obergefreiter* Otto Posacher of the 1/137th Infantry Regiment, 2d *Gebirgsjäger* Division, which was fighting to capture Murmansk in 1941. Death came suddenly and unexpectedly and from an unseen assailant. To say it was unnerving would be an understatement. Fear can increase the desire for self-preservation and Ilan Yakovlevich remembered going thirsty despite a nearby well: "Once there was an episode. We were sitting in a trench. Felt thirsty, but couldn't drink anything, needed water. Someone went out to the well; one guy was shot, another guy was shot, no one else went."[62]

The knowledge that there was an enemy sniper reduced the effectiveness of an opposing unit. At least if one suspected where a shot came from, an artillery barrage or a smokescreen could help protect the targeted unit. While not a sniper (he was a mortarman), Unteroffizer Hans Rehfeldt from the *Großdeutschland* Division describes harassing the Soviets:

"The intention of my shooting was to demonstrate to Ivan that we were keeping a watchful eye on [a linesmen's house]. Through my binoculars I could see the Russians running out through the front door of the linesmen's house to their position. I got myself a Rifle 98 instead of the shorter Carbine 98. The longer barrel gave a better prospect of success against identified targets at the longer range. For a laugh, I aimed my first round over notch and bead at the cross-frame of the window. What else would I aim at from a distance of 1,800m? Aiming at the center of [the] house the shot rang out. My messenger watching through binoculars, reported that the bullet had fallen 100m short. 'I saw the water spray up.' With the third or fourth round, holding the barrel higher, I hit the door while aiming at the chimney. Bubi with the binoculars watched the door and waited. 'Bubi, if you see somebody coming out of the door or going in, let me know and I'll put a slug in him. Ha ha ha!!' I aimed calmly at the chimney, waited a while.

"'*Unteroffizier*, the door is opening! Somebody is coming out.' I took a deep breath, aimed precisely at the chimney and fired.

"'Ha-ha! that gave him a shock!' my observe[r] called out. Whenever there was any movement at the door, I fired. I didn't hit anybody, but they didn't use the door any more. 'Sniper!' they were probably thinking."[63]

Using the same reasoning German super sniper Matthäus Hetzenauer once shot at a standing Russian at 1,100m distance. "I was not likely that I would hit him at that range, but the shot was necessary under the existing circumstances in order to make it clear to the enemy that even at that range he should not feel safe."[64] Harassment has its own value and effect on the opposition.

"Death came suddenly and unexpectedly from an unseen assailant." It's unsurprising that so many war diaries and veterans' accounts talk of snipers. Hearing a single shot ring out and seeing a comrade fall would unnerve anyone. *NARA*.

During the breakout from the Korsun-Cherkassy Pocket, the SS Assault Brigade Wallonia was harassed by an unseen assailant. Léon Degrelle remembered:

"Bullets kept coming every minute or two from the same spot. It took us a quarter of an hour to find the place where the marksman must have been hiding. He had slipped silently away and posted himself in another watery, shadowy hole. We had scarcely moved off when the bullets began whistling past again, sharp, brutal, nerve wracking."[65]

The result speaks for itself and no doubt the Belgian volunteers received little respite. Similarly, when USMC correspondent Sgt. Bill Allen asked one unit, "What element of battle causes you the greatest strain?" "Sniper fire" was the predominant response over "night" or "riding the assault boats from ship to shore."[66]

Lyudmila Pavlichenko grasped how to unnerve attacking soldiers by shooting at the abdomen. Sometime in May 1942, there was an attack on the Soviet defenses at Sevastopol (then, Sebastopol). She was with Sgt. Fyodor Sedykh when their part of the line was assaulted by two waves of Germans. Instead of aiming at the first wave, she suggested to Sedykh that they shoot the second wave in the abdomen. They then proceeded to do so, aiming at the belt buckles to inflict mortal injury but not immediate death. Their victims howled in agony and the cries unnerved the first wave.[67] Similarly, defending against a Russian assault, German sniper Sepp Allerberger applied the same tactic against the Soviet fourth wave with similar unnerving results. Only when the first rank reached 50m did he begin shooting them, too—all with head shots.[68]

Ordered to attack a town near the Arno River, the American 100th Infantry Battalion, 442d Infantry Regiment, was in the lead. The uphill road went around a blind curve that had stone walls on both sides. No one wanted to chance going around it to reach the objective. Finally, a platoon sergeant volunteered and went around the curve and was halfway up the hill when he was shot—probably by someone in the church steeple. After the sergeant was slain, the battalion refused to advance for the entire day because of what could have been a solitary rifleman.[69]

Normandy: "The country south of Bayeux was rather park-like, cornfields interspersed with clumps of tall trees. These trees, bring in full leaf, were ideal cover for the enemy 'stay behind' snipers. In the first few days snipers were a perfect menace and accounted for many casualties."[70]

Five days after D-Day, on June 11, the 6th Green Howards (69th Brigade, 50th Infantry Division) advanced against German lines. Pvt. William Cheall had been with them when they evacuated at Dunkirk in 1940, fought in Tunisia (1943) and Sicily (1943), and was eager to even the score. It was his first time setting foot in France since evacuating in 1940. Cheall recalled:

"C Company was moving forward in our usual extended line across fields and, upon reaching a cornfield, continued to walk through the corn which was waist high, until we were half across. Then all hell let loose upon us from trees a hundred yards ahead, among which were snipers and machine-gun posts. The snipers were after the NCOs and officers and they were very successful, too. It happened so suddenly and the first officer to be killed, by a shot in the head, was our company commander, Captain Chambers, who had taken over charge of C Company on the beach when Captain Linn was killed. We also lost a Norwegian officer attached to us—we called him Norgy—a first-class officer and a gentleman. Several NCOs and other ranks

This church tower in Bénouville, on the canal between Sword Beach and Caen, has suffered the fate of so many in Normandy. Having been used by a sniper or artillery observer it has been cleaned out by shell fire. *British Official.*

were also the victims of the attack, including Major Honeyman and Corporal Alexander, Major Young, Burt Hall and a score of others were wounded. Our Company Sergeant Major was shot through the throat. It was quite a nightmare while it lasted."

Cheall and his mates dropped to the ground and crawled out of the cornfield.[71]

On the extreme east of the Allied lodgement, British 6th Airborne was still holding firm. From the land around Château Saint-Côme, the British controlled the Ranville Plain and the Orne bridges. It was essential to hold it and 9th Parachute Battalion, reinforced by the 5th Black Watch, and men of 1st Canadian Para Battalion, held it for a week against enemy attacks of increasing strength. The unit was relieved by the Ox and Bucks on June 13. There was no shortage of sniping activity from either side. Snipers from the Ox and Bucks were summoned to silence their German opponents. To do this, they found secluded spots and began scanning the trees for the telltale sign of gunsmoke. Once located, artillery would be called down. Sometimes that didn't work and the snipers had to remove the German themselves. This, of course, invited return shots from other concealed Germans so necessitated changes in position after firing. Using smoke grenades to hide their movement proved to be dangerous too. The Germans would mistake it for cover for an attack and bring down mortar or artillery fire on the area.[72]

Alongside 6th Airborne were men of the RM Commandos, who worked in pairs under centralized control rather than with their individual units, usually in front of the British lines often firing at 300–400yd. One of them related:

"'It isn't right to regard every mediocre rifleman the Germans leave behind, as a trained sniper.' The true German snipers showed lots of ingenuity— one house had a chalked notice on the door that read, 'Danger—booby traps. Do not enter', and it was D+10 before an English-speaking German sniper was discovered upstairs."[73]

The Canadians found an innovative way to silence a German sniper on June 15. They used a PIAT on him.[74] Precedent may be found in Italy, where 1st Special Service Force man Canadian Cpl. Gott used a bazooka to eliminate a German sniper who had killed many Canadians. According to a grinning Sgt. Kenneth Chapman, "That surprised the Germans and they wondered where we got the artillery."[75]

Two days later (June 17) while still in the vicinity of Château Saint-Côme, the Ox and Bucks snipers went to a listening post. While not seeing anything, they heard armor moving around. When they decided to retire, one man was hit in the leg. He was dragged to safety by Pvt. Edwards and another sniper. After he was safe, they returned to hunt for the German, but could not locate him.[76] The German sniper fully appreciated that he was in a life and death struggle and rather than risk retaliation, either withdrew from his position or refrained from any further shooting that would divulge his location.

The Allies had been aware of the bocage. Montgomery said during the planning stage, "Ideal infantry country. There was excellent concealment for snipers and patrols, while defensive positions dug into the banks were well protected from tanks and artillery."[77] The trouble was that it worked both ways and perhaps the Allies hadn't anticipated how difficult the fighting among the century-old hedgerows would be. It proved ideal for defensive fighting and the Germans used the bocage to their advantage. They had had four years to prepare their defense and hone their tactics. With pre-prepared fire plans and heavy use of mines to channel attacks, they would hold an outpost line of foxholes manned by infantry, light mortars and machine guns, some 400yd ahead of their main line of resistance. It was from these foxholes that much of the "sniping" took place by ordinary German infantrymen, dug in well in hedgerow and copse. Tanks could not penetrate them either and if they tried, they exposed their vulnerable underbellies to anti-tank weapons. The advance slowed to a crawl as the Allies slowly pushed the Germans back from hedgerow to hedgerow. A number of hedge-clearing methods were tried, including the best known, the pronged Culin hedgerow device (named after its creator, Sgt. Curtis G. Culin) attached to the front of American armor by reusing the German seashore defenses.[78]

Pvt. Cheall of 6th Green Howards describes the danger:

"Whenever we halted, as we did not know how close we were to the enemy, patrols went out to probe the land. On one of these, on 26 June, Corporal Miller went out with six men and was killed by a sniper—poor lad—but we had become so used to seeing sudden death that it did not play on our thoughts for long. We also lost good old Corporal Shaw around this time."[79]

Cheall's luck ran out on June 30 when he was hit by a shell splinter. Evacuated to Scotland for treatment, he did not return to the front until March 30, 1945.

Unpleasant and difficult though the fighting in the bocage proved to be for the Allies, for the Germans it was every bit as attritional and tough. The hard yards made by First (U.S.) Army against German Seventh Army, laid the foundations for Operation Cobra that would break the stalemate in Normandy.

On June 27, a few days before Cheall was injured, the men of 101st Airborne were at Tollevast near Cherbourg. A lieutenant from another unit was lecturing on German sniper technique and held aloft a captured sniper rifle. Bill Galbraith's buddy in Co. I, Pvt. Stan Fadden, recognized it as Bill's war trophy (see p. 111). When the lecture finished, Galbraith approached his company commander who understood the situation. A meeting was made between the lieutenant, named Danny, and Captain Shettle where Galbraith asserted his claim to the rifle. The lieutenant stuck to his story but then was asked to strip the rifle. Unable to do it, Galbraith "told everyone there was a particular cut underneath the stock that was only visible when the weapon was dismembered. Because Danny had lied in a way that was unbefitting of an officer, his commander took a dim view of things." Galbraith recovered his prize from Danny "the sniper killer" and took it back to England where the

division rested before their next jump—Operation Market Garden.[80]

* * * * *

In the drive to capture Caen, the British occupied Hill 112 on the high ground to the southwest of the city near Esquay-Notre Dame. It took ten weeks and 10,000 casualties before it was completely in Allied hands, the Germans throwing two SS panzer divisions (9th *Hohenstaufen* and 10th *Frundsberg*) as well as the Tigers of 102d Heavy SS Tank Battalion into its defense. Once taken, for ten days afterward, the British troops were subjected to harassment fire from a German sniper who remained undetected. Pvt. Denis Edwards traced the source to a foxhole that was hidden in a mound. They called upon the sniper to surrender and when he refused, tried to flush him out with a grenade. The throw missed the embrasure and the grenade exploded harmlessly outside the hole. So, a Bren gun was shoved into the foxhole and the magazine emptied into it. The German was quite dead but had won the admiration of Edwards and other troopers for having held his post for ten days.[81]

Like some German snipers on the Eastern Front, Edwards wanted additional firepower and carried

Sgt. Curtis G. Culin who is credited with designing the hedge-cutting device that permitted American tanks to cut through Normandy's hedgerows, and an example attached to an M5A1 light tank. *NARA.*

Left: A wary British patrol in the hedgerows. *Battlefield Historian.*

Left and Below left: Squad weapons—the BAR and Bren for the Allies, the MG34 and 42 for the Germans—and rifle grenades were essential to provide covering fire and keep defenders' heads down. *Battlefield Historian.*

Bocage

Hedgerow fighting favored the defender. Advance was slow and the fear of hidden machine guns and snipers made men wary. There was always the threat that an observer could call down mortar or artillery fire—and the Germans had had a long time to prepare fireplans. Tanks had problems with the ancient embankments that had thickened with age. Snipers in the trees could dominate an advancing enemy. Even the training in similar countryside in Devon and Dorset didn't prepare the Allies for the problems. It took adaptability, guts, and clever tactics to push the Germans out. The losses were large, but while the Allies had large reserves, the Germans didn't. As their top tank men died facing the anti-tank weapons of the British and Canadian troops around Caen, so the U.S. Army wore down the defenders in the west. When the right moment came, Operation Cobra broke the defenders and allowed the Third (U.S.) Army to be pushed through the gap to exploit the target-rich environment behind the front lines.

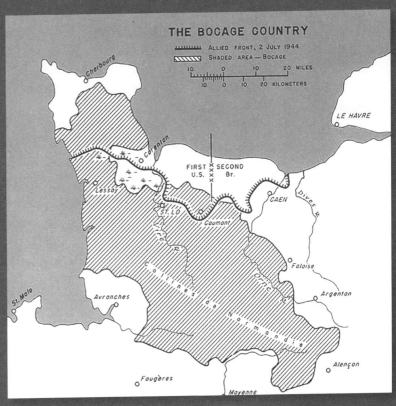

THE BOCAGE COUNTRY

ALLIED FRONT, 2 JULY 1944
SHADED AREA — BOCAGE

Above: Map showing the spread of bocage in northern France. The small fields make the area similar to the southwest of England where U.S. forces had trained before D-Day. *U.S. Army.*

Left: Tempting a German sniper with a helmet on a rifle—although this one looks a bit obvious. *Battlefield Historian.*

Left: The fields and hedgerows of northern France were a defender's joy. *NARA.*

117

Canadian or British sniper lining up a target in Caen. *British Official.*

captured enemy equipment including a MP40 submachine gun as well as a Walther P38 9mm pistol. One thing that made his sniping easier was the German habit of leaving their trenches after the rain to dry themselves. Edwards and his mates took advantage of it as he described here:

"All was peace and tranquillity until Wall let fly at an excellent target. By the time he hit the ground the rest had dived for cover. It was a long time before they began to reappear, probably assuming that a man had been hit by a stray shot. I took careful aim at a hole in the hedgerow. It was well lit by the lighter background. Soon it filled as someone peered across the orchard toward us. I held my fire, hoping that it would encourage others to surface. After a short time the hole reappeared as the man moved away. Then it filled again. This time I gently squeezed the trigger and the target crashed backwards.

"Paddy should have been next to fire, but as I was closing the bolt on a fresh cartridge which I had just loaded into my rifle I saw a well-built German out in the open and exposed to my view from his head to his knees. I waited for a few seconds for Paddy to fire, but assumed that he could not see this target who began to move. I fired and almost certainly winged him as he

let out a loud yell and disappeared from sight. Paddy was furious, and all the more so when I whispered, 'I think that I only winged him!'

"It was several hours before they got over the shock of two kills and a wounding. We had to wait until getting towards lunchtime before, once again, they began moving around, probably on their way to the cookhouse, and at last Paddy was rewarded for his long vigil."

With three kills to their credit, Edwards and his mates called it a day.[82]

* * * * *

S/Sgt. Herman Theodore Vander Laan of U.S. 359th Infantry Regiment, 90th Infantry Division (Texas-Oklahoma or "TO" and nicknamed "Tough 'Ombres"—*hombre* is Spanish for man) landed at Utah Beach on D-Day. It took four days for the entire division to land and afterward it crossed the Merderet River and captured Pont l'Abbé. The division next attacked through Pretot to the Forêt de Mont-Castre (Hill 122), clearing it by July 11, and two of its units earned Presidential Unit Citations: 1/359th Infantry Regiment for Pretot and 3/358th for the forêt. Sgt. Laan wrote home to Marcia, his wife in Iowa:

"Our several encounters with 'Heinie' has given me the impression that he's nothing more than a coward. He snipes behind our lines from well concealed places. He throws lots of lead at our troops but when he's cornered, comes out, hands high, calling 'Kamerad.' Some of our men ignore it and just let him have it anyway.

"We do still find an occasional 'German civilian' sniper. These snipers cause a few casualties but are generally nothing more than a nuisance behind our lines. When he runs out of ammunition he'll give up or quit. He generally doesn't live that long."[83]

It didn't take long for GIs like S/Sgt. Laan to catch on to German attempts to slip away unnoticed by wearing civilian clothes. In fact, their footwear always betrayed their military status and being out of uniform, they could be shot as spies.

Further west in the fighting to capture Saint-Lô, the American 2d Infantry Division was attempting to capture Hill 192 as it commanded the terrain east of the city. *Fallschirmjäger Oberjäger* Paul (of 4th Regiment, 12th Recce Group) fought as a sniper who delayed elements of the 2d Infantry.

"Our battalion had been ordered to hold an area surrounded by hedges and to protect a road along which our supplies would come. A sunken lane ended up directly on the American front line and lost itself in the thick forest. Hidden on top of the escarpment lining one side of the road, I watched from my *Fuchsloch* [foxhole] with my rifle fitted with telescopic sights. I watched the sunken lane but also the tops of the highest trees which could hide a sharpshooter or artillery spotters. This situation lasted for about two days until a machine gun opened with trace bullets. I was not sure whether or not I had been spotted. Once I had located the enemy and his machine gun, I aimed carefully then with a bullseye, I destroyed the water-cooling system of the Browning machine gun.

"The bullet ricocheted and finished right in one of the crew's face. After that we had a bit of peace and quiet. During the night we went to see the result of my shot. The corpse of an American soldier lay near the machine gun. But we had no time to think about this as we had to continue our *Scharfschützen* missions."[84]

The men of the American 2d Infantry Division were not idle. Many of them were behind the front lines being trained in combined-arms tactics for hedgerow fighting to capture Hill 192. After a bombardment of 25,000 shells, they would do so in two weeks' time. To their right (west), infantry scouts of the 29th Infantry Division advanced under the protection of their snipers. Rudi Frübeisser (of German 13/9th Parachute Regiment) remembered the first hours of July 17: "Cautiously the GIs moved forward staying in contact with each other with their Walkie-Talkies. Had they not had the support of their courageous snipers, they would have been obliged to remain where they were. Some of them got as close as 200 yards to our positions. They fired and then disappeared back to their initial positions."[85] The scouts' withdrawal was followed by a bombardment. The next day the 29th Division entered Saint-Lô and despite its almost complete destruction, some French civilians survived and emerged from their cellars to greet their liberators.

* * * * *

On July 15, back near Château Saint-Côme, Ox and Bucks Pte. Edwards was stunned by a shell that landed a few yards from his trench. After recovering, he ventured out alone and spotted a solitary German who stepped out between hedges. Apparently a new unit had relieved the one they had been fighting. It

Posed view of a sniper in Caen with the Church of Saint-Pierre in the background. *British Official.*

became apparent to Edwards that unlike the British practice, the Germans didn't necessarily caution their relief as to the presence of snipers or dangerous spots. Since it was his birthday, Edwards took the shot and brought him down. Despite waiting all day, no new target presented itself.[86]

It was four days later on July 19 that Edwards added to his tally. An unwary German walked into a gap and both Edwards and his sniping partner fired simultaneously. Contrary to practice, they afterward peppered the hedge with more bullets to simulate preparatory fire for an attack. After remaining motionless for a while, they had elected to retreat when Edwards spotted another German. Edwards fired as the German "flitted across two small gaps in his hedgerow" and the German let out a yelp before crashing to the ground.[87]

Returned to service after recovering from his injury (see p. 103), Sgt. Harry Furness was posted to the Hallamshire Battalion of the York and Lancaster Regiment when he was ordered to scout forward of the battalion.

"The C.O. had sent me forward to report back any enemy movement and if I could spot any dug-in tanks or artillery before we put in a battalion strength attack … As I very carefully moved around crawling to get ever better concealed positions, I used my x20 telescope to get better clarity of where the German soldiers were likely to be concentrated. Soon I found something very unusual, a group of enemy were partly hidden behind a hedgerow with trees near them, they were very obviously all officers, so a priority target. As I looked at them intensely the officer in the center of their group received deference from the others as they often looked at him as he was looking towards our positions through field glasses. To spot such a rare grouping was an opportunity I couldn't possibly let pass by and I had to be fast. I put down my x20 and picked up my 4T rifle, I was lying prone, and quickly estimated the range which I thought was around 600 yards. Fortunately I had loaded some long-range ammo I had managed to get from the 2nd Battalion of the Kensingtons who were supporting the Hallamshires with Vickers machine guns.

"Previously I had zeroed my rifle for high-precision hits with this type of ammunition, so when I fired I was confident I had secured a good solid hit as the officer in the center was dropped. I knew that he must have had high rank as he held that Order-Group, but was too far away to identify rank insignia or much else. As I fired I lost my sight picture through the rifle recoil, but was quickly back on target, he was down and the officers surrounding him were in uproar I could see with arms pointing, and I knew then they must have spotted my muzzle flash as most of them had been looking towards our frontlines, and I was concealed in their line of sight. I started immediately to try and crawl out of the way, I didn't attempt to stop any longer to shoot at the other officers, I knew I had to get away fast. The sheer speed of their retaliation was staggering, it seemed to be almost immediate. Which I expect followed so fast in view of all their units receiving immediate fire orders from senior officers."

Furness managed to escape but not without injury. The blasts were so close to him that his nose and ears were bleeding. He was carried by the stretcher-bearer to the regimental aid post where he was debriefed by the intelligence officer. Thanks to the information Furness gathered, the Hallamshires' attack was called off and they prepared for a German counter-offensive instead. While it was later confirmed that a high-ranking officer was slain, the identity was never divulged to Furness. It didn't matter to him since he thought it best if he never knew.[88]

Back at Saint-Lô the First (U.S.) Army had captured that crossroad town but had not taken Périers or Lessay to the northwest. The 39th Infantry Regiment, 9th Infantry Division, was led by 56-year-old Col. Harry Albert "Paddy" Flint. A veteran of World War I and cavalryman, he initially commanded an armored infantry regiment before becoming a staff officer. Seeking a combat command, he took over the 39th Infantry in Sicily. Under his leadership, the battalion became a formidable fighting unit. On July 23, Flint's second battalion had been advancing up the Périers–Saint-Lô road when it stalled. Irritated, he went forward himself and got them moving. When Flint came across a stopped Sherman, he ordered the commander forward. The commander protested he had turret trouble at which point Flint retorted, "It isn't often you have a colonel for a bodyguard!" Flint climbed aboard and operated the commander's machine gun and sprayed German positions while they advanced. Dismounting from the tank, Flint resumed advancing with his infantry.

Later, while standing in the doorway instructing a sergeant on infantry tactics, Flint suddenly fell forward. He was shot in the head. The sergeant with whom Flint was speaking spotted the responsible German who was aloft in a tree. Working his way

forward, the sergeant finally positioned himself for a shot and killed him. However, the 39th had lost its beloved commander.[89]

Breakout from Normandy
(July 25–31, 1944)

Operation Cobra saw the Allies' strategy pay off and Bradley's First (U.S.) Army break through the German defenses. Patton's Third Army—activated on August 1—was immediately fed into the gap and thrust forward against weak opposition. With the Germans line broken, a pell-mell rush through France convinced soldiers and generals alike that the war would be over by Christmas.

> "In our drive across France, the Germans couldn't set up an effective defensive line, but they sure as hell did everything they could to hurt and delay us. Their actions consisted of a good deal more than just mines and booby traps. For starters, they used snipers liberally. Our training never included anything at all, not even a mention, about snipers. We learned about them through experience and heavy losses. There was always something especially eerie about these well-hidden, silent killers. They had an aspect of grotesque, like a spider popping out of its hole to snatch and devour its prey."[90]

Many of the German "snipers" were youths or older soldiers who were instructed to stay behind so that the fitter fighting men could withdraw safely.

Michael Bilder was like most young Americans of the era. He believed President Roosevelt's reelection assurances that America would not be involved in the war. Bilder attended the cinema, watched the Cubs baseball team play at Wrigley Field, danced to the music of Glenn Miller, Tommy Dorsey, and Les Brown, and like other teenage American boys, chased girls. Torn from his happy life as a youth, Bilder was now a private in the 11th Infantry Regiment, 5th Infantry Division, that had landed in France on July 9. Their division belonged to Third (U.S.) Army's XX Corps and was about to take part in the break-out. During Operation Cobra, Bilder and his friends learned fast how to minimize exposing themselves and improve their chances for survival. Those who didn't became casualties. Bilder recalled one incident where a senior officer neglected to conceal himself with fatal consequences:

> "I can't begin to describe how often replacements came into our ranks only to be killed a day or two later by snipers. We knew what to do and how to

survive through our experience, but these green kids served as nothing more than target practice for German snipers. Yet despite their experience, even veterans made fatal errors on occasion. I remember one lieutenant colonel who was always preaching cover and concealment when it came to snipers. He forgot his own teaching one day, and stepped from the jeep and walked across an open field rather than hugging the tree line around it. He was struck by a sniper's bullet and dead before he hit the ground."[91]

Also part of Third Army, the 80th Division (XX Corps) had landed in France on August 5. By early September, it had reached the Moselle River. Pvt. Warren Kenneth Coomer, Co. G, 319th Infantry Regiment, was busy digging a foxhole behind a boulder when a sergeant nearby decided to study the German position across the river. Pvt. Coomer looked up and for the first time witnessed the death of an American soldier. "There was just a slight rise on top of this hill, and Sgt. Bissonet lay down and, taking a pair of field glasses, looked across the river. A German spotted him and I heard the bullet hit him in the forehead. He didn't even groan."[92]

On August 6, Task Force Weaver of the 90th Infantry Division was pushing east in a 37-mile

Mobile operations

Mobile warfare offered more dynamic challenges to the snipers. Pavlichenko recognized that the sniper had to study the new front line, the no-man's-land, and memorize it. Potential hides had to be located as well as back-ups. Egress was a consideration and quick egress to avoid retaliatory fire. The fluid battlefield meant there was less time to study enemy lines or to prepare firing positions. Lest one was overrun or cut off, the ability to evacuate quickly was now a consideration. She also resorted to using rambling roses for concealment. Its thickets were useful for concealing the sniper and any smoke from the rifle's discharge was quickly dissipated in them.[93]

drive from Fougères toward Mayenne. Reaching Mayenne would place the Americans 30 miles from Avranches, a key point in the encirclment of German Seventh Army. Pfc. C. M. Goodson, 358th Infantry Regiment, was in a unique position to see an oncoming bullet.

Celebrating liberation too early, Parisians seek shelter as German snipers open up, August 26, 1944. The same thing happened in Notre Dame cathedral during a Thanksgiving Service. Gen. Charles de Gaulle remained standing throughout, afterwards blaming French Communists rather than Germans or collaborators. *NARA*.

"I saw a bullet coming at me. I was just frozen and it came in like slow motion, it was turning over end to end. It hit my jacket covering my chest. I thought I was a dead man for sure. And it just dropped from there to the ground. Probably a sniper from far away. It was just spent."[94]

Capt. Ivan Schoch led the Reconnaissance Troop of the "Tough 'Ombres." Two bridges were blown but one remaining bridge stood. Watching the last bridge for over an hour, an American sniper saved it from demolition: "A Nazi ducked out of a building and tried to run over to the bridge. One of our riflemen knocked him off. When we crossed the bridge later we found tons of explosives, all fused and ready to be set off. That one shot did the trick." Ignorant of the town's capture, dozens of Germans entered still believing it was in German hands. They were captured by the 90th Division.[95] After the capture of Mayenne, the division pushed on to Le Mans and then north to Chambois to seal the Falaise Pocket.

Eighty days had elapsed since D-Day during which six armies (two German and four Allied) had clashed in hotly contested battles as the Germans struggled to contain the invasion. The battle for Normandy had ended in a significant Allied victory. The German armies were largely destroyed with 500,000 casualties at the cost of 200,000 Allied casualties.[96] Now freed from the confines of Normandy's bocage, the race across France began. Many believed that the war would be over soon.

Operation Dragoon
(August 15, 1944)

Originally planned to be simultaneous with the Normandy landing, the landings in southern France were delayed until August 15, 1944, when sufficient landing craft became available. The Seventh (U.S.) and First (French) armies landed and fought northward and then east toward Germany with major thrusts. Fleeing north, the German army often left stay-behinds as it did in Normandy whose job was to snipe, harass, and delay the pursuing columns. The Americans were prepared to deal with it but sometimes had help from the French locals. As one newspaper man who accompanied the advancing Americans wrote,

"The life expectancy of any such sniper, once he fires into an American column, generally is less than 10 minutes. French patriots take care of that. Nevertheless the speed of his demise doesn't help whoever he has hit, so the safest policy is to keep highballing."[97]

As its 3d Infantry Division fought its way through the Vosges Mountains in Alsace, two men of Co. D, the heavy infantry company of 1/15th Infantry Regiment, were killed by a sniper. Both had been shot in the forehead. Sgt. Audie Murphy received permission from his company commander to stalk and kill the sniper. His captain advised him to take two men with him and he got two volunteers: Owl, a Cherokee Indian, and Barker, both riflemen.

Crossing a wooded ridge, they halted at the edge of a clearing. Owl pointed out where on the trail the two men were killed. The bloodstain marked where the men had fallen. Because the area was forested, Owl suggested that the trees would interfere with a long-distance shot and therefore he must be close at hand. "If he's at his old post, he can't be far way. He couldn't get much range through the trees."

Barker adds, "I'd say he was uphill. Those guys were shot right after they stepped into the open. If the kraut had been on either side, he would have waited until they got further into the clearing."

Murphy surmised that the Germans expected the Americans to come up the trail again, and would therefore lie in wait. He explains what he did:

"Keeping under cover of the brush, I skirt the clearing and move towards the boulder. An acute sense of loneliness comes over me. I and my enemy, it seems, are the last two men on earth.

A U.S. Army unit in Brest works its way into the city street-by-street, watching for snipers. The city was a hard nut to crack—as had been Saint-Malo—and such was the level of the casualties that the Allies "masked" other similar locations, such as Lorient, Saint-Nazaire, Dunkirk, and the Channel islands. *NARA.*

I pause; and fear makes my body grow limp. I look at the hills and the sky. A shaft of sunlight pierces the clouds, making the wet leaves of the tree glisten goldenly. Life becomes infinitely desirable.

"The hill now becomes infested with a thousand eyes peering through telescopic sights, with cross-hairs on the center of my head. Terror grows. I crash my fist to my forehead. The fantasy passes. I inch forward.

"At the boulder I stop. My straining ears catch no sound. I get to my feet and with my left hand against the rock for support step into the open. It happens like a flash of lightning. There is a rustle. My eyes snap forward. The branches of a bush move. I drop to one knee. We see each other simultaneously.

"His face is as black as a rotting corpse; and his cold eyes are filled with evil. As he frantically reaches for the safety of his rifle, I fire twice. He crashes backwards. I throw two hand grenades to take care of any companions lurking in the area. Then I wilt.

"When Owl and Barker reach the scene, I am mopping the cold sweat off my forehead.

"The sniper is sprawled on the ground just beyond the old machine-gun position. The two bullet holes are in the center of the forehead; and one of the grenades has torn off an arm."[98]

Since Murphy didn't want the sniper rifle, Owl kept it instead. After they returned to their lines before a prearranged mortar bombardment of the area commenced, Murphy retired to clean his carbine.

The 15th's sister regiment in 3d Infantry Division, the 30th, was approaching the Belfort Gap from the direction of Lantenot. That town had been captured by the 30th's 1st Battalion on September 15 and defended against German counterattacks the next day. On September 17 its 2d Battalion passed through the area and was advancing when Co. H was halted by sniper fire. Sgt. Al Brown led an HMG section when it ran into a sniper:

"Our lead troops were coming out of a stand of trees and entering a clearing. When our lead scout was some distance into the clearing, a shot rang out, and the scout went down. A sniper claimed another victim. The scout was not killed. We could see he was trying to crawl back toward us.

"His platoon medic raced out to treat him. The medic was well identified as a noncombatant. He had a Red Cross insignia on all four sides of his helmet and Red Cross armbands on both arms. Also, all frontline medics wore two large pouches filled with medications and dressings, one on each hip. They resembled the pouches you see on the back of motorcycles. Even at night, medics stood out from other soldiers by their silhouettes.

There is no mistaking one of our medics for a combatant. The sniper picked him off before he could reach the man he was going to help.

"Then the most amazing thing happened, a second medic dashed out in spite of having just witnessed the sniper's lack of respect for the Red Cross symbol. He was also shot.

"Our advance was halted, and a search for the sniper began. After about 10 minutes, his hiding place was discovered. Our troops kept firing on his position to keep him pinned down while two of our men moved in close and took him prisoner.

"The prisoner was brought in to the edge of the clearing. As the German stood with his hands in the air, the sergeant of the men he had shot walked up to him, and with his rifle, delivered a horizontal butt stroke that removed his ear and a portion of his face."

While disfigured, the prisoner was escorted to the rear where he received medical treatment from an American doctor. Sgt. Brown was wounded soon afterward and sent to the same hospital where he was placed in the bed next to that of the German sniper. After telling the doctor the German's story, the doctor said to Brown, "When you see the sergeant again, tell him to aim about here. [The doctor indicated a point on his head by tapping his finger.] He will save us from having to use our precious blood plasma the next time."[99]

Much less dramatic than either Murphy's or Brown's encounter with a sniper was that of Platoon Sgt. John B. Shirley. Both Murphy (Co. B, 1st Battalion) and Shirley were staff sergeants at the time in the same regiment (15th Infantry), but Shirley was in Co. I, 3d Battalion. On September 28 Co. I was ordered to attack a farmhouse and they began their assault early in the day when the morning fog made visibility very limited. Shirley deployed his platoon in a skirmish line and moved through a plowed field. As they reached the edge of the forest near their objective, dawn was just about to break. That was when Shirley had his encounter:

"Suddenly right in front of me, was a German soldier sitting on a stump. He had a sniper's rifle in his left hand, the rifle butt was on the ground … We saw each other at the same moment! He didn't make a move. I covered him with my M-1 rifle, and he surrendered to me."

It was a good thing the sniper's commander didn't realize that guard duty is far from optimal use of a sniper.[100]

The newly arrived 100th Infantry Division had just joined the Seventh (U.S.) Army. On November 8, Co. L, 3/399th Infantry Regiment, was ordered to relieve a 45th Infantry Division company. Only seven days before they had landed in France and now they were to face combat in the lower Vosges Mountains. Hailing from Brooklyn, Pfc. John M. Khoury was the son of a Syrian immigrant who established himself as a wholesale linen importer. Far from his home now, he was with his company as it advanced under small-arms fire from unseen Germans. Pfc. Khoury remembers what it was like to be under fire for the first time:

Shooting medics

After a medic was found dead with a bullet hole beneath the Red Cross emblazoned on his helmet, Timberwolf Pfc. Charles Duke's company commander didn't want snipers taken prisoner anymore. He issued a standing order: "You've got five minutes to get that man back to the CP ... I want you back here in five minutes."[101] A similar hostility towards snipers arose in the British Army too. For example, after their section corporal was killed, Pvt. Bill Cheall and the men of the section of 6th Green Howards were filled with a bloodlust and took no prisoners. Instead, they shot every Italian they chanced upon in that battle.[102] A more drastic example happened in the vicinity of Monte Cassino where Germans, camouflaged with leaves and fighting from trees as rearguard snipers, surrendered only after exhausting their ammunition. Their British captor radioed for and received permission from company headquarters to execute them.[103]

While many believed that medics were regularly—and deliberately—shot by the Germans, postwar, the official U.S. medical history took a more conciliatory view:

"[The] killing and wounding of aidmen, litterbearers, and aid station personnel

by aimed rifle fire, usually from snipers, raised the question whether the enemy, as general policy, was respecting the Geneva Convention rights of unarmed Red Cross-marked medical personnel. After two months of combat and careful analysis of many incidents, most corps, division, and lower-echelon surgeons and medical unit commanders concluded that, except for isolated cases, the Germans were following the rules. The commander of the 4th Medical Battalion, which had had men killed and wounded and ambulances damaged by artillery and machine-gun fire, summed up the prevailing opinion: 'It is the consensus ... that little of this damage was deliberate and that for the most part the enemy respects the Rules of Land warfare ...'. According to German prisoners, sniper incidents often resulted from difficulties in seeing Red Cross arm brassards on men moving along the hedgerows; medics in some divisions noted that a high proportion of their small-arms casualties were shot from the unbrassarded right side. Aidmen and litterbearers accordingly began wearing brassards on both arms and painted nonregulation red crosses in white squares on their helmets. The XIX Corps surgeon late in July officially authorized these and other measures to make Geneva Convention markings on men and vehicles more conspicuous."[104]

Of course, on the Eastern Front rules of war were seldom followed, as the story of Zina Aleksandrovna Samsonova makes clear. Immortalized by the poetry of Yuliya Drunina,[5] Samsonova attended nursing courses at the Yegor'yevsk Medical School, before joining a unit at Stalingrad. She tended to the wounded and had been recommended for the award of the Gold Star and title of Hero of the Soviet Union for her bravery and coolness under fire. Alas, it was not to be. During the fighting for Kholm on January 26, 1944, she went into no-man's-land to tend an injured soldier. Instead of waiting for darkness to set in, she decided to reach him in daylight. She did so and, having dressed his wound she was about to drag him toward the Soviet positions when a German sniper—who must have been aware that she was a nurse and was bandaging a wounded man—killed both of them in cold blood.[106]

Medics were always well marked in theaters where rules of war were accepted. On the Eastern Front and, particularly, the Pacific the Red Cross meant less. *NARA.*

"I lay behind a tree with my 1903 sniper's rifle trying to see something to aim at. Nearby I could hear an M1 rifle going full blast … Then I heard someone yell, 'Medic! Medic! I'm HIT!' At the same moment, I heard and felt the crack of a rifle bullet fly right by my head. Instinctively I looked up into a tree directly in front of me about 50 yards away and saw a puff of smoke. Though I could not see anyone, I aimed my sniper's rifle at that spot and fired each of the five rounds in my rifle.

"Now I had to reload my bolt-action rifle. Because of the telescopic sight mounted over the breech opening, I could not feed the clip of five rounds at one time. I had to take each round off the clip one at a time. As I was doing this, the firing all around me kept up at a furious pace. Suddenly I heard a voice almost in a whisper say, 'Nicht schiessen! [Don't shoot]' I looked to my right, and there was a German soldier not more than six feet away, staring me in the face! 'Nicht schiessen?' I wondered! My rifle wasn't even loaded! He could have easily shot me or bayoneted me before I could defend myself."

Grateful that he himself had just been spared, how could Khoury kill him? Khoury took the German prisoner and motioning with his rifle, escorted him to the rear. While passing the 45th Division area one GI said, "Let me see how big a hole you can put in his back." As murder was not in his heart, Khoury demurred and continued escorting his prisoner to the holding area. After delivering his prisoner, Khoury rejoined his platoon and learned that others had seen a German fall from the tree from Khoury's first bullet.[107] In subsequent skirmishes, Khoury exchanged his sniper rifle for a M1 Garand.

Unfortunately, Khoury did not know 99th Division sniper Earle Slyder who mitigated slow reloading by having ammunition literally in hand.

"I carried the ammo in eight-round Garand clips. That's the way the ammo was issued to us. Whenever I had the opportunity I would load my rifle with six rounds: one round in the chamber and five in the magazine. In a fight, I would also put one round between each finger in my left hand so I could just click them right in."

Slyder was the only soldier to mention this speed-reloading technique.[108] Slyder was able to do this because the Springfield's magazine cut off switch prevented fresh rounds from being pushed up by the follower.

Pvt. George T. Sakato was fresh to 2/442d RCT, the regiment composed of Americans of Japanese descent. Along with 671 other replacements, he filled the depleted ranks of the 442d which for now was attached to the 36th Infantry Division. They had landed in southern France, and were engaged in hand-to-hand combat to capture Bruyères in the Vosges Mountains. Ordered to search for the Germans, Sakato's squad moved out.

"We go out a thousand yards and a machine gun opens up. I hit the deck, rolled over, got behind a bush. George F. is out in the open. Ben M. is out in the open. And F. is out there in the open. It so happened that the machine gunner had a sniper with him. He had telescopic lens. As soon as George F. looked up, Pow! [A shot to the forehead]. Oh Jesus Christ. And the Ben looks up, and his helmet goes flying off, and Friday looked up, and the bullet went right through his helmet. Those three guys are dead and that guy is looking for me; and he can't see me because I'm behind this bush. So I had to back up, crawl back and tell the platoon back there … We had to leave the three bodies there."

When they returned, only two bodies remained.[109]

A few days after Sgt. Audie Murphy had stalked and killed the sniper (October 14), he was commissioned as a second lieutenant. As with any other American infantry unit, casualties were high and survivors were promoted. Another effort was made to eject the Germans and capture the Belfort Gap. Murphy's platoon withdrew before an impending barrage descended upon the Germans. While they were hugging the earth and waiting for orders another lieutenant walked by.

"'Where do you think you are going?' Murphy asks. 'After rations. I'm looking for a short cut for my jeep.'

"'Not up that trail. It's a short cut to hell.'

"'Did you just get up, lieutenant?'

"'We just got shoved back. I'm telling you this area's swarming with Jerries.'

"'Thanks. I'll keep an eye open for them.'

"'Not for long, if you stick to that path.'"

Brushing off Murphy's suggestion, the lieutenant proceeded up the trail anyway. He didn't get far before he dropped from a headshot fired by a sniper. Murphy's platoon dug in for the night and in the morning, was ordered to advance under the cover of a walking barrage. Murphy describes what happened next:

German rifles

Gewehr 41(W)
Caliber: 7.92mm Mauser
Weight: 11.08lb (5.026kg)
Length: 44.25in. (1.124m)
Barrel: 21.5in (54.61cm)
Magazine: Non-detachable 10-round staggered box
Operation: Bang gas-operated semiautomatic
Muzzle velocity: c. 2,550ft/sec (772m/sec)

Gewehr 43
Caliber: 7.92 x 57mm Mauser
Weight: 9.5lb (4.309kg)[110]
Length: 44in. (1.118m)
Barrel: 21.62in. (54.91cm)
Magazine: 10-round detachable staggered box magazine
Action: Gas, semiautomatic
Muzzle velocity: 2,550ft/sec (777.2m/sec)

Mauser K98k
Caliber: 7.62mm x 57
Weight: 9lb 0.6oz
Length: 43.7in. (1.11m)
Barrel: 23.62in. (60.0cm)
Magazine: 5-round internal magazine
Operation: Bolt-action
Muzzle velocity: 2,493ft/sec (760m/sec)

1: Walther G41 magazine-fed, semiautomatic rifle with ZF-4 scope. *J. Terrill Biedenharn Collection.*

2. G43 7.92mm rifle with Gw ZF 4x scope. The 10-round box magazine is detachable and makes reloading quicker. *Image courtesy the National Infantry Museum Collection, U.S. Army.*

3. Waffen-SS K98k with long-rail scope mount.

4. Late short-rail K98k.

5. K98k with high-turret mounted Dialytan 4x scope.

6. K98k with low-turret mounted Dialytan scope. Note winter trigger guard that allowed the sniper to Shoot with gloved hands. *Images 3–6 courtesy Dave Roberts.*

7. K98k Mauser fitted with reproduction swept back mount and scope. The only known original with provenance is in the U. S. Army's collection. *Jarrith Kiel collection.*

Austrian sniper Helmut Wirnsberger of Styria found the G43 to be less accurate than the K98k. When asked the furthest he ever shot at, he replied, "About 600 meters, rarely more. I usually waited until target approached further for better chance of hitting. Also, confirmation of a successful hit was easier. Used G43 only up to about 500 meters because of poor ballistics." Fellow Austrian Matthias Hetzenauer expressed similar views although was less optimistic about the performance: "It is suitable only up to about 400m; inferior precision."[111] The G43 was inherently less accurate because it had more moving parts than a K98k. If there is any inconsistency in parts' movement that will affect the harmonics of the rifle and changes can shift the point of impact.

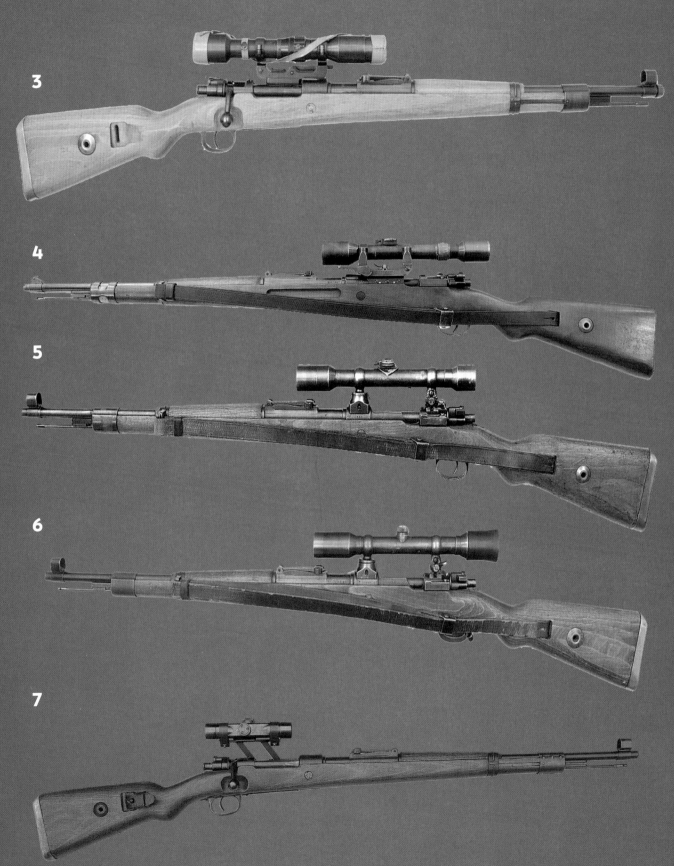

3

4

5

6

7

"We leave the trail and push directly through the woods. Except for sporadic mortar fire, the enemy is quiet, too quiet to suit me.

"Crack!

"Paderwicz is dead before his body thuds against the ground. The sniper's bullet got him just above the left eye. I leap behind a tree.

"Crack!

"It is like being struck with a ball bat. The ricocheting bullet digs a channel through my hip and knocks me flat. The sniper throws his camouflage cape back to get a better view and drills my helmet. That is his last mistake he ever makes. My head is not in the helmet.

"I raise my carbine and with my right hand fire pistol-fashion. The bullet spatters between the German's eyes. It was his brain or nothing. He would not have missed the second time."[112]

Murphy was hospitalized but recovered later to reassume command of his platoon. He kept this sniper rifle as a souvenir and it is presently displayed at Audie Murphy American Cotton Museum in Greenville, TX. It is a high-turret mount with 4x Dialytan scope.

As scout-sniper, Bob Flagg was leading his company. The division had relieved the 3d Infantry Division on November 8, and began attacking at Saint-Dié-des-Vosges on November 16.

"My job as a combat infantryman of the 103d Infantry Division was first scout-sniper. My mission was to advance well in front of my company, spot the enemy and fire tracers from my '03 to point out where he was. Then my guys were supposed to join the firefight. About 300–400 yards ahead I saw irregular mounds of dirt, pretty good evidence of dug-in Germans. Were they there, or had they pulled back? I flopped down, just like it says in the Infantry Manual, and fired off a five-round clip of tracers from my '03 rifle, just like it says in the manual. Then I saw a German get up—probably an officer because he was wearing a long, gray overcoat. So, I banged away two more tracer clips, rolling sideways, just like the Infantry Manual. Don't know whether or not I hit him.

"Then the whole damned Germany army opened up on me. First with small arms fire. Then automatic weapons. Then mortars and, finally, an 88, the most feared weapon in the entire German army. Those buggers would fire with extreme accuracy at a single soldier (like me).

"How did they spot me? I was concealed behind trees, rocks and ridges, changing place every time I fired. What the range sergeant, the lieutenant, the company commander, and the Infantry Manual never told me was that if our guys could see my traces, so could the bad guys!"

Flagg's buddies caught up with him and in a running firefight they chased the Germans a mile.

"Finally, we stopped in a wooded area. Some guys from the company weapons platoon said 'Flagg, we sure knew where you were, thanks to those tracers. But you were moving around so fast, we couldn't keep up with you.' It was only then I realized why I attracted so much fire. Those damned tracers! And that's the only kind of ammunition I had. So I picked up an M1 and ammunition from a soldier who wouldn't need it anymore, leaned my Springfield carefully and almost lovingly against a tree, draped my remaining bandoleers of tracers around the stacking swivel and walked away."

Forty years later Flagg returned to the same tree but, unsurprisingly, his Springfield wasn't there.[113]

The 3d Division finally reached Strasbourg and its 7th Regiment was fighting its way into the town center. Former ordnance man turned infantry squad sergeant Murray Soskil had already earned a Silver Star for destroying a German bunker. He was now leading his squad in house-to-house fighting.

"At the outskirts of town a soldier next to me was hit by a sniper. The bullet sliced across his stomach, spilling his intestines on the ground. I yelled for the medics and tried to gather his insides together. He lived for a while but died later. The sniper who shot him was hidden in a church but we found him and killed him to avenge our companion."[114]

On November 20, 1944, Combat Command A of 14th Armored Division entered Gertwiller near the Rhine and took the town in daylight. It was during the night that the Germans emerged from their hiding and engaged the Americans. Hugh West remembered how his division responded with superior firepower.

"They [the Germans] were directing accurate mortar fire from their hidden perches, and we were losing men in the streets, as snipers picked them off. Our tanks fired their 75mm guns as fast as they could be loaded, and if a single German sniper was spotted in a top floor window, he got a round that blew him and the top of the building apart. Later, when we began to collect German prisoners, one of them asked me about this strange American habit of using a heavy gun to kill a single man. I told him we were there to do the job and save lives, and if it took a howitzer to kill every single sniper, we were glad to oblige."[115]

They were facing a major counterattack and the fighting was so intense that a retreat was ordered. The next day, after a very intense artillery barrage, the division reentered the town and captured it for good.

In the subsequent fighting at Strasbourg, soldiers of the 7th Regiment learned to use their bazookas to blast holes into walls, enabling them to capture a building without going into the street where German machine guns and snipers were waiting for them. Similarly, the supporting M4 Shermans helped by blasting new holes into buildings. This practice not only stunned the defenders, it also gave the infantry fresh, undefended entry points.

Leclerc's 2d (French) Armored Division liberated Strasbourg, rushing across the Alsatian plains and entering the city on November 22. Most Germans were forced out by November 23 and the Tricolor flew over the city's cathedral that day. However, German resistance remained in the form of snipers. In response, Leclerc announced on November 29 that for every French soldier killed by a sniper, five German hostages would be shot. He also announced that any sniper caught would be shot. The courtesy of the firing squad was extended to anyone found assisting or harboring a sniper. His last measure was that anyone bearing arms without a permit would be arrested and court-martialed.[116]

After a year of combat beginning in Sicily and then Italy, "Thunderbird" Pfc. Stan Richardson became fatalistic about snipers and resigned himself to his fate.

"The duty of the first scout is to lead the squad by going out in front about 30 or 40 yards to see if he can draw any enemy fire. The second scout follows by a few yards and tries to ascertain where any fire may be coming from … Like night patrols, serving as first and second scout was also rotational. I think I had a fatalistic view about my turns as first scout. Having learned that the German snipers were excellent marksmen, able to kill you with one shot to the head, I figured that if one got me, I would never know what hit me.

"One time when I was first scout, a sniper decided to let me get closer so he could shoot and kill the second scout, who was about 20 yards to

my rear, and then knock me off, an easy mark since I was even closer. When I heard the second scout get hit, I immediately hit the ground and rolled a few times. I think the sniper took off after the first shot, realizing his plan had failed. The second scout had been killed instantly. I guess it was by the grace of God that the sniper had decided to take out the second scout rather than the first."[117]

While in a foxhole on a hill that overlooked a valley that led to the Siegfried Line, Richardson's foxhole buddy Phil came under rifle fire. Richardson advised his buddy to dig a bit deeper on his end to be safe

131

from the German who was slightly higher than they. After a while, their platoon leader ordered the platoon to charge. It was during this assault that Richardson was hit.

"At first we were running as fast as we could, zigzagging this way and that because we were getting shot at. However, because of the distance across the valley, maybe 3,000 feet, we tired in short time. I didn't see anyone get hit as we crossed the valley, and I slowed down to a walk, still in a zigzag pattern. Lefty, who was in great physical shape, had run all the way across that open expanse and was halfway up the big hill, calling to the rest of us to hurry it up.

"Suddenly we drew fire from an unseen gun position, and I saw Lefty hit the ground. I hit the ground in the same instant. Just as I looked up to see where he was crawling to, he got hit in the head by a bullet. He died instantly. A split second later, I got hit in the back of the head by a bullet.

I was knocked out for several minutes and when I came to, I felt that if I checked the back of my head I was going to find a hole big enough to put my fist in. I was scared, and it was a minute or more before I dared to put my fingers to the back of my head. To my huge relief, I could tell it had just grazed my head and I wasn't bleeding all that bad. I figured I'd try to get the medic to bandage it up, but first I needed to retrieve my rifle and helmet. The force of that shot had knocked me a few feet away from my gear.

"I started to move and got shot at again. The dirt was kicked up about a foot from my head so I knew a German had me, and anyone else near me, in his sights. I played dead until dark and then felt safe in getting my gear and heading back down the hill to a trench we had crossed coming up. I scared the hell out of a couple of GIs who had taken refuge in the trench, apparently to avoid the same gunner that got me. They told me that they thought I'd been killed along with Lefty."[118]

100th Infantry Division Sgt. Horace T. West initially served with the 45th Infantry Division. After being reassigned to the 100th Infantry, he fought in the Vosges Mountains where he became a sniper. Sgt. West survived the war and was honorably discharged. *Author's collection.*

Sgt Horace T. West And His Faithful "Mabel."

Photo by P.e Vernon Biccer, Staff Photographer.

Sniper Picks Off 17 Krauts To Square Things for 'Kid'

No stranger to combat, Seventh (U.S.) Army's Sgt. Horace Theodore West was a seasoned soldier. His childhood in Wagoner, OK, taught him to shoot squirrels and rabbits on the run. Before joining the 100th Infantry Division, he fought in Sicily as a member of the "Thunderbirds," putting his childhood experience to use in combat. He was credited with slaying over 120 enemy soldiers with his Thompson SMG. Now a member of the 100th Infantry Division he was fighting in Alsace and added 17 to his score with an M1903A4 sniper rifle. Reluctant to brag, he told the reporter:

"A man shouldn't be too proud of killing another man. I know it ain't exactly right. But the Germans started it.

"Coming up here on a train from south France, I rode with a young boy I got to like. I told him as much as I knew about war—the right and the wrong things to do. 'Bud, never get out of a hole once you've got a good one. Do that and a Jerry sniper has done got you.' Well I guess the kid forgot. About a month ago he got out of his hole and sat beside it—and there was another gold star mother back in the United States.

"I didn't know about it until that afternoon when the captain pointed to a rifle with telescopic sights leaning against a tree. It was the kid's rifle.

"'West,' the captain says to me, 'Can you shoot that rifle?'

"'I reckon so,' I told him.

"Then he told me about this boy and it went plumb against my liver."

Despite not having any training as a sniper, Sgt. West did the next thing a sniper would do. He searched for witnesses. "I talked to the boy's buddy, found out where he had been sitting and how he had been hit. I figured awhile and decided the sniper must be in a tree 300 yards away. I just sat and watched that spot until I saw something move. Through the sights I saw a Jerry standing behind a stump. I killed him. The captain let me keep that rifle."[119]

As the Seventh (U.S.) Army raced north into Alsace, it linked up with Third (U.S.) Army, pushing the *Wehrmacht* almost into Germany. Their costly fight in the Vosges Mountains spanned four months before bringing them near Germany's doorstep.

In the north, Belgium was being liberated by 21st Army Group. One British company had stopped and was being harassed by a sniper. The message went up to battalion to send a pair of snipers. Cpl. Arthur Hare and Pvt. William Packham along with Lt. Harding who was serving as an intelligence officer were sent. Lt. Harding ignored Hare's advice to stay with them. They were, after all, experienced soldiers and snipers unlike Lt. Harding who was fresh from Sandhurst. After a day without seeing anything, Hare and Packham signaled for Lt. Harding to rejoin them. When he failed to respond, they stalked their way over to his position and found the lieutenant had lost his duel against the sniper they were sent to kill. After recovering his rifle, they returned to battalion and reported his death to the colonel. Hare and Packham returned to their hide for three consecutive days without firing a shot. On day four, Hare was spotting and Packham taking a break when Hare spotted something.

> "'See that dead tree standing to the right of that hayrick, just on the edge of the wood? Two fingers from there to the right.'
>
> "'No, can't see a thing,' Packham replied

adding, 'What am I looking for?'

"'Smoke, the bastard's having a fag.'

"Packham spotted the smoke but couldn't get a clear shot. 'Who's going to have him?' he asked Hare.

"'You fire,' Hare responded."

They didn't have an opportunity to fire that day and rather than chance a shot on luck, they waited until the next day. The German was late to his hide and his head and shoulder appeared briefly among the foliage. Packham fired and the German's rifle flew in the air. "Got him," Packham announced proudly. There was no time to celebrate. The Germans retaliated immediately by opening up with small-arms fire all along the line. Before sliding down to the bottom of their hide, Hare noted the German firing positions and reported them to the colonel for a good plastering by the artillery.[120]

Stay anonymous!

That snipers went first for battlefield leaders (and political commissars) was not lost on his platoon, when American Lt. George D. Miller was shot after making himself conspicuous by his hand signals.[121] Realizing that officers were targeted, one of the first things Capt. Arthur Kaiser (Co. A, 1/121st Infantry Regiment, 8th Infantry Division) told his newly arrived executive officer, 1Lt. Richard Blackburn, to do was to remove his insignia.[122] Fighting in Normandy was so bad near Saint-Lô that soldiers of the 29th Infantry Division including "sergeants, corporals, technicians and even the one stripe of private first class" removed their rank.[123]

Graduates from the 3d Kuibyshev Infantry Military College also learned the hard way that their rate of survival was not very good. Zabolotnyi Ivan Dmitrievich recalled:

"After a six-month course of study they were supposed to send us to the front, where we would get the rank of Junior Lieutenant. How many of these lieutenants were killed at the front—oh! Not many survived! As soon as you got [to] the front you would run into a sniper for sure. We didn't care enough to protect people properly: officers had different military jackets, and combination caps rather than field caps. German snipers aimed well."[124]

In the Soviet Army rain capes were issued only to officers and inadvertently made their wearers a target.

Two snipers Bernard Machin and Joe Leedham are briefed by No. 3 Commando commanding officer Col. Peter Young, Bréville, Normandy June 17, 1944. Apart from the Combined Operations shoulder patch, there are few indications of rank visible. *Battlefield Historian.*

Operation Market Garden

(September 17–25, 1944)

The combined airborne and land offensive to bounce the Rhine saw three airborne divisions—1st (BR), 82d and 101st (U.S.)—and the 1st (Polish) Independent Parachute Brigade were to capture the bridges leading to Arnhem (Operation Market) linking up with a ground advance by the XXX Corps (Operation Garden) of the British Second Army. Proposed in the optimistic period after the success in Normandy, it failed for a number of reasons but mainly the thickening German defense that was helped by fast rail reinforcement.

As a buck sergeant (1942) and officers' payroll clerk in 101st Airborne, Sgt. Donald L. Deam was not airborne-qualified. This irked him so while typing up a list of men scheduled to attend jump school, he simply added himself to it. Deam attended, qualified, and only afterward did the 501st PIR commander, Col. Howard R. Johnson, learn of Deam's action. He exploded. "Those were not your orders Sergeant!" Deam admitted that they weren't but asserted that he wanted to be a fully fledged member of the regiment. "You made this decision all by yourself?" asked Johnson. "Yes, Sir." Turning away from Deam and addressing the platoon Johnson announced: "This is the kind of man I want in my outfit, one that can see an opportunity and take advantage of it." Now addressing the adjutant Johnson ordered, "Notify his commander and make him a staff sergeant!"

Deam was promoted not only to staff sergeant but subsequently to first sergeant in Regimental HQ Company. He jumped in Normandy where he suffered a gunshot wound but was discharged from the hospital in time to jump in "Market Garden." An engineering lieutenant was assigned to jump with Deam and before they departed Deam said, "I suggest that you remove your insignia. A sniper with a telescope sight could quickly pick those out." Grinning, the lieutenant took the advice and survived.[125] After a couple of weeks on the ground, Deam joined a patrol of 12 enlisted men led by another lieutenant.

"Ahead of us on the right was a small knoll covered with wild persimmon trees. On our left was a small group of men and women working in a beet field. Suddenly, a shot rang out and one of our men fell, shot in the head. We all hit the ditch for cover and there was a cry up and down the ranks calling, 'Sniper!'

"Our attention was drawn to a knoll up ahead. One of my men raised up, fired his M1 rifle and shot one of the supposed civilian workers out in the beet field. The rest of the people in the field scattered and ran.

"The Lieutenant came running up screaming, 'Soldier, that was a civilian you killed. I'm charging you with murder!'

"'I thought I saw that he had a rifle,' the soldier said.

"'You probably thought you saw a rifle, you probably saw a garden hoe,' the Lieutenant said.

"I piped up, 'Lieutenant, that's one of my men you've charged with murder. He's been a good soldier and never been in the habit of shooting civilians. With your permission, sir, I would like to go out and check what happened.'

"'The sniper fired from the knoll on the far right,' the Lieutenant said.

"'That's probably so sir, but let me go check,' I said."

Deam ascended the knoll, located the *franc-tireur* attired in civilian clothes as well as a recently fired Mauser K98k rifle which he brought to the lieutenant. "That was the sniper out there, sir." Happily, the subsequent hearing cleared the soldier.[126]

The 101st Airborne's 506th PIR dropped near Eindhoven. Their mission was to capture the bridges in the immediate area and move into the city. In the early morning hours of September 18, its three battalions began its march to Eindhoven and met light resistance along the way. As it reached Zon (American sources use Zon for today's Son to the north of the city), resistance stiffened. Capt. John Kiley was conspicuous as an officer could be with shiny bars on his helmet, map case, and binoculars around his neck. It didn't help that he exposed himself fearlessly. "God damn Kiley! What the hell are you doing up here. You shine like a f***** officer. You know the Krauts are waiting to kill officers," shouted his friend Lt. Charles "Sandy" Santasiero. Kiley brushed Santasiero off, telling him he was concerned for his safety since he led the point platoon. Pvt. William Galbraith was serving as Kiley's runner and had just returned from a mission when he spotted Capt. Kiley. "Kiley was standing behind a burned out German truck and next to a small cottage with a little courtyard in front. I was lying down on the left side of the road. I told Kiley he better get down. He said, 'If I get down, so will everybody else.' He no more than got the words out when a bullet hit him in the throat, killing him instantly." Galbraith thought the bullet came from Woensel church and fired at the tower and the windows before attempting to storm it alone. The door was bolted from the inside and he was unable to gain entry.[127] A bazookaman retaliated with a rocket.[128] Unfortunately, the Germans were able to

Per 4 Commando First Troop Sgt. Don Martin, "Pte Bill Johnson, one of the snipers in 1 Troop, 4 Cdo. It was taken in Flushing, Holland on or about November 3, 1944, after the successful assault. Bill died some years ago in Canada, but I met him two or three times in Normandy on visits with my late uncle. He rejoiced in being known as the scruffiest and dirtiest man in 1 Troop but that probably went with the job!" Johnson's spotter, Sammy Ryder is seen directly behind Johnson. The third man who is seen lying down was sent to retrieve them. Image from the John Martin Collection. *Commando Veterans Archive. https://www. commandoveterans.org/.*

blow the bridge at Zon before the 101st reached it. A Bailey bridge was thrown up in ten hours, but the delay was another nail in the operation's coffin.

Also jumping with the 506th was Trooper Donald Burgett. His first sergeant was unique in that he jumped with his personal sporting rifle.

> "As our first sergeant, Burley Sizemore, stepped through the gate carrying his personal, highly accurized, bolt-action 30-06 Springfield rifle, the trooper with the camera took his picture. Sizemore told me in Aldbourne some time before we knew that we were going to jump in Holland that he'd had his dad send his personal rifle from home. He said he wanted to make sure he could hit an enemy at long distance as well as up close. I told Sizemore that might be a waste. If he got wounded, as I had in Normandy, he would have to leave his weapon behind. They would not let him carry it through the aid stations or the hospitals, and he would lose his prized rifle. I told him he would be better off using an M1. It was a hell of a good rifle: semiautomatic, accurate at long distances, carried an eight-round clip, and, if he lost it, it would be replaced. Still, he insisted on carrying his own weapon. That was how 1st Sgt. Burley Sizemore came to have his

photo taken with his personal 30-06 Springfield as he passed through the farm gate to enter the Zoenche Forest."[129]

Burgett was right and Sizemore was injured at Zoenche Forest. His rifle was left somewhere there when he was evacuated.[130]

Serving in Co. D, 2/501st was machine gunner T/5 Glen Derber, who was also adept with rifle grenades and fancied himself as a sniper. They were fighting around Heteren when Derber volunteered to eliminate a German machine gun. Going forward alone, he had bracketed the gun with his rifle grenades but having exhausted his supply, resorted to accurate rifle fire to disable the machine gun. The machine gunners escaped but the next day a German sniper replaced them. His mission was to kill Derber for destroying the machine gun. His presence was announced when he killed two troopers with headshots. Realizing that a sniper was hunting for him, Derber took it upon himself to eliminate the German.

> "Having previously knocked off a Kraut at 700 yards, I thought it would be easy. I tried the old trick of putting my helmet in view at one location and observing with field glasses from another but it didn't work and I gave up when a bullet hit the

opposite side of the road, just six inches higher and there would have been three casualties shot through the head. And I never heard where the shot came from. I was brave but I wasn't foolish. Anyhow, my sergeant reprimanded me for leaving my gun position to go hunting Nazis on my own."[131]

Dropped northeast of the 101st, the 82d jumped over Groesbeek, Overasselt, and Grave. Lt. John W. Spooner was in the 82d's Co. A, 1/504th PIR. When they encountered a German sniper they couldn't neutralize, he summoned a 75mm artillery battery which fired ten rounds for him. It worked, but Spooner was later chastised by his colonel for expending $1,000 of artillery shells to kill one sniper from 8,000yd. The colonel reasoned that if an infantryman had killed the sniper, it would have cost the taxpayers only 5c. In an editorial comment, the *Hutchinson News Herald* editor supported Lt. Spooner's calling down artillery fire to plaster the German, made the suggestion that Americans would be happy to spend the money to save one of their boys and suggested that the colonel could pass the hat in any town to easily collect that $1,000.[132]

The bridge at Nijmegen didn't fall until the 21st and offensive momentum was lost when the British armored column was stopped a mere 11 miles from Arnhem—but by that time 1st (BR) Airborne had lost control of Arnhem bridge. Landed too far from their objective, too few of the Paras had been able to reach the bridge to hold out for longer. This didn't mean the fighting ceased. On September 27, Co. I, 504th PIR, 82d Airborne found itself at the edge of Devil's Den Woods—as the Americans called Den Huevel Woods southeast of Nijmegen. Pvt. Albert Essig was a pathfinder—part of a team who dropped first to set up beacons for subsequent drops. Called upon to approach Devil's Den Woods, he overheard an officer screaming over a phone, "If you order I Company down into the wooded area with no withdrawal route and they get massacred there, I'll see to it you're court-martialed." The officer made no impression on the listener on the other end. Essig moved out and made a remarkable shot. He recalled:

"I moved to the front line. I just lay down on the ground right at the front edge of the woods, approximately two feet back from the open field.

"Things remained quiet all day, except for the occasional crack of a German sniper's rifle. I heard someone shout out that one of our I Company had been killed. I crawled over to see who it was and discovered it was a guy I knew.

Suddenly I was angry. I didn't have a sniper's rifle or sights, but I started firing my Thompson submachine gun across the field where I thought the sniper was lying, and another guy started blasting away with his M1.

"I lay at the edge of the woods for about two hours. It was still daylight when I saw a small figure—I'd say about 1,000 yards out—walking across the field from my left to my right. I took my M1 [he had swapped his Thompson for a Garand] and aimed about one inch above the figure as he was walking. Then I squeezed off a round. I knew that, at that distance, the bullet might fall a little short. But the figure dropped to his knees. I wondered if I'd hit him. I lowered the rifle another quarter inch and fired another round. The figure fell flat on the ground and never moved again."

Essig modestly admitted it was a lucky shot but his hold (over) was correct. Unfortunately, Essig was injured during a bombardment and captured in the woods that day. He finished the war 50lb lighter as a PoW.[133]

When "Market Garden" finished, lack of manpower meant 82d and 101st Airborne had to stay in the line. They were ordered forward to the dikes by the Neder Rijn close to Arnhem. Donald Burgett came across a novelty by the British Royal Engineers which he described:

"South of the river our battle lines were separated by a dike running parallel to the river with the Germans on the north side of the dike and us on the south. On the south side of the dike the Allies and German forces were separated by a railroad, which ran south to north over the Neder Rijn, the Germans on the east side and us on the west side. ... [A] truck pulled in next to our outpost to take four of us to man a listening post close to the railroad bridge. Except for one or two men, that was our whole squad, what was left of it. At midnight Bielski, Phillips, Speer, and I boarded the truck and were driven to a lonely spot near the water's edge. One of the men on the truck led the way. We waded through knee-deep water to a small house nearly abutting the dike. Inside we found engineer tape stretching across the room at angles from all directions.

"When one of us asked what the tape was for someone explained that it had been put there to keep our men from wandering into that space, which was visible to snipers on the dike. The Germans had dug tunnels through the dike from their side, leaving small apertures on our side from which they could snipe undetected at individuals on this side. Three men had been killed in this house and several Englishmen had been killed in the surrounding area. The British posted their own snipers to look for the German shooters but none had been detected yet. They were still sniping and killing. Many men have been shot and wounded by ordinary enemy foot soldiers and later claimed it was a sniper who wounded them. They're wrong, though. Snipers don't wound; they *kill*."[134]

At the end of October, the 101st moved up near Arnhem. Co. E of the 506th relieved Co. B. Edward "Babe" Heffron and his machine-gun squad set up in a roofless barn whose sole occupant was a dead SS officer who had the night before demanded Co. B's surrender. Their response was to shoot him. The Co. B troopers left the officer's body by the cow because they figured that's where he belonged. This was the condition when Co. E relieved them. In the morning, a German a long distance away stood up from his foxhole, put his thumb on his nose and grabbed his crotch to taunt them. He did it again the following day. Co. E called for snipers and got two British snipers. Heffron and the rest of the machine-gun squad anxiously watched: "The morning after that, we had two British snipers sent to our line to take him out. They set up positions twelve hundred yards away, he did his nose-thumbing thing, and they shot, and missed!" Twelve hundred yards was pushing the .303 Enfield bullet to the extreme. Six to eight hundred yards would have been more reasonable. Heffron tells how their tormentor was finally dealt with:

"A sergeant with the 377 Para Artillery that was attached to us devised a plan to get rid of him. He said, 'I'll have a surprise for him tomorrow morning.' Next morning, the kraut stood up and did his thing. The sergeant picked up the phone, called in the coordinates, and said, 'Fire,' and the shells flew over our heads. They gave him what they call 'air burst.' The shell blew up before it hit the ground, and took the German soldier with it. We were all hooting and hollering. ... We have a law in combat: If you're a wise guy, you're on your own."[136]

Hürtgen Forest
(September 19–December 16, 1944)

After "Market Garden" failed, as U.S. airborne troops battled in the north of the salient, British and Canadian forces fought to clear the Scheldt and expand the bridgehead east to the Rhine at Overloon. To the south Lt. Gen. Courtney Hodges' First (U.S.) Army was faced with the city of Aachen and then the Eifel Region's Hürtgen Forest—the staging area for the Ardennes counteroffensive to be launched in December. With inadequate intelligence, the Americans confidently believed that the Hürtgen Forest would be lightly defended and would take only a few days to cross. Unknown to planners there were minefields, poor roads, hills, and as the Westwall (mistakenly called the Siegfried Line by the Allies) ran through it, no shortage of fortifications. These factors, German determination, and the forest itself ensured that those few days would stretch out to become three dreadful months before the Americans conceded defeat.

On September 12, 1944, Taskforce Lovelady of the American 3d Armored Division or "Spearhead" was conducting a reconnaissance in force and had entered Roetgen, Germany (nine miles southeast of Aachen) and was breaching the Westwall. Resistance was encountered and a German assault gun was quickly knocked out by a Sherman tank. Some pillboxes were destroyed and their occupants captured but not without a price. Capt. Almiron P. Hall, Co. E, 36th Armored Infantry Regiment, wore a brown leather jacket that distinguished him from his men who wore tan field jackets. Capt. Hall was picked out and killed (September 12, 1944).[137]

Among one of the first Americans to fight at Hürtgen was Pvt. Donald Lavender, Co. I, 39th Infantry Regiment, 9th Infantry Division. While a college coed, he received a draft deferment that permitted him to complete his first year in junior college. Now, instead of attending classes and dating coeds, Lavender found himself in the gloominess of Hürtgen. He left an excellent description:

"The Hürtgen Forest was like many other German forests. The pines were about fifty feet or more in height and were very close together. The heavy boughs made the forest area dark even at noon. In many of these forests, the trees had been planted some years earlier and they stood in long rows like rows of corn. Darkness and heavy undergrowth made visibility very poor. At regular intervals throughout the forest, there were some fire breaks, about the width of a country road. These were the only bright spots in the entire forest area."[138]

Fighting in the forest was especially difficult and favored the defender. Lavender recalled:

"The dark night in the forest was almost beyond description. A man couldn't even step out of his foxhole to relieve himself with any certainty that he would find his way back again. Trees less than five feet away were not visible. It was not possible to throw a grenade at night without the fear that it would bounce off a tree and come back into the foxhole. Resourceful GIs overcame this problem by placing stones on the edge of the hole in daylight so that they could tell by feel the direction of a safe throwing lane in the dark."[139]

At the outbreak of the battle (September 19), 19-year-old Platoon Sgt. Arthur Staymates of Co. B, 1/26th Infantry Regiment, 1st Infantry Division, was leading the remnants of his platoon when they came under sniper fire from a long distance.

"We were trying to move forward and there was a blown out building [They were trying to exit with a block wall on both sides of the exit.] but any time my boys, any of us tried to move out of the building, there was a sniper probably a mile away or maybe even more, but we didn't know about it, but he would just pick one off. Pichum! and the guy would be hit and drop. Finally we caught a glimpse of where he was shooting from. It was a third floor of a building about a mile away."

In his interview, Sgt. Staymates says his men were being picked off at one mile's distance. While the 8mm Mauser will carry well over a mile, it is highly improbable that it has any degree of accuracy at that distance. It is more likely that the platoon came under fire at half a mile's distance. With his platoon reduced to between 15 or 18 men (normal strength was 40), Staymates asked for suggestions. The soldiers suggested rushing the house but Staymates demurred, saying that the distance would allow all of them to be picked off. Instead, he decided it was a one-man job, gave his Thompson SMG to Wally Morgan, and took Morgan's BAR.

Stripping himself of helmet and canteen and anything that would make noise, he backtracked half a mile away from the sniper before entering the woods. Staymates stalked his way forward silently and approached from the flank to within 150 yards of the sniper.

"I'm sneaking through the woods and probably get to halfway through the woods … and there's a small river … too wide for me to jump, and so I crawl and get down in it, crawl through and hold the BAR up so it stays dry … I get through it and I get out to the other side. No Germans so far and in my mind I know the woods is full of Germans. So I'm expecting I can get killed any minute. I kept crawling on my stomach and finally get out to where I was probably 160–150 yards from his

building. Just when I did, I saw him look to see if any of our guys were moving. I said Oooh hooh, if he looks out again … so I waited and waited and finally he looks out again to see if any of our men are moving and he gave me a good shot this way [pointing at his temple]. Fortunately I made the shot which is a terrible thing but had to be done."

Despite fear of being killed by the sniper's buddies, Staymates managed to run two miles back to his platoon. He was physically and mentally exhausted from the ordeal. Moments later he was injured by a mortar round. For his feat, Staymates was awarded the Bronze Star.[140]

On November 10, the 4th, 28th, and 90th Infantry Divisions were ordered to relieve the exhausted American forces in the Hürtgen Forest. After capturing Grosshau by skirting around the German defenders and entering the town in the rear, on November 20 Co. F, 22d Infantry Regiment (attached to 4th Infantry Division) was ordered to advance through an open field to capture a ridge southeast of Grosshau. Lt. George Wilson was certain that the enemy was on the hill, and that night observed Germans moving into position and requested artillery to drive them off. His request was refused as it was believed that the 5th Armored Division occupied the hill. A patrol was sent out and positively identified them as Germans by their helmets and long-handled shovels (something the GIs didn't have). Another request for an artillery bombardment was met with an order that a second patrol be sent out. The second patrol got close enough to hear German being spoken. Still, Wilson's request for artillery was denied and the Germans were allowed to peacefully entrench. The next day, when Wilson and his company were ordered to cross an 800yd-long open field and seize the hill beyond Grosshau, they gained 300 yards before being plastered heavily with mortars and artillery. Caught in the open, men sought what little cover the ground offered. Wilson himself was tracked by an artillery observer who identified him because of the radioman who accompanied him. Wilson would leave his position and within 20–30 seconds an artillery or mortar round would land there.

During a lull in the firing, Wilson was trying to get his company to move again. We let Wilson tell of his brief encounter with a sniper:

"About a half hour later this new sergeant came over to me and pointed to the only building left standing on the hill to our left. He asked if we had anyone in there. He said it looked like someone was up in what was left of the chimney. I raised my field glasses and sure enough spotted a sniper as he was pointing his rifle our way. I yelled at the sergeant to duck and instinctively pulled him down into a shallow trench dug by the Germans, just as the sniper's bullet kicked up the dirt beside us. Then I told the Sergeant to get some of his [men] shooting at the SOB.

"He got up and walked nonchalantly about twenty yards to his nearest men, knelt down, and pointed up to the chimney. This was repeated to the next group of men, and then he casually walked over to a shell hole for himself.

"Just as he reached the tip of his hole the sniper dropped him with a bullet to the head. Damn it, why hadn't he hustled? The sniper might well have missed. His men quickly got the sniper, who also must have been the mortar FO [forward observer], because after that the mortars didn't bother us any more."[141]

The American offensive operations in the Hürtgen Forest ceased when the Germans launched an attack through the Ardennes. The Germans under Field Marshal Walter Model enjoyed a rare late-war victory at Hürtgen, although both sides suffered heavy casualties. It was depleted units from the Hürtgen battles—particularly the 4th and 28th Divisions—that were sent to recuperate and bed in new men in quieter sectors of the front: Luxembourg and the Schnee Eifel in the Ardennes—just in time to be pitched into the Battle of the Bulge.

While the First Army offensive stalled in the Hürtgen Forest, immediately to its south Ninth (U.S.) Army's 104th Infantry Division, nicknamed the "Timberwolves," crossed the Inde River in Belgium, entered Lucherberg on December 2, and held it against enemy counterattacks the next day. During a lull in the fighting on December 4, Pvt. Charles Davis and a buddy saw a "dead" German leap up and run.

"It was almost half an hour later that another one of the 'dead' Germans leaped up and took off down the street. I was the only one to fire at him. It was no trouble to get him in the scope. The crosshairs centered in the middle of his back and I squeezed it off just as he started to cut to the left to make the opening between the houses. At the same instant he stumbled, fell over a pile of bricks and disappeared from sight. Sergeant Smart later reported seeing the body."[142]

Lucherberg was cleared of Germans but the men prepared themselves for other counterattacks. Several efforts were made to recapture Lucherberg but the men of the 104th stubbornly held them back. Davis set his rifle down and when he returned, it was missing. A buddy told him an officer had picked it up and declared, "This is a German sniper's rifle." Luckily for Davis, his supply sergeant was extremely adept at procurement (albeit sometimes not legitimately) and within a few hours a new M1903A4 was in Davis's hands. Now Davis had to sight in his rifle again and the longest range available was a mere 40yd. Happily for Davis, a few days later he was promoted to private first class. It meant extra pay.[143]

Reflecting on killing, Pfc. Charles Davis wrote:

After Operation Market Garden, the Allies expanded the salient they had created toward the Maas and the Rhine. On the west bank of the Maas, men of the Royal Scots hunt for snipers, December 5, 1944. *GF Collection.*

"When I was shooting to kill my only thought was self-preservation. I knew that if I did not stop the enemy from coming at me then I would be killed. There was no hesitation or trembling as I squeezed off the shot to take a human life. The misses or near misses that I made were not caused by buck fever. I attribute them mainly to tough shooting conditions and an improperly sighted rifle, plus my inexperience with a scoped gun."[144]

South of the stalled First Army, Third Army's thrust into Germany was blunted at Metz, a heavily fortified and well-defended city that held out from September 27 to December 13, 1944. Even after it was pacified, resistance continued in the form of *francs-tireurs*. When the 26th Infantry Division arrived after December 13, they were fired upon. 2Lt. Lee Otts of the 328th Infantry Regiment recalled how they deterred this: "The sniping ceased a few days after we got there because whenever one of our men was shot at he would get some of his buddies and take the building apart."[145]

On December 6, 1944, the 90th Infantry Division crossed the Saar River and breached the Siegfried Line into Germany. Their mission was to clear a path for 10th Armored Division. By December 15 the GIs of the 90th were fighting house-to-house to capture Dillingen, Germany. One GI, Pvt. Dale Lundhigh, decided to play sniper only to learn the German response when they didn't have a sniper of their own to counter him.

"From the house I occupied I could watch German soldiers moving about in the trenches between pillboxes. I made the decision to snipe at them with my M1. Wiser soldiers had decided not to. From the upstairs kitchen of our house I began firing at the targets as they briefly exposed themselves. Although I was not accomplishing much, I continued my personal harassment as the bodies exposed themselves dashing between the trenches and pillboxes. A fellow platoon member joined me in the kitchen, where he voiced he was less than enthusiastic about my sniping. He proved correct. The sniping drew an impressive response from the Germans in the form of a mortar barrage. Mortar rounds smashed into the yard and garden in front of the kitchen. Although I was not hit by the streams of shrapnel from the mortars my fellow GI was not so fortunate. He was standing near a window. The shell blasts and shrapnel poured through the opening and hit him. Suffice it to say I ceased sniping."[146]

Earlier, on September 29, 90th Infantry Division T/Sgt. Herman Vander Laan had been promoted to second lieutenant. His division crossed the Sarthe river and cooperated with the 79th Division to liberate Le Mans (August 8). During a lull, he wrote home to his wife Margie:

"We do still find an occasional 'German civilian' sniper. These snipers caused a few casualties but are generally nothing more than a nuisance behind our lines. When he runs out of ammunition he'll give up or quit. He generally doesn't live that long. There's no such thing as a captured sniper. We've had occasion to see some dead women snipers too."

They later helped close the Falaise Gap before racing across France. On December 15, 1944, while fighting in the bridgehead north of Saarlautern, Lt. Laan was killed in an action that won him a Silver Star.[147] The citation reads:

"The President … takes pride in presenting the Silver Star (Posthumously) to First Lieutenant (Infantry) Herman T. Vander Laan … for gallantry in action while engaged in military operations involving conflict with an armed hostile force while serving with Company L, 3d Battalion, 359th Infantry Regiment, 90th Infantry Division, in action against the enemy on 15 December 1944 in the vicinity of Dillingen, Germany. When intense fire from two pillboxes temporarily halted the advance of a company, First Lieutenant Vander Laan skillfully led his platoon around one of the fortifications and successfully captured it along with 18 enemy. Again pinned down by machine gun fire from a position outside of the second pillbox, he, at risk of his life, crawled to within 20 feet of the fortification and with accurate carbine fire killed the machine gun crew. Although First Lieutenant Vander Laan was mortally wounded by sniper fire while in prosecution of his courageous act, the capture of the pillbox and its 23 occupants was subsequently accomplished with a minimum of casualties. His gallant actions and dedicated devotion to duty, without regard for his own life, were in keeping with the highest traditions of military service and reflect great credit upon himself, his unit, and the United States Army."

The next day on December 16, 1944, German Field Marshal von Rundstedt launched *Wacht am Rhein*— the Battle of the Bulge. The 90th Infantry Division was pulled back and redirected north into the flank of the attacking German Seventh Army.

6 To the Rhine and the Elbe

"When the Americans start using 155s as sniper weapons, it is time to give up!"[1]

German commander at Aachen

The "Checkerboards"—99th Infantry Division shoulder sleeve insignia. *Snubcube/ Wiki Commons.*

The Combat Infantryman Badge was awarded in World War II to infantrymen ranked colonel or below who fought in active ground combat between December 7, 1941, and September 3, 1945. *Ipankonin/Wiki Commons.*

In the aftermath of the fighting in the Hürtgen Forest, Middleton's exhausted VIII Corps was moved to the quiet Ardennes sector. They were joined by the newly arrived and untested 106th Infantry Division. It was a calculated risk by Bradley and Hodges, who reasoned that should the Germans attack, VIII Corps could not hold its ground but that the furthest the Germans could advance would be the Meuse. Strongly concerted counterattacks against the flanks would drive the Germans back.[2]

As part of Hodges' First (U.S.) Army, the V Corps' 99th Infantry Division—the "Checkerboard" Division because of its emblem (taken from the heraldic crest of the Earl of Chatham, William Pitt, for whom Pittsburgh, PA, was named)—took up positions north of Malmedy, Belgium. The 99th had landed at Le Havre in Normandy between November 3 and 7, 1944, and was still green and untested when it deployed along its 20-mile front. It began patrolling along the Siegfried Line south of Monschau on November 9. Along with the 2d Infantry Division to its north, it was to bear the brunt of the assault of the Sixth Panzer Army's 12th SS Panzer Division *Hitlerjugend*, re-formed after having been nearly destroyed in Normandy.

Before the German offensive, there was a lull where a lot of patrols took place and casualties arose either from patrolling or from mines. "Checkerboarders" Jack Prickett and Leslie Miller of Co. I, 3/393d Infantry Regiment were approached by an M1903A4

sniper rifle-armed major who wanted to fire a few shots at a German pillbox and thereby earn the coveted Combat Infantry Badge for himself. Refusing, Prickett explained, "If you fire, in three minutes they'll mortar the hell out of us." The major tried to brush them aside. "If I decide to fire, I'll fire." Officer or not, neither Prickett nor Miller were about to have the Germans provoked at their expense. Prickett warned the major, "If you do, we're going to kick the shit out of you." Knowing the threat was earnest and that Prickett and Miller would carry it out, the major left with a threat, "I'll have you court-martialed!" They weren't![3]

Among the replacements to the "Checkerboard" was 394th Infantry Regiment's Pvt. Max Gendelman. He had been attending sniping school in England and rejoined his division only after finishing training— thus he was spared some of the earlier skirmishes the division had experienced.

"The casualty losses affected all of us at the school for snipers. Sniper losses were extremely heavy. My training intensified, and the day when I would be sent across the channel was rapidly approaching. The entire group with which I had come to England was already in France. I had only to await my turn. I was assigned to the Checkerboard Division, the 99th Infantry, Company L, 394th Regiment, part of the 1st Army … The 99th were extremely shorthanded, having suffered many casualties. Company L was short a sniper, so I was very welcome in my new company and fit in well. Their other sniper didn't last too long."[4]

Gendelman's predecessors included Pvt. Milton Crawford, Pfcs. Walter Beard, John Cunningham, and Pvt. Alfred Slaybaugh, all of whom graduated from the regimental sniping school on June 1, 1944.[5]

Since there was no German sniper threat that demanded counter-sniping, Gendelman followed the American doctrine for a mobile sniper and ventured out on his own, seeking targets of opportunity: "Being a sniper, I was not chosen for these patrols. I had other duties and went out by myself, thus giving me a better

Max Gendelman. The story of his amazing friendship with a German Luftwaffe lieutenant and their mutual escape from the war is told in the book, *A Tale of Two Soldiers*. Decades later, after the German lieutenant emigrated to California, they renewed their friendship. Max's medals were:

Top row (L–R): Middle Eastern Campaign, Good Conduct Medal, World War II Victory Medal, American Campaign, PoW, PoW. Second Row: PoW Ribbon and beneath it Purple Heart Ribbon, duplicate Good Conduct, blue Combat Infantry Badge, collar tab for US Infantry (crossed rifles), "U.S." collar tabs, Army Corps of Engineers collar tab, and beneath it his discharge pin (irreverently called the Ruptured Duck). Beneath his Combat Infantry are his PoW tags issued by the Germans at Stalag IVB. Patches (L–R): Army Specialized Training Program, 44th Infantry Division, hash marks indicating one year overseas, Eighth Service Command (eight-pointed star) for troop movement and covered Arkansas, Louisiana, Texas, New Mexico, and Oklahoma; Seventh Air Force, 99th Infantry Division.

(L–R): Purple Heart, La Légion d'Honneur (French), Bronze Star and miniature Purple Heart.

Nina Endleman.

chance to seek cover and to fulfill my designated missions." December 16, however, was very different to the other days. He described it as follows:

"At 6:30 a. m., the shelling stopped. The German infantry advanced, coming out of the fog and the mist. Our communication with headquarters was disrupted by shelling. The radios were jammed. We had no officers left to lead and direct … With the enemy coming, I had to move fast. I grabbed two rifles: my sniper rifle (a 1903 Springfield with telescopic sights) and my M1. I also grabbed some ammunition, C-ration, backpack, and shovel. Then I quickly bade farewell to my wet, miserable home of six weeks. Personal items, such as photos, letters, and the package from Captain Ferguson, had to be left behind. I hoped our troops would later find it and get it to his wife. The package had her name and address on it … My duties as a sniper had me often going out alone, thinking for myself in order to fulfill my mission and at the same time stay alive. Once again, my training kicked in. The attack was coming from both sides. I decided to go straight—straight to and through the middle of the approaching juggernaut … I used up most of my ammo, shooting at approaching troops. Hundreds of isolated clashes were going all around me. Hit and run … The Germans, too, were shooting at you. You had to shoot back but be more accurate and deadlier. Most of that first day, December 16, became a blur. Shooting, running, hiding, advancing, and fighting, and then escaping again to shoot, and run and hide." [6]

By the second day, Gendelman had exhausted his ammunition. He found a pillbox occupied by other Americans and, being exhausted, slept there. Failing to receive the order to fall back, part of the 394th Regiment was overrun and captured. Among the captured (December 18) was Pvt. Gendelman who luckily hid his Jewish identity from his SS captors. He was to endure privations and hard labor until he and a Luftwaffe pilot collaborated on escaping to the Allies. [7]

A survivor who wasn't captured was John Wearly of Co. K, 3/394th Regiment:

"Just before we moved into our new CP [command post] I was returning about dusk to our CP on the forward slope of the hill and I made a big mistake. I crested the hill and made a perfect silhouette when I heard a loud crack by my right ear that I was unable to hear out of for several seconds. I knew right away what it was and hit the ground

like I was hit. The snow was still deep. A German sniper had taken a shot at me and he came so close that another inch or so and I would have been shot on the right side of my face. Jim Whitaker was sitting in his hole a few feet away and hollered to see if I was hit. I told him no, so he covered me while I made a dash to my foxhole. Sliding into the back side of the hole I knocked over a small can we were using to heat rations over and spilt gasoline all over the bottom of the fire, but what a mess! The sniper in front of us at the bottom of the hill was protected by the edge of the woods and try as we may we could not locate him. In a period of two months, he killed two men and wounded eight others."

Wearly survived and was involved in the January 31, 1945, effort to drive the Germans off the Elsenborn Ridge. [8]

A strange story was reported about a German who aspired to shoot five Americans to win a one-week furlough. He told the interrogators: "The Americans were easy marks because they exposed themselves carelessly." Lt. James Butler felt it was unsubstantiated but did note about his prisoners: "The jerries we are fighting are paratroopers, young, surly and tough." He added, "The Germans generally are poor snipers, but not these paratroopers. They shoot as accurately as we and most are equipped with snipers' rifles." [9]

Guarding Monschau and north of the 99th Division was the 9th Infantry Division. In the desperate days of the German offensive, Sgt. Lewis Creddo and his men were in dire straights. They were down to a single K-ration and 12 cartridges per man per day. On December 28, 1944, a sniper in a tree only 35–40yd away fired at them. His bullet hit Creddo's helmet and then deflected into Creddo's right eye, blinding him and causing him to pass out. The assistant squad leader retaliated by shooting the German out of the tree. [10]

Also caught in that assault was VIII Corps' 28th Infantry Division which was south of the 99th. After being decimated by the fighting in the Hürtgen Forest, the 28th was pulled out of the line and redeployed to a "quiet" region in Luxembourg where it was to rest, be reinforced, and recover. As an example of the attrition, earlier on November 7, while still in Hürtgen Forest, Pfc. William F. Meller of 2d Platoon, I/110th Infantry Regiment was sleeping in his foxhole when he was awakened by his squad leader and told that he was now assistant squad leader and a sergeant. Meller didn't even know the squad leader's name to thank him for the promotion when the squad leader himself was killed by a shell. Instantly, Meller became the squad leader. Just over a month later, S/Sgt. Meller found himself and his squad of 12 other soldiers, all that was left of the platoon, defending a mile of ground near Weiler. Meller wasn't the only one in a bad position. Only two battalions of the 110th were on a front line that covered 25 miles. Its third battalion was held as divisional reserve between Doennange and Wiltz. Up till then, Meller's platoon had received very few reinforcements, three of whom were convicts released from prison provided they serve in the Armed Forces.[11]

On the evening of December 15 the 2d Panzer Division moved into its assault positions and began advancing in the early hours of December 16. The infantry of Heinrich Freiherr von Lüttwitz's XLVII Panzer Corps—26th *Volksgrenadier* Division—advanced across the Our and Clerf rivers. Meller attempted to call Company HQ to get the bridges blown, but communications were cut and he had no runner to relay the urgent message. Lüttwitz's corps crossed uncontested.

Now Meller's company was going to suffer the penalty. Advancing against Company I were five companies of the 26th *Volksgrenadier* Division. As the fog lifted, Meller could see the Germans approaching.

"I automatically picked up Slim's M1 rifle. Again I look at the Germans, almost in a single line. I push up the rifle sight as far as it goes. There is no need for windage. I lean the rifle on the windowsill and unlock the safety … In basic training we weren't shown the maximum range of this piece. Maybe it will shoot eight hundred yards. Now I will know. The sight is on the first German in line. I move it just in front of him to compensate for the distance. He will walk into the bullet, if it carries that far. I fire. He goes down and they all scatter out of sight."[12]

For hours Meller and his men fought a desperate holding action and even captured a German captain and medic before being captured themselves. Miraculously, only one soldier in Meller's squad was

The German Fifth Panzer and Seventh armies' attacks. *Greene Media Ltd.*

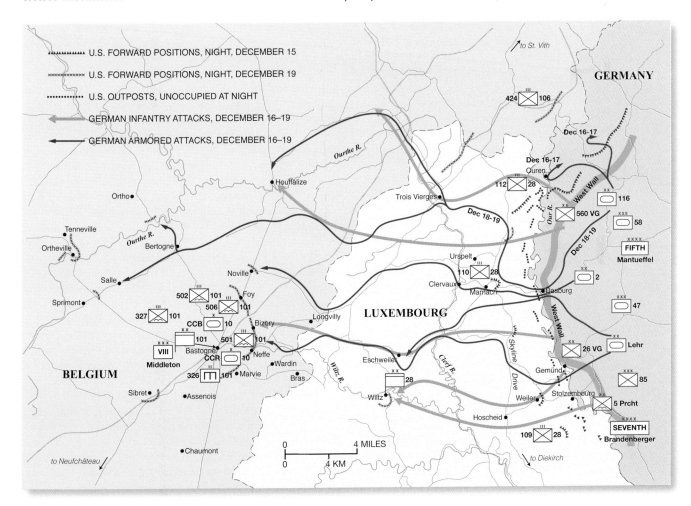

Clervaux after the heroic defense. *NARA.*

killed. After being taken prisoner, they saw a very angry German officer clad in a long leather coat and wielding a baton yelling at his officers. One GI who understood German interpreted for Meller. "The general is giving them hell for allowing eleven American soldiers to hold this road junction all day. We should have been wiped out first thing this morning. He wants to know why the Americans have no casualties." Meller and his men were not executed because the German captain whom he had captured spoke favorably on their behalf. As for the general, the baton suggests that it was Army Group B commander *Generalfeldmarschall* Walter Model who had a reputation for yelling at his officers.

Nearby, the town of Clervaux was defended by 110th Infantry Regiment—Companies E, F, and H of the 2d Battalion, as well as HQ company scouts, cooks, clerks, and other personnel trapped there. They were supported by the 707th Tank Battalion's three surviving Sherman tanks and a few anti-tank guns. With a total strength of around 450 men, they were attacked by 5,000 infantrymen and 120 armored fighting vehicles of the 2d Panzer Division. On December 17 Clervaux was isolated and enveloped by the German columns. Supported by assault guns, the *Panzergrenadier* unit attacked. Some GIs sheltered themselves in the 15th-century castle. Also seeking refuge there was 16-year-old Jean Servé. Why he was not ordered to the cellar is unknown, but when the German infantry and assault guns got closer, events became as surreal as a Hollywood movie. Servé watched from a window while Sgt. Frank Kushnir, who had a cigarette hanging from his mouth, used a sniper rifle to shoot down German infantrymen.

In the same room an unknown GI, ignoring the murderous gunfire and artillery, played the piano. The tune is unknown, as is whether, if parts could be heard over the din of battle, it exerted a calming effect.[13] After the attack was driven back, the overconfident German assault-gun crews dismounted their vehicles to smoke cigarettes and relax. Unwittingly, they had halted their vehicle and dismounted within range of Kushnir who sniped a few before the survivors fled to safety of their vehicles.

The overwhelming fire of the German anti-tank and tank guns made quick work of the three Shermans that were supporting the infantry. Clervaux was burning as the Germans advanced, taking out each GI's outpost as they came across it. Their advance slowed from street to street, then house to house, and finally room to room as the GIs stubbornly held on. At 1845 hours, regimental commander Col. William Hurley Fuller requested permission to withdraw his survivors but was ordered to hold on. With his HQ under direct fire from German tanks, Fuller escaped from the second story via a steel ladder while the Germans stormed the lower level of the house.

While Fuller and other surviving GIs retreated west to avoid capture, in another part of town the chateau was still held by about 50 men under the leadership of Capt. Clark Mackey and Capt. John Aiken. They continued firing on the Germans while the 2d Panzer raced westward, leaving an infantry battalion behind to mop up the small American holdout. Finally, in the morning hours of December 18, their ammunition was exhausted and they had no choice but to surrender. Sgt. Kushnir led a German sergeant out at gunpoint to see if the Germans would accept their surrender. A German colonel asked the now liberated German sergeant, "What was the treatment?" The German sergeant replied, "Well, they didn't mistreat us, they fed us good, they took care of our wounded, and they also protected us within the chateau so we wouldn't be under our own fire." Satisfied, the German colonel spoke to Kushnir in English, "You men are so lucky. My intention was to shoot all of you for the dead comrades [who] are strung throughout the compound."[14] Thanks to the determined stand of the 110th Infantry Regiment, 2d Panzer was two days behind schedule and 15 miles from Bastogne—more importantly, the delay had allowed 101st Airborne to reach the town. It came at the expense of 80 percent casualties to the 110th.

The green 106th Infantry Division was cut to pieces in the first days of the offensive. The division only had sufficient ammunition for one day of combat. It had only just taken up its positions and was spread very thinly. According to American doctrine, an infantry division should only defend a five-mile front—the 106th was stretched across four times that, in an exposed salient which had its back to the Our River. While spanning only 50ft across, the steep banks on both sides made it unfordable and only two crossing points were available: the bridges at Schönberg and Steinebrück. Another disadvantage was the lack of communication equipment. Because of the radio silence imposed on the 106th as it relieved the 2d Division, the signalmen had not calibrated their equipment.

When the Germans attacked, they poured through the Losheim Gap that was defended only by a reinforced squadron of the 14th Cavalry Group. South of the Losheim Gap in the Schnee Eifel was the 422d Infantry Regiment. Being a sniper, Herb Sheaner belonged to the HQ of Co. G, 2d Battalion and was excused from camp duties (he stood guard only once a day for five nights from 2400 to 0400 hours). While he had both the scoped M1903A4 Springfield rifle and an M1 Garand at his disposal, he hadn't received the manuals on the Springfield and its scope. Worst of all, he wasn't given access to a range so he could sight it in. In fact, the range was ten miles away, no transportation was offered, and Sheaner wasn't going to hike 20 miles. Anyway, since he could hit a man's head at 500yd with an M1 Garand and was very confident with it, he grabbed the Garand and as much ammunition as he could and ran out of the log hut inherited from 2d Infantry Division. His decision

Pvt. Herb Sheaner in happier times at camp before arriving at the ETO and fighting in the Battle of the Bulge. *Herb Sheaner.*

147

not to have a scoped Springfield probably helped spare his life when he was captured on December 21.

Also encircled was the 422d's sister regiment, the 423d. The next day both regiments attempted to break out toward St. Vith. By December 19, the 423d had reached Hill 504 south of Schönberg. Sgt. Russell Lang of I Co., 423d Infantry went ahead of his mortar squad to find a position to set up their mortar to support their infantry attack. He was followed by his friend, Sgt. Marvin (Sammy) Pate who had similar orders. Sgt. Lang and his buddy encountered a sniper.

"There was a small clearing in the woods that would allow us to set up the mortars. I ran out into the field and I dropped the gunsight box at the location where I wanted my crew to set up the gun. Then I continued to run ahead to take up a position to observe and direct the mortar fire. While running to about the middle of the clearing, with my binoculars now pulled out from my jacket and hanging from my neck, I came under sniper fire from the left side of the field.

"I dove for the ground. Each time I raised my head attempting to see where the fire was coming from, the sniper would fire at me, the bullets whistling by my helmet. When the sniper was firing at me he was firing to my rear, at Sammy I thought. I had assumed that Sammy was behind me and I thought that he was doing the same thing I was doing. I don't know how long I was out there, but it seemed like a very long time. Someone from the rear yelled at me to keep my head down. Finally I heard a small explosion that came from the direction of where the sniper was and then a call came from the rear to crawl back. The sniper had been killed. I began to crawl back through the snow to the cover of the woods when I noticed that Sammy was not moving, he was lying perfectly still. As I drew next to him my worst fears were confirmed, he had been shot right between the eyes, the sniper's aim was flawless. Sammy was white and there was nothing that could be done."[15]

Years later Lang learned from a buddy, Howard "Sparkie" Songer, details about Sammy's death and how the sniper was killed. Sparkie told Lang:

"When the sniper started shooting, Colonel Cavender our Regiment commander was in our area and he spotted the sniper location. None of the crews had left the woods yet and Sammy was close by. He told Sammy and our crew to 'Get that God damn Sniper that is in those bushes over there.' Sammy and his crew moved out into the clearing to set up the mortar. The range was too short to use the standard elevating mechanism. Sammy, my squad leader, was trying to aim the mortar tube by elevating the tube by holding it vertically with the bottom resting on the ground. It was while he was doing this that he was killed by a bullet to the temple. At the same time, I was hit but the bullet lodged in my mess kit spoon that was in my shirt pocket. Then another mortar man ([Murray] Stein) and I grabbed the mortar and dropped three shells in the area of the sniper, killing him."[16]

The 422d and 423d regiments were trapped by the Our River. They had exhausted most of their ammunition, had no means of escape, dwindling rations, no relief forthcoming and dimming hope for resupply—an air drop had been arranged but was turned back as an air traffic controller had no idea where to direct them. The two unlucky regiments had no choice but to surrender. The Germans captured over 6,000 prisoners from the 422d and 423d Infantry Regiments.

The 106th's survivors, mostly from the 424th, withdrew over the Our River and joined in the defense of St. Vith where the division's 81st Engineering Battalion earned a Distinguished Unit Citation for gallantry. One of the 424th Infantry's snipers was Co. I's Pfc. Paul J. Chodera, who recalled his experience:

"We were in a defensive position somewhere in Germany along the Siegfried Line until just before the break through. It was not so bad as we were pretty well dug in and in no great danger. We used to go on patrols in enemy territory to gain information and pull guard duty so no Germans would infiltrate through our lines. Then all at once one morning about 3 a.m. they shelled us with everything they had and just about daylight they hit our lines. We stood them off pretty well, but some broke through the line on our right and found shelter in some buildings. All the time our artillery and mortar were dropping close fire on our wire to keep them back. Their heavy stuff was also dropping on our lines. You can't imagine how much noise there was—it was awful. Talk about hot rifles—we all had them.

"My sniper's rifle had stood by me OK until now. I needed something that could be reloaded faster and fire faster, so I got rid of the '03 and got an M1 from one of the boys who would never use it again.

"Things sure were hot. I was acting assistant squad leader then and believe me you not only have to look out for yourself, but half the squad also. Some men just have to have someone to prod them along and keep them going. I remember one fellow who was in a trench close to me. When things got about the worst he dropped his rifle and started to pray. It was OK to pray, but you can't lay down your weapon to do so. You learn to pray, shoot, swear, and load your rifle all in one breath. By noon or a little later we had everything under control except the Germans that got in our building.

"Our platoon was going to clear those buildings, but after we got reorganized it was just our squad that cleared those buildings. We didn't have too much trouble. We had a couple of guys hit, but we took about 150 prisoners and sent them back. That took about the rest of the afternoon. We spent the night in one of those buildings with our platoon lieutenant and another staff sergeant. We took turns pulling guard, including the lieutenant. They shelled us some but not much.

"After a long night, daylight finally came. We were afraid of another attack but none came. After a 'K' ration breakfast, I was told to get all the Germans automatic weapons I could find and get them in working order so we could use them in case of emergency. With the help of another man we soon had enough automatics and ammunition in every foxhole. For myself I saved a machine gun which is capable of firing 1,000 to 1,200 rounds of ammunition a minute. That heavy shelling the day before put out some of our communications so I had another job to do. Sometimes I wish I was twins.

"I laid some new lines and fixed some of the old and we were all set again. By that time it was 2 p.m. and I needed a rest and something to eat, so I went to my foxhole, ate a 'K' ration, cleaned my '03, checked my machine gun and got a few more hand grenades. While getting the grenades hell broke loose again and the big push started. They were not like the Germans that hit the line the day before. These panzer troops were really tough. One must not underestimate them as they are deadly killers and don't give up easily. They just keep coming and coming.

"I held my own with them until they served a mortar in on the foxhole I was in. The machine gun I guess had them worried. All I remember was an explosion and everything went black. When I came to I was 10 feet from the hole. Whether I crawled out or got blown out I don't know. I had an awful headache. My right hand was awful numb and I was pretty well covered with blood.

"I got up and went back to the hole to see how my buddy was—he wasn't. The shell must have hit him square. That accounted for all the blood all over me.

"I then went back to the command post and a medic patched up my hand. The lieutenant in charge told me as long as I could walk I should go back to the Bat. Aid station and leave. I told him I thought I could still fire left handed and went back to the line. I cleaned the dirt out of the machine gun and got it working, but I couldn't hold it down with one hand. It jumped all over. I tried loading the M1 one handed and that didn't work. I was through.

"At this time I reported back at the C.P. You had to sneak along hedgerows and crawl in ditches because there were German patrols all over. I never really got as shaky as I did then; Germans all around, me without a weapon and even if I had one I couldn't use it. But all went well.

"The Bat. Aid station was four miles away and I made it all right by 9 p.m. They gave me a tetanus

1/506th PIR, 101st Airborne, heading out to Noville to support Team Desobry. *NARA.*

American troops of the 506th PIR, 101st Airborne, recaptured Noville on January 15, 1945. Note the knocked out Sturmgeschütz 40 Ausf G. *NARA.*

shot and just then someone came in and said, 'Pack up, the Germans are coming.' We left in jeeps. That sure was a tough wild night also, but we got out OK."[17]

Pvt. Chodera was wounded on December 19 and evacuated to England for hospitalization. He survived the war and became a grader and excavation contractor, passed away in 1997, and is interred at Hinckley Ridge Cemetery in Medina County, OH. As for the 106th Infantry Division, it would be rebuilt by assigning the 3d and 159th Infantry Regiments to replace the captured 422d and 423d. The division finished the war in Germany.

The 101st Airborne Division had been rushed to reinforce the existing defense of the crossroads at Bastogne. After fighting on the Betuwe north of Nijmegen for some weeks, they had been sent to the French barrack town at Mourmelon for rest and refit. Along with 82d Airborne they constituted Eisenhower's strategic reserve and both divisions were hurriedly put into trucks and driven to support Bastogne (the 101st) and the northern flank (the 82d). Those on leave in Paris were hustled out of bars and restaurants by the MPs and sent to the assembly areas. Many did not even have weapons and took the liberty of relieving retreating soldiers

of theirs. Few had snowpacs (cold weather footwear) and many lacked overcoats with which to keep them warm. White camouflage clothing wasn't issued, so their olive drab uniform and equipment would stand out in stark contrast against the snow-covered environment they were about to be thrown into. Indeed, they didn't have their CO—so quickly had they left that Maj. Gen. Maxwell Tylor hadn't time to return from the United States and Brig. Gen. Anthony McAuliffe took over.

The 506th PIR held the road from Houffalize to Bastogne including the villages of Noville and Foy. They fought off numerous attempts to break into Bastogne. On December 29, while men from Easy Company were on patrol, legendary sharpshooter (no sniper rifle was ever issued to the company) "Shifty" Powers' observation skills proved especially valuable. Powers recalled:

"A couple of days later I was out on patrol near Noville and spotted a tree that hadn't been there before. It was maybe a mile away, but I'd memorized the line of foliage the day before and knew what I saw. A little gully ran down left-handed, you know, and I could look off to my left and see that gully and a fence line. Well, that tree was brand-new. So I went back and reported to Sergeant Lipton. He brought out his binoculars and studied the spot. Sure enough, the tree moved. Krauts were bringing in gun barrels—88s, the sergeant guessed, big artillery pieces, firepower that could bring down a plane. Sergeant Lipton got on his radio and described the target to some upper brass back in Bastogne. They gave the okay, and we brought in our artillerymen. They gave a few blasts and scattered those big German guns. Pretty soon the place where that new tree had been staked was completely deserted. I felt fine about that."[18]

On arrival at Bastogne on December 19, the 502d PIR was sent north to guard the approach from Longchamps. During the siege the regiment beat back German armor and infantry thrusts. On January 4 they were ordered to advance and Sgt. Ahzez Karim of the 2d Battalion remembered a sniping incident:

"The next day, we moved again. Lt. Phipps took squads 3 and 4 and Capt. Homan moved out with squads 1 and 2. I didn't understand the reason for moving us across some open fields. This never made sense to me but we followed the captain until we came to a dead end. Now, as we had forest on three sides of us, and the Germans somewhere ahead of us, the captain said to dig in along the edge of the forest. Then with two troopers, he went back the way he came. Now, we thought, what the hell is this? Two 81mm mortars with no outposts and nothing to fire at. I had a map. I opened it, spread it out on the ground to find out where we were and which way the Germans were located. A couple of guys knelt next to me on[e] my left and one to the right. We were looking at the map when a single shot rang out. It hit the trooper to my right. The bullet hit him square in the chest. He fell forward on top of the map I had laid out.

"At the sound of the shot, all the troopers hit the ground, put a tree between them and where the shot came from and tried to spot the sniper but in vain. ...

"That sniper must have had a scope on his rifle, to pick out a target through all those trees. Grogan said, 'That's a hard way to find out where the Germans are!'"[19]

On the southern edge of the Bulge, the 80th Infantry Division had recently been transferred from Third (U.S.) Army's XII Corps to the First's III Corps. Still in the Ardennes Forest, its 317th Infantry Regiment was west of Kehmen and protecting the approach to Luxembourg City about 25 miles to the south. Lt. A. Z. Akins of 4th Platoon, H Company, and some men were on a hilltop. Beneath them was a pair of King Tiger tanks probably from the German army's Heavy Tank Battalion 506 which had been involved in the fighting at the Losheim Gap and Bastogne. They were abandoned for the want of fuel.

"We had been receiving sniper fire for a while, but we couldn't tell where it was coming from. After a few days we found that the German would sneak into one of the abandoned tanks just before daylight. He would wait until one of our men got out of his hole for one thing or another, and then pick him off. He killed or wounded several men in this manner. We had some tank destroyers sitting on that hill with us. After we realized where the bastard was, they opened on the tank and blew the hell out of it. That sniper didn't bother us again."[20]

The German Seventh Army was mostly composed of infantry and had a limited objective. It was to support the offensive and protect its flank from an attack from the south—exactly the direction from which Third (U.S.) Army was advancing. 41st Armored Infantry Regiment Commander Col. Sidney Hinds had emphasized marksmanship and sniping in his regiment. He proudly describes one of his snipers, Pvt. Ray M. Register:

"During the recent unpleasantness in the Ardennes, it was our job to hold the line of a certain sector. We were having the hell torn out of us by Jerry snipers. Life was pretty unpleasant.

"One of our observers finally went out and came back with the report that he thought he knew where one particularly bothersome sniper was hiding out. But he wasn't sure. The platoon leader sent Register to see, if possible. He watched the wood where the sniper was possibly hiding for about six hours. Not a peep out of Jerry. But just about dusk he spotted the Kraut—well camouflaged in a tree about 400 yards away. He got off one shot. Register reported back and his comment is a definite part of the regimental history.

"'I got him right between the eyes,' he proudly said. 'I think his vision is permanently obscured.'"[21]

Another rifleman in Col. Hinds's regiment, Pfc. Virgil Slover, was distinguished as "the only guy in all Kentucky who couldn't hit a dime at 600 yards with

Above: Pfc. Roland V. Blackburn was serving as a sniper in the 55th Armored Infantry Battalion, 11th Armored Division when he was killed in Belgium on December 31, 1944. Besides his parents, Mr. and Mrs. C. M. Blackburn and many siblings, he left behind his wife and three sons. *Author's collection.*

Below: Snow camouflage suit-clad 6th Airborne Division sniper in the Ardennes, January 14, 1945. *British Official.*

a blindfold over one eye." That was before he was trained as a marksman by Col. Hinds. During the Battle of the Bulge, Slover spotted a German patrol at 400yd. Using Kentucky windage, he fired six shots and accounted for five Germans.[22]

Within the 407th Infantry Regiment of 102d Infantry Division, "Officers and sergeants removed their rank or grade designations in order to lessen the possibility of being a sniper's target. There was no uniform standard for combat troops in the front line."[23] Commander of the 106th Infantry Division, Brig. Gen. Herbert T. Perrin, was seen by his men during a trip to the front line without any insignia on his helmet or field jacket.[24] Similarly, the officers of the 11th Infantry Regiment, 5th Infantry Division also took off all insignia. However, Pvt. Bilder of that unit said that the NCOs could not.

"Officers serving on the frontline normally wore no insignia, diligently scrubbed the white vertical line off the back of their helmets, and threatened any soldier stupid enough to salute them. All of the above were considered invitations to enemy snipers. Sergeant and corporal stripes also drew the additional interest of snipers, but NCOs did not have the luxury of being able to hide their status from the enemy."[25]

Despite being poorly supplied, under-equipped, and surrounded by the enemy, the troopers of the 101st and other units held on tenaciously until the Third (U.S.) Army broke through on December 26 and lifted the siege. Even then, the fighting around Bastogne continued and the resupplied 101st began pushing its perimeter out. In the house-to-house fighting around Foy, the 101st used rifles, tommy guns, bazookas, LMGs, mortars, and grenades to drive the Germans out. Sgt. Don Malarky who commanded a mortar section narrowly missed being killed when a corporal insisted on going first, turned a corner and was shot dead. Malarky hopped over the dead corporal and dashed around the corner, spraying a barn window with his tommy gun, striking the German with two or three bullets. Elsewhere though, high-placed Germans couldn't be reached easily; especially with a pistol-caliber submachine gun. Sgt. Malarky recalled: "Snipers, well placed in high positions, were picking off our guys left and right. Finally, Shifty Powers spotted them and opened fire with great success."[26] The Germans were ejected from Foy.

Hitler's gamble proved to be a costly failure and he typically underestimated the fighting ability of his enemies and overestimated that of his own. The Germans losses are estimated at between 81,834 and 98,024 men and this figure may well have been over 100,000 when Luftwaffe personnel are included. Losses in tanks and assault guns were around 600–800 vehicles. Allies' losses were 80,897 men along with 733 tanks and tank destroyers.[27] Unlike the Germans though, the Allies could make good their losses. Eisenhower wrote that, in hindsight, had the Germans withdrawn across the Rhine instead of attacking, it would have been more costly for the Allies to force a crossing.[28]

The Allies advance into Germany

The British and Canadian armies renewed their advances into Germany. The Canadians did not take kindly to being shot at from a house. If they were fired upon, they burnt the house to the ground in retaliation. If, however, the Germans refrained from fighting from a house, the Canadians left the house untouched. It was a heavy price for the civilian to pay if German soldiers decided to fight from their home.[29]

The Lake Superior Regiment was a motor battalion equipped with Universal carriers and M3 halftracks and attached to the 4th Canadian Armoured Division. When holding the banks of the Meuse, it could observe an enemy headquarters in a hotel in Hedel on the other bank. Lt. D. Marcotte sent his snipers to disrupt traffic to the hotel. Pte. Mike Delorme had

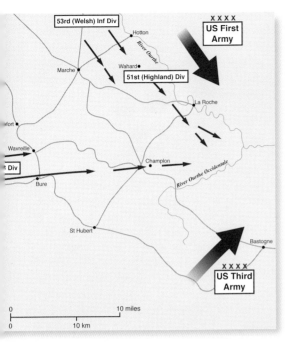

hunted as a civilian and became a sniping instructor. He instructed, "Stalking an enemy sniper is just like hunting." It is also known that—as it did before and during World War I—the Canadians recruited among its native people for scout-snipers.[30] DeLorme added: "The Germans used snipers extensively, so we had to adopt counter measures. We would take up our positions and wait until he fired. After we had located him, we would let him have it."

Between March 31 and April 19, 1945, the 4th Canadian Armoured Division advanced to and crossed the Küsten Canal near Oldenburg, Germany (Küsten Canal was awarded as a Battle Honour to the units that took part). Pte. Delorme teamed up with a FOO, Lt. Charlie Conquest of the 23rd Field Regiment, who acted as his spotter. He picked off 20 Germans on the first day and eight the next, along with bagging six prisoners.

* * * * *

By the end of January 1945, the Americans were pushing the Germans back to the Siegfried Line and eradicating the "Bulge." Co. A, 1/363th Regiment, 99th Infantry Division swept down from near the Elsenborn Ridge and advanced toward Krinkelt before abruptly swinging north toward the woods. Radioman Tom Lacey of Co. C was on the right flank of Co. A.

"As we were halfway through, 'A' company ran into sniper fire, and halted. Before I, or anyone

else, could get a handle on what was really going on, Lieutenant Henderson had borrowed an M1 from one of his riflemen, and from a standing position, knocked that sniper out of his perch in one of the many trees that peppered the area … The rest of the advance was almost without resistance."

Henderson wasn't always a lieutenant. About six weeks earlier on the opening day of the Battle of the Bulge he had earned a battlefield commission

Top Left: The attacks by British XXX Corps. *Greene Media Ltd.*

Top: Camouflaged 6th Airborne sniper (left) and his companion fighting in the Ardennes, 1944. *Battlefield Historian.*

Above: Sniper and Bren gunner providing cover in the Ardennes, 1944. *Battlefield Historian.*

and demonstrated his worth again when he used a bazooka to knock out a Tiger tank.[31]

After penetrating the West Wall, the Americans raced to the Rhine but met brief resistance at Prüm. Part of that resistance was a lone German gunman. Nicknamed "Hoffman" by the GIs, he had killed five of their number and from a church dome controlled the traffic on the main street which had been nicknamed "suicide lane" by the GIs. Three panzers on the overlooking hill along with a huge shell hole in the middle of the main street prevented the Americans from bringing up a tank or tank destroyer to shell Hoffman out too. One GI who dashed across a road and was missed attributed it to: "Hoffman must be getting sleepy. He missed me." Battalion Commander Maj. James Kemp said: "That dirty so-and-so is sure earning whatever pay he is getting, but we'll get him." How Hoffman was dealt with or whether he eluded the Americans was not reported, but it demonstrates the effectiveness of a single sniper.[32]

Ninth (U.S.) Army (Lt. Gen. William H. Simpson) drove into the Rhineland as part of Operation Grenade and its 84th Infantry Division cleared out Dülken. Pfc. Roscoe Blunt of 3/333d Infantry Regiment's anti-mine platoon, when not preoccupied with detecting and disarming booby traps or mines, fought like any other infantryman. He arrived on the continent in November 1944 with the rest of the 84th and had been captured once by the SS during the Ardennes Offensive. In a masterful bluff, he convinced his SS captors to surrender to him on the promise of safe crossing as prisoners into the American lines. Now Blunt was going door-to-door clearing houses and had just entered one when he was shot.

Snipers force Allied soldiers to keep their heads down during Operation Grenade. *Battlefield Historian.*

"As I entered the front door, a violent blow punched me in the side, spinning me around and dumping me in a heap of shattered masonry. A sniper had been following me in his sights and my preoccupation with the dying old man made me careless in a city that had not yet been declared safe … Instinctively I felt for the wound. I couldn't understand why there was no pain, just a dull ache as if I had been walloped hard in the side by someone. There was no wound. The sniper's bullet had severed my cartridge belt and hit my M1 ammo pouch. The cartridges had been flattened and twisted but not one had exploded. Another close call with death.

"I crawled to a window and shot nervous glances out at the street. I even dangled my helmet out the window on a piece of wood as a ruse but the cagey sniper didn't bite. I heard the roar of a Sherman tank approaching and I yelled at the sergeant crouched in the turret. 'Sniper, sniper over there,' and pointed at the building across the street. He heard me and instantly 'buttoned up' his turret.

"I hadn't noticed at first but the tank was equipped as a flamethrower, similar to the British 'Crocodiles'. The tank turret slowly ground to its right and in the next moment, the building across the street disappeared in a massive sheet of fire. I watched the building consume itself to a pile of burning debris. But I also knew that a sniper would most probably move to the cellar and wait the fire out. Then he would resume his deadly game.

"When it was safe, I climbed over the rubble and, not finding a charred corpse inside, tossed a grenade in the cellar. I didn't bother to check if anyone was there."[33]

Ninth (U.S.) Army awarded a commendation to the 84th Division for its execution of Operation Grenade, the bridging of the Roer River and the capture of towns on its eastern bank.

* * * * *

As part of 21st Army Group's crossing of the Rhine—Operation Plunder—on March 23–25, 1945, the 51st Highland Division crossed in Operation Turnscrew opposed by 8th *Fallschirmjäger* Division. The Gordon Highlanders fought to clear Rees in the face of persistent and accurate sniping. The OC of B Company, 1st Battalion, Gordon Highlanders, Maj. George Morrison, had his batman killed alongside him—but was able to despatch the sniper. The

market place and cathedral square of Rees were dominated by snipers until the 3.7in. mountain guns of 454th Mountain Battery, 3rd Mountain Regiment, RA, were called into action. While this meant that bridge building could take place without enemy sniping, the Scots:

> "ran into very stiff opposition from a machine gun emplacement … supported by a number of snipers … In a short period of time three B Company officers became casualties. Lieutenant V M Halleron was shot in the back by a sniper and died; Second Lieutenant A K Macdonald was mortally wounded by a burst of Spandau fire from the pill box and Lieutenant P G Burrell, a B Company spare officer called up to replace Halleron less than an hour before, was shot in the head and appeared to be fatally wounded.
>
> "Major Morrison was himself hit on the head by sniper fire but his helmet deflected the round and he was uninjured. Lieutenant Burrell recovered after hospitalisation."[34]

By March 26, 1945, the 5th (U.S.) Infantry Division reached the southern outskirts of Frankfurt. There was a four-day fight against elements of the German LXXX Corps before the 5th Infantry, with the support of the 6th Armored Division, was able to push the Germans out. Pvt. Michael Bilder, 5th Infantry Division, had shot "expert" at boot camp and at one point was temporarily issued an M1903A4:

> "While the Germans were retreating out of Frankfurt, I was selected with three other men to occupy a tower for sniper duty against the fleeing foe. The Germans were racing to evacuate the city and the surrounding area, but were slowed by the civilian foot traffic that clogged the roads. Our mission was to shoot as many German soldiers as possible, using Springfield bolt action rifles equipped with telescopic sights. It didn't matter whether we killed or wounded them, just so long as we hit them. In either case our victims would be out of the war. Our actions left a number of *Wehrmacht* bodies littered about … The others knew that I was aiming at the trunk of my targets. I didn't want to shoot anybody in the head or see their faces in my sight."[35]

In April 1945, Hugh West's recon unit was assigned to protect the engineers who were tasked with protecting the engineers assigned to clearing the roads. They had tank recovery vehicles fitted with bulldozer blades and M3 halftracks.

Charles Henry Byce

Charles Henry Byce's father, Harry, was awarded the Distinguished Conduct Medal—and a French *Medaille militaire*—for leading an attack on a German machine-gun post during World War I. He had married Louisa Saylors, of Cree descent, from Moose Factory, Ontario, before leaving for war and their son—born while Harry was still in France—lived up to his father's example.

Sgt. Charles Byce went to war in 1940 with the Lake Superior Regiment (motorised)—the "Lake Sups"—and won a Military Medal on the Maas in the Netherlands in January 1945. On March 2, 1945, the action that saw him awarded a DCM took place during the Rhineland Campaign in the Hochwald Forest. His unit was decimated by an artillery bombardment during which all the officers were killed. As tanks approached the position, Byce ordered the retreat of his men, remaining behind as a rearguard, sniping at the enemy infantry. He killed eight and wounded 11 and held them off long enough for his men to get away. His citation reads, "The magnificent courage and fighting spirit displayed by this NCO when faced with almost insuperable odds are beyond all praise. His gallant stand, without adequate weapons and with a bare handful of men against hopeless odds will remain, for all time, an outstanding example to all ranks of the Regiment." He died in 1994.[36]

Charles Henry Byce, Indigenous hero of WWII, commemorated in bronze, Chapleau, Ontario. Sculptor: *Tyler Fauvelle.*

"My outfit had to stand guard over these roads as they were being cleared, because sometimes kraut snipers fired at the bulldozer drivers. By this point in the war, we went into a bloody rage when a sniper fired. We became absolutely determined to kill him."

Lacking the tank support they enjoyed earlier, West's unit developed new tactics to locate and destroy snipers. It became standard operating procedure to send a few scouts forward to invite a shot while the rest of the unit provided covering fire.

"There seem to be snipers in every town at this late stage in the war, which infuriated me. When they fired at our bulldozer drivers, however, they never hit them. A steel bulldozer scoop makes a great shield when it's raised.

"We performed our highway patrolling in peeps. [Peeps was the cavalry's and armor's nickname for the jeep.] I drove down the road at a good clip while another fellow sat in the back, manning the mounted machine gun. I drove at fifty to sixty miles per hour down these roads, while the gunner fired in every direction. It sprayed a lot of bullets and used up lots of ammunition, but we didn't care. The Germans didn't know what to make of it though.

"There were times when we knew where a German sniper hid. We liked to dupe them by pretending to do road repair work, while sending a small unit around and behind to get him. This worked more than once.

"It was always a good feeling."[37]

The 1st (U.S.) Infantry Division breached the Westwall and crossed the Roer River on February 23, 1945. In its drive toward the Rhine, its 26th Infantry entered Wesseling. Pfc. Charles W. Foxx was the sniper of 3d Platoon, Co. I, 3d Battalion, and manned an upper-story room from which he could scan across the Rhine to German-held territory. Foxx focused on two haystacks and was rewarded when a German emerged from one of them. Lining up the unwary enemy in his crosshair, he squeezed off a single shot and killed him at 450yd. Unfortunately for Foxx, he did not survive the war and he is interred in Green Castle, PA.[38]

Desperate, the Nazis impressed teenagers of both sexes to fight and armed them with rifles and *Panzerfäuste* before leaving town. The lucky ones were disarmed by older Germans who administered punishment. According to Maj. Mercer Sweeney of Seventh Army's 101st Cavalry Group:

"We've confiscated, in towns we've gone through, hand grenades and sniper rifles with instructions to the Hitler Jugend to use them. One thing we found was that as soon as SS men got out of town the old folks gave the kids a spanking and told them to behave. The old folks appear to have received quite a kicking around between SS men and Hitler youth and now they are taking the bit between their teeth again."[39]

Better a spanking than an American bullet, grenade, or artillery shell. Unfortunately, that was not always the case and some youths fought and died.

M36 of 628th Tank Destroyer Battalion, in Rheydt, Germany, on March 1, 1945. The tank destroyers had open turrets and postwar they were given armoured turret tops. To protect against sniping in the last days of the war some modifications were made to the turrets. *NARA*.

On March 1, the 99th Infantry Division was near Düsseldorf and within 17 miles of the Rhine River. Sgt. Frank Tezak of Easy Company, 2/395th Infantry was fired upon by a sniper and shot in the left temple. Easy Company immediately sheltered itself in a ditch, but every time a soldier raised his head to locate the sniper, he was killed with a headshot. Four men were shot successively. Easy was pinned for the rest of the day until Baker Company flanked the area and drove the sniper out.[40] One month later the 2d Battalion of its sister regiment, the 394th, captured Dietfurt in southeast Bavaria. Sentries were posted on the hills that overlooked it. One man who was posted as a sentry, Pfc. Michael Popinny, was shot by a sniper. Two squads moved out immediately and flanked the hill that the shot came from but the German sniper slipped away unpunished. After coming up empty handed, the battalion then mounted tanks and drove to Kelheim.[41]

Another division crossing the Rhine, 3d Infantry had enjoyed a short rest around Strasbourg before it advanced on December 15, as part of the Seventh (U.S.) Army's push into Germany. When the German offensive on December 16 caused the Third Army to swing north, the Seventh continued its slow advance before pulling back to fill the space created by the Third Army's departure. By February the situation was restored and on February 4–7, Seventh Army attacked and captured the fortress town of Neuf-Brisach, just a few miles from the Rhine. On March 15, they assaulted across the Rhine between Worms and Mannheim. They came under fire at Sandhofen from *francs-tireurs*. 7th Infantry Sgt. Soskil described the Americans' response: "As we reached the other side, civilian snipers targeted us. Anyone shooting at us was fair game so we killed them."[42]

Leading elements of the 87th Infantry Division (VIII Corps, Third Army) first reached the Rhine around March 10–15. Nineteen-year-old S/Sgt. John Moran of Co. K, 3/347th Infantry and other elements of his regiment were trying to stop the Germans from escaping across the Rhine. At Oberspay near Boppard they fought building to building to reach the waterfront. Squads were deployed every fourth or fifth house for a mile's distance.

"One of our kids found a motorcycle and he was on the back street of Niederspay [This is incorrect: actually Oberspay] driving this motorcycle down the street doing about 20 mph and a German sniper on the other side of the river knocked him off the motorcycle. He's firing at 600 yards and hitting a moving target. That's pretty good shooting. The next day one of our lieutenants

was running across from one building to another, and I say run, you never walked. You left one building, boom, you zipped to the next one. He's running across to get to the next building and he gets hit right behind the ear and it came out here [points to cheek near the left nostril]. It missed his brain and his spinal cord so he survived. But that told me that sniper, he wasn't just standing around, he saw somebody run and he'd pick up his weapon. He was laying in a shooting position looking through the scope and had his finger on the trigger, partially pulled, and the second he spotted something he'd hit on it. It was amazing how accurate they were shooting at that distance and they could hit moving targets."[43]

A few days later their division crossed the Rhine under German fire.

To be or not to be

Robert L. Anderson was a sniper in Co. E of 86th (U.S.) Division's 341st Infantry. Assaulted in barracks by an inebriated sergeant, he fought back and got the better of his assailant, but was court-martialed. He had to explain his actions—a private striking an NCO was not looked upon favorably by any army. Anderson explained he had been writing letters home when the sergeant came in, yelled profanities at him, grabbed him by the tie, and yanked him to his feet. The sergeant cocked his arm to strike but Anderson was faster. Boom! His left fist went straight into the sergeant's chin, snapping his head back. Right fist followed and then another left. It was the old 1-2-3 masterfully delivered. When Anderson revived him with water, the sergeant swung again. Anderson blocked and hit the sergeant in the face while he was down. Look ma! No front teef.

The colonel told him to wait outside, from where Anderson heard the board roar with laughter and he was soon told that they had decided he had acted in self-defense. To avoid charges, he was promoted to corporal with the promotion backdated to before the incident; at the same time the sergeant had a backdated demotion, also to corporal. Anderson was transferred to the radio section of Company HQ and away from the offending "corporal." This was all before the unit departed for the ETO, too.

Months later, around April 13, 1945, the 341st was fighting the real enemy in Attendorn, Germany, where four GIs were shot down by German snipers. "Andy!" his lieutenant—who was aware Anderson had trained as a sniper—called, "Go get those snipers!" Dashing into a damaged building, Anderson went up into the attic. Remembering his training, and remaining in the shadows, he was ready when a German appeared and leaned forward to look for the GIs below. Using the sling to steady his offhand hold, Anderson applied pressure on the trigger. As instructed in his training, the gun's fire should surprise him. It did and both the German and his rifle fell out of the window. Instantly, Anderson ducked to avoid any return fire and shifted to the another window where he shot with his left hand at two more Germans. An alert GI below killed one and Andy shot the other. He then picked the better of the two scoped Mausers for himself. Sniper turned radioman had become a sniper again.[44]

Urban fighting[45]

"Sniping from Houses, Buildings, Behind Walls, Etc.

During open warfare snipers must be prepared to take advantage of any position which may help to inflict casualties on the enemy and open the way for the advance of our soldiers, not only in open country when enemy machine guns are holding them up, but also in villages—outlying buildings, rooms in houses, cellars, walls, chimney-pots, and through the roofs of houses which have been partly demolished by shell fire, etc.

Rooms in Isolated Houses or in Streets

Whether sniping from rooms in isolated houses or houses situated in streets, it is not advisable for the snipers to occupy rooms on the ground floor. These can be mopped up systematically and quickly by our own infantry. Until the advance troops arrive, snipers should go forward and attempt to establish themselves in the nearest house or houses, preferably in the second storey. If they occupy ground-floor rooms they will present an easy target to the enemy provided with hand grenades. Our snipers should carry at least two grenades for their own protection and to clear enemy snipers out of rooms if they are unable to do so by rifle fire. These grenades also may be of much service should our sniper have been discovered and an attempt made in force to kill or capture him.

Rooms—out of Windows—Second Storey.

Select, if possible, rooms in the second storey. In most cases all glass will be shattered from the windows and only frames left. Window space may be wide open and no frames left. In any case the sniper must never expose his head or any part of his body out of the window for the purpose of sniping. He should take up a position in the room which will give him an oblique line of fire protected by the wall of the room and well clear of the window. If unable to get a good view while standing on the floor of the room, the sniper can pull out a bed or chair or table, and for protection may possibly use mattresses, pillows, furniture, etc.

Removing Bricks.

If it is possible to do so the sniper may remove a few bricks in the wall for loophole purposes. These should be in the lower part of the wall so that the aperture may be fired through either in a prone or kneeling position.

Line of Retreat.

When occupying a room of this description the sniper should not overlook his possible line of retreat in the event of being spotted and finding it necessary to move to another position. Both in occupying the house and leaving it, the sniper must be on the alert, keeping close to the walls, watching carefully any houses on the opposite side of the street, making use of doorways for temporary observation, being careful about his own shadow if in sunshine and turning a corner, when it is best to go down on hand and knees or crawl.

Walls—unless breached by Shell Fire.

Selection of walls remaining after shell fire, or low walls bordering gardens or roads. Unless these have been breached by shell fire, snipers should never fire over the top—unless, of course, the tops of the walls have been knocked about, leaving a very uneven surface so that the sniper, while keeping close to the wall, can fire over the top at an oblique angle, while his head and body are protected from a shot fired at right angles to him.

In most instances it will be found that a prone position on the ground at either end of the wall may give better results. Here the sniper must keep very low and be careful about his steel helmet if wearing one, as the outline will be dangerous.

Roofs of Houses.

When houses have been shelled and portions of the roof knocked in, snipers should climb into the rafters or get behind the remains of brick chimneys passing through the roof and take up a positon for sniping; these form excellent sniping posts.

Chimney-pots.

Our sniper on several occasions in 1918 placed themselves behind rows of chimney-pots, firing between the various chimneys. These were most effective sniping posts and hardly ever spotted.

To Sum Up.

In open warfare small villages and small towns are mopped up in more or less quick time, so that snipers are usually able to move fairly rapidly from one position to another and thereby try to cover the troops who are operating in the streets and among the ground-floor rooms and houses. Snipers should keep a sharp look-out for enemy snipers who may have concealed themselves (very often in cellars) from the first wave of troops passing through villages, and who then emerge and proceed to snipe our men in the back with unpleasant precision, and then surrender themselves when they cannot safely kill any more.

Approach Work.

Sniping from buildings is dangerous work for snipers, not so much the actual firing from buildings but in approach work—in occupying positions. It must be realized that one sniper could cover any movement up a long open street without any turnings in it, and that by two snipers working together, one on either side of the street, severe casualties could be inflicted. It is therefore far better to select an approach by a back door instead of the front—much more cover may usually be found on premises behind houses than in front. Only the most expert snipers should be detailed for this kind of work."

Opposite, above: Arthur Godin of the Canadian Le Regiment de la Chaudière is seen here sniping in Zutphen, the Netherlands. Note his distance from the window, which offers him better concealment. *British Official.*

Opposite, below: This Commonwealth sniper has made some effort to camouflage his post with foliage. While resting it on the window sill is steadier, his exposure is much greater than that of Godin's. *British Official.*

Below: Canadian sniper of C Coy., 5th Battalion Black Watch in Gennep, Holland, February 14, 1945. *GF collection.*

the occasion required, well-placed salvos. In addition to their long-range cultural mission, the memorials also had a very salutary immediate effect. It was found they appreciably expedited surrenders and discouraged sniping."[46]

One American sniper, Pfc. Charles Davis of the 104th Infantry Division, recalled that some of the last casualties in his unit were inflicted by snipers in late April.

"The first few days we were opposed by the remnants of the great or once great German *Wehrmacht*. They threw some mortar fire and they did some long-range sniping. Our last two casualties were hit by snipers, accurate shots through the neck. The men of course were killed."[47]

The shots were probably fired by fanatics who hadn't given up on Hitler or the Third Reich. Most Germans gladly surrendered themselves in the west but those in the east fought tenaciously as they feared their fate if captured by the Soviets.

Adding to the confusion was the brutal Nazi regime's use not only of children but also girls. Those who demurred were often hung by the SS for their refusal to die for the Führer. The sad ending of one fanatical child is told by Pvt. Michael Bilder:

"Surrender, however, could be a tricky thing. One town in Germany had all white flags out as we approached. They hung from every window in every building. It was an historic town, and the burgermiester had persuaded the German army to leave it to us without a fight. Despite the obvious lack of resistance, we moved into the town cautiously, hugging the sides of the buildings on both sides of the street.

"The lieutenant leading us nevertheless walked right down the middle of the main drag. He was gutsy and exemplified real qualities of leadership and command. A shot rang out from a high point and he fell over, wounded in the groin. About eight of us rushed the house where the shot had originated, freely throwing grenades into the window. When the smoke cleared, we found the body of a girl in her mid teens. She may once have even been pretty, but now she looked like she had been fed through a meat grinder. I could only think she had been a committed Nazi. Her action was a near guarantee of suicide, and she was wearing numerous swastika armbands. She was

Above: *Run fast!* A GI dashes across an open intersection in Cherbourg, France to avoid sniper fire. *NARA.*

Below: Postwar Sgt. Harry Furness kept his skills honed by hunting for game he gave to starving locals. *AFPU.*

Opposite, above: Cpl. Arnold of the Canadian Cameron Highlanders with a No. 4 Mk. I (T) sniper rifle. *LAC.*

After crossing the Rhine, the Third (U.S.) Army decided to leave "memorials" to mark their wake. Third Army's G-2 Intelligence Officer Col. Robert S. Allen remembered they served a dual purpose:

"[T]o bring the war home directly to as many Krauts as possible, and to enable future Kraut generations to trace readily the course of the Third Army's triumphant sweep through Germany. The memorials were very simple. They consisted of plastering every village and town in the zone of advance with several or more as

determined to die for her cause, and she did. Fortunately, our officer survived."[48]

Clearly she was no sniper but she paid the ultimate price for her misguided dedication. Other cases of non-military women taking up arms to shoot at Allied soldiers have been recorded, too. The 99th Infantry Division's newspaper, *The Checkerboard*, even has photos of women prisoners who had shot at them.[49] Even young children were called upon to "die for the Führer" and the 9th Infantry Division's Co. B (2d Infantry Regiment) reported capturing an 11-year-old with a telescopic rifle who was in a tree in Lorraine.[50]

On May 6, Capt. T. Moffatt Burriss of 82d Airborne's 504th PIR decided to ignore orders and taking a sergeant and a lieutenant, hopped in a jeep and sped eastward across the Elbe. With a white flag flying from the jeep, they drove 40 miles until they bumped into a German column. The German captain asked him what he wanted to which Burriss responded, "I'm here to accept your surrender." Seeing no one behind him, the German captain balked causing Burriss to warn: "I have a whole army of paratroopers and tanks behind me, and you have the Russians right behind you. You're about to be sandbagged. Do you want to surrender to me or to the Russians?"[51] The German captain excused himself and walked back to a Mercedes and consulted with its occupant. Emerging from the Mercedes was

SS Lt. Gen. Felix Steiner who surrendered his III SS-Panzer Corps. Steiner was driven across the Elbe in Burriss's jeep with his men following behind.

Meetings between the victorious Western Allies and the Soviets were always joyful; especially for the Soviets. As mentioned earlier, the Germans fighting the Russians feared capture and fought stubbornly until they were either killed, reluctantly captured, or were able to flee to the west. The significance to a Soviet soldier of meeting with a Western ally meant more than an end to fighting—it meant he survived. Germany capitulated unconditionally to the Western Allies on May 8 and on the following day, May 9, in Berlin to the Soviet Union. After almost six years of war, the guns fell silent over Europe again.

Below left: German sniper trainees—rather older than many in the last days of the war. *Nik Cornish at www.Stavka.org.uk.*

Below: Canadian snipers Sgt. H. A. Marshall (left) and Cpl. S. Kormendy of HQ Coy., Calgary Highlanders, cleaning their No. 4 Mk. I (T) sniper rifles. Note both men are wearing Denison smocks. *Lt. Ken Bell, LAC.*

7 Drang Nach Osten[1]

"'This way, comrades,' shouted Ballers, proud of his exploit. 'There's nobody in there.' We all stood up, prepared to join him. He was laughing nervously. A crisp detonation whistled through the leaves, followed by two more. Prinz was running toward us, but Ballers wasn't. He was walking hesitantly, stretching one hand toward us. Then he fell."[2]

Guy Sajer
Großdeutschland

Blitzkrieg in Poland

German unpreparedness for sniping first evidenced itself during the invasion of Poland. While the speed of the German advance and conquest of the country caught the world by surprise, there was one stumbling block that would recur repeatedly to haunt the Germans. In this case, it involved a sole Polish rifleman against an unwary panzer unit.

"Not all the sniper's work will be at short and mid-ranges. There are many types of terrain in Europe and Asia where long-range shots will be possible and tactically useful. Published photographs of enemy troops in action, and reports from both United Nations and Axis sources prove this assertion. The crews of German tanks have consistently left the shelter of their vehicle to make repairs to damaged treads, in utter contempt of the possibility of being liquidated by long-range small-arms fire. In at least one reported instance, some unnamed Polish sniper disorganized a German tank group and delayed their forward progress for almost a half-hour by killing or wounding the entire crews of two German medium tanks when they exposed themselves to make exterior repairs. One of the men killed happened to be the Lieutenant in command of that particular tank group. This incident was reported by German, not Polish, sources, and was cited as evidence of the unsportsmanlike conduct of the Polish."[3]

Experience in Poland caused a clamor among the German infantry for a designated marksman's rifle with a low-powered scope that would enable the user to silence a pillbox or a machine gun. Development was started on the Zf41 long eye-relief scope.

Finnish prelude

On November 30, 1939, the Soviet Union invaded Finland. Misled by reports from the Soviet Embassy in Helsinki, Stalin expected the Finnish proletariat to rise, overthrow the government, and finish the revolution that started in 1918. Because of this, many of the divisions sent were reserve units that expected to be welcomed as liberators. The Finns thought otherwise.

If anyone stands out as a sniper in that war, it is the Finn Simo Häyhä. Prewar, he volunteered in the Civil Guard where he perfected his marksmanship under the tutelage of World War I veterans. The guard met on weekends and its members were free to return to home and work during the week. By contrast, the Finnish Army had no equivalent training program and very few scoped rifles. Without the budget, the army lacked equipment and what it did have was obsolete. This didn't discourage Häyhä. Nicknamed "Dead-Eye Dick," he was also called the

Right: Unwary Soviet as seen through a sniper scope. *SA-kuva.*

"human machine gun" for his prowess. He disliked scoped rifles because using one caused his head to be slightly higher and more conspicuous as a target. Thus throughout his entire brief career as a sniper he relied on the iron sights of his SAKO-made M28-30 (serial #60974). Clad in white and camouflaging his rifle similarly with gauze, Häyhä once prevented an artillery bombardment by shooting out the two lenses of a spotter's telescope.[4] Häyhä killed as many as 23 Soviets on one day and at one point had 259 confirmed kills.[5] With the unconfirmed or those killed in regular combat, Häyhä's unofficial tally is as high as 542. He modestly admitted, "But I got some of them with machine pistols and machine guns in pitched battles when the Russians attacked en masse, and a fellow shouldn't count those. There's no sport in that."[6]

When the scoped rifle-armed Lt. Juutilainen was unable to kill a Soviet sniper, Häyhä was summoned to help.

"This Russian had taken up position about 400 metres from us and was constantly shooting towards our lines. After a while, the Lieutenant sent for me and showed me approximately where he knew the enemy sniper's position to be. One of our 2nd Lieutenants was with us, acting as spotter, when our duel begun. At first, I did not see a trace of him, just a small rock where he was supposed to be. After careful investigation, we spotted him behind a little hump of snow near that rock. I took a careful aim with my trusty M28-30 and the very first shot hit the intended target."[7]

In another incident Häyhä experienced Soviet retaliation for winning a duel against a Soviet sniper:

"Soon heavy artillery started sending their roaming regards. There was this forward observer and his crew nearby, and once I knocked out their sniper, they sent a swarm of shells in my direction from a rapid-firing cannon shooting direct fire. About fifty shells landed around my foxhole but in vain. Many of them sent clouds of sand on my face, but nothing worse than that was received."[8]

Most of the time Häyhä fought alone but there were a few times he partnered up with Cpl. Yrjö Malmi.

"In early February (1940), Corporal Malmi and I spotted a new area of enemy accommodation bunkers. The two of us set out to an observation to learn what was going on there. We moved

Victorious Finnish soldiers enjoying a smoke break as one man recounts the capture of a Soviet sniper rifle (August, 1941 near Kurkijoki). *SA-kuva.*

silently through the forest and got within 150 meters of the enemy bunkers, which were located between the front lines. We spent the whole day in our position and killed nineteen Russians. They never learned where we were and dared not to send a patrol out under those circumstances."[9]

The most Häyhä killed on any single day as a sniper was 25. Being a sniper didn't exempt him from close-in fighting, however, and Häyhä also used a Suomi submachine gun and grenades to kill the Soviet invaders. His combat career ended on March 6, 1940, when, while repelling a Soviet assault as a squad leader, he was struck in the jaw by an explosive bullet. He survived the wound and despite numerous plastic surgeries, remained disfigured the rest of his life.

Häyhä's amazing tally has come under some scrutiny. He began his combat career on November 30, 1939, and ended it on March 6, 1940, when he was injured. Within a mere span of 97 days of combat, depending on the total used, he either killed an average of 2.67 Soviets per day (259 victims) or 5.63 (542 victims). By his own admission Häyhä resorted to both an LMG and an SMG for repelling an infantry assault. Considering other snipers like Zaitsev, Allerberger, and Furness also carried SMGs at times, this is not at all unusual. Still, the figure of 542 kills is extremely high over such a short period and bears further investigation.

Another Finn is touted as a successful sniper: Sulo Kolkka, who is credited with over 400 kills. While it is said that Kolkka penetrated behind Soviet lines and hunted in areas the unwary Soviets thought were safe, and his most famous sniper duel involved

Finnish rifles

M1928/30
Caliber: 7.62mm x 53R
Weight: 9lb 10oz
Length: 46.75in. (1.19m)
Barrel: 27in. (68.58cm)
Magazine: 5-round internal
Operation: Bolt-action
Muzzle velocity: 2,297ft/sec
   (200 grain boat tail spitzer)

M37PH (M27PH)
Caliber: 7.62mm x 54R
Weight: 9lb 0.6oz
Length: 46.85in. (1.19m)
Barrel: 27in. (68.5cm)
Magazine: 5-round internal
Operation: Bolt-action
Muzzle velocity: 2,297ft/sec

M39PH
Caliber: 7.62mm x 54R
Weight: 9lb 14.4oz
Length: 46.75in. (1.19m)
Barrel: 27in. (68.5cm)
Magazine: 5-round internal
Operation: Bolt-action
Muzzle velocity: 2,297ft/sec

Below: Finnish sniper team on the River Svir in July 1942. The weapon is a captured Soviet SVT-40 sniper rifle. *SA-kuva.*

Bottom: Finnish sniper taking aim with captured Soviet M/91-30 PEM-scoped rifle, June 30, 1943. *SA-kuva.*

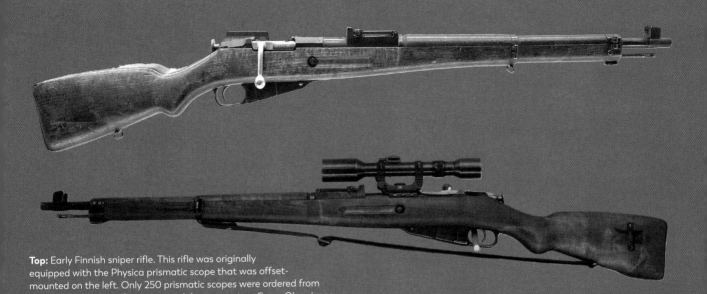

Top: Early Finnish sniper rifle. This rifle was originally equipped with the Physica prismatic scope that was offset-mounted on the left. Only 250 prismatic scopes were ordered from Physica Oy and even fewer survived. *Image courtesy Georg Oberaigner.*

Above: Finnish reworked Mosin-Nagant M39/43 into sniper rifle configuration. Besides a superior barrel whose bore was .310in. (7.9mm) it was required to shoot a three-shot 1.3in. (33mm) group at 100m for acceptance. The sling swivels are suitable for both infantry and ski troop use. Scope is a German Ajack 4x 90 on a top mount. Besides the locking lever on the right side, there is a centrally mounted tension screw that prevents slipping. *Image courtesy Alan Lundberg.*

Below: M/33 rifle with side-mounted Zeiss Zielvier 4x scope, August 1943. *SA-kuva.*

Bottom: Sgt. Maj. Vääpeli Varkila using an M39PH sniper rifle in April 1943. Note the Physica 3x24 sight. *SA-kuva.*

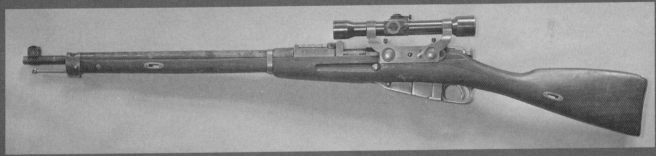

165

Explosive rounds

Two international agreements banned the use of explosive bullets against people. The first, 1868's Declaration of Saint Petersburg, was the first ever formal proposal to prohibit the use of a type of weapon in war. The declaration, which still has the force of international law, confirms the customary rule: the use of arms, projectiles, and material of a nature to cause unnecessary suffering is prohibited. It was later laid down in Article 23 (e) of the Hague Regulations on land warfare of 1899 and 1907.

Designed primarily for use by aircraft or antiaircraft weapons, though explosive rounds were banned by the Hague Convention this didn't stop them being used during World War II in sniper rifles. The main users were Russia and Germany, although both Finnish and Japanese snipers employed them too. Both sides accused the other of first use, and both used very similar types of round: a standard ball round with a steel pin and tetryl-filled primer that explodes 3–5 inches after impact. Japanese calibers were 7.7mm rimmed navy, 7.7mm semi-rimmed army, and 7.92mm rimless army bullets.

The Germans' bullets were known as B-Patrone rounds (B for *Beobachtung* = observation as they were primarily intended for Luftwaffe use); the Russians', PZ. Perhaps the most famous casualty of an explosive round was Simo Häyhä, whose career was ended after being severely wounded by one. It took 26 operations and 14 months' recuperation to rebuild his shattered face.

Availability was problematic and the Germans—who often used captured Russian sniper rifles—hoarded any explosive bullets they could find (see Roth and Allerberger story on p. 231).

Armor-piercing rounds were developed during World War I and also used in World War II to deal wih armored shields. Anti-tank rifles could prove highly effective as sniper rifles although the quality of the ammunition meant they were not always the most accurate of weapons.

Tracer and incendiary rounds were also used but, again, the St. Petersburg and Hague conventions had pronounced them illegal for anti-personnel use.

using an iron-sighted rifle to kill a Soviet sniper at over 650yd, no verifiable evidence of his existence or victims can be found.[10]

Besides deploying its own snipers, the Red Army also resorted to propaganda that included encouraging articles making the killing of Finnish snipers seem simple. The "cuckoos"—as the Finnish snipers were called—were easily shot from their trees. In reality, it was Finnish artillery observers who ascended trees and not snipers. By far the highest casualties in the Winter War were the Soviets', whose performance was not helped by Stalin's purges of the Red Army, particularly its officers, that started in 1937. One Soviet infantryman complained about fighting the Finns, "They cut us down like a sickle." By contrast,

Above right: Finnish sniper surveying the battlefield from ruins. If this were a combat situation, he would not have silhouetted himself against the sky. *SA-kuva.*

Right: Finnish sniping team. Finns were not adverse to using a spotter to help them locate targets. *SA-kuva.*

a jubilant Finn effused, "I like fighting the Russians, they fight standing up."[11]

As successful as the Finnish infantry were, they could not stand up to the overwhelming Soviet resources. Shortly after Häyhä's wounding, the Soviets compelled Finland to the negotiating table and in the Moscow Peace Treaty, Finland ceded 11 percent of its land to the Soviet Union. As one Soviet general bitterly commented, "We gained 22,000 square miles of territory. Just enough land to bury our dead."[12] In an unsuccessful bid to regain its lost territory, Finland would later ally itself with Germany in what the Finns called the Continuation War. Häyhä attempted to reenlist but was refused. His injuries were too serious to permit him to serve again. However, in recognition of his bravery, he was awarded Finland's highest honor: the Mannerheim Cross.

Russian sniping

As we have seen in Chapter 1, the Soviet Union was an early adopter of sniping as part of its defense efforts. Prewar Soviet doctrine emphasized sniping and there were extensive programs to train soldiers and civilians alike. However, Stalin's purge of the army (1936–38) eliminated many forward-thinking military leaders, the best known of whom was Marshal of the Soviet Union Mikhail Tukhachevsky. There's little doubt that this—and the subsequent reorganization of the Red Army that was underway when the Germans attacked—had an effect on every level of the army. To what extent it affected Russian sniping is difficult to quantify. However, the demand for snipers became so great that ad hoc field schools had to be established as an expedient means to increase the availability of snipers. This undoubtedly led to inconsistent training and meant that some Soviet snipers lacked a common knowledge base or skill level. This could well explain the poor shot witnessed by Capt. Clifford Shore and his suggestion to divide Soviet claims by 100![13] On the other hand, the Russians proved extremely fast learners, and by mid-1942, many first-class snipers were being produced.

"It was our first attack, for which we had meticulously prepared. Company commander Kruglov had split up the snipers, assigning one pair to each platoon. Ulyanov and I joined Vladimirov's platoon in the attack.[14]

"Major Chityakov ordered Senior Lieutenant Kruglov to send forward a group of snipers, in order to pick off enemy machine-gunners ensconced in the buildings. While successful, one was killed and another injured."[15]

Left: Finnish sniper seen here with either PE or PEM-equipped M91/30. While the Finnish snipers had the upper hand in the Winter War, the Soviets dominated the Finns in the Continuation War. *Author's collection.*

Below left and Below: Simo Häyhä (1905–2002) was one of the most remarkable snipers of the war, whose career was cut short when he was badly wounded in the face by an explosive bullet on March 6, 1940—less than a month after he had been honored to receive a nameplated SAKO M/28-30 "Pystykorva" honorary rifle. He recovered from his wound and died, aged 96, in a veterans' nursing home. *SA-kuva; Klokster/WikiCommons (CC BY-SA 3.0).*

Soviet snipers were issued white camouflage clothing for winter warfare. Sgt. Khidov fought on the Northern Front and has camouflaged with SVT-40 Tokarev with white cloth. *Author's collection* .

Within a company, snipers could be divided among platoons. After Joseph Pilyushin's battalion (105th Separate Rifle Regiment) was disbanded, its members were absorbed into the 14th Regiment, 21st NKVD Division, and the snipers became regimental assets who were parceled out among the regiment's battalions. At other times Soviet snipers operated alone: "as close as possible to the German lines, settle into our favorite shellhole or other convenient hiding place and, before the sun was fully up, manage to camouflage ourselves, take a good look around and make ourselves at home. The front line was our second home, one in which we spent more time than in our own dugout."[16]

When units were replaced, the snipers remained behind temporarily to orientate their relief:

"When sub-units were replaced on the sector where we were located, one or two snipers who had made themselves thoroughly familiar with the enemy defences were left behind as 'over-timers.' Their job was to help the fresh sub-unit to adjust to the new location and come to terms with the environment. But, as a rule, we stayed on as part of this new company or battalion until the next shift arrived. And this was all repeated with the following shift. The troops went on leave, but the snipers continued working without a day off."[17]

In anticipation of an ambush mission, Yevgeni Nikolaev (154th NKVD Rifle Regiment) cleaned his rifle and carefully loaded up with different ammunition. While a mission might only be a day's length, Nikolaev carried enough ammunition for a week. He did not limit himself to ball cartridges but carried all types (tracer, armor-piercing, explosive). Each cartridge was inspected and wiped down before inserting them in his pockets. His ammunition belt was also filled. Other equipment included high explosive and anti-tank grenades, a Finnish knife, gas mask, a smaller sapper shovel, and two handguns. The last things he packed were bandages. Food and water were left behind because he felt that food could make a soldier drowsy. Nikolaev wore a padded jacket and left his greatcoat behind as it inhibited mobility.[18]

Prior to leaving, the company commander, scouts, and military security needed to be informed. This was to ensure that no one would become a victim of friendly fire when returning from their stalk. Having done this, Nikolaev would discretely slip past their lines. Once at the desired location, he spared no effort in digging a hole. A good hole made the difference between life and death. Then from his camouflaged hide hours were spent studying the enemy's position. Once, Nikolaev identified what he thought was an enemy HQ bunker. He estimated the distance to be some 750yd and waiting for machine-gun fire to mask his shot, he confirmed the distance by firing a tracer round [Not always a good idea! A tracer works both ways and could have divulged his location to the enemy]. With the final adjustments made to his scope, all he had to do was to wait for a target to appear.[19]

With regards to the deployment of female snipers, if they graduated from a women's sniping school, they were sent out in platoon strength. If they trained individually before the war through the *Osoaviakhim*, then they could be integrated into any infantry unit. Such was the case of Lyudmila Pavlichenko and Zina Stroyeva—see pp. 190–2.

* * * * *

When the Germans attacked the 602d Rifle Regiment near Leningrad, the Russians launched a counterattack—including the snipers. Joseph Pilyushin participated in close-quarter combat and bayoneted a German.[20] After crossing the Dnieper River in March 1944 the Azerbaijani 416th Rifle Division was depleted and a regimental commander ordered forward his reserve of anti-tank gunners, scouts, signalmen, and snipers fresh from sniper school. Adjutant Isiah Bondarev knew better and said:

"The sniper's task is to choose a special position and shoot, but we threw them into the attack, like ordinary soldiers. When we went on the offensive, there was, of course, bitter resistance.

Again, there was no artillery; there was nothing to suppress the enemy's firing positions … At this time, I looked around, and many of these young guys … [these] poor young snipers were killed."[21]

Soviet female sniper Roza Shanina also joined in infantry attacks instead of supporting them. Finally, for her own safety, a battalion commander and a political commissar chased her away.[22] At other times snipers were used in support of an infantry attack. In this case, snipers were ordered to eliminate enemy snipers, machine-gunners, and—naturally—leaders.[23] It was not unusual for snipers at close quarters to carry additional firearms. When noted sniper Vassili Zaitsev found himself at close quarters, he along with another sniper used submachine guns to repel a German attack. They also had plenty of grenades.[24] When the Red Army launched Operation *Iskra* ("Spark"— January 12–30, 1943) to lift the siege of Leningrad, not only did sniper Mark Epshtein join in the infantry assault, he and his comrades were offered pure alcohol (many diluted it with snow) to stiffen their resolve.[25] In the final approach to Berlin, Soviet snipers also rode atop tanks. Their purpose was to shoot down *Panzerfaust*-armed German infantrymen.[26]

Around Rzhev-Bryansk, the Soviets introduced a novel (to the Germans) method of moving snipers.

A German radio broadcast mentioned, "White polar dogs [Samoyeds, some huskies, and Yakutian Laikas] pulling white sleds on which were Siberian snipers dressed in white coats and masks." The same mode of transportation was used by machine-gunners on both sides. While the Finns used dogs and reindeer to move equipment, they did not use them in a combat capacity as the Soviets did. One German complained: "They came like a flash, emptied machine guns against our lines and before we could reply they were out of sight."[27]

As in most World War II armies, Soviet snipers were used to eliminate signals or communications men.[28] Soviet scouts and snipers knew that if a telephone line was cut, a signalman would come along to repair it. It provided an opportunity for a scout to nab a "tongue" (Soviet slang for prisoner) or for a sniper to rack up a kill.

Soviet female snipers

The Soviet Union used women in front-line roles to a greater extent than other combatant nations. However, as well as nurses, stretcher-bearer, medics, artillerists, pilots, and tankers, the Red Army employed female snipers. It deserves more than a cursory look.

In an incident related earlier (see p. 68), a company of Dutch volunteers attached to the 5th SS Panzer Division *Wiking* was temporarily halted by a female sniper which took a German sniper three days to locate and eliminate. She was only one among thousands of women who fought as snipers. Patriotism and love of country is not exclusive to men, as that unknown Soviet woman proved. In the 1930s, Nazi ideology viewed women's place in society as in the home as mothers

Left: Roza Shanina. Also called the "Terror of East Prussia" she wears the Order of Glory 2d Class and Order of Glory 3d Class. She was wounded while trying to protect an injured officer and died in a hospital in Ilmsdorf, East Prussia, on January 28, 1945. *Courtesy the Central Museum of the Armed Forces, Moscow via Stavka.*

Photo from 1944 *Izvestia* (Information) Newspaper shows four PU scoped armed Soviet female snipers. *GF Collection.*

Deserters and shirkers

Desertion was a problem in every army—the Allied figures for the Italian campaign are eye-opening—but in the vast battles on the Eastern Front the numbers were of a significantly higher magnitude. Part of the reason for this is the death rate of PoWs on both sides. Offered the "choice" between a 50%+ death rate and working for the Germans, unsurprisingly many Soviets "deserted." An estimated 588,400 Soviet soldiers deserted to the Germans and another 994,300 were convicted of intent to desert. In either the German or Soviet armies, desertion meant execution. Keenly aware that some Slavic prisoners became German *Hilfswillige* (volunteers)—*Hiwis*—who performed auxiliary service in the rear areas and that the Germans recruited non-Slavic minorities into their own fighting units, desertion was not something the Soviets took lightly. It represented not only a loss of manpower, but also a substantial increase in the enemy's. Soviet officers were fearful if a man deserted that it was viewed as a failure on their part to control their men and prevent the desertion. After a tribunal, an officer's punishment included being demoted to private and transferring to a penal battalion. Junior Lt. Boris Gorbachevsky prevented desertion in his company by mixing his men according to nationalities so the likelihood of conspiring to desert reduced. He also designated two men as snipers whom he equipped with scoped rifles and instructed them to shoot at any movement (German or otherwise) in no-man's-land.[29]

Enemy snipers and the shirkers

While opposing snipers were generally hated and had to be eliminated, there was one group appreciative of their presence—shirkers. In the presence of a German sniper, Soviet men as well as other nationalities exposed their hand (or another body part) above the trench in anticipation of receiving a wound that would entitle them to leave the front. Soviet doctors, officers, and political commissars were always suspicious of non-lethal hand or foot injuries.[30] Americans and German officers were suspicious, too, of deliberate injuries or self-inflicted wounds, and in both the German and Soviet armies, soldiers who deliberately wounded themselves could be punished by execution.

Pfc. John M. Khoury of the 399th Infantry Regiment, 100th Infantry Division, spied a German foxhole that was across the open field that was no-man's-land. He then noticed a buddy in an adjacent foxhole waving at the German. Instead of shooting, the German waved back! Curious, Khoury called out to his buddy, "Why are you waving at the German? Or is he waving at you?" "I want to get a million dollar wound in my arm," came the response. It didn't work.[31]

insisted that they were nurses and auxiliaries and denied that the captured women were soldiers. It was finally decided in Berlin that if a woman was captured in uniform, she would be treated as a prisoner. If she was out of uniform and caught taking pot-shots at the Germans, she would be tried and executed. Of course, a much worse fate could await any Russian woman regardless of the capacity in which she served if she was captured by the Germans. As a female sniper, Yulia Zhukova feared being captured and explained that it was common knowledge that a female sniper would be tortured and abused before being killed. Zhukova saw the results of one dead comrade. Years after the war Zhukova was haunted by nightmares about being captured.

As the war progressed, more Soviet women entered the army as snipers. Initially, the first were graduates of the *Osoaviakhim*. They were later joined by those trained in a field school or women from the Central Women's School of Sniper Training. Nina Alexeyevna Lobkovskaya and Vera Ivanovna Artamonova were graduates of the latter. While other female snipers in adjacent battalions began scoring, Lobkovskaya and Artamonova couldn't spot any Germans to shoot. Their dry spell was eventually broken:

> "Finally, we spotted a soldier who was emptying water out of the trench. Every once in a while, he popped out to empty the bucket. We both took aim and shot at the same time. Chernykh, who was watching through his binoculars, yelled out, 'Yeah! Now that'll show you're supposed to shoot!' Immediately came to the question, 'To whom do we attribute the kill?' We decided to split it, half and half."[32]

Lobkovskaya racked up another six kills before being transferred to another division. Before the war ended, she and her classmates were fighting in Berlin.

One of the most enigmatic Soviet snipers is known to history only as the "black Marfusha." Krakow-born 21-year-old Fred Virski was studying chemistry at Jagiellonian University when the war broke out and interrupted his studies. He was working at a factory in Soviet-occupied Poland when he found himself drafted into the Red Army where he became a driver in an artillery unit. After many adventures, he found himself outside of Taganrog, a port city on the Sea of Azov near Rostov.

> "The room was gray with smoke and extremely noisy. Suddenly a hush fell over it. All eyes were turned toward the entrance. In the doorway stood a girl in uniform with a sergeant's insignia on

not warriors. This may have left the SS men mentally unprepared to see female combatants. They would see a lot more before the war was over. By 1944–45 German female could be found on the front line, particularly in the air defense of Germany as *Flakhelferinnen*.

When the Germans first came across Russian women in uniform a legal issue arose. Were they soldiers or not? What status should be accorded to them? The Russians

her collar. She wore a black fur cap [caps of Red Army soldiers are gray] and was accompanied by a major. When the couple had seated themselves, the babble of voices broke out again.

"'Who's that?' I asked my friend the lieutenant.

"The answer was a strange story. The girl's name was Marfusha, popularly known as the 'black Marfusha' on account of her cap. Like thousands of Russian girls, she had volunteered for front-line service. Unlike most of them, Marfusha had a fiancé from whom she never separated. The boy was young, handsome, and courageous. Together they went off on patrols, deep into no-man's-land, even behind the German lines. The girl was a first-class sniper, with more than a few kills to her credit. During the first day of the Rostov offensive, they had both fallen into the hands of the Nazis. The Germans, realizing that they were dealing with lovers, first raped the girl more than a dozen times under the boy's eyes, and then, bringing her back to consciousness by douching her with water, they tortured the youth to death. Thanks to an almost superhuman constitution, the girl lived through the ordeal and by some miracle managed to escape. Having wandered about the snow-covered steppe for two days and nights, she'd been picked up by Soviet sentries in a state of utter exhaustion. Back in her own regiment she had regained her physical health, but the experience had proved too much for her nervous system. She was definitely not quite sane. But it had not prevented her from her career as a sniper. Working all alone now, she still managed to penetrate behind the German lines, picking off Nazis while hiding in ditches or in the tops of trees. During the last few days she had become an almost legendary figure on our sector of the front. Some stories had her in two places at once, others that she disposed of a hundred Germans in a week. In appearance Marfusha was definitely beautiful, with bright golden hair over distinctly tragic features. *Her* eyes were never still, she kept looking from face to face, as though still in search of her boy whom, so the lieutenant told me, she refused to believe dead."[33]

While nothing else is known about her, she was likely a graduate of the prewar *Osoaviakhim* sniper program either at a university or a factory.

Twenty-year-old Klava Loginova and her partner Tosya Tinigina were in a trench observing the German lines. Klava already had 16 kills to her credit and, unlike her partner, was no stranger to combat. They were in an area where several Soviet soldiers had been shot by a sniper and they were looking for him. Klava

scanned for clues to his location. Using her scope, she spotted an embrasure camouflaged with leaves. Scrutinizing it, she spotted a rifle but held her fire. She had to be certain he was present. A slight twitch of the leaves alerted her. She could see her adversary and even his ginger hair. They fired almost simultaneously. Her recoil knocked her back (slightly) and saved her

Below: German officers check the papers of a Russian nurse. Neither side treated female combatants well. *NARA.*

Bottom: Czech sniper Marie Ljalková and her SVT-40. *USSR Information Bulletin.*

Soviet female snipers from the Third Shock Army, First Byelorussian Front, May 4, 1945. From front to back, L–R:

Front row—Guards Sr. Sgt. V. N. Stepanova (on her account, 20 kills), Guards Sr. Sgt. Yu. P. Belousov (80), Guards Sr. Sgt. A. E. Vinogradov (83);

Second row—Guards Jr. Lt. E. K. Zhibovskaya (24), Guards Sr. Sgt. K. F. Marinkina (79), Guards Sr. Sgt. O. S. Marienkina (70);

Third row—Guards Jr. Lt. N. P. Belobrova (70), Guards Lt. N. A. Lobkovskaya (89), Guards Jr. Lt. V. I. Artamonov (89), Guards Sr. Sgt. M. G. Zubchenko (83);

Fourth row—Guards Sgt. N. P. Obukhovskaya (64), Guards Sgt. A. R. Belyakov (24).
GF Collection.

172

life. His bullet cut the strap and the wood forearm of her rifle. While credited with a kill, it took a long time before she stopped shaking from that experience.

Anya Multova was another female sniper. Like her male counterparts, she also became engaged in sniper v. sniper duels. In early July 1944, Anya Multova was near Minsk and advancing with the infantry when a Soviet horseman was shot. Scanning the woods, she saw the muzzle flash as another Soviet fell. Dashing into the woods, she flanked the position and then began crawling with her pistol toward the suspected location. She got within 30ft of him before jumping up and rushing him at gunpoint. In her butchered German she commanded, "*khende hokh, shmutsige shavaine!*" (Trans: *Hände hoch, schmutziges Schwaine*. English: Hands up, dirty pig!). His rifle was resting on a mound and being defenseless, he raised his hand to surrender. She shot him anyway and only afterward thought of taking him prisoner.[34] On October 17, 1944, Anya Mulatova was with her partner in the trenches at the Lithuanian town of Raczki. They got bored looking for the Germans and decided to amuse themselves by firing tracers into a barn to burn it. Tracers have a disadvantage in allowing the enemy to locate the firer's position and in this case, a German sniper spotted her. While Anya was reloading, she heard a gun report and sand flew around all. Blood started flowing and Anya began crying. Her partner also broke down and cried. Luckily the bullet had struck the barrel and shattered the stock. A piece of the stock struck Anya's forehead and injured her.

Another pair of female snipers who were school classmates, Natalia Koshova and Maria Polivanova, convinced a commissar to allow them to fight. Soviet sources say that, during their first six days of battle, they killed 36 Germans. Together they are credited with 300 kills before succumbing themselves. Both were posthumously awarded the Hero of the Soviet Union.[35]

Sniper Yulia Zhukova ended the war with eight confirmed kills, one of which was a sniper v. sniper duel. In this, she and her partner were ordered to eliminate a German sniper. Highly elusive, he had no observable pattern and after firing, would disappear for a few days only to fire from a fresh post a few days later. To find him, Zhukova enlisted their scouts to help locate where his shots came from.

"Then came the deciding day, when we went out to the front line with a clear goal—to stalk a German sniper. We took up our positions; I was in a machine-gun nest, and in a trench a little further away from me was my partner. We stood there, waiting and observing. Time passed slowly. It was getting cold, but running on the spot or even moving was out of the question—you could miss the enemy or give yourself away. Our 'neighbors' were silent—no movement, no shooting. Given the frost we had, they were probably freezing too. We were already tired and chilled to the bone, and our eyes had begun to water from the tension. Suddenly I had an idea. 'Lift your cap up over the parapet,' I told my partner. Quickly cottoning on what to do, she walked three or four metres away from me, put some sort of cap on a stick, raised it slightly over the parapet, lowered it and raised it again a few steps away, as if to represent somebody walking along the trench. The distinct, dry crackling of a shot rang out—a direct hit on the cap. Just a single shot; it was not followed up. It was him! From the sound I was able to determine roughly where the shot came from. I looked in that direction. In no-man's-land, at a slight angle from me, a bush seemed to sway a little. But no, it wasn't even a bush; rather, a shadow on the snow which flashed by and froze. So, that was where he was! I took aim and fired. Immediately I changed my position and pressed against the window in the gun-port. Now I could clearly see the bush sway and snow drop from it. Then it swayed once more and that was it. My partner and I continued our observation, and the soldiers in the trench also waited with interest to see what would happen. Nothing. All was quiet and peaceful. Nobody on the other side responded to my shot, even though our shots usually drew a volley in response."[36]

The next day the Germans released a barrage on the trench where Zhukova and her partner operated. To spare them from retaliation, no sniper was allowed to go forward that day.

First Sgt. Klavdia Grigoryevna Krokhina recalls an event that is testimony to the effectiveness of one female sniper:

"Our scouts took a German officer prisoner, and he was extremely surprised that so many soldiers had been killed at his position, and all with shots in the head. Almost in the same spot. A simple rifleman, he insisted, would be unable to make so many hits to the head. That's certain. 'Show me,' he asked, 'the rifleman who killed so many of my soldiers. I received a large reinforcement, but every day up to 10 men fell.' The commander of the regiment says: 'Unfortunately, I cannot show you. It was a girl sniper, but she was killed.' It was our

While there is abundant evidence of female snipers in the Soviet Army, this photograph of E. Popova of Astrakan was released for propaganda purposes. The rifle's small ejection port suggests it is a 22 LR and not a "three line" M91/30. *Author's collection.*

Sasha Shlikhova. She died in a snipers' duel. And what betrayed her was her red scarf. She liked that scarf very much. But a red scarf is visible against the white snow. When the German officer heard that it was a girl, he was staggered, he didn't know how to react. He was silent for a long time. At the last interrogation before he was sent to Moscow (he turned out to be a bigwig), he confessed: 'I've never fought with women. You're all beautiful … And our propaganda tells us it's hermaphrodites and not women who fought in the Red Army …' So he understood nothing. No … I can't forget."[37]

While serving as a hidden lookout, Krokhina saw a German who was barely exposed. She shot him and he fell. Krokhina paired up with another sniper as this allowed one to rest while the other maintained a vigilant watch for targets. Even then, her eyes and the eyes of her partner could get watery, the hands devoid of feeling, and the body numb. In the spring, the snow would melt beneath them, forcing them to lie in water. At dusk, it would freeze, sticking them to the ground. It was especially hard in spring. The snow melted and they spent whole days in water. They'd remain still in their nest, a tree or a rooftop as close to the enemy as possible. Sometimes they would be as close at 500yd and could hear German voices. By war's end, her tally stood at 75. While she returned home safely, she learned that her brother had been killed.[38]

While snipers in many armies were excused from standing guard, this was not necessarily the case in the Red Army. Sasha Yekimova and Dusya

Kekesheva were on sentry duty at night when their throats were cut to the point of almost decapitating them.[39] Besides fighting as snipers, Klava Loginova and Tosya Tinigina dragged 22lb crates of shells to the front line.[40] More humiliating was when a combat-proven female sniper squad was ordered to provide women to wash the headquarters floor. They refused and were sent to the guardhouse for which there was some compensation when the female cooks prepared special meals for them. Their refusal was not held against them when the regiment was preparing to invade East Prussia.[41]

Another platoon had just finished two and a half day's fighting when the deputy political officer ordered Lida Bakieva to provide two female snipers to wash his floors. Lida tried to wake them but they were dead asleep. Summoned by the political officer who demanded why no one had arrived to wash his floor, Lida Bakieva honestly replied that they, like the rest of the battalion, had been fighting for two days, were exhausted and sleeping. He immediately sentenced her to five days in the guardhouse which she mused would afford her an opportunity to sleep. While being escorted by a guard they ran into the Chief of Staff who asked where they were going. Lida explained what had happened to which he responded, "Forget it. Go back and rest."[42]

When there was a shortage of trained nurses, male or female, the all-female sniper platoon that Yulia Zhukova belonged to was pulled off the line and dispatched to various hospitals as nurses.[43] While this was far from the optimal use of snipers, what Zhukova didn't realize at the time is that the presence of a woman in a hospital improved wounded men's morale and with it their recovery rate.[44] The shortage of stretcher-bearers also resulted in Nina Lobkovskaya's entire female sniper platoon being made temporary stretcher-bearers.[45]

It was not all bad and there were advancement opportunities. Jr. Lt. M. Nicholas met a Voroshilov Marksman badge-holding Ukrainian Jew who also won a gold medal for German language, literature, and poetry before volunteering in the Soviet Army. She served two years as a sniper, and because of her knowledge of German was transferred to intelligence where she was among the best interrogators in the Second Guards Tank Army. While primarily a staff officer, she could be called upon as a scout who, along with other intelligence personnel, crossed the lines to capture prisoners.[46] Another example was Irinia Botnar who graduated from the Central Women's School of Sniper Training and afterward transferred to the NKVD where she worked as a censor. Despite her training, she never fired a shot.[47]

The worst was when a commanding officer demanded sex or forced himself upon a woman. One female sniper was locked up for two days before escaping with the help of her platoon. Another had a bald, middle-aged lieutenant colonel attempt to rape her.[48] Vera Barakina and her squad were assigned to 715th Infantry Regiment. While their commander was delighted to have them and respected them as soldiers, some of his subordinate officers did not. Vera refused the advances of one officer who began threatening her. She produced a grenade and threatened to throw it into the stove if he didn't desist. He left rather than be blown up.[49] When the Soviet 331st Infantry Division (Thirty-first Army) reached Poland, the petite and slim sniper Zosia from Samoteka was grabbed and dragged by a lieutenant toward his dugout. Luckily, outraged male soldiers disregarded the consequences and punched him numerous times to free her.[50]

Lt. Moisey Abramovich Chernoguz led a penal platoon composed of freed murderers, rapists, and robbers who had been released on parole provided they enlisted. Despite the reputation of Chernoguz's men:

> "the women's company commander asked me to send my criminals to keep the girls from getting harassed. I had to be a peacekeeper and protect the girls from our front-line soldiers. People got out of control. You see, our environment was completely unpredictable. So the reconnaissance soldiers raced to see the girls, and my soldiers, who were huge guys, wouldn't let them through. My soldiers were mature; they understood."[51]

During the 1945 New Year's Eve celebration Captain Pdznyakov made advances on female sniper Dogadkina. When she declined, he ordered her to stand at attention and verbally abused her. "We know why you have been sent here. You are all whores and prostitutes and you have been sent for us to ..."[52] Even the Soviet counter-intelligence officers of *SMERSH* (*Smiert' Shpionam*—death to spies) were not above attempting to force themselves on the female snipers. Happily, they were turned back by the timely arrival of a defiant company commander and the *Komsomol* instructor.[53] Roza Shanina knew female snipers who had been raped. She herself turned away advances by many men.[54] Additionally, if Shanina's views are representative of Soviet women, women who lacked carnal knowledge were girls and those who experienced it during service as women. In her platoon within the 157 Infantry Regiment, only five out of 27 remained virgins.[55] Yulia Zhukova was transferred out of her all-female sniper platoon to an all-male artillery battery where she refused the drunken advances of her commanding officer and in so doing, earned the admiration of the men in her battery who adopted her as their own *fille du regiment* and protected her.[56]

After Germany surrendered, some female snipers were sent to the Far East for the war against Japan. Once there, Zoya Mikhailoa and other female snipers became telephone operators before being demobilized. Postwar the female snipers (and other female soldiers) were often shoddily treated after discharge. Post-traumatic stress disorder affected them, too, and adjustment for them was no different from any other combat veteran. Sniper Bella Epstein remembered:

> "I came back different ... For a long time I had an abnormal reaction with death. Strange, I would say. They were inaugurating the first streetcar in Minsk, and I rode on that streetcar. Suddenly the streetcar stopped, everybody shouted, women cried, 'A man's been killed! A man's been killed!' And I sat alone in the car. I couldn't understand why everybody was crying. I didn't feel it was terrible. I had seen so many people killed at the front ... I didn't react. I got used to living among them. The dead were always nearby ... We smoked near them, we ate. We talked. They were not somewhere out there, not in the ground, like in peacetime, but always right there. With us."[57]

Of the 1,885 women who graduated from the Central Women's School of Sniper Training, over 250 were killed in combat. Collectively though, they were credited with killing over 10,000 Germans.

Despite Soviet assertions of having an egalitarian society and the treatment of women as equals, women who served in the Soviet Armed forces in any capacity were viewed suspiciously as front-line whores. Dubbed *Pokhodno-Polevye Zheny* (PPZh or "marching field wives" or "campaign wives"), Soviet citizens were suspicious of women with medals. When the medal for military service, the *Za Boyeve Zaslugi* was seen worn by a woman, it was derisively called, *Za Polyovye Zaslugi* (for sex services).[58] Prospective in-laws viewed it degrading if their son chose a soldier wife. Many successful female snipers hid their military achievements and honors; especially if they wanted husbands. It wasn't until many decades later when they began receiving the recognition and acceptance they deserved.[59]

Operation Barbarossa

On June 22, 1941, in an unprovoked attack to fulfill the Nazi quest for *Lebensraum*, the German

Non-Russian female snipers or female *francs-tireurs*

Private Sam Burns recalls the capture of a female "sniper" to the newspapers: "One day we captured a sniper who turned out to be a woman about 23 years old. Boy, was she mad when we got her. Maybe it's a good thing I don't understand German or French. She had plenty to say. She wore a regular German camouflage suit."[60] Canadians captured a Frenchwoman who was, according to intelligence, the leading quisling in the village.[61] Another newspaper reported a German female prisoner who sniped at soldiers. The article added, "Among the many women snipers in France, Irma, Myra, Erna—whatever her name is—is said to be the second woman sniper taken prisoner, but I'm assured by the men back on brief leave that she was the only woman sniper captured."[62] She may be the same "Myra," who claimed to be of Polish descent and was forced into German service as a cook, and who was later sent to an enemy internment camp on the Isle of Man.[63]

The female wing of the *Hitlerjugend*—Hitler Youth—for teenage (14–18-year-old) girls was the *Bund Deutscher Mädel* (BDM—League of German Girls). It did not include small-arms training for its members and emphasized health. Nazi ideology held that women's place was in the home: marriage and having children were their duties. Only a handful of BDM leaders (200) received marksmanship instruction (as did female concentration camp guards). As Germany's position worsened, so women and girls became involved in the fighting. By April 1945, when collapse was imminent, Goebbels asserted his plenipotentiary powers over Berlin's defence as Reich's Defense Commissar for *Wehrkreis* III (Berlin) and ordered the SS to give housewives five hours of rifle instruction.[64]

Yet there were strange cases of armed women being captured. Thirty-one-year-old Frenchwoman Audette Chraud was (she claimed) hired by the Nazis to shoot Americans. She was incarcerated aboard the hospital ship whose commanding officer, Maj. Edward Wagenaar, said, "Our own men over there have told us of squads of Frenchwomen who get so much a head for a Yank. You'd be surprised at the number of casualties that were hit by women. It just looks like in that particular area there are too many Frenchwomen who are pro-Nazi."[65] Pfc. Joseph Motil of Co. L, 3/22d Infantry, 4th Infantry Division remembered the killing of a woman who was shooting at the Americans from a tree in Normandy.[66] A 56-year-old woman in Normandy was caught by one patrol after shooting at Americans.[67] The numerous reports of female snipers prompted the British to send an officer to Normandy to investigate them. The unnamed officer couldn't sustain a single allegation.[68] In clearing out Cherbourg, grenades flung out of a second-story window prompted the 39th Infantry Regiment, 9th Division GIs including Andriello Sebastian to storm the house. Rather than assault up the staircase and into the room, they sprayed the ceiling with gunfire. After the uniformed bodies were rolled over, it was discovered that they were German female auxiliaries.[69] In Sicily, Sicilian women shot at Canadians and when captured, were treated like any other PoW.[70] When Lt. Alexander M. Mather (378th Infantry Regiment, 90th Infantry Division) was fighting at Falck (SW of Saarlautern, today's Saarlouis), they came across the body of a woman dressed in *Flecktarn* (mottled camouflage).[71]

In France, Italy, Yugoslavia, and Greece, female fighters were known to take up arms and fight the Germans.[72] A 23-year-old Marseille Frenchwoman known only as Genevieve shot two Germans. She said, "I think women can kill Germans just as well as the men. After all we were oppressed by the Germans just as much, if not more, than men. The home is all right for women in peacetime but in war they should help kill the enemy, especially if that enemy invades your hometown."[73] Combat Engineer Pfc. Fred Kelly was with Fifth (U.S.) Army fighting in Italy when he wrote home about the Italian partisans:

"There were 12 Partisan girl snipers there that could out-shoot many a good man. They were also the cooks for the Partisans. One girl there had killed over 25 Jerries and had destroyed three tanks by replanting Jerry mines where their own tanks were sure to run over them. She also destroyed an ammunition dump by using a mine and a pull string that set it off. She was a very nice girl, rather attractive and with a sweet smile. The Jerries had killed her brother and parents because they had aided the

Partisans, and when she escaped she vowed she would shoot 10 Jerries for each one of her family they killed."[74]

With the exception of the American islands of Attu and Kiska, the American nation was in no danger of invasion. Prewar American Naval War College studies revealed that no major power had either the amphibious capability to attack the American continent or sustain an invading army if it should arrive on American soil. Most Americans weren't aware of that, though. In New Jersey, a female defense unit—the Molly Pitcher Brigade—was raised and drilled and practiced rifle marksmanship.[75]

Reports of female fighters were not limited to Europe, and there are details of them in the Pacific theater. Marine Sgt. Lee Ann Cassity told of a naval officer on Guadalcanal who encountered a female sniper. He said the navy man whirled and drew his pistol and fired it off at the sniper in three seconds. Her only garments were sections of coconut bark which also served as camouflage.[76] At Tulagi, 1st Sgt. Matthew Gerschoffer, USMC, reported:

"A number of Jap women snipers, prostitutes imported from Korea, were engaged in the fighting and would sometimes come out of the caves trying to entice the marines within range of the guns of their hidden comrades. It may seem cruel, but there was nothing to do but to shoot them. They were just as dangerous as the men."[77]

Pfc. John C. Bruns was one of fighter ace Capt. Joe Foss's squadron ground crew. He also reported coming across a female sniper at Guadalcanal.[78] Despite all these reports, no photographic evidence has yet to be produced to support the proposition that Japanese women fought as soldiers, yet alone as snipers. We do know that before their surrender, the Japanese militarists were quite willing to arm mainland Japanese women with bamboo spears to attack the Occidental invaders. Thankfully, capitulation precluded this drastic measure.

A partial explanation of the women among Japanese garrisons may be explained by Japan's practice of forcing Korean, Chinese, and others into slavery as "comfort women" or at Tulagi where nurses who were dressed in white, exited a hospital, and enticed marines to step

Apart from the Soviet Army, other nations did not use female combatants. Irregular forces like this woman were the exception and the vast majority of women who picked up a rifle fought as a *franc-tireur*.

On Okinawa USMC Pfc. Gosch shot a rifle-armed woman when she was running across a rice paddy. He examined her body the next day and took her hat as a souvenir. Gosch described the shooting, "At that point I didn't know if it was a he or a she. Didn't make any difference. Bingo! [Indicating with his hands that he had fired his rifle.] I went out the next morning and sure enough here it is. A woman. Japanese." *Author's collection.*

into the open where they were gunned down by hidden Japanese soldiers.[79] The Stockholm Syndrome comes to mind where the hostage identifies with and ties their survival to the survival of the captor/hostage taker. Another arises from Buna, New Guinea, where Sgt. Ralph C. Spencer found another plausible explanation: "When I shot the sniper, I discovered it was a woman—a Jap nurse."[80] Finally, it is possible the Japanese "women" snipers were not women at all. Capt. Siegfried F. Lindstrom who was fluent in Japanese did some investigation and on Makin he questioned Japanese and Korean prisoners about a long-haired female sniper. They explained it wasn't a woman at all but rather a transvestite who wore his hair long and applied rouge and powder on his face daily.[81]

It is highly unlikely that other than the Soviet Union or guerrillas in the Balkans that Western women or Asian women who took pot shots at Allied soldiers were trained snipers. Rather, they are more akin to informal *francs-tireurs* with no military training approaching the level of boot camp, yet alone sniper school.

Wehrmacht plunged into the Soviet Union in a three-pronged attack: northeast toward Leningrad, formerly St. Petersburg, capital of Russia 1712–1918; east toward Stalin's capital, Moscow; and southeast into the Ukraine, Russia's breadbasket, and toward the Caucasus oilfields.

Army Group North

Under the command of *Generalfeldmarschall* Wilhelm Ritter von Leeb, Army Group North attacked the Baltic states. It was spearheaded by Panzer Group 4 (*Generaloberst* Erich Hoepner) and planned to cross the Dvina River and ultimately capture Leningrad. To accomplish this mission, it had two panzer corps—*Generalleutnant* Georg-Hans Reinhardt's XLI and *General der Infanterie* Erich von Manstein's LVI. Attached to Manstein's corps was a company of Brandenburgers, a specialized unit that relied on deception to capture key points such as bridges in advance of the tanks.

The Soviets dug round one-man foxholes or climbed trees and were cleverly camouflaged. They permitted the vanguard and tanks to pass by unmolested and waited for the service troops (cooks, supply, support vehicles) to appear before they began firing. This required some German front-line units to return to support their service troops. As it was difficult to force out the well dug in Soviet infantry, tanks sometimes span over the foxhole, burying the soldier alive.[82]

The Brandenburgers had just captured the bridge to Josvainiai in Lithuania and had suffered very light losses: three men. *Gefreiter* Sepp De Giampietro was among the victorious men and described what befell them:

"The first day, full of adventures and excitement, drew to a close. We sat on the embankment, close to the junction, like swallows on a telephone wire; we smoked and reviewed what had happened. Meanwhile, below us, the advance detachment kept rolling towards the east. Some random shots still reverberated through the night, but we didn't much care—for us, the work was finished

"Suddenly, one of our comrades flinched and tumbled down the embankment. A shot had hit him right in the neck, and he was dead on the spot. No time was wasted, and a troop was put together to comb the terrain. But we returned from our search none the wiser. It had probably been a chance hit, an errant bullet, particularly bad luck.

"In the meantime, some comrades had already dug a grave at the junction. Four bodies next to each other and wrapped in tarpaulin were lying there in the pit. A field priest had also arrived.

"'I'll go back for some planks to make a cross,' said a comrade, and he climbed up the embankment and approached a house that stood in a small orchard. We heard another shot, and this comrade too fell down, dead. We were seized by an indescribably fury.

"'There must be a sniper holed up over there, we'll smoke the swine out,' we said. We got hold of our weapons, circled the house, and threw hand grenades through the window. 'He's up there, up in the loft,' shouted a comrade. 'I got a clear view of him in the dormer window.' A volley of fire put an end to the nightmare. Just like in a Western, the Russian soldier fell from the dormer window.

"We buried the fifth comrade."[83]

In the initial stages of "Barbarossa," Battle Group Raus, 6th Panzer Division, XLI Panzer Corps advanced into Lithuania with its initial goal of Raseinai. Emerging from the swampy forested area east of Paislinis, it entered a meadowed area covered with fruit trees. As it moved into open country, a shot rang out: "The first victim of the ambush was the company commander, who was driving at the head of his column. Before he even had time to shout an order, he was shot through the forehead by a Russian sniper." Morale was high and the Kampfgruppe responded by attempting to flank and cut off the Russian retreat. *Generalmajor* Erhard Raus attributed most German casualties in this period to snipers and wrote that most casualties:

"resulted almost exclusively from snipers, concealed in the tops of the fruit trees and aiming at their targets from close quarters. These snipers

Capt. Grigoriev meeting workers from the October Factory. Grigoriev and his people are hosting a delegation of communists from the October District of Leningrad, who came to raise the fighting spirit of the soldiers. Shoulder straps were introduced to the Red Army in 1943. *From the fonds of the RGAKFD in Krasnogorsk via Stavka.*

remained in their hiding places even after the main body of the enemy withdrew, looking for worthwhile victims—primarily officers. The use of cover fire by regular Russian infantry helped to conceal the activity of the snipers.

"As long as the snipers fired during the height of the battle, they remained unnoticed, and it was not until they continued firing after the noise had died away that we discovered them and brought them down with machine-gun fire. The last of them tried vainly to flee, but immediately spotted in the open, they were killed by the fire of the nearest machine gun before they managed to reach the cover of the forest."

The removal of German officers slowed the advance and Raus commended his Soviet counterpart.

"The plan to have his snipers concentrate on eliminating our officers was especially clever. The commander and his numerically weak unit could take pride in the success of the ambush. It had forced our advance elements to interrupt their rapid motorized progress and caused a delay of more than one half an hour, as well as inflicting the casualties enumerated above."[84]

Raus elaborates on their camouflage:

"Artificial camouflage was another device used by the Russians. Even at the beginning of the war the Germans came across Russian troops wearing camouflage suits dyed green. Lying prone on the grass, these soldiers could be spotted only at a very short distance, and frequently were passed by without having been noticed at all. Reconnaissance patrols frequently wore 'left' suits of green cloth patches, which provided excellent camouflage in the woods. Russians wearing face masks were no rarity.

"The Russians enforced strict camouflage discipline. Any man who left his shelter during the day was punished severely, if it was forbidden for reasons of camouflage. In this way the Russians were able to conceal the presence of large units."[85]

Later, an infantry battalion sent to clear some woods was cut up:

"Several weeks later, while combing a forest for enemy forces, a battalion of the Infantry Regiment 465 was attacked from all sides by Russian tree snipers and lost seventy-five dead and twenty-five missing. ..."[86]

"The utmost caution had to be exercised when passing through unknown terrain. Even long and searching observation failed to reveal excellently

Two snipers on the Leningrad Front (1942). On left, Cpl. I. Plekhov armed with a top-mounted PEM-scoped M91/30. Leading him on the right is Sgt. P. I. Bedash whose M91/30 has a side-mounted PEM scope. *From the fonds of the RGAKFD in Krasnogorsk via Stavka.*

Leningrad postcards honoring snipers

1. Happy New Year! Smiling sailor sniper sends his greetings and in the lower image his bullet's trajectory passes through ten Germans.

2. Sniper Antonov is credited with 171 kills.

3. "Snipers."

4. Watercolor postcard honoring Hero of the Soviet Union Sr. Sgt. P. I. Golichenkov.

5. Sr. Sgt. M. Ia. Miranov, credited with killing 233 Finns.

6. Sr. Sgt. N. T. Rogulin, credited with 125 "Hitler-serving" Finns.

All photos Blavatnik Archive Foundation (http://www.blavatnikarchive.org).

1

Красноармеец - снайпер
Н. Т. ДОБРИК

2

Снайпер младший лейтенант
В. И. КУТАШКИН

3

Герой Советского Союза
П. Т. СОКУР

1. N. T. Dobrik is credited with 302 kills. He wears the Order of Lenin and the Order of the Red Banner.

2. Sniper Jr. Lt. V. I. Kutashkin was credited with 132 kills and wears the Order of Lenin. Postcard is dated 1944.

3. Naval infantryman scout-sniper P. T. Sokur is credited with killing a dozen men and capturing three in one battle.

4. The caption reads, "I raise my rifle like a sniper. For my native land I celebrate the anniversary of the Red Army today." The 273 references the tally of "Fritzes" killed.

5. The rhymes in this Russian poem are lost in translation: "In Leningrad style, acting skillfully, I will sum up my sniper result. While my letter was flying to you, another invader lay in the ground."

6. Sailor sniper Noah Petrovich Adamia in 1942. His Hero of the Soviet Union medal in the center. He died on July 4, 1942, during the siege of Sevastopol.

All photos Blavatnik Archive Foundation (http://www.blavatnikarchive.org).

4

5

6

As a member of a platoon guarding 86th Rifle Division HQ, Mikhail Liderman remembers female snipers being used there for sex. *Blavatnik Archive Foundation (http://www. blavatnikarchive.org).*

camouflaged Russians. Frequently our patrols passed by the immediate vicinity of Russian positions or individual riflemen without noticing them, only to be taken under fire from behind. Caution had to be doubled in wooded areas, where the Russians often had to be driven out individually, Indian fashion. There, sniping from trees was particularly favorable."[87]

After fighting in France, *Gefreiter* William Lubbecke's regiment became part of the army of occupation in Belgium. Their peaceful existence was disrupted when they were sent to Prussia as part of the XXXVIII Army Corps, Eighteenth Army, Army Group North. By September 15, they had passed Uritsk and could see the Gulf of Finland and were within seven or eight miles of Leningrad. Ordered to lay siege, they dug bunkers and fighting positions. Now serving as a forward observer, Lubbecke was promoted (October 1) to *Obergefreiter* (senior lance corporal) and found himself skiing a few hundred yards between the rear bunkers to the forward observation post. Skiing was faster and reduced his exposure to snipers. It was during this siege that Lubbecke first noted the presence of Soviet snipers:

"These sharpshooters had been posted in large numbers among the multi-story buildings at the edge of Leningrad's suburbs, approximately a mile away from our front line at Uritsk. This situation reflected the Red Army's effort throughout the war to field larger numbers of better-equipped, well-trained snipers than the *Wehrmacht*. Our snipers considered the Soviet scoped rifles superior and preferred to use captured Russian weapons rather than the equivalent German rifle. When I once had the opportunity to test one, its precision amazed me.

"The accuracy of sniper fire meant that the number of killed relative to wounded was much higher than with other weapons. Our helmets protected us pretty well from glancing bullets or shrapnel, but if a bullet hit one squarely it would easily penetrate the steel. Being six feet tall, I soon learned to keep my head down and travel quickly through any area where I might be vulnerable."[88]

In response to the German conquest of the Baltic States, on December 17, 1941, a new Soviet defensive line was set up by the Volkhov Front which was composed of the Twenty-sixth (later renamed Second Shock) and the Fifty-ninth armies. It would later be reinforced by the Fourth, Fifty-second, and Forty-fourth armies. It was anchored at its south on Lake Ladoga and deployed over 150 miles to Leningrad. One of the defenders was a female sniper known as Catherine, from Dimi near Leningrad, who killed at least 39 Germans. She acquired her marksmanship training in the field under combat conditions.[89]

As a boy, Vladimir Pchelintsev won many shooting awards. This proved useful when he became a soldier. Originally not a sniper, he approached his commanding officer and told him, "I am a good shot and I want to kill our enemies. Make me a sniper," and just like that, his commander issued him a scoped Simonov rifle. His first shot went wild, but after he became familiar with the weapon, he bagged four Germans that day. It was the beginning of an auspicious career, by the end of which he would be credited with 456 kills (including 14 snipers).[90] Pchelintsev once hid in a house across a stream where the Germans were about 330 to 380 yards away. Knocking a hole in the space between the ground floor and the upper level, he studied the houses that were across the stream. When someone appeared in an attic window, Pchelintsev shot him. When the German's companion tried to flee out the door, Pchelintsev shot him too. In another incident, Pchelintsev was leading a squad of snipers to a hill that overlooked the Germans on the other side of a stream. Eleven Germans began crossing and Pchelintsev instructed his squad to wait until he fired. When they fired, seven Germans were killed outright, two wounded and two escaped. Shots fired: 13.[91]

182

Pchelintsev learned to prepare at least four firing positions which were carefully camouflaged. To do this, he would dig them at night, haul away the dirt afterward so there would be no signs of excavation. He also learned to hunt at key spots such as water sources and farms (foraging points). While German snipers later learned to befriend artillerymen (especially to borrow officer jackets to construct decoys), Pchelintsev got binoculars or spotting scopes from his. For night shooting, especially known machine-gun loopholes, he had another technique:

"It's best to stick forked sticks [wooden slingshot-shaped sticks] at the firing position, on which you will put a rifle in the dark so as not to lose direction. The scope is pre-set, the goals are known. Besides that, the Germans themselves come to the aid of the sniper: they continually launch flares, and shoot with tracer bullets to detect targets. As soon as the firing points of the enemy come alive, aim and shoot at their loopholes."[92]

Not surprisingly, Senior Lt. Pchelintsev was involved in a sniper duel which he described:

"The antagonists sighted each other simultaneously. The German immediately dropped behind a stone and the Russian lowered himself into a shallow hole. They lay like this for four hours, without once shifting from their positions. The slightest movement of either would have brought a bullet from the other. Finally, the German moved behind the stone, exposing himself for a second, long enough for the Russian bullet to find him …

"Sometimes it is necessary to stay motionless for hours in a pouring rain, water running down one's face, under one's clothes and into one's boots. Sometimes in winter in a heavy frost one must be in the snow all day without eating. The only way to get warm a little is to wiggle one's fingers and toes. But movement is death and so one waits for the enemy to move first. Snipers must learn to shoot under most awkward conditions, lying behind tree stumps, sitting in the branches of trees, standing in a pit, stretched out on the open ground or doubled up for concealment. I once picked off an enemy corrector of artillery fire while I was lying in a swamp, my gun resting against a dry hummock, the rest of my body in the water. I shot at the enemy while I was practically swimming."[93]

Leningrader Mark Epshtein began the war in the ninth grade by digging defensive works for Leningrad. After graduating school he] became a member of the 78th Infantry Reserves Company during which he attended a two-month long sniper school before receiving basic training. He received a concussion during Operation *Iskra*, an offensive designed to break the siege of Leningrad. Following recovery he was transferred to the 123d Rifle Division and helped liberate Siverskaya. After being wounded in the fighting over Sizran, he was transferred to administrative posts. *Blavatnik Archive Foundation (http://www.blavatnikarchive.org).*

In another incident, a Soviet machine-gun embrasure was struck three times in succession. Alerted that they were faced with a sniper, the machine gunners reported it and Pchelintsev was summoned. Using binoculars, he began his hunt.

"[I] looked closely to every bush, hollow, and hill. It was winter time. In one place, the snow suddenly rose like a fan, a short flash flickered, the bullet hit our embrasure again. There is surely a fascist sniping. Mentally, I drew a line from that place to the embrasure. In relation to this line, the gunner must lie at an angle to the left. Now it was clear to me where to aim the rifle … Once again the snow fan rose. In response to that shot, I shot twice. There was no sniper in that place anymore."[94]

Originally Yevgeni Nikolaev belonged to the 154th NKVD Rifle Regiment. Upon its disbandment, its members were transferred to the 14th Red Banner Rifle Regiment of the 21st NKVD Division. At that time (June 26, 1941), it had no sniper detachment until 5th Company commander Lt. Vasily Butorin suggested raising one. This was approved. After training the snipers, he divided them into pairs and assigned them to specific parts of the line.

Ivan Dobrik was paired up with Yevgeni Nikolaev. The two had served together earlier on the Karelian Isthmus. Before daybreak they had been lying on the ground behind a snow parapet watching the German lines. It was getting dark, visibility decreased and

Dobrik began to grow impatient and suggested they leave. Nikolaev demurred, stating it was still too light and they could get a bullet if they moved. Then Nikolaev saw three Germans. Adjusting for crosswind and movement, Nikolaev aimed for the last German and pressed the trigger. After the German dropped, his two comrades continued on without noticing. Nikolaev aimed for the next German and killed him too. This time the surviving German took notice, looked back and stood over his fallen friend, gesturing for him to rise. This gave Nikolaev the time needed to work his bolt back, eject the spent cartridge and chamber a fresh round. Aiming again, he dropped the third German who collapsed on top of the second one.[95]

Nikolaev once went out alone and dug himself a hide in front of a tram. He spotted three Germans, two of whom were cleaning themselves with snow while a shirtless third began exercising. Nikolaev shot the shirtless man who was doing squats and had just lowered himself in another squat. He did not rise. His comrades noticed that he was down and picked him up. At that point, they realized he was dead but it was too late for one man. Nikolaev fired again and dropped one of them. The third man was shot down in quick succession.

A motorcycle with sidecar approached the HQ dugout that Nikolaev had ranged at 730yd with a tracer bullet earlier in the day. The overweight passenger was having difficulty dismounting from the sidecar and a tall German who was riding on the pillion jumped off to assist him. Nikolaev killed the driver first, who slumped over the handlebars as if he were asleep. The tall German got the sidecar rider out who then began stamping his feet. Nikolaev shot the sidecar passenger next while the tall German turned to speak to the driver. Getting no response from the driver, the tall German nudged him and then fell from Nikolaev's third shot. Six Germans had been killed from the same hide.

An officer then emerged from the HQ dugout and called for help. Two more officers emerged and began picking up the sidecar passenger. All three died. Nine dead from the same hide. An hour passed without anything happening. Suddenly, two Germans dashed for the motorcycle. Both fell to Nikolaev's bullets. Eleven dead from the same hide and it was enough for the Germans to have spotted his location. Rather than summon a German sniper to duel Nikolaev, the Germans called in artillery. The first two went over. The third one hit near Nikolaev's hide, knocking out and wounding Nikolaev and destroying his rifle in the process.[96]

During the winter of 1941–42, German sharpshooters began appearing on the Leningrad frontline. They were first noticed when observers were killed while peering through a pillbox view slot. Then, on January 15, 1942, 13th Division sniper Feodosy Smolyachkov, who had 125 kills to his credit, was himself killed. Swearing revenge for Smolyachkov's death, Nikolaev spent three days in the rear practicing his marksmanship on matchboxes tied to a piece of straw. He would hang these at 100yd and practice knocking down the matchboxes by cutting the straw. When he became proficient, he would increase the distance. Confident after three days of practice, he got permission from his battalion commander, Major Morozov, to duel with the German sniper. Morozov desperately wanted Nikolaev to prevail in this match where the loser's prize was death. When he asked Nikolaev how they could support him, Nikolaev asked that the men remain hidden but to continue firing. This would keep the German sniper searching for a target.

The next thing Nikolaev did was to determine the path of the bullets fired by the German sniper. This enabled him to narrow down the lair to an area near the tram line in front of the 3d Platoon. He also concluded that from the potential positions the German had, he could fire blindly into the Soviet trenches. The German didn't necessarily have to see a Soviet to hit one. Covering himself in a snow-white smock over his padded clothing, Nikolaev crawled out at night and positioned himself in no-man's-land. Then he waited for daylight. Neither Nikolaev nor his German opponent fired a shot that day. Nikolaev's ungloved right hand was stiff with cold as were his feet. Suddenly, he spotted an area that was slightly grayish. He made note of it and would return to it after scanning other areas. Then suddenly a white object emerged from it. It moved a couple of yards to the left and then disappeared. That was the German and he had just escaped retaliation.

Nikolaev pulled out some white sticks he had brought with him. He marked out the space where the German appeared and then disappeared. He then set up forks to support his rifle. One on the left, one in the center, and one on the right. He would focus solely on the areas between his white marking sticks tomorrow. Rather than disturb the snow, Nikolaev burrowed his way back to the trench. Frozen, he needed assistance to be lowered into it. The medic rubbed his feet until he could feel tingling and then advised him to cover them in grease before going out tomorrow.

It was four in the morning when Nikolaev was awakened. After eating, he rewrapped his rifle in white cheesecloth. He had procured boots two sizes larger to allow him to slip on wool socks over his greased feet, newspapers for insulation, and then double foot wraps. After donning his white smock over his padded jacket, Nikolaev retraced his path back to his hide.

Despite the known area he would concentrate on, Nikolaev did not break from the practice of scanning for other dangers. Scanning the terrain before him, he looked for any changes that would suggest that something was afoot. Hours passed before a German's head appeared in the same location as yesterday.

"The Nazi's face, firmly held in the sights of my rifle, was distinctly visible through the eyepiece. His eyes looked furtively at our trenches, from which he could naturally expect all sorts of unpleasant things. He did not even glance in my direction. 'That means he can't see me and he doesn't imagine there could be anyone here apart from him. That's good!' I thought I could have pulled the trigger and fired, but I didn't feel like doing that; for then the Nazi would fall into his trench and that did not suit my plans. I had to bring him down and show everyone that he was lying fallen on our land. And I was almost certain that any second now he would leap out. He was all ready for it and he had no other course. He was bound to repeat his maneuver from yesterday. Only now I knew about it and was expecting it.

"Unsettled by the silence around and hurried along by the intensifying frost and gathering darkness, with one short jump the Nazi landed up on the surface of the ground. Stooping low, he managed to take his first and last step. The

shot long awaited on our sector resounded. Like the crack of a whip echoing in the frosty air, it brought the Nazi down onto the snow. His rifle, now a danger no longer to our troops, slipped out of his hands and fell at the feet of its dead owner."

Seeking confirmation, Nikolaev first warmed his hands up by rubbing them with snow to restore the circulation. Then he crawled out to the fallen German and noticed the bullet hole in the temple. After cutting open his white camouflage suit, he stripped the uniform of its awards, collected the documents, letters, and photographs, as well as any foodstuff. Finally, he took the binoculars and the rifle and returned. Glancing into the German's lair, he noticed it had double cheesecloth concealing its firing slit. The German's mistake was not to dig a tunnel to his lair. This necessitated his brief exposure which allowed Nikolaev to spot him on one day and kill him on the next. For this achievement, Nikolaev was given two days of leave—all of which he spent sleeping.[97]

Greater recognition came when Nikolaev was promoted to Deputy Regimental Political Advisor. While this reduced his opportunity to snipe Germans, he began training sniper candidates. Near the end of 1942 Nikolaev's score stood at 324. His sniping career ended when he was transferred to the counter-intelligence organization, SMERSH.

Joseph Pilyushin also served in the 154th NKVD Regiment but at a later date than Nikolaev—hence neither man mentioned the other in their memoirs.

Born in 1903 in Belorussia, Pilyushin was a welder who had served in the Red Army in 1926. Discharged and placed in the reserves, he learned to shoot at the *Osoaviakhim*. It is unknown whether he earned the Voroshilov Marksman badge before being called up in 1941 as part of the 105th Separate Rifle Regiment. He was then transferred to the 14th Red Banner Regiment of the 21st NKVD Division. While deployed at the Narva River, he used his scoped Mosin-Nagant to kill his first German, who was disguised as a laundress to spy on the Soviet defenses. Later, when the Germans attacked Ropsa with a tank and infantry force, the panzers stopped briefly and a tank commander appeared from a hatch. An infantry officer ran up to the tank and began speaking with the tanker. He was obviously a command officer. A shot from the Soviet side caused him to collapse into the turret. The attack faltered and a counterattack by a Soviet submachine gun company drove the attack back. The opening and crucial shot was fired by Zina Stroyeva, who was trained as a sniper before the war at the *Osoaviakhim* and demanded to be accepted into the Red Army.[98]

In preparation for building a hide, Pilyushin and his comrades would spend the day gathering and preparing materials. After sunset, they would camouflage themselves and haul their materials to the site and under the cover of darkness construct the new hide. So as not to betray it, any dirt that was excavated was carried back to the trench.

Soviet snipers were asserting themselves all along the Leningrad front. M. Ivanov announced that on May Day, 1942, he had killed 122 Germans "as a May Day present for the country." This spurred other snipers to organize a May Day competition to see who could kill the most Germans.[99] Alexander Kalinin crossed the front line 20 times, spent 107 days operating behind German lines, slew 115 Germans and on February 6, 1942, he was awarded the title of Hero of the Soviet Union.[100]

* * * * *

In March, the German 58th Division was ordered to move from its position near the Gulf of Finland inland to south of Leningrad by the Volkhov River. Lubbecke continued his duties as a forward observer and was near a MG42 machine gunner (June 1942). A half hour of peace was disrupted by a Soviet infantry attack. Lubbecke called in artillery to within 25yd of their line. When the Soviets got too close, he dropped his telephone and grabbed his submachine gun and joined the machine gunner in sweeping the field with bullets.

"Perhaps half an hour passed with no let-up in our fire. Upon emptying my third or fourth 32-round clip, I again ducked down behind the wooden walls in order to avoid exposing myself as a target during the 15 seconds it took to reload another magazine into my weapon. At that moment, I became aware that the machine gun had grown silent, but assumed that the gunner was also reloading or again switching his barrel.

German armed with M91/30 with PEM scope mounted on siderail mount. Note third German in dugout entrance. Sign reads *Vermittlung Zutritt verboten* or "Switchboard, No Admission." *Image courtesy Georg Oberaigner.*

"A glance to my right revealed the gunner crumpled on the ground beside me. A second later, I spotted blood running from a hole in his temple just under the rim of his helmet. The shot that killed him had not been audible in the din of combat, but its precision made it instantly obvious to me that it came from a sniper's rifle."[101]

As an observer, Lubbecke could leave the line without being accused of desertion. Before he did though, he sprinted to the next infantry position 50yd away to warn them that their machine gunner was dead.

* * * * *

Still on the Leningrad front near Ligovo, Pilyushin discerned a dummy being used by a German sniper. One of his students was duped though and gestured toward it. It was a convincing dummy with a moving arm. Pilyushin saw through the deception and asked his partner if he'd been to a puppet show. He then explained that it was a dummy that was being used to entice a Soviet sniper to take a shot. After a lengthy search, Pilyushin noticed a hump near a beam that moved. Its size varied from big, to small, to disappearing altogether. He finally identified it as the head of the observer (there was no rifle).

"The enemy sniper was lying right up against the beam. I could see the barrel of his rifle and the top of his helmet. The German was holding his weapon at the ready. I cautioned Naydenov not to open the embrasure of the gun port under any circumstance, while I then crawled away into the trench, in order to shoot the fascist from a reverse position.

"From my new position I could see the upper part of the helmet, but the beam was concealing the German's body. I waited for him to raise his head, holding the crosshairs of the sight on his helmet. Time passed slowly, ponderously. My hands were growing numb, tears were interfering with my vision, and the blood was pounding in my temples like the blows of a hammer. I began to count, reached the number 1,000, lost count, and started again. But my adversary continued to lay there without moving. In our trench someone began to cough loudly and the fascist slightly raised his head, exposing his entire helmet. I fired and quickly moved to rejoin Naydenov.

"'Got him!' Sergey exclaimed 'He's lying there motionless.'"[102]

German *Oberfeldwebel* (master sergeant) examining a Soviet SVT-40 sniper rifle. *Image courtesy Georg Oberaigner.*

Pilyushin was with Zina Stroyeva searching for a German machine-gun embrasure. To assist them, they placed a reference stake in the ground. They searched for hours, checked the position of the reference stake and searched again. Finally, it was located behind an armored shield. The shield was painted in earth and sand on one side and white on the other (for winter use). Impossible to detect by eye alone at 400yd, what helped Pilyushin was the wind. "It was the wind that helped us spot it. There was a narrow strip of ground, where tall blades of grass were waving in the wind on either end. But the grass in the middle wasn't moving."[103]

Now attached to the regiment's administrative platoon, Pilyushin was prohibited by order of the regimental commander from visiting the front line. When he was needed, his major turned a blind eye to this order.[104] On one such visit he was greeted by Zina Stroyeva who was reassigned from sniping to being the bodyguard for Maj. Ogurtsov, the battalion commander. She complained to Pilyushin about the German snipers who killed three men in their attempt to reach their outposts. They had to be stopped. Pilyushin accompanied Stroyeva to the sniping nest on the second floor of a ruined structure. As a valuable observation point, they rarely shot from there. After extensive searching Zina spotted them and told Pilyushin to examine the shaded area of a birch tree.

"Many times I had looked at this birch, which a shell blast had uprooted. Its dried-out roots now stirred in the wind like the legs of an enormous, overturned beetle, looking to right itself.

"This time I hadn't given the birch my customary attention … I examined every piece of the toppled birch tree, from its top to its root, and each clump of scorched grass, searching for the concealed enemy."

He confirmed her observation but suggested that she refrain from shooting them there. [Pilyushin realized the importance of the post and did not feel it was worth betraying and losing it just to kill a few snipers.] Leaving Zina behind with instructions not to shoot but to keep them under observation, Pilyushin departed for the backup position and while en route, heard two shots. A retaliatory barrage fell upon the observation post occupied by Zina. Returning to the observation post when the barrage lifted, he found Zina curled in a fetal position nursing a wounded arm. She was removed for medical care and recovered sufficiently to return to duty.[105]

A sniper from the regiment's first battalion, Pilyushin's old friend Ivan Dobrik, approached him with a plea for assistance against the German snipers. "Yesterday evening they killed two of our rifleman, Ivanov and Smirnov. The snakes, they're nestled in some spot from where they can see our trenches and lines of communications, and we can't detect them!"[106] Having fought alongside Dobrik, Pilyushin held him in high esteem. "Dobrik was an outstanding sniper and as slippery as a fish. When 'on the hunt', he typically liked to creep out into no-man's-land, set up on the edge of a shell crater, and from there he would hunt down enemy observers, and sometimes kill the sentries at machine guns as well. But Ivan knew that a particularly dangerous struggle was now in front of us."

Urging Dobrik not to take them on by himself, Pilyushin replied that he would be there with a team of snipers the next day. The next day, Pilyushin led Tolya Bodrov to the 1st Battalion sector and joined Zina Stroyeva who was already there. Dobrik wasn't. He had been wounded by mortar shrapnel. They took their positions and began scanning the ground slowly. Before them, the German side was cluttered with an array of junk including rags of various colors, bottles, cans, bricks, plywood, bones, helmets, barbed wire, and other refuse of war. After hours of scanning, Zina produced her notebook and passed it to Bodrov, suggesting that a fresher pair of eyes may detect some changes from yesterday.

The two snipers spotted a potential sniper who was on the shady side of a tree. They watched as a rat cautiously approached it, sniffed the chin and then the nose. Suddenly, something startled it and the rat scurried down the shirt! It was a well constructed dummy that was placed there to entice a less observant sniper to shoot. Since it was a decoy, some German sniper or snipers must be lying in wait. They would continue their search.

Soviet discipline and patience

When former submachine gunner Gorozhaev complained that sniping was complicated and that peering through a periscope all day searching and studying the German positions was monotonous, he was told that sniping needed awareness and self-control. Additionally, patience and observation included memorizing the terrain so as to detect any slight change, which although seemingly insignificant, could be a prime target.[107]

American sharpshooter Darryl "Shifty" Powers and USMC scout-sniper Lawrence Kirby were both gifted in that regard. Snipers had to have the observation powers of "Sherlock Holmes along with the patience of a fisherman."[108] When a well-camouflaged German machine gun that gave the Soviets a lot of trouble could not be detected, sniper Ipatov was summoned and he watched for hours before being rewarded by observing wilting and drooping leaves. The German machine gunner had failed to refresh his camouflage (which itself could dangerously expose him). Ipatov fired a few shots and silenced the hidden machine gun.

Semyon Tkachenko spent 12 hours in a narrow and damp trench waiting for some Germans to leave their posts for the shelter of their bunker. When all three were exposed, he fired three shots over 40 seconds and killed all three.[109] In a front-line conference to share experience among the soldiers, Jr. Sgt. Galyushin described his patience and endurance in bagging four Germans.

"During my first three days in this sector, I bagged three Hitlerites. Then came a blizzard that nearly carried me under the snowdrifts. But I stuck it out patiently, knowing that after the storm the Germans would begin clearing their trenches and leveling off their parapets. I got four more Germans after that."[110]

After a lengthy search, Pilyushin spotted a real sniper hidden among the rubble 35yd away from the dummy. He was shrouded with a cloak and they had originally assumed he was dead. Refraining from shooting, he shared his finding with Zina and Bodrov. The potential for another sniper was real and he had to be located first. A cough from the Soviet side spurred the German to move. In response to the cough, the German was slowly gripping the rifle and raising it to firing position. He was about to shoot at unsuspecting Soviets who were moving to an outpost. Pilyushin had no choice and fired to save a comrade's life. The German's rifle jerked upward before dropping to the ground. Closing the loophole to his firing port, Pilyushin began searching with a periscope for the other sniper.

Hours passed and it was now afternoon. Zina spotted the second sniper first. "Guys! [S]omeone else has appeared by that clump of sage." Turning the periscope, Pilyushin spotted a head. Studying it, he could make out the rifle and the sniper's arms—and finally his eyes. The German was looking at the loophole Pilyushin had fired from. Bodrov volunteered to move out of the trench to entice the German to move. Zina attempted to discourage him but he would not be dissuaded. Steadying his scope's post on the sniper's eyes, Pilyushin waited for his opportunity. The German spotted Bodrov's movement. Pilyushin could now see the blond eyebrows of the German who hadn't yet raised his rifle. Instead of taking a shot, the German waited as if he knew that Bodrov was playing the role of a lure and that there was a sniper laying in waiting for him. Unwilling to shoot, the German now began creeping backward as if to exit a play he grew weary of watching. Applying pressure to his trigger, Pilyushin dropped the curtains on him. The other member of the audience, the rat that gave away the decoy, scurried away.[111]

* * * * *

Having finished a three-week leave (including travel time, it was between August 19 and 30) during which he enjoyed the company of his parents and his sister, *Obergefreiter* Lubbecke returned to the Leningrad front. Upon return (September 1), his division had moved from its position along the Baltic coast to the north shore of Lake Ilmen and was on the outskirts of Novgorod. In late April, they were fighting at Demyansk and were subject to regular sniper fire that forced them to remain inactive and hide in their bunker during daylight. Frustrated, Lubbecke decided to take matters into his own hands.

"Grabbing a Mauser rifle, I made my way from our bunker to the snow rampart. Crouching down on my knees, I carved out a small aperture through the wall with my hands. Scrutinizing the winter landscape, there was nothing that gave away the location of the enemy sharpshooter.

"Suddenly, a shot burst through the snow wall, passing just over the top of my helmet. Accepting my defeat in our brief duel, I pulled my rifle from the hole and quickly ducked back into our bunker. As far as I was concerned, we would have to learn to live with the threat of the sniper."[112]

Sniping, Lubbecke conceded, was something best left to professionals.

Also serving in the Leningrad area was the 132d Infantry Division which had recently been transferred from the warmer Crimean region and now belonged to the German Eighteenth Army. They had been on the front since September 1942 and after exhausting themselves in a futile assault, were defending the same ground a month later. *Gefreiter* Arno Sauer was in an outpost with his friend, Robert Kleinz. Sauer remembered the death of his friend.

"In the fourth week Robert was lying watch in the foremost ditch with me. He was very restless and stared time and again out of our trench across the raised protective earth wall toward the enemy positions. I said to him several times: 'Just stay put down here under cover. If the Ivan attacks, we will notice and learn this early enough.'

German officer examining a K98k equipped with a Soviet 4x PEM scope. *Image courtesy Georg Oberaigner.*

189

Kyra Petrovskaya Wayne

Born in 1918 in the Crimea to a noble family (her grandfather was Czarist General Baron von Haffenberg), her father was an aviator for the Czar and was executed during the Revolution. Her mother never remarried and they moved to Leningrad where her talents as a child got her admitted to the Leningrad Academic Capella. As a child performer, she was not exempt from marksmanship training and earned a Voroshilov Marksman badge in school. After graduating she enrolled in the Institute of Theater Arts to further her skills as an actress and singer. Her talent spared her from duties as a medic and she was given command of a performing arts troop which entertained the troops. Following her war service, she continued as a performing artist and, being multilingual, represented the Soviet intelligentsia in diplomatic receptions. It was during one such meeting that she met an American diplomat. They married in the first official church service in Russia since the October Revolution. In 1946 they moved to the United States where she attempted to resume her performing arts career but failed because of her Russian accent. For a while she had her own television show but after her divorce, moved to Los Angeles. She wrote her autobiography in 1959 which launched her career as a writer. In 1960 she married Dr. George Wayne and she became a lecturer for a cruise line. She and Dr. Wayne had one son and five grandchildren. She passed away in 2018.

Lt. Kyra Petrovskaya posing with a commercially gunsmithed (not a M1903A4) scoped Springfield M1903 indicates that this a postwar photo likely taken in the United States. *By kind permission of Dr. R. Wayne.*

"Yet Robert ignored my warnings. Suddenly I heard a dull impact. When he had lifted his head once more above the protective wall, a shot hit him full frontal in the forehead through the steel helmet. The Russian sniper had done a perfect job. Robert was killed immediately."

After pulling the alarm string that connected to the rear, Sauer closed Robert's eyes and waited for help. Some comrades arrived and assisted in carrying Robert's body away.[113]

* * * * *

Initially trained for two months as a *druzhinniza* (medic)[114] and serving (after more training) as a nurse at a soldier's hospital in Leningrad, Lt. Petrovskaya commanded an entertainment troop on the Leningrad front. On the anniversary of the siege of Leningrad and following a performance during the "Kill a Nazi" campaign, a soldier pointed at her Voroshilov Marksman badge and challenged, "It is very well for you artists living in safety at your headquarters to go about telling other people to kill Nazis. If you're such a fine sharpshooter, why don't you go and kill one yourself?" She accepted the challenge and the men cheered.

While she was shooting champion in her school days before the army, she had never trained to be a sniper. To assist her, she was mentored in a field school by an experienced sniper credited with 114 kills, Sgt. Nikanorov. Nikanorov didn't ask for the assignment and begrudged having to instruct Petrovskaya. When she challenged him as to why he hated her, he responded that he didn't but resented having women doing a man's job. Petrovskaya asked if it had ever occurred to him that women would prefer not to fight but were compelled to? Taken aback, he conceded such was the case. Afterward, he had her practice her marksmanship but didn't teach her sniping techniques such as camouflage, stalking, observation, or the sniper's mindset. When Nikanorov was satisfied that she could hit her mark, they went on their hunt and Petrovskaya showed how naïve she was about sniping when she asked how high they had to climb a tree.

Pre-dawn, they went to a ruined house and watched from a cellar window. Since she lacked the upper body strength to hold up the rifle, Nikanorov used straw to build up a rest for her. Then they waited and when she spotted a German, she failed to fire. Petrovskaya wrote: "Nerves taut, straining my eyes, I waited a long time, yet, when the figure of a Germany finally appeared, dashing, crouching across the clearing, I failed to fire." (Lt. Pchelintsev's comment that a target shooter is not necessarily good material for a sniper comes to mind.) Petrovskaya had all the training to shoot, but had not reconciled herself with taking a life.

"Why didn't you shoot?" asked Nikanorov, who warned, "Do that again and I'll report you to the commissar. I could have shot him myself."

Incentivized, Petrovskaya apologized and asserted that she would not miss the next man. "We waited, silently, for what seemed an eternity and my arms began to tremble from tension. Then, at last, another soldier showed. I caught him with my telescopic sight, squeezed the trigger slowly—and saw him fall, face downward."

Nikanorov congratulated her on making good her promise to kill a Nazi. Afterward, he relieved her and waited for his turn at the cellar window. Petrovskaya sat against the cellar wall, her body trembling from the adrenalin that coursed through her veins. As an actress and singer who lacked a killer's mindset, nothing in her experience or training had prepared her for what she had just done.

Ignoring her, Nikanorov was in his own world and concentrating on the kill zone. Bang! "Another bastard," he grunted. There was no time to celebrate. The second shot had enabled the Germans to spot the hide and they retaliated with artillery. Both Soviets were wounded: Nikanorov mortally. Petrovskaya was hit in the leg and used her *druzhinniza* training first to bandage Nikanorov and then herself. Soviet counter-battery fire replied to the Germans but it wasn't until dark that Petrovskaya began trying to drag the now unconscious Nikanorov back to their lines. Luckily for them, another *druzhinniza* arrived, applying more bandaging before dragging him back. Naturally, the weapons were not left behind (that was part of a *druzhinniza*'s training). Unfortunately, despite the surgeon's care, Nikanorov died on October 29. Petrovskaya recovered and returned to the theater, but did not fight again.[115]

* * * * *

On 1943's Red Army Day (February 23), Joseph Pilyushin's sniping school was suspended and his students went to the front lines to hone their skills. The effectiveness of the Soviet snipers caused the German machine gunners around Leningrad to cease using tracers because they made them easier to spot and kill. The Germans learned to move their machine guns at night after a few bursts. Around that time, armored shields were manufactured in Leningrad for the snipers. On August 23, 1943, Pilyushin became marksmanship instructor for the 14th Red Banner Rifle Regiment, 21st NKVD Division, and command of the new sniper

platoon went to Lt. Yuriy Grudinin.[116] Shortly after that, the shorter 3.5x PU scope entered service.

Now free to roam, Pilyushin returned to the front of his own accord. One day, music carried over from the German line. Pilyushin searched for the source and discovered the slight movement of an embrasure on a camouflaged shield. Slowly, a rifle emerged from it. Sensing an urgency to spare an unknowing comrade, he fired and watched as the rifle jerked upward before sliding back into the loophole. After shooting, Pilyushin withdrew his rifle, covered the firing slot, and remained there observing in case there was retaliation.[117]

The Red Army slowly began to push back the Germans besieging Leningrad. On January 24, 1944, Ropsha was recaptured and Pilyushin's unit moved west, fighting in the vicinity of Mestanovo where he once again fought alongside Zina Stroyeva. The snipers were ordered to suppress the machine guns and German snipers. While changing position, they came under German machine-gun fire and Zina was killed.[118] Pilyushin's combat career ended on February 5, 1944, when an artillery shell struck a tank he was standing next to. Wounded, he was hospitalized and did not return to frontline service. He had killed 136 Germans and was awarded the Order of the Red Banner. Postwar, he returned to his welding job but his war wounds finally blinded him and forced him into retirement where he dictated his memoirs.

Army Group Center

In 1941, as the German panzer groups were trying to capture Moscow in a pincer attack, the residents of the city were called upon to form new defensive battalions. Many dug anti-tank ditches and other defensive works. While many women became nurses, radio operators, or operated the antiaircraft guns, some went into the labor battalions including 19-year-old Natalie (or Natasha) Kovshova and 17-year-old Maria Polivanova. Together, they approached Col. Petrov Sokholovsky to enlist them, and he attempted to dissuade them. "You are too young and innocent for the bitter battle of Moscow that's coming." Both women had received prewar training in the paramilitary *Osoaviakhim* where they not only qualified as snipers but became sniping instructors within that organization. One replied, "You have no right to refuse us; we'll complain. We are snipers." Sokholovsky enlisted both but had no sniper rifles for them. They drilled and trained alongside the men. When the sniper rifles finally arrived, they were detached to the sniper squad "for special duties." They instructed many of the new snipers.

1944 Soviet postage stamp showing the last moments of the Soviet Union Maria Polivanova and Natalia Kovshova. *Author's collection.*

A rivalry began between them. Natasha reached 34 kills; Mary 30. Both were wounded in battle and when they recovered, the sniper commander was wounded leaving Natasha in command of the sniper squad. During one attack, the squad was whittled down to themselves and one man who was wounded. He asked, "Do you think we'd better fall back now?" Natasha responded, "Not one step back!" Both women were soon wounded and incapable of firing their rifles. When the Germans shouted for them to surrender, they refused and prepared their grenades. They died along with the Germans standing over them. Pvts. Natasha Kovshova and Maria Polivanova were posthumously awarded the Gold Star of Heroines of the Soviet Union.[119]

The stand of the Red Army outside Moscow and the weather stopped the *Wehrmacht* cold in its tracks. They were exhausted by losses and unprepared for winter warfare. Whereas *Blitzkrieg* had previously proved itself so successful, and after the early successes no one believed that the Soviets could withstand the Germans—but they did.

Odessa and Sevastopol

Lyudmila Pavlichenko was one of the first female Soviet snipers to see action. She helped defend Odessa, besieged by the Romanians between August 8 and October 16, 1941. She and other snipers had specific orders from the Odessa Defense District to occupy key positions that afforded good observation and an opportunity to snipe and dominate the enemy. So, the first enemies to fall to her were Romanians who would lose over 93,000 in the siege, many to snipers.[120] Pavlichenko toured Canada and the United States in 1942:

"People say I am manly because I am a sniper in the Red Army, but they don't

know. A woman remains a woman first no matter what she does. When the war began, I had to do something and could serve best by shooting. When it is over, I want to get married and raise a family. I like to look nice. It is only normal and natural for a woman to want to please. But people asked if I wear lipstick at the front."

She added sarcastically, "I supposed I should carry a compact instead of a cartridge case and attract the fire of the Germans with a mirror. That would be fantastic." She also contrasted the mindset of the two nation's women. "The difference between Soviet women and American women is that we think chiefly of strength, but Americans appear to think chiefly of beauty. We exercise to be strong. You exercise to reduce."[121]

She described her experience to an American audience. "I was a soldier like the rest and took part in the defense of Odessa. I lay there and watched the Romanians dig in. Only 300 or 400 yards away. We were strictly forbidden by the commander to shoot without his permission." She asked for permission and was granted it. Pavlichenko continues: "Are you sure of hitting them," he asked. "Yes." Permission was granted. "I got a grip on myself. I forced myself to be steady and cool, take careful aim and fired. I waited

First kill

Antonina Kotliarova

Antonina Aleksandrovna Kotliarova left school to be a turner in a factory. When it was evacuated, she choose to remain behind, joined the *Komsomol*, and worked in a mine. When the sniper school opened, she enrolled, and was thereafter sent to the First Belorussian Front with the 143d Division, Forty-seventh Army. Her female sniper squad was kept together instead of being broken up among the companies.

Upon arrival one woman wanted to study the Germans and peered through an embrasure in the trench. "When she looked through the embrasure, a bullet ricocheted and hit her right under the eye. So our wartime experience began with a funeral." Kotiarova killed her first German after that and couldn't eat or sleep afterward. The same thing happened with her second one. She recalled, "When I killed the second one, I was in a horrible state again. Why? Because I saw him through my optical sight: a young officer. He seemed to look at me and suddenly I killed him. But he was a human being!" She eventually became desensitized.

When working as snipers, they kept communication to a minimum:

"Olga and I lay at arm's length from each other. We spoke quietly because the Germans would be there not far in front of us. They were listening to everything. Their outposts were better organized, after all. We tried not to move, to say something quietly, find a target. Everything would grow so numb! For example, I would say: 'Olia, mine.' She would already know—she wouldn't kill that one. After the shot I would help her by observing. I would say, for example, 'There, behind that house, behind that bush', and she would already know where to look. We took turns shooting. During the daytime we were always in position, came and left at night. Every day. No days off."

In the liberation of Warsaw, she often fought with a submachine gun. "Our sniper skills did not work there. Because, first of all, while you aimed, you could get killed."

When asked about their treatment by the male soldiers, Kotiarova replied, "Very well. Soldiers treated us well. They were protective, didn't do anything to harm us. Sometimes they would find us a chocolate, or something else."[122]

Alexandra Medvedeva-Nazarkina

After graduating from the Central Women's School of Sniper Training, *Starshina* Medvedeva-Nazarkina was assigned to the 508th Rifle Regiment, 174th Rifle Division that was fighting near Orsha (today in Belarus). The *frontoviks* and especially the soldiers were fatherly toward them. She remembers her first kill:

"Together with my partner, Zina Vershinina, we occupied our sniping positions. While observing enemy positions, I

spotted a machine gunner. I aimed and shot. It was unclear whether I hit him or not. But when I returned to the detachment, everyone already knew I'd killed an enemy. An artillery observer reported this. He saw it in his periscope, how the enemy machine gunner was killed. Everyone was joyous, they hurried to congratulate me And I wept, for I had to kill a man ... I— a common girl— had a hard time getting accustomed to the front and shooting at people, although I understood I was shooting at the enemy. Soon there was a crisis in my conscience. Seeing people's sorrows, the tears and blood of my native land, I understood there could be no pity for the invaders. For the killing of my 10 first Hitlerites I was awarded with the medal, 'For Courage.'"

She tells of a duel three of them had against a solitary German sniper.

"Among many battle episodes the following one was the most memorable to me. In autumn 1944 there was heavy fighting in Poland. An enemy sniper appeared in one location, and we suffered appreciable losses: our commander, a scout, and many signalmen were killed. Then came an order: 'Destroy the fascist sniper!'

"Three of us went to carry out the order. Nina Isaeva, Lena Akulova, and I. We settled upon our positions and started shooting at roofs with armor-piercing [and] incendiary bullets. Thatched roofs caught fire fast, the Germans started escaping those houses with their mortars and machine guns. And we shot on and on ... We were so carried away with this, that we completely forgot about staying cautious. And the German sniper noticed us. He hit Nina Isaeva right in the eye by a well-aimed shot. Luckily, she stayed alive, although she lost her eye and vision was significantly impaired.

"Having concentrated ourselves, we still discovered the lair of the enemy sniper and eliminated him, as well as other firing positions of the Germans. Our task was fully accomplished! For this successful battle operation I was awarded with the Order of Glory, 3d Grade."

By the time the war ended for her in Czechoslovakia, she had 43 kills to her credit and another Order of Glory, 2d Grade.[123]

for a fraction of a second; another head appeared over the top. I got that one too."[124] She coldly told her audience, "Every Nazi who remains alive will kill women, children and old folks. Dead Nazis are harmless. Therefore, if I kill a Nazi I am saving lives."[125]

As Pavlichenko developed a reputation as a sniper, she and Sgt. Fyodor Sedykh were ordered to instruct new sniper students on the care and the maintenance of the SVT-40 rifle, of which Sevastopol received 8,000. Among them were eight sniper versions with the 3.5x PU scope. They were instructing soldiers on field-stripping it when they were ordered to report to the regimental command post. Once there, Pavlichenko learned that a German sniper had appeared in the area of the 2d Battalion and had killed five men, including two officers. It was suspected that he was operating in the area of a wrecked bridge that was 650–900yd away. She now had her first counter-sniping mission.

Unlike the enemy-held northern end of the bridge which remained intact, the destruction of the southern end made it an unlikely sniping post. An inspection confirmed this, so a sapper company dug a trench and camouflaged it. Additionally, a decoy with a rifle was prepared. When Pavlichenko was ready, she signaled Sedykh with a whistle. He began moving the dummy as if it were a soldier returning to the rear. The German took the bait, fired, and hit the dummy. But he had been spotted and Pavlichenko fired back. The German tumbled down in to the gully. Much to Pavlichenko's and Sedykh's surprise, his rifle was not a scoped K98k but a Soviet M91/30 with a PE scope. His decorations, *Soldbuch* (soldier's pay and record book carried by every German soldier), and rifle were recovered and he was identified as *Oberfeldwebel* Helmut Bommel, 121st Infantry Regiment, 50th Infantry Division.[126]

While she hated the German invaders, she acknowledged that she also learned from them.

"It was the German snipers who taught me caution, endurance and restraint. If I so much as stirred a finger, a bullet would whistle just over my head or at the back of my legs. Occasionally a German tin hat would appear, just a fraction of it, and I would think, 'Aha! I'll get that Jerry.' Then I would fire, and the hat would waggle like a head of a toy elephant and disappear. It was only a German decoy to make the sniper betray his position.

"Then the Germans would open such a squall of fire that I dare not raise my head. It was just terrible. Out of sheer fright I would call out to the machine-gunners. Then the gunners would open fire and quieten the Germans down a bit, and I would be able to crawl back, more dead than alive, for a breathing space."[127]

She wasn't always lucky and Pavlichenko suffered a concussion, had shrapnel in her cheek, and—according to her—half her ear off. She was among those who escaped the German entrapment at Sevastopol. It had been ordered evacuated on July 3, 1942. With a tally of 309, on July 16, 1942, she was awarded the Order of Lenin for her actions in Odessa and Sevastopol and promoted to junior lieutenant.[128] She didn't know it just then, but her combat career was over. She and Leningrad sniper Lt. Vladimir Pchelintsev were sent on a propaganda tour to the west in 1942 to encourage a second front. Both were offspring of NKVD officers and considered reliable (unlikely to defect). Because female soldiers were a novelty, Pavlichenko found herself thrust into the media limelight and overshadowed Pchelintsev. As American First Lady Eleanor Roosevelt acknowledged, "Lt. Lyudmila Pavlichenko, the Russian girl sniper, attracts the most attention because she represents something so unusual to us."[129] Unused to public speaking, Pavlichenko soon mastered questions from American reporters and the public. American students of both genders were fascinated by the female sniper. "It is not easy especially for women, to sleep on the earth in the rain and the snow. But still they fight because they are sure that with the United Nations they will crush fascism," she lectured.[130] When asked about her tactics, she told them: "You get up before daylight, move into position and stay quiet until you get the enemy where you want them. You get out while it is dark, at 4 or 4:30, and come back late at night. You need great self control, will power and endurance to lie hours at a stretch without moving. The slightest start may mean death."[131]

Upon return, Pavlichenko was ordered to report to the Kremlin to debrief with Stalin, who was very curious about Roosevelt. Afterward, she asked to be returned to the front: Stalin balked. He explained that she could return and kill another hundred but could be killed herself. However, if she trained a hundred snipers and each of them shot ten Nazis or a thousand Nazis altogether, that would be more valuable to the Soviet Union. Having explained how her services were more important as an instructor than as a sniper, Pavlichenko acquiesced.[132] Before being made a permanent instructor, Pavlichenko asserted that she had trained 80 snipers since the war began.[133]

There are problems with Pavlichenko's account and Lyuba Vinogradova points them out in her book.[134]

The most glaring is Pavlichenko's assertion that shrapnel wounded her right cheek and cut her ear lobe. An examination of photographs of her during her visit to the United States or postwar does not suggest a facial wound. For a discussion of this subject see box on pp. 196–7.

The Soviet Union understood the psychological and propaganda value of snipers and promoted the cult of the sniper. Vasily Grossman, a reporter for Soviet Armed Forces newspaper *Krasnaya Zvezda* (Red Star—first published in 1924) described the inauspicious start of 19-year-old Anatoly Ivanovich Chekhov:

"A notice appeared on March 29, 1942, and I volunteered for sniper school. In fact, I had never shot anything as a child, not even with a slingshot. My first experience of shooting was from a small-calibre rifle. I scored nine out of fifty. The lieutenant got very angry: 'Excellent marks in all subjects, but you shoot badly. We'll never make anything of you.'"

Despite this lackluster start, Chekhov applied himself and soon mastered the rifle. He also taught himself distance estimation by eyeball alone.[135]

Theory and practice are distinctly different, and knowledge of the former does not automatically impart one with marksmanship skills. For the latter there must be practice, practice, practice. Even with practice the top shooter may not make a good sniper. If a shooter cannot cross the threshold that separates the target range from battlefield killing, then that shooter is unsuitable for sniping. Hence the shooter must believe in the necessity of taking lives to reduce the casualties among his own comrades. Chekhov accomplished his objective and inspired others to try to become snipers. The response to Grossman's article was a flood of new recruits and the need for more training schools. Having read Vasily Grossman's articles, Pvt. Stepan Vernigora aspired to become a sniper.

"I was in an infantry company, and after reading in the newspapers about the exploits of Chekhov and other snipers I decided to become a sniper too. When I told my platoon commander, Second Lieutenant Ignatov, that I wanted to be a sniper, he granted my request and straight away fetched me a sniper's rifle, serial number 3165, from the armory. I immediately set about sending Nazis to their deaths. They were very close by, so I got to kill a lot of them. Instead of drinking water from the Volga I made them drink lead. By the time

the rout of the Germans in the Stalingrad region was complete, I had sent 142 Fritzes to their deaths, and the rest will remember me and know what to expect if they ever try messing with our 13th Guards' Division again. But I'm not going to stop now. I'll carry on killing them until they have been completely smashed."[136]

It is highly unlikely that Pvt. Vernigora was responsible for killing over 100 Germans. While he may have learned camouflage on his own or through experience (many Russians were adept at camouflage), he did not undergo any selection process for marksmanship, received no instruction on how to care for and use the scope, distance estimation, or other things associated with sniping.

While the Soviets understood both the force multiplier the sniper represented as well as the propaganda value to instill fear in the enemy and as encouragement for its men, Soviet doctrine did not spare the sniper from assaults against the enemy. Ordered by their platoon commander, Pvt. Pilyushin and four others crawled toward German tanks with grenade bundles.[137] To stop another German attack supported by three tanks, the Soviet infantry counterattacked and joining them was a female sniper platoon. They succeeded but suffered two killed and four wounded.[138]

Lyudmila Pavlichenko's scorecard

Among the controversies surrounding the top female sniper of the war, Lyudmila Pavlichenko, is her claim of 309 kills. Pavlichenko served in the 25th Chapayez Division that fought first in Odessa and later in Sevastopol where it was destroyed. There were survivors like Pavlichenko who were evacuated, including Fifty-first Army commander Maj. Gen. (promoted postwar to lieutenant general) Trofim Kolomiets, who observed,

"I don't know who, when and for what deeds nominated Pavlichenko to the title of Hero of the Soviet Union … But neither the commander of the 54th Regiment nor the command of the Chapayez Division made such a presentation, since there were absolutely no grounds for this."[139]

Pavlichenko felt some jealousy (or envy) at the time of her visit to the West toward her fellow traveler, Vladimir Pchelintsev, who not only had a lower sniper score but was senior in rank to her and was a Hero of the Soviet Union. This raises the issue of Soviet policy of awarding medals and inconsistency of it within the Red Army. Leningrad was a power center in the Soviet Union and the Communist Party there fully appreciated the value of propaganda. The postcards of snipers reproduced elsewhere in this book are evidence of it. The need to buoy morale in their besieged population was one reason to promote the cult of the "noble sniper." Leningrad needed heroes and found them among its local defenders. Like Napoleon who contemptuously remarked on medals, "With such baubles men are led," the Communist Party in Leningrad was eager to recognize heroes and promote them. Under these conditions, Pchelintsev became a favored son honored with rank and with the Hero of the Soviet Union award.

Incidentally, Soviet awards conferred benefits upon the holder. Easier promotion, favors, postwar preferred housing, and in some circumstances, no waiting in line. Recipients of a Hero of the Soviet Union also enjoyed a lifetime pension. There were certainly incentives and motivation to earn (or acquire) them.[140]

Some of Lyudmila Pavlichenko's stories seem odd. As an example, she talks about receiving a sniper rifle on July 26, 1941, that was covered in grease and needed cleaning. She didn't limit herself to cleaning it:

"I had to strip the rifle completely and do some work on its components. For example, I removed the wood along the whole length of the handguard groove, so that the woodwork no longer touched the barrel, I had filed down the tip of the gunstock, so the barrel fitted snugly, bedded the barrel properly to the fore-end, and inserted padding between the receiver and the magazine. To ensure that the various parts of the bolt mechanism worked properly, it was recommended that they were carefully worked over with a small needle file. The trigger mechanism of the rifle needs to be efficient, reliable and stable."[141]

This is suspect, and in most armies, soldiers were not permitted to alter their firearms and those who did it without permission in advance were subject to disciplinary action. However, in Pavlichenko's favor it should be noted that a 1934 manual included instructions on accurizing the M91/30.[142] *Vladimir Nikolayevich Ivanov/visualrian.ru/ media/40015, Public Domain/WikiCommons.*

Unlike Leningrad, elsewhere some commanders conferred awards reluctantly, were too busy for baubles, or worse, reserved them only for favored toadies or for themselves. One officer observed that medals went to officers who led from the safety of their headquarters while their men shed blood and lives for those officers' medals.[143] Those who deserved it were dead, unrecognized, or forgotten, while those who did little actual fighting were showered with glory and positioned themselves for future advantages. Who has not witnessed something similar in their own lifetime? Additionally, as Isaak Kobylyanskiy observed, if an officer fell from favor, his recommendations for medals were "turned down."[144]

Pavlichenko's commanders were not generous, and she wrote that whereas others received awards or medals, she was only presented with a personal rifle. Furthermore, she initially fought in Odessa which had been a possession of Romania until 1940 when it was ceded to the Soviet Union. This circumstance meant that Odessa's local Communist Party was relatively new and never approached the influence that Leningrad's had. Considering the short span of time it was Russian territory, there was no time to allow the party there to rise to prominence. Similarly, while significant as a seaport, Sevastopol was never a rival to Leningrad and was never the capitol of Russia. The political conditions in the locations where Pavlichenko fought were not inclined toward conferring medals or awards.

Continuing his criticism, Kolomiets wrote:

"Only on April 28, 1942, Pavlichenko was awarded a medal for military merit 'by order from the Primorsky Army.' This award was as a result of an order by the Field Administration of the Primosky Army that a sniper who killed 30 fascists should be awarded a medal 'For Military Merit' or 'For Courage.'"

He added that any newspaper article was written without confirmation and is not alone in questioning Pavlichenko's score. Veteran Vasikovskii of the Chapayez Division wrote of that she, "ascribes herself non-existent feats." He went on:

"[S]ince she did not perform any feat during her service with the regiment, I began to look in the documents in the archives. The archives in the documents of the division does not say anything of Pavlichenko. I had to ask for the GUK37, they told me there were no documents on Pavlichenko's representation in the GUK. Requested by the Presidium of the Supreme Soviet, there is nothing there either. No, no telegram, no digits (letters), no telephone conversations."

It is entirely possible that a Russian chauvinistic male attitude toward female soldiers led to the distrust of Pavlichenko. Additionally, most writers of divisional histories were men like Sgt. Nikanorov (who had trained Kyra Petrovskaya for her sniping mission) who were resentful of a woman's presence on the battlefield. Another possibility is that while she did kill Romanians and Germans, her overall score could be a product of Soviet math (discussed elsewhere) that inflates figures for propaganda purpose. Kills had to be witnessed and when Pavlichenko worked as a lone sniper, which wasn't unusual for snipers, there were no witnesses. In her defense Pavlichenko complained,

"The Central Committee of the *Komsomol* has been gossiping about me for a long time. Until a certain period, I put myself above them and repelled from them. This attitude of mine led to the fact that in the eyes of the workers of the Central Committee of the *Komsomol*, I became a 'prostitute' and a 'fake hero.' It turns out that is why I am not invited to receptions, rallies, meetings and congresses. Therefore the press is silent about me ... [T]he *Komsomol* even instructed to remove my portraits from the exhibition of '*Komsomol* of the Patriotic War.' I am deeply offended both as a decent woman and a warrior."

She added ruefully, "If there is a war again, then women should avoid the army in every possible way to maintain their reputation."[145]

Early war female snipers were a rarity as there was reluctance to accept them as soldiers. Women like Lyudmila Pavlichenko and Leningrad's Nina Petrova constituted some of the first female snipers who struggled to even receive a sniper's rifle. They were slowly joined by field school-trained female snipers who trickled into the ranks. The next generation of female snipers emerged only after the Central Women's School of Sniper Training began operating. Before that though, there was likely a lot of resentment and prejudice against any woman who fought. That a woman may have successfully undergone six months of grueling training at the school did not affect the male soldiers or Soviet society's attitude towards the women. This is reflected in both their treatment at the front during the war and postwar.

So what is history's verdict on Pavlichenko? That she fought as a sniper and received the Hero of the Soviet Union is undisputed, and there is no scarcity of publicity photos of her with a sniper rifle. Her total score is at issue and inconsistency between her accounts—both published during her wartime tour in the West and postwar—raises issues. To the world, the Soviets presented themselves as an egalitarian community that granted women full participation in all aspects of Soviet society. It was, therefore, a well-calculated and deliberate move in selecting her as their female student representative to the International Student Conference. Apart from being a warrior, her greatest contribution was as the Soviet female representative who promoted the second front to the West. A novelty, her message generated support for defeating Nazi Germany. She also became as a role model to other Soviet women who became soldiers and snipers. Those things cannot be denied to her.

Tsyrendashi Dorzhiev

Siren Dordziyez, more modernly spelled Tsyrendashi Dorzhiev, came from the poor village of Barai Adag in Buryatia. Born in 1912, at age 14 he began tracking and hunting the *taiga* (forests). When the war broke out, he enlisted in the Red Army and to his chagrin, was initially driving a food wagon. After pleading with his company commander, he was transferred to a rifle company and practiced for a day with a sniper rifle before turning his rifle on the Germans. He was nominated for the Order of Lenin for his 174 kills and a Messerschmitt Bf109. He was awarded the medal, "For Courage" for his 216th kill. Depending on the source, his final tally was somewhere between 270 or 297 before he succumbed to his wounds on January 3, 1943.

Fighting on the Leningrad front, Sgt. Tsyrendashi Dorzhiev is credited with 270 kills before being killed in January, 1943. *Library of Congress via ww2db.com.*

Army Group South

The Axis forces in the south included Panzer Group 1 (*Generaloberst* Ewald von Kleist), three German (Sixth, Eleventh, and Seventeenth) and two Romanian (Third and Fourth) armies and, from early July, the Carpathian Group of the Hungarian Army. This was attached to the German Seventeenth Army and advanced into south Ukraine.

The Hungarian mechanized group formed the southern pincer that cut off the Soviet Sixth Army. Its initial success began to meet stubborn resistance. Cpl. Istvan Daloga of the 2d Battalion, 1st Hungarian Motorized Brigade, recorded in his diary:

"Sad notes: many Hungarian comrades are watering the soil with their blood. We cannot even evacuate our wounded fast enough … Russian snipers firing well … They pick us off as soon as we should show ourselves. They seldom miss … The Russians are excellent shots. Their best divisions are here—Siberian sharpshooters."

While it is unknown how he died, Cpl. Daloga never saw Hungary again.[146]

Among the Soviet snipers who enjoyed success against the Germans was Sgt. Siren Dordziyez, who had 181 kills to his credit on July 25, 1942. Kill 175 was his most difficult after the German sniper had shot off his *ushanka* (fur hat). Dordziyez lay in snow at -40°F for two hours watching. When another German brought food to the sniper, it revealed that he was high in a pine tree. Round two went to Dordziyez.[147]

Another successful Soviet sniper, Vasily Komaretsky's score as of July 20, 1943, stood at 170. He would slip out at 0300 hours with a partner, set up within 300yd of the Germans, and carefully camouflage themselves. They would then get to work. His achievements were recognized by Lt. Gen. Pavel Belov who presented Komaretsky with a Tula Arsenal-made rifle.[148]

As part of the German drive into the Caucasus, the German 97th *Jäger* Division (originally a light division but redesignated as *Jäger* in July 1942) had the Belgian Walloon Legion attached to it. Initially a battalion strong, they were cut to pieces during the winter fighting of 1941. In 1942, they participated in Army Group A's attempt to capture the Caucasus. The Walloon commander (and postwar neo-Nazi), Léon Degrelle, recalled reaching the Caucasus mountains.

"August 16, 1942. The great mountains of the Caucasus looked down on us, blue-black at first, then white and pink, very high in the sky … We arrived at a large green river that surged through rubble of a dynamited bridge. A soldier advanced, straddling the jagged platform. A rifle shot rang out from a tree on the other side, the man fell into the river.

"A second man tried. Then a third. They fell, hit in turn.

"The mountains were still twenty kilometers away, but already the Caucasus was sending us a warning."[149]

How they managed to cross Degrelle is not mentioned, but they were stalled again at Tyeryakov where they fought for 126 hours to capture the village. Furious Soviet counterattacks to recapture it ensued. It was during the five days of fighting that the Belgians came up against Soviet snipers again. Degrelle says:

"Elite Soviet marksmen climbed in the trees like jaguars Sometimes we could make one of them out, then take careful aim. The body would topple to the earth or dangle in the branches. But most of these Bolshevik climbers were invisible. A dozen of them interdict all movement. It was impossible to make 10 meters in partially wooded terrain. Tyeryakov was surrounded by marksmen, sparing of their cartridges and astoundingly skillful."[150]

Eventually the Belgians prevailed and retained their tenuous grip on Tyeryakov. From it the Germans would launch their bid to capture the Caucasus.

During the invasion of the Soviet Union, the SS Division (mot.) *Leibstandarte*-SS Adolf Hitler (LSSAH) was attached to XIV Panzer Corps of the *Generalfeldmarschall* Ewald von Kleist's First Panzer Army of von Rundstedt's Army Group South. In 1942, it helped to capture Rostov. Because of the Soviet counterattack that threatened the German forces in the Caucasus, the Germans and LSSAH were compelled to retreat. Among its ranks was Berliner Erwin Bartmann, who as a child witnessed an LSSAH changing of the guard ceremony and aspired to become a member. Now, the former apprentice baker found himself a member of the heavy weapons company and in a freezing foxhole in the Mius–Sambek Line of the Donbass region. He was stomping his feet to keep them warm when he spotted a figure "hobbling from foxhole to foxhole."

It was a man whom he recognized as a senior sergeant. Bartmann greeted him, "*Oberscharführer*, you're taking a risk."

"Naja. Ivan's been quiet today," replied the former senior sergeant who had been demoted to private. The two chatted and the former sergeant announced it was his birthday. Before he departed for the next foxhole, Bartmann became uneasy and he recalled what happened next:

"As he made to leave, a feeling of intense unease gripped me and I hooked a hand on his shoulder to restrain him. 'Watch out, you were a sitting duck when you came over. This still air is perfect for a sniper—no need to allow for wind when he aims.'

"'You worry too much,' he said, shrugging his shoulders before scrambling out of the trench.

"He took a few paces back the way he had come and then turned and stood for a moment, lost in some private thought, gazing across the frozen fields before slinging his rifle over his shoulder. There was a metallic clink. His head swayed under the weight of his steel helmet then his arms fell limply to his sides. The rifle slid from his shoulder and he slumped to his knees like a

burst sack of flour. He groaned something—it might have been his girlfriend's name—before falling face first in the snow. His helmet rolled away from his head and rocked back and forth a few times before coming to a rest on a patch of ice. Bright blood spread under his face, freezing in seconds into a congealed mass, its redness intensified by the purity of the snow. At the front of the helmet, exactly in the center, was a perfectly round hole."[151]

Incapable of fighting back, Bartmann kept his head down for the rest of the day. At night the medics removed the body for burial. A few days later, they retreated to the new line at Sambek near Taganrog. Christmas was approaching and the captain, knowing that Bartmann was a baker, asked him to bake cakes for the company. Lacking baking powder, he made biscuits instead. Despite the celebratory Christmas shelling by the Soviets, Bartmann finished his task and went from post to post to distribute the fresh treats to the company. When he got to one bunker, he found one man laying on his stomach, propped up on his elbows and writing a letter. His friend greeted him.

"'Listen to this Erwin,' he said. Then, reading from the letter, 'Have been shot through both cheeks but can still talk. The bluebird is coming home. See you soon.'

"'What happened?' I asked.

"'Sniper caught me having a shit.'"[152]

Bartmann and LSSAH were sent to France where they were rebuilt and converted to a panzer division.

Snipers in the Caucasus mountains. As the German *Anleitung für die Ausbildung und den Einsatz von Scharfschützen* (see p. 70) says:

"A good sniper gets better if he knows how to dig himself in and to camouflage himself skilfully in every situation.

"He must be a master of terrain and camouflage. The sniper must choose or build his positions so that he can stand, sit or lie comfortably. Nothing reveals more than careless movements ... must be able to quickly disappear into the ground, camouflage himself with grass, leaves, twigs, snow, etc. He has to find a well-camouflaged position in crouches, bushes, trees, ditches and holes and in the skylights of houses.

"In doing so, he must always remember that he has to move his position in houses deep into the room so that gun smoke and muzzle flashes do not give him away."

USSR Information Bulletin.

| 8 The Stalingrad *Kessel*

"The Russians have remarkable marksmen. God don't let me be their target."[1]

Cpl. Balogh

Hungarian Army at Stalingrad

Situated on the Volga River, the city that bore Stalin's name was also an industrial center. Its importance was secondary as the primary goal of the German offensive of 1942 was the capture of the Caucasus oilfields and to deny the Soviet Union its access to petroleum. Stalingrad (renamed Volgograd in 1961), however, became an obsession to Hitler who wanted it captured and humiliated. As it turned out, it was Hitler and not Stalin who was humiliated at Stalingrad. As the German Sixth Army lost momentum among the streets and buildings, the Soviets launched a counteroffensive which broke through the Hungarian, Italian, and Romanian armies that guarded the flanks. When the two Soviet pincers met, the Sixth Army and its allied armies were isolated.

Soviet 1034th Infantry Regiment of the 293d Infantry Division (Twenty-first Army which faced the westernmost position held by German Sixth Army) had among its soldiers Tartar mortarman Mansur Abdulin. Breaking from traditional practice, his 82mm mortar section was detached from its company and assigned to support a regular infantry company. The company's 50mm mortar was ineffective against heavier German field fortifications and if machine guns or snipers were to be eliminated, the heavier 82mm mortar could deliver greater fire power on demand.

Abdulin was a miner from Siberia. He grabbed a rifle and earned a "For Bravery" medal for being the first soldier in the regiment to kill a German. There was no fire mission for them and the front had stabilized except for sniper activity. When seven soldiers of the 1034th Regiment were killed by a German sniper, Abdulin badly wanted to find the sniper and was chided by his comrade who dismissed his ambition as wishful dreaming. Undeterred, Abdulin went hunting and in his words described his action:

"The only way of finding the sniper's position was by using a scout's periscope. I took one, returned to the rifle company, and began a long and laborious survey of No Man's Land: shell holes, corpses, debris … To catch a sniper in that chaos

would be like finding a needle in a haystack! For the hundredth time I swept the endless plain with my periscope, trying to remember the outlines of suspicious looking hillocks: 'He can't stay in the cold forever,' said someone behind my back, 'he'll have to leave sooner or later!'

"I was jumping up and down in the trench, trying to keep warm, when a young company commander, following my example, also took the periscope. But he soon tired of squinting, and assuming the air of a man with more important things on his mind, walked away, sternly snapping out orders: 'Be careful! Stay low! Understand?'

"Meanwhile, I got excited by the game, and took the periscope once more. Soon I knew all the minute details of the terrain, as if it was on my own palm. Restlessly scrutinizing the ground from left to right, I began systematically eliminating the possible number of hiding places, all the time narrowing the circle. By noon I was concentrating my attention on one particular 'hillock', when suddenly it moved! I couldn't believe my eyes—it was him! Now I was terrified that after all my efforts I might lose him. What if he crawled away to safety before we had [a] chance to do something?

"Suvorov appeared in the nick of time. Without looking away from the periscope, I reported the situation. We decided to use a rifle belonging to an old soldier from Siberia: 'My gun always gets the bullet home,' said the private, handing me the weapon, 'I wish they'd give it to me after the war, to take back to the forestland! I don't want no orders or medals, just my rifle!' I carefully aimed the gun on the parapet, while Suvorov thought how to best provoke the sniper into firing, so that I might take advantage of the 10 'dead' seconds it would take him to reload.

"With no time to lose, Pavel wrapped an entrenching shovel in a piece of cloth, marked two eyes and a mouth with mud, stuck his cap on top, and cautiously lifted it above the breastwork. The 'hillock' gave a start, and the shovel clinked. I instantly put the rifle butt against my shoulder and fired. The 'hillock' sank down. Then, there was a burst of automatic fire from the enemy lines, and our machine-guns snapped back.

"Soon afterwards, when everything was quiet again, we spotted two figures crawling like lizards from the enemy lines towards the 'hillock'. These Nazis also got their due, and when night came, some of our more daring men approached the dead sniper and brought back some booty. This included a notebook, which contained a chilling piece of accounting: the figure '87'."[2]

Commanding the Soviet forces within Stalingrad was General Vasily Ivanovich Chuikov. Chuikov was of peasant stock and as a child worked in a factory that made spurs for officers. During the Russian Revolution, he enlisted in the Red Guards and rose to regimental command. Between the wars he attended the M. V. Frunze Military Academy where, among other things, he studied Chinese. In 1939 Chuikov commanded the Fourth Army when it invaded Poland, and later the Ninth Army when it attacked Finland. Afterward, he went to China as the chief military adviser to Generalissimo Chiang Kai Shek until the Soviet Union recalled its military mission. Chuikov next commanded the Sixty-fourth Army then on the west bank of the Don River—later it was on the west bank of the Volga and encircled the German Sixth Army south of Stalingrad. It was pushed back toward Stalingrad during the fighting, and Chuikov was then appointed command of the Sixty-second Army. During the fighting retreat, Chuikov studied the German tactics and developed countermeasures which he describes:

"Analysing the enemy's tactical and operation methods, I tried to find counter-measures and counter-methods. I thought a great deal in particular, about how to overcome or reduce the importance of German superiority in the air, and its effect on the morale of our troops. I remembered battles against the White Guards and White Poles in the Civil War, when we had to attack under artillery and machine-gun fire, without any artillery support of our own. We used to run up close to the enemy, and his artillery would be unable to take fresh aim and fire on rapidly approaching targets. A short, sharp attack would decide a battle.

"I came to the conclusion that the best method of fighting the Germans would be close battle, applied night and day in different forms. We should get as close to the enemy as possible, so that his air force could not bomb our forward units or trenches. Every German soldier must be made to feel that he was living under the muzzle of a Russian gun, always ready to treat him to a fatal dose of lead."[3]

Camouflaged German sharpshooter. The German armament industry could not meet the demand for scoped rifles. *Narodowe Archiwum Cyfrowe.*

Arrival in Stalingrad

When Jr. Lt. Alexander Gak arrived at Stalingrad, he was sent to the village of Kotluban' (today part of the expanding city), and was directed through various HQs to his battalion in the 115th Rifle Regiment, 38th Infantry Division. "When I first laid my eyes upon the battlefield at Stalingrad I was horrified. There were damaged tanks standing abandoned ... As I was walking down the road between the division and regiment HQs, I witnessed Katyushas in action for the first time." He was given command of a

Lt. Alexander Gak led an infantry platoon of the 115th Rifle Regiment, 38th Infantry Division, that was fighting in Kotluban, just outside Stalingrad. At his request, the sergeant gave him a sniper rifle which he cleaned and sighted in and later killed a German at 450–500m distance. At age 21, he became a battalion commander in the 421st Rifle Regiment, 119th Rifle Division. After being wounded and losing use of his fingers he was discharged in 1944. He reenlisted in 1945 as part of the Soviet Army of Occupation in Germany. *Blavatnik Archive Foundation (http://www. blavatnikarchive.org).*

rifle platoon, where, at first, the old hands were somewhat patronizing toward him. However, he was given a new sniper rifle shortly after his 19th birthday and some two or three days after receiving the rifle, he put it to use.

"The German front lines were 500–550yd away. I saw a door open into a ravine, that they also used to travel down, and two Germans walked outside. One was carrying a bucket of water and the other, an officer, was shirtless. The two men stopped and the man with the bucket began pouring it on the officer so he could wash. I took aim and opened fire for the first time. The German fell and the second grabbed him by his legs and quickly dragged him back into the open door before closing it. Later, the position that I had set up near the tank was shelled by a massive mortar barrage. It seems that they had already been aware of certain firing positions and assumed that someone was firing from under the attack. Of course, I got out of there. I managed to escape the heavy fire from the mortars and made my way back to the trench."[4]

Having proved himself, he was accepted and led his platoon until he was wounded. After recovering, he was promoted to first lieutenant and given command of an infantry company. In early 1943 he commanded a battalion before being wounded for a second time—on this occasion with an explosive bullet that ended his days as a fighting man. He remained in the army and served in the Soviet Occupation Army. Postwar, Gak learned that only two of his classmates had survived.

One of the units sent to bolster Chuikov's army was Col. Gen. Alexander Rodimtsev's 13th Guards Rifle Division (formerly the 87th Rifle Division). Among Rodimtsev's guardsmen was Anatoly Ivanovich Chekhov who initially served as an infantryman. After Chekhov proved his bravery in combat, and since he had been trained as a sniper by the army, he was issued a sniper rifle.

"When I was given a sniper's rifle, I chose a place on the fifth floor. There was a wall and its

shadow concealed me ... I went out at four in the morning. It starts to get light at this time. The first Fritz ran to get some water for the chiefs to have a wash. The sun was already rising. He ran side-on to me. I didn't look at their faces much, I looked at their uniforms. Commanders wear trousers, jackets, caps and no belts, privates wear boots ... I'd arranged my rifle behind the grill so that the smoke would drift along the wall. At first they walked. I knocked down nine on the first day. I knocked down seventeen in two days. They sent women, and I killed two out of five. [German women did not serve on the front line so it is likely they were Russian women in German service.] On the third day I saw an embrasure! A sniper. I waited and fired. He fell down and cried out in German. They stopped carrying mines and getting water. I killed forty Fritzes in eight days."[5]

Chekhov's division and its commander, Alexander Rodimtsev, received a lot of media fanfare from the Soviet press and General Chuikov grew envious. Possibly motivated by his jealousy, Chuikov promoted his own favorite sniper, the 284th Division's Vassili Zaitsev. At war's outbreak, Zaitsev was a bookkeeper and clerk serving in the Red Navy's Pacific Fleet. Along with other sailors, he volunteered to fight at Stalingrad and was transferred to the 1047th Rifle Regiment, 284th Rifle Division, Sixty-second Army under Chuikov. When it came to selection of men, all the other sailors were chosen before him. His short stature and status as a clerk made him shunned by the army officers who selected the biggest and strongest sailors for their units. While frustrated and angry at being passed over so often, he was finally accepted into a machine-gun platoon. His unit arrived on September 21, 1942, and he initially fought as a rifleman until October 5, 1942, when his marksmanship was noticed by the regimental commander, Metelev. Metelev witnessed Zaitsev shoot three Germans at 600yd with his iron-sighted Mosin-Nagant. Impressed by Zaitsev's marksmanship, Metelev ordered that Zaitsev be given a sniper rifle.[6]

Zaitsev received rifle #2826 the next day and Sr. Lt. Bolshapov taught him how to use the scope. Sniper Kalentiev mentored Zaitsev for three days. He soon mastered his weapon and his techniques. When the building he was fighting from was surrounded on three sides, Zaitsev climbed a ladder to an upper level. Through a crack in the brick wall he spied an HMG over 500yd away. He adjusted his scope and studied the rising smoke to check the wind. It rose straight, indicating none. Zaitsev worked his bolt, inserting a cartridge into the chamber. He centered the post of his scope between the German's eyes. A squeeze of the trigger sent the bullet on its path, killing the German instantly. When the two assistant machine gunners ran up to man the gun, they too were shot down.[7]

His kills taught the officers the value of their clerk turned sniper. Formerly scorned by everyone because of his small stature, Zaitsev was now a cherished and desirable asset. When their regiment was ordered

Zaitsev seen here with his M91/30 equipped with a side-mounted 4x PEM scope. *Mil.ru/WikiC (CC BY 4.0).*

to retake Mamayev hill from the Germans, one of the challenges it faced was the German machine gunners. The light machine gunners' actions were coordinated by radio so that their fire remained optimal. To combat them, the regiment's political instructor ordered him to raise a sniper unit. Zaitsev selected sailors whom he thought had potential. Besides teaching them how to use their sniper rifles and scopes, he also taught them tactics. His training was mostly hands-on. Among his pupils was Mikhail Ubozhenko. With his sharp eyes, Ubozhenko was the first to spot two Germans who were digging a trench. Asking Zaitsev what to do, Zaitsev estimated the distance at 400m and gave instructions on adjusting the scope. Zaitsev then followed with instructions not to shoot just yet.

He explained to Ubozhenko that sniping could be approached like billiards. It is not enough to score, but to set up for the next shot. Wait, Zaitsev told him, for the German to face them. That way the shovel will stay in the embankment and another German will retrieve it. Ubozhenko waited and when the German drove the spade into the embankment, he pulled the trigger, bowling the German over. Zaitsev was startled by the shot. It was all the difference between being a shooter and an observer. Being behind the barrel meant the report is not as loud but to an observer off to the side, the report is louder. The same effect is heard between a modern flash suppressor and a muzzle brake. A flash suppressor disperses the gases in the direction of its milled out slots. With a muzzle brake, the cutouts direct the gases to mostly to the left and to the right. Thus the report is louder. Moments later, the second German exposed himself to retrieve the spade whereupon Ubozhenko slew him with his second shot. His pupil had downed two men under guidance of the master. Noticing they were spotted by Germans, they scrambled down before the enemy could retaliate. [8]

As the Soviet snipers asserted themselves, some Germans began to retaliate. Among them was *Leutnant* Adelbert Holl who commanded the 7th Company 2/276th Infantry Regiment which had been temporarily detached from the 94th Infantry Division and attached to the 24th Panzer Division. Holl originally enlisted as a private in 1937 and was commissioned on July 1, 1940. His battalion was fighting at the Barrikady Housing District when they were subjected to sniping.

> "We had to be on our guard every second here because carelessness could mean death or a severe wound … Several aimed shots from the enemy's side confirmed the presence of snipers. What they can do, we can do too. I would look for a suitable spot at dusk so that I could give them an answer tomorrow … I would prove that I had not worn my 'Schützenschnur' [lanyard awarded for marksmanship] after my first year of service for nothing."

On October 2, 1942, after instructing his runners not to disturb him unless something extraordinary was happening, Holl went beyond the front line before daylight and ascended the loft of a wood house that was about 10yd above ground. A hole in the wall afforded him a view from 100yd to the left and 300yd to the right. He had with him binoculars, an ordinary rifle, and ammunition. Then he positioned himself 10ft back from the loft window where he was hidden by the darkness. Holl continues his narrative. "One of the most unsettling things for every soldier is the call: 'Look out, sniper!' One shot, the target goes down, and nobody knows a thing. Where had the shot come from? Every soldier on both sides is rattled."

Looking straight, he could see at 200yd the Russian command post. That would be his priority. To his left he saw a machine-gun post 100yd away. Finally, to the right at 300–350yd there was what Holl thought was a well. He would wait for his prey.

> "Here comes one! Not on, he moved out of the zone too quickly. But he surely had to come back. I was now completely focused. Had it been 10 to 20 minutes? I didn't know. His return run from the company post was slower. Pressure was applied, my finger slowly pulled back, the shot struck home, hit."

German Army sniping team with turret-mounted K98k. The *Anleitung für die Ausbildung und den Einsatz von Scharfschützen* (see p. 70) says:

"It is advisable to assign an observer with binoculars to the sniper. Both have to move like hunters and lie in wait. The observer supports the sniper in observing the enemy territory and in watching the gunshots. If the enemy does not offer a target for a long time or if he is also on the lookout, shooters and observers must try to lure the the enemy into firing by cunning deceptions, but only if they are performed skillfully and reasonably. Example: the observer appears for a moment in a trench, then reappears again for a short time in order to draw the attention of the opponent. A few minutes later, the observer pushes a helmet or a helmet-like object over the cover, causing the opponent to shoot in most cases. A straw doll can also be used. The more varied the deceptions, the greater the success for the sniper will be." *Narodowe Archiwum Cyfrowe.*

"Target Number 2: I adjusted the sight for 100m. The observation post for the machine-gun position was well camouflaged. Only after observing the spot for a long time with my binoculars could I see a slight head movement. I carefully marked the position and looked with the naked eye. I could still see it. I again practiced my aim; it would have been easier with a telescopic sight. Over my head I could hear the howling of the Stukas as they plunged headlong down on the Barrikady and Red October factories, unleashing the destructive force of the payloads. All this, combined with the noise of fighting from near and afar, could not distract me. The only thing that mattered to me now was to take out the designated target with a single shot. Even the daily 'afternoon-greeting' from the impacting shells of the 'Stalin-Organ' landing in our sector could not deflect me from the task. A deep breath, take up pressure, calmly exhale, hold my breath and gently pull back my index finger. I looked through my binoculars: the target had vanished. Despite the battle noise going on outside, I was certain the shot had hit."

Holl tried for the longer-range 300–350yd shot but missed. He then sketched the enemy positions and, unwilling to invite retaliation from either artillery or a sniper, he returned to the safety of his company.[9]

Oberleutnant Wigand Wüster was commanding the 2d Light Battery of the 171st Artillery Regiment (71st Infantry Division) deployed among the ruins of Stalingrad along the banks of the Volga. He recalled:

"You have to be extremely careful because numerous Russian snipers with telescopic rifles—or even anti-tank rifles—were lurking everywhere, and many lone soldiers fell victim to them. Only when you knew what areas were overlooked by the enemy could you feel relatively safe in the ruins. Still, it was wise to sprint from cover to cover. In the meantime, many things had also been done to improve safety: warning signs were put up and screens were erected to allow positions under observation to be crossed. Nevertheless, you had to orient yourself carefully or—even better—have soldiers with good local knowledge guide you."[10]

Mamayev Hill is a prominent terrain feature of Stalingrad. It reaches a height of around 300ft and offers a commanding view of the city. Today's visitor cannot help but notice the inspirational monument of the sword-bearing woman, *The Motherland Calls*, beckoning people against the invaders. Sixty-second

Army commander General Chuikov remembered the fighting on that hill.

"The enemy realized that mastery of Mamayev Kurgan [hill] would enable him to dominate the city, the workers' settlement and the Volga. To achieve this aim, he spared neither men nor material. We decided that we would hold on to Mamayez Kurgan whatever happened. Many of the enemy's panzer and infantry divisions were destroyed here, and our less-than-a-division withstood the fiercest battles, battles to the death, unparalleled in history in their stubbornness and ferocity."[11]

Today, the serenity of Mamayev belies the carnage, death, and destruction when Zaitsev and his comrades were sent to fight there.

On October 24, Zaitsev and his pupils were needed at an adjacent regiment that was also fighting on Mamayev Hill. The anti-tank unit holding the sector they were sent to support was being decimated. It was pointed out that there was a spring that both sides wanted to deny the other access to. Zaitsev decided to dominate it with his men. Any German approaching it was shot down day or night, "It was shooting fish in a barrel." When the Germans brought up anti-tank guns, they shot the gunners and forced the survivors to abandon their guns. After four days, they were relieved by a penal company, and sent to the rear for a day's rest and fresh clothes. They were less one man—Sasha Gryazev—who was killed by a German sniper.

Zaitsev noted the difference in tactics used by the Germans and the Russians. Whereas German snipers operated deep within their own lines, the Soviets would work from the very front if not beyond. Like the Soviets, the Germans set up numerous firing positions and used decoys to entice the Soviets to reveal their position by shooting. To overcome this, Zaitsev recommended using good observation and a lot of restraint. Given time and patience, one will be able to discern a decoy from a real target. Lacking patience and shooting early served only to divulge one's location.[12]

Zaitsev and his team searched all day for the German sniper who had shot Gryazev. Boredom set in. Then Zaitsev noticed some shell casings and being bored, began counting them. There were 23 in all. He studied them individually and suddenly it became apparent that one was missing its bottom. Raising himself slightly for a better view, he saw a flash and a bullet struck the dirt behind him. One of Zaitsev's snipers asked him if he was OK. Shaken but otherwise unharmed, Zaitsev replied that the German earned the honor of the first shot and

Soviet Sniper Vassily Faronov is seen posing behind a tree with his Tokarev SVT-40 sniper rifle. Note the camouflage netting draped over his helmet and shoulders. He defended the area around Stalingrad and is credited with 136 Germans. *Author's collection* .

Sniper patience

The life expectancy of snipers drawn from soldiers without front-line combat experience could be measured not in days but by round count, which averaged from 15 to 20 rounds. The inexperienced snipers generally chose poor hides, did not preplan an escape route invisible to the enemy, failed to zigzag in sprints (to avoid mortar fire), and fired too many rounds without moving.[13] It should be noted that the army sniper manual allowed for anything from three to six shots from the same position before changing position.[14] In a sniper duel, this could be fatal. The *Anleitung für die Ausbildung und den Einsatz von Scharfschützen* (see p. 70) says:

"The marksman must be a master at stalking his opponent at close range. In his approach and in the selection of the position he needs to use all imaginable cunning in order to deceive and mislead the enemy (e.g. pushing a bush ahead of himself).

"All kinds of preparatory work are to be practiced in a drill-like manner in changing terrain, preferably in the form of small competitions by several shooters next to each other ... the sniper must be particularly skilled in the patience and perseverance, often laboriously stalking long distances to a position and then sitting for days in an advanced hole, in a tree or behind a skylight and never letting go of observation. The trust in his ability, the certainty of being able to make himself invisible, will raise his self-awareness."

took it. He recalled what Chuikov told him: the job of the sniper is to make the other sniper expose himself first and then to kill him. Returning with an artillery periscope the next day, Zaitsev counted the shells and noticed one was missing. He began diligently searching for it and finally found it in a small depression near a hill and hidden by an embankment. Having located the sniper, he waited.

To entice the other sniper to expose himself first, Nikolai raised a helmet on a stick a few inches above the embankment. Amazingly, the German took the bait and fired. He must have been equally strained from hours of watching to have taken the first shot. As the German was reaching to retrieve the spent cartridge, he raised his head up and forward of the scope. Zaitsev fired, hitting his opponent in the head. The German slumped, his rifle barrel still partially in the shell.[15]

It was on Mamayev that Zaitsev again demonstrated the virtue of patience and its reward. He had spied a German soldier carrying pails of water in excess of that needed for hydration. Deferring his shot, he observed that it was for junior officers to wash. Zaitsev desisted again, anticipating bigger game. Including himself, there were six snipers whom he divided into three pairs, each using a different vantage point to shoot from. The next day, their patience he was rewarded. First,

a German cap was clumsily raised. Recognizing it as bait, Zaitsev's men withheld their fire. After a while, a slovenly German soldier appeared with a pail. Too low ranking to bother with, they continued waiting. After ten minutes, two colonels appeared, followed by a sniper, who was their escort, and a major. This was their moment and Zaitsev gave the signal. Three volleys of two shots rang out and all four Germans dropped from head shots.[16] Along with mortars, artillery, and the Luftwaffe, the retaliation knocked the snipers about but also uncovered the wood panels that masked the German artillery which allowed Zaitsev and his men to pick off artillery officers.

When a Soviet lieutenant was shot in the back, he complained that Zaitsev wasn't doing his job. This set off Zaitsev and a new sniper, Gorozhaev, in search of the German. First, they found a witness who told them that the lieutenant had been shot before entering a boiler room. Furthermore, three other soldiers had been shot there previously. Deploying near where the boiler room entrance was, they waited for hours.

The German sniper was operating under the cover of submachine gunners and could not be enticed to fire. Finally, a political officer came by and was encouraged by Zaitsev to use his megaphone to shout German insults through it. That only drew machine-gun fire, but allowed Zaitsev and his pupil to dispatch the gunners. German artillery fired in retaliation and the political officer dropped his megaphone. When he reached to retrieve it, his arm was exposed and the sniper fired. Zaitsev spotted the German between the wheels of a railroad car. Zaitsev's student took the shot but missed, alerting the German sniper that a Soviet counterpart was onto him. He shifted position. Nothing happened for the rest of the day.

The next day, Zaitsev and his student took up their position. Zaitsev switched on the megaphone and shouted a German obscenity. A bullet barely missed his ear. He was pinned and for two hours could not move. Finally, he instructed his student to use a mirror and blind the German with it. It worked and Zaitsev escaped. He then placed a dummy he had prepared earlier into the spot where he was trapped. They could see the German between the wheels of a railroad car, but had to change position to get a shot at him. They choose a tar vat that stood above ground. Using an inconspicuous hole, they waited. A half hour passed before the German emerged from beneath the car. Slinging his rifle over his shoulder, he walked to the trench where he was greeted by a comrade. While the sniper began describing and reliving his shot, he unslung his rifle and was demonstrating his action when he spotted the glint from Gorozhaev's scope. His expression changed from joy to fear as he realized he was being targeted. He never had a chance as Zaitsev's student shot and made his first kill. Zaitsev followed up by taking out the other German. The pupil had learned and killed his first German, and a sniper at that.[17]

In another incident on Mamayez Hill, Zaitsev was speaking with Lt. Shetilov when the latter was hit with an explosive bullet. Zaitsev dug three hides and intending to make a proper dummy, propped up a helmet as a temporary decoy. He didn't have to make a dummy as the helmet was shot. Examining the helmet, he figured the sniper was in the same location as when Lt. Shetilov was wounded. Using an artillery periscope, he located the German sniper behind a camouflaged Maxim machine-gun shield 600yd away.

Every now and then Zaitsev saw the muzzle of the sniper's rifle, but held back from shooting, fearing his bullet would only strike the barrel and alert the sniper that he was being hunted.

"I would have to wait until my opponent stood up, or at least raised his head. Fortunately on this occasion, I didn't have long to wait. Another German delivered the sniper's lunch. Two helmets surfaced above the shield. But which of these belonged to the sniper? Just then something flashed in the sunlight—a cup a thermos. Aha, I said to myself, they've brought the sniper hot coffee. Now who's going to take a drink? Not the fellow who had just made the delivery. The coffee had to be intended for the thirsty sniper. He of the two threw back his head. He was drinking down the last drop. Ever so gently, I squeezed my rifle's trigger. The sniper's head lurched backward. A shiny little cup dropped in front of the shield."[18]

Vasily Grossman also reported that Zaitsev shot a female collaborator. "Zaitsev has killed a woman and a German officer: They fell across each other."[19] This incident was omitted in Zaitsev's autobiography—possibly censored, as was shooting Soviet children who collaborated. Since the Germans couldn't collect water without exposing themselves, they instructed or paid children to fill their canteens. Considering how the hapless Soviet citizens caught behind the German lines (Stalin had previously issued a "no retreat" order compelling people to remain in situ) were starving, the payment could have been as little as a piece of bread. Those children were also killed by Soviet snipers.

The most famous story about Zaitsev is his duel with Maj. Erwin König, the subject of Hollywood epic *Enemy at the Gates*. From a captured German, it was learned that a German super sniper had been sent from the Berlin sniping school to deal with Zaitsev.[20] Having learned about his new enemy, Zaitsev needed

to locate him, so he began questioning medics and witnesses to sniper casualties to determine his possible locations. Once these were identified, he began studying the terrain for possible hides. For two days he and Nikolai Kulikov watched. On the third day a commissar, Politruk Danilov, joined them. He spotted the German—or at least thought he did—and raised himself to point out the lair. He was rewarded with a bullet wound. It confirmed the German's presence—but where?

Zaitsev and Kulikov continued scanning. Before them, among the ruins, were a wrecked tank, a pillbox, and the open space of no-man's-land between the German and Russian lines. In that open space and adjacent to a pile of bricks lay a sheet of iron. Zaitsev pondered whether there was a sniper's nest beneath the iron sheet. It broke the usual German practice of deploying behind their lines. Because it was unorthodox for the Germans, Zaitsev grew suspicious of it.

Zaitsev placed his mitten on a board and raised it to invite a shot. His opponent took the bait and put a bullet through it. Removing the mitten, Zaitsev examined the board and saw that the bullet bored a hole straight through and confirmed the sniper's lair. Zaitsev and Kulikov remained in position throughout the night. When day came, they fired one shot to draw the sniper's interest. Then they waited for the sun to shift to a favorable position. Zaitsev described what happened next:

"[A]fter lunch, our guns were completely in the shade, while the direct rays of the sun fell upon our

Soviet sniper in the Caucasus holding a decoy aloft to entice a German. His rifle is has a side-mounted PEM 4x scope. *Author's collection*.

Hero of the Soviet Union *Starshina* Nikolay Yakovelich Ilyin of the Sixty-fourth Army fought at Stalingrad and was credited with 494 kills. He did not survive the war. He's seen here aiming his SVT-40 semiautomatic rifle. His other awards include: Order of the Red Banner, Order of Lenin and Medal for the Defense of Stalingrad. He was also memorialized on a postage stamp. *Author's collection* .

rival's position. Something glimmered beneath the edge of the iron plate—was it a random fragment of glass, or a rifle's scope? Kulikov took off his helmet and slowly raised it, a feint that only an experienced sniper can pull off credibly. The enemy fired. Kulikov raised himself up, cried out loudly and collapsed. 'At last, the Soviet sniper, their "main rabbit" that I've hunted these four long days, is dead!' the German probably thought to himself, and he stuck his head up behind the sheet of iron. I pulled the trigger and the Nazi's head sunk. The scope of his rifle lay unmoving, still flashing in the light of the sun."[21]

There are doubts about this story, starting with Zaitsev's account. First, timings: if Zaitsev's and the other Soviet snipers' guns were in the shade, that would indicate a morning sun and not an afternoon sun. Generally, the Germans were facing west at Stalingrad and the Soviets facing east. How then could there be a glint of light from the German sniper's scope if it was an afternoon sun that was against the German's back? Second, would a super sniper be so gullible as to be duped by the mitten? Third is an issue raised by noted British writer and researcher Anthony Beevor who contacted the Russian authorities and was told that they could not find records of the duel. Beevor pointed out that no reports of it were submitted to Alexander Shcherbakov, Head of the Political Department of the Red Army in Moscow.[22] Fourth, British sniper and researcher Harry Furness found no evidence of a Maj. König or a Berlin sniping school.[23]

General Vasili Chuikov, the commander of the Sixty-second Army, mentioned the story in his memoirs.[24] Beevor suggests that Chuikov's promotion of the duel was born of jealousy over the fame showered on the commander of 13th Guards Division, Colonel General Alexander Rodimtsev, and his sniper, Anatoly Ivanovich Chekhov, by *Krasnaya Zvezda* (Red Star) military newspaper.[25] Zaitsev claimed to have recovered the body and the papers of the fallen German major. If he did, the *Soldbuch* (soldier's pay/record book) should be in the Russian archives and would remove the doubts about whether such a duel actually occurred or was merely propaganda to steal the limelight from Rodimtsev and Chekhov.

Zaitsev was wounded soon afterward by an artillery explosion and nearly lost his vision. With a final tally of 242 kills, he was considered too valuable to risk and he became a sniping instructor. He was awarded the Hero of the Soviet Union. Chuikov also credits Zaitsev with founding the sniper movement in Col. Nikolai Filippovich Batyuk's 284th Infantry Division. "Zaitsev trains his young hares and Medvedev his young bears. They all kill Germans and never miss." This was a play on their names since *zaitsev* means "hare" and Medvedev is derived from the Russian word *medved*, meaning bear.[26]

Even though he was not the highest scoring sniper in Stalingrad, Zaitsev's fame endures today and the duel is mentioned in numerous books and, of course, the movie. One sniper who is said to have killed more Germans at Stalingrad was known only as Zikan. He was credited with 224 kills by November 20, 1942. More modest was Kucherenko with 19 kills. Commissar Ilin was credited with 185 kills and would often shoot through a pipe. Sniper Kovbasa of the Sixty-fourth Army had clever lures. He dug dummy hides in front of adjacent platoons and then placed white flags that he could raise with levers attached to strings or with wire. An unwary German who spotted a flag would raise his head and shout, "*Rus, komm! Komm!*" Instead of a prisoner, he got Kovbasa's bullet. Dummies were used by 161st Rifle Regiment Danielov who shot the Germans who revealed themselves by shooting his dummies.[27]

Serving with Zaitsev in the Naval Brigade was Kazakh Mikhail Memkov who, prior to becoming a gun layer on a destroyer, was a hunter. Fighting now in Stalingrad, he led six other snipers. He led his group within 75–100ft of the Germans. They set up dummies to entice the Germans to shoot and if one did, they would study the dummy to determine the German sniper's location. Using this technique, they slew four snipers and three machine-gun crews. They also used their numbers to their advantage as he describes himself.

"Sometimes we had to seek out the enemy by more complicated means. One time we put a sniper in the center of town, knowing that his shots would attract the attention of the enemy to a dressed dummy which we placed not far from our man's foxhole. To the sides were two observers whose job was to spot the German when he shot. Once we knew where the fritz was located, we closed in on him secretly and took him out. Over the course of six weeks, we killed eighteen snipers, thirteen tommy gunners, six machine-gun teams and seven anti-tank teams.

"I gave each sniper in my group a kill sector of his own—an area of anything from 50 to 1,200 metres. Every one of us had reserve firing positions, at least four, so if we thought that we had been spotted at one location we could move unnoticed to another. As a rule you would always be spotted by the time you had killed five or six Fritzes from the same lair. The Germans would then usually try to flush you out with mortar or artillery fire.

"In the last days of the battle for Stalingrad we were surrounded by Germans. They were very nearby, and more than once we had to stand up and fight them face to face or attack with hand grenades. In these skirmishes, four of my

Snow camouflaged Soviet sniper team moving among the ruins of Stalingrad. *Russian International News Agency via ww2db.com.*

Heroes and heroines of the Soviet Union

Established on April 16, 1934, the title "Hero of the Soviet Union" was given a combat perspective on August 1, 1939, when the Gold Star medal was established. The recipient of the title received this medal, the Order of Lenin, and a number of privileges—preferred housing, tax, transportation, and medical treatment. There was no gender distinction but the English-speaking world tends to differentiate between heroes and heroines. There were 11,635 winners, 119 double, 7 triple and 1 quadruple winner. Of these, 92 were women and 50 of the awards were made posthumously. Female aircrew, medics, and resistance fighters were well represented, as were snipers, six of whom received the award. Of these, only Pavlichenko survived to receive hers.

Name	Date of award
Cpl. Tatyana Nikolayevna Baraminza	May 24, 1945
Jr. Sgt. Tatyana Ignatovna Kostyrina	May 16, 1944
Pvt. Natalya Venediktovna Kovshova	February 14, 1943
Cpl. Aliya Moldagulova	March 24, 1945
Maj. Lyudmila Mikhailovna Pavlichenko	October 25, 1943
Pvt. Mariya Semenovna Polvanova	February 14, 1943

Of the 11,635 winners of the Gold Star, the majority were men—Russians or Ukrainians—and 8,447 were army, the majority infantrymen. Amongst the 81 male sniper winners were:[28]

Cpl. Ivan Filippovich Abdulov	October 26, 1943
Khusen Borezhevich Andrukhaev	March 27, 1942
Sailor Ivan Petrovich Antonov	February 22, 1943
Lt. Mikhail Ignatievich Belousov	October 26, 1943
Sgt. Mikhail Ivanovich Budenkov	March 24, 1945
Lt. Leonid Vladimirovich Butkevich	October 25, 1943
Sr. Sgt. Fyodor Trofimvich Dyachenko	February 21, 1944
Lt. Vassili Ivanovich Golosov	October 26, 1943
Sr. Sgt. Piotr Alekseyevich Goncharov	January 10, 1944
Jr. Lt. Ivan Pavlovich Gorelikov	April 28, 1943
Guard Sgt. Maj. Ilya Leonovich Grigoriev	June 15, 1944
Sr. Sgt. Abukhadzhi Idrisovich Idrisov	June 3, 1944
Dep. Pol. Ins. Nikolai Yakovlevich Ilyin	February 8, 1943
Sr. Lt. Mikhail Adamovich Ivasik	March 24, 1945
Sr. Sgt. Vassili Shalvovich Kvachantiradze	March 24, 1945
Lt. Ivan Ivanovich Larkin	January 15, 1944
Jr. Lt. Alexander Pavlovich Lebedev	June 4, 1944
Sgt. Victor Ivanovich Medvedev	February 22, 1944
Sgt. Fyodor Maveyevich Okhlopkov	May 6, 1965
Lazar Khaimovich Papernik	July 21, 1942
Lt. Vladimir Pchelintsev	February 6, 1942
Guard Sr. Sgt. Stepan Vasilievich Petrenko	March 24, 1945
Petty Officer Philip Yakovlevich Rubakho	January 22, 1944
Capt. Ivan Mikhailovich Sidorenko	June 4, 1944
Sgt. Maj. Zhambyl Yesheevich Tulaev	February 14, 1943
Moisey Timofeevich Usik	October 17, 1943
Sr. Sgt. Gennady Iosifovich Velichko	October 26, 1943
Jr. Lt. Vassili Grigoryevich Zaitsev	February 22, 1943

The Gold Star was the highest state decoration in the former Soviet Union. With the decoration came the title Hero of the Soviet Union. *Fdutil/WikiC CC BY-SA 4.0.*

Marine Filipp Yakovlevich Rubarko is credited with 346 kills and one tank. He is seen here with a M91/30 equipped with a 4x PEM scope. *GF collection.*

1. V. Lugovsky in Leningrad. *USSR Information Bulletin.*

2. Memorial in Kerch to Jr. Sgt. Tatyana Ignatovna Kostyrina. © *Kerch.com.ru.*

3. Memorial honoring Hero of the Soviet Union, Viktor Ivanovich Medvedev (1922–68). He fought in the 216th Guards Regiment, 79th Guards Rifle Division, Eighth Guards Army (formerly Sixty-second Army) in Stalingrad and as a sniper is credited with 232 kills there. Like Vassili Zaitsev, he also trained snipers amid the ruins of that city. Medvedev also fought in Warsaw where he was wounded, but not before his score rose to 362. After recovering, he was sent to fight the Japanese and postwar worked as a machinist in the Troitsk State District Power Plant. *Andryusha Romanov/ WikiCommons.*

4. Soviet sniper Sr. Sgt. Maxim (sometimes spelled Maksim) Aleksandrovich Passar. Hailing from a family of hunters, as a child he learned to save as much fur as possible by hitting squirrels in the eye. He also learned patience which would serve him well as a sniper. He fought in Stalingrad and like Zaitsev and Medvedev, Passar also trained other snipers. Three of his trainees are credited with 100 kills each and Passar had a bounty of RM100,000 on his head. Credited with having killed 237 enemy soldiers, Passar himself was slain on January 22, 1943. He was posthumously made a Hero of the Russian Federation on February 16, 2010. *Courtesy the Central Museum of the Armed Forces, Moscow via Stavka.*

comrades were killed, and I too was wounded by shrapnel. The battalion commander ordered me to the field hospital in the rear, but my wounds were light so I didn't go. I could still shoot. In the next three days my team wiped out 165 fascists."

In recognition of his service, Mikhail Memkov was awarded the Order of the Red Star and credited with killing 261 enemy combatants. Cumulatively his sniping group is credited with 1,002 kills total.[29]

* * * * *

From the German perspective we have non-commissioned officer Josef Schaffstein who recorded in his diary:

"Gorodische, near Stalingrad. This is real hell! … I saw the Volga for the first time today. Our attacks are having no success; we began our attack successfully, then retreated … Heavy bombing at night. I thought our end had come … Our next attack was again unsuccessful. Bitter fighting. The enemy is firing from all sides, from every hole. You must not let yourself be seen."[30]

General Vasili Chuikov is best remembered for having defended Stalingrad (Volgograd today) against the German Sixth Army. In honor of their victory, his Sixty-second Army was renamed the Eighth Guards Army and Chuikov awarded the Order of Suvorov, First Class. Along with other Soviet armies, they fought their way to Berlin, a fitting end for their fighting career. He was awarded Hero of the Soviet Union twice and made Marshal of the Soviet Union in 1955. Before he passed on 18 March, 1982, Chuikov asked to be buried on Mamayez Kurgan so that he could be among his men. This memorial is in Volgograd. *Leha-11/WikiCommons (CC BY-SA 4.0)*.

Operation *Uran* (Uranus), the Soviet counter-offensive that isolated and trapped the Sixth Army, was launched on November 19. The Germans surrendered on January 28, 1943.

* * * * *

There were many other Soviet snipers who only had brief moments of fame. One was P. Mushtochkin who was known for his novel method of enticing his foe to expose himself. Mushtochkin stole a rubber squeeze type horn from a German car. Then he crawled within 150ft of the German's lair. "Toot! Toot!" enticed the German to raise his head to see who was visiting him. Instead of a hot meal, he got Mushtochkin's bullet.[31]

In fighting on the steppes outside of Stalingrad, German snipers took advantage of disabled or destroyed tanks, vehicles, planes, broken equipment, and anything that offered cover on the flat steppes. Their Soviet counterparts did the same and the fighting between them was said to be closer to that on the American frontier than modern mechanized warfare. At night, the Germans fired flares or lit bonfires to illuminate the battlefield.[32]

Outside the Stalingrad ring but still on the Volga was the Soviet Twenty-ninth Army. As a rifleman in the 375th Infantry Division, Yakut Siberian Fyodor Matveyevich Okhlopkov was already an experienced hunter and tracker. There, Fyodor lost his brother, Vasily, to an explosive bullet. He swore revenge and it wasn't long before his success was noted by the regimental commander. He was wounded three times in 1942 (March 2, April 3, and May 7) but refused medical care and cauterized his wound with a flaming pine branch. His luck ran out when he was wounded and knocked unconscious. This time he was sent to a hospital. Upon recovery, he was reassigned to the 234th Regiment of the 178th Division.

Okhlopkov's regimental commander welcomed him as a sniper and tasked him with eliminating a German sniper who had already killed seven Soviets. Like Vernigora, Okhlopkov was unschooled in sniping. The latter at least had the advantage of being a hunter. Okhlopkov studied the landscape and, knowing that Germans liked shooting from trees, focused on one pine tree. At a prearranged time, 0812 hours, an infantryman would raise his helmet 300ft from Okhlopkov's position. A shot rang out and the helmet was hit. Okhlopkov didn't see where it came from, but continued studying the tree. Then at 0842 hours, a glove was raised from where the helmet was exposed; suggesting a wounded man attempting to raise himself. It was followed by a second glove. The

German fired. This time Okhlopkov spotted part of a face as well as the muzzle of the gun. He fired twice and toppled the German, who fell headfirst to the ground. It would be the first of many German snipers who would fall to him.

Okhlopkov once feigned dead and lay among the bodies in no-man's-land. The smell from the decomposing corpses sickened him but he was rewarded when he killed a German sniper who was hiding behind a drainpipe. Being in the open, he could not return to Russian lines until after darkness. His luck was legendary and despite 12 wounds, he seemed immortal; that is, until he joined in an infantry attack against Vitebsk (north of Minsk) on June 23, 1944. He was shot in the chest. With an admirable tally of 429 kills, he was not allowed to return to the front and instead instructed aspiring snipers. Among his instructions:

- Don't imitate others but instead develop your own technique to fight the Nazis.
- Find new shooting positions with new camouflage.
- Fight from behind the enemy's lines.
- Use finesse, if you don't have an exit, don't go in.
- "In our business, anything can serve a useful purpose: a damaged tank, the hollow of a tree, the frame of a country well, a stay of hay or straw, even the oven of a burnt-down house or a dead horse."[33]

There were other accomplished Soviet snipers who were naturals and unschooled in sniping (see box p. 63). Included among them is Ivan Mikhailovich Sidorenko. Dropping out of Penza Art School, he was drafted into the Red Army graduating from the Simferopol Military Infantry School in 1941 straight into the battle of Moscow. A lieutenant in a mortar company, he taught himself to snipe and by the time he was promoted to Assistant Chief of Staff of the 1122d Infantry Regiment (334th Infantry Division, Fourth Shock Army, First Baltic Front) he was credited with 500 kills as well as preparing more than 250 snipers for the front. On June 4, 1944, he was awarded the title of Hero of the Soviet Union.

After the capitulation of the German Sixth Army on February 2, 1943, 91,000 men shuffled into captivity. Of them only around 9,000 would return after the war. Among them were *Hauptmann* Adelbert Holl and *Oberleutnant* Wigand Wüster, both of whom survived captivity and returned home (Wüster was captured by Soviet infantry on January 31). Chuikov's Sixty-second Army was rewarded by being renamed the Eighth Guards Army. Mansur Abdulin's regiment was also recognized by being retitled the 193d Guard Rifle Regiment and his 293d

Red Sniper Gets His Man

Before snow fell around Stalingrad, Soviet snipers helped reduce the German Army. This sniper had his kill filmed by a cameraman. *Author's collection*.

Infantry Division renamed the 66th Guards Division. More than just a title, Guards units received more (if not better) equipment and finally, all Guards were entitled to wear a Guards' badge on their uniform to distinguish them from regular soldiers.

In the wake of the Sixth Army's destruction and the Fourth Panzer Army's retreat from the Caucasus, the German army regrouped and at Kursk attempted to pinch off a large salient, thereby destroying a sizable portion of the Red Army. Instead, the Germans suffered irreplaceable losses with little gain to show for it. Their offensive was halted by layers of minefields defended by field fortifications held by a Red Army that was growing more skillful and confident. Finally, there was also the diversion of German units in response to the Allied invasion of Italy. This rendered the remaining units, which were now depleted, incapable of further offensive operations. From this point on, Germany would be on the defensive on the Eastern Front and the Soviet Army would push westward, liberating land that was captured in 1941–42.

Männer gegen Panzer

This old German training film—*Men against Tanks*—instructed infantrymen how to overcome the iron beast, and there were instances where a lone marksman accomplished something that other means (anti-tank, another tank, artillery, or mines) failed to do.

During the war, many American GIs mistakenly identified any German tank or even an assault gun as a feared Tiger. Similarly, almost any unseen rifleman becomes a sniper. Someone to be dreaded, feared, and shown no mercy once located.

During the Ardennes offensive, the shortage of infantrymen compelled the Americans to scour the rear areas for men. Among them was a dump truck and bulldozer operator who learned to shoot in boot camp. Placed in a truck, they had no idea where they were or where they were going. When they reached their destination, they found themselves parceled out among the paratroopers. With dawn came the Germans. A PzKpfw IV with its long-barreled 75mm gun led two armored halftracks and a line of infantry. The GIs had some comfort in being supported by two Shermans, but neither tank would engage and remained hidden behind some houses.

"I looked around to see what everybody else was doing, and everyone was sitting tight. The paratroopers never moved, so no one else did either.

"I kept expecting the two Sherman tanks to appear and start shooting; but nothing happened, and the German tank just kept coming, at the same pace as the infantry.

"Sticking up, out of the top turret hatch, was the head of the German tank commander. He was wearing their standard steel helmet, and he only showed enough so his eyes could see over the hatch rim. In this way, he was very well protected.

"About this time, I figured that if I was going to die, I was going to try to take this bastard with me. So I whipped up the Garand, and rested it on top of the wall, and everything kind of went into slow motion. I suppose that this was because I was scared so bad. But I remember feeling very calm as I snapped the safety catch forward, into the off position.

"At this same time, the Kraut raised his head well up above the hatch rim and turned to look back to his left rear to see how the infantry was keeping up. He was a little over a hundred yards from me now, and as he turned back to look forward, he was right in my sights. I took up the slack in the trigger just like I had practiced a thousand times before pulling the trigger.

"The bang of the rifle was louder than hell, and as it recoiled up off the wall he disappeared down into the tank. At the same time, the tank lurched, turned about a quarter turn to the left, and nosed down off the high crowned road into the snow-covered ditch. It stopped with its nose pointing down quite a bit and we could hear the driver trying to restart the stalled engine. In a second or two, it caught, and was spinning the treads trying to back up onto the road again.

"At this time, our guys down on the right put the water cooled .30 up on the top of the wall without its tripod, and with a couple of them holding it there on both sides, they went to work on the infantry caught right out in the open field. They just knocked the hell out of them.

"Suddenly, there was a long hell of a bang behind us. What had happened was that one of the Sherman tank crew had been hiding and watching for an opening to attack the infantry. He sprinted back and the two Shermans pulled up and slammed two rounds into the MK-4's right rear quarter section. The first round penetrated and knocked out the engine, and the second blew the bogie wheel and the right track. The two half-tracks were caught flat-footed, as the tank had the narrow road completely blocked, and the fields were too soft to support them at this time. The Shermans made very quick short work of them, too."

The Germans retreated to the woods and a white flag appeared. A German officer stepped out along with a soldier who bore the white flag. They were met by an American officer and a German-speaking trooper. The German officer asked for a truce to remove their dead. This was granted.

Crying and moaning was heard emanating from the disabled tank. The German-speaking trooper approached and demanded the crew's surrender. The tank quieted. The trooper warned that if they refused to surrender, the Shermans would shoot again. This time hands appeared and four crewmen emerged; one of whom had a bandaged head and helmet with a bullet hole in it.

It was learned that the bullet had entered the helmet's rim and exited the rear. When shot, the injured commander fell into the turret, knocking the loader over who in turn slammed into the driver, causing the driver to lose control and drive the tank into the ditch.

The American officer who agreed to the truce went back to the men and asked, "Who fired that first shot?" As everyone else knew, the culprit identified himself and explained why. The officer gazed at him silently before responding, "Good shooting."[34]

During the American counter-offensive, a German tank column attempted to push them and destroyed two tanks. The lead German tank was knocked out but an open-topped self-propelled gun charged out from the side. S/Sgt. Robert Lotz damaged the periscope which caused the commander to expose himself to direct the vehicle. Lotz shot him down too and his squad flanked it and disabled the crew with hand grenades.[35]

The Americans were very aware of how tank commanders endangered themselves by exposing their heads from the hatch. This gave them a better view of battle and allowed them to direct their tank driver and gunner better. Unfortunately, the trade-off was exposure to small-arms fire. Early in the war the old mirror-style periscope needed replacement and a laminate plate-glass prism was developed by the Libby-Owens-Ford Glass Company for tanks that offered 50 percent greater visibility.[36] While this improved visibility, it didn't stop commanders from exposing themselves. For example, on April 24, 1945, near Nattheim, Germany, Lt. Bill Chapman (4th Infantry Division) mounted a Sherman tank to confer with its commander who was standing in his hatch. A bullet struck the hatch rim, causing the commander to drop down into the turret and almost slamming the lid on Chapman's hand. Chapman saved his hand by diving off and behind the tank.[37]

Sepp Allerberger's battalion was attacked by Russian infantry who were riding American-made M3 halftracks into battle. Examining one through his binoculars, he observed the driver's viewing slit. From a distance of 60m he fired at the slit and the vehicle slid into a shell crater where it became stuck. He then proceeded to do the same to another seven out of 12 halftracks that day with similarly gratifying results.[38]

When the Tiger I was first introduced in combat, it was sent to Heavy Tank Battalion 502 under the Leningrad Front. They fought south of Lake Ladoga near Sinyavino and south of Krasny Bor between January 12 and March 31, 1943. On April 12, during a probe of the Russian positions, a Soviet anti-tank man armed with a 14.5mm x 114mm caliber PTRD anti-tank rifle achieved something that the 76mm-armed T-34s had failed to do: turn back a Tiger. With nerves of steel,

the unknown Russian fired a single shot that penetrated the vision glass of the armored cupola. It killed the commander, *Stabsfeldwebel* Sanderring. Afterward, the Tiger retreated.[39]

Soviet defense against the Panzers

Soviet doctrine called for the anti-tank rifleman to kill the tank commanders and an examination of the photo of *Hauptmann* Lange's cupola on his Tiger I in Richard Freiherr von Rosen's book, *Panzer Ace* shows evidence of several hits by a 14.5mm anti-tank rifle. Panther radio operator/bow machine gunner Henk Kistemaker acknowledged that the commander was always the most vulnerable crew member to the sniper.[40] Leaflets identifying vulnerable spots for anti-tank riflemen were distributed. Heavy Tank Battalion 507's Tiger No. 311 was being driven by Siegfried Beck when the viewing slit shield deflected an anti-tank rifle's armor piercing round. On July 2, 1944, near Polonka (today in Belarus), Tiger crewman Ludwig Hagenberger had his nose shot off when a bullet fired from an anti-tank rifle pierced his viewing slit.[41] While the anti-tank rifle disappeared from the inventories of armies worldwide, heavy caliber anti-material weapons would reemerge as sniper rifles decades later.

Shooting exposed tank commanders or tank periscopes was not unique to the Soviets. When Americans lacked anti-tank weapons, they fired at Japanese tanks' periscopes with small arms.[42] Similarly, the Japanese did likewise to the American tanks. In New Guinea, Australian-manned M3

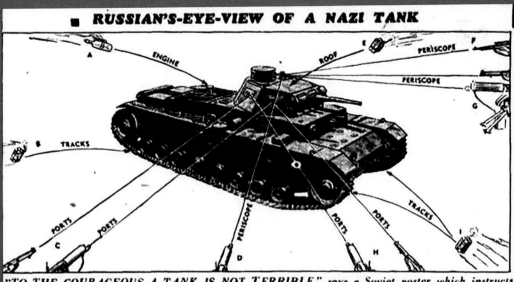

Soviet defense against Panzers—Soviet anti-tank riflemen, infantry, and snipers were instructed on the vulnerable points of German tanks. Snipers were to aim at the periscopes to blind them. The tank here is an early 37mm-armed PzKpfw III. *Author's collection* .

Caption within image:

RUSSIAN'S-EYE-VIEW OF A NAZI TANK

ENGINE · ROOF · PERISCOPE · PERISCOPE · TRACKS · PORTS · PORTS · PORTS · PORTS · PERISCOPE · TRACKS

"TO THE COURAGEOUS A TANK IS NOT TERRIBLE." says a Soviet poster which instructs citizens how to fight tanks, urges them to study the vulnerable points of tanks and do this at these points, from all angles:—

A.—Throw fire bottles into engine.
B.—Throw hand grenade bundles under tracks.
C.—Direct fire from rifles and machine guns on the ports.
D.—Fire at the gunner's periscope.
E.—Throw bundles of hand grenades on the roof.
F & G.—Direct sniper fire at gunner's periscope.
H.—Fire on the ports from this angle, also.
I.—Throw bundles of grenades under the front tracks.

Stuart light tanks opened the assault against the Buna Mission. They were closely followed by Australian infantry who kept the Japanese at a distance from the Stuarts. Two M3s had just smashed the strongpoint at Cape Endaladere when they were summoned back to assist the Americans who were stopped by two pillboxes that had been overlooked. Dutifully, the two Stuarts retraced their steps and blasted the pillboxes at point-blank range. The captain commanding one tank was tossing grenades into the trenches when a bullet smashed through the glass visor, causing an injury to his hand. He was replaced by a lieutenant colonel.

"It was not easy going for us, however, for, with coconut trees every 12 feet and a year's jungle growth among them we could never tell what was ahead, and continuously had to feel our way. When the captain was shot the visor was damaged, and would not close. A sniper shot me through it, as I was dropping grenades into a weapon pit. My steel hat saved me, but I got a black eye and cuts which filled my eyes with blood. The gunner put a dressing on my head, and I continued in action directing the tank advance until weakness through the loss of blood made me a burden to the tank and the force." One Stuart machine gunner "never stopped crooning, and his crooning took on the tone of a pleased puppy every time he saw a Japanese sniper in the trees. We had our casualties, but, fortunately, none of our men had been killed."[43]

Above: The length of the PTRD-41 anti-tank rifle and size of rounds (14.5mm cartridge) is well shown here. *Unknown author - http://waralbum.ru/8375/, Public Domain, https://commons.wikimedia.org/w/index.php?curid=31154373.*

Right: Soviet anti-tank gunners equipped with a PTRD-41 anti-tank rifle. Occasionally because of its range, they would attempt to snipe individual Germans with this rifle. *Courtesy the Central Museum of the Armed Forces, Moscow via Stavka.*

9 Nach Berlin![1]

"Snipers made every step out of the trench a race against death."[2]

Leutnant Martin Pöppel was in the MG Battalion of 7th Flieger Division, which was redesignated 1st *Fallschirmjäger* Division in 1943. He fought in the Soviet Union until he was injured on January 8, 1942, returning to his unit around Demidov (near Smolensk) on October 19. In February 1943, *Unteroffizier* Idzykowski was using a scoped rifle to shoot at Soviet sentries. Evidently confident that they were immune from return fire because of the distance, *Obergefreiter* Fuchs and *Leutnant* Pöppel were both standing upright and outside the trench to observe when Fuchs was unexpectedly hit. Pöppel wrote:

> "When Fuchs grabs himself around the heart I'm sure that he's done for and start to drag him into the trenches. But he manages to hobble to the bunker under his own steam—I can hardly believe my eyes—and removes a 14mm anti-tank rifle bullet from his shoe! We're both stunned at his incredible luck."

Apparently the Soviets didn't have any snipers to duel *Unteroffizier* Idzykowski and, not wanting to start a battle, called upon the only long-range weapon immediately available—an anti-tank rifle. While effective at short ranges against tanks, poor quality-control of its ammunition made the rifles inaccurate at longer range. Soviet sniper Vassili Zaitsev attempted to create a longer-range sniper weapon by attaching a PEM scope to an anti-tank rifle. He abandoned his project after he, too, found that the ammunition lacked the accuracy required.[3] Whoever the Soviet anti-tank rifleman was, he finally figured out the hold and scored a kill. Lt. Pöppel recalled:

> "At 11:00 hours Obergefreiter Waldfried is hit at the entrance to the bunker. Though I get to him straight away, there's nothing anyone can do to save him ... Unfortunately, incidents such as those are greatly on the increase at the moment."[4]

Sepp Allerberger was a machine gunner with 7th Company, 144th *Gebirgsjäger* Regiment. While recovering from his wounds he was on light duty assisting the regimental chief armorer by repairing broken K98k Mauser stocks.[5] He found a Russian Mosin-Nagant 91/30 sniper rifle and began practicing

Goliath

Wars brings about innovations. As an example, to remove Soviet bunkers or strongpoints, the Germans introduced a small remote-controlled land caterpillar, the Goliath, that carried a 220lb explosive charge. First issued to panzer and engineer units, it could be devastating against a tank, pillbox or strongpoint. However, it was slow (6mph) and its 10mm armor plate and exposed control cables made it vulnerable to countermeasures. When the Soviets learned of their nefarious nature, snipers were instructed to destroy them before they could reach Soviet positions. Many were found in Normandy after the invasion, but there are few records of them being used in action.[6]

Goliaths were found on American and British Normandy beaches, June 6, 1944. NARA.

with it. His skill impressed the chief armorer who consented to Allerberger returning to the front with it. His company commander needed snipers and gave Allerberger free reign to hunt.

He began by interviewing his fellow soldiers to learn about enemy activity. Most were glad to see him with a scoped rifle. Using an eight-power binocular issued to him by his commanding officer, he surveyed the terrain through a gap in the parapet logs. Seeing nothing, he rolled up a tent, propped a hat onto it and raised it above the log. The Soviet sniper took the bait, fired at the decoy, and from his muzzle flash, revealed his position to Allerberger. Allerberger learned two lessons almost immediately. Never fire at anything

German soldiers in happier times. Note scoped SVT-40-armed *Landser* on the left. Lacking German sniping equipment, the Germans equipped themselves with captured Soviet sniping rifles. *Image courtesy Georg Oberaigner.*

gun was sniffing out a target. Satisfied that there was no threat, the turret hatch cracked open. Allerberger immediately sighted in on the opening, hoping that a target would emerge.

"I aimed the crosswires of my telescopic sight at the lid. [This is likely the translator's error. German reticles were not crosswires but a heavy post that comes to a point near the center and two side bars with one at three and the other at nine o'clock.] A head protruded two hands' breadth above the rim, and a pair of hands raised binoculars to the head's eyes. I calibrated my weapon on a pinpoint at 120 metres [130yd]—if he raised himself much higher I would be bound to score. In this situation it was absolutely essential that the shot was good, for it would signal the fire-fight to begin. I hesitated briefly, during which time it occurred to me that the individual was probably not only the commander of the tank, but possibly the entire attack. His death might decide the affair in our favour. I took a deep breath, concentrated, put myself into a calm frame of mind, drew back on the trigger evenly, and the shot cracked out. Through the sight I saw a torrent of blood spatter the hatch lid, after which the head disappeared. Seconds later everybody began firing. The three tanks, immobile, raised a harmless fire above our lines; after a few minutes their motors started up and the colossi reversed, confirming my assumption. The Soviet attack was now leaderless, and when the Soviet follow-up began an hour later it lacked impetus and conviction. A single bullet had rendered the enemy assault literally leaderless and in all probability enabled us to ward it off."[8]

until the target is positively identified. Second, after firing, either desist from firing any further from that lair or move to a secondary position.

After placing his rolled blanket on the parapet as a rest, Allerberger rested his rifle on it and allowed the muzzle to protrude between the logs. Since the logs prohibited the use of the telescopic sights, Allerberger used his iron sights. His opponent was only 100yd away. Since everyone was focused on him as if he was a performer on stage, Allerberger felt very nervous. He focused carefully on the target, squeezed the trigger, and fired. Another *Jäger* joyfully shouted, "You got him!" In the eyes of his company, Allerberger was now a genuine sniper and all felt better about having a real sniper among them. He had learned a lesson too:

"War is a merciless system of Killing and Being Killed. In action sympathy for the enemy is ultimately suicide, for every opponent whom you do not kill can turn the tables and kill you. Your chances of survival are measured by the yardstick of how you compare in skill and objectivity as against your opponent."[7]

Allerberger did not betray the trust of the regimental chief armorer or his company commander. He went on to kill two more Soviets who had carelessly exposed themselves that day.

Later, while Allerberger and his comrades scanned the enemy lines, a new threat emerged in the form of three T-34 tanks that stopped 500yd from the German trenches. One tank rotated its turret, as if its

Allerberger was not infallible and one mistake cost a comrade's life. The fighting had quieted down and was limited to raids. As there was no opposing sniper, Allerberger made a hide beneath a burned-out T-34. Its steel bulk offered him shelter from artillery but since the Soviets had no artillery, he was relatively safe. However, he made the mistaking of firing from it continuously for four days straight and his hide had been identified. A Soviet sniper was called upon to eliminate him. On the fifth day Allerberger returned but with a friend, Balduin Moser.

Beneath the supposed safety of the tank, they began scanning the Soviet lines. Allerberger with his scoped rifle and Moser with binoculars. A glint of light reflecting off the binoculars probably betrayed Moser's presence. He was pointing out a suspicious location, "Two fingers near the little hump there's a movem …"

Moser didn't finish his sentence as a bullet struck the binoculars before tearing into his mouth and blowing away his lower jaw. Another explosive bullet followed, blowing up the ground between them. Allerberger pulled Bauldin down into the darkest and deepest hole beneath the tank. Allerberger watched helplessly as his friend's breathing grew increasingly difficult. He gave Allerberger one final look, extended his hand to say goodbye, and died in Allerberger's arms.[9]

Being the sole sniper, prior to Matthäus Hetzenauer's arrival in March, sometime in January 1944 Sepp Allerberger was transferred from his company to the battalion where his skills would be available to the entire unit.[10]

On January 16, elements of the 282d Infantry Division fighting near Marianovka (north of Rostov, Ukraine) found themselves under a bombardment which lasted for two days. Soviet infantry began its attacks. As a radioman, Funker Georg Rauch found himself in his first battle, busy replacing telephone lines that had been broken by enemy fire. After the Soviet attacks were halted, Rauch recalled that they had brought out their anti-tank rifles which they then used with deadly effect. "These fast and low-shooting weapons could draw a bead on each separate man, on every house, on every hole with a German inside. This knowledge had a horrible psychological effect on our troops. The Russian guns produced very high casualties."[11] Rauch survived and later won an Iron Cross, First Class, when he reestablished contact that allowed his surrounded unit to break out. He was captured afterward but being Austrian, was released in 1945.

In the summer offensives that followed German failure at Kursk, the Soviets attacked the salients from which the Germans had launched their attacks. Lt. Evgeni Bessonov was now a *desanti* (tank-mounted infantry) in the 2d Platoon, 1st Company, 1st Motor Rifle Battalion of the 49th Mechanized Brigade, 6th Guards Mechanized Corps, Fourth Tank Army. They attacked south on the Bryansk Front and drove the Germans back. Having been a sniper instructor, Bessonov knew better than to distinguish himself from his men. He therefore declined the light-coloured sheepskin coat offered to officers as it would immediately mark him as a target.[12] After that campaign, his unit was transferred to the Kiev area where they attacked the Germans in the western Ukraine. By March 14/15, 1944, they were fighting the Germans for Skalat. During this fight his marksmanship skills were called upon.

"German snipers arrived on the scene. My soldiers tracked down one of them—he was firing from a window of a high house. Shakulo's

German soldier armed with a high-turret mounted K98k. *Nik Cornish at www. Stavka.org.uk.*

platoon had a Soviet-made sniper rifle. I got a commission to get the guy. I was looking out for him for a long time and when his head popped up in the window, fired a round. Soldiers, who were observing our duel through binoculars, told me that I got him. The German never popped up again."[13]

Skalat was captured and the Soviets advanced. By March 27 they had established a bridgehead over the River Strypa.

* * * * *

Machine gunner Hans Kahr was a farmer's son from East Styria. A farming school student, his pre-military service included working an auxiliary in an AA battery and the *Reicharbeitsdienst* (labor service). After training, in November 1943 he was sent to Nikopol to join 4th (Heavy) Company 1/138th Regiment,

German officers with scoped rifles

Five examples have been found where German officers possessed a rifle with telescopic sights. As their job was to lead rather than fight, it is unlikely that officers would be trained as snipers. Research has divulged several incidents that should be explained. Normally, a sniper rifle was issued in two ways. A prospective sniper attended a sniping school and then left with the rifle he had used in training. The other method was described in Sepp Allerberger's example where he worked with the regimental armorer and was allowed to take a captured Soviet sniper rifle with him when he returned to the front. Should a sniper be killed or disabled, his rifle normally should have been returned to the regimental armory. In the confusion of a retreat, it may have fallen into the hands of an officer. Alternatively, the scoped rifle remained with the company and was probably not in the hands of a trained sniper. So, when the officer needed it, he called for it and used it.

During the breakout from the Korsun-Cherkassy Pocket, *Oberstleutnant* Gerhard Franz (Kampfgruppe Stemmermann, XLII Corps) had a rifle with telescope sights. How he got one is unknown but no one cared. Everyone was desperate

to escape. He and other survivors were in the woods when shots were heard. Belgian SS Walloon Legion men appeared and reported, "An enemy machine-gun is blocking the way out from the forest across a clearing. We can't get through. We've already suffered casualties—killed and wounded." Franz took his rifle and accompanied them forward so that they could point out the machine gun to him. Peering through the scope, Franz estimated the distance to be 300m (330yd). He fired three times, killing the machine gunner and his two assistants. Franz stepped first into the opening and after going five paces, the rest of the column followed him southwest.[14] Franz survived the war as a general commanding 256th *Volksgrenadier* Division.

Oberstleutnant Joachim Heidschmidt was another German officer known to use a scoped rifle—a Mauser K98k with a turret-mounted Ajack 4x 90 scope. Like Franz, Heidschmidt survived the war, having served throughout in the 508th Infantry Regiment, 292d Infantry Division. He began the war as a *Hauptmann* (captain) and finished as a *Oberstleutnant* (lieutenant colonel) with the same regiment. His Knight's Cross was earned on August 27, 1944, while he was serving as a major commanding the battalion.[15]

During the siege of Festung (fortress) Poznan, a Soviet sniper had been wreaking havoc on the Germans. Tiger tank commander Richard Siegert watched as *Leutnant* Pehle took up position next to him in an attic. Lt. Pehle removed some tiles to create a firing port. Taking up binoculars, he studied the windows of a building the Soviet was known to be shooting from. "Suddenly Pehle picked up his rifle and I watched as he put the barrel through the roof opening and waited. I tried to hold my breath, but it was impossible: the incessant shaking caused my hands to tremble. At that moment, I saw his finger flex as the recoil forced the rifle butt back into his shoulder. Without a word, he handed me his binoculars and pointed to the mansion on our left. I scanned the area and suddenly spotted a dead Russian hanging from a small staircase window, his rifle still in his hand."[16]

Richard Law's book, *Backbone of the Wehrmacht, Vol. II*, has a photo of Maj. John Lee of 6th Battalion, Argyll & Sutherland Highlanders, looking through a turret-mounted K98k sniper rifle which was "latterly the property of a German major, who no longer had a use for his rifle."[17]

7th Infantry Regiment, 252d Infantry Division, Third Panzer Army, found itself fighting in western Russia and later Lithuania. Among its men was 20-year-old Lt. Armin Scheiderbauer, who led a company reduced to a mere 20 men. Around January 16, 1944, they had been forced to retreat and just repelled a Russian attack with well-aimed gunfire. As their reward, the Russians treated them to an artillery

Knight's Cross-wearing German officer—probably *Oberstleutnant* Joachim Heidschmidt—with a turret-mounted K98k and Zf39 scope. He was awarded the Knights Cross on August 27, 1944, while commanding the 509th Grenadier Regiment, 292d Infantry Division, in its defensive actions on the Eastern Front.

bombardment. Scheiderbauer described his response:

"I scanned the farm with my binoculars and discovered the advanced observers. There were two men with wireless sets, whose heads, shoulders and equipment could be seen behind low cover. I asked to be handed a rifle with a telescopic sight and for a runner to observe through the binoculars. Then I pushed myself carefully over the parapet of the trench and calmly took aim. There was a soft pressure as I fired. The observer's head sank on to the cover and that of the second man disappeared. My runner saw through the binoculars the dead man being dragged back to cover."

The distance to the farm was about 650yd (600m). During his training as an officer-cadet, Scheiderbauer scored 55 points while shooting prone at a target 230yd (200m) away. His training paid off but unfortunately for his company, another Russian observer was able to direct fire onto them that inflicted casualties before they were ordered to withdraw.[18]

With the exception of Scheiderbauer, who was never a hunter, no pattern may be discerned explaining how the other officers came about a scoped rifle or were skilled in their use. It is likely that in the prewar peace they were sportsmen hunters.

General of Infantry and commander of the XXXVI *Gebirgsjäger* Army Corps Karl Weisenberger visits his Finnish "brother-in-arms" and examines a captured Soviet M91/30 with side-mounted PEM 4x scope. Weisenberger's corps was supposed to capture Murmansk. He commanded the corps December 1, 1941–August 1944. *NARA.*

3d *Gebirgsjäger* Division. They were attacked almost immediately and barely held off the Soviets.

The 138th's sister regiment in the division, the 144th, was even harder-pressed in the fighting. Kahr's boyhood friend and neighbor, identified only as Toni M., was equipped with a K98k and Zf41 scope. The only advantage the long eye-relief scope gave him was that he could still use stripper clips for faster reloading.

"As I mentioned, my school friend Toni served with this unit. He witnessed and survived the battles that day. During one of our chance meetings at the front, he told me more about it. It turned out that, after a long, hard struggle, the enemy finally succeeded in breaking through the lines around the village of Stachanov. The main battle line had soon been broken, and wild carnage set in. Just as Toni wanted to push a new loading strip into his sniper rifle, a Russian had jumped on him with a bayonet. Quickly turning

aside, he had barely been able to dodge what would have been a fatal blow and, in return, he had smashed his rifle butt into the Russian's head. With all the comrades around him already fallen, he had fought his way back to the company command post, running alongside Russian tanks."[19]

Around April 20, 1944, while 3d *Gebirgsjäger* was holding a defensive position on the Dniester River, Sepp Allerberger learned that snipers could be unpopular among their own men. He climbed a hill and saw some Soviets bathing in the river below. He killed one at 600yd before scrambling down the hill. Mortar fire crashed down upon his firing point while Allerberger fled back to the trenches where he received a hostile reception from the occupants who knew there would be retaliation. It came in the form of machine-gun fire and artillery shells and after it lifted, Allerberger absented himself to avoid further verbal abuse.[20]

Eighteen-year-old ethnic German Czech-born John Steiber had been raised in Ireland. Besides being fluent in German, he spoke English with an English accent, and as a teenager was sent to Germany for schooling. Caught up in the war, Steiber as a youth served in a Luftwaffe AA unit as a *Luftwaffenhelfer* or *Flakhelfer* (Luftwaffe auxiliary) before turning 18 and enlisting in the Hermann Göring Division. After training, he joined one of the division's AA units. After the fall of Rome, the division transferred from Italy and was sent southeast of Warsaw in the vicinity of Magnuszew. A Soviet penetration that crossed the Vistula River had to be contained. Steiber was ordered to go to a forward observation post to relieve another solider. The post was sited to observe the Soviets and give notice of any impending movement. Warned by the soldier he relieved that the post may have been spotted by the Soviets, Steiber held the post for an hour before it came under fire. Pressing himself against the bottom of his hole, Steiber endured hours of shelling. At dusk, with no relief forthcoming, Steiber decided to return to his battery. No sooner had he begun returning when gunfire erupted around the battery. They started their engines and left without him. Abandoned, Steiber began trekking west toward the German lines.

At nightfall, he bedded down among the undergrowth in the woods. He continued his journey the next day. Sunrise allowed him to get his east/west bearings and Steiber tried his best to remain under cover. There was one point when he had no choice but to cross open ground. Thankfully it was only for half a mile. As he stepped out in to the open, he became exposed to a Soviet sniper. He relates his experience:

"I held my helmet close to my body in the hope that only somebody with binoculars could recognize me as a German soldier, and set off quickly. I must have got to within 200 yards of safety when I heard a bullet hit a bush close to me. From the vibration of the branch and the sound of a rifle I knew that it had not come from ahead of me. It had to be from behind me and somewhere to the right and seemed to come from a sniper fairly far away.

"Anticipating that there would already be a second bullet in the air and a third one just leaving the sniper's rifle, I automatically dropped to the ground and began to crawl swiftly to my left; hoping that the sniper had lost sight of me when I dropped down. I waited for the third shot and then sprang up and ran for a few seconds in the direction of the wood before dropping down again. Once more, I crawled to the side waiting

for the next few shots to be fired and then leapt up for another sprint. This time I could keep my run shorter as I managed to reach an area covered with ferns about two feet high. I was now able to cover the last stretch by crawling, but had to be careful not to disturb the ferns too much, because the sniper was still taking the odd pot-shot at me. Having safely entered the edge of the wood I did not stop for a breather, but immediately hurried on. I decide to make a slight detour, although I did not think the sniper could alert anybody to try to intercept me."

In the safety of the woods, Steiber discarded his helmet and gas mask as impediments to mobility. He escaped the sniper but on the third day almost walked into a Soviet column. Backing into the woods, he waited for them to depart before continuing. His food was exhausted (day four) and Steiber was living on snow melted in his canteen. On the fifth day he found a destroyed cottage that had a barrel of pickled tomatoes. He ate some and placed some in his bag before heading west. Hearing gunfire, he took this as a good omen that he was approaching the front line. Following a logging road, he came across a German truck and circled around it until he could identify the men. Happily for him, they were from his own division! To avoid being shot (as Russians were known to master the German language), he began to shout in the Hamburg accent[21] known throughout Germany and unlikely to be used by a Russian, as he approached. He was welcomed back and fed.[22]

Steiber's odyssey was a minor episode in the Soviet Lvov–Sandomierz offensive which in itself was part of Operation Bagration that destroyed much of Army Group Center and forced the Germans from the Ukraine and Eastern Poland. After the liberation of Lvov (July 27, 1944), Bessonov's battalion was ordered to attack toward the Polish town of Przemyśl (Peremyshl in Ukrainian). By July 30, they were on the right bank of the Dniester and in a village near Sambir. Once they crossed the Dniester, they would be in Sambir proper but first they had to enter the village. Bessonov remembers what happened:

"A threatening silence hung in the air. I was used to relying on intuition, and I did not believe that there weren't any Fritzes in the houses. Machine-gun platoon leader Lieutenant Petr Malyutin from our MG company, however, did not agree with me, saying: 'There are no Fritzes in the village, because it is quiet.' It was this very quietness that scared me. I was about to send a squad of soldiers to check what was going on in the village, when Malyutin went out to the middle of the road and started to inspect the village through his binoculars. A shot sounded—the bullet hit him right between the eyes and the binoculars fell apart into two pieces."[23]

Instead of storming the village, their battalion commander had it bypassed with a flanking maneuver. As they did, the Germans emerged from behind to attack. Many Soviets panicked at the sight of the Germans and fled. Level-headed Soviets like Bessonov fired at the Germans to stem the tide. Bessonov had a close call before being compelled to retreat.

"As I fired, my garrison cap fell from my head, I put it back on and continued to fire, before I ran out of ammo … When I ran out of ammo, I withdrew, sometimes sneaking and sometimes in short rushes to the rear, where the fighters ran, or rather, frightened soldiers, one could not call them fighters—they had got scared by a bunch of 40 or 50 Germans." Gradually, after the Germans escaped, Bessonov and the other officers rallied their men. "We were all hungry after the skirmish and arranged some snacks. During the meal one of the officers asked me: 'Where did you tear your garrison cap?' I took it off and saw two torn holes in it—in the front and the back. It was only then that I recalled that the garrison cap had fallen from my head as I heard the machine-gun and told the story. The guys told me: 'You were really lucky, Bessonov, if that sniper had aimed several millimeters lower, you would have been dead.'"[24]

* * * * *

In what seemed like endless retreats, the 3d Gebirgsjäger Division finally stopped at the foothills of eastern Carpathian Mountains. Machine gunner Kahr had set up his weapon with a boulder behind him and, as customary by then, carefully camouflaged his post. Their lieutenant came up and urged him to shoot at the (unseen) Russians who were thought to be a couple of hundred meters away. Kahr was hesitant and his lieutenant goaded him:

"'Well, what are you waiting for, are you too much of a coward to shoot?'

"I heard a restrained, 'Why don't you shoot!' coming from behind. I immediately recognized the voice of the Alsatian, who had grown accustomed to our dialect. And the lieutenant would not be embarrassed in front of us. Without further ado, he got a carbine, climbed onto the

boulder and fired across to the other side. He did not have a chance to fire a second shot. What was probably a sniper's bullet pierced his left shoulder and threw him off the rock. There he was. With a pained face. Dazed, but alive. A Jäger ran over to him immediately and began to bandage his shoulder. The lieutenant stared in disbelief at his shattered shoulder joint and with the next onset of pain he finally fainted. For him the war was over."[25]

A few days later on August 19, 1944, the Soviets bombarded their sector and on the following day, launched a major offensive which pushed the Germans out of Romania. Additionally, the Romanians had switched sides, trapping many German divisions. Kahr's Gebirgsjäger division escaped into Hungary.

Fighting on the northern sector near Leningrad was 7th Panzer Division. Combat engineers Helmut Jung and his friend, Hans Meier, were both sent to a sniping school in the rear. Upon return from the school, they were transferred from their platoon to the regiment where other specialist troops were assigned. Almost immediately they were called upon to an area where a soldier a day was being lost to Soviet snipers. Another pair of sharpshooters had been sent earlier, but they had fallen victim to their prey.

Jung learned that the Soviets had been shooting in the morning when the Germans were blinded by the rising sun. He reasoned that in the evening when the Germans enjoyed the advantage the Soviets would hide until it was too dark to shoot. However, even when the sun was low on the horizon and in his favor, the Soviets were still able to see and hit their targets. One Landser who was helping by trying to spot the Soviets was shot and killed. Another was suspicious that the shots originated from a rooftop or from a tree, but even when using his higher power binoculars, Jung was unable to discern the Soviet's location.

Camouflaged Gebirgsjäger uses his skis as cross sticks to support his rifle. *NARA*.

Attitude toward opponent

While the Soviet press was guilty (as was everybody else) of mocking the enemy, Pavlichenko did not agree with the writers who mocked the enemy's appearance. To her, they were the enemy to be driven from the Motherland. No glorification or exaggeration was needed nor should a sniper, in her opinion, put too much thought into it.[26] Similarly, German sniper Sutkus did not feel contempt towards the Soviets. Sepp Allerberger witnessed two Soviets torture and execute two soldiers. Rather than kill them in a heat of passion, he shot them professionally.[27] Englishman Sgt. Harry Furness felt sniping was a specialist duty and to "switch off" his emotions and concentrate on making the shot.[28]

"Live baiting," c. 1942. *Blavatnik Archive Foundation (http://www.blavatnikarchive.org).*

· Рис. Бор. Ефимова.

The two snipers needed help. They were both inexperienced and their opponent very skilled and experienced. Help was forthcoming from the *Landser* whom they were charged with protecting. One man raised an object which drew fire. Neither Jung nor Meier spotted where the shot came from and they shifted positions to observe different potential hides.

They instructed the *Landser* to raise the decoy again. The Soviets refused to be baited again and withheld their fire. Finally, as darkness approached, one soldier asked if he could try to spot them with the binoculars. So that both snipers could concentrate on their scopes, Jung handed them over to the soldier who went down the trench and propped himself up. Bang! A bullet narrowly missed him but he cried out, "He's on the left corner of the roof. On the house on the left!"

Jung had scanned the roof area earlier and now, scrutinizing it more closely, made out the Soviet and fired. Unsure whether he had hit him or not, they called it quits and retired for the night. It was too dark to do more.

Returning to the trench before dawn, they began studying the terrain in search of their opponent. A dummy was raised by a *Landser* to simulate a soldier who was getting up. It failed to draw fire as the Soviets were now wise to them and knew they were up against another sniper. A long period passed before the dummy was tried again. This time it was hit. They were joined in a battle of wits; a sniping duel with each side attempting to induce the other to shoot. Both were keenly aware of the other's presence, and patience and cunning came into play. Jung and Meier didn't located their opponent that day and one soldier who was helping them was shot and killed.

"The following day was almost my last day on Earth. It began just like the day before, teasing and spotting for shots from the Russians. The hours were passing very slowly and there is no way for me to describe the tension that kept every nerve in my body as tight as wire. I was looking with my field glasses every chance I got. That meant peaking over the edge of the trench for just a moment and then dropping back before the Russian could send a bullet after me. There was one spot I hadn't paid a great deal of attention to, a big broad-leaf tree. I took one more look at the tree and when I did, a bullet snapped the air as it went within an inch of my ear. I felt the wind."

It was a close call that almost cost Jung his life. Instead of being scared, which Jung admitted should have been his reaction, Jung became mad, real mad. He now knew that the Soviet was in the tree, but what to do?

"The Russian sharpshooter was in that tree. Then I began to play a real guessing game with myself. The Russian had seen me too, that was obvious, and if I was going to try to shoot him I should move to a new position in the trench. I thought,

'Wouldn't the Russian expect me to move, wouldn't he be looking for me somewhere else?' I decided, very quickly, to shoot from where I was, without re-positioning myself. I would get only one chance and this was it.

"Hans had watched all this time and when I started to get up so I could train my rifle over the trench he began to yell at me. He told me to get down, the Russian had me spotted. I heard those words but I was already in motion. I found the Russian in my scope. He saw me a moment later but he had been looking for me at another point in the trench. I could watch him move, he was swinging his rifle around to aim at me. The picture in my mind is vivid and it seems like slow motion. The Russian was leaning his eye to his scope when I fired. Immediately after my shot, I fell back to the floor of the trench."

The Soviet fell from his perch and the *Landser* let out a cheer. The pest was finally gone and Jung had his first kill.[29] It was not the end though: the Soviets dispatched another pair of snipers. They were less experienced than the snipers they replaced and both were killed by Jung and Meier. Jung reflected, "Sometimes these sharpshooter-vs.-sharpshooter contests would last a week or more. I never got into a stand-off which was that bad but I heard about them from other sharpshooters. Those experiences were kill-or-get-killed in the simplest form."[30] Months later, Meier was killed when he exposed himself over a trench. Jung's career ended when his rifle was destroyed during an artillery barrage.[31]

*   *   *   *   *

When the Soviet Army entered Poland in April 1944, some tank regiments in Rossokovsky's First Belorussian Front were being reequipped with the new 122mm-armed Joseph Stalin II tank. Former Central Sniping School student Lt. Leonid Solodar finally managed to leave his post as a sniper trainer and join a combat unit. His infantry platoon was tasked with protecting the regiment from *Panzerfaust*-equipped infantrymen. Solodar was eager to fight and used an optically sighted gun. He spotted some soldiers clad in Soviet uniforms—including *ushanka* fur hats—at 800m. Dismounting the tank, he steadied himself and fired two shots. Luckily the person he shot was the artillery spotter who had been directing fire against the tanks. The artillery fell silent and the tanks were able to save a motorized infantry regiment from encirclement.[32]

In July 1944, the Soviet Thirty-first Army received a 23-strong female sniper platoon freshly graduated

Leonid Solodar (R) was born in Vakhnovka in Ukraine. He was among the 400 Communists and *Komsomol* members Stalin ordered to be trained as sniping instructors and attended the Central Sniper School in Moscow. After graduating, the school director Col. Busyatsky retained him as an instructor. He only left his teaching post when a Human Resources Officer from the Department of the Ministry of Defense came by seeking volunteers for the front. Solodar commanded a *desanti* platoon attached to the 79th Guards Heavy Tank Regiment. He finished the war in Berlin and later emigrated to Boston, MA. *Blavatnik Archive Foundation (http://www.blavatnikarchive.org)*.

from the Central Women's School of Sniper Training. Upon learning of their assignment, the *Komsomol* leader told his men that he had a hands-off policy towards them and promised to demote and beat (since Czarist days and throughout the history of the Red Army beating was an acceptable punishment) anyone who did. Two of the division's best male snipers, Lt. Zhora Kasimov and *Starshina* Nikodim Ivanovich were assigned as their platoon leaders. Lt. Kasimov allowed them two days' rest before assigning them. He used that period to test their knowledge of sniping, optics, camouflage, sniper tactics, and especially marksmanship. Satisfied, he shared some advice. "When you go to meet the adversary, you must respect the sniper's two basic principles. First: the sniper must have confidence in his or her every shot. Second: shoot sparingly, but accurately!"

An older man, Ivanovich had fathered two girls and treated the platoon as if they were his own daughters. He arranged for a Polish family to give them access to their bath in exchange for stew. When the platoon had to march to Prussia, he procured a cart for their weapons. He also inspected their rifles daily and knew each rifle by sight and could identify the sniper by her rifle. The platoon in turn grew to love him like a father. Besides being a father figure, Ivanovich also worked on the men's attitude and they came to respect the women as snipers and not just as women to be conquered.

They suffered their first casualty when "Natasha from Krasnaia Presnnia" (today, Krasnaya Presnya, just outside Moscow) slipped while descending a slope and was killed by a machine-gun burst fired during her descent. The day after her funeral, two of her comrades killed three Germans. "Klava from Chulinka" had a premonition of her death and was shot the next day.

In one duel against a German sniper, "Liuba from Sretenka" made a mistake and thought her opponent had spotted her. Unable to extract herself, she remained motionless in the snow for hours. Well into the evening, she was so stiff she could not move and *Starshina* Nikodim crawled up, tied a rope around her ankle and dragged her to safety. She was more fortunate than "Dina from Oruzheiny Pereulok" (a street in Moscow) who was shot through the head while moving.

On New Year's Day the platoon had 15 kills to its credit and was transferred to another division. By then they had been reduced to 17. Three had been killed, one hospitalized, and two sent home pregnant. A greater tragedy was to strike when a Panzer counterattack penetrated the division's rear area. Seven of the women and *Starshina* Nikodim were in a bunker when a grenade was tossed in. This was followed by a burst from a flamethrower. *Starshina* Nikodim's body was found clutching one of the women snipers. He died trying to protect her with his body.[33]

Fighting in Prussia was Arkhangelsk (Archangel) school teacher-turned sniper Roza Shanina. Over her mother's objection her father named Roza after Polish Marxist Revolutionary, Rosa Luxemburg.

Marie Ljalková (later Ljalková-Lastovecká by marriage), a Czechoslovak from the Ukraine, fought from March 1943 first as a sniper and then an instructor. During the battle of Sokolovo (March 8–12, 1943), she knocked out four Nazi machine guns. Her front-line experiences won her the Czechoslovak Cross and Soviet Order of the Red Star. She ended the war as the medical officer for a Czech tank battalion. Postwar she was awarded the Order of the White Lion, a year before she died at the venerable age of 91. *Courtesy the Central Museum of the Armed Forces, Moscow via Stavka.*

As a child, Roza was the only girl in her seventh grade class to earn a sharpshooter badge. When she turned 19 she was drafted and trained at the Central Women's School of Sniper Training.[34] The Soviet media tells that Shanina would crawl through a muddy communication trench to her camouflaged pit that overlooked the German line. She once saw a German crawl out from a pillbox to make his way to the rear. She killed him, and when two of his comrades rushed out to investigate she slew them too. When another pair showed themselves, they too were killed—five dead in one day.[35]

Dubbed by the Soviet propagandist as the "Terror of East Prussia," Shanina was uncomfortable with the media attention. Obviously her photogenic qualities endeared her to the propagandists. Roza Shanina's all-female platoon in the XLIXth Rifle Corps, Fifth Army was a corps' asset and its members were moved around to wherever there was a need for snipers. The 1942 Soviet goal of nine snipers per company or 87 per rifle regiment proved too idealistic and Roza and her snipers were shuffled around the corps to whatever division or regiment needed them. Her diary identifies no fewer than eight divisions that she fought alongside: 144th, 157th, 159th, 184th, 215th, 277th, 338th, and 371st Infantry divisions.[36]

On December 12, 1944, she was wounded:

"Yesterday I got hit in the shoulder. The night before, I dreamed that I got hurt, and it was my shoulder. Yesterday I was in my shooting position and I remembered my dream. Just a few moments later, I jumped. The bullet from the German sniper hit me in the exact spot as in my dream. I didn't feel any pain; I only felt my shoulder filling with warmth."[37]

Almost a month later she rejoined her unit. Unfortunately, we don't know whether she had made a mistake. It might have been a camouflage issue. Did she arrive too late giving her opponent the advantage, or use the same position too many times? Had she had shot several Germans from a position, bringing herself to the attention of the Germans who summoned their own sniper?

Her last diary entry was on January 24, 1945. On January 27 she was near Ilmsdorf, south of Bürgel, in Germany when she was wounded by a shell fragment and died the next day. Her papers were collected by Pyotr Molchanov who kept them in Kiev for 20 years before sending them to her home town, Arkhangelsk. Excluding her time in the hospital, in the three months of combat, depending on the source, she was credited with between 54 and 59 kills.

Unlike Helmut Jung, Günter Koschorrek remained a machine-gunner throughout the war and like Allerberger was at the Nikopol bridgehead. As a *Landser* of 21st *Panzergrenadier* Regiment, 24th Panzer Division, he was close to the division's supply vehicles and joined it in its flight to safety before the jaws closed on the Sixth Army. Now sheltered in a foxhole at the Nikopol bridgehead, he was manning a tripod-mounted MG42. The high visibility of these weapons made them a target for a Soviet sniper. Koschorrek could see the Soviets moving back and forth with impunity, but because of the sniper's presence, was powerless to intervene.

> "[S]omewhere, in front of us, a sniper has dug himself in, so well camouflaged that I can't pick him out even with my telescopic sight. I am aware of his presence only because of the dangerous explosions all around our position which have a noticeably higher tone, which continues to ring in the ears."

His assistant machine-gunner, Paul Adams, grew uncomfortable from the sustained kneeling. "Stay down!" Koschorrek told him. Paul caught a glimpse of the Soviets brazenly setting up mortars right in the open. Learning this, Koschorrek pushed Paul aside and grabbed the machine gun in anticipation of firing. Just as he was about to let loose, he spotted a movement of the sniper and darted back down. Lucky for him, too, as an explosive bullet barely missed him. Huddled in the bottom of their hole, a grenade landed right on the edge and harmlessly exploded above them. Once again Paul tried to rise but an explosion forced him down. Fresh scratches scarred their machine gun. Koschorrek looked carefully and now spotted the heavy shield of a Maxim machine gun rising above the snow. He mentioned it to Paul who impetuously wanted to rise again. "Stay down." Koschorrek ordered, but Paul did not heed him.

> "'Keep down, damn you!' This is the first time since Paul and I have been together that I have raised my voice to him. I'm angry because he is so stupid—remember the promise I gave Katya that I'd look after him.
>
> "When I again glance over towards the Russian machine-gun position, I notice two figures crawling up towards it and two figures retreating. So—they are changing shifts. If the snipers were not out there I would fire off a few rounds. But at the moment I won't risk anything and would rather bide my time. I lower the entire machine gun on its mounting, to one side, in order to get

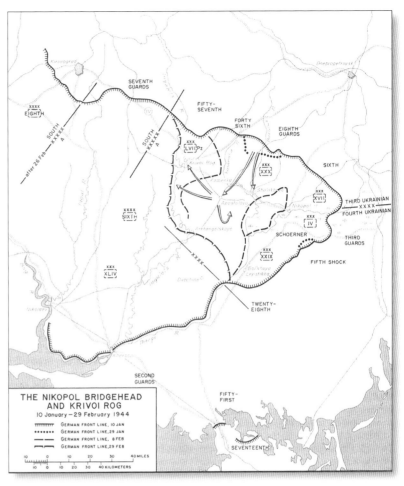

Map showing the Nikopol bridgehead. *U.S. Army.*

a wider view, and then there is another sharp crack! right in my eardrum. Quick as a flash, I duck down and then freeze. With his eyes wide open, as if struck by lightning, Paul slumps in a heap down at the bottom of the foxhole. He must have popped up behind me in spite of my warnings not to do so.

> "I stare aghast at the fist-sized hole in Paul's head just above his left eye, from which blood is leaking in dark red streams on to his steel helmet and from there right over his face and into his mouth, which is moving up and down."

That Soviet sniper would claim four more victims of which only one survived.[38]

Soviet pressure against the Nikopol bridgehead gradually forced the Germans to evacuate across the Dniester River. Fighting as one of the rearguard units, 3d *Gebirgsjäger* Division pulled back stubbornly. To delay the advancing Soviet reconnaissance platoon, Sepp Allerberger stayed behind his company to bring up the rear. Watching the Soviet vanguard leap, Allerberger correctly identified their leader:

Soviet rifles

Famous Soviet sniper Vladimir Pchelintsev described the M91/30:

"The sniper's rifle differed from the standard one in only a few details. Firstly, it had an Emalyanov (PE) telescope sight mounted over the barrel—a fairly long metal tube (274mm with a weight of 598g) with two regulating drums. In the second place, this modification meant the scope prevented the magazine from being charger loaded; the cartridges had to be put there one at a time. Thirdly, the handle of the bolt stem was bent sharply downwards. Here were also differences not visible to the eye: the barrels for the sniper rifles were manufactured from the best steel, processed on precision lathes for greater accuracy, while the components were assembled by hand and adjusted in a special way."[39]

Top female sniper Lyudmila Pavlichenko voiced her opinion about the SVT-40:

"There were different views about the 'Sveta.' They [the gasses] entered a gas port situated over the barrel and pushed against a cylinder with a long rod. The rod was joined by a tappet, the other end of which rested against the bolt. But someone rightly criticized the excessive complexity of this device and the difficulties of looking after it in field conditions ... [O]n the Black Sea steppe, in trenches dug out of dry, soft, crumbling earth, the risk of dirt in the mechanism—which consisted of 143 small, fine and very fine components—was quite large.

"The rifle would begin to 'snap' (for instance, it would not reload or it would barely expel the used cartridge) if the pressure of the powder gases changed. It also depended,

1. Lyudmila Pavlichenko carrying a PU 3.5x-equipped SVT-40. Note the camouflage smock. She belonged to the 25th or "Chapayev" Rifle Division which was named after the Civil War hero, Vasily Ivanovich Chapayev. The division was destroyed at the siege of Sevastopol. *From the fonds of the RGAKFD in Krasnogorsk via Stavka.*

incidentally, on the weather, on the air temperature. In that case the marksman had to regulate the aperture in the gas port manually, to make it bigger or smaller. Apart from that, the 'Sveta' also misbehaved when covered with thick grease or if dust got into its mechanism. Among the deficiencies of the SVT-40 I would also mention its bright muzzle flash upon firing (on account of the barrel that was 100mm shorter than the Three Line) and its loud sound, which immediately gave away one's location. It was superbly suited to clashes with the enemy in the field, when artillery, machine guns and mortars were operating. However, to put it bluntly, it increased the danger of a marksman being detected by the enemy in a single person-hideout, in a forest, for example. Among the sniper fraternity, though, the 'Sveta' had its admirers."[40]

2. Left side of AVS-36 showing side-mounted PE scope. *Image courtesy Georg Oberaigner.*

3. Left-side view of top-mounted (over receiver) PE-scoped M91/30. *Image courtesy Georg Oberaigner.*

4

M91/30
Caliber: 7.62mm
Weight: 8.7lb (3.95kg)
Length: 49.5in. (or 1.257m)
Barrel: 28.7in. (72.9cm)
Bore: Four-groove, right-hand twist, .007in. deep and .0310–.0311in. land-to-land (though some as large as .0314in. have been found)
Magazine: 5-round, non-detachable
Operation: Bolt, manually-operated
Muzzle velocity: 2,838ft/sec (865m/sec)

AVS-36 with PE scope
Caliber: 7.62mm
Weight: 8.93lb (4.051kg)
Weight w/scope: 10lb 9oz (4.791kg)
Length: 48.4in. (1.23m)
Barrel: 24.16in. (61.37cm)
Magazine: 15 rounds, detachable box
Operation: Gas-operated selective fire with locking block with secondary locking flappers
Muzzle velocity: 2,576ft/sec (840m/sec)

SVT-40 with PU scope
Caliber: 7.62mm
Weight: 8.35lb (3.787kg)
Weight w/scope: 9lb 9oz (4.332kg)
Length: 48.3in. (1.226m)
Barrel: 24.6in. (62.5cm)
Magazine: 10-round detachable box
Operation: Gas, semiautomatic
Muzzle velocity: 2,720–2,760ft/sec (830–840m/sec)

4. Left-side view of M91/30 with 3.5x PU scope. *Image courtesy Trinidad State College.*

5. M91/30 with side-mounted and detachable PEM scope. *Image courtesy Georg Oberaigner.*

6. Left-side view of SVT-40 with 3.5x PU scope. *Image courtesy Georg Oberaigner.*

5

6

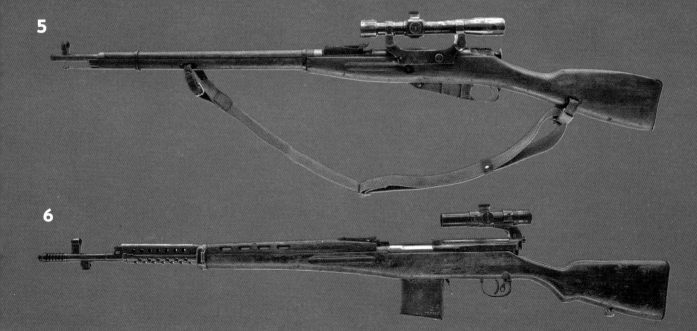

"[I] lined the crosswires of the telescopic sight at his chest and watched his passage through the dense vegetation. The right moment came. For a second or so he was exposed between bushes. I squeezed the trigger and saw the impact of the projectile hurtle him backwards into the brush. His platoon was sufficiently astute to recognize the work of a sniper and splayed out in all directions for cover. I got off two more rounds without definite result, although one hit a field flask and kept all of them low for the next half hour, gaining precious time for my retreating group."[41]

Allerberger learned that a sister battalion in the 144th Regiment—American and German infantry regiments were similarly organized, each having three battalions with three infantry and one heavy weapons company—had a self-trained sniper, Josef Roth. As both men enjoyed the confidence of their battalion commanders, they soon partnered up and were freed from tasks like trench digging, sentry duty, and other menial chores. They conducted joint reconnaissance and later cooperated in eliminating a Soviet sniper threat. The battalions were engaged in digging trenches for a new line of defense. One *Jäger* screamed before collapsing on the ground. Save for one man, most of the other *Jäger* dropped to the ground. A bullet ended the life of the standing man and a runner was sent to the battalion for help. Both Allerberger and Roth were present when the runner arrived and reported the incident. The battalion commander turned to them and laconically told them to solve the problem. Following the runner back to the trench work, they spoke with an *Unterfeldwebel* (sergeant) who filled them in with the necessary details. They then worked their way to a camouflaged observation post where they could begin their vigil. For hours they scanned the terrain before them, searching for potential hides. Another *Jäger* helped break the silence when he rose to empty a can of excrement over the trench. A shot rang out from the Soviet side. It hit the *Jäger*'s helmet and deflected into his arm—luckily for him, only a flesh wound.

"At that very moment, Joseph and I were observing the enemy front line through binoculars. We both noticed now the tall grass fronting a low undulation parted briefly under the pressure wave of the shot. We had to admire the ingenuity of our opponent in creating such a neat lair: he must have burrowed through the elevation from the back. The question was, did he have enough experience to abandon the position, or would he stay? The latter seemed more likely,

since all three of our victims had been hit from roughly the same direction."

Allerberger and Roth wondered if the Soviet was still in his same lair. They decided to entice him out with a decoy. A dummy was constructed and Roth moved down the trench another 50yd. Roth handed the dummy to a *Landser* and instructed him to wait ten minutes before he raised it. This would give Roth time to reach his post and settle in with his rifle aimed at the sniper's hide.

"Our two rifles were focused on the presumed hide of the Russian sniper, waiting for the scarecrow to make his debut. When it rose, the Soviet made his fatal error. He was over-confident, and that was what killed him. Clearly he had already dismissed from his mind the idea of a lure, and was therefore not even certain of

Lone wolf sniper or sniping pair?

As an experienced and successful sniper, Yevgeni Nikolaev knew at times it was better to operate alone, but was aware of the advantages of operating in pairs. Besides being easier for the lead sniper, the other sniper can also critique the firing position as well as the camouflage. Each season in the Soviet Union presented its unique problems. Winter meant lying motionless for hours in snow or ice. Spring meant the ice or snow you dug your hide in could melt and leave you laying in a puddle, only to freeze at night when the sun set. Spring and summer also meant a lot of distracting insects like mosquitoes, bees, wasps, flies, ants, and even field mice who took advantage of your inactivity to climb into your clothes.[42] Famed Stalingrad sniper Vassili Zaitsev worked with others but sometimes had to work alone. The same may be said of Lyudmila Pavlichenko. Allerberger worked mostly alone but when there was another sniper available, he thought it was good to cooperate as partners. Helmut Jung worked with his partner, Hans Meier, until the latter was killed. Ox and Bucks sniper Denis Edwards also had a partner in Normandy and British sniper Cpl. Arthur Hare often worked with another sniper.

his target when he fired from an unchanged position. Hardly had his shot run out than we replied, each using one of our precious captured explosive rounds. I watched the drama through the sight: a flurry of hectic activity and then something heavy being dragged away."[43]

A Soviet with binoculars carelessly exposed himself to search for Roth and Allerberger. It was as if he was spotting for artillery or another sniper. Before he could spot them, Roth and Allerberger quickly laid him to rest. The rest of the day was quiet. From this experience Allerberger and Roth learned the advantage of having an observer who was a sniper. They dug a series of six hides that covered the front of both battalions. This allowed them to shift position after firing and avoid retaliation. The regiment was finally ordered to abandon the Nikopol bridgehead on February 12, 1944. During the retreat to the Inhul River they fought as part of the rearguard and held up the advancing Soviets. The line at Ingulez held until March 16 when intensified Soviet pressure forced that to be abandoned. Allerberger fought again as a member of the rearguard. This was always a dangerous duty. One had to give the impression that the line was held in strength, remain in constant contact with the foe and delay his advance for as long as possible. The main force withdrew under darkness, leaving the rearguard behind. Since they had to engage without being pinned, camouflaged positions with invisible retreat routes had to be prepared in advance. Abandoned positions had to be booby-trapped to delay the enemy.[44]

The Soviets were now more cautious in their advance and Allerberger could score once or twice daily before going to ground for fear of being counter-sniped. Once he spotted the Soviet observer who betrayed his presence by inopportune movement. He took the shot and the trembling of the bush confirmed a hit. What happened next came as a surprise. He waited for over an hour, patiently scanning the terrain for the sniper. Sensing something wasn't right, Allerberger continued studying the landscape. Then he made his mistake. In moving his right foot, he invited a shot from the Soviet opponent who shot off the right heel of his boot. Allerberger balled up in his rifle pit to make himself smaller and remained in his hole until darkness allowed him to retreat to the German lines. He remained alert to the Russian sniper's presence but saw nothing the next day and two days later they retreated across the Bug River where the Russians gave them a respite while they built up forces in anticipation of a river crossing.[45]

On the night of March 26, 1944, the Soviets stealthily crossed the River Bug and overpowered the sentries.

This allowed more men to land and form a bridgehead. Their nocturnal activity ended when an alert machine-gunner noticed a raft being lowered into the water and scanned around him. Spotting Russian helmets above the trench, he sounded the alarm. A firefight ensued and the Soviets began gradually to expand their bridgehead. Allerberger occupied himself with shooting the Soviets who were crossing in the boats when a sergeant brought to his attention a Soviet with a white fur cap who was apparently the group commander. The sergeant suggested that Allerberger shoot him to remove their leadership.

> "'Sepp, he's making to the right, wait a bit and you'll see the cap appear above the trench.' I had worked out the rhythm of my opponent. He would soon pass across the sapper's entrance giving me a split second to shoot him. I aimed the crosswires of the sight on the entrance at head height and awaited the decisive moment. Suddenly, at 120 metres distant, the target head filled the sight, my shot rang out and hit. Through our respective optics, the NCO and I saw the white fur cap swell like a balloon, then burst like an overripe water melon."

Russian resistance became disorganized and the German assault team was able to reenter the trench and recapture it, killing every single Soviet in the process.[46]

On April 7, Allerberger's *Oberst* (colonel) withdrew the survivors of his regiment on his own initiative. The previous day's fighting had whittled them down from an already weak 300 men to a mere 168. When 11 men and two company commanders of the reserve

On the left, Semyon Nomokonov, a Hamnigan Evenk, came from a family of hunters. He started shooting at age seven and hunted sable, Manchurian wapiti, and elk. When not hunting, he practiced carpentry. He is credited with slaying at least 368 enemy soldiers which includes seven or eight Japanese. On the right is Boris Kanatov, also of the 163d Rifle Division. Kanatov was from Ossetia. *Courtesy the Central Museum of the Armed Forces, Moscow via Stavka.*

battalion were shot with head shots or chest shots, the men of the reserve battalion realized they were facing snipers and took shelter in the ruins of a collective. A desperate call went out to the regiment for artillery support with which they could counter the Soviet menace that was decimating them. As no artillery was available, the regiment sent Allerberger. He arrived three hours later and was briefed by a sergeant who was leading the remains of the battalion.

Allerberger needed to safely study the woods that were 300–350yd away. He spotted a shallow depression with a bush at the edge which he crawled to. Before departing though, he prepared five decoys which were distributed among the *Jäger*. They were instructed to raise them as if a helmeted head was about to peer over a wall. Allerberger pulled a half-umbrella with handle out of his pack. He stuck grasses into it to make a screen from which he could scan the enemy positions from concealment using binoculars. After 20 minutes Allerberger was in position behind his screen. He gave the hand signal and a decoy was raised. The Soviets fired, allowing him to spot movement among the branches which divulged their positions. That all five decoys drew fire told Allerberger that while his opponents were skilled, they lacked fieldcraft.

He crawled back to discuss a plan with the sergeant. Positioned with good arcs of fire, five machine guns would sweep the wood line. The *Jäger* with the decoy would raise one and after the Soviets fired, the five machine guns would retaliate with a burst. Under the cover of a burst, Allerberger would shoot one bullet and the pattern would repeat itself. He then returned to his position behind the bush.

"The tactical battle began. The lure rose and received three rounds as if to order. I saw the movement in the trees, took aim, waited for the MG to fire, then pulled the trigger. One by one the Russian snipers dropped from the trees, dead. After a quick change of position, a new round of the duel began. Within an hour I had reckoned on eighteen kills but still the lures drew fire. It was about five in the afternoon, and an hour since the last shoot had been loosed from the woods, that the sergeant decided on storming the woods under the cover of the two MGs and myself. They reached the woods unopposed, looked with astonishment at the corpses and gesticulated wildly for us to join them."

What Allerberger saw shocked him. His opponent was a female sniper platoon. They had heard of female soldiers, but this was the first time they encountered them in combat. One was just barely alive and when a *Jäger* turned her over, she pulled a Tokarev and mouthed, "Death to Fascists!" before pulling the trigger. The *Jäger* rolled out of the line of fire and the bullet barely missed the seat of his pants. The *Jäger* sprang up with his submachine gun in hand and delivered the coup de grace.[47]

Allerberger was not always successful over his Soviet counterpart. While accompanying the battalion commander, *Hauptmann* Kloss, on an inspection tour, a machine-gunner who was new to the front, was almost killed with a head shot. Seeing Kloss, he stood and began to point at the direction of the shot. Allerberger immediately tackled him, but not before the sniper fired and hit the *Jäger* a glancing blow. While the inexperienced *Jäger* was not killed, he suffered a fearful wound requiring him to be evacuated. Allerberger went to his hide and began searching no-man's-land. It continued until darkness fell but the wily Soviet refused to fire again.[48]

Driven from the Ukraine into Poland, Allerberger's regiment settled down around Bielitz (the German version of Bielsko). There Allerberger found a house whose loft made an ideal nest. He removed tiles from different spots on the roof to conceal his actual shooting hide. After a few days of sniping, the Soviets brought up their own sniper who couldn't, because of the numerous tiles removed, identify Allerberger's loophole. Frustrated, on the third day they brought up an anti-tank gun to silence him. The Soviets calmly unhooked the gun from their truck and began unloading ammunition. Others began tending to the gun by opening its trail, installing its sight. They worked nonchalantly, as if they were on a training exercise instead of combat. Allerberger aimed above the head of the man installing the sight and fired. The bullet caused him to double up and fall. Allerberger shifted to the next Soviet and slew him too. The third Soviet picked up the second one to carry him away to the barn where his comrades were storing the ammunition. He didn't get far either before being shot. Since no more Soviets exposed themselves, Allerberger aimed at the gunsight itself and shot. The rest of the day was quiet and there was no further activity on the Soviet side. Later that evening, battalion intelligence intercepted a message confirming that the gunsight was destroyed.[49]

* * * * *

When the war started, Siberian Alexander V. Pyl'cyn had just completed tenth grade and since his father was a railroad worker, wanted to follow in his footsteps. He applied for the military institute for railroad engineers. Instead, he found himself drafted and sent to the Far East Army where he received his military training. Later, Pyl'cyn was sent to the 2d Vladivostok Infantry Academy for six months where he graduated with a lieutenant's commission. Afterward, he became a platoon leader in the 29th Independent Rifle Brigade. After a few transfers, he found himself in command of a platoon in a penal company. Shocked, he asked why and was told, "You are asking the wrong question, Lieutenant. Not why, but what for. You will lead the *shtrafniks* [Common name for soldiers and officers serving in the penal battalion]." Now in 1944, while fighting on the Narew River in Poland, he had a brush with death.

> "I can well remember the death of one *shtrafnik*, Kostya Smertin. I only remember his ex-officer rank. He was either a Lieutenant or a Captain. He was one of the observers in our company. On that day, I stood in the trench next to him, and was observing German positions through binoculars. I thought I managed to spot a well-camouflaged position of a German sniper. I warned Kostya about it, telling him not to stick out of the trench as the sniper could be hunting for one of us. My assumption proved to be true only a second later. Immediately after I sat down in the trench a bullet whizzed over my head. I was lucky, as often happened. I did not have time to order Smertin to sit down. But apparently he wanted to seize the opportunity and see where the sniper fired from. The second bullet hit the middle of his forehead, immediately after the first, a bit above his eyebrows. He slowly went down to the bottom of the trench. He did not drop, but gently sat down. His eyes looked up and started moving quickly, while his lips whispered something I could not understand. His face went very pale. I put a bandage over his very small wound. The blood did not flow a lot. I recalled how we were trained to put a bandage on a head that was called 'Hippocrates's hat.' The strange eye movements and whispering lasted for about a minute. Then, after convulsions that shook his entire body, all his muscles suddenly tensed and he went silent. He died. I closed his eyes. He was not as lucky as I was."[50]

German distribution of scarce sniping equipment was inequitable and (thankfully) not optimal to the German war effort. During one retreat, Sepp Allerberger saw a Waffen-SS company entirely equipped with scoped Gewehr 43 semiautomatic rifles and two scoped StG44 assault rifles. Among them were 16-year-old teenagers who had two weeks

The ten commandments of German sniping

1. Fight fanatically.
2. Shoot calmly and carefully. Fast shots lead nowhere, concentrate on the hit.
3. Your greatest opponent is the enemy sniper, outsmart him.
4. Always fire only one shot from your position, if not you will be discovered.
5. The entrenching tool prolongs your life.
6. Practice judging distance.
7. Become a master of camouflage and terrain usage.
8. Practice your shooting skills constantly, behind the front and in the homeland.
9. Never let go of your sniper rifle.
10. Survival is 90 percent camouflage and ten percent firing.

of training as snipers before being sent to the front. Allerberger thought it was sheer folly and predicted their combat career would be short.[51]

Bruno Sutkus, it will be remembered, was sent to the 169th Grenadier Regiment, 68th Infantry Division which was attached to the First Hungarian Army. In his first battle he was among his comrades in their defensive positions. After being softened by Soviet artillery, their tanks and infantry attacked. Sutkus remembers his first kills.

> "Amongst the Soviet infantry I saw an officer of Asiatic appearance driving his men forward towards our trenches with pistol drawn. I shot him down. I kept firing. Each round was a hit. The infantry was forced to seek some cover. Anyone who stood up and attempted to advance was hit. The commissars remained behind their soldiers, herding them forward into our defensive fire. I aimed first at the commissars and shot them all down. When the leading ranks of infantry noticed that the commissars were out of it they turned and went back to their own lines."[52]

As he was fighting like an infantryman, none of these battlefield kills were counted towards his sniper score. That would begin soon. His performance did change Sutkus's standing with his comrades though. "At first my presence in the ranks as a sniper was

Bruno Sutkus in the Carpathians. He's holding a K98k with a Zf42 scope. *Sidas8888/WikiCommons (CC BY-SA 4.0).*

hardly noticed. Only when it began to be realized what a sniper could achieve and how much depended upon him did the opinion of my comrades change."

Before the battle Sutkus had 120 rounds of ammunition and the attack was furious enough that he now required a resupply. He then noticed that many soldiers had their sights adjusted for 600yd and neglected to adjust them when the Soviets closed the distance. The second attack, a combination of tank and infantry, now approached.

> "The enemy had certainly noticed that a sniper was operating in the sector of the front directly opposite them, for now they moved about more cautiously. I could have taken out quite a few more of them but was anxious not to betray my position. First I took a very good look at the terrain and estimated the distances. No Man's Land was about 500 meters wide. There was a Russian sniper ahead of their trenches and well camouflaged. He had a good view of our lines and had inflicted losses on our men."[53]

Sutkus's sniping score began on May 8, 1944. He had spotted the enemy sniper's lair by the impressions of the sniper's boots in the grass. He determined that the sniper had created a rifle pit in which he could lie. The pit was some distance from the ruins of a house that was being used as an artillery observation post about 500yd from Sutkus. The Soviet sniper's imperfect camouflage allowed Sutkus to discern his camouflage face mask and jacket. Those things only supplemented but did not replace fieldcraft. The Soviet sniper knew that the ruins would attract his counterpart's eye and wanted not only to protect the officers using that post but also eliminate any sniping threat to them. Sutkus took the bait. As one officer was in the communications trench, Sutkus shot him down. The second officer was too stunned to move and a second bullet quickly found him too. "The Russian sniper I had detected earlier identified my position from these two rounds. He made a slight turn to fire at me and I hit him at the same instant as his bullet hissed passed my head."[54] Sutkus was both skilled and lucky.

Working in Sutkus's favor during his sniping career was an intuitive sense of the enemy's location even when he was being glassed. "It was obvious that I was getting on their nerves, for they called up one sniper after another to winkle me out. I could always sense, however, where they had concealed themselves. I could literally feel it when I was in their sights." It would ensure his survival in his numerous encounters against his Soviet counterpart. Sutkus added: "I am sure I had a sixth sense that enabled me to spot enemy snipers very rapidly."[55] Additionally, Sutkus was adept at identifying decoys. "I was often shown a lure but never fell for one. Now and then they would raise a mannequin in officer's uniform. It had a lifeless face and so I was not deceived."[56]

In October 1944 Sutkus's depleted battalion received reinforcements, including another sniper. "The new sniper received an order to engage enemy snipers. He found himself a position. His first shot missed, and it was his last because the enemy sniper shot him in the head." Another new sniper was dispatched but was wounded and invalided out of service.[57] The inexperience of the new snipers at the front strongly suggests they should have been partnered with an experienced sniper before being left on their own.

Regarding his Soviet counterparts and their tactics, Sutkus noted:

> "Soviet snipers had no compunction about shooting our soldiers wherever the chance presents itself. That is the way of warfare. I received the orders to spot these snipers and kill them. According to the Russians this was a war crime. I was actually an auxiliary in the foremost trenches saving our grenadiers' lives. I risked my life for them. The enemy was equally ruthless, but I had more luck than they did, even though they often had me in their sights."[58]

It should be noted that Sutkus also shot targets of opportunity and his effectiveness in killing machine gunners, snipers and high-ranking officers brought him to the attention of the Soviets. To say that they wanted him eliminated would be an understatement. Thus it came to pass that the Soviets deployed two snipers simultaneously against him.

"On 22 November, 1944 I was in 7 Company sector and saw two Russians bailing water from their trench 450 metres away. I shot one and another who came on the scene to render him aid. At first light I made out an enemy MG position which had advanced to within 250 metres of our lines and was well camouflaged. I shot the gunner through the head. I spotted the gleam of the sun on an optic and had the sensation that I was in somebody's sights. Suddenly a shot rapped out that narrowly missed my neck. It was the Russian sniper's last shot, for I soon had him in the crosshairs and squeezed the trigger. That same moment a second sniper fired at me, but his aim was a little too high, and the bullet glanced off my steel helmet. Both of these snipers had concealed themselves behind a wall. I shot the second in the chest from 200 metres. Thus I had shot two enemy snipers the same morning, a rare occurrence."[59]

* * * * *

The 52d Rifle Division, Third Ukrainian Front, was fighting in Yugoslavia. Having been trained at Leningrad's Artillery Specialist School, then 2Lt. Petr Alexevich Mikhin was initiated into combat as a battery commander in the 1048th Artillery Regiment and saw savage fighting near Rzhev. He survived three years of war, had numerous brushes with death, and was now a captain commanding the battalion. He had recently disposed of a useless, alcoholic, battery commander and received as a replacement Sr. Lt. Raskovalov, a high-school principal and math instructor from Siberia. Described by Capt. Mikhin as tall, slender, and nice looking, at age 33 Raskovalov was ten years older than his CO but inexperienced in combat. Mikhin tried to impart to him the knowledge that would keep him alive. Raskovalov's battery had to be positioned to lay direct fire on the German lines. This meant that the battery's detection would be easier and was very dangerous. Knowing this, Raskovalov asked Mikhin for assistance in placing his guns to have the most cover. It was dark when they were examining the ground and beginning to get light when Raskovalov noticed a ravine from which tanks could approach unseen. Scanning it, Mikhin

concurred and suggested that they return to the safety of the trench. Raskovalov demurred, suggesting they should go and study it some more. "No," responded Mikhin who complained it was getting too light—as it was. Still, Raskovalov delayed and Mikhin remembered what happened next:

"All of the sudden there was the crack of a single rifle shot from the German side. We both dropped to the ground. I called over to him, but he was silent. I crawled over to where he was lying, and I saw a stream of blood shooting from his forehead like a fountain. I clasped my hand over the wound in an attempt to staunch the bleeding and immediately reached for a bandage in my pocket before it occurred to me that the battery commander was dead. Only a sniper could score such a precise hit from such a distance. It was a sniper that got him … I was overwhelmed by pity towards my friend and the bitter hatred for the German that had killed him. I hated myself as well, for I had failed to keep the Senior Lieutenant alive. I imagined his wife receiving the death notice and his small children crying—and my heart sank, my sight darkened. I couldn't move, we were both nailed to the ground, but I was alive and he was dead."

Survivor's guilt overcame Mikhin and he pondered over why he had survived and Raskovalov had died. Then he had an epiphany.

Soviet Red Army Infantryman with M91/30 and 3.5x PU scope. His lack of camouflage and concealment indicates this was a souvenir photo not taken under combat conditions. *Image courtesy Georg Oberaigner.*

"When I regained my senses, I grabbed him by his shoulders and dragged him into the bushes. I caught my breath a bit, but I still had the German sniper on my mind: for days he'd been watching our lines from his concealed position and finally in the dim light of early dawn, he spotted two men through his optical sight. But he only had time to kill one of us. Why had he selected Raskovalov as his target? Did the sniper manage to see our faces and notice that the Senior Lieutenant was older than me, and thus probably an officer of higher rank? Raskovalov was not all that heavy, but his feet were dragging on the ground as I walked and I recalled that Raskovalov had been a half-head taller than me. That's why the German sniper had selected him. He was taller and older, and these two factors sealed his fate: the German chose the taller and older man, thinking he was the higher ranking officer."[60]

* * * * *

In December 1944, 3d *Gebirgsjäger* Division found itself in Hungary's Slovak Ore Mountains. Many of its rear echelon troops were fighting against Hungarian partisans. It was just before Christmas when *Gefreiter* Hans Kahr had a chance reunion with his schoolmate, Toni M., a sniper with the 144th Regiment. Kahr tried to engage Toni M. in conversation but he seemed distant and kept muttering about having to repay the Russians. They parted and Hans grabbed an unidentified *Jäger* and asked,

"'Tell me, what's the matter with Toni?'
"'Oh him, yes, since Miskole he's been completely done in. Thinks he has the death of a little Hungarian girl on his conscience. A Russian sniper had been after him but caught the girl instead. Headshot. She was trying to bring him a jug of milk. Now he's constantly on the prowl. Doesn't sleep anymore. He's gone through three spotters in the last four weeks. Nobody wants to go out with him anymore.'"

It is unknown whether Toni M. ever repaid the debt, but he survived the war.[61]

Gefreiter Bernhard Averbeck fought in 95th Infantry Division, XXIII Army Corps, Fourth Army, Army Group Center. They had been pushed out of Russia and into the Ukraine. The Soviets were regrouping for the next offensive, giving the Germans a much needed breather. It was past Christmas and Averbeck went outside to make a holiday drink by melting artificial honey to mix with vodka. When he finished, he returned to the cottage. What happened next was unexpected.

"I returned from one of my visits outside to discover that Ludwig Kluge had taken my place in front of a blacked-out window. I didn't comment on it because Ludwig and I were close friends and had been together ever since we had first met while training at Herford.

"We were all feeling pretty good, and in the candlelight that flickered over our faces, gathered inside. All of a sudden a sniper's tracer bullet ripped through the window opening, striking the ceiling. Everybody jumped up looking for pliers or some other tool to pull the thing from where it had lodged in a wooden rafter before it caught fire. Ludwig remained seated the whole time so when I came back I asked him what was the matter?

"'I think that I am wounded,' he said. I opened his shirt and sure enough, I discovered the bullet had entered his back, angled down towards the ground, and ricocheted up to the ceiling. He had unwittingly exchanged places and the risks that went with it."[62]

Ludwig Kluge was sent to a field hospital where, despite orders to the contrary, he waited for the medics' attention to be drawn elsewhere when he grabbed some water and gulped it down. It was his last drink.

* * * * *

After completing their nine-month study at the 14th Sniping School, Nadol'ko Nikolai Dmitrievich was assigned to the 585th Rifle Regiment, 213th Novoukrainka Rifle Division. Partnered with Volodia Churikov (or Churmikov), they found themselves in the Sandomierz bridgehead over the Vistula River (September–October 1944). Besides improving their defenses, their first task to was to eliminate a pesky German machine gun. Dmitrievich wrote:

"That damned machine gun had several positions prepared beforehand and he skillfully changed them. Our company commander told us: 'We must overcome him.' Volodia, my fellow sniper, and I stepped forth along the trenches and fitted out our firing positions about 20 meters apart. Initially we just observed the area through our optical sights. In order to not decamouflage ourselves, we did it only when under a shadow or during an overcast day. After we got to know the locations of his firing positions, the order of his placements, and some of his habits, we started to hunt.

"My fellow sniper was watching, while I tried to stimulate the machine gunner to fire. The usual method was to lift my helmet a little over the parapet for some 20 seconds and then to hide it for a minute or so. During my third attempt the machine gunner fired a burst towards me, but Volodia was ready to fire and didn't miss."

Their machine gunner's death by sniper resulted in the Germans summoning their own sniper to even the score by picking off unwary Soviets. Alerted to his presence, Dmitrievich and his partner were called upon to neutralize him. "Volodia and I used the same tactics of hunting. There was, however, only one difference; the day was sunny, therefore I slightly rocked my rifle with the optical sight over the parapet to motivate the German to fire." It worked.[63] Dmitrievich's sniping career ended in January 1945 when he was sent to the Odessa Order of the Red Banner Infantry School as a cadet. It is likely he was spared the Vistula–Oder Offensive (January 12–February 2, 1945) that drove the Germans out of Poland and into eastern Germany.

Now part of the Fourth Tank Army, Evgeni Bessonov's 35th Guards Mechanized Kamenets-Podolsk Brigade was ordered to support Marshal Georgy Zhukov's offensive to capture Berlin. Along with other units, they would encircle Berlin from its south and western approaches. It was warm in late April and they came across a fruit garden on the outskirts of a village.

"Popov's platoon and our company did not go further but lay down in the orchard. The enemy's snipers were delivering aimed rifle fire. The tanks also stopped, fearing *Panzerfaust* attack. They did not want to die, but did we, the infantry, want to? As it turned out later, there were no *Panzerfäuste* there, just eight or twelve snipers. Popov's machine-gun platoon opened fire on the forest edge, and half of the company, some twelve to fourteen soldiers rushed to assault on my command, while approximately the same number of men gave their fire support. There was an open field up to the forest. The soldiers ran into the German trenches, and killed some of them; others fled, while one Fritz was taken prisoner. The Fritz was a stubborn one; when my soldier ran up to his trench, he fired at him at point-blank range, but luckily wounded him in his forearm. They pulled the Fritz out of his

Unknown gloved Soviet sniper aims his M91/30 on an unwary target sighting through his side-mounted PEM scope. *Courtesy the Central Museum of the Armed Forces, Moscow via Stavka.*

foxhole and brought him to me; he was armed with a sniper rifle. I was stressed and angry after the assault and shouted at the German, mostly in Russian, and then hit him twice on his ear."

The German was highly decorated and when Brigade intelligence rushed up to grab him, Bessonov told them to go to hell, but was overridden and had to relinquish his prisoner to them.[64]

While Soviet snipers practiced their art to help drive the Germans into Berlin, German snipers did their best to keep the Soviets at bay. One was noted for his eccentricities. When off duty, he would don a civilian top hat and matching tailcoat upon which he affixed his German Gold Cross—an important award ranked between the Iron Cross First Class and the various Knight's Crosses. Because of its star shape, the Germans nicknamed it the "fried egg." As with many German snipers in Stalingrad, he generally took his position behind the German front lines and often fought from a barn. Others would spot for him and he had an impressive score of 130 kills.[65]

To capture Berlin, the Soviets crossed the Oder River and fought a major battle against entrenched positions on the Seelow Heights April 16–19, 1945. Capt. Alexander Pyl'cyn crossed the Oder under machine gun and artillery fire. Of his entire company, only 20 men landed successfully on the west bank of the river. Not a single platoon leader was among them. Since his radio operator was injured and the radio damaged, Pyl'cyn fired a green flare to signal that they landed successfully. His landing force stormed the German trenches and by the time they reached the second trench, only 12 men remained with him. Being too weak to advance further, he ordered his

Right: In Finland, the Continuation War had seen Finns and Germans ranged against the forces of the Soviet Union. It came to an end with a ceasefire on September 5, 1944. German forces had to leave the country and so Twentieth Mountain Army, under *Generaloberst* Lothar Rendulic, began moving toward Norway, as did all the German forces in Finland, following carefully laid down plans. Finnish snipers were forced to turn their weapons toward their erstwhile brothers-in-arms. *SA-kuva.*

Below: Snipers from 1st *Fallschirm-Panzer* Division *Hermann Göring* in Kubschütz, a suburb of Bautzen, which had recaptured from Soviet troops in one of the last German victories of the war; April 25, 1945. The man third from right carries a Soviet Mosin-Nagant PU sniper rifle. *GF collection.*

men to halt and to prepare for the inevitable German counterattack. Because he distinguished himself as a leader, Pyl'cyn drew the unwelcome attention of a German sniper.

"I ordered the evacuation of two heavily wounded shtrafniks [*shtrafniki*] to the boat, in order to send them to the rear for medical treatment. They would not have survived there [on the west bank of the Oder]. Before we managed to carry the wounded to the bank, I leaned down to the radio operator, when suddenly, again suddenly! I did not even hear, but rather sensed a loud bang at my right ear and I immediately fell into a bottomless black hole. Much later, when I regained consciousness, I thought that it was a lie about your life flashing in front of you the moment you die. It was not like that at all. I think the only thing I thought was, I am killed. That was it. As it turned out later, I was hit by a bullet in my head which was later described in [the] hospital, as a wound certified as 'penetrating bullet wound of the right temple area. The wound was received in battle at Oder River on April 17, 1945.' I think it was a German sniper who got me."[66]

It was during their fight toward Berlin that Red Army American volunteer Jr. Lt. M. Nicholas noticed a dead German lad—no more than 13 or 14 years old—missing the left side of his face. The force of the bullet's impact had thrown him back from his shallow foxhole, leaving his arms outstretched and his helmet a short

distance away. Outside the foxhole was his unfired *Panzerfaust*. A former sniper explained to him that, "A Soviet sniper used an explosive bullet." She went on to explain that snipers accompanied tanks to protect them from *Panzerfaust*-armed Germans.[67] This is confirmed by Bogachev who added that flamethrower crews, machine gunners, mortar men, and anti-tank riflemen also accompanied the tanks.[68]

The Red Army overwhelmed Berlin's outer defenses and drove the Germans into Berlin itself. Since the Western Allies had already agreed to stop their advance well to the west, the prize belonged solely to the Red Army. Berlin and the remnants of the defenders surrendered on May 9, 1945.

Victory in Europe

Amazingly, Capt. Pyl'cyn survived his head wound and rejoined his battalion on May 1. While not leading his company, he was present when most resistance in Berlin was crushed on May 2. Pyl'cyn remained in the Red Army and retired as a colonel.

Postwar Lyudmila Pavlichenko finished her studies and was consulted on the Dragunov rifle which was to become the standard semiautomatic sniper rifle for decades. She retired as a major in the Soviet Coast Guard.

Her travel partner to America, Vladimir Pchelintsev returned to combat and ended the war with 465 kills. Postwar he graduated from the Leningrad Military Academy of Communications, served in Egypt as the colonel commanding the electronic warfare unit during the War of Attrition (after the Six-Day War), and afterward (1976) worked in Balashikha (near Moscow). Pchelintsev passed away in 1977.[69]

Stalingrad sniper Vassili Zaitsev returned to work in a steel mill until he was disabled by blindness due to injuries suffered from the war. The other famous Stalingrad sniper, Anatoly Ivanovich Chekhov, ended his combat career in 1943 near Kiev when an explosion tore off both legs. He finished the war with 265 to his credit. He was supposed to be awarded the Hero of the Soviet Union but the plane carrying the papers for his award was shot down. He passed away in Kazan in 1967.[70]

When Yulia Zhukova returned home, she discarded most of her memorabilia and did her best to forget the war. She became a school teacher, mother, and later a grandmother.

After victory in Europe Capt. Mikhin and the 52d Division were transferred east to fight the Japanese, but Japan capitulated before they arrived. He met his wife while his unit was en route to the Far East. They were married and postwar he taught mathematics.

After the war Jr. Lt. M. Nicholas became a dramatist

As a *Komsomol* member, Irina Botnar attended the Central Womens' School of Sniper Training in Moscow, completing a six-month course in 1944. Post graduation, she was recruited by the NKVD where she worked as a censor at the Second Ukrainian Front. Postwar she worked in the police department of Bendery, Moldove. Photo dated 2013. *Blavatnik Archive Foundation (http://www. blavatnikarchive.org).*

and director and after the fall of the Soviet Union he returned to his native United States.

Léon Degrelle fled to Spain to avoid a death sentence imposed on him by his native Belgium. He remained an unrepentant Nazi until his death.

LSSAH's Erwin Bartmann was captured by the British and was imprisoned in Scotland. Postwar he naturalized, married a Scottish lass, and became a baker in Scotland.

Bruno Sutkus's tally ended with 207 kills when he became a sniping instructor. Postwar he was discharged but ended up first in Eastern Europe and later worked as a coal miner in Siberia. The Soviets only learned later that he was a sniper but by then, since he was a quiet, unassuming, and willing worker who wasn't a threat to the Soviet system, he did not suffer from it. However, he wasn't allowed to return to Germany until after the Soviet Union collapsed.

Sepp Allerberger eluded Soviet capture and surrendered to the Americans.

Helmut Jung was captured by the Soviets, escaped, fled westward, and surrendered.

Matthäus Hetzenauer, Hans Kahr, and his sniper friend, Toni M., were less fortunate and became Soviet prisoners. Kahr was released in 1947, Toni M. in 1949, and Hetzenauer in 1950.

| 10 Far East

"So, just as we're beginning to get ready to move that morning, Frankie gets up and lets out a roar. 'Hey you guys,' he yells, 'I am eighteen years old today. Happy birthday, Frankie Benshadle!' Bang. It's from a sniper. Down goes Frankie. It doesn't look as if he'll make nineteen."[1]

Cpl. John Thompson
B/1/26th Marines

Japanese thoughts on U.S. snipers as published in *Intelligence Bulletin* Vol. III No. 3 of November 1944:

"The Americans prepare fields of fire in front of their positions, and establish four or five rows of barbed wire entanglements in this same area. When advancing Japanese units destroy these entanglements and approach the positions, the American try to halt our attack with sudden artillery, light-mortar, and machine-gun fire at minimum range.

"In jungle areas they place fallen trees in front of their positions and snipe at our men who are obliged to clamber over these trees, stumbling in the process. For this purpose, U.S. snipers take up positions in standing trees nearby." *U.S. Army.*

It is far too easy to attribute fire from an unidentified source as that coming from a sniper. In addressing the war against Japan, the words of Capt. Clifford Shore should be kept in mind:

"The average Japanese sniper was a rifleman, and not always a good one, who had selected for himself an advantageous position from which to fire at his enemy. The true Jap sniper suitably camouflaged, specially armed and equipped with concentrated rations was responsible only for a very small amount of that which was so-often termed 'sniper fire.' It was noticed that these snipers seldom fired at parties of men larger than two or three along the jungle tracks because they feared detection by the remainder of the group, and parties of three and four men searching for these snipers by maintaining careful watch or by patrolling action had a deterrent effect."[2]

Shore is quite correct and in many cases it was a sergeant or an officer who ordered some poor private to ascend a tree or descend into a spider hole and lay in wait for an opportunity to kill. Many who obeyed those orders did not survive.

As far as the Chinese and many in southeast Asia are concerned, World War II started in 1937 when Japan invaded China, committing acts of great brutality on the civilian population. It was not unknown for the Japanese to retaliate with poison gas against a Chinese village if a sniper or *franc-tireur* fired at them. On September 27, 1940, Japan signed the Tripartite Pact with Italy and Germany, and after a year of preparation attacked in December 1941—the United States by sea at Pearl Harbor on the 7th and then both the Americans and British on land on the 8th, when they invaded the Philippines and British Malaya.

The Japanese attack on the Philippines had two purposes: to prevent the American military from using the islands as a base to stage an attack against the empire, and to have their own base from which they could invade the Dutch East Indies. Lt. Gen. (promoted to general on December 20) Douglas MacArthur had hoped to stop the Japanese on the beaches but belatedly conceded his coastal defense plan had failed and ordered a withdraw to Bataan. The capitol Manila was declared an open city and abandoned. Despite pulling back to the more defensible Bataan Peninsula, there were still infiltrations by the Japanese and United Press correspondent Frank Hewlett found himself targeted by a Japanese sniper. He reported his encounter:

"My experience with the sniper came when I accompanied Maj. Joseph Cabot, New York, and Maj. John Pugh, Washington, D. C., to investigate a sector where a small group of Japanese had been cut off.

"A lieutenant colonel advised the American officers to wait until dark to make the trip, but they were anxious to get the desired information so we started out. We were in sight of our destination when we stopped to talk with a tank corps lieutenant.

"'Any snipers around?' asked Major Pugh.

"'I haven't heard of one on the path,' the lieutenant said, and with this information we stepped into the middle of the trail to talk. Just then a bullet kicked up the dust a foot from where we were grouped. Another whined past my ear and then two more shots whizzed past.

"Before the third and fourth bullets whined past, however, the four of us were rolling in the brush. I saw the officers crawl behind trees and I followed their example.

"'Anyone hit?' asked Major Chabot.

"All had escaped injury so we started squirming through the brush, flat on our bellies. It isn't pleasant to burrow through jungle, but you're glad to have such a cover when there's an enemy waiting to pick you off if you show yourself. When we were out of range we got to our feet again and compared notes. No two could agree on where the shots came from."

While none of them were equipped to eliminate the sniper, riflemen were summoned. Hewlett tells of the sniper's fate.

"The snipers are still around, though, but they're hard to find. The one who shot at me and the officers was killed later. When we saw him we understood why we hadn't been able to determine where he was firing from. He wore a green uniform that blended perfectly with the foliage of the high tree he had climbed. His face was painted green and he wore green shoes. He wore linesman's climbers to aid in scaling the trees and his ammunition was smokeless.

"Our sniper is still up that tree. He had tied himself to a limb and when an American rifleman picked him off his body remained high in the branches."[3]

The Japanese were extremely adept at night penetration and would work themselves behind American lines, ascend trees and snipe at the unwary. One newspaper man who was reporting out of the Philippines remembered:

"The Japanese are especially adept at sniping. Carrying only a handful of rice plus their arms, they sneak through the lines and hide high in the trees, and remain motionless for hours awaiting their chance. The average Japanese is not an expert marksman, but their snipers are especially chosen crack shots. This American unit flushed six snipers out of a single tree yesterday."[4]

Japanese snipers climbed trees using instep crampons such as these demonstrated by an American serviceman. *U.S. Army.*

Shod in *tabi* split-toed rubber shoes and using tree spikes, the Japanese made great use of trees. One possible victim was Brig. Gen. Clinton A. Pierce, who was shot in the foot by an unseen foe.[5] This suggests either a stray bullet or high-angle shooting where the shooter was unfamiliar with adjusting for difference in elevation. It made no difference where the shooter was to General Pierce, whose toe was shot off. Filipino high-ranking officers—including generals—soon learned that they were prime targets for snipers and removed their insignia from their uniforms to conceal their leadership role.[6]

Another American elaborates on the Japanese sniping tactic: "Their training called for absolute control of motion. They never attracted attention by swinging a gun barrel to a new bear[ing]. If you cross a man's line of fire, the gun spoke—but walking between the line of fire you might go right up to the tree itself." *Palay na Ikaw* (you're dead)!

It was against infiltrators like these that Capt. Arthur W. Wermuth would earn his reputation as "MacArthur's One Man Army." Wermuth and men like him were needed as there were no sniper-trained soldiers in either the American or Filipino armies. Wermuth was a graduate of North Western Military and Naval Academy (Class of 1932) where

Japanese Equipment

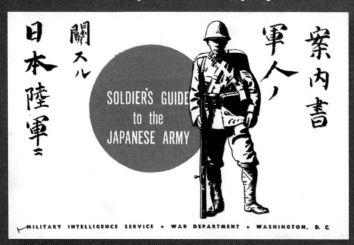

SOLDIER'S GUIDE to the JAPANESE ARMY

關スル 日本陸軍ニ 軍人ノ 案内書

MILITARY INTELLIGENCE SERVICE • WAR DEPARTMENT • WASHINGTON, D. C.

Above and **Below right:** The Japanese coconut cape as shown in this U.S. Army manual. These manuals were often derogatory about the fighting skills of their opponents. This one observes: "Japanese units by no means always have been steadfast under fire; on occasion they have been routed 'squealing like pigs!!' ...

"The Japanese soldier is a notoriously poor marksman; even snipers who are specially picked and trained men fail to capitalize upon the advantages which their infinite patience and skill in concealment otherwise would afford. In some combat areas it has been reported that Allied troops enjoyed virtual immunity to casualties from this type of fire at ranges greater than 50 yards, and snipers seldom have fired at moving targets." *U.S. Army.*

Far right: The real thing: Japanese two-piece coconut cape, 7.7mm Type 99 sniper rifle and scope, split-toe shoes (*tabi*), and transit case for the scope. *Image courtesy the National Infantry Museum Collection, U.S. Army.*

Other equipment a (real) Japanese sniper may carry is described in one newspaper article:

"A gas mask; a green combination mosquito net-camouflage hood covering his helmet, head and shoulders; a green corded net to camouflage the rest of his body; a black wire eyescreen to protect him from sun glare; a coil of rope for miscellaneous uses, including climbing trees and tying himself to the trunks and branches to prevent the rifle's recoil from dislodging him; a 5 inch long sack of rice; a small bag of hardtack; a half-pound of hard candy; a package of concentrated food; a can of field rations; a small can of coffee; vitamin pills; a can of chlorine to purify water; a messkit; a canteen; an antidote for mustard gas; quinine, stomach pills; game pads; roll and triangular bandages; spare socks; gloves, a

toothbrush and a flashlight.

"The flashlight has rotating vari-colored lenses, one color apparently intended as a sign of recognition, a visual password.

"A half-dozen spare lenses for eyeholes of the gas mask include some usable in zero and sub-zero weather, possibly indicating that the troops either served previously in Manchukuo or North China or that the equipment originally was intended for those northern fronts.

"The medical supplies are packed in a nest of wicker baskets and in the gas mask.

"Despite the number of articles, the packs are far from bulky. Most of the equipment is not very substantial, testifying to Japan's lack of material."[7]

The Japanese machine gunners were known to hang sacks camouflaged with leaves and vines over the barrels of their guns to help conceal the muzzle flash.[8]

While it is known that the Japanese had special rubber-soled sneakers with a separate appendage for the big toe, it was reported that sometimes the Japanese removed one shoe to assist them in climbing trees.[9] They also had tree climbing spikes which they attached to their footwear to assist in tree climbing.

he was on the rowing, baseball, and football teams. After college he received his commission in the Filipino Army's 57th Scout Regiment.[10] Using both a Tommy gun and a rifle, he personally accounted for 116 Japanese soldiers (unofficially 129). Wermuth preferred revolvers over semiautomatic pistols since he experienced the latter jamming on him once.[11] Accompanied by Cpl. Crispin "Jock" Jacob, he raided Japanese lines and wreaked havoc by surprise attacks. One time he fired from a foxhole near a ridge where a long line of Japanese were passing. "I worked them over with my tommy-gun and got at least 30 like ducks in a Coney Island shooting gallery." Wermuth also organized from members of the Filipino Scouts an 84-strong "suicide anti-sniper" volunteer company of picked marksmen that cleared up a 300-strong Japanese group that had penetrated American lines and hid itself to snipe at Americans, particularly at officers. They were credited with killing 250 Japanese.[12] Of course, there is no way to verify the authenticity of these numbers and it is very possible that the American media was not exempt from artistic license to buoy American public morale. At one point he was also joined by marines including Carl Sheldon, who used their three-day pass to hunt Japanese with him. The following are excerpts from Wermuth's diary:

> "January 6—Went out to locate and lead back the outpost which had been cut off for six days. Went on patrol with six men against snipers. Established order and drove Japs back 200 yards.

> January 10—Killed 21 Japs with tommy gun. They were moving along a trail at perfect range.

> January 1—Killed Jap lieutenant with revolver at short range. Took top of his head off slick as an Indian scalper. Took his sword and papers [which were of great importance, it proved]. Led small patrol 2,500 yards through enemy line. Located 400 enemy in camp. Sent runners back to our artillery and watched Japanese being blown into air. Patrol got into trench and rice field and surprised long line of Japanese crossing ridge just ahead. Like shooting ducks at Coney Island."[13]

On one patrol, Wermuth was ordered to observe and not engage the enemy. He had penetrated very far into Japanese lines and was reprimanded by his colonel who angrily shouted, "I told you to go on a reconnaissance, not to the Manila Army and Navy club for a drink!" In helping to repel a Japanese landing on Bataan, he and his comrade once walked into a Japanese machine gun. Wermuth's rib was nicked and the bullet exited his back. This required hospitalization but after two days, he left to return to his men.[14]

While dubbed "MacArthur's One Man Army," Wermuth attributed most of his success to the cooperation of the Filipino Scouts. Wermuth's final injury occurred when he fell down a ravine. His injuries required hospitalization and he was captured there by the Japanese. It was only after some months in captivity that the Japanese realized who he was and what he had accomplished against them. Amazingly, he survived Japanese captivity.

Also distinguishing himself against Japanese infiltrators and snipers was Lt. Alexander "Sandy" Nininger and the 57th Filipino Scouts. Twenty-three-year-old Nininger was a West Point grad (class of 1941) who was barely one year out of the academy.[15] A devout Christian, he wore a black cross given to him by his father. He often led a team of hand-picked men to destroy the Japanese who penetrated American lines. Armed with grenades, a rifle, and either a Thompson or a BAR, on January 12, 1941, Nininger led volunteers on anti-sniper hunts and at one point became separated from them in the jungle. He was found dead with his empty pistol and three fallen Japanese nearby. In recognition of his gallantry, on January 29 he was posthumously awarded the Medal of Honor and became the first recipient of the war.[16]

Bataan fell on April 9, 1942, and its gallant defenders were forced to walk to PoW camps. Conservative figures suggest between 5,000 and 10,000 Filipinos and 600–650 Americans died on the journey known today as the Bataan Death March. The Japanese conquest of the Philippines ended on May 8, 1942. Not among the prisoners was MacArthur, who had been ordered out of the Philippines to assume command of the forces in Australia.

Timor

(February 19, 1942–February 10, 1943)

On February 20, 1942, the Japanese landed on Portuguese and Dutch Timor. It was opposed by Sparrow Force—mainly composed of the Australian Army's 2/40th Infantry Battalion, 2/2nd Independent Company (commandos), and 2/1st Heavy Battery of artillery, and the British 79th LAA Battery—and the Dutch garrison of 2,050. The fighting on Timor was minor in comparison to New Guinea, but the continued Australian commando presence drew off Japanese resources that would otherwise have been used on New Guinea.

Sparrow Force's sniper was an ex-kangaroo hunter who was mentioned by Clifford Shore:

U.S. rifles

1903A4 Springfield with M73B1 scope

Caliber: .30in.
Weight: 8.8lb
Weight w/scope: 9.38lb (4.254kg)
Length: 43.5in. (1.11m)
Barrel: 24in. (61cm)
Magazine: One round at a time: scope blocked usual 5-round, charger-loaded box
Operation: Bolt, manual
Muzzle velocity: 2,805ft/sec (854.964m/sec)

During the war the Remington Arms Company sponsored a centerfold information bulletin in the NRA monthly publication, *American Rifleman*. The August 1944 centerfold discussed the 03A4 sniper rifle and quoted an anonymous American officer:

"Trained ordnance observers returning from overseas and reporting enthusiastically on the Remington made rifles.

"This rifle is essentially the same as the 1903A3—Official designation of the Springfield—the chief differences being a half-pistol grip on the stock and a Weaver telescopic sight carefully adjusted for extra accuracy.

"One officer reported: 'Captured Germans cannot understand how American parachute infantry riflemen can face a spray of 40 or 50 rounds from lightning-fast German sub-machine pistol, then coolly dispose of his enemy with a well aimed shot. Infantry paratroopers armed with Springfields equipped with telescopic sights were regarded with special awe and the Germans who admit that one bullet was often enough for these sharpshooters at distances of 500 to 600 yards.'

"All of which indicated that Uncle Sam's army have superior equipment—plus fellows who know how to use it."[17]

Another officer, a Fifth (U.S.) Army ordnance colonel with 39 years of service, tested the M1903A4 at the range and disliked it. Under the pretense of taking it to Anzio to allow the men to test it, he took a regular unscoped M1903A3 instead to bag a German.[18]

During the war competitive shooter and gunsmith Roy Dunlap served in the Army Ordnance Corps. Dunlap's comments on the 03A4 were equally unfavorable.

"I never considered the Remington-made 1903A4 sniper rifles very accurate, although I must confess I did not get a chance to shoot them with good ammunition. Most of these rifles were equipped with Weaver 330 scopes, in Redfield Jr. mounts, a poor choice for the Pacific, as the Weaver just was not designed for that kind of a beating. When they came in to our instrument repair men, water could actually be poured out of many of them. They just were not weatherproof enough."[19]

Another of the M1903A4's disadvantages is that—other than the barrel—little care was given to the assembly of guns by Remington to be scoped. Many of the modifications done by the Marine Corps on their sniper rifles were known to Remington, but the company didn't have the time. Pfc. Robert Emary of Co. I, 3/506th PIR, jumped into Holland with an M1903A4 and fought at Bastogne with it. In the sniper school in England he had shot up to 500yd with it and knew what settings to use, but was wary of shooting beyond 200yd in combat lest he miss and his target shot back at him. Most of his shots were at only 150yd distance. In training, he felt that if a three-shot group could be covered with a quarter (.955in. or 24.26mm), it was as if he'd reached Mecca. Neither he nor anyone else in his sniper class ever did.[20]

Garand M1C

Caliber: .30in.
Weight (M1): 9.5lb (4.309kg)
Weight w/scope: 11.75lb (5.328kg)
Length: 43.6in. (1.107cm)
Barrel: 24in. (61cm)
Magazine: Eight round en-bloc clip
Operation: Gas, semiautomatic
Muzzle velocity: 2,805ft/sec (855m/sec)

Because of the lag time between production and delivery, very few M1Cs arrived in time to see service in World War II in the European Theatre of Operations. When *Obergefreiter* Allerberger was captured by the Americans, he noticed that one of his captors was armed with an M1C. He thought it appeared very robust and was surprised how low the scope was to the bore.[21] This was in contrast to the German practice of mounting the scopes high above the receiver.

1. Fifth (U. S.) Army Pvt. Charles Cooper poses with his M1C. *NARA.*

2. Looking down the M1C makes clear the offset scope. *Image courtesy Jim Tomkiewicz.*

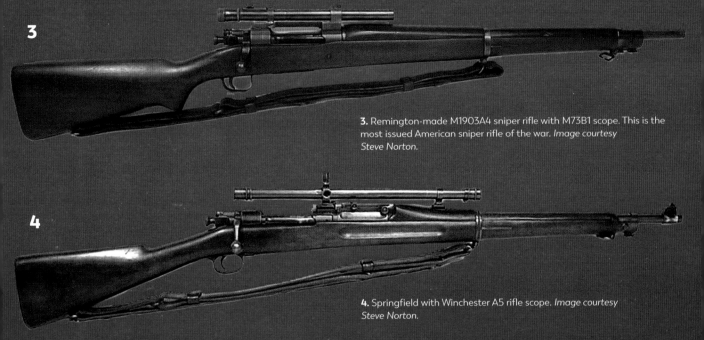

3. Remington-made M1903A4 sniper rifle with M73B1 scope. This is the most issued American sniper rifle of the war. *Image courtesy Steve Norton.*

4. Springfield with Winchester A5 rifle scope. *Image courtesy Steve Norton.*

Like the Japanese, Australians were taught to snipe from trees. This sniper is training somewhere in northern Australia. *Argus Newspaper Collection of Photographs, State Library of Victoria.*

"In Timor one of these Kangaroo hunters had a great sporting time, whether right or wrong, he played sportingly with the Japs, and never used his telescopic sights on his rifle when the Nips were at less than 300 yards range! He was credited with 47 Japanese killed, but with characteristic modesty claimed only 25 certainties, remarking that 'In my game you can't count a 'roo unless you see him drop and know exactly where to go to skin him.'"[22]

Among the first of the 47 killed was a Japanese officer who led his column mounted on horseback. After he was unhorsed, two more conspicuous officers were admitted into the afterlife. The sniper responsible was Pte. Doug Wheatley who also proved the viability of a sniper rifle in guerrilla operations.[23] Wheatley was

nicknamed "Doc" and eschewed using the telescopic sight at distances closer than 300yd and relied on his iron sights instead.[24]

When rumors spread that Gen. Tomoyuki Yamashita, the "Tiger of Malaya," had been sent to Timor (in fact, after Malaya Yamashita was sent to Manchukuo and in September 1944 to the Philippines) to tame the Australian commandos, the Australians decided to bushwhack him. Sgt. Ray Aitken was placed in charge of the detail assigned responsibility for the hit.

> "Aitken instructed his snipers—all ace marksmen—to pick off the four officers as they rounded the bend 200 yards away. Bren gunners covered the rest of the party. As the enemy party cleared the bend, the four snipers shot the four officers. Bren gunners blazed away and then the traditional Australian withdrawal without a casualty."

The identities of the four officers are unknown, but it's known none was Yamashita. However, while in this instance Yamashita was never in danger, he wouldn't escape justice and was hanged for war crimes in 1946.[25]

The campaign ended on February 10, 1943 when the last of the survivors of Sparrow Force were withdrawn. The Allies suffered approximately 630 casualties to an estimated 4,000 Japanese. The civilians on Timor would pay the price: between 40,000 and 70,000 died under the barbarous Japanese regime.

Borneo
(December 16, 1941–April 1, 1942)

Invaded by the Japanese who landed at Seria on December 16, 1941, disparity in strength and equipment made the conquest of Borneo a foregone conclusion. The British governor surrendered on January 19, and the remnants of the British and Dutch forces fought on until April 1, 1942. During this period a Dutch guerrilla leader played *franc-tireur* and selected as officers the "plump" Japanese who looked best fed and shouted the loudest. One said:

> "We give the Japs no rest, night or day. We swarm round their camps, fire a few shots, and then disappear into the jungle. We always pick off a few. Our Indonesian sergeant, who has a passion for officers, once shot three at the window of a house. He shot the first, who was looking out, and then the second, who came up to investigate. A third one showed up and was shot dead. The rest fled out the back door."[26]

11 Southwest Pacific Theater

"I caught a rifle bullet in my shoulder from a Jap sniper. He must have been at least four hundred yards away when he shot me. My first reaction was, 'Wow! What a great shot!' So much for the baloney about all the Japs having buck teeth and bad eyes. I don't know about that Nip's teeth, but there was nothing wrong with his eyesight."[1]

Maj. Samuel B. Griffith
1st Marine Raiders

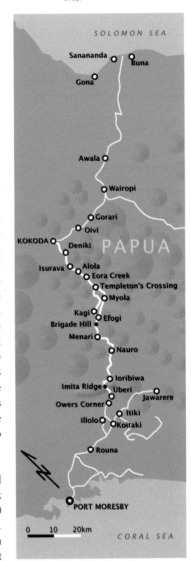

The Kokoda Track or Trail ran from the Solomon Sea to the Coral Sea through the Owen Stanley mountains in Papua New Guinea. *Chris Rees/ WikiCommons (CC BY-SA 3.0).*

New Guinea
(January 23, 1942–September 9, 1945)

After capturing Rabaul in New Britain on January 23, 1942, Japan launched a two-pronged attack—one against New Guinea (Operation Mo) and the other into the Solomon Islands to isolate Australia from America. Port Moresby was only 340 miles from Australia's Cape York Peninsula and would be an ideal point to invade Australia should the opportunity arise. Operation Mo was stopped at the battle of Coral Sea (May 4–8, 1942) which saw the U.S. Navy prevent the Japanese landing at Port Moresby. Their amphibious operation having been stymied, the Japanese had to attack New Guinea overland across the Owen-Stanley Mountain Range that rose over 13,000ft at its peaks and ran east to west along the length of the island. The route through the mountains, the Kokoda Track (or Trail as the Australians tend to call it), was a 60-mile-long red dirt path impassable to vehicles, requiring an ascent to 8,000ft.

The Japanese sent an infantry column to cross the mountains and also landed at Milne Bay on the eastern shore of New Guinea. From there, they advanced along the coast toward Port Moresby. On July 21, the Japanese landed at Buna, Gona, and Sanananda. Almost immediately the 5th Sasebo Special Naval Landing force (Lt. Col. Hatsuo Tsukamoto) began marching to Kokoda high in the Owen-Stanley Range. After three clashes with the Australian 39th Battalion, they captured Kokoda village.

Prior to the war's outbreak, Australia, acting on British suggestion, began raising independent companies in the Territory of New Guinea. They were organized into the 39th Battalion under Lt. Col. Ralph Honner, a former schoolmaster, and would be the first units to fight the Japanese. At times they would operate behind Japanese lines. As Australia's first Special Forces, they were trained in commando-type tactics that included raids, demolition, and sabotage as well as supporting local resistance. Their weaponry included a P14 sniper rifle.

On July 30, the 8,500-strong Japanese reinforcements of the crack 144th Regiment of the South Sea Detachment, under Maj. Gen. Tomitaro Horii, began advancing inland along the Kokoda Track. About six miles past Kokoda, at Isurava, they unexpectedly ran into the 39th (Australian) and Papuan Infantry battalions. Serving as a sniper in the 39th, Pte. Don Latimer had been trained at the Guerrilla Warfare School. It did not include sniper instruction, but he was selected because he had been a rifle club member before the war. "My mates dobbed me in and I was told to report to the Sergeant Armourer [as] he had just taken delivery of 3 sniper rifles and was looking for someone to use them." He was issued a P14 rifle with a Pattern 1918 scope. Often he left it behind at base, as the jungle warfare they were engaged in was more suited to the Owens SMG. There were times, however, when he was called upon to use the P14.

"Sometimes the patrol leader would tell me to bring the sniper rifle. I could pick off a few Japs at long ranges, 600–800 yards [550–732m], across a valley … I would not stay any more than half an hour popping away and then get out while I was still lucky. I was also used a bit when we were watching the Japs in a village … they would turn me loose … After a dozen shots you would have them [the enemy] running around like ants. If they had a clue as to your whereabouts they usually started the mortars going … You had no mates when you were sniping because you drew the crabs so quick."[2]

The marksmen of these independent companies became the first Australian snipers to confront the Japanese.[3]

"The Japs had a camp in a native village and we decided to stir them up a bit. The Intelligence section had a portable range finder and the night before an escort took me there and I selected a possie [position] overlooking the village. The range on the range-finder was 800 yards and I got set up and they left me to it. I stayed most of the next day shooting up the village and anything that moved. I know I got 6 definite hits which was my best day ever, but I really stirred the Japs. They used a lot of mortar ammunition to find me."[4]

Sniper Wally Roach belonged to 2/6th Independent Company commanded by Maj. Gordon King. Unusually, the company had eight snipers on its roll, and they helped as it distinguished itself by killing approximately 300 enemy soldiers during the course of two days of fighting. Roach killed several at 300–400yd. Fighting alongside, Acting Sergeant Katue of the Papuan Infantry Battalion earned the Military Medal, the first Papuan to be so honored. The citation for his medal includes:

"In the Awala-Buna area (Northern Papua) during the night of July 22–23, 1942 at great personal risk and alone, NCO Katue penetrated to the rear of the enemy lines for a distance of several miles and returned to his headquarters with valuable information of the enemy strength and disposition, thereby enabling his unit to take up a strategic position and greatly slow the enemy advance. This NCO repeated his feat again on July 26 and 27, 1942."

Katue was a sniper and killed 26 Japanese during the operation that slowed the Japanese advance significantly.[5]

Capt. T. Grahamslaw briefing Sgt. Maj. Katue, New Guinea, October 1942. *Australian War Memorial collection/WikiCommons.*

The Australian and Papuans held out against frontal assaults for four days before being forced to fall back on the Kokoda Track. The exhausted battalion had only retreated a short distance when they ran into Brig. Gen. Arnold W. Potts with an almost battalion-strong vanguard of 7th Australian Infantry Division—Western Desert veterans—who were part of two brigades being sent to push across the Kokoda Track towards Buna. The Japanese fought Potts's men who, although experienced, were untrained in jungle warfare.

Japanese flanking attacks forced Potts to fall back. The Japanese succeeded in capturing Ioribaiwa Ridge and from it, could see the sea. "The sea!" some cried. "Look! It's the sea of Port Moresby!"[6] Now they were only about 26 miles from their goal.

However, the terrain that had worked against the Australians now worked against the Japanese whose supplies ran out. Furthermore, the strategic situation had changed. First, the amphibious invasion at Milne Bay had been defeated so there was no pincer attack on Port Moresby. Second, starting on August 7, 1942, the Americans began their counter-offensive by landing in the Solomons on Tulagi, Gavutu, Florida, and Guadalcanal. New Guinea in the eyes of the Japanese Imperial High Command became a secondary theater and Horii's reinforcements were diverted to Guadalcanal. Third, under the misconception that MacArthur was planning an amphibious attack on Buna to cut the Japanese off, Horii was ordered to return and fortify Buna. Withdrawing was no easy task and a bitter pill for Horii and his men, but Horii stealthily withdrew on September 24. Two days later MacArthur, ignorant of the Japanese withdrawal, counter-attacked along the Kokoda Track and found nothing.

Milne Bay (August 25–September 7, 1942)

On August 25, concurrent with Horii's advance on the Kokoda Track, the Japanese landed almost 2,000 men of its Special Naval Landing Force on the eastern coast of New Guinea at Milne Bay. Poor intelligence led the Japanese to believe they would be opposed by a few militia companies. Well aware of the significance of Milne Bay, MacArthur ordered in May the establishment of a base there and an American engineer battalion was dispatched to work on airfields. When Allied intelligence warned of the Japanese attack, reinforcements were sent to boost the militia. These included some artillery as well as two brigades of the Australian 7th Infantry Division.

Initially, the Japanese were resisted by Australian militia but then they ran into the Australian and American regulars. The Japanese deployed light tanks, some of which despite being tracked, bogged down in New Guinea's mud. When one tank commander exposed himself from the turret hatch, an Australian sniper shot him immediately. The tank moved off aimlessly until some crew member gave the driver directions.[7] In another incident an Australian sharpshooter was faster on the draw than his Japanese opponent.

> "In the mopping up operations at Milne Bay an A.I.F. sniper along the jungle track, looked up suddenly, saw a Japanese sniper taking careful aim at him along the telescopic sight of his rifle. Quick as a flash the Australian swung round, took aim and fired before the surprised Jap. could press the trigger. The Jap. fell dead from the tree."[8]

The Japanese were reinforced by 800 men under Commander Yana who then assumed command. Even with new leadership and more men, no progress could be made and the Japanese retreated on September 5. It was the first time a Japanese amphibious assault had been repelled and Australia's first victory over Japan.

While the ground was recaptured, it was not secured as there was a Japanese combatant who lingered on at Milne Bay. Cut off from retreat, he decided to sell himself dearly. The following is related in an *Intelligence Bulletin*:

> "A Jap, camouflaged as a tropical bush, crouched for 2 days without moving, on the edge of an Australian jungle outpost, to learn the names and nicknames of members of their detachment and their particular habits. One day, in a perfect Australian accent, he called out, 'Say, Bill, where are you? This is Alf.' When Bill shouted in reply, the tropical bush suddenly arose and shot him dead. The bush immediately dropped back into the foliage. The sniper was wounded only after the area had been completely raked by machine-gun fire. The Jap, wounded severely, told his story. He had fully expected to die after the shooting."[9]

Because Milne Bay remained in the Allies' hands, it was finished as a base to support a counter-offensive against the Japanese-held northern coast of New Guinea. More runways were built to support a base for aircraft operations. Milne Bay port facilities were improved with the benefit being the reduced workload on Australian ports and shorter supply chains.

MacArthur's offensive on New Guinea (November 16, 1942–January 22, 1943)

Early in September units of the American 126th and 128th Infantry Combat Teams, 32d Infantry Division, were ordered to Port Moresby. Their transfer was

Australian sniper with rifle. Note his observer off to his left. His shirtless condition as well as exposure suggests this photo was taken during a training exercise. *Author's collection.*

complete by September 28. The presence of American units made the Allies strong enough for a counter-offensive. By early November, both regiments had crossed the Owen-Stanley and reached Soputa. Airstrips were built and more men were flown in along with supplies. Allied forces began concentrating to capture Buna.

The Australians under Maj. Gen. George A. Vasey advanced down the Kokoda Track and recovered the ground ceded earlier in the campaign. Fighting there the Australians learned to keep their rifles and grenades at hand as the Japanese were predisposed to night raids. One dead Australian was propped up on the trail. The sniper then lay in wait and fired at other Australians who approached to investigate.[10] Other tricks tried on the Australians included calling out an English Christian name or with a general question like, "Hey Bill! Is the corporal there?" If an Australian was duped and stepped into view, he was machine gunned or killed by a sniper. "Harry" was another name used to lure out the unsuspecting.[11] Others would call for medics or stretcher-bearers. One Japanese even tried, "Where are you Digger?" to which an unconvinced and hidden Australian replied, "I'm here, Tojo."[12] Sometimes they even called for the chaplain hoping he'd expose himself. "Padre!"[13]

Returning home because of a shoulder wound, Sgt. Jim Coy angrily spewed: "They are more like wild animals than men." Sgt. Coy had been speaking with his commanding officer far from the beach where the fighting was taking place when he was struck by a bullet that was fired 1,000yd away.[14] Similarly, at the Faria River when an Australian officer stood up to organize an attack, he was promptly shot down. When another soldier ran out to help him, he too was shot down. Command fell upon a corporal who led the men out.[15]

Being a sniper wasn't always about shooting the enemy. On the Kokoda Track an Australian soldier was wounded and captured by the Japanese. During a firefight, he managed to crawl away from his captors and hid himself. He was spotted by an Australian sniper who directed rescuers to him.[16]

The attack on Buna, begun on November 19, was problematic and the Allies were only successful in early January 1943. During the battle, snipers played an important role. Outgunning an enemy worked in one incident at Cape Endaiadere (near Buna) when a pair of intrepid Bren gunners used their weapons against the top of one coconut tree until it broke off and fell crashing to the earth taking with it the Japanese sniper.[17] Sometimes aircraft were summoned to strafe the treetops. Not only would the treetop crash down, so would the sniper.[18] When it came to ground fighting though, the most formidable man in the Australian Infantry Force was Lt. Don Taylor. In three days of fighting at Buna, he was credited with slaying 36 Japanese.[19]

When faced with snipers, neither division had its own snipers to counter them. Spraying treetops with gunfire was the countermeasure most often used. A pair of American heavy machine gunners learned of an annoying Japanese in a tree. They fired off bursts against the treetop with no visible results other than to provoke the Japanese to return fire. In cooperation with one another, both guns fired at about six feet below the tree top, blasting the top off and bringing the Japanese crashing down to his death.[20] In another incident after an intense bombardment on Japanese lines, Army Captain Millard Glen Gray spotted a Japanese climbing a tree at 250 yards distance. He shot him and modestly told reporters who arrived at his location just after the act, "You watch them climbing trees, through binoculars, wait till they are nearly at the top, then you draw your bead."[21]

One pair of Americans who were good at hunting Japanese were Pfc. Charles Zuke and Pvt. John Combs, both of 126th Infantry Regiment. Zuke's childhood squirrel hunting skills showed when he used his M-1 Garand to shoot 22 Japanese. His buddy Combs was no slacker either at 17. Their captain, Melvin W. Schulz said of them:

"They're both wonderful boys and I am proud of them. But I owe Zuke the most because he saved my life at least twice. Zuke is a quiet youth who talks little, but he is a shooting fool. I remember

the first Jap he got because he saved my life. We were near the front lines when suddenly Zuke stopped, pointed ahead a ways and said, 'Captain, there's a Jap out there and I can't get a grenade out.' The Jap apparently heard us because he began cutting loose. All the cover I could find was grass, and those bullets were coming close. Zuke slipped away and I watched him. He slithered through the grass to the side of the Jap, stood up, walked forward like he was hunting rabbits and shot the Jap through the head. From then on there was no stopping him. I kept him close by me after that. Every once in a while he would stop short and I would hear the crack of his rifle and would say; 'Now what, Zuke?' He would point to a tree and I would see a Jap hanging down a little ways. His biggest day was December 8 when he got nine. All of these Japanese were seen by at least one other person."

On December 8, the Americans finally received their flamethrower. Their first attempt at using it failed with the operator, the two soldiers covering him, and the chemical officer supervising them all slain. The 126th Regiment could do no more and the 127th Regiment relieved them. Embedded with the 127th Regiment was AP reporter Murlin Spencer. Led to the front by a corporal, he was introduced to the men with a quick, "This correspondent wants to see the battle zone." With that, the corporal vanished, leaving Spencer literally among a squad that was hunting Japanese. 1Lt. Francis J. Endl touched Spencer to catch his attention. Pointing to a tree, he said, "I see a sniper there." While Spencer tried to locate the sniper, two shots rang out from Endl's Garand. "I think I got him," announced Endl as he pointed again. While Spencer strained to see, two more shots rang out from Endl's rifle. "The bullets knocked him into a leaning position and about all you can see is his rear end. If I dared I would use a tracer to warm his pants for him but that would show our positions." Borrowing field glasses from Endl, Spencer was finally able to see the rear end of the dead sniper.

It was quiet for a few hours and some men tried to get some sleep; but only two at a time since the Japanese were adept at night infiltration. Suddenly, the corporal who led Spencer to the front returned. He was holding his neck to stem the flow of blood. It was a signal for the men to spring for the trenches and to start shooting. The men began firing at trees and whatever else they thought was a target. Sgt. Ronald McCann soon returned to get more ammunition. He was asked, "You get one?" "Damned right I did and he's my eighth." Pvt. Stanley Orlowski jubilantly cried out, "I loosened one.

He is slipping." Determined to finish the work, Orlowski fired again. "There, I got the _____! Now he's hanging by his feet." From the darkness an unidentified soldier shouted, "I got one!" By now, the men had advanced beyond the trench and were at the edge of the jungle looking in Buna village. Artillery fell on it and nothing stirred within the village. [22] On December 14, their regiment entered Buna. The Japanese had abandoned it the day before.

Regarding Combs, Capt. Schulz described him as a short, husky lad with a hard eye when he is talking about shooting Japanese.

"Combs really walked into something the day he got his seventeen. We were on the Buna trail when a bunch of Japs tried to cut off one of our platoons. They took up their positions behind a bunker. But Johnnie got inside them and came up on one side. He got a direct bead with a tommy gun and cut loose. He had a drum of fifty shells and he used all of them. As he began firing the Japs shouted and there was the damndest mess in that place you ever saw. But Johnnie just stood there and kept firing. Other boys finally came up to him, but I think Johnnie got all seventeen. At least there wasn't a live one left when he finished."[23]

While seriously wounded, Pfc. Charles Zuke, along with Capt. Melvin Schulz survived the war.[24] Schulz later retired as a colonel in the Michigan National Guard.[25] No further information was found on Pvt. Combs.

In a incident reminiscent of the World War I rifle batteries, one Japanese sniper baffled the Americans and Australians for a week.

"The sniper operated two .28 caliber machine guns planted on the ground but manipulated them by wires from his position at the top of a coconut tree. Each machine gun was loaded with 25 trays of ammunition, each tray having 25 shells. The trays were interlocked so that when one was exhausted, the next in line would come into place. The sniper stayed up in the tree all day, tied securely to the treetop, and would come down only at night to reload his machine guns. We tossed plenty of hand grenades at that machine gun nest but couldn't put it out of action. Finally, someone spied the camouflaged Jap in the treetop and he was brought down with a cannon shot. Thereafter we blew the tops off of all coconut trees."[26]

This was not the first time that remotely operated machine guns were found. Sgt. Roman Wisniewaki reported that after his unit had shot one Japanese down from a tree, they found four long strings attached to one hand. By bending a finger, a hidden machine gun would be fired. Hidden Japanese were nearby and reloaded the machine gun when it was safe. As a countermeasure, all trees in the vicinity were liberally sprayed with machine gun fire before bivouac was set up for the night.[27]

Thinking that tanks could not be used in the jungle, the Americans did not have any available. Unlike the Americans, the Australians brought their Stuarts—Lend-Lease M3 light tanks—which proved useful. Earlier they had attempted to use five Universal Carriers to support an infantry assault but they were quickly disabled or destroyed by the Japanese who resorted to sticky bombs, grenades (they were open-topped), mines, and tree snipers who fired down at the exposed crews. While M3 Stuarts were only thin-skinned light tanks, they had a 37mm gun and were completely armored. During the mopping up around Buna Point, when Australian stretcher-bearer and aid men were being shot down with alarming frequency, a tank was called up. Its commander, Lt. Philip Tucker, began to methodically spray every coconut treetop with machine-gun fire until a Japanese equipped with a scoped rifle came tumbling down.[28] Another Stuart tank rammed a tree with sufficient force to knock the Japanese, if not tied down, from his perch.[29] Unfortunately, being thin-skinned light tanks built for speed, the Stuarts were vulnerable to the small Japanese anti-tank guns.

One Japanese sniper was fond of shooting at stretcher-bearers. Lt. Philip Tucker of Sydney responded and described his action:

"This sniper would wait until a stretcher-bearer bent to pick up a wounded man then would pick

Stuart light tank of B Squadron, 2/6th (Australian) Armoured Regiment, accompanied by men of 2/12th Infantry Battalion, assault Buna on New Guinea. Note hull .30 machine gun pointing upward. The contemporary caption asserts that the squadron's tanks fired 10,000 rounds while clearing treetops of snipers by systematic spraying of trees. *Photo taken by Australian Department of Information photographer George Silk. Australian War Memorial collection/WikiCommons.*

Marine sniper with his Unertl equipped M1903 fighting at Tarawa. Note the American M3 37mm anti-tank gun on his right. USMC.

him off. Finally I got the general direction from which he was firing and systematically sprayed the tops of every coconut palm. Very soon a Japanese toppled from a palm about 70 yards ahead and with him a rifle with telescopic sights. Sniping on the stretcher bearers in that area then ceased."[30]

On December 28, 1942, along the Sanananda front, an unidentified Japanese soldier shot Padre Clive Cox while he was burying a dead soldier. He was the first Australian chaplain to be killed in the war. After that a special group of marksmen was raised to hunt the Japanese. Their motto was, "One shot, one sniper."[31] Two men who distinguished themselves during the mopping up operation on that front were Pte. Bill Paull and Cpl. Clement Maloney. Paull did not survive. Lt. M. W. Power's condolence letter written to his parents reads:

"The attack was most successful and the battalion earned a name which will not be forgotten in New Guinea history. We were mopping up the area for four days afterwards and killed hundreds of the swine. In that stunt young Bill was well to the front and later did a marvelous job of offsiding for Clem Maloney on the Bren gun. They accounted for a great number of Japs. While covering the platoon after we had cleaned up three pillboxes, and were waiting for further orders, they also killed a Jap sniper who had accounted for at least 20 of our men. The Jap was well camouflaged in a tree. No one else could pick him up, but Bill was on to him. I believe Clem had to fire about two magazines of Bren ammunition to cut a piece out of an intervening tree so that he could get a good aim and finish the blighter off."

The unit then relieved another battalion and while digging a new foxhole, Paull and Maloney were gunned down by a machine gunner.[32]

Finally, when machine gun and gunfire couldn't bring one sniper down, a digger known only as Scotty, a 34-year-old former businessman, dashed up with a machete and under the covering fire of his mates who prevented the Japanese from exposing himself to shoot down the tree, hacked at the tree with a machete. When the Japanese came down, Scotty throttled him.[33]

Big-game hunter Sgt. Harold Pointer applied his skills to hunting Japanese instead of animals. Venturing out on his own in the jungle muck and waist-deep water, Pointer would hide himself, wait for a shot to divulge the general area of the sniper and then slowly approach the location and wait for a shot. For two weeks Pointer used this techinque and accounted for 19 Japanese.[34] Another sniper-hunter said, "The best way is to sit tight and watch the leaves being cut from the tree by the bullets. Then you can find out the direction from where the Japanese is firing."[35] When his company commander learned what Pointer was doing, he had him leading patrols with the purpose of teaching the patrol members on his hunting techniques. Pointer at times used an SMLE but preferred a Springfield with the stock shortened.[36]

As a former power company lineman, Sgt. Rupert Henneman felt he could climb trees better than his men. So, slinging his M1 Garand, he ascended a palm tree to spot for the mortars. He was ready when the mortars ceased fired. "When the firing was over, three Japs came out of a pillbox. I fired three shots with my M-1 and got two of them. The third got away but I think I winged him." Some retribution had been exacted.[37]

Army Cpl. Glenn Wehrli and his sergeant were resting in the shade when they saw a Japanese soldier climb a tree. Wehrli dropped him but he wasn't done yet. Another Japanese was seen approaching his fallen comrade to render assistance and Wehrli dropped him too.[38]

As the Allied forces continued to clear New Guinea, there were still vestiges of Japanese resistance. Wewak was captured from the Japanese on May 10, 1945, and the Australian Sixth Division made its HQ near there. C-47 Douglas planes were used as couriers and cargo planes to Wewak airport for the Australians. A lone Japanese rifleman earned the moniker "Two-Shot Pete" for his practice of taking two shots at each aircraft before running away to another hilltop. No pilot took Two-Shot Pete seriously until he scored two hits on the tail of a C-47. The Royal Australian Air Force mustered six Beaufort twin-engine fighters that kept a holding pattern in his area of operation. The next time Two-

Shot Pete fired at an aircraft, all six Beauforts dove down and saturated the area with machine-gun fire. Two-Shot Pete shot no more.[39]

The capture of Buna village by the Americans and the joining up with the Australians who fought their way over the Owens-Stanley Ridge removed the threat of the Japanese using New Guinea as a staging area for invading Australia. The victorious Americans at Buna, of course, were more concerned about souvenir hunting than cleaning up Japanese remnants. Their colonel ordered them to cease their souvenir hunting and hunt for stragglers and snipers instead.[40]

A new Japanese deception was used late in New Guinea. A dummy dressed in a Japanese uniform was tied up in a tree and used to draw enemy fire. This helped the Japanese on the ground to locate their enemy or to deceive the Americans into thinking they had killed their sniper.[41] Some soldiers of the 41st Infantry Division took a cue from the Japanese playbook and adopted some Japanese tactics including using trees from which to shoot unwary Japanese.[42]

Of the two American divisions (all of the 31st and elements of the 32d) present with a combat strength of 13,645, they suffered 671 killed, 2,172 wounded, and 7,920 sick. Including the 116 deaths from other reasons, the total casualties were 10,879.[43] At almost 80 percent casualties, it was a victory won in hell at a high price. New Guinea would not be secured until September 9, 1945, when the Japanese finally capitulated. Ironically, it was a week after the Japanese formal surrendered on September 2 and almost a month after Emperor Hirohito announced the surrender (August 15).

Solomon Islands campaign
(August 7, 1942–August 21, 1945)

Guadalcanal (August 7, 1942–February 9, 1943)
To isolate Australia from communication and supplies from the United States, the Japanese captured Guadalcanal and then began constructing an airfield at Lunga Point. American planners realized its strategic implication and to secure the lines of communication, marines landed on August 7, 1942. The fighting lasted for months.

Col. John S. Arthur describes one Japanese tactic:

"The Japs infiltrate in the night, hide out in the tree-tops, and although it's suicidal they continue such tactics day after day. The Japs are good fighters, but poor soldiers. They won't surrender. It's a fight of extermination. Even when we have the yellow bellies downward we have to blow them out of their fox holes, shoot them down, blast them out of caves, and bayonet them."

Night infiltration tactics were first used in the Philippines to penetrate MacArthur's defenses.

Another Japanese sniper survived for a long time because he would only fire when his own gun's report would be masked by that of a machine gun. Nineteen-year-old marine Pfc. Murrell Eugene Davis camped near him for three days without suspecting his presence. Davis survived and was credited with slaying 47 Japanese on Guadalcanal.[44]

One strange anomaly from Guadalcanal is the report by Lt. Paul R. Brantigen. One of his men spotted a sniper in a banyan tree and fired eight to ten shots at the sniper. He then ascended the tree to cut the body down. "To everyone's surprise it was the nude body of a woman—painted green in the usual Jap camouflage custom. The woman had not so much as a sarong to cover her. She was slender, and no more than five feet tall."[45] Lt. Brantigen attributed the death or wounding of 11 Americans in the vicinity of her hide. Lt. Brantigen's account isn't isolated either.

Pvt. Harlan J. Hinkle enlisted in the USMC the day after Pearl Harbor. He attended boot camp at San Diego and received further training at Bremerton, WA before attending the Scout-Sniper school at Camp Elliott, CA. Hinkle "served on 10 islands and in one engagement shot a Japanese woman sniper. Before dying she told Hinkle that she had lived in California for sixteen years and was a graduate of the University of California She also told him she had returned to Japan to visit relatives and they forced her to join the army."[46] Apart from the Soviet Union and guerrillas on the Eastern Front, no major power used women as front line combatants.

Marine Carl A. Russell, Jr. fought on Guadalcanal from November 1942 to March 1943 and almost lost his life. Russell had climbed a tree and was serving as a "sniper" when his shooting caught the attention of the Japanese, who released a fusillade of bullets in retaliation. In trying to shift to another limb, Russell fell and broke his arm. "Those Japs thought they had killed me and I aided that belief by remaining as still as possible." Russell was rescued by other marines and told a reporter, "[T]hose Japs can't see 300 yards in the day time so we just hide out and pick them off like Panhandle hunters shoot cottontails." He added, "Those little men see like owls at night and, Mister, that's when we do some cautious hunting." In being shipped out to the hospital, the scalp he had collected from a victim of his hunting was confiscated. "I still think that scalp would have helped boost fighting morale in the States."[47]

USMC Pvt. Carl. A. Russell, Jr. fought as a scout-sniper on Guadacanal. He climbed a tree and shot a Japanese as far as 300yd away before his location was identified and he himself was shot. Russell feigned dead or as Americans say, played possum until he was rescued by his fellow marines. The newspaper dubbed him Russell the Scalper because the corps denied him permission to return stateside with a scalp. *Author's collection.*

In the fighting around Hill 208, MGySgt. Lou Diamond found one Japanese youth particularly formidable:

"Few Jap snipers were taken alive. There was one, though—a kid who looked to be about sixteen years old—whom we found in a cave under Hill 208. We had hit that cave with everything—TNT, grenades, mortar projectiles, Bangalore torpedoes, and gunfire—but bullets kept coming out of it and some of those bullets found good Marine targets. Finally, a venturesome Marine dashed in. There were two live Japs in the cave. One, who had been firing from a position under the bodies of his own dead, unable to turn his rifle in time, tried to reach the Marine with a sword. He failed; but the second sniper, the sixteen-year-old kid, shot the Marine through the head.

"Following Marines took care of the man under the dead bodies. A BAR gunner put a whole burst of machine-gun slugs through his head. Those Marines were justifiably irritated at that particular sniper. He had shot about eight men during the fight for the cave under Hill 208—or so we thought at the time. I believe now that it was the sixteen-year-old who did most of the damage. We got him alive. He said he was an aerologist. The cave was equipped to back up that statement. Whatever he was, he was a good shot; too good!"[48]

In another incident, Diamond remembers another Japanese sniper who was caught by surprise.

"Strange things happen, sometimes, to Jap snipers. I saw one, lying at the base of his tree, wearing his climbing irons and all tangled up in the wreckage of his boatswain's chair, who had been stabbed to death with a knife. Some Marine must have spotted him, must have lain in wait for him, and caught him there as he came down out of his tree, probably to return to his unit."[49]

Marine tanker Cpl. Robert Kohl used his tank to ram a tree and knock it down. He then drove over the sniper and crushed him.[50] Less orthodox were other American tankers who used another method other than its firepower against an isolated sniper.

"When a palm tree concealing a Jap sniper was located, a tank crew would drive forward and hit the tree in such a fashion that it was bent backward and then suddenly released. When that trick was done (care had to be taken not to knock the tree down), the sniper was snapped from his perch and went sailing, sometimes as much as 40 feet from the tree. The tank crew bouncing a sniper the greatest distance won the game—and the bets."[51]

To do this, the tankers had to be protected from infantry by American infantry or marines. Among trees, the palm tree is noted for its flexibility which is required to withstand typhoon strong winds that would snap other trees. Some marines took advantage of the flying Japanese and per Col. Leonard Rodieck, "Shooting Japs on the wing like you do clay pigeons is the most popular sport on Guadalcanal."[52] Other times the marines would examine the tree bark for scarring, suggesting that a Japanese had climbed up the tree. A tank would be summoned and a rope tied to the tree. The tank would move away and when the tree was bent, someone would cut the rope, catapulting an untied man into the air.[53]

When not piloting his aircraft, marine Lt. R. B. Fleener used flashing lights to help guide planes that were landing after dark. While so engaged, he was shot at by a Japanese soldier. Instinctively Fleener dropped to the ground. Seeing him drop and thinking he had been hit, other marines rushed over to help Fleener. Now reinforced, Fleener promptly organized a sniper hunt.

"We spotted his position from his gunflashes over on the edge of the field and crawled up toward him. Every time he'd shoot we knew he would be blinded for a moment, and we'd scramble closer. Finally we were right upon him. I fired one shot and he dropped like a rock. Pretty lucky. He was across a little ravine from me, and I was tired and didn't like the idea of scrambling around in the dark, so I shouted to the others that I was all right and had hit him, and we went back to camp. We buried the sniper and many others the next day."[54]

Another marine's poor gun-handling habits resulted in a score. When his rifle went off "accidentally" a dead Japanese rolled out from a coconut tree. Unless malfunctioning, guns generally don't "go off" on their own. He probably had his finger on the trigger and if he did have poor trigger discipline, it was fortunate.[55] Much more skilled was Pvt. Hiram Brooks. As a boy scout, he had earned a merit badge for stalking (badge was discontinued in 1952) and used those scout skills to hunt and kill Japanese.[56]

In November, marine scout-sniper Pfc. Lloyd D. Gunnels was out on patrol and described his encounter against multiple Japanese. "I was a sniper, so I operated alone," he said. From his hilltop perch, he was watching Japanese torpedo planes attacking five American supply ships. After taking some shots at a single plane that was circling over him, Pvt. Gunnels decided to return to camp. He describes running into and stopping a company-strong Japanese force.

"Then I moved down hill and had just reached a spot in the clearing when this Jap outfit—about 75 or 100 of them—pushed out of the tangled jungle. They were headed for the bivouac area above where my buddies were. A dozen plans flashed through my mind. To make a break for camp would lead the enemy directly to my mates. I spotted a foxhole and made for it. And as I did, shots zoomed over my head. Fortunately, the Japs were as surprised as I was and their shots were hurried.

"I expected them to encircle me, but they didn't. They just kept coming straight ahead. In the grass they were more of a target than I, and as each showed his head I let fly. They were only about 30 yards away now and I could see them roll over as I connected. I fired about 20 shots and I'm sure I didn't waste more than three or four.

"After about 10 minutes their firing ceased. The Japs were withdrawing. Why, I'll never know. As they withdrew I raised my head a little, and when I did a Jap, who had worked his way around behind me, sent shots whizzing by my head. I swung my rifle around in his direction, but couldn't locate him. I turned slightly toward the main Jap body and as I did the sniper's second volley caught me in the temple, injuring my right eye.

"The firing attracted the attention of my men above, and when I was hit they were only a short distance away. This is the last thing I remember. My buddies claim that as I was hit I threw my rifle in the direction of the retreating Nips and swore a bloody streak at Japs in general. Then I passed out. One of our boys finished off the remaining sniper, and, you know, it's funny about that foxhole! It was dug by the Japs because our lines didn't extend that far. Their digging sure backfired."[57]

Pfc. Gunnels survived but lost his right eye. After being treated aboard ship, he was sent to a naval hospital near San Francisco. Following his recovery, he was discharged from the Marine Corps.

The marines were not alone in conquering Guadalcanal and the U.S. Army also fought there.

Army Col. Russell P. Reeder commented on the Japanese rifleman.

"He is plain lousy and his snipers have been overemphasized. The Jap has a flair for concealing himself in a tree trunk, in a maze of banyan roots, or in a coconut tree top. He shoots at our men from these concealed positions, and his little .25 caliber rifle doesn't make much noise or give out much smoke. It's hard to track down these snipers. But because of their poor marksmanship their value is more a nuisance than real. So well concealed are they that our men frequently go past them and find themselves attacked from the rear."[58]

While Col. Reeder was not impressed by the Japanese riflemen, the same could not be said of the division's soldiers. While the article is unclear where one company suffered grievous casualties, it did prove at least one Japanese sniper was very effective.

"Not always are eight or ten Japanese killed for every dead American. During three days of fighting one company of the 37th Division dwindled from 137 men and four officers to 76 men and two officers. One sniper was responsible for dozens of casualties. They couldn't find him. One day he wounded four Yanks and killed one. Two patrols hunted a hillside with no luck. The next day he killed a bulldozer operator and seriously wounded his assistant. The patrols hunted again. Finding the Japanese was like picking up quicksilver with boxing gloves. So they called in a tank. It sent fifty rounds of 75s into the hillside cutting down trees, plowing up landscape. Two cases of machine gun ammunition was sprayed over the hillside.

"Almost at his wits' end, the company commander set out another patrol. The leading sergeant was in front. He raised up over a knoll—rolled back dead. But Captain Edward Nicely, Akron, Ohio, spotted the location that time, a tree deep in the gully. They blew Japanese and tree to smithereens. But the price was stiff."[59]

Another army division fighting at Guadalcanal, the 25th Infantry was led by Maj. Gen. Joseph L. Collins. When Lt. Gen. Millard F. Harmon, the Army Commander in the South Pacific, learned that Collins had used eight shots to kill a Japanese "sniper" he reprimanded him and ordered that in the future, all major generals were limited to two rounds of ammunition and mentioned something about damaging a coconut tree. In response, General Collins blamed his poor marksmanship on

On Guadacanal Marine scout-sniper Pfc. Lloyd David Gunnels was returning to camp when he ran into a Japanese company. He shot about 20 shots and probably killed 16 or 17 of them before he was flanked and shot in the eye. He survived and was sent to Oakland Knoll Naval Hospital, CA. After recovering, he was discharged from the Marine Corps. *Author's collection*.

"old age, failing eyesight and buck fever" and then gave an accounting for all eight bullets: 1. Nicked the sniper's trigger finger; 2. tore off his cartridge belt; 3. grazed his left eyebrow; 4. splashed dirt in his face; 5. missed entirely; 6. carried away the big toe of the right foot; 7. removed an ear, and; 8. "a silver bullet which I had carried for just such an occasion, plunked him squarely between the eyes."[60]

Harmon rejected the "explanation based on circumstantial evidence. Policy on major general stands." He added, "consider damage to the coconut tree … may later develop into a claim against the government."[61] That Collins was not one to sit behind a desk and would position himself on the front was confirmed by McManus.[62] Collins later commanded VII Corps in the invasion of Normandy, was responsible for the breakout that enabled Patton to sweep behind the Germans in Operation Cobra. Additionally, the Germans regarded Collins as one of the more competent American corps commanders. Of the two opponents, Collins considered the Germans more skilled as a professional army and better with handling combined-arms operations. To their credit though, the Japanese were more tenacious.

When the Marine Corps landed on Guadalcanal, its snipers were equipped with Winchester A5 or Lyman 5A scopes that were older than the men themselves. *USMC.*

Tulagi Island (August 7–9, 1942)

The Japanese construction of an airfield on Tulagi represented a threat to the planned use of the airfield on Guadalcanal which in itself threatened American supply lines and communication with Australia. Recognizing this, on the same day 7,000 marines landed on Guadalcanal, 3,000 marines from Lt. Col. Merritt A. Edson's 1st Raider Battalion and 2/5th Marines (Lt. Col. Harold E. Roserans) landed unopposed at Tulagi. The raiders moved southeast while 2/5th secured the northwest part of the island before joining the raiders. After Tulagi was secured, the raiders moved to Guadalcanal. On Guadalcanal, raider Cpl. William Griffiths had shots come uncomfortably close and when he looked up, spotted a tree sniper whom he eliminated.[63]

Gavutu Island (August 7–9, 1942)

On May 3, as part of the Coral Sea campaign that was to extend the defensive ring of islands outward, the Japanese landed naval forces on the southern end of the Solomon Islands at Tulagi and Gavutu-Tanambogo (almost two separate islands, they are joined by a causeway). Tulagi was part of the Guadalcanal Campaign. The 3/2d Marines along with two M3 Stuart tanks landed on Gavutu. One tank became stuck on a stump and isolated from its supporting infantry. Inside it was loader/radio operator Pfc. Eugene Oliver Moore who shares his experience:

"We were advancing up the beach in front of the infantry. They were moving very slowly as a result of sniper fire, when we stopped to fire a shot with the cannon. We were firing at a pillbox a couple of hundred yards away, when I heard our tank commander yell and fire his .45 up through the turret. I looked out of the peep-sights and saw what looked like an army of Japs."

A mob of about 60 Japanese airmen (ground personnel) swarmed Moore's tank. Pfc. Moore continues his story:

"We all drew .45's, cocked them and posted ourselves to keep the Japs from coming down the turret. One Jap rammed a pitchfork down the turret, and another started swinging a long knife. The tank commander shot him in the hand and they both withdrew. They were making a lot of noise and after looking out again I found that someone was firing at them. I got up next to the sergeant who was guarding the turret, and one of the Japs stuck his head down inside the turret. I knew one of them would sooner or later, and was ready for him. I shot him between the eyes.

"About that time the tank commander ordered the driver to move up the beach. The tank jumped ahead a few feet and we realized that they had put a brace between the wheels. I poked a submachine gun outside the tank and started firing but they cleared away.

"Suddenly there was a terrific explosion and I saw the tank commander go down—then I felt a burning rain in my neck and realized they must have thrown a grenade down the turret. A few moments later they set fire to the tank. Smoke and fumes were terrific, and the driver and I figured it was better to get outside the tank and get shot rather than burn to death. So the driver poked his head outside the front hatch. They shot him.

"I figured it was better to go out feet first, so I piled out of the tank and one of them helped me along. I remember one of them climbed on my back and started walloping me on the head. They were banging me all around the place and I was bleeding and every one of them was trying either to kick me, punch me or knife me, and about that time I passed out. When I came to, they had me in the naval shack which served as a hospital."

Watching the hapless Stuart and Pfc. Moore was marine Pfc. Kenneth Koon, who sprang into action.

"Somehow I got ahead of my platoon and was forced to take cover by snipers. Up ahead was a bomb shelter and beyond it was a Jap pillbox. I saw a [M]arine [C]orps tank come lumbering up from the beach, heading for the pillbox, and at the same time a howling herd of Japs came pouring out of the bomb shelter.

"They threw a brace in the wheel and stopped the tank, and then swarmed all over it. During this time I was banging away with my rifle, and several times, I am convinced, I got two Japs with one shot. They were so intent upon getting the guys in the tank that they didn't notice their men going down.

"I could see one Jap on top of the tank with a pitchfork, jamming it down the turret and trying to get at the marines inside. Several others were brandishing long knives, but they didn't seem to be getting to first base. Finally one of them threw a hand grenade into the tank. I figured the marines were done after that, since there was a pretty big explosion, but I kept firing and they kept dropping.

"They still couldn't get inside, since the men were evidently alive, so they got some gasoline, threw it on the tank, and set fire to it. The tank started burning and throwing up big clouds of smoke and I was wondering whether the boys inside were dead or supermen.

"I saw one of them come out and they promptly shot him. Another marine (this was Moore, I later learned), came out of the front hatch, and in all my life I never seen one man take such a beating.

"They kicked him in the face and stomach, they pulled his hair, smashed him with their fists, jabbed him with a pitchfork, knifed him, and one of them got him by the arms and another by the legs and bounced him off the tank. They finally moved away from the tank and let him lay where he was.

"After the Japs left the tank they took off toward the pillbox."

Moore only witnessed a part of Koon's action to save him. "One of the Japs I thought was dead came to life. But one of our snipers saw him and killed him while the Jap was raising his rifle to let me have it. I recall that pretty vividly." Slipping in and out of conscious, Moore recalled the marines rushing past him and someone paused to offer him some water. "I heard marines talking again that night. I made my way toward their outpost. I was dopey, all right, and just didn't seem to give a damn whether I was shot or not. Finally, I got close enough to yell, 'For God's sake, don't shoot!' Then I fell down again. Next time I came to I was shipboard."[64]

Koon himself was injured later and was at the same naval shack that served as a hospital that Moore was initially treated at. An officer came by and told Koon there were 31 dead Japanese around the tank. Discounting at least two killed by the tank crew, the rest were killed by Koon.[65]

Elsewhere Sgt. Harry M. Tully spotted gunfire coming from a small embrasure. Firing a tracer round, he calculated the range, adjusted his sights and—as if he were on the range—calmly began shooting into the aperture. It was later found that he had killed three Japanese.[66]

By noon on August 9, the twin islands were secured by the marines who suffered 70 casualties. Of the garrison of 496, only 20, all of whom were Korean laborers, were captured. The rest were killed.

Almost a month later, MM2c Bernard Riley landed on Gavutu and witnessed the high degree of alertness possessed by some marines.

"Marines were walking along the beach only a few feet from us. Frequently one would kneel and fire at some target we couldn't see. Five Raiders came along the beach and suddenly opened fire with tommyguns at a coconut tree. We thought they'd gone crazy. A few coconuts dropped from the tree. Then a dead Jap fell down, and we decided they weren't crazy."[67]

Following the liberation of the Solomon Islands, the natural anchorage of Tulagi was used as a naval base and refueling station. From it American PT (patrol torpedo) boats operated and harassed the Tokyo Express that supplied the Japanese on Guadalcanal.

On October 27, 1943, the 29th Battalion, 3rd New Zealand Division, landed on Mono on the Treasury Islands, as part of the larger Solomon Islands campaign. The Treasury Islands were to be used as a staging area for the attack on Bougainville. The 29th's landings went

After his M3 Stuart tank was disabled, Marine Pvt. Eugene O. Moore was beset upon by about 60 Japanese. He survived partly because scout-sniper Kenneth Koon slew over 25 of his assailants. *Author's collection.*

well until casualties started to be taken from snipers. The Japanese turned out to be be holed up in a weapon pit that had survived the bombardment and soon another victim, Pte. Gray, was mortally wounded.

"A section of carriers, guided by Privates E. V. Owen and E. C. Banks, of the I section, reached the scene and grenades were thrown into the pit. Silence followed, and the section continued to search through the village. Perhaps 40 minutes later, further fire came from the enemy position, and this time no mistake was made. An American bulldozer turned the process of death and burial into a simple one-piece job."

Pte. Owen was awarded a Military Medal for his coolness under fire.[68]

Bougainville Island (November 1, 1943–August 21, 1945)

Part of the Solomon Islands chain, Bougainville was administered as part of the Australian Territory of New Guinea. When the Japanese landed there in March 1942 as part of their expansion to protect Rabaul, they built up airfields as well as a naval base at Tonolei Harbor. Adm. William F. Halsey and his Third Fleet had the task of recapturing it for the purpose of isolating Rabaul. The 3d Marine Division landed on November 1 at Cape Torokina and were later joined by the U.S. Army's 37th Infantry Division.

As a distraction for the landing at Bougainville, Lt. Col. Victor Krulak, commander of 2d Parachute Battalion, led his 2,000 marine paratroopers to Choiseul Island and through aggressive action, gave Tokyo the impression that they were fighting a 20,000-strong force. One trick Krulak's men used was to embed their own razor blades into trees that the Japanese were likely to climb. Per Krulak, "When we opened fire the Japs assigned to sniper duties leaped for the trees. They would climb about 10 feet up the trunk, drop back and look at their bleeding hands in amazement. And then the marines knocked them off."[69]

On November 1, Allied forces landed at Empress Augusta Bay. Marine Pvt. Claude Murphy teamed up with a buddy to kill a Japanese sniper who had been shooting at marines for two days.

"We kept passing a point where Marines were beating the dense undergrowth trying to locate the sniper. On a return trip to stand by for another load, I was sitting on the top of the cab of our vehicle. I am used to using my eyesight on the Texas Plains. It was lucky I was on top of the cab, for the sniper couldn't be seen from the ground, he was so cleverly camouflaged. I got a brief glimpse of what looked like a face and movement of one leg in a tree about 35 feet off the trail."

Murphy tapped on the cab, alerting his buddy, Cpl. James H. Tatum, to stop the truck. Two machine guns were swung at the suspected location and Murphy fired two bursts. The sniper slipped but being tied to a tree did not fall. The next day Murphy cut down the body and learned it had been riddled with his bullets.[70]

After marine Sgt. H. S. Barnabee was shot, he feigned death. "I lay there quiet until two came out of the tall grass. Another climbed down from a coconut tree and all three walked toward me. They were less than 25 feet away when I leaned up and got all three with my gun."[71]

When the telephone line from the front to a marine artillery unit was cut, Cpl. Byron J. Griffith, Cpl. Robert H. Hagarther, and Pfc. Carsten D. Leikvald went out to restore communications. Cpl. Griffith described their experience:

"The lines led smack thru the jungle. We started moving up the wire trail we'd cut thru the bush. It was dark, but just ahead of us there was a small clearing. We figured the 'short' on the line was a little ahead of us. Suddenly we got a notion that the 'conked out' wire might be a trap. So, instead of going to the 'short', we brought the 'short' to us. Sure enough, the wire had been snipped by the Japs, the insulation torn, and the bare ends twisted together to create 'short'! Just then we heard a noise in the trees about 30 yards ahead. We looked in time to see a Jap. You can't see more than a few yards ahead of you on the ground. The smart Jap cut the wire and put the ends in the clearing, lining us up for a sweet target when we came to repair it. When we didn't fall for it, he fell out of the tree trying to shift so he could get us. We fooled him."[72]

It was at Bougainville that the Marine Corps introduced a new ally: the K-9s [canines] of the War Dog Platoon. The 1st War Dog Platoon became part of the 2d Raider Battalion, but were not as well trained for Marine Corps purposes as they had been trained by a Hollywood dog trainer. On D-day at Bougainville a Doberman Pinscher named Andy alerted its handler to the presence of snipers, saving marine lives. On D+7 Rex, also a Doberman Pinscher pointed out a tree to a BAR man who sprayed the top, bringing down a concealed Japanese. Despite their good performance, the marines thought it could be improved upon.

Lessons were learned and more military specific training was given to the subsequent dog platoons.

Dogs were classed into three different types: messengers, mine detectors, and finally scout dogs. Specifically, the USMC used Doberman Pinschers, German Shepherds, and a few other breeds as war dogs. The dogs were donated by patriotic Americans and were to be returned to their owners after the war was finished. The first dogs were acquired from the army which had initiated its own war dog program. After being physically examined for fitness (one to five years old, 25in. high and a minimum of 50lb blood tests, and quarantined for incubating diseases), the dogs were tested for suitability. As with cowardly dogs, the overly vicious animals that could not be controlled by their handler were rejected. Dogs were housed in their brick kennel with wood floors with tongue and groove flooring to prevent drafts. Each dog was allotted 5sq. ft. in the 200ft. long, 12ft. high by 20ft. wide structure.

Included in the landing force was Lt. Cylde Henderson's war dog platoon of 32 canines; specifically, 29 Dobermans and three German Shepherds. One Doberman, Gentleman Jim, was on patrol when he suddenly stopped. The marines accompanying him also stopped and were fired upon by a machine gun that missed. The patrol returned with reinforcements and destroyed ten pillboxes and many Japanese. Less fortunate was the war dog Otto, who was shot and injured. Otto limped up to a tree and glared upward. The marines fired into the tree top and the next day a dead Japanese was found at the foot of the tree.[73] When not fighting, the dogs were kept penned up in a cage area that featured a wood fire hydrant that was painted red and white. The hydrant was made by a police sergeant near Camp Lejeune as a gift to the War Dog Platoon. While the paint did not withstand the frequent dousing with urine, the dogs didn't mind.[74]

Dogs trained at the War Dog Training Company (Capt. Jackson Boyd, USMCR) in Camp Lejeune for 12 weeks. They were first taught obedience and simple commands (heel, sit, down, stay) and then the hand signals that accompanied them. Hand signals were needed so they could operate silently. Commands could also be given by the handler's silent whistle. Dogs were trained not to bark when wearing a leather leash. If a dog was on sentry duty, barking would alert the enemy that they were detected. The marines wanted the enemy to walk into a trap and silence was necessary. Training also included an obstacle course and crawling beneath a barbed wire while under dummy machine-gun fire. Scout-dog handlers were first trained to become expert scouts. Their dogs, in turn, were trained to lead patrols, to detect ambushes, and to locate men hiding behind bushes or trees, in foxholes, caves, or even up in trees.

Dogs and scouts on Bougainville. *USMC.*

"Once, for instance, two dog handlers were preparing to bivouac for the night. A Japanese sniper fired, wounding one of them. The dogs immediately went to one of many trees—an ironwood with a great spreading base—and pointed. Several Browning automatic bursts were fired into the leafy portion. The next morning blood dripped down, demonstrating that the sniper had been killed."[75]

Detecting human scent was essential for sniper detection and it was thought that no amount of camouflage could prevent the dogs from locating a human. All dogs received training in sentry duties to detect Japanese night infiltrators. Messenger dogs could also serve as ammo carriers and to guide first-aid units to injured marines. Messenger dogs also required two handlers; one to send the message and the second to beckon the dog. The command "report" was used to send the dog on its way. Rarely used as intended, it was recommended against training any further messenger dogs. It was ignored.[76] The last type of marine war dogs were the mine/explosive detection dogs. Their handlers were first sent to engineer schools to learn mine detection. Afterwards they were to train their dogs, all of which were Doberman Pinschers selected for being "absolutely sound, emotionally stable and have an exceptionally good nose."[77] As for rations, the dogs ate whatever the marines had.[78] By war's end, each marine division could boast of having its own war dog platoon.[79]

Also using dogs was the U.S. Army's 164th Infantry Regiment. A Chow/German Shepherd mix named Hey was handled by Cpl. Pasquale Forte and used to locate hidden Japanese. Hey had arrived with the 164th from Hawaii along with 14 other dogs.[80] Besides Guadalcanal, war dogs were also used on Tinian, Saipan, Guam, Philippines, and Tokyo.

Another soldier knew from childhood how sharp-eyed parakeets could be. Clinton Wistner and his buddies were guarding an airfield and every night some Japanese would infiltrate, ascend a tree, and in the daylight pick off unwary Americans. Wistner had a friend in South America send him half a dozen parakeets.

> "Their keen, sharp vision immediately detects the slightest movement in a tree even hundreds of yards across the airfield and the birds immediately become agitated and put up a soft warning squawk while cocking the head in the direction from whence the movement is detected. That slight warning is all the expert sharpshooter needs and he trains his telescopic sight on the spot as he halts and keeps watch in the direction the parakeet is looking. The Jap sniper is doomed."

In the beginning Wistner and two buddies would each have a parakeet in a small wood case fastened to their shoulder. This prevented the gun-shy birds from flying away. As they became accustomed to gunfire, they were content to remain perched on the soldier's shoulder. It was estimated that the use of the birds helped in the elimination of over 150 Japanese infiltrators.[81]

Lt. Ray Ross proposed to the battalion that he raise his own snipers. Not only was the battalion receptive, so was the regiment.

> "So I got the Battalion Commander's permission to organize a club of snipers. Regimental Headquarters thought it was a good idea and gave me the pick of the regiment. We asked for volunteers and, of course, got more than we could use. I wanted nine men to make three teams, with myself as C.O. Picking the men was tough. I checked them on their jungle work, got their reaction timing on various courses, and tested their shooting ability. We dropped five of the very best prospects because they didn't know how to handle their guns. We wanted experts. Without exception, a man builds up a lot of cool confidence in himself if he's a good shot."

They named themselves the "Dime a Dozen Club" because Ross paid a magnificent bounty of a dime for every confirmed dozen Japanese killed. That's all Ross considered the Japanese were worth.

> "We organize into three-man teams. One member of the team is the observer. He lies out in front with a pair of field glasses and watches the area we're going to hit. The second man is the sniper. The third man, in the rear is for security and flank coverage. Many time we've lain right in the middle of a Jap bivouac area, with Japs coming and going all around us. We've been able to do it because this calm division of labor takes some time of the strain off the individual. If you don't split up the duties, if every man is trying to look in all directions, if each man is tensed up for a shot, you won't last long. You sweat, then you get a headache, and then you get weak. But this way, with these cool and well-trained men, it's comparatively safe and easy.

> "Generally we'd go out and work our ways into a Jap area. We'd lie there studying the situation; then the teams would withdraw and we'd make our plans. Sometimes we'd spend two whole days just scouting around to find out where their trail blocks were, where they ate, drank, what trails they used. The next morning we'd get up about 4 A.M. and move into position. The teams would be perhaps 150–200 yards apart. Around 6 A.M. the Japs will start wandering around, getting chow, and so on. Quite often they'll come along unarmed, not dreaming that there's an enemy within a couple of miles. But armed or not, they're duck soup. A couple of shots ring out from one team, then two from another, and we fade back into the jungle, leaving some dead Nips for live Nips to bury and to worry about.

> "I'd get a big kick out of working on their morale this way. I honestly don't believe they've ever seen us in all our trips; and that's nerve-racking. Sometimes after we'd fire we'd hear them scurrying around, forming a combat patrol. When this happened, we'd just pull out over the ground we'd guerrillaered, and stir them up somewhere else.

> "Every time we went out we got Japs. It was easy! As long as you've got a good bunch of men, men you know you can count on, and as long as you've got a couple of yards of jungle between you and the Japs, you're plenty safe. It did a lot for our morale, too. This gang of mine can go anywhere.

"Ross says that, when they were formed, the order was to use the sniper's rifle, the M1903A4 Springfield—an '03 with a Weaver 330 scope. They trained with these and took them out on one trip, but later dropped the '03A4 for the M1 and the carbine.

"Staff Sergeant McLean, of Grafton, North Dakota, got two with a sniper's rifle. It was about 7 A.M., on a patrol working back of Hill 600. McLean and others of the patrol were extended in a skirmish line, moving in on a trail. When McLean hit his part of the trail, he stepped out almost into the arms of four Japs. He got two of them. Distance? Twenty feet. 'I think I could have got all four if I'd had an M1. For that kind of work, the sniper's rifle isn't fast enough.'"

While scoped rifles were not popular with the "Dime a Dozen Club," S/Sgt. McLean used an M1903A4 sniper rifle to kill two Japanese soldiers who had stepped onto the trail at 20ft distance. He speculated that had he been armed with a M1, he could have gotten all four. T/Sgt. Cottrell also got one kill with a scoped rifle.

"He was sitting out on the nose of Hill 600 before we had taken over and noticed a grass shack about 250 yards away and well beneath him. Off on one side two Nips were cooking supper. One shot was enough to finish the first one but Cottrell says the second one took off before he could reload and get a bead on him."

Due to the nature of the jungle, long-range shots like those in Europe were rare for the "Dime a Dozen" men and Pfc. C. Phillips made one of the longest.

"I was a lanky boy who has been shooting .22's for small game ever since I can remember. While laying on a bank above the Laruna River, he and Lt. Fossan spotted five Japanese walking Indian file.

"They were a pretty good piece up the valley. I wasn't sure they were Nips at first. They wore raincoats and the light was pretty bad. But just then the clouds parted for a minute and a little of the late afternoon sun came shining in on 'em … Lieutenant and I figured it was about 400 yards to them, so I took the rear sight on the M1 up to twenty-two clicks. It takes twelve to give it its 200-yard zero. At that distance the front of the sight is a couple of times wider than a man, but I held centered as best I could on the middle of the back of the last man. When I touched her off he just sort of sagged frontally and fell on his face. He never

budged. But the rest of them were around the bend before I could get off another shot." [82]

In the area around Empress Augusta Bay on the western side of Bougainville Island, company runner marine paratrooper Pfc. Tony Stein proved himself an adept stalker. He would approach close enough to see the whites of their eyes before killing his victim. "The snipers could hide everything but their eyes. They couldn't shoot with them covered, so I just waited till one raised his head and then I let fly with a burst before he could fire." [83] One of them didn't need stalking. Stein spotted him in time to knock his company commander out of the way to take a shot. When he did, the Japanese fell at their feet. [84]

Americans continued fighting on Bougainville until relieved by Australian II Corps. They would be fighting the remaining Japanese until V-J Day. However, the capture of key parts of Bougainville allowed airfields to be constructed at Torokina and Piva, both of which allowed fighters to escort bombers strikes against Rabaul and Japanese bases on New Ireland and New Britain. It also helped with the cooperation between the U.S. Navy and Marine Corps.

New Georgia

(June 30–October 7, 1943)

After the completion of the Solomon Islands Campaign, Operation Cartwheel was initiated to isolate the Japanese naval base at Rabaul and cut it off from supplies. The lack of landing craft meant a direct attack against Rabaul was unfeasible. As an alternative, the United States attacked and captured several islands in the Central Solomons which included New Georgia.

Landing at various points on New Georgia, Vura on Vangunu Island was captured on June 30. A June 21 landing force on Lambeti on New Georgia itself captured Viru Harbor. Landing at Zanara on July 3, Munda Point was captured on August 4. After difficult fighting, a northern landing force on and around Rice Anchorage on New Georgia (July 4–5) captured Bairoko (August 24).

U.S. Marine Raiders gathered in front of a Japanese dugout on Cape Torokina on Bougainville, January 1944. *NARA.*

Cooperation between tanks and infantry in removing pillboxes was soon extended against snipers. Writing for the North American Newspaper Alliance, reporter Ira Wolfert witnessed an incident.

"One sniper action I watched centered around a very tall coconut tree. Two of our men worked over the tree from behind and before long that tree trunk was cut in two by their shellfire. The sniper shot frantically and often. But he was a poor marksman and that cost him his life. But the poor marksman seemed to know it would— the more he shot the wider his shots got. Our men moved up carefully, their faces blank as they squinted through their sights. They aimed at the palm leaves and shot them off one by one, peeling the cover off the sniper.

"The sniper twisted and squirmed from side to side but finally exposed he was killed and fell crashing through the boughs of the surrounding trees a shower of leaves twirling slowly and silently downward for some time after his dead body had landed on the ground. The sniper was a very young boy."[85]

One GI, Pvt. Frank Rasonsky, was fighting at Munda when he and his squad opened up on a tree. Out tumbled a Japanese soldier who fell ten feet in front of Rasonsky. Rifling through the body for intelligence, Rasonsky came across a Japanese war bond that was fully paid for.

"I don't know if I was the one who kept him from going back to Tokyo to collect it. You never know if you kill a Jap sniper. They tie themselves to trees so the enemy won't know if the danger is past or not. Somebody's shot clipped the rope that held him up, and when he tumbled, I got to him first."[86]

Marine Pfc. Cecil W. Swiness said the same thing about credit for killing snipers. "I fired at one sniper who was up in a tree 30 yards away, and his rifle dropped down while he hung limply in the tree. We fired volleys and killed other snipers, but we couldn't be sure whose bullet did the job."[87]

Tennessee-born Pfc. Windom Guinn Craig found himself targeted by a rifleman but survived.

"I recall one time in particular when my buddy and I were on patrol duty. We were some distance from our camp when all of a sudden we came in contact with a Jap sniper who had concealed himself in a palm tree. We were cracking jokes to pass the time when we heard the unmistakable crack of a rifle. The Jap's aim was not perfect for all he did was knock my steel helmet off. I fell from the impact of a bullet and was deaf for a few seconds but otherwise I was O.K. Thanks to Uncle Sam for giving his boys steel helmets. I owe my life to one. I brought back some souvenirs I took off that Jap."

It was fortunate that the bullet was the lower energy 25-caliber Arisaka. However, Craig did not leave Munda unscathed and was evacuated with a bullet wound in his thigh.[88]

Twenty-two-year-old Pfc. James O. Walker accounted for seven Japanese. He saw a Japanese raise his head above a log, heard a bolt being operated, and stealthily flanked their position. He stopped within five yards of their log and saw them side by side with two machine guns. One burst of his BAR eliminated them as a threat. While returning to his squad he was fired at. Ducking down behind a brush, he remained hidden, waiting for the assailant to move. A gust of wind blew the leaves of a nearby tree, revealing a platform. He raised his BAR and fired, causing three Japanese to fall dead from it.[89]

In the summer of 1942, Pvt. Bernard A. Shanahan was involved in a mopping up Japanese outposts when he stepped into a small clearing.

"Private Shanahan spied a Jap sniper in a tree. He crept forward a few feet, got into position and fired. Then, just as the sniper dropped from the tree dead, another Jap sniper hit Shanahan with a bullet in the right leg above the knee. As he fell he turned to fire at the second sniper, only to find that another Marine whom Shanahan had not noticed before, nor seen since, had cut the sniper out of the tree with a Browning Automatic rifle."[90]

The fighting in New Georgia ceased on October 7 when the Japanese successfully evacuated their remaining troops. American casualties were almost 1,200 with less than a hundred aircraft lost. The Japanese lost over 1,600 men and over 350 aircraft.

New Britain
(December 15, 1943–August 21, 1945)
In addition to attacking around New Georgia to isolate Rabaul, elements of the 1st Marine Division landed on New Britain itself, the very island that Rabaul was located on. The purpose was not to capture it by landing at Cape Gloucester on the opposite side of the island but to seize the airfield there. By capturing

the airfield, Rabaul would wither from isolation. When Pvt. Jim Burke took advantage of a lull to get a canteen cup of water, it was shot from his hand. Both he and Pfc. R. V. Burgin reacted immediately. Burgin recalled:

> "Whoever had taken a shot at us was up somewhere in the trees. Jim and I fired several rounds into the trees, but we never hit anything, so I called for a machine gunner and told him to rake the trees over to get the sniper. He took that .30-caliber machine gun and raked the trees. Bits of leaves and branches showered down. Then the Jap fell about halfway out and jerked to a stop twenty feet above ground. He had tied himself to the tree with a rope around his waist and a rope around his rifle. We left the body there swinging."[91]

Wakde Island

(May 18–21, 1944)

As part of an American offensive to protect newly liberated Hollandia in New Guinea (captured April 22–27, 1944), a landing was conducted on Insoemoar Island (one of the two Wakde islands but generally called Wakde Island by the Allies). The Japanese had 800 men—infantry, naval troops, artillerymen, and other personnel. The smaller, unoccupied, Wakde Island was captured without opposition (May 17) and would serve as a mortar and machine-gun base against the larger island. On May 18, four companies of the 163d Infantry Regiment along with two Sherman tanks landed (two other Shermans were lost in accidents before landing).

War correspondent George Lait was witness with Co. C during the assault to capture the aerodrome.

> "I saw one company commander hit in the back of the neck. His body did a double somersault and when we reached him he was dead. But we located the sniper who got him and blasted him out of his leafy bower in the top of a tall coconut palm. He crashed to the ground as dead as the many birds lying nearby; all the victims of the concussion of our bombardment. We crept cautiously towards the drome, moving through tangled undergrowth waist deep in mud with water-filled bomb craters making the going difficult … I crouched behind a fire-blacked gasoline drum and laid some cigarettes on top of the drum to dry in the sun. Just as I was laying out the smokes I heard the crack of a sniper's rifle and felt a searing pain in my left hand. I saw blood spurt and thought: 'How in hell am I going to typewrite with one hand?'"

The USMC took to sniping to a greater degree than the U.S. Army, using better set-up equipment. This is a Korean War shot of a USMC sniper armed with a Springfield 1903A1 and Unertl 8x scope. *USMC*.

Corpsman Lawrence Malanca rushed to Lait's aid and using forceps, removed metal from Lait's hand and bandaged the wound. The advance continued and Co. C came within visual distance of the airfield. A banzai charge led by a sword and grenade-wielding officer followed by four soldiers was stopped by the GIs' rifle fire and grenades. The 161st Regiment pressed on and in capturing their objective, shot down a few more Japanese snipers from their trees. One injured soldier needed assistance and Lait, having seen enough for his story, volunteered.

> "We started out but hadn't crawled more than 50 yards when a sniper spotted us and shot the wounded man again—this time in the heel. I dragged him into a shallow depression and yelled to nearby soldiers, explaining that the sniper was nearby. Half a dozen of our men crept over to us and we peered at the tree tops for fifteen minutes before one guy exclaimed: 'See the reflection of the son of the B----'s glasses?' He pointed to a tall palm and sure enough, occasional flashes came from the depth of the palm fronds as the evening sun glinted on his spectacles. One soldier crawled off and soon returned with four Browning automatic riflemen. All four aimed their deadly weapons at the sniper's nest and at a single command opened up with thunderous fire.
>
> "The Jap reacting to the impact of scores of .30 caliber bullets leaped into the air like a jack-in-the-box, soaring 20 feet from the tree top, going into a graceful swan dive and landing in the undergrowth 75 feet below. The boys ran up to make sure he was deceased. He was."[92]

Japanese rifles and scopes

Type 97
Caliber: 6.5mm
Weight: 9.25lb (4.196kg)
Weight w/scope: 11.2lb (5.08kg)
Length: 50.2in. (1.275m)
Length of pull: 13.5in. (34.29cm)
Barrel: 31.4ft (79.76cm)
Magazine: 5-round internal
Operation: Bolt, manual
Muzzle velocity: 2,400ft/sec (731.5m/sec)

Type 99 Short Rifle
Caliber: 7.7mm
Weight: 8.5lb (3.856kg)
Weight w/scope: 9.8lb (4.445kg)
Length: 43.9in. (1.115m)
Barrel: 25.8in. (65.53cm)
Operation: Bolt, manual
Magazine: 5-round internal
Muzzle velocity: c. 2,360ft/sec (719.3m/sec)
Length of pull: 12.75in. (32.39cm)

Lt. John George recovered a new one packed in cosmoline at Guadalcanal. After checking samples of the 6.5mm ammunition for sabotage, he set up a makeshift range and tested it.

"I fired at the short ranges first, taking the initial five shots at a five-inch bull on the target closest to me—as near 100 metres as I could estimate. All of those shots were bulls. The sixth was a bad hold and went out at three o'clock—just where I called it. A walk to the target and a look at the first group convinced me that the rifle I had was a good shooting weapon. The entire six shots had an extreme of less than four inches—enlarged by an inch and a half by a single wild hold.

"At 200 meters the weapon kept almost everything inside eight inches, even with some bad holding involved and I found that the reticule [sic] holdover mark for that distance was perfectly placed. I fired shot after shot at that range because I wanted to be especially sure of that setting.

"To make a long story short, the gun continued to behave beautifully, not missing any of the settings for ranges up to 400 metres. Beyond that I didn't bother to test the weapon. By firing 100 rounds I had adequately tested the worth of the scope and rifle and I was satisfied that it was a surprisingly good outfit.

"To check the zero-return qualities of the scope mount, I took the scope mount off the rifle several times during the firing, with no noticeable change in the point of impact. There were no ready adjustments on the scope, which I naturally recognized as a fault, but at least the Jap soldier would not be able to ball up what zero his rifle had been given at the arsenal. That was more than could be said for our Weaver-Springfield."[93]

That was quite a compliment from an American competitive shooter turned soldier. One advantage of the Type 97 rifle as a sniper weapon was its low muzzle blast and hard to detect smoke signature. This gave the sniper a greater ability to remain undetected when he fired. The disadvantage was its low power. There were numerous cases of the bullet being defeated by the GI's helmet.[94]

1. Type 97 6.5mm Ariska sniper rifle. Note brass muzzle guard and transit case. Missing is the rubber eyepiece for the scope. *Image courtesy Mark Darnell.*

2. Japanese Type 99 rifle with 4x 7 adjustable scope. Unlike other rifles, this had limited adjustments for windage and elevation. The detached scope is shown with the mount locking system in the neutral position that allows the scope to be removed or secured on the mount.

3. Type 97 6.5mm sniper rifle serial with 2.5x 10 Nikko telescope.

4. Japanese Type 99 7.7 x 58mm sniper rifle with Kogaku T99 2.5x 10 scope. This rifle was manufactured at the Nagoya Arsenal's Toriimatsu Factory. The scope's rubber eyepiece is missing.

5. Type 97 2.5x 10 side view. Note the mount locking system is in the locked position here and in **6**.

6 and 7. Type 99 4x 7 side and top views. *Images 2–7 courtesy of the National Infantry Museum and Collection, U.S. Army.*

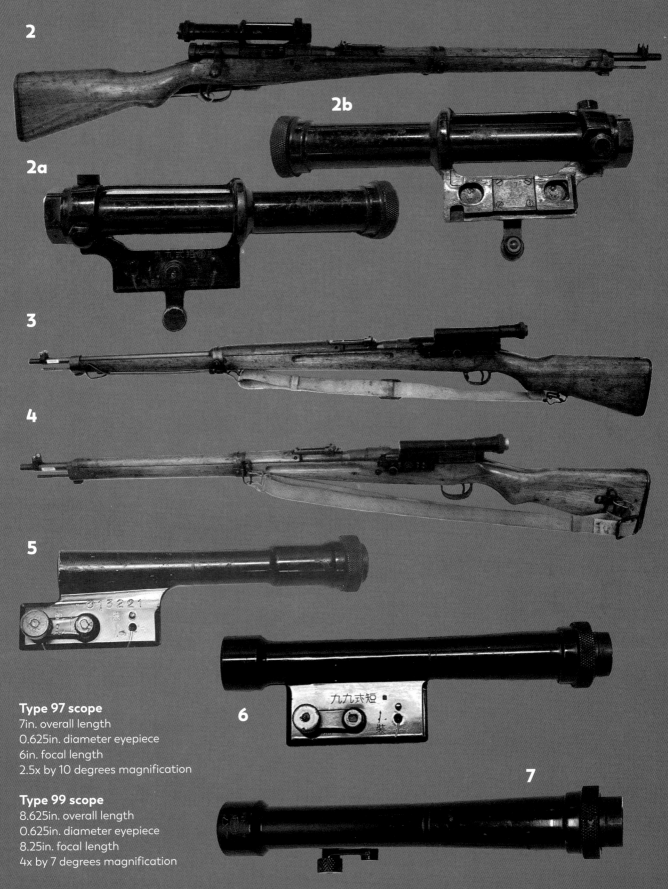

2

2b

2a

九九式短①号

3

4

5

313221

Type 97 scope
7in. overall length
0.625in. diameter eyepiece
6in. focal length
2.5x by 10 degrees magnification

Type 99 scope
8.625in. overall length
0.625in. diameter eyepiece
8.25in. focal length
4x by 7 degrees magnification

6

九九式短

7

Liberating the Philippines
(October 20, 1944–September 2, 1945)

On October 17, 1944, elements of the American Sixth Army landed on Leyte in the Philippines. Lt. Col. Kenneth Cramer, Deputy Commander of the 24th Infantry Division, found himself drawing fire. His habit of visiting the front line drew a lot of fire and his men pointed out that Cramer's bald head was a shiny, tempting target that attracted bullets. Cramer promised not to remove his helmet.[95] Three days after the landing, MacArthur waded ashore and announced, "I have returned."

In the battle for the Shimbu line east of Manila, T/5 Louis F. Korinek, Jr., a medic with the 38th Infantry Division, was wounded. He was being treated for a minor scalp wound when he asked, "Say, Doc, which way did the bullet hit my head?" The doctor told him it had penetrated the steel helmet above the left ear, creased the scalp and came out above the right ear. "Call the sergeant right away. Tell him that sniper is right where we thought it was." Undoubtedly the sniper was disposed of.[96]

One man who didn't believe the legend that the "squinted vision and thick glasses" made Japanese poor snipers was machine gunner Pvt. Vernon R. Thompsons. While fighting near Luzon, a phosphorous grenade that was outside of his foxhole was hit, causing burns to both Thompsons and his machine-gun crew. Thompsons said of the Japanese snipers,

> "The snipers have developed a number of crafty tricks. Sometimes they fire tracer bullets into an American flame thrower. The chemicals in the flame thrower are exploded by the tracer. They especially like to wait until a group of men come out to rescue a wounded soldier. Like waiting until a medic and corpsman come out. Then the sniper will [kill] them all off. You could never see the snipers. They were all well hidden."[97]

Also fighting in the Philippines was the 40th Infantry Division which landed at Lingayen on Luzon on January 9, 1945. After seizing the airfield, it occupied the Bolinao Peninsula and San Miguel, opening the path to Manila. While on patrol, Pfc. Manuel S. Gomez's steel helmet was creased by a Japanese bullet.

The patrol returned to American lines but Gomez was incensed. He approached his commanding officer, saluted and said, "Sir, please let me go out and put that quietus on that so-and-so." Permission was granted and Gomez stalked his way back into the jungle and after a long spell, returned victorious.[98]

Squad leader Sgt. Raymond E. Jennings was able to locate hidden Japanese snipers. He would figure out the direction of the bullet and from it, the likely location they could come from. He would then stalk to the area and wait. One time after staring at a tree for half an hour, he saw a movement and with his M1 fired at 200yd distance. He was rewarded by a seeing a Japanese fall from the tree perch.[99]

On May 16, 1945, 25th Infantry Division Assistant Commander Brig. Gen. James L. Dalton, who had commanded the 161st Infantry Regiment at Guadalcanal, was killed near the Balete Pass on northern Luzon Island. West Point class of 1933, General Dalton wanted to visit Col. Hayashi's headquarters and had taken the precaution of removing his insignia. He was escorted by Lt. Col. J. D. Vanderpool and seven other men.

> "Along there the trail goes through a narrow canyon. This Jap rifleman was hidden in a knoll beyond, commanding the canyon. A Filipino laborer had told us a Jap was somewhere ahead and we all had our guns ready. Capt. [Robert E.] Lane was in the lead with an enlisted man, a guerrilla and laborer when the Jap opened fire. The bullet ricocheted from the canyon wall and went over Lane's head. They pressed against the wall and got partial cover. The Jap fired again and just missed the guerrilla. I thought I could see where the sniper was and I moved past the general. But I found the Jap could cover both sides of the canyon so I decided this was no place to be exposed. I jumped sideways and rolled under an outcropping of rock. The general at once did the same thing. Just as he jumped the Jap let go. The general fell against my leg and rolled back in the line of fire.
>
> "I didn't know how badly hit he was, so I crawled down and dragged him back. Lane's sergeant was yelling, 'Get back. You can't do him any good!' But I got him back a way. Then I could see that the bullet entered above the temple and come out at the base of the skull. He was dead."

The sergeant collected some men and went hunting for the shooter. It was unknown if they were successful.[100] Dalton was 35 years old when killed, making him the youngest American general killed during the war.

When the U.S. Army returned to the Philippines, it had sniper rifles. A few units transferred from the ETO to the Pacific at the end of the war in Europe. One of these was the "Blackhawk" Division—the 86th Infantry—which was the first to return from Europe to the United States, arriving on June 17, 1945. After a month's training, the 86th was sent to the Pacific. Robert L. Anderson—now a sergeant—was with them, having survived Germany (see p. 157). The 86th was deployed in the Philippines and on his last patrol, Anderson killed a charging Japanese soldier. Postwar he was a psychotherapist in Los Angeles before passing away in 2017. *U.S. Army.*

12 The South Pacific Theater and Asia

"Sniper Alley is its own main event, although the Japanese along this stretch are not snipers at all. They are Japanese riflemen, pure and simple. That the marines call them 'snipers' gives them almost a bogeyman quality—a mythos that doesn't belong. That the Jap 'sniper' is somehow more trained or more motivated than the marine is up for debate."[1]

Pfc. Eugene Sledge
Co. K, 5th Marines, 1st Marine Division

Adm. Chester Nimitz was Commander-in-Chief, Pacific Oceans Area. His goal was simple: drive the Japanese back, destroying their navy in the process, and capture Japan. Instead of going straight for Japan, which would have been exactly the war the Imperial Japanese Navy (IJN) had planned for, Nimitz island-hopped his way forward, isolating bypassed islands and starving their garrisons in the process as well as slowly grinding down the IJN. Simultaneously, Nimitz ordered unrestricted warfare to his submarines to destroy the Japanese merchant fleet and any elements of its navy they could find. By war's end, over 90 percent of the

Japanese merchant fleet had been sunk and, deprived of food imports, the Japanese were beginning to starve.

Aleutian Islands campaign
(May 11–August 15, 1943)

After the Doolittle Raid on Tokyo, the IJN was extremely embarrassed and devised a plan to lure the American carriers into combat where they would be destroyed. A large invasion fleet supported by four of the six Pearl Harbor carriers were to strike Midway Island, so named because it was midway between Asia and North America. Prewar, Midway was a refueling

Kiska Island was assaulted by the 1st Special Service Force (FSSF) in Operation Cottage—with landings in the south on August 15, 1943, and north the next day. The southern beaches were secured by 1st Regiment, FSSF; those in the north by 3FSSF. 2FSSF was held in reserve ready to parachute in as necessary. In fact, they were more at risk from jittery U.S. trigger fingers as the main body of troops arrived rather than the Japanese who had evacuated the island. Note the FSSF badge (as above) and plastic-covered rifle of the man in the center. *NARA (left); U.S.Army (above)*

Taking cover from a Japanese sniper after landing on Attu. *NARA.*

Map showing U.S. operations May 11–30, 1943. Clevesy Pass is at **A**. *U.S. Army.*

marksmanship on May 16 of one anti-tank company against the Japanese.

"The war for the 2d Battalion consisted of blocking Clevesy Pass, and life for us just amounted to sniping back and forth and trying not to get blasted out by mortar fire and slowly freezing. This gunner sat talking idly with a couple of riflemen for quite a while not paying any attention to his business at all; then, all at once he began to twist wheels and peer through his sight and urgently juggled around to beat hell. I looked out across the pass and there, running up the hillside, was a Jap sniper. The muzzle of the 37 moved smoothly under the gunner's manipulation, and suddenly he pressed the trigger. The shell streaked across the pass and hit the Jap squarely between the hips. He just disappeared in the explosion. The gunner was serious. He looked at his friends and with a gesture of absolute perfection he said, 'I led him just a hair.'"[3]

stop for the Pan American Airlines' China Clippers. The Japanese carrier strike was dubbed Operation MI and Midway's capture would bring Japan closer to America but more importantly, compel the U.S. Navy to commit its carriers to battle.

As a diversionary attack, on July 6–7, 1942, the Japanese landed on two American islands that were part of Alaska: Attu and Kiska. Having cracked the Japanese naval code, the Americans were not distracted by this. All four Japanese carriers involved in the attack on Midway were destroyed for the loss of only one American carrier (USS *Yorktown*). Left alone, the Japanese on Attu and Kiska had almost a year to entrench themselves until May 11, 1943, when the Americans landed 15,000 men on Attu to retake it from the 2,900-strong Japanese garrison. It was on Attu that the Americans learned that the Japanese dug caves with tunnels leading to numerous fighting posts which allowed their soldiers to withdraw from heavy fire only to emerge and fight from another post.[2]

The 2d and 3d Battalions, 17th Infantry Regiment, landed at Massacre Bay; the 32d Infantry Regiment at Casco Cove to support their left flank. The Japanese withdrew on May 16–17 to reinforce the defense of the Massacre-Sarana Pass (**A** on the map above). This is now called the Clevesy Pass, named after Lt. Samuel W. Clevesy, Jr., Co. H, 2/17th Infantry, who was killed by a Japanese sniper while he organized his HMG platoon. (The nearby Jarmin Pass was named after Capt. John E. Jarmin, CO of Co. L, 3d/17th Infantry who was killed on May 14.) The 2/17th Infantry—including its 37mm-armed anti-tank company—with the 2/32d in support—began to clear the pass. Lt. John W. Erdington of Co. F of 17th Regiment recalled the

On May 17, 17th Infantry pushed up Cold Mountain towards Holtz Bay. The Heavy Company—Co. D—of 1st Battalion was challenging the Japanese machine guns for domination. Pfc. Melvin J. Nelson recalled:

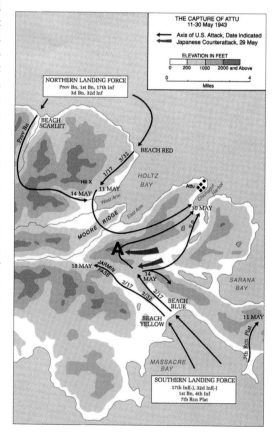

"Our gun was in position over near the left flank, and the gunner was raking the Japs on the hills to the left front without a letup. He was getting in some good licks too, from what we could see through the fog, and the men were getting positions they could fight from, and then the damned fog broke over our left flank. A sniper over there somewhere fired and got our gunner right through the head. Mel Nelson jumped behind the gun and continued to fire, while the section sergeant tried to spot the sniper. He saw him when the Jap raised up and fired at the gun again. Nelson was hit in the stomach, and it hurt and he was furious. The sergeant hollered where the sniper was and pointed. Nelson kicked the gun onto free traverse and swung it over, just as the Jap raised up again. He fired a long stream of tracers right into the sniper's head and chest; then he laid back, and a couple of boys carried him away from the gun. 'The little sonovabitch' he said, 'I guess that'll teach him.'"[4]

Clevesy Pass was cleared by May 21 and the Americans began to push on.

While the 17th was securing Clevesy Pass, the 32d attacked the adjacent Fish Hook Ridge. May 24 was particularly tough going for them. Sgt. Donald W. Wonn and his buddies from Co. I found themselves under sniper fire and Sgt. Wonn recalled:

"We started out from around Hill 4 and moved along the ridge line through the damned wind and cold until we got squared off above the basin, and then we got orders to attack the Japs in the basin and on the hill behind it. We moved out on the right of company K and got out maybe five or six hundred yards. Then suddenly all hell broke loose on us. I remember running through several large explosions and hearing lots of bullets crack around, and then I was on my belly behind a rock with Staff Sergeant James R. Carney, Dick Schuester, and a couple of others. The next thing I knew Carney was taking off his helmet. There was a hole in the front and a hole in the back, so far down that I kept looking at his head. I didn't think the bullet could go that way and not hit him. Carney swore. 'The damned little yellow sonuvabitch! Now I can't even wash my face.' 'Hell, you're damned lucky fellow,' I told him, and about that time there was a crash around my ears and my helmet gave a lurch. I pulled it off and a bullet had gone through my own helmet in a similar place, ripping my wood cap clear through and not even touching my head. We compared the holes

quickly and lined up where the sniper should be. The sniper fired again, and we saw him, but Schuester fell dead beside us with a bullet hole low on his helmet. The Jap was 300 yards away and had a telescope sight on his rifle. One of the men had a BAR and the next time the sniper stuck his head up the BAR almost cut it off."[5]

Without being snipers themselves, the two sergeants knew enough to triangulate and locate the position of their sniper. Excellent marksmanship later removed the threat.

One Japanese, nicknamed Itchymoto, had been holding the Sarana Pass and shooting down stretcher-bearers. To clear out Itchymoto required teamwork between infantry scouts, the signal corps, and mortar men. The scout platoon formed a skirmish line and worked their way uphill. When a machine gun opened on them, the radioman and the telephone layers provided communications which allowed the mortar men to wipe out the machine gun nest. With the machine gun silenced, the scout platoon continued its advance.

Correspondent Russell Annabel accompanied the officer in command and wrote:

"Presently we heard a burst of rifle fire but no word came from Lieutenant Murphy. Worried, [Maj. Ernest] Bearse began requesting information. 'Are you all right, Murphy? Come in please,' he repeated again and again. The mortar crew knelt tensely and everyone was quiet.

"I thought that damn Itchymoto was alone on the crest and Murphy must have walked into a trap. The machine gun tipped the Japs off and they were laying for him, I imagined.

"It wasn't the first time we cursed Itchymoto. Of course, this wasn't his name and I don't know who first started calling him Itchymoto, probably one of the medics he fired upon so often. We all hated him because he had his rifle targeted on the trail the stretcher-bearers used and he fired on these people so often the medics refused to mark their dressing stations with the Red Cross, knowing it would draw fire.

"A half hour passed before a single rifle shot echoed down the canyon walls, sounding faint and far away. Bearse reached swiftly to turn up the volume on his walkie-talkie.

"'I got him,' he said. 'Here's your target.'

"The climax was swift, noisy and very efficient. The mortar went pow pow as fast as the crew could load, its reports mingling with the sound of the shell bursts high on the unseen ridge crest. The firing continued until Maj. Bearse

USMC Sgt. Robert L. Kleinknight served as a scout-sniper when he earned his Silver Star at Tarawa. His award read: "For gallantry and intrepdity during action against enemy Japanese forces in Tarawa, Gilbert Islands, November 20 to 24, 1943. He, for three days and nights without sleep and under the most trying battle conditions, destroyed with his unit many enemy emplacements in the central sector of Betio Island. With the greatest of personal valor and military skill, he attacked an emplacement by crawling under heavy enemy fire to a gunport of the position and destroyed it by the use of grenades and demolitions. He then entered the position and killed the remaining enemy personnel. Later while his unit was attacking another position he exposed himself to heavy enemy fire to support more advantageously with fire the advance of one of his comrades to the entrance of the emplacement. By his absolute coolness, tireless energy, fearless devotion to duty, and extraordinary example he was an inspiration to our troops and contributed greatly to the success of his regiment. His actions were in keeping with the highest traditions of the United States Naval Service." *Author's collection.*

After Marine 1Lt. William Deane Hawkins was killed on Betio Island, Platoon Sgt. Morris. C. Owens assumed command of the scout-sniper platoon. *Author's collection.*

announced that the target was destroyed.

"Itchymoto was finished."[6]

In another incident, Col. Lawrence V. Castner's scouts composed of indigenous Inuit men, nicknamed Castner's Cutthroats, located a Japanese foxhole high up on a snow slope. The site was well selected and the scouts' attempt to assault him from below failed. Finally, they circled around to get above him but even then they could neither shoot him nor toss a grenade into his hole. So, one scout took a canvas shelter-half and spread it out on the snow. He pulled the front end up and between his legs. His buddies gave him a good shove and he went, using his feet to guide him while he slid down towards the hole. As he passed it, he threw in a grenade and slid down out of danger. The grenade did its work.[7]

By February 15, the liberation of Attu from the Japanese was completed. The high casualties (many attributable to inadequate equipment) always made Admiral King regret his decision to retake it. On August 15, 1943, a joint Canadian and American force landed on Kiska. They found only abandoned dogs as the Japanese had been successfully evacuated. Despite the absence of Japanese, nervous Americans and Canadians suffered 313 casualties thanks to friendly fire, booby traps, mines, accidents, and frostbite.

Tarawa
(November 20–23, 1943)

After leaving Guadalcanal, the 2d Marine Division was sent to New Zealand to recuperate and be reinforced before attacking Betio, part of Tarawa Atoll in the Gilbert Islands. Occupied by the Japanese since September 1942, the Gilberts were strategically located and needed to support American operations in the mid-Pacific and the Philippines. They were also 800 miles closer to Tokyo and the capture of the Japanese airstrip on Betio would provide an airbase for Allied aircraft. An American presence would also help isolate the Marshall Islands, which had been mandated to the Japanese after World War I.

Preceding the landing on Betio, 2,700 tons of ordnance was fired or dropped on Betio but the small Japanese garrison, swelled to 2,600 men by the 7th Sasebo Special Naval Landing Force and the 3d Special Base Defense Force along with over 2,000 Korean and Japanese laborers, was protected by coconut-log bunkers buried in the sand. They had had a year to fortify the island and made the attackers pay dearly: one in four of the marines who fought on the atoll became a casualty. Of the defenders, only 146 soldiers and laborers survived.

Betio had a coconut seawall that offered shelter to the marines. *Time* magazine reporter Robert Sherrod was present on Betio and near Maj. Henry P. Crowe who led one of the assault battalions. Sherrod saw for himself how deadly it was on that tiny island.

"A handsome young Marine walked briskly toward Maj. Crowe's headquarters, grinning in greeting to a pal. There was a shot. The Marine spun round, fell to the beach dead.

"He had been shot through the temple. A Jap sniper had waited since early morning for just such a shot at a range of less than 10 yards.

"A bit later a voice called: 'major, send somebody over to help me. The son-of-a-bitch got me!'

"Two men crawled over the retaining wall, dragged back a Marine shot through the knee. Then a mortarman 75 yards down the beach rose to a kneeling position, tumbled back with a sniper's bullet through his back. The wounded man's companion popped up to help, got a bullet through the heart."[8]

In the vanguard of the 2d Marine Regiment's assault was half of its 35-strong scout-sniper platoon led by Lt. William Deane Hawkins. He had graduated from high school at age 16, earned an engineering degree from the Texas College of Mines, and at age 21 was working as an engineer. After Pearl Harbor, he attempted to enlist in the Army Air Corps and alternatively as a naval aviator. Both rejected him and Hawkins enlisted in the Marine Corps Reserve on January 5, 1942. He graduated from the Marine Scout-Sniper School at Camp Elliot and was retained as an instructor. Bypassing both the lance corporal and corporal ranks, Hawkins was promoted to sergeant and served in the Solomons at Guadalcanal as the assistant chief of scouts and snipers.[9] He was commissioned as a second lieutenant while overseas (November 17, 1942). He led several patrols and after being promoted again (first lieutenant on June 1, 1943) he was given command of the sniper platoon on September 1943.

Along with half of his platoon and a squad of demolition experts, the engineer lieutenant wielding a flamethrower, they were to assault a 500ft pier that jutted out to sea. Built on the pier were numerous shacks that were suspected of being a machine-gun nest. Although injured by a grenade in the initial landing, Hawkins shrugged off his injury and led attacks against machine gun-armed pillboxes. He fired point blank into them and finished off any survivor with grenades. Hawkins was killed while assaulting a pillbox. He and 31 of his men received decorations.[10] However, it must be said that although courageous and heroic, using snipers as assault troops was not the optimal use of their training or ability. Hawkins's death reflects this only too clearly.

Along with two of his buddies, mortarman Pfc. Robert Louis Lutz responded to a call for volunteers as replacement riflemen to replenish the depleted infantry ranks. According to Lutz, on the second day, "[t]here was a sniper firing at us from a tree. We got him." While fetching ammunition for a machine gun, he saw a field gun destroy a tank that a Japanese rifleman was using as a shelter. He also witnessed several small banzai charges in which all the attackers were cut down with gunfire.[11]

Another mortarman, Pfc. Burton Hanchette, recalled the time his unit was summoned first to take out some machine guns and later a sniper: "That was on the second day [November 21] right after we got a chance to go to work for the first time. This particular sniper had been covering the far end of the Betio Island airstrip and we had been ordered to work on a couple of machine gun nests a bit farther along." After finishing off the machine guns, the spotter pinpointed the "Jap in the tree." "We lined up on it and sent two mortars toward it in quick succession. They both plopped right onto the tree-top and that was that."[12]

Marine Pfc. Frank J. Poppay described a novel and horrific method used to take down tree-mounted snipers. "I saw this Marine with the flame thrower go after a Jap sniper, hidden in a tree. He started to shoot

1Lt. William D. Hawkins USMCR

"For valorous and gallant conduct above and beyond the call of duty as commanding officer of a Scout Sniper Platoon attached to the Assault Regiment [2d Marines, 2d Marine Division], in action against Japanese-held Tarawa in the Gilbert Islands, November 20 and 21, 1943. The first to disembark from the jeep lighter, 1st Lt. Hawkins unhesitatingly moved forward under heavy enemy fire at the end of the Betio pier, neutralizing emplacements in coverage of troops assaulting the main beach positions. Fearlessly leading his men on to join the forces fighting desperately to gain a beachhead, he repeatedly risked his life throughout the day and night to direct and lead attacks on pillboxes and

1Lt. William D. Hawkins is buried in the National Memorial Cemetery of the Pacific in Honolulu. *NARA; Bilestone/WikiC (CC BY-SA 4.0).*

installations with grenades and demolitions. At dawn on the following day, 1st Lt. Hawkins resumed the dangerous mission of clearing the limited beachhead of Japanese resistance, personally initiating an assault on a hostile position fortified by five enemy machine guns and, crawling forward in the face of withering fire, boldly fired point-blank into the loopholes and completed the destruction with grenades. Refusing to withdraw after being seriously wounded in the chest during this skirmish, 1st Lt. Hawkins steadfastly carried the fight to the enemy, destroying three more pillboxes before he was caught in a burst of Japanese shellfire and mortally wounded. His relentless fighting spirit in the face of formidable opposition and his exceptionally daring tactics served as an inspiration to his comrades during the most crucial phase of the battle and reflect the highest credit upon the United States Naval Service. He gallantly gave his life for his country."[13]

flame into the tree, then instead cut the tree down with the flame. The tree crashed and so did the Jap—with a scream—as the tree fell on top of him. That was the end of one sniper."[14] Sherman was right when he said, "War is hell."

Hollywood Actor Eddie Albert was allowed to resign from the Coast Guard to accept a commission in the Navy Reserve.

> "Lt. Eddie Albert, the film actor, who participated in the conquest of Tarawa, tells of the marine sharpshooter who was picking off snipers. 'How'd you like to be going back?' Albert asked him. The marine looked through his telescope sight, fired, watched a sniper drop, and answered: 'No. I'd rather stay here.' 'Been away long?' Albert continued. The marine again sighted his gun, dropped a sniper, and replied: 'Comin' on two years, sir.' 'I guess you're cured of homesickness,' said Albert. 'Yup,' said the sharpshooter studying the palm trees, finding his target with the telescope sight, and dropping another sniper. 'Yup. But … er … well,' he said, aiming, firing and killing another sniper, 'mebbe I'd like to be back home in Louisville right now. You see, sir,' and the marine—aiming, firing, killing, 'it's the squirrel-huntin' season.'"[15]

Makin
(November 20–23, 1943)

Three days after the attack on Pearl Harbor, the Japanese landed on Makin unopposed. They established a seaplane base from which aircraft could patrol eastward to Allied-held islands. This would give the Japanese advanced warning of an approach from that direction. As the northernmost of the Gilbert Islands, Makin needed to be captured not only to neutralize the seaplane base there but also to bring the Allies closer to the Marshall Islands.

On November 20, 1943, while the 2d Marine Division was fighting on Tarawa, the U.S. Army's 27th Infantry Division assaulted Butaritari Island in the Makin Atoll. Like the marines, the soldiers of the 27th were trained in amphibious landings. Lt. Col. James Roosevelt, USMC, accompanied the landing as an observer. According to reporter Leif Erikson:

> "For half an hour he and I were targets for unseen Japanese snipers, and one of their bullets killed a staff officer who stood nearby. A group of American soldiers and marines were advancing when we ran into heavy sniper fire coming from an apparently well-protected nest. A bullet from this nest killed Col. Gardiner Conroy, commanding the 69th Regiment of World War I fame."

The "Fighting Irish"—69th New York Infantry—became the the 165th Infantry Regiment in World War II. Brooklyn-born lawyer Conroy was busy directing tanks to support his infantry.[16] He had been at the front earlier and was under the impression that the advance was delayed by a lone Japanese rifleman. When he returned, he was upright and shouting at 1st Battalion commander Lt. Col. Kelley to get his men moving. Kelley motioned for Conroy to take cover. It was too late. Conroy was shot in the forehead and died before he hit the ground. Eyewitness Col. James Roosevelt, the president's eldest son, said: "The colonel stood up straight, and I pleaded with him to get down. He was so interested he forgot his own safety." Because Col. Conroy's body lay out in the open, it could not be recovered immediately. That would wait for nightfall.

Newsman Leif Erikson had accompanied Roosevelt to the front and described the colonel's reaction to the slaying of Conroy.

> "Col. Roosevelt, about 20 feet from me, took a shot, aiming at what he believed was a sniper in a nearby tree. He said later he wasn't sure a sniper was there. Anyway nothing fell from the tree. After half an hour had passed, Roosevelt suggested, 'Let's try to make it out of here. You and I can't do any good here.' Erikson concluded, 'I agreed.' Roosevelt stood up and in a dodging, zig-zag course from one tree to another. I followed in the same manner. I will never forget how I could feel taut nerves relax when we reached a point where we were satisfied we were out of sniper range."[17]

Sgt. William Schliessman, also of 165th Infantry Regiment, found a simple way to clear the jungle. When they went on two or three-man patrols, they sprayed every treetop with two or three bullets; and so it went on with a methodical approach to clear Makin.[18] Using joint tank and infantry attacks, each strongpoint had to be reduced individually, and Makin was only secured on November 23. Of the 400-strong Japanese garrison, 395 were killed; U.S. casualties were double that. However, with the capture of both Tarawa and Makin, the sea lanes between Australia, New Zealand, and the United States were free of Japanese. Airbases were expanded for the Army Air Force to threaten Japanese bases and ships.

Kwajalein
(January 31–February 3, 1944)

Following the conquest of the Gilberts the invasion of Kwajalein Atoll in the Marshall Island chain was the next step in the Navy's island-hopping campaign. Pfc. Henry C. Rabideauv was searching the treetops for a Japanese sniper when a marine tank with "Lady Killer" painted on its side came along.

> "I was on the ground, looking up into the trees for snipers when the tank came along. I had my eye on this one tree at the time. I could swear that no one was in it. When the tank got near, I got a quick look at a Japanese face which peeked out to see what the noise was all about. That's when I shot him … Bullets and mortar shells were coming at us all the time, from both directions. We were never more than 15 yards from the Japanese and we had to be as careful about being hit by our own men as by the other side. I'm pretty sure I got a few more snipers before we finished fighting."[19]

Marianas and Palau Islands campaign

Saipan (June 15–July 9, 1944)

The next objective was the Marianas Islands in the Central Pacific: Saipan, Guam, and Tinian—the Allies' first incursion into Japan's outer defenses. Held by the Japanese since 1920, Saipan was garrisoned by about 30,000 Japanese troops under the leadership of General Yoshitsugo Saito.

The 2d Marine Division landed first and established the beachhead. Among their ranks were the 6th Marine Regiment and the 40-strong scout-sniper platoon it raised in Hawaii. Nicknamed the "Forty Thieves," they began immediately neutralizing any Japanese soldier in a tree. Spraying one tree, scout-sniper Tipton was rewarded with a Japanese who fell from it. Each of the Forty Thieves carried 3lb of TNT along with a detonation cord. Scout-sniper Smotts used his to blow up the trunk of one tree. They were shocked to find the soldier was a teenage Japanese girl.[20] Other members of the Forty Thieves destroyed a Japanese trench with grenades and gunfire. After checking the dead foes for intelligence, they sniffed them so as to learn the distinct smell of the rice-fed Japanese soldier. This would be useful later in the jungle.

Two other Forty Thieves, Evans and Mullins, were armed with Unertl-equipped M1903s. They had approached to within 1,000yd of a road leading up to Tipo Pale, one of the two mountains on Saipan. From their vantage point they could see bicycle-mounted Japanese riding down toward the beach. A U-turn curve in the road required the Japanese bicyclists to slow, creating a bottleneck. After adjusting their scopes, they began shooting the Japanese. "Just like a carnival game," grinned Mullins. Unknown to them, it would be the last time they would use those scoped rifles in battle. The next day moisture rendered their scopes useless.[21]

On D+1, the threat of an approaching Japanese relief fleet caused an expedited unloading of all troops, their equipment, and supply ships to avoid a repeat of Guadalcanal where the marines were stranded without supplies. Hence the 27th Infantry Division landed earlier than scheduled. The exigency of the circumstances resulted in a misuse of three members of the Forty Thieves. While assisting unloading supplies, the three Forty Thieves were shocked to find among the equipment a piano meant for the officers' club. They accidentally threw it into the ocean.[22] Further inland, other members of the Forty Thieves found themselves fighting off a tank assault. They scrounged all glass bottles they could find along with gasoline. Attaching a rag to the bottles, one of them would shoot the tank commander and another would toss the Molotov cocktail into the tank. After their first success, they began to methodically hunt down the Japanese tanks. When one surviving tank became stuck near the regimental HQ, a Thief shot a crewman who attempted to escape through a belly escape hatch. Kuppel, a member of the Forty Thieves, then stalked up to the immobilized monster and inserted a grenade past the dead crewman into its escape hatch. Cries from startled Japanese tankers were muffled by the grenade's explosion.[23]

On the third day (June 17) the Forty Thieves had been relieved of protecting regimental headquarters and were sent to assist a pinned company. So far they had not suffered any casualties, but while en route one member who was a veteran of Guadalcanal and Tarawa lost his nerve and turned back. Save for three of their members who were carrying a wounded marine on a poncho, the platoon reached the summit. Being burdened with a wounded marine from another unit, the Thieves had barely moved when dust spouts began appearing near their feet. One Thief, Mullins, immediately recognized that they were being fired upon by a rifleman who had an incorrect hold. Using sound as a guide, Mullins looked uphill to a cliff and spotted at about 100yd distance a barrel protruding from a stump. The Japanese fired again and this time Mullins saw the barrel jump. His keen eyesight allowed him to recognize the Japanese's shoe; the only thing visible to him. Taking careful aim, Mullins fired off one shot, striking the Japanese in the foot and caused him to jump up and down. With his opponent now fully exposed, Mullins shot him.[24]

Day four saw the Forty Thieves finally being sent on a patrol. Camouflaging their faces and hands with black shoe polish, they exchanged their boondockers for sneakers. Stealth was required for their mission.

Vacuum is your friend

Expert Rifleman and BAR operator Pfc. Tommy Clayton had killed four men, one of whom he mistook for a Japanese sniper. He was covering a hedgerow when he spotted someone in a tree. Clayton sprayed it with his BAR and the "Jap" tumbled out. He had used sound to locate him.

"When a bullet passes smack over your head it doesn't zing; it pops the same as a rifle when it goes off. That's because the bullet's rapid passage creates a vacuum behind it, and the air rushes back and with such force to fill this vacuum that it collides with itself, and makes a resounding 'pop.' Well Clayton learned that the pop of a bullet over his head preceded the actual rifle report by a fraction of a second, because of the sound of the rifle explosion had to travel some distance before hitting his ear. So the 'pop' became his warning signal to listen for the crack of a sniper's rifle a moment later. Through much practice he had learned to gauge the direction of the sound almost exactly. And so out on this animal-like system of hunting, he had the knowledge to shoot into the right tree—and out tumbled his Jap 'sniper.'"[25]

They passed through the lines at night and were soon deep in the jungle. Carefully they worked their way forward, stopping frequently to listen for any sound suggesting the presence of an enemy. It began to rain as they moved along a trail that led them to some huts, one of which had a Rising Sun flag draped over the door. While one Thief was sketching a map beneath a poncho, the raindrops on the poncho alerted one Japanese officer who approached to investigate. Before he could sound an alarm, he was garroted. With the map finished, they began moving off when they saw a squad of Japanese cooking their meal. They were spotted and the Japanese, thinking they were other Japanese on patrol, called out to them. One marine waved back after which more greetings were shouted by the Japanese. "*Dah-mah-ray!*" (Be quiet!) one marine responded. His accent must have been off and the Japanese grabbed their rifles.

Scurrying away, the Thieves ran down the path and around a bend. Then they hid. They could hear the Japanese approach. One called out in English but the deception didn't work. Discouraged, the Japanese turned about to return to their meal. They prodded the bushes and slashed away with machetes when one soldier grazed a Thief. Discovered, they had no choice but to quickly overpower the squad. After disposing of their bodies, they found rations in a Japanese cave and ate lustily. The Thieves returned the next day with their intelligence, which was used for a naval bombardment to destroy the Japanese post. They had many other encounters on Saipan and suffered four killed and eight wounded before the island was captured.

One Japanese rigged up six dummies that he could drop from the trees. He would fire at an American and when they fired at a tree, he would release a dummy as if it were a fallen sniper. The Americans would relax and the Japanese would wait before shooting another victim. He finally ran out of dummies and the Americans ended his career.[26]

Sgt. Robert L. Richmond was shot by a sniper:

"I was on the island five days before I was hit. We were preparing to attack a ridge on the island that was thick with Japs, and as I was assistant squad leader, it was my job to observe the enemy and decide what direction we should fire in. I was shot while observing by a Jap sniper who was tied up in a tree (the kind you can't see anything in, but can see it moving). I heard voices before I was hit and I'm sure there were at least three Japs in the tree, probably arguing which one was going to shoot me.

"I fired eight rounds of ammunition on the Jap sniper that shot me and I'm sure that Jap won't fire again."[27]

Disabled by a shot in the thigh, no medic would expose himself to aid Richmond since it was known the Japanese did not respect the Red Cross emblem. Knowing this, Richmond dragged himself to safety after killing his assailant.

While on Saipan, marine scout-sniper Pfc. Hiram W. Westbrook II was credited with the longest American shot of the war. He and other members of his platoon were on the high ledge on the northeastern side of Mt. Tapotchau (this suggests that Westbrook belonged to the 8th Marines). Looking down the valley, Westbrook spotted a Japanese. He had his sights set at 600yd and adjusted it to 900. Afterward he held high, squeezed off the trigger and moments later the Japanese dropped. "I am fairly sure

I got him," Westbrook modestly asserted. His section leader, Sgt. Donald F. Allen and another sniper, Sgt. Charles B. McGinnis, were eyewitnesses and both gave Westbrook full credit for it. Allen said, "Westbrook is one of our best men. He's quiet and unassuming and you wouldn't know he was around most of the time. It's kids like him that are winning this war."[28]

With no hope of reinforcements, on July 7 at 0445 hours the Japanese launched the largest banzai charge of the war (about 4,000 men) against the Americans. They struck two Army battalions of the 105th Infantry Regiment and came close to annihilating them. Determined resistance along with marine artillery repelled the Japanese and by 0700 hours, it was over. By the time Saipan was declared secured on July 9, it had cost the Americans over 3,000 dead and over 13,000 wounded. As usual, 29,000 of the 32,000 Japanese defenders died, 5,000 at their own hand. Lengthening of the airfield by the SeaBees enabled the B-29 to reach Japan. The loss of Saipan also led directly to the fall of the Tojo government.

Guam (July 21–August 10, 1944)
The 3d Marine Division landed on Guam on July 21, 1944. Marine Sgt. Bill Allen described how two marines rewarded themselves after killing a sniper.

"Marine Private Conridge C. Thomas … and his buddy, Private First Class Roy H. Mardia … were in a group of 10 Marines sent to flush out a Jap sniper hidden in a thicket 150 yards from a motor transport center. The two men zig-zagged toward the clump of trees believed to conceal the sniper. Then Thomas and Mardia disappeared in the thick undergrowth. Their companions heard several shots. There were a few minutes of silence. Then there was a strangle rustling of brush and rapid running of feet. Presently, Thomas and Mardia emerged from the thicket. They were hiding something under their coats and were strangely uncommunicative as to what took place in the brush. They admitted having gotten a Jap sniper, but refused to explain further."

It turned out that they came upon a chicken, caught it, and seasoned it with bouillon powder and salt from their K-rations.[29]

On Guam, the 2d and 3d War Dog platoons landed as part of the invasion force. The dogs proved their worth when they detected hidden Japanese. Some paid for it with their lives. They also alerted marines of night attacks and one dog died when a grenade was thrown into his handler's foxhole. One dog, previously owned by the Japanese, was lured to marines by 2d Division Pfc. Carl E. Bliss. "Here boy! Here boy!" An MP taught Bliss some Japanese words which Bliss used to alert him and other marines of the presence of Japanese and "Boy" helped them avoid an ambush.[30]

Similarly on Guam a black German Shepherd captured from the Japanese was found to have only been trained as a guard dog. Renamed Lady, she was retrained by the marines as a scout dog. Another dog, a Doberman named Emmy, flushed out a Japanese who killed four Americans.[31] It is known that the Japanese occupation troops in Hong Kong had dogs but the nature of their training is unknown.[32]

When one Japanese who fired at marines only when he saw one pass could not be dealt with conventionally, the marines unleashed a clipped-eared Doberman after him. Rather than try to shoot the dog, the shooter smacked a grenade against his helmet and blew himself up.[33]

Trained as a scout-sniper, because of his small size and his scoring on the aptitude test, Marine Lawrence Kirby served mostly as a scout. He was with the 3d Marine Division when it landed on Guam.

"On August 22nd, long after I had been wounded and returned from the hospital ship, the island was declared secured. As part of our 'mopping-up' procedures I was in charge of a detail working with the 19th Engineers at Ritidian Point, blowing caves where defiant Jap soldiers were holding out. The enemy troops refused to surrender and were creating casualties with sniper fire. Men of the 19th were in close, setting charges at the mouths of the caves. We were providing fire cover for the demolition teams.

"I happened to turn and look behind me. I looked again, but this time I snapped my head around to see the imposing figure of Colonel Wexell standing on a promontory overlooking the area of action. The colonel held his field glasses to his eyes. A cold chill went through me at the sight of this ominous figure. I mumbled to one of my cohorts, 'Now that it's nice and safe, the bastard comes out to see what the real war is like.'

"At just that moment, a Japanese sniper, and a damn good shot, took an odds-on gamble … The Arisaka had an unusually long barrel. With an extra set of lands and grooves and a muzzle velocity of over 3000 feet per second it could carry a 7mm bullet a lo[n]g distance with great accuracy and solid impact. The colonel had to be at least five or six hundred yards away. The soldier took a deep breath, exhaled about a third of it, froze every muscle, steadied his left arm propped under the rifle and squeezed off a round. The round ripped into Wexell's upper right leg and painfully shattered the thighbone. From this day on the colonel would, forever, walk with a limp."[34]

While the Japanese marksman didn't kill Colonel Wexell, he did render him *hors de combat* and probably underestimated the distance.

With Guam in American hands, it became an airbase.

Tinian (July 24–August 1, 1944)
Tinian was garrisoned by an 8,000-strong Japanese force. On July 24, 1944, the 4th Marine Division assaulted. Naval aviators flew as spotters for the marines. Lt. Raymond Globokar was skimming along the treetops in his Grumman TBF Avenger when he killed a Japanese sniper in a novel manner:

"I felt the plane strike something. My immediate impression was that we had been hit. The plane shuddered and seemed to stop—but then it kept on going. I looked back to see what was left: A wooden platform with a piece of tin. To my surprise a Jap sniper was falling out of the tree."[35]

The crew reported that the sniper had been decapitated by the plane. It is unfortunate that the thoughts of the crew chief aboard the carrier were not recorded. Like Guam and Saipan, Tinian was turned into an airbase for the Twentieth Air Force.

Strategic decision
As the Americans were pushing back the Japanese, two different strategies were proposed. Nimitz wanted to bypass the Philippines and capture Taiwan and Okinawa before going directly for Japan. Capturing Taiwan would shorten the supply line for the Nationalist Chinese. MacArthur argued for the capture of the Palau Islands as a prelude to the liberation of the Philippines before attacking Japan. The Palaus were to the east of the Philippines and flanked it. Recapture of the Philippines would deprive Japan of the resource-rich South Pacific. The two theater commanders met with President Franklin Roosevelt for the Pacific Strategy Conference at Hawaii (July 26–27, 1944), and Roosevelt decided in favor of MacArthur.

Angaur (September 17–October 22, 1944)
Angaur is a small 3sq. mile-long pork chop-shaped limestone and coral island in the Palau Islands chain and is 7 miles from Peleliu. Halsey's argument that Angaur should be skipped was ignored and the green 81st Infantry Division, the "Wildcats," was tasked with capturing it. Its 322d Infantry Regiment landed on Red Beach in the northeast and sister regiment, the 321st, on Blue Beach in the east, while the division's third regiment, the 323d, remained afloat as the

divisional reserve. They were facing 1,400 Japanese of Maj. Ushio Goto's 29th Infantry Regiment, 14th Infantry Division, which had previously fought in China. Both the 322d and 321st plowed through the choppy surf and landed on September 17, 1944.

Overcoming the initial Japanese resistance, the two regiments fanned out and moved inland. After meeting, the 321st swept south and cleared out that portion of the island. The 322d advanced toward Lake Salome and the hill that overlooked it. Nicknamed the Bowl or Suicide Hill, Goto and his men made their last stand there.

Among the 81st Wildcats fighting on the island was Pfc. Joseph A. Koetz who remembers one incident when a Japanese sniper was killed.

"One day I saw my squad leader, Sgt. Louis Bauman, lie and watch a tree a half hour for a Jap sniper to show himself. Sgt. Bauman was a farm boy from Aitkins, Ark, and he had sharp eyes. Finally he saw the leaves move in one place, and even then he didn't take any chances on stirring up something for nothing. He kept his eyes on that tree, 100 yards away, for another 15 minutes before he opened fire. When he did open fire with his M1 rifle, he shot 14 rounds and we saw the sniper come tumbling out of the tree."[36]

Pfc. Jack M. Wheeler was neither a sniper nor a rifleman when he took out a Japanese sniper. He had the especially dangerous duty of being a flamethrower operator. When one sniper pinned down a squad leader, Wheeler sprung into action.

"It was shortly after we had landed on the island and we were on patrol over terrain which was unfamiliar to us. The thick foliage gave the Nips plenty of concealment and snipers were giving us plenty of trouble. One sniper in particular had pinned down the patrol leader and was banging away at him, coming closer with each shot. Because the Japs used smokeless powder [probably the 25 cal Type 97 rifle] it was difficult to locate the sniper. The patrol leader didn't dare move because the Nip would surely have knocked him off. I volunteered to take off and see what I could do about finding the Jap rifleman. I finally got him spotted by the sound of his shots and got close enough to kill him."

Pvt. Wheeler commented on his weapon. "The flamethrower, incidentally, is a wonderful weapon. It's one thing that absolutely terrorizes the Jap. And don't think I didn't get a sense of satisfaction from using it on

dugouts and pillboxes from which the fire had killed some of my best friends had come." Unfortunately for Pvt. Wheeler, he did not escape unharmed:

"We were digging in for the night and we believed the immediate area had been cleared of Japs. But what happened just goes to show you can't be sure of anything in the jungle. One minute I was digging a foxhole and the next I was flat on my back. I had been knocked over by a rifle bullet from an unseen sniper. Later I found that he had been up in a tree, apparently waiting all day on the chance that American troops would come into the area. After he hit me one of my comrades sprayed the tree with a Tommy gun and killed the Nip."

Besides earning the Purple Heart, Pvt. Wheeler received a Bronze Star for his heroism.[37]

Pfc. David Kong grew up in Arizona where he was a ROTC cadet in high school. He attended basic infantry training at Fort MacArthur (San Pedro, Los Angeles) where he shot expert with the M1 Garand. Afterward Pvt. Kong received his advanced infantry training at San Luis Obispo (also in California). Before entering combat, the division received additional jungle warfare training on Guadalcanal.

ROTC Cadet David Kong before he enlisted. On Anguar he shot a Japanese officer at 700yd. *Dr. Stephen Kong.*

As a scout and observer, Pfc. Kong landed on Red Beach as part of the first wave on Angaur with HQ Company, 3d Battalion, 322d Infantry Regiment. On their approach to the beach, the LCVP was pelted by small-arms fire, causing the sailor piloting the craft to become nervous. He dropped the ramp 50yd from the beach and told everyone, "Go!" Following his 6ft 4in captain, McChanles, who instructed, "Stay with me on the shore," Pfc. Kong ran off the ramp and like McChanles, promptly sank into eight feet of water. Kong held his breath and jumped up for air as he waded ashore.

Almost a month later, Pfc. Kong was patrolling on the Bowl (patrols were generally three- to four-men strong and were out for three days) with other scouts. While observing the Japanese lines, they spotted a group of Japanese moving a large camouflage net at 600–700yd distance. Afterward a large artillery piece was wheeled out from a tunnel. They called in artillery but the Japanese wheeled the field piece back into the safety of the tunnel. This went on for two days and every time the Japanese attempted to push the gun out, Kong and his comrades would call artillery down on it. Frustrated, an artillery officer suggested he could set up a small cannon at their observation post and sight it in on the tunnel. Kong protested that if the cannon were fired from there, their observation post would be compromised. The officer suggested that they find another way to neutralize the gun.

"We kept watching the cave and notice[d] a Japanese officer coming out every morning and directing his men to wheeling out his gun and back into his cave. I thought it might be possible to take them out with a sniper rifle with telescope, but we could not find a sniper gun. The following day I took my M-1 Garand and shot a white phosphate rock from another position and [the] same distance away. I raise[d] the peep sight up till I started to chip the white rock with every shot. The following morning when the officer [came] out of his cave I was ready and when he stood up I took the shot. My observer said I got him and blood was gushing from his chest. Some Japanese soldiers carried him back into the cave."[38]

Pfc. Kong neither knew nor cared about the officer's identity. Kong had a job and did it.

Later, Kong was off duty on Palau when he and a friend decided to swim in the Pacific. They were spotted by a sentry who didn't know them. While Kong gave the correct password, the soldier suspected him of being a Japanese infiltrator. Tense moments that seemed an eternity passed before someone who knew Kong vouched for him. When Capt. McChanles learned of it, he feared for Kong's safety and made him the company cook on the spot. Kong protested that he didn't know the first thing about cooking but his captain said that he'd learn. The Wildcats helped liberate the Philippines and Kong was promoted to staff sergeant and returned home, where he married and raised a family in San Francisco.

After 36 days of fighting, Angaur was secured on October 22. Stubborn Japanese resistance resulted in the Wildcats suffering more casualties (260 killed and 1,354 wounded) than they inflicted (1,350 killed and 50 captured). Even before the 322d finished mopping up (the 321st was redeployed) the Japanese resistance, the engineers completed two 6,000ft airfields from which B-24s could operate.

Peleliu (September 15–November 27, 1944)

As part of the Mariana and Palau Campaign, the marines landed on Peleliu on September 15, 1944, and were later joined by the army's 81st Division. Its capture would protect MacArthur's right flank as he drove toward the Philippines. It was garrisoned by 11,000 Japanese soldiers and laborers. Japanese defense tactics changed from stopping the landings at the beach to an in-depth defense consisting of bunkers, caves, and underground structures many of which were interconnected by tunnels. The fighting posts had interlocking fields of fire and its infantry force was supported by 17 tanks. Rather than futile banzai attacks, the Japanese relied on attrition against the invader. Fire discipline was excellent, too: the Japanese would wait for the Americans to close in before firing.

After the 1st Marine Division was withdrawn from Guadalcanal, it returned to Australia where it received replacements. Among the replacements to Co. K, 3/5th Marine Regiment was Pvt. R. V. Burgin. The third of seven children, he and his siblings worked their family farm in Texas where he helped grow corn, sorghum, sugarcane, and for cash, cotton. After planting and before the harvest, they'd fish for perch or catfish. Burgin enlisted into the marines on November 13, 1942, and went to boot camp in San Diego. The battle-experienced veterans began immediately passing on tips to keep them alive. Burgin recalled being warned that, "Jap snipers would tie themselves to treetops. You couldn't see them, but they were there, watching and waiting. They'd cut fire lanes through the trees, narrow breaks about three or four feet wide at right angles to our line of march." He added, "What the Guadalcanal veterans had said stuck in my mind. Watch your back. Watch your sides. Watch everywhere."[39] He would learn that the Japanese picked off officers, medics, and stretcher-bearers and carelessly exposed marines.

To capture Umurbrogol Mountain, rather than approach it from the south, they reembarked and landed on the north part of Peleliu to attack it from there. Burgin's battalion was among them.

> "From the top of our hill we looked across a sixty-foot drop-off to the valley floor. On the hills opposite we could watch for Japs to appear in the cave openings and pick them off. And they could pick us off. There was a man on my left that afternoon, sitting about three or four feet away. I heard the whack of the bullet even before I heard the rifle shot. I knew instantly he was dead. I'd shot enough deer on the farm to know what a bullet sounds like when it hits. It got him about half an inch above his eyes, dead center."[40]

Marine 2Lt. Clinton Eugene McKnight commanded a platoon of combat engineers. Part of their job was to blast out caves from where Japanese infantry and snipers fought. Rather than methodically approaching every cave to set up explosive charges, he decided to bring a 1,300lb M1 75mm pack howitzer up a sheer cliff. His men anchored one end of a cable around a coral pinnacle and the other around a "dead man"—a telephone pole sunk into the ground. They then set up a block and tackle which was attached to a truck. As the vehicle went forward, it pulled the field gun up the hill. After it was manhandled into position, they set up a tripod at the foot of the ridge and ran another line through it. A block and tackle was also used to haul a basket of ammunition up until they were well stocked. After everything was ready, the gun was trained at each cave and after a few rounds, would seal the defenders inside. The adage of bringing a bigger gun to a gunfight was certainly applied by Lt. McKnight and his platoon.[41]

Besides the 1st Marine Division, elements of the army's 81st Infantry Division also fought on Peleliu. T/5 Maurice Clark recalled how Japanese set up rope bridges of twin cables that supported foot boards between treetops. This allowed them to move from one tree to another; perhaps giving them another chance to shoot another American.[42]

Peleliu was finally captured on November 27, 1944. Of the 11,000-strong garrison, only 202 allowed themselves to be captured. The Americans suffered 2,336 killed and 8,450 wounded. Of those, 3,300 were suffered by the 81st Division. It had been a very costly battle and 1st Marine Division would not see combat again until Okinawa. The high casualties exceeded other invasions and the marines questioned whether it was worth the cost.

Iwo Jima
(February 19–March 28, 1945)

Almost halfway between the main islands of Japan and the Marianas Islands, Iwo Jima would be a convenient place for crippled bombers to land as well as an airbase for the P-51 fighters. Japanese strategy by now had changed. Instead of contesting a landing, the Japanese instead dug into mountains and fought from tunnels and pillboxes; American intelligence optimistically calculated that Iwo Jima could be captured in a week.

Commanding the 3d Marine's engineering company, mustang 1Lt. Lemuel Wylie landed on Iwo Jima on D+4 and helped the infantry eliminate an estimated 1,000 Japanese who were hiding in caves. While Wylie is modest about his kills, his men told a different story of how he shot a Japanese sniper after a two-hour cat-and-mouse game:

> "It happened near the rough terrain at the southern tip of Iwo. A Japanese sniper—hidden in the mouth of a cave between two cliffs—was holding up the advance of two platoons of marines. Behind a rock, 20 feet above the Japanese sniper, Lt. Wylie was concealed at the only point where the sniper was visible between the cliffs. It was a veritable baseball game with both the Jap and Wylie tossing hand grenades at each other, according to marines who witnessed the event. With his carbine, Wylie took pot shots at the sniper. Finally, the Jap got careless and exposed his head over some rock. It was the break the marine engineer had waited two hours for. His first shot killed the sniper."[43]

Pfc. William M. Maples served with Co. A, 3d Engineer Battalion, 3d Marine Division. They landed on the fifth day and were assigned to protect the caterpillar operators who were hacking roads out of the jungle. Scouting ahead and searching for booby traps, Maples saw his first Japanese soldier behind a rock. Maples warned the working party and then went back to stalk his prey. He got behind him and then shouted in English. This made the sniper raise his head, offering a fine target. As Maples explains, "It was the break I wanted. That Jap never moved his head, because I blew it off with my rifle. When I stopped shootin' that Jap looked like an empty cow-hide." Maples went on to kill two more Japanese including one that fled from the cave the bulldozer was blocking up.[44]

One anonymous American who signed his letter as "Jap Hater" submitted a letter describing how he killed a Japanese sniper to the *Washington Citizen*.

This marine scout-sniper team on Okinawa are using Unertl-equipped sniper rifles. *USMC.*

While it didn't matter in the Pacific Theater as the Japanese would have killed him anyway, Jap Hater's unorthodox tactic would have had him shot as a spy in Europe or elsewhere. Before there is any cry of foul play, American intelligence reported that on Iwo Jima Japanese soldiers would also wear marine uniforms to approach closer. Additionally, during the day they hid themselves with the bodies of dead marines and emerged at night to fire.[46]

Marine Pfc. Milton M. Mitchum was a BAR operator concentrating on a pillbox that was ten yards away. Suddenly he was struck from behind and spun to the ground, causing him to roll twice. Luckily, he had been hit in the helmet and not his head. He immediately sized up that a Japanese had sprung up from a camouflaged spider hole that was behind him.

"It sure made me mad. The Jap figured I was dead and was sighting in on one of my buddies, who was coming over a ridge. I learned to shoot by killing coyotes in the deserts of El Paso. If you wantah score here, you gotta do the same thing—shoot fast and hit the varmint any place you can!"

Mitchum emptied his 20-round magazine into the back of his assailant.[47] The spider hole could have been a 50-gallon oil drum with a hinged lid. Marine Clarence Rea was also on Iwo Jima and recalled:

"There'd be a Japanese soldier squatted down in it with the lid down. They had grass and stuff on top of it, so we'd walk right over it and wouldn't know it. Then, when we were in front of them, they'd raise the lid, get their rifle out, and fire at us, then quickly close the lid again. Many times, you didn't know they were behind us like this. But other times not. You turn around and look back, and all you could see is level ground and weeds. These traps were everywhere."[48]

At Iwo Jima, an army dog discovered Japanese Senior Seaman Tsurju Akikusa unconscious. When Seaman Akikusa awoke two weeks after his capture, he found himself at a Guam hospital where a friend explained that a dog had found him and his handler summoned a stretcher-bearer who took him to a field hospital on Iwo Jima. After being told of lucky survival, he responded, "I owe my life to that American soldier and his dog who rescued me."[49]

The projected week-long campaign lasted 36 days before victory could be declared. It had cost the Americans 6,800 dead and over 26,000 other casualties.

"The reason I did not get my letter off to you last week is because I played a trick on a Jap sniper and the trick backfired on me. I was fired at by my own fellow Americans, but was very fortunate to get no more out of it than a blistered ear and a badly shrunken stomach. I think the sacrifice was worth it as I got the sniper before he got me.

"The sniper had been hanging around for weeks and we never did get at him. One morning I rubbed my head against a caneo tree and devised a scheme to fool him. I pulled the uniform off a dead Jap and slipped it over my own, practiced how to make a rice-eater's squint, and set forth on my mission. The sniper, who was hidden about three miles away, saw me approach. Thinking I was a brother Jap, he stepped out of his hiding and made toward me. Then I let him have it. My trouble started after that. While I was making my way back to the camp, some of our men thought I was the sniper. They all fired, and I ducked. One bullet got me in the ear. The only thing that saved me was quick thinking. When I ripped off the Jap uniform and began singing 'Pistol Packing Mama,' the boys rushed up and hugged me."[45]

Okinawa

(April 1–June 22, 1945)

Okinawa was part of Ryukyu Islands, southwest of Japan itself. It was the final stepping-stone before the Japanese home islands could be invaded. Garrisoned by the 67,000–77,000-strong Japanese Thirty-second Army as well as 9,000 IJN personnel and the indigenous Rukyuan militia, it was faced by Lt. Gen. Simon Buckner's XXIV Corps composed of four army divisions and the III Amphibious Corps consisting of three marine divisions.

A son of a marine, officer candidate William Manchester refused a corporal's "chickenshit" order to clean his clean rifle, was court-martialed out of Marine Corps OCS, and subsequently became a corporal and then sergeant with 1/29th Marine Regiment (6th Marine Division). It was his first time in combat and he was among the marines who were near the village of Motobu. He had witnessed two B Company men of the 1st Battalion drop and knew the shots had been fired from a fishing hut. As a sergeant, Manchester could have ordered his men to storm the shack, but instead instructed one marine to cover him while he dashed in a zig-zag pattern toward the hut. Manchester reached the hut safely and described confronting the sniper:

> "Utterly terrified, I jolted to a stop on the threshold of the shack. I could feel a twitching in my jaw, coming and going like a winky light signaling some disorder. Various valves were opening and closing in my stomach. My mouth was dry, my legs quaking, and my eyes out of focus. Then my vision cleared. I unlocked the safety of my Colt, kicked the door with my right foot, and leapt inside. My horror returned. I was in an empty room. There was another door opposite the side I had unhinged, which meant another room, which meant the sniper was in there—and had been warned by the crash of the outer door. But I had committed myself. Flight was impossible now. So I smashed into the other room and saw him as a blur to my right. I wheeled that way, crouched, gripped the pistol butt in both hands, and fired.
>
> "Not only was he the first Japanese solider I had ever shot at; he was the only one I had seen at close quarters. He was a robin-fat, moon-faced, roly-poly little man with his thick, stubby, trunk-like legs sheathed in faded khaki puttees and the rest of him squeezed into a uniform that was much too tight. Unlike me, he was wearing a tin hat, dressed to kill. But I was quite safe from him. His Arisaka rifle was strapped on in a

Okinawa

Lt. Col. Robert C. Williams produced a report on Operation Iceberg. It covered the period March 3–April 9, 1945, and was based on interviews with officers and enlisted men of all units in XXIV Corps. There were three mentions of sniping that show that the skills remained less developed in the Pacific theaters than in Europe. It touches on the introduction of the Sniperscope M1 with infrared sighting (see p. 316):

"The sniperscopes were well liked. The idea of sending trained crews out to demonstrate new equipment and weapons meets with everyone's approval. They suggest, however, that these crews always include a maintenance expert. The sniperscopes are especially good in the perimeter defenses, where the troops are sold on them."[50]

"It is not feasible to have infantry ride on the rear of tanks here as there are too many [Japanese] snipers in depth."[51]

"No special sniper units were organized. Smaller units used their own methods and organization. Sniper posts were not used outside the perimeter at night but were always inside. The sniperscopes were used very successfully on Okinawa. When the Japs made a night attack two sniperscope men fired tracers, and all the other riflemen fired at the point where the tracers intersected."[52]

sniper's harness [climbing sling], and though he had heard me, and was trying to turn toward me, the harness sling had him trapped. He couldn't disentangle himself from it. His eyes were rolling in panic. Realizing that he couldn't extricate his arms and defend himself, he was backing toward a corner with a curious, crablike motion.

"My first shot had missed him, embedding itself in the straw wall, but my second caught him dead-on in the femoral artery. His left thigh blossomed, swiftly turning to mush. A wave of blood gushed from the wound; then another boiled out, sheeting across his legs, pouring on the earthen floor. Mutely he looked down at it. He dipped a hand in it and listlessly smeared his cheek red. His shoulders gave a little spasmodic jerk, as though someone had whacked him on the back; then he emitted a tremendous, raspy fart, slumped down, and died."[53]

Manchester emptied his magazine into the sniper's stomach. Manchester survived both his first encounter and Okinawa. Postwar he became a successful writer.

Less fortunate than Manchester was Marine Fred Boenisch who played football for San Mateo College and the University of California. He was shot in the jaw, shoulder, and chest. Boenisch and his buddies blasted the trees and brought down three Japanese snipers.[54]

The most senior Allied casualties of the battle of Okinawa were Lt. Gen. Simon Bolivar Buckner, commander of Tenth (U.S.) Army, and Brig. Gen. Claudius M. Easley who instructed his division—he was assistant divisional commander of the 96th, the "Deadeyes"—in marksmanship. He once used an iron-sighted rifle to kill a Japanese sniper at 500 yards. Easley was directing a light machine gun and attempting to flank the enemy when he was struck by a machine gun bullet. Just moments before he was killed, he was shaming some soldiers in a fatherly manner reminiscent of Civil War Maj. Gen. John Sedgwick at Spotsylvania Court House. "You should be ashamed to let one Jap make you take cover."[55]

The hard fighting and casualty levels at Okinawa led the Allies to anticipate a million casualties from an invasion of Japan itself. The dropping of two nuclear bombs, along with the Soviet invasion of Manchuria and Sakhalin Island, brought the Japanese to terms and they surrendered.

Burma

The Japanese conquered Burma between December 1941 and May 1942. Limited Allied counter-operations in 1943 were unsuccessful but included the first of the famous Chindit raids behind Japanese lines that achieved little militarily but gave a big boost to morale.

The Chindits weren't the only long-range operations. The American Merrill's Marauders fought with skill and bravery, using Kachin scouts. The Office of Strategic Service's Detachment 101 trained and equipped Kachin guerrillas to operate behind Japanese lines. The weapons included M2 Thompson SMGs, rifles, M1 carbines, pistols, light mortars, and machine guns. Additionally, a few M1903A4 Springfield sniper rifles were distributed. Tactics called for the Kachin to hold no ground but rely on stealth and mobility for survival. OSS Lt. Richard Hilsman describes their organization and armaments.

"Our solution was to organize each of the companies into four platoons. Each platoon in turn was made up of three light-machine gun squads and one 60-millimeter mortar squad. One of the eight to ten men in a machine gun squad carried a Bren gun, a British light machine gun; one carried a sniper's rifle with a silencer on it; and the others carried the British Sten gun, a submachine-gun that was very light. They all carried ammunition for the Bren … The men armed with a sniper's rifle, a telescopic sight, and a silencer were to be used in a variety of special circumstances—to harass an enemy installation from a distance, for example, or to pick off the enemy machine-gunner in covering a withdrawal."

Hilsman was dispatched to coordinate four OSS groups. The American leader of one was a Middle Eastern American, nicknamed the Arab, whose group fought the Japanese but also rescued downed American aviators. Hilsman reported that when one village headman succumbed to Japanese bribes for an American aviator, the group leader decided to execute him. Several attempts to capture him failed and it didn't help that the village was surrounded by Japanese installations. Unable to approach him, another method was needed. Lt. Hilsman described what happened: "So the Arab persuaded headquarters to send him a high powered sniper's rifle with a telescopic sight. A Kachin sharpshooter on a nearby hill drilled the headman from a range of a thousand yards while he was sitting on his front porch."[56]

Another OSS soldier, William Disanza described a similar incident:

"We had one guy one time who was a sniper and we called him in one time. He was able to get into us and we wanted to knock off a Japanese high ranking officer. We knew who he was and we've seen him but we could never get close enough to [his] camp to do it. Of course you've got to be careful. You go in to raid a camp and you got to know that you can get in and get out. But this particular camp we couldn't. But anyway we radioed for a sniper and he came in. We pointed [out] who the guy was, oh it had to be more than half a mile, and he got him. We were very fortunate. Of course they came after us but we took off like birds."[57]

While thousand-yard hits can be obtained today, there is probably some exaggeration as to the distance in both of foregoing incidents.

Besides the OSS, General Frank Merrill had two scoped rifles airdropped so that he could give them to the Kachin hill people who fought the Japanese. Some training was sometimes supplied, as reported by one OSS man: "I have had a man trained to use the telescopic sights you sent us. He is to join Kiwi near Chipwi as a lot of long-range sniping can be done in this area."[58]

To support the OSS-led Kachin guerrillas and Americans fighting in the jungles of Burma, T/Sgt. Robert J. Fiske was a pilot who flew ambulance planes for injured or sick men for hospitalization in India. While flying his ambulance plane he spotted a Japanese sniper firing at him from a tree. Pulling out his handgun, Fiske fired "a single bullet from the pistol brought the Jap down from his perch in a tree."[59] That was a remarkable one-handed shot from an airborne airplane.

Maj. John Jones, an observer with Merrill's Marauders, reported a withdrawal across a river while under attack:

"Six hundred yards north of Walawbum, Lt. Weston's intelligence and reconnaissance platoon began taking a heavy pounding from Jap mortars just after daylight. …

"The combat team commander decided to withdraw the platoon immediately. He told Lieutenant Weston by radio to withdraw under the cover of a squad on the south bank and a smoke barrage on the Jap positions overlooking the river. …

"The Japs had anticipated this withdrawal and had placed two Nambus (light machine guns) near the bank. The BAR's opened up on them, however, and the Nambus didn't fire more than 10 shots at the men withdrawing. One of Lieutenant Weston's snipers, Chief Janis, a full-blooded American Indian, picked off five Japs who had crept to the river bank and were firing from close range at the infiltrating members of the platoon.

"Lieutenant Weston was the last man to cross the river."[60]

India

On April 4, Japan launched a major, two-pronged offensive. Operation *U-Go* attacked India with an immediate goal of taking the Kohima ridge. Its capture would sever the British supply lines to IV Corps at Imphal. Operation *Ichi-Go* was a massive attack on the Chinese Army. Capt. Clifford Shore relates a sniping incident.

"During the Kohima affair a British sniper in the half light of early morning, saw movement in a deep, narrow nullah which led to one of our forward localities. The range from his own position was only about 100 yards. With eyes riveted to the spot he saw a number of Japs crawling up the steep slopes of the nullah. This was certainly a pleasant job of work, and

Merchant Seaman turned OSS Detachment 101 Sgt. Albert Van Arsdale armed with a scoped rifle, scanning the Japanese-held village of Lawksawk. Reconnaissance revealed it was defended by an entire regiment! Besides Merrill's Marauders, the OSS also used the M1903A4 sniper rifle and one is slung over Van Arsdale's back. *Hoyt Hillsman.*

he immediately settled down and with a stifled grunt of satisfaction, and proceeded to pick them off one by one. Immediately the first Jap had fallen to the sniper's first shot, the second man proceeded to crawl over his comrade's prostrate body. The sniper shot him, and the third man and the fourth and so on. The sniper was amazed to see that the Japs were apparently quite incapable of appreciating what was happening … they just continued to advance, crawling over the mounting mass of corpses. The sniper finally claimed 27 killed, and when daylight came the nullah was piled high with dead bodies."[61]

Complicated by the Chinese fighting between Nationalists and Communists and politics between Nationalist leader Chiang Kai-shek and the American General Joseph Stillwell, the Allies were unable to prevent the Japanese winning a pyrrhic victory in China. However, under General "Bill" Slim, the Fourteenth Army in Burma turned the tables on the Japanese, inflicting on them their largest land defeat so far in the war. With help of the Detachment 101-led Kachin guerrillas who harassed Japanese supply lines and rear areas, the British and Indian Army counter-offensive forced the Japanese back, followed up in 1945 by a deep thrust into Burma, that liberated Rangoon before the monsoon season could halt the attack. When the war ended, the British had retaken much of the country.

Part III The Weapons
| 13 Guns and Equipment

"Without my rifle, I am useless."

U.S. Marine Corps rifleman's creed

Britain & the Commonwealth

Rifle No. 3 Mk. I*(T)

During World War I, demand for rifles for the army exceeded the production capability of British industry. The government ordered the Pattern 14 (P14) rifle from various American manufacturers. They entered service late in 1916 and a few were sent to the sniping schools for evaluation. To everyone's surprise, the P14 was more accurate than the SMLE. Some sniping students actually shot better with the P14 than a scoped SMLE (the P14's heavier barrel, one-piece stock, and rear aperture sight were probably contributing factors). It was decided that a scoped P14 would replace the scoped SMLEs. Additionally, these newer rifles would have their scopes mounted over the bore.[1] Quite a number were produced, but they arrived too late for the war. Placed in storage, many were distributed throughout the Commonwealth during the interwar years.

At the outbreak of World War II, Britain still had a supply of post-World War I P14 sniper rifles fitted with the Pattern 18 3x scope that had a 7.5-degree field of view and a cross-wire with pointed-post reticle. Mounted over the bore, the forward scope base was similar to the German double-claw mount. After the front claws were dropped in, the rear single claw was dropped into the rear mount which was attached to the left side of the rear sight. It was then locked into place by means of throwing a lever. The scope mounts were high enough to allow use of the iron sights.[2]

Scope
Weight: c. 12oz (340.2g)
Magnification: 3x
Reticle: Pointer with crosswire
Objective lens: 19mm
Field of view: 7 degrees 30 minutes

Rifle No. 3 Mk. I*(T)A

More sniper rifles were needed and some of the 10,000 Winchester-produced P14 rifles were selected for conversion. Winchester-produced rifles were made to a closer tolerance than either Eddystone or Remington and shot better. The P14 was selected over the available SMLE Mk. III because of the P14's stronger action—it had a heavier barrel and better short-range accuracy. To convert the P14, Aldis Pattern Nos. 3 and 4 scopes were soldered onto the offset mounts which were then attached to the left side of the P14 receiver to create the Rifle No. 3 Mk. I* (T)A. As the rear-aperture sight was removed to make space for the scope, a fixed rear sight was installed in its place. Since the Aldis did not have internal adjustment for the reticle, windage was done by loosening the screws on the rear mount. The clamping plate for the rear mount was not marked for windage and movement of $1/24$in. changed the deflection about 4.5in. at 100yd. The final addition was a wood cheekpiece that was attached by a single screw. Conversion to sniper-rifle configuration was by Alexander Martin which produced 421 of these rifles.

Scope
Weight with mount: c. 20oz (567g)
Magnification: 3x
Reticle: Pointer with crosswire
Objective lens: 19mm
Field of view: 8 degrees 30 minutes

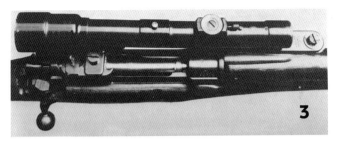

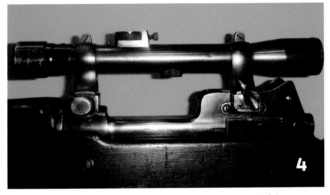

1. Top view of P14 action with scope removed. Note the offset rear scope mount. Because of the dogleg shape of the rear mount, the scope was still mounted over the bore's centerline. *Courtesy Doug Peel.*

2. Left-side view of the No. 3 Mk. I* (T) without scope. The offset mounting system still brought the scope centerline to the bore.

3. Rifle No. 3 Mk. I* (T) A. Note how the scope is offset and also the fixed iron sight that characterizes the weapon from its superior predecessor, Rifle No. 3 Mk. I* (T).

4. Close-up showing some offset in the rear scope mount and the thumb lever that secured it to its base. Too late to see service in World War I, the P14 was converted to a sniper rifle by addition of an claw-mounted overbore scope that permitted the use of the iron sights. Of the different makers of the P14, the Winchester was regarded as the most accurate of the P14s and was selected for conversion. As newer rifles were unavailable, these were issued in World War II. *Courtesy Doug Peel.*

5. Late-war Australian target rifle based on a prewar heavy-barreled target rifle that was fitted with a scope.

SMLE Mk. III* (HT) (Australia only)

The origins of the SMLE Mk. III* (HT) may be traced to the interwar period. During the Depression, the Australian Small Arms Factory at Lithgow produced heavy-barreled SMLEs for rifle clubs and for competitions. They were stamped with an "H" on the stock to distinguish them from ordinary rifles. The shortage of sniper rifles led to their recall for conversion to sniper configuration. All their receivers were of World War I British or Australian production—the selection based on the belief that their steel was superior and "flexed better," which was more conducive toward accuracy. Aldis Pattern 1918 3x scopes left over from World War I or new Australian production of them, solely because no other pattern was available at that time, were fitted to these rifles.[3] Some 1,612 rifles were made of which 1,250 had high-scope rings that allowed for using the iron sights and 362 had low-scope rings. (Daniel Cotterill gives figures of 1,131 high mounts and 481 low.) Because of production delays only a few reached front-line troops in the Pacific before the war ended.[4]

A newspaper reported the cost of conversion. "One Australian sniper in action carries a rifle and ammunition worth £11. The money must be there behind the Services of Australia to win the war … We can't give a sniper a rifle and ammunition worth only £4 and expect him to achieve the services he would with equipment worth £11."[5]

There is some difficulty in determining when the refurbished rifles were issued to the troops at the Port Adelaide Rifle Range. The July 17, 1941, *Adelaide News* reported that "for the first time since the outbreak of the war, special snipers' rifles fitted with telescopic sights were fired in South Australia yesterday afternoon." The shooters were under the direction of Maj. A. E. Gurner.[6]

Scope
Weight: 12oz (340.2g)
Weight of mount: 3.5oz (99.2g)
Magnification: 3x
Reticle: Pointer with crosswire
Objective lens: 20mm
Field of view: 8 degrees 30 minutes

6. Close-up of iron sights of prewar heavy-barreled Australian target rifle. *Images 2, 3, 5, 6 courtesy Ian Skennerton.*

Rifle No. 4 Mk. I (T)

Prior to the Mk. III development above, there was some effort to redesign the SMLE with a rear-aperture sight. Additionally, it would have a heavier barrel—less affected by heat—and a stiffer action. Production techniques were to be modernized. This would eventually become the No. 4 Mk. I. At the time it was believed that a semiautomatic rifle would become the future service rifle for the UK and very little effort was made beyond that. The efforts to improve the SMLE were not wasted, though, and were adopted into the No. 4. Experiments continued on refining the No. 3 Mk. I and included attaching a third sling swivel to the front of the trigger guard, a wood cheek rest on the stock to assist with the cheek weld, and a rubber recoil pad.

In September 1939, 3,500 of the interwar pre-production No. 1 Mk. VI and No. 4 trial rifles were pulled from storage and reconditioned to No. 4 standards; 1,400 of these were set aside for scopes. The process of converting them entailed stripping the action down to the receiver which was then mounted in a jig. This ensured that holes could be precisely drilled and tapped for screws and pins to secure the pads upon which the scope base could be fixed. A new buttstock with a raised wood cheekpiece was also fitted. Surplus Aldis scopes left over from 1918 were fitted to these early guns. On March 20, 1940, the telescopic sight for the Bren gun was approved for use on the No. 4 rifle. This was the No. 32 Mk. I scope. Unlike other scopes used by the British Army, the No. 32 Mk. I was adjustable for both elevation and windage. Initial models had elevations adjustable in 50yd increments and ranged from 0 to 1,000yd. Windage was 16 MOA left or right of center. Over the course of the war the No. 32 was to go through three marks. The No. 4 rifle did not enter production until mid-1941.

RSAF Enfield began converting rifles, and on September 22, 1942, Holland & Holland began producing them. Canada also began producing their version at Long Branch as well as a handful (1942 only) in the United States (which because of Lend-Lease were marked "U.S. Property"). Conversion began by selecting rifles that were more accurate than others during the sighting-in process. These were pulled aside and stripped. Two steel pads were fitted to the receiver and secured by screws. The action was then carefully restocked for tighter fitting. The buttstock was marked with the scope's serial number so as to keep the scope mated with the rifle.

Scope
Weight: 1lb 11oz (481.9g)
Weight of mount: 10oz (283.5g)
Magnification: 3x
Reticle: Crosswire and pointed post
Objective lens: 19mm
Field of view: 9 degrees

No. 4 Mk. I* (T) with C No. 32 T. P. Telescope
Weight of Lyman Alaskan: 11.75oz (331 g)
Weight with G&H style mount: 1lb 2.75oz (531.6g)
Overall Weight: 11lb 7.75oz (5.209kg)

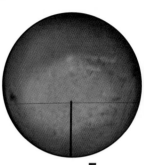

Canada

On September 1, 1937, the British Army Council Instructions ordered, "8 rifles, No. 3 Mk. I* (T) for each Infantry Battalion." Canada's had only two such rifles and resorted to issuing World War I rifles. Thus, despite its poor reputation for jamming under muddy conditions, the shortage of sniper rifles in the Canadian Army resulted in the Ross being pressed back into service. Master-General of Ordnance Major-General Clyde Caldwell proposed to the Chief of the General Staff:

> "As the conditions under which these sniping rifles would be used would be very different from those under ordinary service use, possibly considerable training could be obtained, and we could put into use nearly 400 of these rifles if required. Possibly it would pay the Department to provide additional stock of sights and utilize the long Ross Rifle for sniping purposes, otherwise it will be necessary to provide in estimates, some time in the future, for the supply of the No. 3 Mk. I* (T) rifles for practice and for mobilization purposes."

Canada at that time had 385 Warner & Swazey sights at hand. Apart from training, no evidence has been found to support that the Ross was sent overseas. However, the Warner & Swazey sights were remounted on No. 3 Mk. I* rifles and saw service with the Canadian 1st Infantry Division in Italy as late as 1944.[7]

In addition to the No. 3 Mk. I* rifle Canada also produced the No. 4 Mk. I (T) with its version of the No. 32 scope. The rifles were produced by the newly created Arms Limited (originally named Dominion Small Arms) at Long Branch, Ontario, with manufacturing equipment provided by the United States. It is estimated that 1,588 sniper rifles were manufactured here. Of these, 350 were set up with the Lyman Alaskan scope in lieu of the No. 32. Since the body of the Alaskan scope was narrower than the No. 32, two bushings were used to secure the Alaskan to the mount intended for the wider No. 32 scope.

Initially, the most accurate rifles were pulled aside for conversion. Problems arose in that the receivers of the finished rifles were already hardened, making it difficult to drill and tap for the scope mounting brackets. This was solved by drilling and tapping of selected receivers first. The receiver was afterward assembled with other components to finish the rifle. In an innovative departure from the British practice, SAL developed an oil-soluble dye that was applied under pressure to the wood furniture. Depending on the density of the wood, it could penetrate up to $^3/_{16}$ in. The metal parts were degreased and sprayed with Silico which was then baked and afterward left an olive drab color that was "resistant to corrosion, abrasion, heat and organic solvents."

Not all scopes were mounted using the cast-iron bracket of the No. 4 Mk. I* (T). A one-piece bracket that required four screws and two pins was also made at Long Branch. Like the Griffin & Howe (G&H) scope mount, it required two levers to be thrown to secure the scope to the

7

1–6. No. 32 Mk. III scope on a No. 4 Mk. I (T). Note the case for the sight (4) and the side-mount lugs. Reticle seen in 5. *Images 1–4 and 6 courtesy SniperCentral.com. Image 5 courtesy National Infantry Museum Collection, U.S. Army.*

7. Canadian No. 4(T) with licensed Griffin & Howe scope mount and commercial Lyman scope. *Image courtesy Ian Skennerton.*

bracket. It was clearly an infringement on G&H's patent but the firm was patriotic enough toward an allied nation to grant very lenient terms of either $0.75 per sight or 10% of unit cost; whichever was less. G&H's motive was not profit-oriented but protective of its patent rights.[8]

To provide the necessary optics, Research Enterprises Limited (REL) was founded in Leaside, Ontario in August 1940. Since it was started from scratch, it was decided to combine American manufacturing equipment and practices with British techniques. As the Canadians were ignorant of the latter, a senior officer and two technicians were sent to the optical glass-making firm Chance Brothers in the UK to study their techniques. They returned with 18 workers, among them some Canadians who had worked at the company. By June 1941, REL was up and running and produced not only its version of the No. 32 sighting telescopes, but also its own 25x sniper spotting scopes for its snipers and tank periscopes along with other instruments. REL also produced a refined sniping scope but that was too late to see service. British tests comparing their Type 32 with the REL version proved the REL was equal or better and enjoyed the advantage of being lighter.

A complaint was received in December 1943 that REL scopes fitted to No. 4 rifles would lose their zero. It was discovered that the screws securing mounting brackets had become loose. Tightening the screws down only temporarily fixed it and they became loose again. Center-punching the screws was tried, but the mean point of impact shifted when the rifle warmed up during shooting. It was discovered that some commercial screws lacked tapered heads and thus did not seat well. The final solution was to use the correct screws, fire five rounds to bed the action and then tighten the screws and afterward center-punch them.

6

Finland

Soviet Scopes

When hostilities broke out between Finland and the Soviet Union, there was a shortage of sniper rifles and the Finns resorted to adapting captured Soviet scopes to their rifles. Known as the M39 SOV, 200 rifles were converted by VKT (Valtion Kivääritehdas or State Rifle Factory). Since Finland used both the earlier hexagonal receiver M91/30 and the round receiver M91/30, VKT developed both a hexagonal and round top receiver mount that was attached to the front of the receiver with six screws.

Model 1939-43

In addition to using captured Soviet scopes, Finland turned to its German allies who provided 500 Ajack 4x 90 M43 scopes (4x magnification and 90 indicating its relative brightness). These scopes were also mounted over the centerline of the receiver. The mounting system was based on the topmount used by the Soviet Union for its PE and PEM scopes with one difference: unlike the screw and anti-backout screw used to secure the mount to the base, a throw lever was used instead. The German scoped version was known to the Finns as the M39-43.

The final wartime sniper rifle development involved an indigenously designed scope by Prof. Yrjo Vaisala. Based on the German 4x Ajack scope, the adjustable objective was eliminated and a smaller objective lens (32mm instead of the Ajack's 38mm) was used. Only 50 were produced and when mounted on the M39, was known as the M39-44.

Above: Finnish reworked Mosin-Nagant M39/43 into sniper rifle configuration. Close-up of scoped action—scope is a German Ajack 4x90.

Below. Top view of Finnish M39/43 rifle top mount. *Images courtesy Georg Oberaigner.*

Above and Below. Views of the Ajack 4x90 scope. *Images courtesy Georg Oberaigner.*

M1928/30

After the Finnish Civil War, the Finnish Civil Guards (aka White Guard which was a voluntary militia that during the Civil War fought against the communist Red Guards. Pre-1934 the Finnish Civil Guard was a voluntary part of the army and after 1934 a voluntary defense training organization) adapted the Model 1928, a Finnish variant of the M91/30. Improvements included better rear sight with graduation from 200m to 2,000m and a larger locking device that could be operated with gloved hands. Some M28/30s had sights marked for only 200–1,000m. Improving on the Czarist magazine design, two small indentations on the magazine box guided the cartridges towards the rear of the magazine where it could be picked up more easily by the bolt. Besides a smaller bore of .3082in., the Swiss Schmidt-Rubin practice of bedding the area around the muzzle with an aluminium sleeve allowed the barrel to be free floated between the stock and the upper band. This was critical for accuracy. Eleven were converted into sniping rifles.

Before that, earlier in 1927, Finland purchased Gerard, Goerz, Zeiss, and Hensoldt scopes from Germany. SAKO mounted them on 25 rifles for trials. Only Goerz and Zeiss were found satisfactory and no further acquisitions were made. Being a small country, the military budget was very limited and for almost a decade, neither development nor acquisition was made.

M37PH (M27PH)

The Finnish Mosin-Nagant was not a straightforward copy of the Czarist rifle it had inherited. While the bore diameter remained the original .3095in., the twist was decreased from one in 10in. to one in 9.5in. The barrel was only 27in. long and heavier than earlier Finnish rifles and was easier to carry in Finland's wooded countryside. Being shorter and stouter, it was more rigid too, and this made it more accurate than its predecessors' longer and thinner barrels. The sear was modified to make it crisper.

1. Captured Soviet top-mounted PE 4x M91/30. *SA-kuva.*

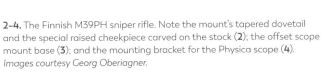

2–4. The Finnish M39PH sniper rifle. Note the mount's tapered dovetail and the special raised cheekpiece carved on the stock (**2**); the offset scope mount base (**3**); and the mounting bracket for the Physica scope (**4**). *Images courtesy Georg Oberiagner.*

5. M27PH with prismatic Physica Oy scope. As evidenced by the lower height of the scope, this is the later Finnish adaption for the Physica Oy. *SA-kuva.*

6. The Physica Oy was an attempt to acquire a universal weapon sight. This photo makes the prismatic nature of the scope apparent. *SA-kuva.*

In 1937 the Finnish Army had a renewed interest in sniping rifles and ordered 250 3x24 prismatic scopes from Helsinki's Physica Oy. Similar to the Warner & Swazey scopes used by both Canadian and American armed forces of World War I, they were originally intended for use on a machine-gun mount. Adapted for rifles, the M37PH had a mounting block welded to the left side of the receiver onto which the Physica Oy could be slid. A lever was thrown toward the front (muzzle) to secure it. The bolt was bent so the sniper's hand would not interfere with the scope. The height of the eyepiece meant the shooter had to use a chin weld on the stock instead of a cheek weld. Also known as the M27PH rifle, its high mount required the sniper to raise his head to use the scope and unnecessarily expose himself. Additionally, the offset placement of the scope required the sniper to accommodate for deflection for windage. This is common with any rifle with an offset-mounted scope. Total production was 150 units.

M39PH

While retaining the 27in. barrel length and twist of its predecessors, the M39's bore diameter was increased to .310in. This was done so that either Soviet or the heavier Finnish D166 ammunition could be used. The normal Finnish bullet was a 170-grain spitzer with a flat base. Other Finnish ammunition was the D46 which was a boat-tail 170-grain bullet that produced a muzzle velocity of 2,528ft/sec. The D166 was a .310in.-diameter 200-grain boat-tailed bullet originally meant for Finnish HMGs. Fired from the M39, it produced a muzzle velocity of 2,297ft/sec. There were other changes including moving the front sight slightly back from the muzzle. Deceptively, this made the barrel appear longer. With 100 of the original order of 250 Physica Oy scopes remaining, it was decided to mount them on the newer M39. A new lower mount was designed and a wood cheekpiece added to the stock to ensure proper and consistent cheek weld. Called the M39PH, the bolt was bent to allow clearance. Only 84 were completed in time for the Winter War.[9]

Germany

In the interwar period, while scoped rifles left over from the war remained in inventory, the *Reichswehr* had little interest in scoped rifles. Concerned over civil unrest and political violence, the *Reichswehr* assembled scoped rifles from among the most accurate available for police work. Those converted from the prewar K98a were designated K98AZ. Conversion was also extended to postwar K98b (b representing *betritten*, or mounted, for cavalry). Both K98AZ and their scoped K98b counterparts had turned-down bolt handles that would not interfere with the scope's eye objective. The scoped rifles had detachable claw-mounted rifles that required milling a dovetail on the top of the receiver for the forward scope base. In 1932 the *Hereswaffenamt* (Army Weapons Office/HWA) ordered the scopes returned to the Spandau Arsenals and instructions were issued for local army armorers to plug the holes in the receiver. In light of the high standard of marksmanship attained in the *Reichswehr*, the scopes were thought superfluous. A new low was reached in 1935 when the army ordered the surplus scopes to be sold to army personnel at the following prices:

Zielvier scope, new	30RM
Container for Zielvier, new	3RM
Zielvier scope, used	12RM
Container for Zielvier, used	1RM
Other telescopic sights without container	5RM

ZF39 (*Das Zielfernrohr 39 für den Karabiner 98k*)

In German eyes the success of the campaigns in Poland, the Low Countries, and France confirmed their assessment that sniping was obsolete and characteristically unique to trench warfare. It did, however, provide impetus for the development of a designated marksman rifle. The German experience in Norway taught them otherwise with respect to long-range sniping. Norwegian sharpshooters with diopter sights used favorable terrain with safe egress to ambush advancing Germans and kill them at 1,200m,

1 and 2. Besides being 4mm taller in height difference, the high turret (left) simplified manufacture with fewer parts. A simple machined spring steel slid into a groove and its tension helped secure the scope. The earlier low-turret scope mount (reproduction seen right) required a plate secured by four screws to mount a scope. *Images courtesy Brian Glenwright.*

3. Overhead view of K98k with low-turret mount and scope removed to show the mounting system. Note the tunnel that allows for the iron sight to be used. Front ring is inserted and pivoted 90 degrees and lever on rear lever thrown to secure the scope.

4. High-turret mount atop of the receiver. Ball mill cutouts on front and back of mount allow the iron sights to be used.

5 and 6. Top view of K98k with high (**3**) and low-turret (**4**) 4x Dialytan scope. Note the scope is in line with the bore. *Images 3–6 courtesy Dave Roberts.*

Close-up of German K98k receiver action with low (**Above**) and high turret (**Below**) Dialytan scope. *Images courtesy Dave Roberts.*

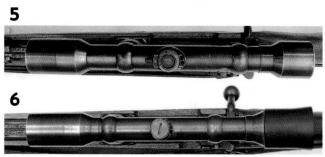

bringing advances to a halt.[10] Artillery, armored cars, and heavy machine guns had to be brought up to drive off the Norwegians who fell back to their next ambush point. Because there were very few Zf39 (4x Zeiss Zielvier) scoped rifles in the *Wehrmacht* inventory (only 200 were delivered), infantry companies privately acquired scopes which their regimental armorers mounted for them. This became so rampant that a special order was issued on February 7, 1941, prohibiting this practice.[11]

The *Wehrmacht* was not against scope-equipped rifles, but rather sought uniformity and discouraged various regiments from cobbling together rifles that could not be serviced later or for which parts might be difficult to obtain. Efforts to develop a sniper rifle started sometime in 1939 and the earliest document found was dated January 18, 1940—before Operation *Weserübung* (invasion of Norway commencing April 9, 1940). Officials from the HWA met with Mauser to develop the Zf39 (*Das Zielfernrohr 39 für den Karabiner 98k*). This was to become the turret-mounting system of which there would be two types both with the same designation (known today to collectors as low- and high-turret mounting systems). The installation of the front turret base on the receiver ring required two holes for the mounting screws. It was then soldered into place.

Rifles that were shown to be accurate during the test firing were set aside for conversion to sniper rifles and by April 2, 1940, 875 rifles with scopes refurbished by Zeiss were supplied to the Ordnance Office at Ulm.[12] Material cost for the rings in 1940 was 38RM per rifle and labor 1,443RM. By May 21, 1940, 1,340 units were delivered by Mauser in Oberndorf.

The lower the scope is mounted on the rifle, the closer it is to the rifle bore's axis which makes it easier for a consistent cheek weld and sight picture. Some modern long-range shooters or snipers want their scope mounted higher for longer-range shooting. Scopes have only a limited amount of internal adjustment for range and by sighting in for a longer range, say 300m instead of 100m, the shooter has a wider range of adjustments his scope permits him to make. This was not on the designers' minds when, in 1943, they decided to produce the high-turret mount that elevated the scope by 4mm.[13] For one thing, long-range shots beyond 600m were uncommon during World War II. Rather, their motivation was to reduce the machining steps and associated costs. By eliminating the low-turret mount's plate and four screws with a machined spring-steel bar that was inserted into a slot in the mount, production time decreased. Finish, though, was cruder than the pre-1943 low-turret mount and machine marks were left unpolished in an expedient measure to deliver more scoped rifles to the troops. By late war, some rings and scopes were delivered unblued! Final deliveries ended

Left (**1**) and right (**2**) side views of Zf41 scope and its transit case (**3**). *Images courtesy National Infantry Museum Collection, U. S. Army.*

by spring, 1945. For either low or high-turret mount, the one-piece solid-steel rings were soldered to the scope. Depending on the scope, this required one of the bells (most likely the ocular bell housing) to be unscrewed so the scope body could be slid through the ring for soldering. On the BMJ scope both ocular and objective bells were removed

There were four major suppliers of scopes and scope tube diameters were not necessarily the same. This required Mauser to manufacture scope ring systems. The major scope suppliers were Zeiss, Ajax, Hensoldt & Söhne Optische Werke, and Dialytan. Other scopes were also used.

Mauser K98k with Zf41

After the Poland campaign infantry commanders asked for a telescopic sight that would allow a marksman to hit smaller or more distant targets and enable infantryman to shoot machine-gunners or into the firing ports of pillboxes. Work began on a low-power, long eye-relief scope and mounting system in early 1940. Originally intended to be supplied to 6% of all K98ks, the Zf41 was not intended as a "sniper weapon" but merely to extend the effectiveness of marksmen. With its quick detachable mount, the scope was mounted over the rear sight and once the scope was removed the rear sight could still be used for rapid shooting. Additionally, the rifle could still be charged with a clip—something needed for rapid firing and close-range combat.

Development of the long eye-relief-scoped Mauser 98K was not at Oberndorf but at Mauser Berlin and Berlin-Lübecker Maschinenfabrik. The low 1.5x Zf41 meant it could not compete

Mauser 'BYF' K98k with Zf41 scope. *Dave Roberts collection. Image courtesy Rock Island Auction Company.*

1. Early short rail K98k and matching transit case for scope. Note the lack of the center tensioning screw used on the late-war short rail fixing.

2. Late short rail K98k close-up. Note the clamping knob in the center of the scope mount.

3. Close-up of late short-rail K98k.

4. Overhead view of late short-rail K98k.

5. Left-side view of K98k with long-rail scope mount. Note how the locking lever has been moved to the center of the mount. *Images 1–5 courtesy Dave Roberts.*

against the various German 4x-scoped sniper rifles let alone against the sniper rifles of opposing armies. Many sniper candidates thought of it as a poor joke. Its extreme eye relief, poor light-gathering ability and low power made it unsuitable as a sniping tool. Despite this, it was the most widely produced and issued optical device used by the *Landser*. 144th *Gebirgsjäger* Regiment sniper Toni M. was known to have used a K98k with the Zf41. By May 1943, 87,396 units had been delivered and production continued well into 1945.

Waffen-SS short and long-rail mounting systems
When the Waffen-SS originally sought scoped rifles, it drew upon the stocks of World War I scoped rifles that remained in inventory. Rather than rely on Mauser as a supplier, the Waffen-SS went to commercial suppliers like J. P. Sauer & Sohn or Gustloff Werke for scope-mounting accessories (base and rail/mounts and scope rings) that could be attached by their ordnance personnel at the SS-*Hauptzeugamt* (ordnance depots).

Known as the *Schiebehalterung (Sauer)*—sliding bracket (Sauer)—the original short-rail scope-mounting system required three holes to be drilled into the side of the receiver. These were then tapped for mounting screws for the bracket. Recoil could shift the rail-mounting bracket and allowed the scope to move. This in turn shifted the point of impact. As a remedy, three more holes were drilled for set screws to keep the screws in place. The final variation had two more holes drilled for tapered pins that went through the mount and into the receiver. The scope mount slid onto the tapered mounting bracket and an offset lever that was mounted near the front was rotated toward the muzzle to lock the scope mount in place. Later versions had a wingnut on top that engaged a pin in the base. The stocks for the short-rail system were relieved such that a portion of the mounting bracket was concealed beneath the stock. It is thought that production of this type of mounting system ceased in 1943.[14]

Even these measures were unsatisfactory and in late 1944 the Gustloff Werke began producing the long-rail system developed by Sauer. The left side of the receiver was made slightly larger so a flat could be machined on the receiver. The receiver was then drilled and tapped for mounting the bracket for the scope base. The longer contact surface meant the bracket was more stable and less likely to "shift" and thereby throw off the zero. The locking lever for the scope mount was centrally located and instead of relieving the stock, it was simply cut away leaving the mounting bracket exposed. Some of these guns were equipped with an extended, modified safety that

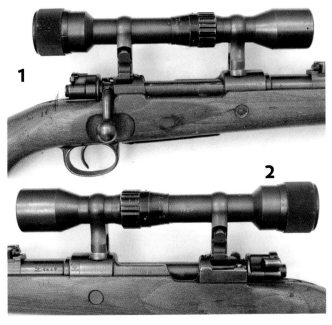

1 and 2. Left and right sides close-up of double claw mount and Opticotechna "dow" scope. Knurled levers on rear scope mount is depressed to dismount the scope. *Images courtesy Dave Roberts.*

3. Scope mounted on single claw Mauser. Pushing the button on the rear scope base allows the scope to be detached and lifted off the rifle. *Brian Glenwright Collection and image courtesy Brian Glenwright.*

4 and 5. Comparison of double (4) and single (5) claw mount base. *Images courtesy Dave Roberts.*

6. Top view of Diatylan 4x scope mounted on single claw Mauser. Note how the scope rings bring the scope centerline with the bore. *Brian Glenwright Collection and image courtesy Brian Glenwright.*

allowed the safety to be engaged while the scope was mounted. Another feature included a recoil collar on the scope body that prevented the scope from shifting in the mount.[15]

Waffen-SS claw mounts

Since World War I, the Austrian rifle maker Steyr had been producing quick, detachable claw mounts for the M95 Mannlicher used in the Austro-Hungarian Army. This system was adapted for the Mauser K98k by the SS during World War II. The two-piece (later three) front scope bases were soldered onto the receiver, obscuring the manufacturer's code and year of manufacture. The rear base was more complicated in that it had the push button release for the claw. This, too, was soldered on the rear of the receiver. The system allowed for quick detachment of the scope and the latter was transported in a special metal tin to protect it when not in use. Since the scope mounts were offset to the left, this allowed the shooter to use the irons sights without removing the scope.

The double-claw mount was adopted from Czechoslovakia in 1944. The major difference in this system from the earlier single-claw mount was that instead of soldering the mount to the receiver, a dovetail was milled into the receiver ring. The front scope base was then pushed into the receiver's dovetail cut. Two slots were milled in the front base for the double claws of the front scope rings. Both front and rear bases had a ball mill passed through to provide clearance to use the iron sights. Similarly, the rear scope base required a dovetail cut into the bridge of the receiver. To install the scope, one tilted the front claws into the front mount and then lowered the rear of the scope down atop of the rear mount. By pushing a button (sometimes two on some models, with one left and the other right) and releasing it, spring-loaded catches locked onto the mount and secured the scope in place. Some of these double claws had a ring that slipped over the objective lens housing that was split at the top and secured with a screw.[16] An early variation uniquely used by the SS was the objective-mount claw mount. This involved soldering the objective lens housing to the scope base. Per Peter Senich, this was a commercial system adapted by the SS.[17]

Swept-back mount

When it was decided to mount the stamped Zf4 scope on the K98k, it became apparent that it could not be mounted conventionally like other scopes because the ocular lens had to be positioned slightly

1. K98k Mauser fitted with reproduction swept-back scope mount and reproduction scope. The only known original with provenance is in the U. S. Army's collection.

2. Reproduction swept-back scope mount and scope. *Images 1 and 2 courtesy Jarrith Kiel collection.*

3–5. Walther G41 magazine-fed, semiautomatic rifle with Zf4 scope. Note bang muzzle cap. *J. Terrill Biedenharn Collection.*

behind the trigger. The problem lay in the K98k's bolt release located on the left side of the receiver. Its presence prevented adoption of the Soviet M91/30's PU mount. The solution provided by Herman Weihrauch of Zella-Mehlis was to develop a swept-back mount. The dovetailed base was on the left side of the receiver and ahead of the bolt release. Produced by J. P. Sauer & Sohn, it required two holes to be drilled into the receiver and the pins installed from the inside of the receiver into the base. Afterward the base was soldered to the receiver. The scope mount was then slid onto the base and the lever thrown forward toward the muzzle, causing two arms to project into a centrally located hole in the base, thus securing the mount to the base. A variant included a mount base that was held by two pins, three screws, and three lock screws. Since only small numbers of either type were made before the war ended, Spielauer suggests the swept-back mounts were only experimental.[18]

Gewehr 41

Since the Kaiser's days, Mauser had been working to develop a semiautomatic rifle. Semiautomatic offered the advantage of greater firepower, less manipulation, and for the sniper, faster follow-up shots. In 1941, German army ordnance asked Walther (Zella-Mehlis) and Mauser (Oberndorf) to develop a self-loading rifle to be designated the Gewehr 41. The order stipulated that there could be no gas port drilled in the barrel and that there must be a bolt handle that could be manually operated. The lack of gas port compelled both Walther and Mauser to adapt the Bang system, named after the Danish inventor, Søren H. Bang. A cap fitted over the muzzle captured the gases and pushed a cylinder back to work a system of operating rods that worked on the bolt carrier.

This, of course, made the system awkward, and the Mauser version, the G41(M), was unreliable when exposed to mud or sand. From the

1. Close-up of the G41's Bang style gas trapping muzzle cap.

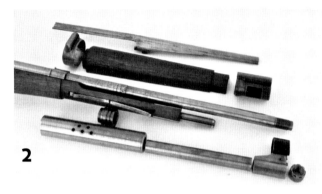

2. After developing the G41, Walther attempted to combine the cylindrical gas piston with a long gas piston rod. It was unsuccessful and Walther adapted the SVT-40's gas system to develop the G43. *Images 1 and 2 courtesy J. Terrill Biedenharn Collection.*

3. View of the G43 rifle showing the scope mounting bracket on the right side of its receiver.

4. Close-up of G43 semiautomatic rifle and its Gw ZF 4x scope. Note the operating handle is worked by the left hand.

5 and 6. Left and right sides of the Gw ZF 4x scope, Sr. No. 36794. Note the stamped steel body construction. *G43 images courtesy the National Infantry Museum Collection, U.S. Army.*

Walther produced a flap-locking bolt that retracted when the bolt unlocked. The system was nothing new and had been used on previous designs—notably Paul Mauser's C98, the Swedish Friberg/Kjellman (1870), Belgium's Karl Bräuning FN Modéle 1914 rifle, and the venerable Soviet Degtyarev DP27 light machine gun.

After firing, the trapped gases act on the cylindrical pistol which forces the piston rod to the rear. The piston rod forces the cover cocking rearward $^9/_{16}$in. at which point the flapping locks unlock, allowing the breech-bolt assembly and cover-cocking to go rearward as a unit. The rearward movement cocks the hammer, extracts the spent cartridge, ejects it, and the forward movement of the breech-bolt assembly and cover-cocking picks up the next round from the magazine and chambers it.

When Mauser's design was compared to the Walther's, it was clear that the Walther was superior and the Walther G41(W) was adopted as the G41. Naturally, the Germans explored the possibility of scoping it for sniper use and—as with the Mauser G41(M)—a 1.5x long eye-relief Zf40 scope was fitted to the rear-sight base. It is unknown how many of these were produced. Much more successful was the receiver-mounted GW Zf 4-fachs (Zf4) sight. By the time at least one example was made, production of the Walther G41 was superseded by the Walther G43.

Gewehr 43 (G43) semiautomatic rifle and other semiautomatics
Walther adopted a rotating bolt in its design along with a gas system similar to that used in the SVT-40 to produce the Walther G43. Besides forgings, the G43 used many modern fabrication techniques including stampings and castings.

It also featured a detachable 10-round box magazine. It fired the same full power 8mm (7.92 x 57mm) Mauser cartridge as the bolt action K98k and was placed into production in October 1943. Innovation did not end with just the rifle. The HWA was tasked with developing a scope that could be used on all weapons.

To facilitate production, the HWA turned to stampings for the scope body to simplify production for the GW Zf4 4x scope. Inspired

outset it was envisioned that it would be scoped for sniper work and a few G41(M)s were fitted with the 1.5x long eye-relief Zf40 scope. As on the K98k, the scope was mounted on the rear-sight base. Only a few experimental models were made and of the G41(M) production, Mauser may have made 15,000 rifles before discontinuing production.

Designation	Weight	Effective lens aperature (E-P)	Light intensity	Dlw	Magnification	Effective lens aperture (E-P)	Dlw from measured values	Light intensity reduced	Magnification (nominal)	Light transmission	Eye relief	Eyepiece opening	Objective lens opening	Field of view at 100m	Light intensity	Diameter A-P	Magnification	Serial No.
Zeiss Target 6	625*	-	-	-	-	31.30	979.8 (2300)	27.2	6	43.2 +/-0.11	8.0	27.0	31.0	3.95	33.6	5.80	5.40	3747
Zeiss Target 4	390 (450*)	31.0	59.3	948.8	4	31.0	966.2 (1020)	60.5	4	48.3 +/-0.16	10.0	34.0	31.0	10.65	63.2	7.95	3.91	13430
Zeiss Target Compact	220	18.0	64	324	2-1/4	17.55	308.0 (342)	60.8	2-1/4	61.2 +/-0.14	11.0	20.0	17.5	11.3	81.0	9.00	1.95	66560
Jackenkroll Ajack 4x90	460 (630*)	37.95	90	1440	4	37.90	1436.1 (1020)	89.8	4	47.8 +/-0.15	8.0	34.0	38.0	10.20	84.6	9.20	4.12	45922
Hensolt-Dialytan	420 (620*)	36	81	1296	4	34.90	1436.1 (1020)	76.2	4	48.8 +/-0.16	9.0	34.0	35.0	9.20	74.9	8.65	4.13	19314
Busch-Parvisar	220 (300*)	31.4	32.5	458	3-3/4	21.60	446.1	33.2	3-3/4	44.7 +/-0.13	8.0	23.5	21.5	9.40	37.2	6.10	3.54	2786
Prismen-ZF (Dr. Jung)	520*	-	-	-	-	19.60	382.3	24.0	4	55.8 +/-0.19	2.5	13.5	20.0	11.40	28.7	5.36	3.65	115
Gw-Zf4 (Voigtlander)	270 (620*)	-	-	-	-	25.10	630.3	39.4	4	45.3 +/-0.14	8.0	25	25.0	8.38	42.3	6.50	3.86	11568
Zf41/1 (Dym)	185	-	-	-	-	10.40	109.9	48.0	1-1/2	51.3 +/-0.19	40.6	14.0	10.5	2.55	44.6	6.60	1.57	366
Zf41/1 (Fzg)	185	-	-	-	-	10.30	106.5	47.2	1-1/2	52.6 +/-0.20	46.0	14.0	10.5	2.65	59.3	7.70	1.34	2570
Russian ZF39	600	-	-	-	-	29.10	845.2 (1020)	53.0	4		9.0	32.5	29.0	9.45	50.4	7.10	4.10	26259
Russian Zf41	250	-	-	-	-	21.50	463.9	37.8	3-1/2	52.7 +/-0.14	8.0	24.0	21.5	8.85	39.2	6.26	3.44	40317
Margin of error	-	-	-	-	-	0.18	0.36	0.36	-	0.31	6	4	4	0.60	0.16	0.10	0.10	-

by the Soviet 3.5x PU, the Zf4 was a departure from previous German scopes and had turrets to adjust for both elevation and windage. When equipped with the scope, the G43 was supposed to be capable of head shots at 300m. The first 500 scopes were delivered to the sniper training companies on May 1, 1944. Newly trained snipers could leave with a scope-equipped G43.

To attach the Zf4 to the G43, a bracket was mounted on the right side of the receiver. When mounted, the Zf4 was slightly offset to the right to provide clearing for the cocking handle and for the ejection of spent cases which came out at about two o'clock to the shooter. The scope mount was slid onto the bracket and a lever thrown to clamp it in place. As it was supposed to be a universal scope, a swept-back mount was adopted for the K98k by having a mounting bracket installed on the left side of the receiver. Similar brackets were attached to the right side of the novel Sturmgewehr 44 (MP44) and top mounts for both models of the Luftwaffe rifle, the FG42.

Extreme temperatures
Initially, the Germans had bad experiences with their firearms not working in the Russian winter. Bolts would stick and actions froze. The practice of oiling firearms ceased as the oil would freeze. Even the scopes that were rated for cold weather could not go below -4°C and adjustments could not be made on the scope. The one advantage some German sniping rifles had was the laminated wood stock composed of fir or other woods and bonded with a phenolic resin. Unlike the solid walnut stock, they were less susceptible to warping due to temperature, wetness, or humidity and remained more consistent when the rifle was disassembled and reassembled. While more weather resistant, they were heavier than walnut stocks. Plywood stocks in the Western world would not be popular again until the late 1980s or early 1990s.

German scope camparisons
The table (left) was a German study. It's a comparison of some commercially available German rifle scopes and a few German and Russian Army developments.[19]

Japan
Type 97
Japan fielded two sniper rifles during World War II. The first was based on the 6.5mm Arisaka Type 38 rifle adopted in 1905. The 1905 was itself an improved and simplified Mauser 98 action. When converted to a sniper rifle, it was renamed the Type 97. Mounted offset on the left side of the receiver, the Nikko 2.5x scope attached readily onto the dovetailed base. Throwing the lever-operated latch and spring latch allowed the scope to be slid off to dovetail. When not in use, the scope could be stored in its carrying case. The scope could not be adjusted for windage or elevation.

1

2

3

4

Scope
Scope w/out mount: 14oz (0.4kg)
Scope rail length: 2$^7/_8$ x 1in. (73.025mm)
Magnification: 2.5x
Reticle: Three lines graduated vertically for holdover and horizontally for windage, holdoff, or lead
Field of view: 10 degrees

Scope case
Weight: 12oz (.3402kg)
Length: 9.25in. (23.5cm)
Height: 3.5in. (88.9mm)
Width: 2.5in. (63.5mm)

Type 99

Experience in China showed that the 8mm Mauser cartridge used by the Chinese Nationalist Army was longer-ranged and harder-hitting than the Type 37's 6.5mm cartridge. In response, Japan refined the semi-rimmed cartridge used in the Type 92 HMG into a rimless 7.7mm cartridge. In 1938 Japan adopted the Type 99 rifle that used the new cartridge. Like the Type 97, it had a sliding-bolt cover to protect the action and a folding monopod. Additionally, the rear sight had folding arms as an aiming lead against aircraft. Weighing about 8.6lb and almost 44in. long, the sniper version had a similarly mounted 8in. long 4x scope with a reticle similar to that

1. Japanese Type 97 6.5 mm sniper rifle Sr. #512 with 2.5x 10 Nikko rifle scope Sr. #14889 and transit case. Note dust cover is intact. Rifle was made in the Chigusa Factory of the Nagoya Arsenal. Canvas case was treated to make it waterproof and has a wood insert that acts as a guide for the scope. There is a small canvas pocket inside for a cleaning brush. *Images 1, 3, and 4 courtesy the National Infantry Museum Collection, U.S. Army.*

2. Scope mount rail on the Japanese Type 97 6.5mm Ariska sniper rifle. Note the spring steel retaining band that must be depressed for the scope's removal. It also conceals the screws and pins that hold the scope mount to the receiver. *Image courtesy Mark Darnell.*

3. Top three-quarter view of the Japanese Type 97 6.5 mm sniper rifle with offset mounted 2.5x 10 Nikko scope and dustcover.

4. Close-up of markings of Nikko 2.5x 10 rifle scope. Dust cover for the action is intact.

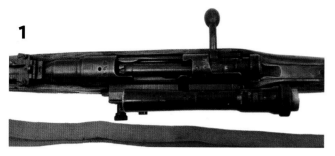

found on the 2.5x scope. There is some dispute as to the field of view. Tantum wrote it has a 20-degree field of view and Pegler asserts 7 degrees.[20] Like its predecessor, the scope did not have any means of internal adjustments for windage or elevation. Some scope mounts had three (unmarked) adjustment knobs. As it would be cumbersome for a sniper to use them in the field for fine tune adjustment, their purpose was probably to help with sighting in at the arsenal. An example is in the National Infantry Museum's collection at Fort Benning, GA.

Scope
Rail: 3in. x 1.25in. (76.2mm x 31.75mm)
Weight: 4x 10 scope 1.2lb (.5543kg)
Magnification: 4x
Reticle: Rangefinding
Field of view: See text above

Both the Type 97 and the Type 99 sniper rifle had a scope mount rail that attached to the receiver by screws. The scope mount itself had a lever with three positions. When facing the rear (toward the butt plate), it was in the unlocked position and the scope could be slid on. When in the center (down), that was neutral. When the scope was mounted on the base, the lever was thrown forward to lock the scope in place.

1 and 2. Views of the Japanese Type 99 7.7x 58mm sniper rifle Sr. #7014 with Kogaku T99 2.5x 10 scope #344. This rifle was manufactured at the Nagoya Arsenal's Toriimatsu Factory. The scope's rubber eyepiece is missing. Note that the scope is offset to the left side of the rifle.

3. Receiver markings partially removed. The words read, "99 Type". The scope and mounting bracket are partially visible.

4. 4x7 adjustable scope on Type 99 Sniper rifle (Sr. #9324). The lever is to the right and the scope mount assembly is ready for removal. The japanned laquer finish is clearly discernable in this photo.

5. Top three-quarter view of the Japanese Type 99 sniper rifle showing the adjustment knobs for the scope. The Imperial chrysanthemum has not been ground off from the receiver.

6. Scope recticle for the Nagaku scope Sr. #344. Recticle was designed to assist in distance estimation and for leading the target. *Images courtesy the National Infantry Museum Collection, U.S.Army.*

Soviet Union

Czarist Russia did not produce rifle scopes. At first, neither did its successor, the Soviet Union. In 1926 the Soviet Union acquired 150 German Zeiss Dialytan 4x scopes and Geschow mounts to build sniper rifles for the NKVD.[21] By 1929 another 350 Zeiss scopes with Walther mounts were acquired.[22] To circumvent the Treaty of Versailles, Germany formed an alliance with the Soviet Union to develop weapons and tactics. A direct benefit to the Soviet Union was the importation of German technology, including a Zeiss optics plant built in the Soviet Union. In 1931, the plant developed the unsuccessful 4x PT scope. It was a start, though, and after examining the Visar 4.5x scope made by Emil Busch of Rathenow, the Soviets asked Busch to redesign it to include lateral adjustment. A hundred of these redesigned scopes were provided and, in 1932, the Soviets modified the design to become the 4x PE adjustable objective scope. It was the first successful Soviet rifle scope.

PE scope
Length: 10.78in. (274mm)
Weight: 1.31lb (598g)
Magnification: 4x

Experience in the Spanish Civil War revealed the PE's adjustable objective permitted dust and moisture to enter the scope tube. By eliminating this, the Soviets simplified the design, made production easier, and gave the scope superior sealing. This improved version, the PEM, began production in 1937. Both PE and PEM were produced concurrently until 1939 when the PE was discontinued and the PEM was produced exclusively. Between 1932 to 1938, while the Western nations were selling their World War I sniping equipment as surplus, the Soviets were arming themselves with scoped rifles and produced a staggering 54,160 sniper rifles.[23]

Serious losses of equipment in the Winter War against Finland resulted in another 53,195 sniper rifles being produced. Production of the PEM ceased in 1942 only after the simpler 3.5x PU scope replaced it. Being shorter, the PU had another advantage in allowing stripper clips for faster reloading—something that couldn't be done with PE or PEM-equipped rifles. Per Martin Pegler, the Soviets produced a total of about 350,000 scoped M91/30s and an additional 52,000 SVT-40s.[24] Lacking optics, the Russians had lagged behind the west in terms of sniper rifles in World War I and the 1930s. They enthusiastically embraced sniping before the Great Patriotic War, and by 1945 the Soviet Army was the best-equipped army in terms of sniping equipment.[25]

1. Mosin-Nagant M91/30 with side-mounted and detachable PE scope.

2. Close-up of mounting bracket for side-mounted quick detachable M91/30 scope mount. Notice the mounting bracket is tapered at its entry point, the stud at the front and the screw hole for the locking screw. Both mounting screws are secured with a smaller locking screw. The mount concept was borrowed from the Germans.

3. Top view of side-mounting bracket on M91/30.

4. Right-side overall view of M91/30 with top-mount scope base. *Images courtesy Georg Oberaigner.*

1. Close-up of top-mounted PE scope on M91/30 receiver.

2. Top view of top-mount scope base. *Images 1 and 2 courtesy George Oberaigner.*

3 and 4. Close-ups of of M91/30 with 3.5x PU scope. *Images 3 and 4 courtesy Alan Lundberg.*

PU Scope
Length: 6.65in. (169mm)
Weight: 9.52oz (270g)
Magnification: 3.5x

Regardless of which of the three major scopes (PE, PEM, and PU) the Soviets fielded, they were not as bright as their German counterparts but they did enjoy one major advantage. They were all better suited for sub-zero fighting conditions that characterized the Russian winter (average -3°C around Moscow). They were easier to adjust and less prone to breakage than their German counterparts. Additionally, in 1941 the Soviets developed a special non-freezing grease for their guns; something the Germans would not do until late 1942.[26]

Mosin-Nagant M1891/1930 with PE, PEM, or PU scope

The Mosin-Nagant M1891/1930 or M91/30 was originally developed and adopted by Czarist Russia. The bolt action was designed by Col. S. I. Mosin and the magazine adopted from the Belgian Nagant design. It was well suited for Russian winter conditions and having fewer parts, less prone to stick under sub-zero conditions. Affectionately called the "Three Line" (*tryokhlinenaya*) after its caliber (each line being one tenth of an inch of an archaic "ligne" measurement system that predated Soviet Union's adoption of metric), this .30-caliber rifle remained the main infantry arm during the duration of the Great Patriotic War. In 1932, as part of the Soviets' Five-Year Plan, the M91/30 was adapted as a sniper rifle.

There are three known mounting systems for the PE or PEM scope. The early ones (1932–35) were mounted directly atop the receiver. Some M91/30s had semi-octagonal receivers and required the scope-mount base to have facets cut to match. Six holes were drilled (three on each side) into the flats of the receiver for the scope base. The scope rings were attached to a base that was slid onto the scope base. Two screws were tightened to secure the scope. Later in 1936 M91/30s were simplified with rounded receivers which made it easier to make the scope-mount base. Like the hexagonal-base version, it too was secured with three screws on each side. A tunnel on the scope-mount base and on the scope mount allowed for the iron sights to be used. The disadvantage, of course, is that with the single mounting point to the receiver the scope is not as stable as a two-point mounting system.

Between 1936 and 1940, a third and easier scope-mounting system was copied from the detachable German side mount. A wedge-shaped dovetailed mounting bracket was fitted to the left side of the receiver and an indexing pin in front of it. The scope mount and scope slid into place and was secured by a thumbscrew. Like its preceding mounts, it also allowed for the iron sights to be used. The disadvantage of this over the previous system was that it increased the weight of the rifle and scope from 9.5lb to 10.5lb. Another disadvantage is that the scope could be attached backwards.

Simonov AVS Model 1936

Like France and the United States, the Soviet Union wanted to reequip its army with a selective-fire self-loading rifle. Full auto was thought to be useful in close quarters and in the semiautomatic mode, the advantage is that the sniper would not have to move to reload after shooting. Movement, as we know, would attract the attention of an observer. Follow-up shots are quicker and they allow for quicker multiple-target engagement. There are inherent disadvantages, too. First, the ejected brass could be spotted by an observer. Second, because of the multiple of moving parts needed to make a semiautomatic work, it is less accurate than a bolt-action rifle.

Work actually started in Czarist Russia and in 1906 a prototype Fedorov selective-fire 6.5mm x Fedorov-caliber rifle appeared. Later rifles were designed around the 6.5 x 50mm Arisaka. Reliability issues (overheating) as well as reliance on foreign ammunition of intermediate power (many Soviet officers could not forsake the 1,200m range the Mosin-Nagant 91/30s was capable of) led to its abandonment in 1924.

Designed by Sergei Simonov, the AVS Model 1936 was the first Soviet attempt at adopting a selective-fire rifle. The selector switch was at the rear of the receiver with the up position for semiautomatic and the down for full automatic fire. The gas block was adjustable for the ammunition and the weapon was fed from a detachable 15-shot box magazine which, thanks to the stripper clip guide on the bolt, could be reloaded in situ. The safety was located behind the trigger and engaging it prevented the rearward movement of the trigger. Striker-fired, it was a complicated design and its action admitted debris and dirt too easily causing jams. It was also finicky with ammunition and its muzzle brake was a failure when the gun was operated on full-automatic mode. Production ceased in 1940 with about 65,000 units made. Some saw service in the Far East when the Soviet Union fought Japan at Khalkhin Gol—the cold caused the grease that wasn't cleaned off to freeze. Others were used in the Winter War against Finland where most surviving models exist because they were captured by the Finns. To accommodate the ejection, the AVS-36 had the PE scope mounted offset on the left side of the receiver. Being offset, the PE scope was lower on the receiver and only slightly above the bore-line and required the sniper to accommodate for deflection for windage. This is common with any rifle with an offset-mounted scope.

Most surviving examples were withdrawn from service in 1941, but Soviet snipers reported scoped versions being issued during the siege of Leningrad. Its most famous user is Vladimir Pchelintsev. A fragile design like the AVS could be entrusted to snipers because part of the Soviet rifle instruction to snipers included meticulous care and maintenance of their weapons.

Tokarev SVT-40

The SVT-40 may be called a product-improved SVT-38 which had replaced the AVS-36. Because of the fragility of the SVT-38, a sturdier and more reliable design was developed. The two-piece stock of the SVT-38 gave way to one-piece, making the firearm more rigid. Internal parts were heavier, making them more robust and less prone to breakage. While superior to the AVS-36, it could jam if dirty and Mikhail Liderman recalled, "They were very capricious weapons. If so much as a speck of dust got in the breechblock, the weapon would not fire."[27] After Kharkov, his men threw their Tokarevs into

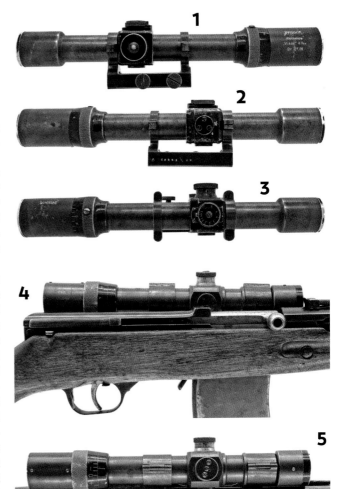

1–3. Busch Visar 4.5x scope with top mount. The Soviets' PE 4x scope was patterned after it. Note the two locking knobs used to secure the scope to the base (**1**) and that the scope rings are conventionally secured with screws (**3**).

4. Simonov AVS-36 selective fire rifle with offset mounted PE scope.

5. Note stripper clip guide milled into the receiver dust cover and hinged scope rings.

6. Rear view of AVS-36 showing offset scope. *Images courtesy Georg Oberaigner.*

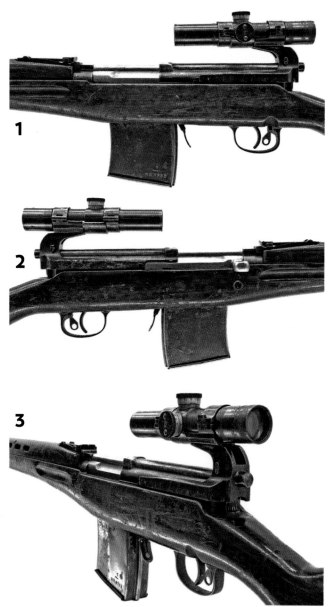

1–3. SVT-40 with 3.5x PU scope. *Images courtesy Georg Oberaigner.*

the lake and got Three Lines (Mosin-Nagant M91/30 rifles) instead. Production ended in 1945 with about 1.6 million made. Wartime production meant that some SVT-40s were poorly bedded. This resulted in the action shifting in the stock which manifested itself with a vertical stringing. About 51,710 sniper versions were made.

Because a top-mounted PE or PEM scope could straddle the ejection port it would be subjected to pounding when an ejected cartridge case struck it. Over time this would cause the reticle to break. Additionally a top-mounted PE or PEM would preclude reloading if the sniper was out of magazines and had to load it with stripper clips.

Soviet engineers could address scoping the SVT-40 in several ways. The first would be to change the ejecting of the cartridge case from the top of the receiver to the side. This required re-engineering the weapon and then having two versions of the SVT-40, which besides slowing down production for retooling was highly impractical and

created a logistical nightmare. Another solution was to adopt a side scope mount as was previously used in the AVS-36—but this created a windage issue for the sniper who had to not only correctly estimate the distance to the target but also account for the scope's offset nature, which required the sniper to compensate for the distance between the center of the reticle and the center of the rifle bore. Soviet engineers struck upon a novel solution by adopting a new, shorter PU 3.5x scope. Being shorter, it could easily be mounted on the receiver cover and still allowed clearance for ejection and for reloading from the top. The Soviets liked the newer PU scope so much they phased out production of the PEM. The scoped SVT-40 were effective out to 400 yards.

U.S. Army
1903A4 Springfield

With the adoption of the Warner-Swazey Model 1908 6x prismatic sight, the U.S. Army was an early adopter of optical sights. American experience with scoped rifles traces back to the American Civil War, when the Confederacy issued Davidson scope-equipped British Withworth rifles to its sharpshooters. Bragging rights as to the first power to issue scoped rifles in the smokeless era belongs to France. Sadly though, the Warner-Swazey adoption was not concurrent with sniper training or doctrine and that would wait until World War I, when British and Canadian instructors taught sniping to Americans. Like most western nations, postwar the Americans sold off their surplus scopes and the Warner-Swazeys were advertised at $7.50 apiece in the January 1939 issue of *American Rifleman* magazine. Since no suitable M1 Garand sniper rifle was available, in January 1943 the army began negotiations with the Remington Arms Co., a commercial arms manufacturer, to develop a new sniper version of the 1903 Springfield Rifle. Remington feared it would slow down production of the unscoped 1903A3 and hurt profits. Instead, they offered their commercial Remington Model 720 rifle with a scope as an alternative. The army rejected Remington's offer and prevailed upon the company to modify the Springfield as the new sniper rifle.

American military small-arms expert Bruce Canfield identifies that, unlike the Soviets or the British, Remington made little effort to select the most accurate rifles for conversion to M1903A4. Instead, rifle barrels from regular production runs were selected "for any items which would affect shooting, such as smoothness of bore and chamber, correct sizes of bore and chamber, etc." Barrels also had to meet the Ordnance Department's standard of a ream diameter of 0.300–0.301in. with rifling not to exceed 0.308–0.309in.[28] Remington used its own gauge to ensure this standard was met. While a barrel is 90% of a rifle's accuracy, a gauged barrel with a shiny bore and chamber does not necessarily make for an accurate rifle. Poor barrel fit to the receiver or bolt, along with fitting to the stock and other parts, can adversely affect accuracy. In short, the best barrel fitted on a poorly assembled gun can still be a poor shooter, and until the assembly was test-fired it was of an unknown quality. By contrast the German, Soviet, or British practice of setting aside the most accurate rifles for conversion to sniping arms at least ensured that the rifle was accurate to begin with. Second, a modified trigger guard with a metal tab between the front trigger-guard screw hole and the magazine well was installed. The raised tab provided a larger bearing surface between the wood and the trigger guard assembly and prevented the trigger guard from digging into the wood. Third, two holes had to be drilled and tapped into the receiver; one in the receiver ring and one in the bridge where the rear sight would have been on an unscoped M1903A3. These holes were tapped and a Redfield Junior one-piece scope base was mounted and secured by two screws. The rear scope rings were retained by two screws with one on each side of the mount. The scope would be inserted into the front split ring set and after the two screws to secure the scope were tightened, the assembly dropped into the scope base and pivoted 90 degrees to bring it into alignment with the bore. The rifle was placed on a rest and the barrel boresighted against a bullseye at 25yd distance. Afterward the rear screws that secured the scope rings were tightened down such that the crosshairs were centered against the target. After adjustments were made, the scope was removed so that the left rear screw could be permanently staked to prevent movement and to help it return to zero if the scope was removed. Sometimes shims had to be installed beneath the scope base to bring the scope into alignment and shims of varying thicknesses were available to raise the base so the scope would not shoot low. After the scope was boresighted, it could then be test-fired and sighted in. Unlike the standard Springfield M1903A3 infantry rifle which had to shoot a one-inch group at 90ft to be accepted, the M1903A4 was required to hit within a three-inch circle at 100yd.[29]

Two commercial scopes were considered for the rifle: the Lyman Alaskan and the Weaver 330C. The army selected the latter to be used in the interim only until Lyman could provide sufficient Alaskan model scopes. The Weaver 330 was designed as a commercial 2.5x power scope and was adopted as the M73B1. It had a 35ft field of view at 100yd and was not the sturdiest scope. Its thin scope body could be bent by a hard knock. The internal windage or elevation knobs could work themselves loose. To meet demand, Weaver initially cleared its inventory of civilian-standard Weaver 330C or 330-M8 scopes with a post reticle for installing on the 1903A4. Besides crosshairs, the civilian Weavers had beveled adjustment knobs that required a screwdriver to adjust. The reticle was a simple crosshair made of titanium which was chosen for its low thermal-expansion property and resistance to rough handling that could break other crosshairs. It was hardly the best American-made scope of the era, and the Weaver's singular virtue was that it was the most readily available. The Redfield Jr. mounting system also had its faults. The dovetail on the base wore, allowing for scope movement. The rear-mounting ring was too soft and the adjusting screws bit into it, causing wear and leaving space for movement.[30]

Lyman was hampered by prior contractual obligations along with the inability of Bausch and Lomb to provide lenses. Thus, the Weaver 330 became the mainstay scope and was adapted as the M73B1. Adopted in October 1944 as the M73E1 (or as the M81/M82 depending on the crosshair), the superior Lyman became the Substitute Standard and was not mounted on any Remington 03A4 for U.S. Army use during the war.[31] Weaver, however, had only limited production facilities and their delay in delivery meant that many unfinished sniper rifles at Remington lingered. Delivery delays of up to four months were experienced while Remington waited for scopes.[32]

It was recommended that snipers zero their scope in at 400yd. At 400yd the sniper was to place the crosshairs on the sternum. Below

M1903A4 Springfield with Weaver made M73B1 scope, Redfield Junior rings and base. *Image courtesy Steve Norton.*

400yd the crosshair was placed one foot below the sternum. If the target was 500yd distance, then the crosshairs were placed at the top of the helmet and at 600yd distance, 52in. (4ft 4in.) above the chest. Distances greater than 600yd required adjusting the sights. If the sniper engaged in city fighting where distances could be shorter, a shorter zero was recommended.[33] The extent to which these recommendations were followed is unknown. The distribution of the manual that recommended it was haphazard. It was unlikely that any newly appointed in-combat sniper was issued the manual, let alone had time to read it. If the sniper was like Pvt. Herb Sheaner (106th Infantry Division), he may never have had the opportunity even to sight it in. Pvt. Charles Davis sighted in his 03A4s at whatever distance was available.

Other modifications to convert the 03A3 Springfield to the 03A4 include forging a concave into the bolt handle to provide clearance for the scope. A regular 03A3 unbent bolt handle would hit the scope body when raised. This could damage the scope. To prevent that, it was necessary to bend the bolt handle during the manufacturing as well as introduce a concave shape. Rifle barrels were selected from stock barrels, but with care taken to ensure that the bore and chamber were smooth as well as the correct bore size. The cost to the government was $1.90 extra per rifle. Like on the Soviet M91/30, the mounting of the over-bore scope precluded use of the stripper clip, making the 03A4 sniper rifle slower to reload. Finally, no iron sights were installed on the rifle, rendering it useless should the scope become damaged.

First deliveries were in February 1943 and by the time production ended, a total of 23,865 03A4s were delivered.

Throughout the war both Weaver and Lyman—as well as Unertl and the 03A4 scope base supplier, Redfield—continued advertising in the *American Rifleman* magazine. It is unlikely that either Weaver or Lyman produced any scopes for the civilian market. Indeed, government demand for scopes was so great that both Weaver and Lyman recalled all unsold commercial scopes (for Weaver it was the 330 and for Lyman its Alaskan scope) from dealers for military use. As mentioned earlier, while no Lyman Alaskans were used on the 03A4, a hundred were sent to the Canadian Ministry of Defense for use on the Canadian produced Lee-Enfield No. 4(T).

Despite Remington and Weaver's glowing advertisements, many soldiers were unimpressed with the Weaver—this includes competitive shooter Capt. Edward C. Crossman who wrote:

"The less said about the 1903 A4 'Sniper' rifle the better. For a country which has developed the telescopic sighted sporting rifle to highest accuracy and general effectiveness, we turned up with the sorriest excuse for a combat man-killer in the war. So help me, the Japs had a better outfit!

"In the first place, the rifles weren't particularly good, not comparable with National Match Springfields, little or no attention was paid to bedding in the stock, and the scope selected—the Weaver 330—was completely unsuited for the job. The scope is a nice little number for a .22 sporter, and a lot of them have been used on .30-06's, but it couldn't stand the rigors of war. I have myself personally poured at least a quart of water from these (collectively) in the Philippines, and never saw any which were in usable condition outside the supply tent … [T]he best report I have is from a rifleman who used one in Germany. He threw away the Weaver and had the Ordnance boys braze on a Russian scope! After this, he got some fair results."[34]

M1C

When issued as a sniper rifle, the M1 Garand was equipped with the Lyman Alaskan scope which, depending on its reticle, was renamed as the M81 or M82 scope. What Pavlichenko described and fired (see caption p. 194) fits the description of experimental M1E2 with offset Stith mounts.[35] Neither National Park Service Ranger Alexander McKenzie at Springfield Armory National Historic Monument nor retired National Firearms Museum Curator Doug Wicklund know of the whereabouts of such a rifle or whether it still exists. It is possible one rifle in the National Park Service collection might have been the rifle fired by Pavlichenko. It has scope rings brazed to the receiver and barrel, but beneath the rear set of rings appear to be filled holes. Similar filled holes appear near the rear sight. This suggests that it once was drilled and tapped for Stith scope mounts. Unfortunately, no photograph has been found showing Pavlichenko shooting the rifle.

Unless a long eye-relief scope was used, the Garand's top-clip loading feature precluded an above-bore scope-mounting system. An attempt to adopt a prismatic scope and straight-tube Weaver 330 (M1E2) was unsatisfactory and another attempt (M1E6) featured an offset mount and a ramp-type rear sight. That, too, was rejected because it would require modifications to the receiver. The commercial firm Griffin & Howe (G&H) submitted a design later called the M1E7 which was a quickly detachable dovetail-mounting system that required five holes to be drilled in the receiver. Three holes were tapped for screws and the last two for pins to prevent shifting. A scope-mounting bracket was then attached. The scope base was slid onto the bracket and by throwing two levers, secured the scope base and scope to the rifle. The commanding officer of Springfield, Brig. Gen. Norman Ramsey

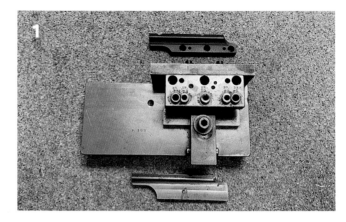

1 and 2. To speed production, drilling jigs were made at the factory and allowed for the uniform drilling and tapping of receivers. Without such jigs preparing a receiver action for scope mounting can be very labor intensive. (**1**) The Garand drilling jig parts: the top piece supports the inside of the receiver and prevents it from being crushed during the drilling process. The bottom piece bears against the right side of the receiver. (**2**) One of the three-part drilling jig required to uniformly drill holes in the unhardened M1 receiver. *Images courtesy Stephan Horak, Griffin & Howe.*

3. M1 Garand with improvised soldered on scope rings. Plugged holes are discernable on the receiver suggesting that another scope-mounting system had been tried. Could this be the M1 rifle fired by Lyudmila Pavlichenko? *Springfield Armory National Historic Site.*

4. Left-hand view of M1C Garand sniper rifle with M81 scope. Note flash suppressor and leather cheekpiece. *Image courtesy. Jim Tomkiewicz.*

criticized the design for being unsuitable for mass production.[36] It required a stripped receiver be sent to G&H for drilling and tapping and mounting of the receiver bracket. Afterward the receiver was

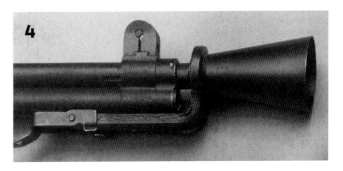

1. M1C detail showing M82 telescope mount.

2. Close-up of G&H base on the M1C. Note two screws and two taper pins that secured the bracket to the receiver.

3. Springfield Armory photo of M1C mount components. *SANHS/NPS.*

4. M2 flash hider.

5. Lyman Alaskan 2.5x M81 and M82 scope details. *Images 1, 2, 4, and 5 courtesy Bruce Canfield.*

returned to Springfield Armory for heat treatment and assembly. This slowed the production time, especially since Springfield Armory was fully capable of drilling and tapping the receivers itself. Additionally, the dissimilar metals used between the receiver and the receiver bracket meant that the bracket could warp during heat treatment, making for an inaccurate rifle. This was solved by heat treating the receiver and the receiver bracket separately prior to assembly.[37]

Another problem was the M1C could be less accurate than the standard M1. The tolerances for the bracket were too loose, allowing the scope mount to shift imperceptibly to the user with each shot. New drawings with tighter tolerances resolved the problem with shifting. The other contributor to inaccuracy was the flash suppressor which, if not tight fitting, shifted upon firing and changed the point of impact from shot to shot. (By the time of the Korean War, this was addressed by the soldiers who simply removed the flash suppressor.) Despite these issues, the M1E7 was standardized as the M1C on July 27, 1944.

Except for the Marine Corps version of the M1C, most were equipped with the Lyman Alaskan 2.5x scope (adopted as the M81 or M82) with a field of view slightly larger than that of the older Weaver 330/73B1 with 40ft at 100yd.[38] When compared to the British No. 32 scope, Canadian Colonel McAvity of the National

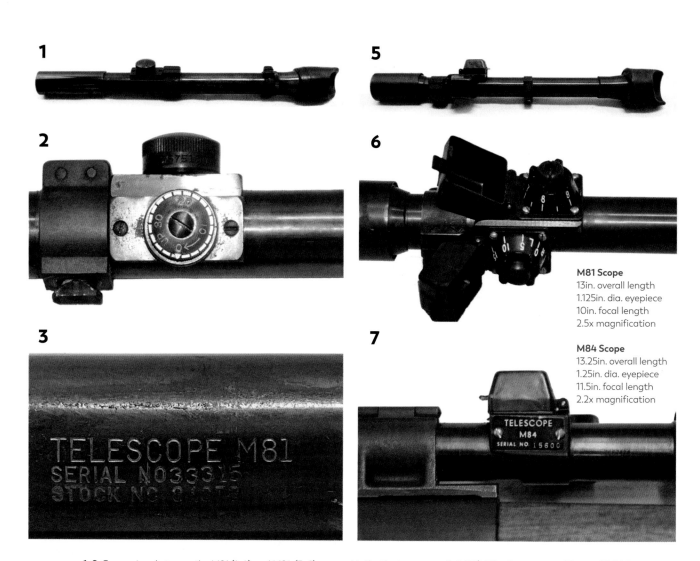

1   **5**

2   **6**

M81 Scope
13in. overall length
1.125in. dia. eyepiece
10in. focal length
2.5x magnification

3   **7**

M84 Scope
13.25in. overall length
1.25in. dia. eyepiece
11.5in. focal length
2.2x magnification

TELESCOPE M81
SERIAL NO33315
STOCK NO.

TELESCOPE
M84
SERIAL NO. 15600

1–8. Comparison between the M81 (1–4) and M84 (5–8) scopes. Unlike the Lyman-made M81/M82, after sustained firing of 3,000 rounds, the optics and adjustments in Wollensak-built M82s came loose. Along with the army's desire for a scope that was fungus-proof, waterproof, and shockproof, work began on a new scope at Frankfort Arsenal. By early 1945, Frankfort developed the 2.2x T134, which was adopted in April 1945 as the M84. With its vertical post and horiztonal crossline reticle, it had a field of view of 27ft at 100yd. To protect it from moisture, it had synthetic rubber gaskets for the lens. It was authorized for the M1C and for the M1903A4. However, only a handful were produced before war's end, and it wasn't until the Korean War that the M84 was used in abundance. With about 40,000 produced, they remained in service until the early 1960s. While capable of being used against targets at 800yd distance, it was considered "pure chance" if the target was struck and generally required several ranging shots first. *Images courtesy the National Infantry Museum Collection, U.S. Army.*[39]

4   **8**

Defence Headquarters wrote, "We consider the Alaskan Lyman best choice. It has tapered posts with cross-wire and luminosity ahead of the [No.] 32. In these tests we were able to distinguish targets 15 to 20 minutes later in the evening than with the 32."[40] Some of the Korean War-era M1Cs had the M84 scope, a military scope of 2.2x with a 27ft field of view at 100yd.[41]

A contemporary design to the simpler M1E7 was the M1E8. Later adopted as the M1D, the design was submitted by John Garand as a competitor to the M1E7. It required turning down the barrel to accept a scope mount base that was pinned to the barrel to secure it. The scope was attached by a mounting bracket which could be hand screwed into the base. As it was easier and quicker to produce, American small arms expert Bruce Canfield suspected that politics—congressional favor toward a constituent—prevailed and Griffin & Howe's design was adopted first.[42] John Garand's design was adopted much later as the M1D.

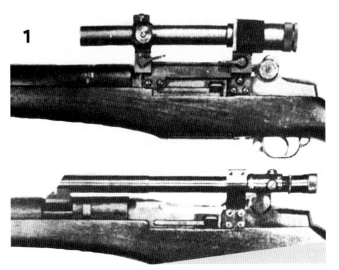

1. Experimental M1E2 Garand with offset prismatic scope. Below is another experimental Garand with an offset Weaver scope. Either may have been the rifle that Soviet sniper Lyudmila Pavlichenko examined and shot while visiting the United States. *American Rifleman, National Rifle Association.*

2. Note the star gauge marking on the bottom of this Springfield National Match rifle used for sniping. *Image courtesy Steve Norton.*

United States Marine Corps

Most USMC sniper rifles enjoyed an advantage over the army's: Springfield rifles converted by the marines into sniper rifles began as either National Match quality rifles or Special Target rifles with the latter being former National Match whose wear (defined as over 1,000 rounds fired through the barrel) required that they were fitted with new barrels that had been gauged to ensure accuracy. The practice of using competition rifles ensured that the corps' M1903A4 rifles were superior to the army's.

The starting point for a rifle's accuracy is its barrel. The best gunsmith who uses a mediocre barrel as a basis of a target rifle can expect the rifle to deliver only slightly above mediocre results. Building a sniper rifle begins with barrel selection, and barrels with smooth chambers and unscratched bores were set aside and star-gauged. The star-gauge system involved using an expandable feeler that was pushed through the bore. Any change in the bore diameter or depth of the groove would appear on a paper graph that documented the star gauge's movement down the bore. Barrels that showed inconsistency were rejected as a National Match barrel. Those that met it were stamped with an eight-point star at the 6 o'clock position on the muzzle.[43]

Starting in 1924, finished rifles were mounted into the Woodworth Cradle that held the rifle. When mounted in this cradle, the rifle had to fire a two-inch group with ten shots at 200yd.[44]

For conversion to a sniper rifle, the marines had the bolts disassembled and blued to reduce any shine that could betray the sniper's presence. The receiver was drilled and tapped for a scope mounting block which was screwed down, barrel-drilled, and tapped for the scope mounting block, and the handguard was cut for clearance for the front scope mounting block. Contact between the wood handguard and the scope base was undesirable since wood can be affected by humidity. This, in turn, could place pressure on the base which would then affect it. While preference was for the pistol grip "C" stock with its higher comb, the straight "S" stock was also used, as is supported by photographic evidence.[45] Trigger housings were fitted to the stock and the screws were either staked to prevent them from loosening or marked with a chisel to show if the alignment was off. Finally, the marines modified the stock further by milling out wood from around the rear sight base to free float it further. More wood was removed from the area around the bolt handle to ensure that the bolt could be lowered into the battery without interference from the stock.[46]

The Springfield M1903 National Match or Special Target rifles were slightly inferior in accuracy to the Winchester Model 70 rifle. The USMC inventory in 1942 included 400 of about a dozen match and 373 commercial sporter variants of the Winchester Model 70 rifles. For the slight improvement in accuracy over the M1903 National Match rifle, it elected not to convert the Model 70s to sniper rifles as it would create logistical issues and complicate the marine armorers' tasks (more training, parts, and tools).

3. Original straight stock.

4. C stock with full pistol grip.

5. S stock with partial pistol grip.

M1903 with Winchester A5 or Lyman 5A scope

Before the war's outbreak, the USMC's Philadelphia Depot had on hand 141 rifles equipped with scopes, as well as 538 receivers drilled and tapped for scope bases and three receivers with scopes mounted on them.[47] Additionally, it still had in its inventory of 887 Winchester A5 or Lyman 5A scopes (probably excluding the 141 already mounted on them). Of the Lyman 5As, it is thought that less than a dozen had been acquired for trials.[48]

First listed by Winchester in 1910, it was unusual in construction. While the scope body was bored through, and therefore very strong, it was handicapped by its narrow field of view—18ft at 100yd—which made target acquisition difficult.[49] Decades earlier, in 1928 Lyman

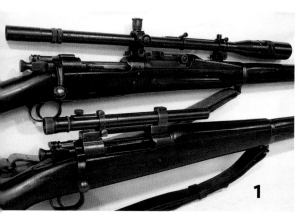

1. Two rifles used by the USMC. On top is the M1903 with Unertl 8x scope and on the bottom an M1903A4 Springfield.

2. USMC 1903 with Winchester A5 Scope. Ammunition usage was still a concern when the M1903 was originally designed. The magazine cut-off is in the off position.

3. USMC 1903 rifle showing scope mount base on receiver and barrel for Unertl scope.

4. To install the front sight base, wood had to be relieved on handguard. *Images 4 and 6 courtesy Mark Darnell.*

5. Unertl scope and rear sight base. *Images 1–3, 5, and 7 courtesy Steve Norton.*

6. USMC 1903 with Unertl Scope. The Marines' fear of the scope's recoil ring (which returns the scope to its position of rest) snagging on jungle foliage resulted in these rifles being issued without the spring. This meant that the sniper had to manually pull the scope back after each shot and with each movement there was a chance of being spotted. *Image courtesy of Mark Darnell.*

7. In comparison, a USMC M1903A1 Springfield with Winchester A5 Scope. *Image courtesy of Steve Norton.*

bought the rights to the Winchester A5 scope and, while it was essentially the same scope, added an external rib to it to prevent it from rotating in its mounts. First sold to the public in February 1929, the modified scope was renamed the Lyman 5A (production ceased in 1937) and—unlike its predecessor—had improved achromatic lenses that eliminated some overlapping colors (blue and red on the edges). Additionally, the groove used on the bottom of the Winchester A5 was replaced with a rib to prevent the scope body from rotating in the mounts. The mounts were also modified for the new rib. Both were limited in their usefulness in low-light conditions. The Winchester A5 and Lyman 5A were easily the worst scopes fielded by any major power during the war, yet sniper rifles with these sights were used both on Guadalcanal and late into the war.[50]

For installation of the rear scope base, holes were drilled into the top of the receiver. The handguard was cut away for holes drilled into the barrel for the forward scope mount. As the Winchester A5 and Lyman 5A did not have internal adjustment knobs, windage and elevation were accomplished by the two knobs on the rear sight. Because of the fragility of the system, the sniper had to take extra care of the rifle, the scope, and the mounting system. Capt. Edward C. Crossman, U.S. Army, had some unkind words to say about the Winchester scope and its sliding mounting system:

"The Winchester scope was never more than a feeble, poorly designed target glass that got by on small bore rifles regularly and lasted for a time on heavy recoil arms because of the sliding feature of the mount. It is about as much of a military telescope as it is of a hunting telescope—and that's nothing. They couldn't even use husky screws to hog-tie their accessories inside the glass, which point the Lyman boys have corrected in their modified scope of this model. ...[51]

"The Winchester A-5 represents a fine composite of things we don't want in the sniper glass, length, fragility, unsubstantial construction, sliding mounts, delicate micrometer, hard to read and easily confused readings. I watched them to the number of nearly 100 take themselves apart at the Small Arms Firing School in the hands of presumably intelligent student officers from the divisions of our Army. In service they would make metallic sights popular."[52]

Forty Winchester A5-equipped rifles were issued to each of the 1st and the 2d Marine Raider Battalions. Whenever possible, the rifles were distributed to trained snipers and if none were available, to the best marksmen (this was done in the 1st Marine Division, too). Experience taught the raiders that the Lyman 5A (and Winchester A5) was undesirable because it was susceptible to rain, fog, and salt.[53] The Raiders' dislike of them would have consequences on the superior Unertl scope.

1903 with Unertl 8x scope
Dissatisfied with the scoped rifles in the marine's inventory, Maj. George Van der Orden proposed to procure the Winchester

Model 70 rifle with a new scope as a sniper weapon. This was rejected by the USMC as it would introduce a new weapons system and the logistics associated with it. Later on January 6, 1943, the commandant approved the purchase of the 8x Unertl target scopes (actually 7.8x but marked as 8x) along with mounts for them. Officially known as the "Rifle, Sniper's Caliber .30 M1903A1, W/Telescope, Sighting, Unertl 8x," it had an 11ft field of view which was narrower than the Winchester A5 it was supposed to replace.[54] If nothing else, while it still required delicate care by the user, the Unertl was a more robust scope than the Winchester A5. Like the latter though, it was not sealed and condensation could build up within the scope body like it did at Saipan. While the Unertl is easy enough to disassemble, no evidence has been found showing that snipers were trained to dismount the

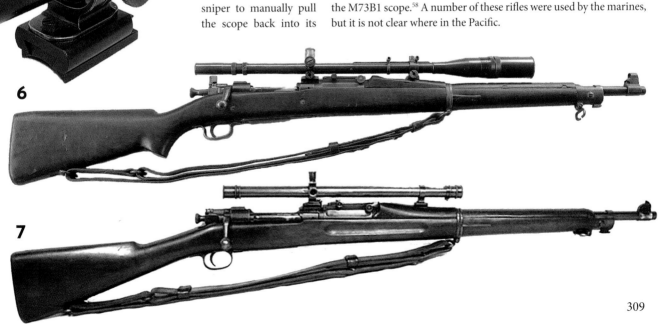

eyepiece to drain the scope body. Each Unertl came with a micarta carrying case that had belt hooks that allowed it to be carried on the pack. However, its length made it impractical for field use and the cases were often left behind. Marine conversions did not include the external recoil spring that was fitted on civilian target rifles. It was feared that sand could get between the spring and scope tube and scratch the scope tube. The spring served to absorb the recoil and prevent damage to the scope. Omitting the spring required the sniper to manually pull the scope back into its firing position. Since movement attracts the eye, the sniper who didn't want to be detected had to be careful.

When the commandant ordered 1,000 Unertl scopes, the USMC had at hand—as already mentioned—1,047 National Match and Special Target rifles, the latter rebarreled at the Marine Depot in Philadelphia. When finished, they were to be distributed to the best marksman in each company.[55] A February 4, 1943, memo from the director of the Division of Plans and Policies stated that each raider regiment should be issued the same number of scoped rifles as an ordinary infantry regiment: 100.[56] That lofty figure was never attained.

Only about 250 Unertl scopes were installed by the corps. This does not mean that all delivered Unertl scopes were actually mounted on rifles. Research by Steve Norton and his associates suggests that by October 1943 the USMC had over 250 scoped rifles of all types (Winchester A5 and Unertl equipped) in service. Late in the war, 100 Unertl-equipped 1903A1 rifles were transferred to the U.S. Navy for use aboard minesweepers. Indeed, at the outbreak of the Korean War in 1950, the corps did not have enough Unertl-equipped rifles to satisfy the ideal target of 100 rifles per division. The Unertl's contract was canceled after an unfavorable report was made by the Marine Raiders against the scoped rifle. Norton found, "It is unclear that the Raiders ever actually received Unertl rifles at all. What is clear is that the Raiders had received 40 rifles equipped with the Winchester A5 scope." The Raiders' dislike of the scoped rifle stemmed from their experience in the jungles of Guadalcanal and Bougainville. It probably sealed the fate of the Unertl and prompted the commandant to cancel Unertl's contract for further deliveries. Scoped rifles would redeem themselves later at Saipan and Okinawa where the terrain was more suited for long-range shooting.[57]

USMC use of the 1903A4

After receiving the Marine Raiders' assessment of scoped rifles, the commandant, Lt. Gen. Alexander A. Vandegrift, canceled the Unertl contract (February 10, 1944). However, there was still a need for scoped rifles—especially on minesweepers where accurate shooting was required to destroy mines. The USMC ordered the M1903A4 with the M73B1 scope.[58] A number of these rifles were used by the marines, but it is not clear where in the Pacific.

Equipment

Ammunition

Different bullets available to the Soviet sniper including yellow-tipped ones for heavy bullets, green ones for tracers, black for armor-piercing (some with a red body), and red-tipped for explosive or incendiary bullets. There was also a light bullet useful only for training.[59] Tracers were useful for identifying targets to artillery observers. Two or three shells and the target was eliminated.[60] When he attended sniper school, Allerberger's instructor told the candidates to ask their armorers for *Anschuß Patronen* (German sighting-in ammunition initially used for testing a rifle's accuracy) cartridges, which were specially prepared and meant for precision shooting. There was never enough of it though to ensure a steady supply to the snipers.[61] *Nah-Patronen* was a subsonic round to be used with the German version of the BraMit suppressor (see discussion on suppressors).[62] The Germans and their Finnish allies also had yellow bullets which indicated that they were prohibited explosive or "dum dum" which were authorized by Hitler for use only on the Eastern Front. Known as "B-Patrone," German sniper Sepp Allerberger admitted using them.[63] Only one incident is known where it was used in the west. An American medic in Sicily claimed that Sgt. Martin Moritz was hit with an expanding bullet that caused the loss of the arm beneath the elbow. In describing the incident, Sgt. Moritz said:

> "It happened at Brolo on August 13. One of the boys got hurt. I cared for him and got him under cover, but then it began to get hot around our position and we had to move. A German sniper caught me in the right arm. He must have been using some kind of dum dum bullet because instead of going through, it mushroomed and tore most of the flesh and bone away."[64]

Desperation caused by lack of ammunition saw the issue of wood practice bullets by the Germans in the west. Inaccurate at long or medium range, they could,

as the American Rangers learned in Normandy, be deadly at close range.[65]

The British developed a special sniper cartridge that featured a blackened case. Marked "DAC VII 1943," they reflected less when ejected and provided one less thing to betray the sniper. However, trials held in Vernon, BC, to determine how effective the blacked case was concluded, "they were of no value for this purpose." With the shooter in the open and observed from a 50yd distance under bright sunlight conditions, the ejected case could not be discerned with certainty. It was concluded that smoke and movement was more likely to betray the sniper's location.[66] Darkened cartridges is a valid concept worth considering today.

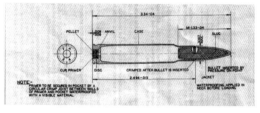

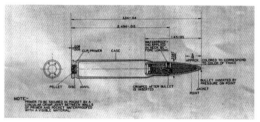

American army snipers were not supplied with special ammunition. What they could select from was regular 150-grain (9.7198g) ball ammunition, black-tipped 165.7-grain (10.73718g) armor-piercing bullets, and orange-tipped 145-grain (9.3958g) tracers. The black-tip armor-piercing bullet fired by the M1 Garand or Springfield rifle was capable of penetrating 4in. of concrete, 12in. of oak, or a steel helmet.[67] It was said to be a favorite as it was more accurate than ball. American arsenals also produced incendiary bullets for air-to-air combat. The early World War I version had a blue tip with a black band beneath it and the later World War II version had a silver band (center had barium with nitrate and magnesium compound). Last, there were blank cartridges for grenade launching. The only evidence this writer has found of explosive bullets being used by Americans in the ETO was during Operation Market Garden when an M2 .50-caliber machine gun loaded for antiaircraft operations (two ball, armor-piercing, explosive) and tracer (blue-tip magnesium) was turned against German infantry.[68]

While tracers were used by the British to designate targets, most battle-savvy American snipers avoided

1. Blank cartridge (*Platz Patrone 88*).

2. Cross-section of ball cartridge (*scharf Patrone S.*).

3. Semi-armor-piercing (*Patronen Spitzgeschoß mit Eisernkern*).

4. Heavy pointed ball (*Patronen schweres Spitzgeschoß*).

5. Armor-piercing incendiary (*Patronen Phosphor mit Stahlkern*).

6. Armor-piercing (*Patronen Phosphor mit Stahlkern*).

7. Observation (explosive) bullet (*Beobachtungsgeschoß Patronen*).
Images 1–7 U.S. Army.

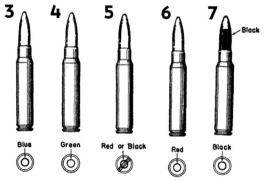

them. 104th Infantry Division Pvt. Charles Davis served as a sniper and recalled:

"I never saw or heard of any other riflemen ever using tracer ammunition in combat. Also, there were very few machine gunners that used tracers that came spaced every fourth round in their ammunition belts. They took tracers out and replaced them with ball ammunition. The only advantage to this practice is that it offered me a source of supply. Tracer ammunition was never issued to riflemen in the ETO … I don't recall ever seeing German riflemen using tracers but then don't forget that we were facing the leftovers from a four-year war. Most of the men in front of us were old men, young boys, and a lot of non infantry soldiers."[69]

This is unlike the experience of another American sniper who was issued only tracer ammunition for his rifle. After one battle, that sniper exchanged his rifle for a M1 Garand.

We know from Capt. Clifford Shore that the British sniper standard load-out included 50 rounds of ball ammunition, five rounds of tracer, and five rounds of armor-piercing (good for taking out machine guns).[70] Shore mentioned that he knew of no example where British snipers actually used tracers.

A problem faced by either the German or Soviet sniper who used both normal ball and explosive bullets is the different weights of the bullet. Consistency is the key to accuracy whether it is in the rifle, the sniper, or the bullet. With the weights varying between the two ball and explosive bullets, the point of impact will naturally shift. If a sniper zeroed the rifle for one type of bullet, (s)he must memorize the ballistics for the other

and adjust the point of the aim. Similarly, the American sniper had two major types: ball and armor-piercing. British sniper Harry Furness kept it simple and tried to find the most accurate ammunition available and stock up the best he could with it.

The Japanese were known to use explosive bullets.[71] Originally manufactured for air-to-air combat, some explosive bullets were found loaded in five-round clips, presumably for infantry rifles. They were 7.7mm (rimmed Navy) with a dull red on the primer cap, 7.7mm Army (semi-rim) with a purple band and a blunt nose that contained an explosive charge; or 7.92mm (rimless Army) cartridges with a white band at the point where the bullet meets the case.

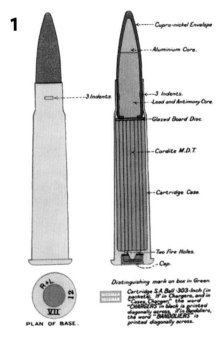

1. Ball cartridge, .303 in. External and internal.

2. Japanese Navy 7.7mm ammo.

3. Type 38 6.5mm explosive ammunition; left practice, right wood.

4. Japanese ammunition packaging symbols. *Images 1–4 U.S. Army.*

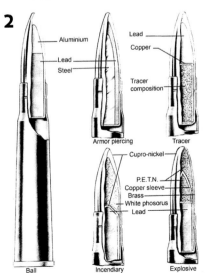

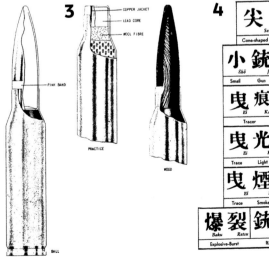

尖 彈	POINTED BULLET
Cone-shaped / Sen / Dan / Bullet	
小 銃 彈	RIFLE BULLET
Small / Shō / Gun / Jū / Bullet / Dan	
曳 痕 彈	TRACER BULLET
Tracer / Ei / Kon / Bullet / Dan	
曳 光 彈	LIGHT TRACER BULLET
Trace / Ei / Light / Kō / Bullet / Dan	
曳 煙 彈	SMOKE TRACER BULLET
Trace / Ei / Smoke / En / Bullet / Dan	
爆 裂 銃 彈	EXPLOSIVE BULLET
Explosive-Burst / Baku / Retsu / Rifle-Bullet / Jū / Dan	

Above: Early in the war the U.S. Army began experimenting with various forms of camouflage. Note the buttoned flap on his pocket, the early WW I style doughboy helmet and uncamouflaged belt by this soldier. *Author's collection.*

Above right: A page from *FM 5–20A* on camouflage: "Skin tone down your face is light in color and, like your canvas equipment, is a beacon to the enemy observer—who usually has the sighting end of a rifle at his eye. Colour your face, neck, and hands to get rid of that light tone. Gloves may be worn." [72] *U.S. Army.*

Below: Two Soviet female snipers and their officer. Note camouflage clothing. *Courtesy the Central Museum of the Armed Forces, Moscow via Stavka.*

Camouflage

While the Japanese used a special camouflage grease to paint themselves green, the Soviets had no such thing and improvised with dirt or mud. The Americans fighting in the jungles of the South Pacific also used mud. Like their forefathers, Americans were also known to use soot to darken themselves. The Forty Thieves (scout-sniper platoon of the 6th Marine Regiment; see pp. 273–4) were known to use black shoe polish to darken their hands and face. During the camouflage training that was part of his scout training, Larry Kirby was given a grease paint make-up kit with various shades of green and black along with a polished metal mirror in the lid.

Germans were known to use loose strings hung over the front of their helmet to make themselves more concealable and a cinematic example from *Fury* showed an SS sniper approaching his prey that way.

British and Commonwealth nations had camouflage cream that could be applied to the skin. At their sniping schools they were given Max Factor makeup kits, but these were not available in the field. In the absence of camouflage cream or makeup, the snipers applied soot or burnt cork to their skin.

Camouflage clothing

Besides improvised camouflage, the Soviets had camouflage-patterned clothing (nicknamed amoeba) with a hood that enclosed much of the head, leaving only the face exposed. A jumpsuit version with hood was also issued. They were available in tan and brown for fall; green and brown for spring and summer. Additionally, the Soviets developed a two-piece uniform and a coverall for spring/summer: it was light and dark green-leaf pattern. A similar brown and green pattern was issued for fall. A brown with white leaf pattern was issued for winter as well as all-white camouflage. Soviet snipers who fought in Finland also used a two-piece ghillie suit.

The *Wehrmacht* began experimenting with camouflage before World War II. Several *Flecktarn*

(spotted camouflage) patterns were developed by Professor Johann Georg Otto Schick for the Waffen-SS and were meant to be seasonally worn/issued: *Platanenmuster* (plane tree pattern from 1937–42); *Rauchtarnmuster* (smoke pattern, of which there was one for spring and summer and another for autumn and winter), *Palmenmuster* (palm pattern) with spring and autumn variant, *Beringtes Eichenlaubmuster* (oak leaf B from 1942 onward), *Eichenlaubmuster* (oak leaf A from 1943 onward), *Erbsenmuster* (44 spot), *Sumpftarnmuster* (swamp pattern). These could be issued to a soldier whether he was a sniper or not. The Luftwaffe also had its own unique Luftwaffen *Splittertarnmuster* (splinter pattern). Sepp Allerberger said that full camouflage (a man camouflaged from head to toe to appear like a bush) was rarely used as it was time consuming to prepare, required a lot of material, and worst of all, restricted movement. The only time he wore full camouflage was when he stole another company's chicken for supper. Most of the time Allerberger wore a smock fashioned from a camouflage tent that was tailored for him by his regimental tailor.[73]

British and Commonwealth forces had special camouflage clothing available to snipers. Unlike the normal camouflage Dennison smocks, those issued to snipers had additional pockets sewn inside for stowing "emergency rations, water, Benzedrine inhalers, field dressings, folded maps, compass, sketchbook and grease pencils."[74] Additionally they had gloves and a scrim (net) that could be used as camouflage or draped over the head. Besides attaching varying colors of burlap to his helmet netting, Harry Furness also sewed burlap to his clothing and sometimes even wore (empty) sandbags over his boots.

As early as October 1940 at Fort Belvoir, MD, the U.S. Army began experimenting with camouflaging

clothing to break up the silhouette of the wearer and give the appearance of tree bark, leaves, and bushy plants. A helmet net was designed so that soldiers could insert small branches.[75] Ultimately, the camouflaged clothing worn by both the U.S. Army and the Marine Corps may trace its origins to a design by Norvell Gillespie, a horticulturist and editor of several magazines including *Better House and Gardens*. It was basically a green spot design that was reversible to brown spot. Issued from August 1942 onward, it was nicknamed the "frog suit" by marines. Originally, it was issued as a one-piece jumpsuit which was disliked by wearers because of the exposure to insects and thorns when answering the calls of nature. Additionally, there was the greater possibility of being spotted while disrobed. A two-piece version was issued from July 1944. The USMC versions of both jumpsuit and two-piece uniform had "USMC" and the marine emblem stenciled over the flapless left pocket. Camouflage was available to army snipers but many, fearing friendly fire, eschewed it. Other army units issued and wore them as standard uniforms. The marines were also provided with helmet covers of the same reversible pattern. The early 1942 version lacked the pre-cut slits for inserting foliage that the 1944 version had. The marines were also issued a reversible poncho that could, if there was a buddy, be snapped together to make a shelter tent. Experience taught the marines that while the frog pattern was good for stationary combats, movement made the wearer more visible and the olive drab was superior.

The U.S. Army field manual *Scouting, Patrolling, and Sniping* had provided practical information about personal and weapon camouflage:

"The straight line of the rifle, or other small arm, may be very conspicuous to an enemy sniper, or other close observer. [Wrap] the barrel and hand guard of the rifle … with tape of a contrasting color to break the regular outline. On other terrain, strips of material normally used for garnishing nets and colored to blend in with the particular background can be used to advantage. Mud or dirt may be used to dull the reflecting surface of a polished stock, or a barrel from which the coloring has been worn. After use, the last six inches of the barrel of the M1 rifle shines brilliantly and is very conspicuous. Some benfit may be obtained by coating this part of the rifle with lampblack."[76]

It may have been from his experience in the Philippines, but MacArthur was aware of the Japanese penchant for green uniforms, shoes, and face cream used by their snipers. While American soldiers were fighting alongside the Australians in New Guinea,

Australian Pte. W. Waters with camouflage head wrapping. The shortage of scoped rifles necessitated his training with a No. 3 rifle. *Argus Newspaper Collection of Photographs, State Library of Victoria.*

Far left: Despite their poor state of equipment, the British Home Guard received camouflage instruction. Rifle is a .303-caliber P14. *Author's collection.*

Left: Two Soviet army snipers with Mosin-Nagant rifles model 1891/30 and optical sights PE. *albumwar2.com Natalia Bode.*

Far right: Canadian Lincs & Welland patrol back from an operation involving canoes (note life preservers). They are dressed in standard British/Commonwealth winter wear. Note scoped No. 4 Mk. III rifle at left. *LAC.*

Right and **Below:** Russian Arctic sniper suit. *GF Collection.*

Right and **Far right:** Finnish soldier modeling a captured Soviet-made ghillie suit. The snaps in the front suggests this was made at some factory and not by the previous wearer. The face veil conceals the eyes and reduces any possibility of eye shine. The Soviets learned well from Hesketh-Prichard's book, *Sniping in France.* The far photo shows a ghillie suit in action. *SA-kuva.*

he ordered camouflage uniforms but none were available. Impression Textiles Pty, Ltd. of Alexandria (Australia) owner, Mr. O. G. Doepel had prepared patterns as early as 1936 and had provided samples to Gen. MacArthur previously. As explained above, the pattern finally settled upon was designed by Norvell Gillespie. When the suits were manufactured, it was with a combination of American material, British dyes, and Australian labor. The suits were packed into bombers which airdropped them over Buna (New Guinea). The snipers who used them "completed their invisibility by blackening their hands and faces and by wearing nets over their faces to screen the give-away whites of their eyes."[77]

By mid-1943, before departing for the Pacific, marines went to Camp Pendleton in San Diego where they were instructed in camouflage. Everyone, including officers, was told to remove their insignia and jewelry (especially rings) and to cover their dog tags with tape. From experience, the marines found that reflection from shiny metal objects drew unwelcome Japanese attention and rifle fire. Instruction also included inserting foliage in helmet netting and camouflaging of faces (and presumably hands).[78]

Of related interest, Capt. John Q. Owsley, CV-6 *Enterprise*'s surgeon, observed that the white label from the plasma bottles for injured soldiers drew fire. At his suggestion, a newer olive drab label was made for plasma bottles.[79]

Winter camouflage

The arrogant belief that the *Wehrmacht* would roll up the Red Army before winter set in meant that the German army was unprepared for the cold of winter

and had to make use of sheets and white material for camouflage. It was only later in the war that proper winter equipment became available.

A similar story was true across the Atlantic. Winter training of the joint American-Canadian 1st Special Service Force saw the first U.S. Army issue of two-piece, white winter uniforms. The jacket was worn over regular clothes and had a button front with a fur collar hood. As the 1st Special Service Force was not deployed as they were intended to be, they never wore those white uniforms in combat. However, in the wake of Operation Cobra, Americans believed the war would be over by Christmas and winter clothing was unnecessary. This led to problems in winter 1944–45, and although some did reach the troops, during the Battle of the Bulge Americans had to improvise snow capes from white bedsheets or tablecloths.[80] Some soldiers from the 2d Infantry Division improvised by wearing white woolen underwear over their olive drab uniforms.[81] Tragically, winter clothing was available

314

in Europe but being a Class II item was given low priority over the big three (food, petroleum products, and ammunition) for delivery to the front.[82]

Snow-camouflage suits were available for the British Expeditionary Force in 1939–40 and the British and Commonwealth units were able to use two-piece winter snow suits that kept them warm and camouflaged.

Dummies and dummy heads

During World War II, the British still had a few dummy heads which were occasionally used. Shore mentions one unit that was troubled by a German "sniper" and borrowed a dummy head from a sniping school to locate him. Six shots were fired by the German and all were misses. Fortunately though, his smoke betrayed his location and he was dealt with.[83] Both the Germans and Russians made extensive use of field-made or improvised dummies or decoys. On the Eastern Front, the Germans would "borrow" an artillery officer's tunic with which they would make a decoy.

About the only major belligerent who didn't resort to dummies was the Americans. Part of this is because of their lack of sniper doctrine and training. Americans, though, were known for using the old cowboy trick of putting a helmet on a stick—something they learned from cowboy movies.

Footwear and tree climbing

In the zero or subzero temperatures that characterized the Soviet Union winter, warm felt boots were necessary. Where they were unavailable, the Soviets resorted to oversized boots with two footwraps (square-shaped linen cloth wrapped around the feet) over their greased feet, with plenty of straw and grass stuffed into the boot to provide insulation.

Besides spikes and special sneakers, the Japanese also used a sling to help them climb trees. Similarly, German snipers were taught to use their poncho. In 1943, the Boston Shoe Company developed a canvas and rubber-soled "sniper boot" that was supposed to make tree climbing easier. It was never adopted.[84] The 6th Marines' (2d Division) scout-sniper platoon wore sneakers in lieu of boondockers (boots) whenever they infiltrated into Japanese lines.

The scout-sniper platoon of the Canadian Nova Scotia Regiment was issued non-slip noiseless footware whose soles were fabricated of rope as opposed to crepe. For winter camouflage they also had white parkas that extended down to the knees and white covers for their weapons. Rain gear and camouflage clothing was issued for non-winter conditions, including helmet covers. Additionally, the men received camouflage paint for exposed skin.

Infrared

In 1935, the Soviet Union—under Professor Pyotr Vailyevich Timofeev, Vyacheslav Ivanovich Arkhangelsky, and E. S. Ratner—began developing infrared vision for the Red Army. A backpack-worn battery powered the infrared lamp that was worn on the user's chest, and the user wore binocular-like goggles that enabled him to see up to a mere 80ft (25m). The truck roof-mounted version saw the goggles also mounted on the inner roof at the driver's eye level. It enabled the driver to go up to 15mph (25km/h) safely.[85] Many night-vision units were sent to the Black Sea Fleet for nighttime entry into ports—daytime invited unwelcomed visits from the Luftwaffe. Larger units were tried by the Red Air Force to assist in nighttime airfield

Diagram from *Sniping in France*—use of a dummy head to determine an enemy sniper's position. *GF Collection.*

Left and **Far Left:** Regardless of type of rifle issued, each Japanese infantry platoon was supposed to have at least one sniper rifle which was normally issued to the best shot. They could be issued tree-climbing spikes—such as these (**Far Left**)—that were attached to their footwear. Palm-fiber capes (similar ones were traditionally worn as raingear in ancient Japan) were fabricated as camouflage. Here, both are demonstrated by an American soldier. *U.S. Army.*

landing. The beacon light could be spotted at up to 25 miles (40km) away and the aerodrome from 2 to 2.5 miles (3–4km). The Soviets, however, did not limit themselves to vehicles, vessels, and aircraft. In 1944 they mounted a similar system, dubbed *Iskra*, on the PPSh submachine gun as well as a M91/30. Effective range was between 55 and 110yd (60 to 100m). The power source was independent of the gun and required a comrade to carry and move the infrared light source.[86] By 1953, the Soviets had developed a one-man unit similar to the American M3 Snooperscope.

Zielgerät 1229 Vampir Infrared

In 1943, German scientists began working on a sight capable of penetrating the night. Based on a 70mm tube, it was produced at the Leitz plant which produced 310 units. For a light source, a 5in. diameter, 35W lamp was paired with an infrared scope and carried in a backpack harness. Weighing 13.63kg (30lb), its effective range was about 70m which, as with comparable Allied units, could be reduced by smoke, fog, or haze. The sight was adapted to the StG44 which, considering the limited range, was an excellent choice.[87] A larger, vehicle-mounted version was developed and possibly used to destroy a Sherman tank belonging to the 756th Tank Battalion, 3d Infantry Division in the Vosges Mountains.[88] Concerned that the Allies would also use infrared sighting devices, the Germans developed an inexpensive paper tube fitted with an infrared lens on one end and a sensitive screen on the other. After exposure to sunlight, for a long time afterward it allowed a soldier to spot an infrared light source.[89]

T3 Carbine with Sniperscope M1 infrared sights

During World War II, the U.S. Army had been experimenting with night-fighting technology, and infrared flashlights were used in the night landings in Operation Torch.[90] In late 1944 it had developed the Sniperscope M1 infrared-based illumination system that was invisible to the human eye

but visible through a special night scope. Its limited effectiveness of 75yd range and heavy weight (28lb or 12.7kg) meant the M1 Carbine was an ideal platform for it. Designated the T3 and sometimes referred to as the "Snooperscope," it was still cumbersome but would have been comforting to a soldier or marine who anticipated a night attack.

Marine scout-sniper Del Schultz was issued the infrared scope and hated it.

"Towards the end of the war, we snipers were issued a 'snooper scope,' allowing us to see images in the dark. Before we put them into use in the jungles, we trained with them in the lower level of our ship so we'd know how to use them. If the enemy captured us, we were supposed to wrap the snooper scope around a tree preventing the enemy from using it. I didn't like this technology and ended up wrapping mine around the tree even though I had not been captured."[91]

While Schultz didn't like the T3, the infrared is credited with "30 per cent of the Jap casualties on Okinawa."[92] The statement isn't qualified, and it likely means casualties from a night battle/skirmish. Infrared was also installed on armored fighting vehicles and at least one M24 Chaffee light tank was equipped with one.[93]

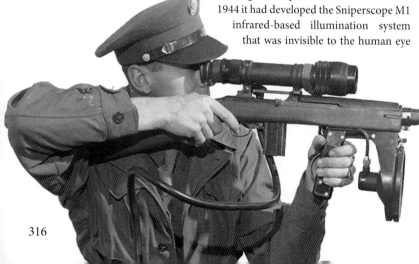

British Infrared

Unlike the Americans or Soviets, while the British were not lagging in development of infrared, they did not mount them on any weapons system. The (British) canteen-shaped Type K Monocular or "Tabby" (Receiver, RG or Red-Green infrared, O. S. 960 G. A., ZA 23119) was a hand-held monocular used by the British Special Forces' Combined Operations Pilotage Parties from 1942–45. Their primary use was to aid in the recovery of reconnaissance teams. They were used in conjunction with an Aldis-type lamp that operated in the 750–950mm IR wavelength. First developed in 1939, it preceded the American M2 sniperscope mounted on the M3 carbine.[94]

Optical devices for spotting

Only the British and the Commonwealth nations are known to use a collapsible three-draw spyglass. The Canadians developed a 25x telescope with a tripod mount that was stored in a cylindrical aluminium case, and the Canadian scope was said to have been easier to use than the British spyglass. The Germans were known to use binoculars and to borrow equipment from the artillery. Unlike other powers, the Soviets issued a small-trench periscope that reached above a trench or hide for observing or studying the enemy position. The Soviet 6x 30 binoculars were capable of being used as a rangefinder. Each small mark represented 5/1000 (5 mils) and each large mark 10/1000 (10 mils). Additionally, some Soviet binoculars had removable yellow-green glass filters that could be mounted to prevent snow blindness.[95] USMC scout-snipers, depending on when and where, could also have spotting scopes for their spotters to locate and identify their targets. Both prismatic spotting scopes with tripods and draw-tube spyglasses were used by the corps.[96] Marine scout snipers sometimes had the USN M7 7x 50 binoculars or when they could get them, the lighter Army M6 6x 30 binoculars.

Shields and screens

The Russians used armor shields with loopholes to protect their snipers. While the *Wehrmacht* did not, it was not beneath the dignity of German snipers to use those captured from the Russians. Most *Wehrmacht* snipers relied on camouflage and deception for their safety. Capt. Shore admitted to having some body armor of 1mm thick manganese plates, but it was intended for ack-ack units and not the sniper or infantryman.

The Germans used half an umbrella to construct screens into which they inserted foliage. While hiding behind it they could observe the enemy with

Top left: Free Polish Forces sniper team being trained in the UK. *Narodowe Archiwum Cyfrowe.*

Top right: In Canada, the Canadians trained the Lovat scouts to ski and fighting in the Canadian Rockies. Mount Andromeda and Mount Athabaska are in the background. *LAC.*

Above: *Scherenfernrohr* or scissor periscopes were also known as "donkey ears" because they rose higher than the user. They were useful for safely viewing the enemy's positions from beneath a trench without risk of exposure. *Narodowe Archiwum Cyfrowe.*

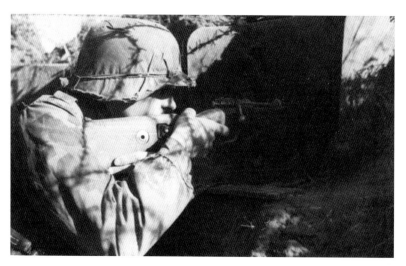

German sniper armed with a Zf41 scoped rifle. Note he is sheltered behind a steel shield. *Bundesarchiv Bild 101L-455-0013-37.*

Below right: Using the sling to provide a firmer base for shooting. *GF Collection.*

Opposite, bottom: Exhibit at the Belarus State Museum of the History of the Great Patriotic War in Minsk, Belarus. Top rifle is a M91/30 with BraMit suppressor mounted on the muzzle. Beneath it is a Nagant 1895 seven-shot 7.62 x 38 mm revolver with a BraMit suppressor. Unlike most other revolvers, the Nagant's cylinder moved forward and engaged the barrel, effectively sealing the gap and allowing it to be suppressible. Beneath it is a RMN-50 (also called PMH-50) 50 mm hand mortar used primarily by Soviet Partisans. M91/30 with Dyakonov 40.5 mm grenade launcher and K98k Mauser equipped with 30mm *Schießbecher* (shooting cup) that fired a grenade up to 280m. *Image courtesy David Golus.*

some confidence that they could remain undetected. Pavlichenko also mentioned using folding metal frames around which a hide could be constructed.

Pchelintsev used (and likely taught the use of) a forked stick as a rifle rest. This offered more support for the rifle, relieving the sniper of the necessity of supporting the rifle for lengthy periods of time. Of course, this is useful when an opponent is known to be in a specific location. Dismounting it would be slow, result in excessive movement and could not be used when there was a chance that a threat could appear from another direction. Similarly, the Germans improvised by making short tripods with materials at hand.

For preparing positions, Pavlichenko used a small sapper's spade. Unlike the long-handled shovel, the smaller spade allowed the user to dig while prone. To deceive an opposing sniper, she placed mirrors on small wooden forks.[97]

Slings

While slings were issued universally as a means of freeing the hands when carrying the rifle, the Americans (and some British) went one step further and used the sling as a shooting aid to steady the shooter. Adopted before WWI, the leather M1907 Gun Sling was a multi-piece leather sling that could be used in various ways (hasty sling, loop sling) to steady the shooter's hold. Its replacement, the M1 Gun Sling, was a heavy cotton that could be similarly used like its earlier counterpart. The M1907 was also used by the British Commonwealth nations. While soldiers in both American Army or boot camps were instructed on the use of the sling, General Patton remarked that his officers reported only seeing them used "on one or two occasions by snipers as an aid to firing."[98] For instructions on how to use either sling, see Edward C. Crossman's *Military and Sporting Rifle Shooting*.

Suppressors

The concept of suppressors predates World War I, when Hiram Stevens Maxim first developed the modern surpressor which he patented in March 1908. His son, Hiram Percy Maxim filed his patent for an entirely different suppressor two days later. The first military field trial of the suppressor was probably by John Pershing's Punitive Expedition to Mexico in 1909 when two Warner-Swazey-scoped rifles with Maxim suppressors were taken along, supposedly to remove sentries silently.

Both the United States and Great Britain were familiar with them and both nations (including France and Italy) had many suppressor patents.[99] Adoption was hampered by the view that they were bulky and impractical for field use. However, among those Western Allies they found a niche on submachine guns

FIGURE 20.—Standing position.

FIGURE 14.—Loop sling adjustment.

or pistols for special operations or silent assassinations. In addition to his sniper rifle, Sgt. Harry Furness briefly carried a suppressed Sten gun, but returned it when he found that the suppressor had been burnt out by the soldier who had it earlier.

In the 1930s, the Soviets began developing a suppressor for the M91/30. Initial tests showed that the rifle's accuracy decreased and that sound wasn't necessarily suppressed. By the 1940s the brothers Mitin designed a suppressor that was attached on the M91/30 like a socket bayonet that slipped over the front sight. Called the BraMit (*Brat'ya Mitiny* or Brothers Mitin), assembled it was 32mm in diameter by 147mm in length (1.26in. x 5.8in.) and was a four-piece steel assembly (excluding the two rubber washers) consisting of a tube (**A** in diagram) that slipped over the rifle barrel like a socket bayonet. The muzzle end of this tube had interior threads. A shorter inner steel tube (**B**) that served as an expansion chamber was dropped into the outer tube. The outer steel tube was threaded to accept a third tube (**C**) that was threaded. This extension was threaded to fit the threads of the first tube (**A**). Part **C**'s outer diameter was the same as that of Part **A** and held the two 15mm thick rubber washers with 30-caliber holes bored into them. These were pressed over each end of the extension. The muzzle end of the extension (**C**) had interior threads for the muzzle knurled metal endcap (**D**). The knurling allowed the suppressor to be easily disassembled and cleaned without special tools. Later postwar versions had a 1mm gas hole drilled into the outer tube as well as the extension tube.

Winter proved harsh for the rubber plugs and they were good for only 15–20 shots. A special winter plug had to be developed but both were soon replaced with a new plug that could be used in any weather from rubber provided under Lend-Lease.

Used in conjunction with a special reduced powder charged cartridge, the BraMit was effective for 100 shots before the rubber inserts would require replacing and the suppressor body thoroughly cleaning.[100] Maximum range with this ammunition was 300m. Green varnish was applied to the bottom of the cartridge case to distinguish it from other ammunition. Subsonic ammunition was produced at Ulianovsk Ammunition Factory #3 and #543 in Kazan. Higher pressure from normal ammunition could damage the unit and was prohibited, but where no subsonic ammunition was available, the bullets could be pulled and the powder charged reduced to one third of the original charge.

Since the reduced powder charge cartridge had a different set of ballistics, the Soviets thoughtfully rolled-stamped on the BraMit's body the sight settings up to 300m. The stampings were 7 for 100m, 8.5 for 150m, 9.5 for 200m, and 12 for 300m. The BraMit was issued with a special metal storage case that contained spare inserts. Several factories made them, including #536 NKV (People's Commissariat of Armament) at Tula and #621 NKLP (People's Commissariat of Light Industry) in Kokchetav (today's Kokshetau). The former manufactured 58,940 BraMits.

BraMits were issued to partisans, scouts, NKVD units, and only rarely snipers. Inevitably some BraMits were captured by the Germans who copied it to make their own suppressors (*Schalldämpfer*) for the K98k Mauser and G43 semiautomatic rifle.[101] The main difference was that instead of using the Soviet socket bayonet method of attachment, the German suppressor was slipped over the muzzle and a clamp was tightened by rotating a lever. A cutaway drawing from Frankfort Arsenal, PA, is reproduced on p. 71 of Truby (1972).[102]

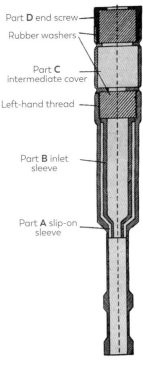

Part **D** end screw
Rubber washers
Part **C** intermediate cover
Left-hand thread
Part **B** inlet sleeve
Part **A** slip-on sleeve

Top: Sniper L. Butkevich with BraMit suppressor. Soviet Sniper L. Butkevich was among the few snipers to be issued a BraMit suppressor which is seen mounted on his rifle. *Author's collection.*

Above: Note the simplicity of the design of the BraMit suppressor with only four metal parts and two rubber washers. The German designation for captured scopes was *Schalldämpfer 254(r). Author's collection.*

| Conclusion

"Suddenly Willi threw up his arms and fell backwards, shot through the heart. His premonition at Quimper had been fulfilled. A single round had ended his life, fired by a Russian sniper from concealment. The Russians had many of them."[1]

Erhard Steiniger

With the exception of the Soviet Union, sniping had a very slow start in World War II. Lacking immunity from the Great Depression, most belligerents were woefully unprepared and sniping occupied a very low priority as armies scrambled to expand, re-equip and train millions of civilians into soldiers.

Harry Furness summed up how views on sniping changed pragmatically through the war:

"Battlefield chivalry is long, long past, though I'm inclined to view it never really existed to any extent, for how is it possible that courtesy can be extended to killing your opponent? Respect shown later for a valiant enemy is commonplace, but chivalry plays no part in that either. So in context it is imperative that snipers accept there will be no quarter given, nor expected in coming battles, take that as a fact of life. Kill or be killed is the very essence of warfare, and for those soldiers whose fate it is to fall in battle and die with a sniper's bullet through the head (and never knowing anything about it) are amongst the fortunate casualties of war, and far sooner a killing sniper's bullet than to die in agony from a flamethrower or to die slowly from horrific bodily mutilations. We all know the old saying that 'all's fair in love and war' so be well prepared in the knowledge that even 'outlawed' cartridges *will* be used against you by very determined enemy snipers. Being forewarned is being forearmed so should increase your motivation to be better than your opponents, so study and practice continually without reservation, that you may make your own luck."[2]

Losses inflicted by Soviet snipers made the Wehrmacht take notice, and in 1943 the Wehrmacht formally began training its own snipers and arming them. Preceding the Germans, the UK and Commonwealth nations began training in anticipation of returning to the Continent. Being the last major power to enter the war, the U.S. Army was the slowest to respond, and when it did, its inconsistency yielded indifferent results. By contrast, the USMC consistently produced skilled snipers who were on par with any of those trained by its allies or by the Axis power. As a skill, sniping surpassed that of World War I, with snipers fighting in both static environments as well as fluid ones.

In 1945 after the last bullet and shell were fired and bomb dropped, the war ended with the Japanese surrender in Tokyo Bay aboard the battleship USS *Missouri*. The battleship itself was no longer queen of the seas, as it has been surpassed by the aircraft carrier. Moreover, the war's impact changed the world forever. SHAEF Commander General Eisenhower's car featured a cellular phone. Radar uncloaked what had hitherto been hidden by the horizon. Jets made their combat debut. Warhead-armed rockets soared through the skies and fell upon unsuspecting populations. Primitive computers cracked codes and directed the long-range fire of battleships' guns. Wire-guided missiles launched from airplanes damaged numerous ships and sank the battleship *Roma*. Perhaps most ominous of all, the atomic bomb ushered in the nuclear era.

After World War I—the "war to end all wars"—everyone hoped for perpetual peace. Military budgets were slashed, programs cut, armies demobilized, and sniping training shelved. Similarly, after World War II, since atomic bombs were capable of annihilating entire armies, what need was there for snipers and sniping? With the exception of the British Commonwealth and the Soviet Union, sniping was thought obsolete and training programs closed and the rifles returned to storage.

Korea proved otherwise and once again the sniper rifles were degreased and cleaned, ad hoc sniping schools established, and snipers called upon to fight once more. This pattern would be repeated until some time after the Vietnam War when sniping was made a permanent part of the American armed forces. Similarly, other nations saw the usefulness of sniping and it is almost inconceivable for an army today not to have snipers.

The best shot

Invariably the question of best sniper arises. Simply put, it is impossible to answer this question. One could go strictly by score—but remember that each nation's method of scoring varies. Many of Simo Häyhä's kills were not witnessed, and some were made in the course of regular combat when he was armed with a machine gun or submachine gun. Soviet claims of each bullet finding its intended mark or incredible scores raise issues of either propagandists' pens or liberal application of Soviet math. Top-scoring World War II German sniper Matthäus Hetzenauer's score is not immune from scrutiny, considering his fellow snipers in the same division fought much longer but had fewer kills to show for it. Another sniper of the 144th Regiment, known only as Toni M., served from November 1943 to war's end and only had around 100 kills to his credit. The disparity between Hetzenauer and Allerberger also raises issues. Could Hetzenauer have included the men he killed in the course of regular combat? Allerberger certainly didn't, but it's difficult to say because, for the most part, Hetzenauer declined to speak about his experiences.

Another more generic issue to the Germans is the requirement of witness signatures. Jealous NCOs could decline signing, leaving the sniper with one less kill. Some artillery officers thought sniping was unethical and similarly refused to cooperate. Part of the animosity could be attributed to the sniper practice of stealing artillery officers' clothing to make dummies/lures. British scores were kept secret to protect its snipers from postwar retaliation and, with some exceptions, Americans didn't care. To most Americans and probably everyone else, surviving the war and returning home was a higher priority. In the case of USMC scout-snipers, the majority of their work involved less glamorous but very important scouting and intelligence collecting.

Furthermore, each sniper fought under unique circumstances. A sniper who excelled in sub-zero temperatures may not be successful in European city fighting or the sort of jungle warfare characterized by the Pacific islands. It is impossible to quantify effectiveness under so many various environmental conditions. Training among the various nations has been covered and shown to be unequal. The Soviets offered excellent schools like the Central Women's School of Sniper Training or the prewar *Osoaviakhim*—but their field schools varied from very effective to, as Kyra Petroskaya experienced, nothing more than shooting instruction. While the U.S. Army didn't adapt a universal curriculum for training its snipers, the USMC had an extensive four–five week course that studied many facets of the sniper's craft.

Unlike today, when snipers can compete in stalking and shooting matches with points awarded for performance, there are no second-places in wartime sniping. The victor won and the loser either died or was wounded. All belligerents eventually fielded effective snipers, some sooner than others. One of Britain's leading snipers, Sgt. Harry Furness wrote:

"With their top shooters we were an even match, each side was a deadly force. The worse of all encounters is one-on-one, sniper against sniper. Such an action can be likened to an intricate chess match where each sniper tries to out-guess his opponent, a match where only one will live. So it doesn't always end with a result. A wise shooter will consider slipping away and knowing he will fight another day, rather than trust to a lucky break. We never, ever, under-estimated an enemy sniper, in a strange way we respected each other. One very important thing we always kept in mind, a re-wording of a religious term: THOU SHALT NOT GET CAUGHT."

Sepp Allerberger would agree and said that a good sniper knew when to exercise discretion and demonstrated it himself after the heel of his boot was shot off. The Soviet had the advantage over him and Allerberger waited for darkness before leaving.

Today, drone weaponry and satellite surveillance present new challenges to snipers and sniping. Heat signatures can be detected from space, and a hidden opponent swiftly dealt with by a soda-sipping drone operator who is comfortably sitting thousands of miles away from the action in a safe and secure air-conditioned office. Additionally, directed energy weapons have yet to reach their full potential, making the individual soldier even more vulnerable. But it is a mistake to think that snipers are no longer needed. Sniping will still play an important role in counter-insurgency operations or urban warfare. After over a century of absence along with fighting tops on warships, sniping again demonstrated its usefulness in maritime operations for both counter-terrorism and as an anti-piracy measure.

In light of this, sniping isn't going away any time soon. Not by a long shot.

Notes to the text

Prelims and Preface

1 Caudill, *The Mountain Eagle*, November 9, 1944, p. 6. Caudill survived the war, became an attorney, politician, and a professor of history at University of Kentucky. Suffering from advanced Parkinson's, he committed suicide in 1990.

2 Waindell (1944), p. 16. Pfc. Osborne was killed on January 23, 1944, and is interred Plot A, Row 7, Grave 177 at Manila American Cemetery and Memorial in the Philippines.

3 The 62nd Regiment of Foot, later renumbered the 60th, and from 1830 the King's Royal Rifle Corps.

Introduction

1 Lambert (2019), p. 179.

2 Kershaw (2019), pp. 209–10.

3 Senich (1982), pp. 140–1.

4 Richardson (2014), p. 104.

5 Bomar, *Burlington Daily Times News*, February 25, 1941, p 7.

6 *The Tiger Triumphs*, Chap. 9, p. 92.

7 Stacey (1948), Chap. 15, p. 265.

8 It said: "The Schmeisser machine pistol has a high cyclic rate of fire, but is by no means accurate. It was used extensively by German snipers who placed themselves 3 or 4 miles outside towns or villages, along the roads leading to these communities. The snipers would cut in on the leading element of a company or battalion in order to hold it back. The would fire until they were out of ammunition, and then would jump out of their trees and come running towards our lines, shouting 'Kamerad!'" *Intelligence Bulletin*, April 1945, p. 64.

9 Nunneley and Tamayama (1992), p. 132.

10 Burgett (1967), pp. 140–1. It should be noted that in Burgett (1999), p. 115, he called a German submachine gunner who was shooting at him from a rooftop a sniper. The meaning of CL used here is unknown. Did he mean common *Landser*? I was told that other editions had GI.

11 Anon., (Danville) *The Bee*, December 19, 1944, p. 11. The term sniping was coined in 1773 by British soldiers but did not enter the American lexicon until World War I. The British began widespread use the term during the Boer War. For a lengthier discussion, see Yee (2009), p. 208.

12 Anon., *Racine Journal Times*, October 15, 1943, p. 7.

13 Anon., *Mason City Globe Gazette*, November 22, 1944, p. 1.

14 Anon., *Escanaba Daily Press*, August 26, 1944, p. 1.

15 Anon., *Sydney Daily Telegraph*, May 7, 1944, p. 19.

16 Anon., *Rolfe Arrow*, January 4, 1945, p. 1.

17 Peters, *Yank*, August 18, 1944, p. 4. For a longer version of this story along with Sgt. Kwiatek's photograph, see *oldmagazinearticles.com/pdf/Sniper-Killer.pdf*.

18 Rehfeldt (2019) Vol. 1, p. 112.

19 Anon., *Fitchburg Sentinel*, March 12, 1943. p. 11.

20 Anon., *Fairfield Daily Ledger*, April 24, 1943. See also *findagrave/memorial/129823154/lloyd-david-gunnels*.

21 Mogan (2020), p. 102.

22 Zaitsev (2003), p. 195.

23 Shore (1998), p. 117 Warfare History Network.

24 Anon., *Sydney Smith's Weekly*, September 18, 1943, p. 7.

25 Anon., *Cumberland Evening Times*, June 11, 1945, p. 8.

26 *youtube.com/watch?v=YYZp8dhLqtM*. Great books about Americans in Stalin's Soviet Union. The quote itself comes from *An American Engineer in Stalin's Russia*. (Zara Witkin).

27 Shapiro, *The Salt Lake Telegram*, November 12, 1942, p. 5; Anon., *Neosho Daily Democracy*, November 7, 1942, p. 4; Anon., *Perth Daily News*, June, 2, 1943. p. 12; Anon., *Ames Daily Tribune*, October 7, 1942, p. 1.

28 Anon., *Auckland Star,* October 9, 1942, p. 3.

29 Morris, *Roma Western Star*, February 19, 1943, p. 6.

30 Anon., *Newcastle Sun*, September 21, 1942, p. 3. See also Anon., *Racine Journal Times*, September 21, 1942, p. 1.

31 Kostia Shalaev was trained as a sniper on the Leningrad Front. For reasons unknown, he was subsequently transferred to an artillery unit. See Moniushko (2005), p. 170.

32 Latimer (2018), Warfare History Network.

33 Anon., *The Mackay Daily Mercury*, June 29, 1942, p. 4.

34 A.L.B., *Melbourne Australian*, August 3, 1940, p. 38.

35 Wright, The World News, April 8, 1944, pp. 12–13.

36 Sasser and Roberts (1990), p. 21.

37 Anon., *Mason City Globe Gazette*, December 22, 1942, p. 4.

Chapter 1

1 Anon., *Mexia Weekly Herald*, December 10, 1943, p. 11.

2 Hesketh-Prichard (1920), pp. 1–2.

3 Anon., *The Land*, May 29, 1936, p. 59.

4 Ladd (1998), p. 147.

5 WO 231/132.

6 ATM No. 29, February 1940.

7 ATM No. 31, April 1940.

8 *Notes on the Training of Snipers* (1940), pp. 1–2.

9 ATM 43, May 1942.

10 WO 27/36, p. 108.

11 *ww2guards.com/ww2guards/WELSH_GUARDS/Pages/2nd_Bn_Welsh_Guards,_1939.html*

12 An article appeared in *The Australasian* newspaper that asserted that Hythe operated a sniping school as early as 1938. The same article also asserted that the *Wehrmacht* had already begun development of a new scope. See *The Australasian*, September 28, 1940, p. 14. Prewar (1938) standards for shooting in the Rifle Brigade was "a least five bulls and four inners out of ten at five hundred yards, and to fire ten rounds a minute. Failure meant encouragement to apply for transfer to another unit." See Gregg (2011), p. 25.

13 Anon., *Sydney Smiths Weekly*, April. 17, 1943, p. 10.

14 Wahlert and Linwood (2014), pp. 101–6.

15 Senich (1993), p. 19.

16 Eisenhower (1948), pp. 2–3.

17 Spickelmier (1971), pp. 101, 106.

18 Ibid, pp. 111–12.

19 FM7-5, §288, pp. 234–45.

20 FM21-75, §165a, p. 169.

21 Anon., *Tipton Daily Tribune*, October 5, 1942, p. 1.

22 Plaster (2008), p. 417.

23 Mogan (2020), p. 13.

24 *blavatnikarchive.org/item13547*. Interview of Mikhail Zamarin.

25 Rottman (2007), p. 10.

26 Underhill, *American Rifleman Magazine*, August 1941.

27 Pavlichenko (2015), pp. 5–6.

28 Blitzstein, *Arizona Independent Republic*, October 1, 1944, p. 2.

29 Pavlichenko (2015), p. 11.

30 Nikolaev (2017), p. 119.

31 Obraztsov and Anders (2014), pp. 30–2.

32 Corti (1997), p. 55.

33 Pegler (2004), Chap 6.

34 Orwell (19), Chap. 12.

35 See: *http://warrelics/eu/forum/japanese-military/evolution-japanese-imperial-army-marksmanship-badges-1882-1945-a-706788/*

36 Williamson (2002), p. 30.

Chapter 2

1 Armstrong (1942), p. 26.

2 Anon., *Brandon Daily Sun*, July 5, 1940, p. 13.

3 Angell (1996), pp. 9–10.

4 Anon., *East Liverpool Review*, July 19, 1940, p. 6.

5 Anon., (Sydney) *Daily Telegraph*, August 27, 1940, p. 1 and Anon., *The West Australian*, August 27, 1940, p. 7.

6 T.H.S.S., *Melbourne Herald*, November 7, 1942, p. 4.

7 Ward (2014), pp. 40–1.

8 Anon., *Perth West Australian*, November 5, 1940, p. 8.

9 Russell (1994), p. 60. Note: this is a fictionalized account of Russell's experience as a World War II South African sniper. As such, only generalities and not specifics were drawn from this work.

10 Armstrong (1942), pp. 2–3.

11 Chandler and Chandler, Vol. 4, p. 87.

12 Ibid, p. 88.

13 Ibid, p. 232.

14 Ibid, p. 93.

15 Ibid, p. 25.

16 Skennerton (1984), pp. 136–7.

17 Anon., *Brandon Daily Sun*, September 16, 1944.

18 July 20, 2020, email to author from Nigel Greenaway. Also see O'Keefe (2019), p. 22.

19 Ibid. As late as Vietnam, undesirable soldiers or sh*tbirds were sent to sniper training if only for the officers and sergeants to be free of them for a few days.

20 Bowlby (1969), pp. 147, 151.

21 Ibid, p. 216.

22 Wynne (1968), pp. 19, 28–9.

23 Allen, *Winnipeg Tribune*, February 5, 1941, p. 7.

24 Anon., *Brandon Daily Sun*, January 8, 1943, p. 8.

25 Mowat (1979), p. 20. Mowat was later reappointed as the battalion's intelligence officer and mustered out a captain.

26 O'Keefe (2019), p. 20.

27 Ibid, p. 26.

28 Mowat (2006), p. 217. After resistance ceased, Mowat and others approached under a Red Cross flag and recovered all the wounded. Pte Sanford was among them.

29 Ross, *Combat Lessons*, No. 4, 1944, p. 50.

30 Folkard, *Newcastle Sun*, January 19, 1943, p. 2.

31 *FM21–75* (1944), p.173.

32 Goodwin (2005), p. 167.

33 Ibid, p. 69.

34 Ibid, p. 200. Kendall's battery was attached to the 103d Infantry Division.

35 Davis (2001), p. 18.

36 Astor (1994), p. 309. Bistrica survived the war and became a cabinet maker.

37 Plaster (2008), p. 385.

38 *ww2online.org/view/daniel-inouye#segment2*. After Inouye was commissioned for helping rescue the "Lost Battalion" (1/141st, 36th Division) he swapped his sniper rifle for a Thompson SMG.

39 *ww2online.org/view/tom-quigley#hill-192-sniping-bar*. Clarence L. Umberger of Tennessee served not only in World War II but also in Korea. He retired as a CWO and passed away on October 17, 1973. See *findagrave.com/memorial/3055270/Clarence-lloyd-umberger*.

40 Roush (1995), pp. 75–6.

41 Goodwin (2005), pp. 70–1.

42 Yee (2017), p. 154.

43 Anon., *Salt Lake City Telegram*, April 12, 1945, p. 13; *veteransday.utah.edu/elbert-t-day/*. Day passed away on June 13, 2008. See also *findagrave/memorial/27611823/elbert-lawson-day*.

44 Sheaner, February 23, 2019, email to author.

45 Gendelman, Max (2013), pp. 20–1.

46 Brotherton (2011), pp. 221–2.

47 Emary, *Guns & Ammo*, 2020; see also Emary, *Outdoor Life*, 2019.

48 Poyer (2012), p. 102. The 551st PIB was later disbanded and its survivors transferred to 82d Airborne.

49 Megallas (2003), pp. 104–5, 250.

50 Pchelintsev (1943), p. 11 there are two known editions of this pamphlet. The author has the shorter 12-page edition. The longer one includes a photograph of Pchelintsev demonstrating his SVT-40 to pupils as well as a passage not found in the author's copy but which is recited on p. 61 of Pavlichenko's book, *Lady Death*.

51 Pavlichenko (2015), pp. 54–5.

52 Gorbachevsky (2008), p. 157.

53 *blavatnikarchive.org/item2422*. Interview of Alexander Gak.

54 *Tactical And Technical Trends*, No. 29, pp. 21–2.

55 Baum (1943), §1.

56 Michaelis (2012), p. 43.

57 Lodieu (2007), p. 38.

58 *Tactical And Technical Trends*, December 16, 1943, No. 40, p. 38.

59 *Wartime Training Guide, No. 1, Sniper Training*, September 29, 1943.

60 *jaegerplatoon.net/RIFLES7.htm*.

61 Leman, (Danville) *The Bee*, May 15, 1943, p. 12.

62 Anon., *Palm Springs Sun*, December 3, 1943, p. 12.

63 *Intelligence Bulletin*, Vol. III, No. 1, September 1944, pp. 48–50.

Chapter 3

1 Chandler and Chandler, Vol. 4, p. 132.

2 Furness, Harry. "The Sucker Shot," in Chandler and Chandler, Vol. 5, p. 90.

3 Ibid, p. 2.

4 Ibid, p. 3.

5 Ibid, p. 3.

6 *ATM* No. 43, May 1942.

7 *Notes on the Training of Snipers* (1940), p. 1.

8 Chandler and Chandler, Vol. 5, p. 209.

9 Ibid, p. 216.

10 Furness, Harry. "The Sucker Shot," in Chandler and Chandler, Vol. 5, pp. 91–4.

11 *Army Training Instruction* No. 9, pp. 1–4.

12 Houghton (2018), pp. 101–2.

13 C.A.B., *Adelaide Advertiser*, July 26, 1941, p. 11.

14 Vernier, *Fremantle Mail*. June 19, 1943, p. 65.

15 Ibid, June 26, 1943, p. 60.

16 Ibid, May 15, 1943, p. 41.

17 Ibid, June 19, 1943, p. 66.

18 Ibid, July 3, 1943, p. 47.

19 Ibid, July 31 1943, p. 54.

20 Ibid, p. 49.

21 Ibid, August 7, 1943, p. 90.

22 Anon., *Mount Gambier Border Watch*, August 17, 1943, p. 4

23 Anon., *Auckland Star*, January 27, 1941, p. 1.

24 Nikolaev (2017), p. 160.

25 Chandler and Chandler, Vol. 4, p. 270.

26 Wynne (1968), pp. 23–4.

27 Leefe (2014), wnsr.ca/history/snipers.

28 Pvt. George N. Burr, son of Walter H. Burr of Pawling, NY was killed in action sometime after the Normandy Invasion. He is interred at Pawling Cemetery in Dutchess County, New York. See also *Brewster Standard*, August 10, 1944, p. 1.

29 Goodwin (2005), p. 169.

30 Anon., *Salamanca Republican Press*, January 8, 1943, p. 5.

31 *FM21–75* (1944), p. 173–4.

32 Goodwin (2005), p. 168.

33 Ibid, p. 69.

34 "Take Care of the Scope," *The Infantry Journal*, Vol. 55, no. 4, November 1944, p. 63.

35 *www.battleofbulgememories.be/stories26/us-army25/663-three-enemies-german-weather-and-fear.html*.

36 Metcalfe, *The Infantry Journal*, vol. 55, no. 2, August 1944, p. 42.

37 Goodwin (2005), p. 111.

38 Plaster (2008), p. 487.

39 Roberts (1992), p. 194.

40 Armstrong, *Port Arthur News*, September 7, 1942, p. 3.

41 Anon., *The Charleston Gazette*, September 13, 1941, p. 4.

42 Aydelotte, Dunkirk (NY) *Evening Observer*, July 18, 1942, p. 14.

43 Anon., *The Cornell Bulletin*, January 14, 1944, p. 5.

44 Hix, *Brookfield Daily Argus*, June 24, 1942, p. 2.

45 *ww2online.org/view/joseph-motil*.

46 Averbeck and Folkestad (2000), p. 28.

47 Anon., *Hope Star*, December 9, 1943, p. 2.

48 Schneider (2017), pp. 74–5.

49 Davis (2001), pp. 55–6.

50 Dixon, *Kingsport News*, May 27, 1944, p. 8.

51 In the days before the superior air gauging, special quality control gauges, called Star Gauges, were used to measure the barrel's land and groove diameter. Depending on the heavy-handedness of the user, it could also give readings thousandths

apart from one part of the barrel to another. Barrels that seemed consistent were stamped with a small "star" on the crown and set aside for National Match and later sniper rifles (see p. 307).

52 ww2online.org/view/theodore-finkbeiner#segment-3. Interview of Theodore Finkbeiner.

53 Khoury (2018), pp. 28–9.

54 Flagg, *American Rifleman*, June 1993.

55 Anon., *Beatrice Daily News*, June, 22, 1945, p. 1. S/Sgt. Melvin J. Treu had been trained as a sniper at Fort Benning, GA.

56 Anon., *Brewster Standard*, August 10, 1944 p. 1. Pvt. George Burr of the 79th Infantry Division received his basic training as part of the 42d (Rainbow) Infantry Division at Camp Gruber, OK. Afterward, Burr was sent to sniper school at Camp Philips, KS and transferred to the 79th.

57 Anon., *Jefferson Bee*, August, 10, 1948. Pfc. Marion Beeebe (KIA November 17, 1944, in France) received basic training at Camp Grant, IN and sniper school at Fort Lewis, WA.

58 Anon., *Moberly Monitor*, September 28, 1945, p. 7. Pfc. Weldon Miller received his sniper training at Camp Mackall, a sub-installation of Fort Bragg.

59 Plaster (2008), p. 482.

60 Johnston (1987), p. 16.

61 Graduates include: Cpl. Joel Thomas Butler of Lakeland, FL—Butler was wounded at Peleliu on D+5 (see Anon., *Portsmouth Herald*, November 3, 1944, p. 3); Pvt. William D. Honaker of Bluefield, WV (see Anon., *Bluefield Daily Telegraph*, July 30, 1944, p. 15; Bud Kingdon of Brimfield, IL (see Anon., October 19, 1944, p. 8).

62 Goodwin (2005), p. 77.

63 Jensen (2016), p. 18. Other graduates of the school include: Pvt. Charles Haynes (Anon., *Coshockton Tribune*, October 25, 1944, p. 2); Pfc. Jerry Chalupnik (Anon., *Cedar Rapids Gazette*, March 7, 1944, p. 12; Pfc. Ed J. Sharp of Co. B, 4th PIB (Anon., *Amarillo Globe*, August 24, 1943, p. 8); Pfc. George Douglas Mets (Anon., *Oxnard Press Gazette*, August 22, 1944, p. 3. Instructors at the school included Sgt. Rudolph Rott who won a Silver Star at Bougainville (Anon., *Madison Wisconsin State Journal*, February 6, 1944, p. 13). Leonard J. Weaver, late of Rock Island Arsenal, IL, completed the school in April, 1943 (Anon., *Daily Dispatch*, Moline, Ill. April 27, 1943, p. 7); Pfc. Clayton T. Barbay of Port Arthur, TX (Anon., *Port Arthur News*, February 9, 1945, p. 9); Pvt. Leslie L. Olson of Ventura, CA (Anon., *Oxnard Courier*, September 16, 1944, p. 5); Pfc. Robert Botton, of Gulfport, MI (*The Daily Herald*, January 26, 1945, p. 6); Pfc. Lloyd C. Fowler was trained sometime in 1944 before being deployed overseas in September 1944 (Anon., *Abilene Reporter News*, April 27, 1945, p. 27). Pvt. William B. Rood also attended the school (Anon., *Ames Daily Tribune*, September. 4, 1944, p. 2).

64 Anon., *San Mateo Times*, July 14, 1943, p. 6.

65 Sasser and Roberts (1990), p. 68. See also Alli, *Lowell Sun*, November 12, 1943, p. 46.

66 Jensen (2016), pp. 17–18. For more insight into Harris's school, see Sasser and Roberts (1990), pp. 23–5.

67 Ibid, pp. 19, 31, 42.

68 Ibid, pp. 75, 79.

69 youtube.com/watch?v=RvqPqqw0O3c. Interview of Larry Kirby at the Morse Institute Library and pritzermilitary.org/whats_on/holt-oral-history-program/lawrence-f-kirby-sergeant/#alt_podcast.

70 Alli, *Burlington Daily Times News*, November 11, 1943, p. 1.

71 Magnan (2003), pp. 189–91, 210.

72 Tachovsky and Kraack (2020), p. 52.

73 Senich (1975), p.9.

74 Walter (2017), p. 210.

75 Bessonov (2003), pp. 31–2, 56.

76 blavanikarchive.org/item5504. Interview of Leonid Solodar.

77 Drabkin and Kobylyanskiy (2009), pp. 154–8.

78 blavanikarchive.org/item5292. Interview of Epshtein.

79 Pchelintsev (1943), p. 10.

80 Nikolaev (2017), pp. 16–7.

81 Ibid, pp. 26–7.

82 Vanach, *Lincoln Evening State Journal*, November 11, 1942, p. 11.

83 Anon., *Medicine Hat Daily News*, January 4, 1943, p. 3.

84 Anon., *Adelaide Advertiser*, March 18, 1944, p. 3.

85 Obraztsov and Anders (2014), p. 48.

86 Zhukova (2019), p. 57.

87 Vinogradova (2017), pp. 61–4.

88 Ibid, p. 68.

89 Ibid, p. 74.

90 Zhukova (2019), pp. 100–1.

91 Alexievich (2017), p. 181.

92 Axell (2001), p. 117.

93 Zaitsev (2003), p. 96.

94 Brontman, *Nevada State Journal*, November 12, 1942, p. 11.

95 Alexievich (2017), p. 7.

96 Pilyushin (2010), p. vii.

97 Ibid, pp. 142–43.

98 Zaitsev (2003), pp. 266–7.

99 Ibid, p. 162.

100 Iremember.ru/en/memoirs/snipers/llavdia-kalugina/.

101 Wacker (2005), p. 120.

102 Jung (2003), pp. 96–7.

103 Ibid, p. 36.

104 This list is incomplete and is based on information in Law (2002), p. 139 accessed via lexikon-der-wehrmacht.de/Wehrmachtbis39/Truppenubungsplatze.htm with extra info provided by ReinhardH.

105 Beevor (2015), p. 58.

106 *Baum Anleitung* (1943), §7.

107 Ibid, §8.

108 Ibid, §C.1

109 Sutkus (2009), p. 8.

110 Ibid, p. 6.

111 Kistemaker (2019), pp. 46–50.

112 Army memo 25b/36 also instructed that snipers were not to be part of an assault force. See Kaltenegger (2017), p. 69.

113 Baum (1944), pp. 30–1.

114 Ibid, p. 28.

115 Ibid, pp. 37–43.

116 Shanke, *Reno Evening Gazette*, September 1, 1944, p. 10.

117 Anon., *Mediterranean Marseilles Stars and Stripes*, December 7, 1944, p. 4.

118 *Baum Anleitung* (1943), pp. 20–1.

119 *Intelligence Bulletin*, Vol. III No. 1, September 1944, p. 51.

120 Ibid, p. 54.

121 *Intelligence Bulletin*, Vol. II, No. 5, January 1944, pp. 75–6.

122 Ibid, p. 56.

123 Plaster (2008), p. 469.

124 *Intelligence Bulletin*, Vol. I, No 4, December 1942.

125 Sandifer (1992), p. 85.

126 *Intelligence Bulletin*, Vol. III, No. 10 June 1945, pp. 6–7.

127 McManus (2019), p. 521.

128 *Intelligence Bulletin*, Vol. II, No. 1, September 1943, p. 33.

129 *Intelligence Bulletin*, Vol. I, No. 4, December 1942, pp. 3–5.

130 *Intelligence Bulletin*, Vol. III, No. 1, September 1944, pp. 54–6.

131 *Intelligence Bulletin*, Vol. II, No. 6, February 1944, pp. 10–11.

132 *Intelligence Bulletin*, Vol. II, No. 2, October 1943, p. 37.

133 Ibid, p. 41.

134 Makos (2013), pp. 164–5.

135 Pegler (2004), p. 219.

136 Fyre, *Hattieburg (Miss.) American*, March 1, 1943, p. 6.

137 *Intelligence Bulletin*, Vol. I, No. 4, December 1942, p. 4.

138 Anon., *Bakersfield Californian*, June 5, 1943, p. 5.

139 Johnston, *Mackay Daily Mercury*, November 20, 1942, p. 6

140 Anon., *Lowell Sun*, April 8, 1944, p. 10.

141 Anon., *Hamilton Daily News*, March 10, 1943, p. 14.

142 Wahlert and Linwood (2014), pp. 131–7.

143 *Intelligence Bulletin*, Vol. III, No. 10, June 1945, p. 36.

144 *Intelligence Bulletin*, Vol. II, No. 5, January 1944, p. 76

Chapter 4

1 Treanor, *Cedar Rapids Gazette*, December 15, 1943, p. 4.

2 Rossino (2001), p. 4.

3 Burkholdt, *Albert Lea Evening Tribune*, April 16, 1940, p. 11.

4 Anon., *The Evening Sun*, April 12, 1940, p. 4.

5 Anon., *Perth Daily News*, January 17, 1940, p. 17.

6 Lubbeck (2006), p. 69. Lubbeck's original name was Lubbecke which he altered postwar after becoming an American citizen. He was tired of the mispronunciation by his fellow Americans. I have reverted to his original name in the text.

7 Ibid, p. 73.

8 Latimer (2018), *Warfare History Network*. Edgar Rabbets's oral history can be found in the IWM sound archives.

9 *Notes on the Training of Snipers* (1940), p. 2.

10 Slessor, *The Morning Bulletin*, Rockhampton, June 14, 1941, p. 5.

11 Anon., *The Courier-Mail*, June 24, 1941, p. 2.

12 Harriot, *Adelaide Advertiser*, July 4, 1941, p. 10.

13 Anon., *Middle East Stars and Stripes*, July 14, 1944, p. 8.

14 Ross (1959), Chapter 5 pp. 89–95.

15 Idem, p. 95.

16 Anon., *The Auckland Star*, October 17, 1941, p. 8.

17 Ibid. A postwar journalist suggested that Hulme was a war criminal for wearing a German smock and wanted his Victoria Cross rescinded. This ignores the many instances when soldiers adopted an enemy appearance as a *ruse de guerre*—such as the German Brandenburger practice of wearing enemy uniforms and operating captured vehicles to infiltrate enemy lines. To evade one encirclement, *Fallschirmjäger* wore Russian headgear while retreating west to safety. See Way (2019), p. 21. In Normandy, Ramcke's *Fallschirmjäger* wore GI clothing to rescue comrades held by the French partisans. Also in Normandy, one German was caught wearing American uniform—see Whitehead in *The Laredo Times*, June 11, 1944, p. 8. More famously, there were many instances during the Battle of the Bulge from English-speaking German paratroopers in American clothing disguised as American M10 tank destroyers. The key thing was not to get caught as retribution was swift.

18 Anon., *Salt Lake Tribune*, November 16, 1941, p. 47.

19 Anderson, *Winnipeg Tribune*, January 3, 1942, p. 15.

20 Anon., *Winnipeg Free Press*, October 2, 1942, p. 3.

21 Anon., *Winnipeg Tribune*, October 2, 1942, p. 4 and Anon., *The Lethbridge Herald*, December 1, 1942, p. 2.

22 Rayburn, *Amarillo Globe*, August 31, 1942, p. 8

23 Figures are from Skennerton (1984), p. 244.

24 Farey and Spicer (2008), p. 132.

25 Anon., *The Evening Tribune*, August 21, 1942, p. 4. See also: Anon., *The Evening Huronite*, August 21, 1942, p. 2.

26 Isby (2017).

27 Alex J. Szima to AmVETS Post #72, *January 30, 1976*, quoted in Henry (1996).

28 Anon., *Launceston Examiner*, January 30, 1941, p. 1.

29 Shore (1998), p. 111.

30 Barker, *American Rifleman*, August 1944.

31 Rochford (2016), pp. 170–1.

32 Wahlert, and Linwood, 113. See also Anon., *Echuca Riverine Herald*, August 2, 1941, p. 2.

33 Gaskill, *Panama City News Herald*, December 12, 1942, p. 6.

34 Anon. *Newcastle Sun*, October 4, 1941, p. 1.

35 Jarrell, *The Charleston Gazette*, November 16, 1942, p. 8.

36 Anon., *The Morning Herald*, January 8, 1943, p. 16.

37 Anon., *East Liverpool Review*, December 17, 1942, p. 5.

38 Pyle (1943), pp. 15–16.

39 Lypka (2007), p. 49.

40 Ault, *Kannapolis Daily Independent*, November 15, 1942, p. 2.

41 Embso, *Freeburg Tribune*, September 10, 1943, p. 1.

42 Scheffel (2007), p. 86.

43 Anon., *Auckland Star*, July 17, 1943, p. 6.

44 Cheall (2011), p. 60.

45 Anon., *Frederick News Post*, March 2, 1944, pp. 1–2.

46 Morriss, *Yank*, August 4, 1944, p. 3.

47 Ross (1959), Chapter 12, p. 270.

48 Shadel (1992), p. 144.

49 Lardner, *The Winnipeg Tribune*, May 12, 1943, p. 1.

50 *Training Memorandum No. 50*, November 20, 1943.

51 Breuer (1983), pp. 130–1.

52 Anon., *San Marino Tribune*, March 16, 1944, pp. 1, 8. Patton survived the war, served in Korea, and left the army as a captain. He was born on May 16, 1916, died on November 11, 1990 and is interred in Arlington National Cemetery.

53 Lypka (2007), pp. 111–2.

54 Pyle, *El Paso Herald Post*, August 21, 1943, p. 2.

55 Wilson, *The Daily News*, July 22, 1943, p. 3.

56 Anon., *Brandon Daily Sun*, August 11, 1943, p. 6.

57 51st Highland Division, *Intelligence from Alamein to Messina* (1943).

58 Sasser and Roberts (1990), pp. 52–4. It is likely that Fulcher actually hit the upper chest region. A stomach wound is painful, causing the victim to scream a lot and taking longer to expire.

59 Treanor, *Cedar Rapids Gazette*, January 3, 1944, p. 12.

60 Carter (1979), p. 75. Casey was killed during the Battle of the Bulge.

61 *ww2online.org/view/theodore-finkbeiner#segment-3* Interview of Theodore Finkbeiner. See also Esfield, 2015, p. 239. The Volkssturm was raised from October 1944 and was composed of anyone from as young as 13 to as old as 60. Impressed into national service to defend the crumbling Third Reich, they were armed with whatever weapons could be cobbled together including sporting arms. There is even an incident where an old man armed with flintlock shot at an American (the GI broke the rifle and sent the old man home). See Scheffel (2007), p. 208.

62 *ww2online.org/view/theodore-finkbeiner#segment-3*. Interview of Theodore Finkbeiner.

63 Ross (1959), Chap 12, p. 286.

64 Wemp, Newspaper unknown, December 21, 1943.

65 Morin, *Abilene Reporter News*, October 3, 1943, p. 9.

66 Houghton (2018), p. 101.

67 Hovey, *Cedar Rapids Gazette*, April 23, 1944, p. 8.

68 Ross (1959), Chap 13, p. 329.

69 Anon., *Medicine Hat Daily News*, November 3, 1944, p. 4.

70 Christopherson, *Winnipeg Tribune*, October 2, 1945, p. 2.

71 Greaves, *Brandon Daily Sun*, October 25, 1944, p. 5.

72 Lovell, *Rapid City Reporter*, November 9, 1944, p. 4.

73 Mowat (1979), p. 198.

74 Anon., *Lowell Sun*, March 8, 1944, p. 19.

75 *Wichita Daily Times*, March 8, 1944, p. 1.

76 Schaps (2003), p. 113.

77 May 8, 2020 email from Philip Rosenkrantz to author.

78 *ww2online.org/view/theodore-finkbeiner#segment-3*. Interview of Theodore Finkbeiner.

79 *Combat Lessons* No. 2, p. 8.

80 Shore (1998), pp. 106–7.

81 Ross (1959), Chap 17, p. 411.

82 Mowat (2006), p. 289.

83 Anon., *Winnipeg Free Press*, January 15, 1945, p. 16.

84 Leefe (2014), *wnsr.ca/history/snipers*.

Chapter 5

1 Blunt (2002), p. 78.
2 Edwards (1999), pp. 127–8.
3 Ibid, pp. 47-8.
4 Horn (2003), p. 146.
5 Ibid, p. 148.
6 Ibid, p. 146.
7 Manning, *Ogden Standard Examiner*, June 16, 1944, p. 3.
8 West (2010), p. 153.
9 July 20, 2020, email from Nigel Greenway to author.
10 Bilder (2008), pp. 131–2.
11 Humphrey (2008), p. 207.
12 Adkins and Adkins (2005), pp. 205–6.
13 Hastings (1984), pp. 209–10. Hastings cites the diary of Bradley's aide-de-camp, Maj. Chester B. Hansen in the collection of the U.S. Military History Institute.
14 Bradley and Blair (1983), p. 221.
15 Farago (1963), pp. 400–2. Patton was later implicated in the murders and an inspector general from Washington visited London to investigate. Patton pleaded that his son-in-law was a PoW and that he refrained from anything that invited retaliation. Patton was exonerated and afterward admonished by Eisenhower who said, "George, you talk too much."
16 Bilder (2008), pp. 218–9. The Polish youth survived.
17 Kaltenegger (2017), p. 64.
18 Wacker (2005), pp. 83, 96–7.
19 Ibid, pp. 21–2.
20 Ibid, p. 136.
21 Altner (2002), p. 210. When his Soviet captor grabbed his arm, Altner feared the worse. Then he realized he was not being led to his execution but being compassionately supported. See p. 229.
22 Pegler (2019), p. 6.
23 Pegler (2004). p. 239.
24 Blunt (2002), p. 75
25 Houghton (2018), p. 119.
26 Koskimaki (2002), pp. 136–7.
27 Slaughter (2007), p. 121.
28 Wurst and Wurst (2004), pp. 121–2.
29 Gavin (1978), p. 103.
30 Goodwin (2005), p. 5.
31 Woolhouse (2013), p. 473.
32 *Hamilton Spectator*, August 1, 1945.
33 Allen, unknown newspaper, June 16, 1944.
34 Koskimaki (2002), p. 227.
35 Burgett (1967), p. 155.
36 Gardner & Day (2009), p. 177.
37 Levitt, *Yank*. July 21, 1944, pp. 8–9.
38 Burgett (1967), p. 157.
39 Burns (2006), pp. 47–9. Burns fought through the war, jumping at Arnhem and fighting in the Battle of the Bulge, without a scratch.
40 Wurst and Wurst (2004), p. 140.
41 Slaughter (2007), p. 123.
42 Ibid, p. 128.

43 Ibid, p. 131. Postwar Couvains rebuilt its belfry.
44 Wurst and Wurst (2004), pp. 149–50. Watro survived the war and passed away on January 5, 2005. Postwar he worked for the Four County Library System in New York State and was, not surprisingly, both a fisherman and a hunter.
45 Pyle (1944), pp. 255–6.
46 *London Stars and Stripes*, July 11, 1944, p. 2.
47 Sasser and Roberts (1990), pp. 47–9.
48 Ibid, p. 59.
49 Shore (1998), p. 231; Baum (1943), §8; Baum (1944), §18.
50 Anon., *Paris News*, September 13, 1944, p. 8.
51 Gardner and Roger (2009), p. 127.
52 Hoge, *European Stars and Stripes*, July 25, 1949, p. 9.
53 Sutkus (2009), p. 13.
54 Ibid, p. 22.
55 Beetz (2018), p. 136.
56 Pyle (1944), p. 181.
57 Guarnere and Heffron (2007), p. 74.
58 Gardner & Day, pp. 287–97.
59 Egger and Otts (1992), p. 49.
60 Hastings (1984), pp. 149, 160–1.
61 Poschacher (2020), p. 118.
62 Chervinsky (2011), p. 25.
63 Rehfeldt (2019) Vol. II, p. 253.
64 Kaltenegger (2017), p. 76.
65 Degrelle (1985), p. 216.
66 Stinnet, *Wilson Daily Times*, December 22, 1944, p. 8.
67 Pavlichenko (2015), pp. 153–4.
68 Wacker (2005), pp. 18–9.
69 *ww2online.org/view/jimmie-kanaya#segment-8*.
70 Mather (1997), p. 269.
71 Cheall (2011), pp. 113–14.
72 Edwards (1999), pp. 88–9.
73 Ladd (1999), p. 197.
74 Edwards (1999), p. 90.
75 Barclay, *Winnipeg Tribune*, January 19, 1944, p. 4.
76 Edwards (1999), pp. 94.
77 Quoted in Horn (2003), p. 145.
78 Hastings (1984), pp. 252–3. 102d Cavalry Recon Squadron (2d Armored Division) commander Capt. Jimmy de Pew asked his men for suggestions on how to overcome the hedgerows at which a Tennessee hillbilly named Roberts wryly responded, "Why don't we get some saw teeth and put them on the front of the tank and cut through these hedges?" Men laughed but Roberts' suggestion inspired Sgt. Culin to fashion his device.
79 Cheall (2011), p. 116.
80 Gardner & Day (2009), pp. 311–2. When Galbraith first found the sniper rifle, the stock was broken. He replaced the stock with one scavenged from another rifle; hence his knowledge of the distinctive cut (see p. 251).
81 Anon., *Brisbane Courier Mail*, July 18, 1944, p. 2.
82 Edwards (1999), p. 114.
83 Letter from S/Sgt. Herman Vander Laan to wife Marcia republished in *Laurens Sun*, July 13, 1944.

84 Lodieu (2007), pp. 89–90. Note: the 2d Infantry Division units in the area included the 1/38th and 1/23d Infantry Regiments.
85 Ibid, p. 147.
86 Edwards (1999), p. 118.
87 Ibid, pp. 123–4.
88 Houghton (2018), pp. 121–3.
89 Hastings (1984), pp. 252-3.
90 Bilder (2008), p. 131.
91 Ibid, p. 132
92 80thdivision.com/oralhistories/WarrenCoomer.pdf.
93 Pavlichenko (2015), pp. 98–9.
94 Sandifer (2012), p. 111.
95 Anon., *Corona Daily Independence*. August 8, 1944, p. 1.
96 Bradley and Blair (1983), p. 304.
97 Dixon, *The Era*, August 29, 1944, p. 6.
98 Murphy (1977), pp. 212–5.
99 Brown (2003), pp. 195–7.
100 Shirley (2017), pp. 60–1. The book mentions a leather cover over the muzzle. Germans sometimes had metal muzzle caps but never leather ones as leather retains moisture and that would promote rust. They did have leather scope covers and his daughter, Jean Otto, in an April 2, 2020, telephone conversation with the Author, agrees he probably meant scope cover.
101 *Youtube.com/watch?v=zTaNjnGc0AA*. Interview of "Timberwolf" Division Pfc. Charles Duke.
102 Cheall (2011), p. 60.
103 Brutton (1992), p. 46.
104 Cosmas (1992), p. 229.
105 Yuliya Vladimirovna Drunina: "Zinka"—in "Memory of a Soldier, Hero of the Soviet Union, From My Unit."
106 Based on Cottam (2000), p16.
107 Khoury (2018), pp. 41–3.
108 Goodwin (2005), p. 168.
109 *ww2.org/view/george-sakato/#fighting-in-the-hills-in-southern-france*.
110 Per W. Darrin Weaver the weight of the scope, mount, and carrying case is 1.3kg. Weaver (2001), p. 245.
111 Ibid, p. 115.
112 Murphy (1977), pp. 221–4. For a variation, see Murphy, *Port Arthur News*, July 19, 1945.
113 Flagg, *The American Rifleman*, June 1998.
114 Soskil (2012), p. 65.
115 West (2010), p. 66.
116 Anon., *Alton Evening Telegraph*, November 29, 1944, p. 1. *The Stars and Stripes* of November 30 doubted whether this would actually take place "since the U.S. Army has taken over the garrisoning of Strasbourg."
117 Richardson (2014), pp. 80–1.
118 Ibid, pp. 94–6.
119 Vermillion, *Racine Journal Times*, February 27, 1945, p. 9. While a member of the 45th Infantry Division, West was involved in the July 14, 1943, Biscari Airfield Massacre. Charged with taking prisoners to the rear, West singled some out and sent them down the road under escort.

He then used a Thompson SMG to murder the remaining 37. What was especially damning against him later was when he reloaded with a fresh magazine and chest shot every fallen man. Concurrently, one platoon of 34 suffered a dozen casualties including medics who rushed to assist the wounded. Thinking they were opposed by snipers, Capt. Compton ordered the 34 prisoners' execution. A firing squad carried out his order. While Capt. Compton was acquitted, West was court-martialed, reduced to private and sentenced to life imprisonment. Collectively the killings became known as the Biscari Massacre.

Probably because of his inequitable treatment (Capt. Compton was acquitted) and the urgent demand for infantrymen, on November 23, 1944, West's sentence was remitted and he was restored to active duty and transferred to the 100th Infantry Division. Postwar West received an honorable discharge. See *military.wikia.org/wiki/Biscari_massacre* and *www.findagrave.com/memorial/14207015/horace-t-west*.

120 Wynne (1968), pp. 21–5. Hare was later awarded a Military Medal for killing four SS officers as they ran out of a house he was watching (pp. 55–6 and 62–3).

121 Miller, *The Daily Iowan*, November 1, 1944, p. 5.
122 Blackburn (2013), p. 152.
123 Cawthon (1990), p. 73.
124 Drabkin and Kobylyanskiy (2009), p. 284.
125 Deam (2008), p. 69.
126 Ibid, 94–95. There were other incidents of German soldiers discarding their uniforms and disguising themselves as civilians. For an incident in "Adolf Hitler Platz" in Thionville, France, see Anon., *Rome Stars and Stripes*, October 4, 1944, p. 6.
127 Koskimaki (2003/1), pp. 109–10.
128 Ibid, p. 49.
129 Burgett (1999), p. 35.
130 Ibid, p. 43. 1st Sgt. Sizemore survived his wound and passed away on January 18, 2000. See *old.506infantry.org/Memorial/lastrollcall*.
131 Koskimaki (2003/1), pp. 361–2.
132 Editorial, *Hutchinson News Herald*, September 26, 1944, p. 4. See also *honorstates.org/index.php?id-76284*. Lt. Spooner was killed in action in Leverkursen, Germany on April 7, 1945. He is interred at Plot N, Row 9, Grave 14, Netherlands American Cemetery in Margraten, Netherlands.
133 Burriss (2000), pp. 151–2.

134 Burgett (1999), pp. 154–6.
135 Arn (2006), p. 105.
136 Guarnere and Heffron (2007), pp. 142–3.
137 Cullen (2018), p. 86.
138 Lavender (1998), p. 26.
139 Ibid, p. 27.
140 *ww2online.org/view/arthur-staymeates-0#bronze-star-and-purple-heart*. Staymates returned to his platoon and served out the war. Postwar he and his men were guards at Nuremberg where he met Herman Goering and other high Nazi defendants. Lt. Arthur Kistler Staymates survived the war and passed away on April 23, 2017.
141 Wilson (1987), pp. 171–2.
142 Davis (2001), p. 58.
143 Ibid, pp. 70–1.
144 Ibid, p. 102.
145 Egger and Otts (1992), p. 93.
146 Lundhigh (2009), p. 65.
147 See *findagrave.com/memorial/112710967/herman-theodore-vander_laan*. He is interred at West Lawn Cemetery in Orange City, Iowa.

Chapter 6

1 Eisenhower (1948), p. 312.
2 This is outlined succinctly and well at the start of Chapter 21 in Bradley, Omar. *A Soldier's Story*. New York: Henry Holt, 1951.
3 Humphrey (2008), p. 77.
4 Gendelman, Max (2013), pp. 21–3.
5 *Checkerboard*, June 1, 1944, p. 2.
6 Gendelman, Max (2013), p. 25.
7 Ibid, pp. 31–7.
8 Wearly, *Checkerboard*, 3d Issue, 2012, p. 13.
9 Anon., *Galveston Daily News*, January 15, 1945, p. 15.
10 Anon., *Naugatuck Daily News*, July 21, 1945, pp. 1, 3.
11 To assist in the American war effort, its prisons paroled non-violent felons who could either serve in the merchant marine, war industries, defense road construction or defense industry. Some entered the armed forces with 200 from the California Department of Correction enlisting. See Anon., *Oakland Tribune*, October 6, 1942, p. 28.
12 Meller (2012), pp. 32.
13 Beevor (2015), p. 44–5.
14 *historynet.com/battle-of-the-bulge-us-army-28th-infantry-division-110th-regimental-combat-team-upset-the-german-timetable.htm*.

15 106thinfdivassn.org/stories/russell_lang-kriege.pdf.
16 Ibid.
17 Chodera, *Medina County Gazette*, March 13, 1945, pp. 1, 8.
18 Brotherton (2011), pp. 143–4.
19 Koskimaki (2003/2), pp. 406–7. The injured soldier was evacuated on a jeep by a medic. They were captured by the Germans who made the medic work at their aid station while a German doctor removed the bullet from the GI. Thanks to the prompt medical care provided by that doctor, the GI survived. The medic was later liberated and told Sgt. Karim of the GI's survival. Powers wasn't the only American who'd commit the trees and bushes to memory. Marine Corps Scout-Sniper Lawrence Kirby also did and would recognize if the Japanese had advanced during the night. Kirby (2004), p. 197.
20 Adkins and Adkins (2005), p. 121.
21 Anon., *War Week*, March 24, 1945, p. 1.
22 Weston, *War Week*, March 24, 1945, p. 4.
23 Wagnon (2016), p. 202.
24 Davis (2001), p. 122.
25 Bilder (2008), p. 132.
26 Malarky (2008), p. 189.
27 Parker (1991), pp. 291–3.
28 Eisenhower (1948), p. 394.

29 Malkin, *Winnipeg Free Press*, April 19, 1945, p. 3.
30 Anon., *Longreach Leader*, February 10, 1940, p. 16.
31 Lacey (2019), p. 40.
32 Anon., *Valparaiso Vidette Messenger*, February 14, 1945, p. 1.
33 Blunt (2002), pp. 209–10.
34 Hope, Maj. N. K. P., *RSigs in BAR*, 2019.
35 Bilder (2008), p. 220.
36 Summerby (2005), p. 24.
37 West (2010), p. 153.
38 Anon., *The Daily Banner*, Green-Castle, April 17, 1945, p. 2.
39 Goldberg, *Phoenix Arizona Republic*, April 15, 1945, p. 71.
40 Humphrey (2008), p. 147.
41 Ibid, p. 277.
42 Soskil (2012), p. 126.
43 *ww2online.org/view/john-jack-moran#crossing-the-rhine*.
44 Anderson (2003), pp. 28–31, 62–3.
45 Armstrong (1942), pp. 29–30.
46 Allen (1947), pp. 356–7.
47 Davis (2001), p. 232.
48 Bilder (2008), p. 223.
49 *Checkerboard*, June 1, 1981, p. 3.
50 *The Stars and Stripes*, December 7, 1944, p. 4.
51 Burriss (2000), pp. 187–90.

Chapter 7

1 German for "Drive toward the East", a 19th-century term coined for the Germanic desire to conquer Slavic territory. The Nazis viewed the Slavs as subhumans and their territories as *Lebensraum*—living space into which the Aryans could expand.

2 Sajer (1971), p. 365.

3 Lister, *The American Rifleman*, September 1942, p. 8.

4 Anon., *The Charleston Gazette*, March 6, 1940, p. 8.

5 Saarelainen (2008), p. 36.

6 Anon., *Victoria Advocate*, Feb. 29, 1940, p. 1.

7 Saarelainen (2008), p. 29.

8 Ibid, p. 30.

9 Ibid, p. 32.

10 Bowser (1998), p. 77.

11 Ibid, p. 174.

12 Ibid, p. 175.

13 Shore (1998), p. 97.

14 Pilyushin (2010), p. 88.

15 Ibid, pp. 94–6.

16 Nikolaev (2017), p. 29.

17 Ibid, p. 45.

18 Ibid, pp. 48–9.

19 Ibid, p. 51.

20 Pilyushin (2010), p. 207.

21 blavatnikarchive.org/12301. Interview with Isaiah Bondarev.

22 Mogan (2020), p. 36.

23 Pilyushin (2010), p. 252.

24 Zaitsev (2003), p. 210.

25 blavanikarchive.org/item5292. Interview of Epshtein.

26 Bogachev (2017), p. 352.

27 Anon., *Albuquerque Journal*, January 1, 1942, p. 1.

28 Pilyushin (2010), pp. 56–7.

29 Gorbachevsky (2008), pp. 180–4.

30 Ibid, pp. 122–3. During the German siege of Sevastopol, Gefreiter Gottlob Herbert Bidermann of the 132d Infantry Division observed: "We experienced rare occasions when individuals fresh to the front would surreptitiously creep along the earthworks, their hands held high in the air above the protection of the berm in hopes of receiving a *Heimatschuss* (lit: home shot—a small wound that would require repatriation) to ensure a ticket home." Bidermann (2000), p. 135.

31 Khoury (2018), p. 55.

32 Obraztsov and Anders (2014), p. 100.

33 Virski (1949), pp. 169–70. Sabina Dent also identifies the Black Marfusa as a character from a Russian Christmas story.

34 Vinogradova (2017), pp. 135–6.

35 Gillmore, *The Decatur Daily*. March 21, 1943, p. 2.

36 Zhukova (2019), pp. 118–20.

37 Alexievich (2017), pp. 10–2.

38 Ibid, pp. 10–12.

39 Vinogradova (2017), p. 244.

40 Ibid, p. 194.

41 Ibid, pp. 157–8.

42 Ibid, pp. 200–1.

43 Zhukova (2019), pp. 140–2.

44 Female presence in hospitals and higher recovery rate was first discussed in SJSU Professor Libra Hilde's book, *Worth A Dozen Men: Women and Nursing in the Civil War South*.

45 Axell (2001), p. 117.

46 Nicholas (2012), pp. 260–5, 295.

47 blavatnikarchive.org/item/23418. Interview of Irinia Botnar.

48 Vinogradova (2017), pp. 122–4.

49 Ibid, pp. 154–5.

50 Gorbachevsky (2008), p. 340.

51 Chervinsky (2011), p. 55.

52 Vinogradova (2017), p. 193.

53 Ibid, p. 194.

54 Mogan (2020), pp. 76, 122.

55 Ibid, pp. 105, 122.

56 Zhukova (2019), pp. 148–51.

57 Alexievich (2017), pp. 320–1.

58 Temkin (1998), pp. 2002–3.

59 Vinogradova (2017), pp. 258–60. See also Beevor and Vinogradova (2005), p. 160.

60 Anon., *Brownsville Herald*, September 28, 1944, p. 36.

61 Anon., *Daily Telegraph*, June 15, 1945, p. 4.

62 Anon., *Sydney Truth*, June 18, 1944, p. 13.

63 Anon., *Yank*, July 7, 1944, p. 4.

64 Altner (2002). Goebbels' order was limited to Berlin's collapsing perimeter.

65 White, *Arizona Independent Republic*, June 15, 1944, p. 19.

66 ww2online.org/view/joseph-motil#anecdotes-from-combat.

67 Anon., *The Stars and Stripes*, June 13, 1944, p 4.

68 Anon., *Cedar Rapids Gazette*, July 4, 1944, p. 1.

69 dmna.nu.gov/historic/veterans/transcriptions/Andriello_Sebastian_D.pdf.

70 Anon., *Lethbridge Herald*, January 10, 1944, p. 5.

71 Anon., *Troy Record*, December 1, 1944, p. 20.

72 Arvad, *Lincoln Nebraska State Journal*, June 27, 1943, p. 2. See also Anon., *Reno Evening Gazette*, October 2, 1944, p. 7.

73 Packard, *Harrisburg Daily Register*, August 28, 1944, p. 1.

74 Anon., *Oxnard Press Courier*, November 1, 1944, p. 1.

75 Anon., *Manti Messenger*, July 19, 1940, p. 7.

76 Anon., *Macon Chronicle Herald*, February. 17, 1943, p. 1.

77 Anon., *Wisconsin State Journal*, August 15, 1943, p. 4.

78 Anon., *Suburbanite Economist*, July 11, 1943, p. 1.

79 Lee, (Lincoln) *Evening State Journal*, September 12, 1942, p. 6.

80 Anon., *Lubbock Morning Avalanche*, Jul 9, 1943, p. 18. Also see Nunneley and Tamayama (1992), pp. 227–42 for first-hand accounts of Japanese nurses in Burma.

81 McManus, *Yank*, January 27, 1944, p .7.

82 De Giampietro (2019), p. 149.

83 Ibid.

84 Raus (1995), pp. 17–18.

85 Ibid, p. 120.

86 Ibid, p. 39.

87 Ibid, p. 4.

88 Lubbeck (2006), pp. 107–8.

89 Kononenko, *Winnipeg Free Press*, January 4, 1943.

90 airaces.narod.ru/snipers/index_m1.htm.

91 Anon., *Yank*, September 23, 1942, p. 4.

92 Pchelintsev (1943), p. 9.

93 Blitzstein, *Nebraska State Journal*, February 26, 1943, p. 11.

94 Pchelintsev (1943), pp. 10.

95 Ibid, pp. 26–7.

96 Ibid, pp. 51–5.

97 Nikolaev (2017), p. 60–72.

98 Pilyushin (2010), pp. 78–80. Pilyushin is the only source for Zina Stroyeva.

99 Anon., *Helena Independent*, May 2, 1942, p. 1.

100 Steele, *Syracuse Herald-Journal*, April 22, 1942, p. 9. See also airaces.narod.ru/snipers/m1/kalinin.htm.

101 Lubbeck (2006), pp. 126–7.

102 Pilyushin (2010), pp. 125–7.

103 Ibid, p. 148.

104 Ibid, p. 155.

105 Ibid, pp. 154–8.

106 Ivanov may be the M. Ivanov mentioned earlier.

107 Zaitsev (2003), p. 178

108 Brontman, *Nevada State Journal*, November 12, 1942, p. 11.

109 Ibid.

110 Anon., *Concord Enterprise*, May 7, 1942, p. 6.

111 Pilyushin (2010), pp. 174–80.

112 Lubbeck (2006), pp. 135–6.

113 Sauer (2020), p. 60.

114 Druzhinnza training included weapons' handling but without endowing the students with a killer mindset. See Petrovskaya (1959), p. 180.

115 Kyra, 265-83.

116 Pilyushin (2010), p. 211.

117 Ibid, pp. 218–19.

118 Ibid, p. 255.

119 Holt, (Hobart) *The Voice*, September 18, 1943, p. 2. See also Nichol, *Winnipeg Free Press*, February 19, 1943, p. 3 and Gilmore, *The Lima News*, March 28, 1943, p. 13. The author has found no such award as "Gold Star Heroine of the Soviet Union." The Mother Heroine gold star was awarded to mothers for having 10 or more children. In Gilmore's article they were posthumously awarded the Hero of the Soviet Union.

120 Pavlichenko (2015), p. 37.

121 Younger, *The Daily Independent*, September 24, 1942, p. 7.

122 *Iremember/ru/en/memoirs/snipers/antonina-kotliarova/*.

123 *Iremember.ru/en/memoirs/snipers/alexandra-medvedeva-nazarkina/*.

124 Anon., *The Evening Sun*, August 29, 1942, p. 3.

125 Anon., *Brownsville Herald*, September 21, 1942, p. 36.

126 Pavlichenko (2015), pp. 118–23. It is unfortunate that the Russian archives were closed while this book was prepared. Examination of Bommel's *Soldbuch* may yield invaluable information.

127 Pavlichenko, (Hobart) *Tribune*, February 19, 1943.

128 Pavlichenko (2015), pp. 161–3.

129 Roosevelt, *Laredo Times*, October 8, 1942, p. 2.

130 Anon., *Barnard Bulletin*, October 22, 1942, p. 5.

131 Anon., *Yank*, September 23, 1942, p. 4.

132 Pavlichenko (2015), p. 234.

133 Pavlichenko in (Hobart) *Tribune*, February 19, 1943.

134 Vinogradova (2017).

135 Beevor and Vinogradova (2005), p. 156.

136 Bastable (2007), pp. 106–7.

137 Pilyushin (2010), p. 26.

138 Vinogradova (2017), p. 86.

139 Regamey (2015).

140 Note: while a soldier may be awarded a honor or medal, it remained property of the state and could be confiscated if the recipient fell from favor or reclaimed by the state if (s)he died. See Taylor (2002), p. 257.

141 Pavlichenko (2015), p. 28.

142 Gebhardt and Tamony (1942), pp. 97–103. USMC Maj. Jacob Dent said the manual with instructions was issued by the Main Artillery Department of the Red Army on Military Inspection and entitled, *Instruction for Troubleshooting Artillery Weapon of the Red Army*. It was published by the People's Commissariat for Military and Naval Affairs, Moscow-Leningrad, 1934.

143 Mikhin (2010), pp. 47, 67.

144 Kobylyanskiy (2008), p. 95.

145 Regamey (2015). It is recommended that reader not only read Pavlichenko's memoirs published as Lady Death but also Lyuba Vinogradova's book, *Avenging Angels*. Vinogradova points out other discrepancies involving Pavlichenko.

146 Morin, *La Crosse Tribune and Leader Press*, February 28, 1943, p. 15.

147 Anon., *The Baltimore Afro-American*, July 25, 1942, p. 9.

148 Morozova, *Bay of Plenty Beacon*, July 20, 1943, p. 3.

149 Degrelle (1985), p. 108.

150 Ibid, p. 125.

151 Bartmann (2013), pp. 72–3.

152 Ibid, p. 77.

Chapter 8

1 Beevor (1998), p. 182.

2 Abdulin (2004), pp. 42–3.

3 Chuikov (1963), p. 72.

4 *blavatnikarchive.org/item2422*. Interview of Alexander Gak.

5 Beevor and Vinogradova (2005), pp. 154–5.

6 Zaitsev gives two different accounts. See Zaitsev (2003), pp. 95–96 and p. 265 for them.

7 Zaitsev (2003), pp. 100–1.

8 Ibid, pp. 113–14.

9 Holl (2005), pp. 89–95.

10 Wüster (2007), p. 125.

11 Chuikov (1963), pp. 97–8.

12 Zaitsev (2003), pp. 148–9.

13 Wacker (2005), p. 29.

14 Baum (1943), §C.2.

15 Zaitsev (2003), pp. 153–4.

16 Ibid, pp. 163–4.

17 Ibid, pp. 179–84.

18 Ibid, pp. 219–20.

19 Beevor and Vinogradova (2005), p. 160.

20 There was no actual Berlin sniping school. The closest was Döberitz which is 15 miles west of Berlin. Other World War II German sniping schools can be found in the table of German sniper training establishments on p. 66.

21 Zaitsev (2003), pp. 233–45.

22 Beevor (1998), p. 204.

23 Furness in Chandler (2001), pp. 94–8. See also Pegler in McKenney (2012), p. 134. Another account identifies the German as Maj. Thorwald. No records of him have been found either.

24 Chuikov (1963), pp. 142–5.

25 Beevor and Vinogradova (2005), p. 160–1.

26 Chuikov (1963), pp. 142, 279.

27 Beevor (1998), pp. 293–4.

28 Info from *warheroes.ru/*.

29 Bastable (2007), pp. 108–9.

30 Chuikov (1963), p. 191.

31 Winchell, *Port Arthur News*, May 1, 1945, p. 4.

32 Anon., Sheboygan Press, October 6, 1942, p. 1.

33 Axell (2001), pp. 110–15.

34 Baumgardner, *Tactical Shooter*, Vol. 3, No. 6, July 2000, pp. 14–16.

35 Shadel, *American Rifleman*, May 1945.

36 Anon., *Morgan County News*, August 3, 1945, p. 4.

37 Chapman (2017), pp. 216–7.

38 Wacker (2005), p. 64.

39 Kurowski (1992), pp. 269–70.

40 Kistemaker (2019), p. 107.

41 Schneider (2020), pp. 104–5, 188.

42 Anon., *Gasconade County Republican*, April 19, 1945, p. 1.

43 Anon., *Mackay Daily Mercury*, January 1, 1943, p. 6.

Chapter 9

1 In a humorous twist, the men of First Byelorussian Army referred to their advance on Berlin in German. Nicholas (2012), p. 206.

2 Reese (2003), p. 81.

3 Beevor and Vinogradova (2005), p. 161. Years later, two Americans, William Brophy and Francis Conway, acting independently of each other, did the same with a .50-caliber barreled weapon.

4 Pöppel (1988), pp. 100–1.

5 The other famous sniper in the 7th Company, 144th Regiment was Matthäus Hetzenauer. He didn't join until March 1944 when he was transferred over from the 379th March Battalion. See Kaltenegger (2017), p. 87. It is curious that despite being in the same company of the same regiment, Sepp Allerberger never mentions Hetzenauer in his memoirs.

6 Anon., *Mansfield News Journal*, August 5, 1943, p. 10.

7 Wacker (2005), pp. 14–16.

8 Ibid, pp. 19–20.

9 Ibid, pp. 31–2.

10 Ibid, p. 42.

11 Rauch (2006), p. 71.

12 Bessonov (2003), p. 44.

13 Ibid, p. 56.

14 Carrell (1994), pp. 425–6.

15 Heidschmidt's image may be seen in Spielauer (2007).

16 Sieger (2021), p. 63.

17 Law (1996), p. 62.

18 Scheiderbauer (2003), pp. 135–6.

19 Hartinger (2019), p. 25.

20 Wacker (2005), p. 80.

21 Historically the northern German dialect was Plattdeutsch or Low German, closely related to Dutch.

22 Steiber (1995), pp. 91–9.

23 Bessonov (2003), p. 133.

24 Ibid, pp. 134–5.

25 Hartinger (2019), p. 75.

26 Pavlichenko (2015), pp. 126–8.

27 Wacker (2005), pp. 100–1.

28 September 7, 2020, email from Harry Furness to author.

29 Jung (2003), pp. 198–01.

30 Ibid, p. 202.

31 Ibid, p. 205.

32 *blavanikarchive.org/item5504*. Interview with Solodar.

33 Gorbachevsky (2008), pp. 336–42, 368.

34 Mogan (2020), pp. 11–2, 19. While weaker in terms of personnel, Soviet corps could have

three divisions and Soviet armies three corps. Chuikov's Eighth Guards Army was structured in this manner.

35 Anon., *Galveston Daily News*, September 24, 1944, p. 14.
36 Mogan (2020), pp. 29, 32, 42, 67, 106, 122, 130, 135, 144.
37 Obraztsov and Anders (2014), p. 81.
38 Koschorrek (2002), pp. 191–215.
39 Pavlichenko (2015), p. 12.
40 Ibid, pp. 60–1.
41 Wacker (2005), pp. 45–6.
42 Nikolaev (2017), pp. 133–4.
43 Ibid, pp. 46–8.
44 Ibid, p. 60.

45 Ibid, pp. 60–1.
46 Ibid, pp. 62–3.
47 Ibid, pp. 69–71.
48 Ibid, p. 112.
49 Ibid, p. 124.
50 Pyľcyn (2006), pp. 110–11.
51 Wacker (2005), p. 134.
52 Sutkus (2009), pp. 10–11.
53 Ibid, p. 11.
54 Ibid, p. 12.
55 Ibid, p. 18.
56 Ibid, p. 14.
57 Ibid, p. 32.
58 Ibid, p. 39.

59 Ibid, p. 42.
60 Mikhin (2010), pp. 149–150.
61 Hartinger (2019), pp. 133–4.
62 Averbeck and Folkestad (2000), p. 60.
63 Drabkin and Kobylyanskiy (2009), pp. 161–2.
64 Bessonov (2003), pp. 214–5.
65 Beevor (2002), p. 162.
66 Pyľcyn (2006), p. 157.
67 Nicholas (2012), pp. 332–3.
68 Bogachev (2017), p. 352.
69 *ru.wikipedia.org/wiki/Пчелинцев,_Владимир_ Николаевич.*
70 *flicker.com photos/36919288%4ONO8/ 3548224139/.* Article on Chekhov.

Chapter 10

1 Berry (1982), p. 336.
2 Shore (1998), pp. 112–13.
3 Hewlett, *Oxnard Press Courier*, February 18, 1942, p. 1.
4 Lee, *Somerset Daily American*, January 26, 1942, p. 3.
5 Lee, *Butte Montana Standard*, February 16, 1942, p. 7.
6 Hewlett, *Montana Standard Butte*, February 1, 1942, p. 12.
7 Lee, *East Liverpool Review*, February 2, 1942, p. 3.
8 Anon., *The Auckland Star*, October 29, 1943, p. 2.

9 Anon., *Abilene Reporter News*, November 16, 1943, p. 11.
10 Benjamin, *Charleston Daily Mail*, March 1, 1942, p. 8.
11 Hewlett, *The Amarillo Globe*, March, 6, 1942, p. 1.
12 Lee, *Valley Morning Star*, February 15, 1942, p. 2.
13 Hewlett, *Moorhead Daily News*, March 6, 1942, p. 2.
14 Lee, *The Evening Huronite*, February 19, 1942, p. 14.
15 Anon., *Oil City Derrick*, January 20, 1942, pp. 1, 7. See also McManus (2019), pp. 97–100.
16 Lee, *Jefferson City Daily Capital News*, February 18, 1942, p. 4.

17 Remington Arms, *American Rifleman*, August 1944, pp. 32–4.
18 Dixon, *Oil City Derrick*, May 6, 1944, pp. 1, 12.
19 Dunlap (1948), p. 302.
20 Venturino, *Guns Magazine*, February 2011.
21 Wacker (2005), p. 140.
22 Shore (1998), p. 117.
23 Wahlert and Linwood (2014), p. 120.
24 Marien, *Peterborough Times and Northern Advertiser*, February 5, 1942, p. 4.
25 Marien, *Proserpine Guardian*, January 29, 1943, p. 1.
26 Anon., (Sydney) *Daily Telegraph*, February 12, 1942, p. 3.

Chapter 11

1 Berry (1982), p. 120.
2 Wahlert and Linwood (2014), pp. 121–2.
3 Anon., *Abilene Reporter News*, March 21, 1942, p. 2.
4 Wahlert and Linwood (2014), p. 123.
5 Anon., *Hobart Courier*, January 4, 1943, p. 3.
6 Mayo (1974), p. 59.
7 Anon., *Adelaide News*, September 9, 1942, p. 1.
8 Anon., *The Warwick Daily News*, October 12, 1942, p. 3.
9 *Intelligence Bulletin*, Vol. 1, No. 4, p. 5. The worst example that almost worked was a pidgin English cry, "Me American soldier. Give me medic—please don't shoot!" Heard by Pvt. William Harris Haarstad, he raised his head to look and was fired on. "When the enemy raised himself, Haarstad fired several shots. "I didn't know whether I hit him or not until daylight. I found the Jap dead in a foxhole several yards away. My bullets hit the mark." Anon., *Fairfield Daily Ledger*, March 18, 1944. The incident took place at Eniwetok. Haarstad belonged to Co. D, 106th Infantry Regiment. Sgt. Haarstad survived the war, passed away on October 27, 1966, and is interred at Washington State's Eatonville Cemetery in Pierce County.

10 Anon., *Sydney Daily Telegraph*, October 3, 1942, p. 1.
11 Anon., *Fremantle Mail*, January 1, 1944, p. 96.
12 Johnston, *Melbourne Argus*, November 10, 1942, p. 5.
13 Anon., *Singleton Argus*, November 6, 1942, p. 1; Johnathan, *MacKay Daily Mercury*, November 20, 1942, p. 6, and Anon., *Lethbridge Herald*, October 13, 1942, p. 18.
14 Anon., *The Record*, December 19, 1942, p. 1.
15 Anon., *Manning River Times*, October 20, 1943, p. 4
16 Anon., *Perth Truth*, January 3, 1943, p. 15.
17 Anon., *Adelaide News*, December 24, 1942, p. 2.
18 Anon., *Brownsville Herald*, September 11, 1942, p. 1.
19 Anon., *Sydney Smith's Weekly*, February 20, 1943, p. 16.
20 Anon., *Edwardsville Intelligencer*, December 23, 1942, p. 1.
21 Anon., *Alton Evening Telegraph*, January 7, 1943, p. 6. Postwar Gray worked for the U.S. Bureau of Prisons and retired as a colonel in the reserves. He passed away on January 8, 1972, and is interred at Schofield Barracks Post Cemetery in Honolulu. See *findagrave/memorial/74930411/ millard-glen-gray.*
22 Spencer, *Beckley Sunday Register*, December 27, 1942. Note: 1Lt. F. J. Endl and and Pvt. Ralph

Erno indicated that they were not marines but soldiers of the 127th Infantry Regiment. Spencer probably misled his readers so as not to divulge useful information to the enemy. Unfortunately, Lt. Endl was killed when he went forward alone to look for more Japanese. See Anon., *La Cross Tribune and Leader Press*, February 4, 1943, p. 15.
23 Spencer, *Reno Evening Gazette*, December 17, 1942, p. 6.
24 Anon., *Cumberland News*, December 22, 1942, p. 2.
25 Pfc. Charles Theodore Zuke passed away on April 24, 1982, and is interred at Forest Hill Cemetery in Evart, MI. See *findagrave.com/memorial/ 79634389/charles-theodore-zuke.* Col. Melvin W. Schulz passed away on February 22, 2001, and is interred at St. Mary's Cemetery, Muskegon, MI. See *findagrave/ memorial/110696220/melvin_w_schulz.*
26 Anon., *Escanaba Daily Press*, October 29, 1943, p. 3.
27 Anon., *Manitowoc Herald-Times*, April 15, 1943, p. 17.
28 Weston, *The Daily Advertiser*, January 8, 1943, p. 2.
29 Anon., *Newcastle Morning Herald and Miners Advocate*, January 9, 1943, p. 1.
30 Anon., *Perth West Australian*, January 8, 1943, p. 6.
31 Weston, *Hay Riverine Grazier*, January 19, 1943, p. 1.

32 Anon., *The Northern Star*, April 30, 1943, p. 6.

33 Anon., *Fremantle Mail*, February 13, 1943, p. 29.

34 Anon., *Alton Evening Telegraph*, January 15, 1943, p. 1.

35 Folkard, *Adelaide News*, January 20, 1943, p. 2.

36 Boni, *The Helena Independent*, January 17, 1943, p. 16.

37 Anon., *Hammond Times*, December 27, 1942, p. 1.

38 Anon., *Lincoln Sunday Journal and Star*, June 11, 1944, p. 4.

39 Barnabus, *Murwillumbah Tweed Daily*, August 15, 1945, p. 2.

40 Anon., *Neosho Daily Democrat*, December 17, 1942, p. 3.

41 Anon., *Perth West Australian*, June 22, 1945, p. 20.

42 Hewlett, *The Corpus Cristi Times*, May 17, 1943, p. 10.

43 Military Intelligence Division, War Department, Papuan Campaign, p. 82.

44 Anon., *Tipton Daily News*, July 12, 1943, p. 4. A member of the 4th Marine Division, Davis also fought at the Solomon Islands, Saipan, Marianas Islands, and Iwo Jima. He passed away in New Orleans, LA on April 13, 2014. See *obits.nola.com/obituaries/nola/obituary.aspx?pid=170698460*.

45 McMurtry, *Arizona Republic*, March 13, 1943.

46 Anon., *Marysville Daily Forum*, June 5, 1943, p. 7.

47 Anon., *Amarillo Globe*, April 2, 1943, p. 1.

48 Diamond (1992), p. 190.

49 Ibid, p. 191.

50 Anon., *Evening Independent*, July 6, 193, p. 6.

51 Anon., *Middle East Stars and Stripes*, June 25, 1943, p. 4.

52 Anon., *Adelaide News*, December 9, 1942, p. 2.

53 Stone, *Valley Morning Star*, January 7, 1943, p. 4.

54 Anon., *Hutchinson News*, May 14, 1943, p. 3.

55 Anon., *Hobart Courier*, October 5, 1942, p. 2.

56 Anon., *Northwest Arkansas Times*, January 27, 1943, p. 1.

57 Anon., *Port Arthur News*, April 13, 1943, p. 3.

58 McCallum, *American Rifleman*, March 1943.

59 Hampson, *The Paris News*, May 30, 1945, p. 5.

60 Anon., *Rochester Catholic Courier*, April 1, 1943, p. 43.

61 Anon., *Cedar Rapids Gazette*, March 23, 1943, p. 3.

62 McManus (2019), p. 357.

63 Remaly, *Endicott Daily Bulletin*, March 22, 1943, pp. 1–2.

64 Anon., *Dunkirk Evening Observer*, October 31, 1942, p. 4.

65 Wright, *Mason City Globe Gazette*, October 9, 1942, p. 3.

66 Tregaskis, *Salt Lake City Telegram*, August 29, 1942, p. 3.

67 Riley, *Phoenix Arizona Republic*, September 8, 1942, p. 8.

68 Sale (1947), Chap. 7, p. 59.

69 Anon., *Madison Wisconsin State Journal*, November 14, 1943, p.4.

70 Anon., *The Amarillo Globe*, January 20, 1944, p. 5.

71 Spencer, *Valley Morning Star*, November 27, 1942. Sgt. Byron John Griffith also served in Korea and passed away on December 21, 2004, in Salem, OH.

72 Hague, *Waterloo Daily Courier*, December 16, 1943, p. 19. GIs in Europe figured out the same trick and if the severed wire was jagged and there were tank tracks or other vehicle tracks over it, it was safe to repair. If however it was cleanly cut, the signalmen repairing the wire suspected an ambush and kept their eyes alert for hidden foe. See Sisson (2020), pp. 41–2.

73 Jones, *Norwalk Reflector Herald*, November 24, 1943, pp. 1–2.

74 Putney (2001), p. 49.

75 *usmc.edu/Research//Marine-Corps-History-Division/Information-for-Units/Shoulder-Patches-in-World War II/War-Dogs-in-the-Marine-Corps/* and Kluckholm *London Stars and Stripes*, February 10, 1944, p. 7.

76 Putney (2001), pp. 43–44. This is the only book I found on the subject of World War II Marine Corps war dogs.

77 Ibid, p. 39.

78 Anon., *Butte Montana Standard*, May 7, 1944. See also: Anon., *Alatoona Mirror*, May 10, 1944, p. 8; Anon., *Burlington Daily Times News*, July 15, 1945, p. 15.

79 Anon., *La Cross Tribune*, August 15, 1946, p. 2.

80 Anon., *Hagerstown Daily Mail*, April 27, 1943, p. 4.

81 Vitale, *Menard News*, January 11, 1945, p. 15.

82 Bright, *American Rifleman*, January 1945, pp. 10–12. Unfortunately, I was unable to identify whether Lt. Ross and his men belonged to the 33d or 37th Division.

83 Anon., *Van Wert Times Bulletin*, December 30, 1042, p. 1.

84 Anon., *Washington Court House Record Herald*, December 30, 1943, p. 1.

85 Wolfert, Pittsburg [Pittsburgh] Evening Eagle, July 22, 1943, p. 16.

86 Anon., *Racine Journal Times*, February 9, 1944, p. 4. Pvt. Rasonsky survived the war and passed away October 7, 1981. He is interred at Graceland Cemetery in Racine, WI. See *findagrave.com/memorial/184182936/frank-w_-rasonsky*.

87 Terry, *Freeport Facts*, March 2, 1944, p. 1.

88 Anon., *The Gastonia (N. C.) Daily Gazette*, February 12, 1943, p. 2. Craig was subsequently promoted to sergeant, survived the war, and passed away on March 9, 1968. He is interred at Friendship Baptist Cemetery in Murphy, NC; *findagrave/memorial/33795980/windom-guinn-craig*.

89 Johnson, *Northwest Arkansas Times*, September 3, 1943, p. 7.

90 Anon., *The Lowell Sun*, November 8, 1943, pp. 1, 3.

91 Makos (2013), p. 112.

92 Lait, *Charleston Gazette*, May 23, 1944, pp. 1–2.

93 George (1981), pp. 296–8.

94 Anon., *Arizona Independent Republic*, December 25, 1943, p. 5 and Anon., *Madison Wisconsin State Journal*, November 22, 1943, p. 9.

95 Anon. *Melbourne Argus*, November 16, 1944.

96 Anon., *Sheboygan Press*, June 9, 1945, p. 3.

97 Anon., *Humboldt Independent*, July 12, 1945, p. 1.

98 Hampson, *Moberly Monitor Index*, January 30, 1945, p. 3.

99 McGurn, *Yank*, January 19, 1945, p. 9.

100 Anon., *Big Spring Daily Herald*, May 21, 1945, p. 1; Miller, *Port Arthur News*, June 1, 1945, p. 4.

Chapter 12

1 Mace and Allen (2012), p. 227.

2 Worden, *Hope Star*, June 2, 1943, p. 1.

3 Mitchell (2000), p. 35.

4 Ibid, p. 59.

5 Ibid, pp. 80–1.

6 Annabel, *Burnet Bulletin*, June 10, 1943, p. 3.

7 Anon., *Troy Record*, January 2, 1943, p. 2.

8 Sherrod, *Time*, December 5, 1942, p. 11.

9 *usmc.edu/Marine-Corps-History-Division/Information-for-Units/Medal-of-Honor-Recipients-by-Unit/1stLt-William-Deane-Hawkins/* and Anon., *El Paso Herald Post*, September 25, 1942, p. 7.

10 Anon., *Sikeston Standard*, May 30, 1944, p. 2.

11 Brunson, *The Daily News*, February 1, 1944, p. 3. See also Zurlinden, *The Port Arthur News*, December 19, 1943, p. 48.

12 Zurlinden, *Madison-Wisconsin State Journal*, April 30, 1944, p. 11.

13 Citation from Congressional Medal of Honor Society (*cmohs.org/recipients/william-d-hawkins*).

14 Anon., *Oakland Tribune*, February 8, 1944, p. 5.

15 Lyons, *Endicott Daily Bulletin*, March 1, 1944, p. 4.

16 Anon., *Gettysburg Time*, December 4, 1943, p. 4.

17 Erikson, *Charleston Gazette*, November 29, 1943, p. 9 and Anon., *North Africa Stars and Stripes*, December 4, 1943, p. 2. See also McManus (2019), pp. 522–3.

18 Miller, *Yank*. December 24, 1943, p. 3.

19 Anon., *La Crosse Tribune and Leader-Press*, March 4, 1944, p. 7.

20 Tachovsky and Kraack (2020), p. 160.

21 Ibid, pp. 160–1.

22 Ibid, pp. 174–5.

23 Ibid, pp. 176–7.

24 Ibid, pp. 185–6.

25 Pyle, *Butte Montana Standard*, November 9, 1944, p. 4.

26 Anon., *Shannon Court Democrat*, September 21, 1944, p. 7.

27 Joseph, *The Raleigh Register*, January 15, 1945, p. 8.

28 Brunson, *Lubbock Morning Avalanche*, July 21, 1944, p. 6.

29. Allen, *Lubbock Avalanche-Journal*, August 27, 1944, p. 2.
30. Anon., *The Daily Messenger* (Canadaigua), March, 26, 1945, p. 2.
31. Anon., *Southern Economist*, September 20, 1944, p. 2.
32. Meyers, *El Paso Herald Post*, August 15, 1942, p. 12.
33. Worden, *The News*, August 8, 1944, p. 1.
34. Kirby (2004), pp. 211–2. There is no Col. Wexell and on p. 252 Kirby admits to changing names. The CO of 19th Marines was Lt. Col. Robert E. Fojt. Prewar Capt. Fojt served in China and Japan and returned to the United States in 1940. Postwar he rose to brigadier general and passed away on December 28, 1994. I could not determine if he was injured at Guam.
35. Anon., *Sheboygan Press*, August 19, 1944, p. 7.
36. Anon., *Dubuque Telegraph Herald*, February 11, 1945, p. 12.

37. Anon., *The Lee County Journal*, June 1, 1945, p. 4.
38. Handwritten note from Pfc. David Kong to author by his son, Dr. Stephen Kong.
39. Burgin and Marvel (2010), pp. 58, 76.
40. Ibid, p. 151.
41. Anon., *The Carbondale (ILL.) Free Press*, December 13, 1944, p. 6. Postwar McKnight became a physician and passed away at home on December 31, 1996. He is interred in an unmarked grave at the Swan Lake Memory Gardens, Peoria, IL. See *Findagrave.com/memorial/138595435/Clinton-eugene-mcknight*.
42. Anon., *Yank*, October 27, 1944, p. 3.
43. USMC Public Relations, *Yuma Sun*, June 11, 1945, pp. 1–4.
44. Weir, *Brownsville Herald*, June 21, 1945, p. 19.
45. Jap Hater., *Washington Citizen*, March 17, 1944, p. 6.
46. *Intelligence Bulletin* Vol. III, No. 11, p. 14.

47. Weir, *El Paso Herald Post*, May 28, 1945, p. 14.
48. Makos (2013). p. 270.
49. King (2014), pp. 183–4.
50. Williams (1945), p. 29.
51. Ibid, p. 40.
52. Ibid, p. 49.
53. Manchester (1979), pp. 5–6.
54. Anon., *San Mateo Times*, October 12, 1946, p. 4.
55. Finstein, *Middle Pacific Stars and Stripes*, June 21, 1945, p. 8. See also Geiger, *The Brownsville Herald*, June 21, 1945, p. 34.
56. Hilsman (1990), pp. 136–7.
57. *ww2online.org/viwe/william-disanza#segment-9*. Interview with OSS soldier Disanza.
58. Dunlop (1979), pp. 224, 309.
59. Anon., *Chicago South End Reporter*, March 28, 1945, p. 1.
60. Shore (1998), pp. 113–14.
61. *Combat Lessons*, No. 5 pp. 87–8.

Chapter 13

Many of the figures in this chapter are drawn from books such as Smith and Edzell (1983), Lapin (2013), and Doug Bowser (1998).

1. Houghton (2018), p. 69.
2. Skennerton (1984), p. 104.
3. Cotterill, *American Rifleman*, August 2003.
4. Ibid, pp. 202–6.
5. Anon., *Goomalling Weekly Gazette*, June 18, 1943, p. 4.
6. Anon., *Adelaide News*, July 17, 1941, p. 2.
7. Law (2004), p. 27–32.
8. Ibid, p. 61.
9. There is some dispute among published works as to the official designation of this rifle. Bowser (1998) refers to it as the M39PH and Pegler (2019) as the M27PH. As Pegler's work is the most recent and relies on M. Palokangas' *Sotilaskäsiaseet Suomessa 1918–1988* (Military Small Arms of Finland, 1918–88), a three-volume set probably not available to Bowser, I have decided to rely on Pegler.
10. Howell, *The American Rifleman*, April 1947, p. 11.
11. Wacker and de Vries (2011), pp. 18–22.
12. Karem and Steves (2017), Vol IIa, pp. 206–7.
13. Ibid, pp. 218–9.
14. Ibid, p. 348.
15. Karem and Steves (2017), Vol IIb, pp. 558–63.
16. Law (1996), pp. 122–3.
17. Senich (1982), pp. 298–9.
18. Senich (1982), p. 367; Law (1996), pp. 189–92, Spielauer (2007), p. 321 (English edition).
19. Karem and Steves (2017), Vol. IIb, p. 231.
20. Tantum (1967), p. 31 and Pegler (2004), p. 219.
21. Pegler (2019), p. 24.
22. Some of the rifles also went to Dynamo, a military-sport organization, and the *Osoaviakhim*. See *m9130.info/sniper-rifles*. Wartime demand resulted in some of these

23. Pegler (2019), p. 25.
24. Ibid, p. 67.
25. Czarist Lt. Col. Modrakh designed a periscope rifle which included a wood stock extension with a metal rod running from the trigger in the extension and connecting to the rifle trigger and a periscope. Two leather straps secured the extension the to M91/30.
26. Pegler (2019), pp. 47–8.
27. *blavatnikarchive.org/item/12271*. Interview of Mikhail Liderman.
28. Canfield (2004), p. 139.
29. Poyer (2012), p. 94. To date this book has the most technical data on the M1903A4.
30. Howell, *The American Rifleman*, April and May, 1947.
31. Poyer (2012), p. 90.
32. Canfield (2004), pp. 139–45.
33. War Department, *FM21-75*, pp. 171–2.
34. Crossman (1989), pp. 357–8.
35. Canfield (2013), p. 394.
36. Ibid, p. 424.
37. Poyer (2014), p. 18.
38. Ramage (1978), p. 143.
39. Sources: Senich (1979), pp. 61–4 and Senich (1996), pp. 3–4.
40. Law (2004), p. 43.
41. Senich (1993), p. 125.
42. Canfield (2013), p. 424.
43. Poyer, pp. 55–6. Star gauge as quality control tool was made obsolete by the Precisionaire air gauge that was easier and faster to use. See Brophy (1985) pp. 209–10. The air gauge is still used today by barrel makers.
44. Brophy, pp. 194–5.
45. Norton, *Garand Collectors' Association Journal*, Fall 2018, p. 19.
46. Norton and Stolinski (USMC NM M1903S).
47. *usmcweaponry.com/usmc-1903-a5-sniper-rifle/*.

units being shipped to the front.

Tim Plowman with Steve Norton and Andrew Stolinski.

48. July 27, 2020 email from Steve Norton to author.
49. Whelan (1944), p. 70.
50. Canfield (2004), pp. 150–3.
51. Crossman (1989), p. 347.
52. Ibid, p. 355.
53. Norton and Stolinski (USMC NM M1903S).
54. Norton, *Garand Collectors' Association Journal*, Fall 2018, p. 20.
55. Chandler and Chandler (1992), Vol. 1, p. 43.
56. Norton and Stolinski (USMC NM M1903S).
57. Norton, *Garand Collectors' Association Journal*, Fall 2018, pp. 16–7.
58. Poyer (2014), p. 69.
59. Nikolaev (2017), p. 48.
60. Ibid, p. 197.
61. Wacker (2005), pp. 100–1 and Pegler (2019), p. 64.
62. Truby (1972), p. 16.
63. Wacker (2005), pp. 88, 91–2.
64. Boyle, *Morning Avalanche*, September 3, 1943, p. 15.
65. Anon., *Cedar Rapids Gazette*, June 11, 1944, p. 1.
66. Law (2004), p. 64.
67. Anon., *East Liverpool Review*, June 23, 1944, p. 10.
68. Koskimaki (2002), p. 375.
69. Davis (2001), p. 53.
70. Shore (1998), p. 290.
71. McManus (2019), p. 322. See also *Intelligence Bulletin*, Vol. III, No. 5.
72. War Department, *FM5-20A*, p. 12.
73. Wacker (2011), pp. 72, 76, 30.
74. O'Keefe (2019), p. 28.
75. Anon., *Jefferson City Post Tribune*, October 23, 1940, p. 4.
76. *FM21-75* (1944), pp. 8, 10.
77. Anon., *Dungog Chronicle*, January 21, 1944.
78. *youtube.com/watch?v=NZqLm_dvU_s*.

Interview of Sam Bernstein, USMC. Bernstein volunteered for the engineers and became a camouflage expert. He received his instruction at Twentieth Century Fox Studio in west Los Angeles where actress Veronica Lake and other actresses instructed them in painting their faces with cold cream. Beige, brown, green, and burnt red were provided by Colby, Max Factor, and Elizabeth Arden.

79 Anon., (Annapolis) *Evening Capital*, December 11, 1943, p. 1. Postwar Dr. Owsley taught at UCSF medical school and passed away in San Francisco on November 3, 2014.

80 Center of Military History (1994), pp. 312, 321, 327–8.

81 Anon., *Greenville Delta Democrat*, December 22, 1944, p. 2.

82 *youtube.com/watch?v=T6WCFwUrKrA*.

83 Ibid, pp. 294–5.

84 Anon., *Hagerstown Daily Mail*, August 24, 1943, p. 10.

85 *designyoutrust.com/2017/09/futuristic-prototype-of-the-first-soviet-night-vision-goggles/*.

The website has deleted it but in December 2020 it was be recovered: *webarchive.org/web/20201020062344/https://designyoutrust.com/2017/09/futuristic-prototye-of-the-first-soviet-night-vision-goggles/*.

86 *russianengineer.narod.ru/tank/russianfrarot.htm*. See also Ponomarenko and Filachev (2007), pp. 2–7.

87 Weaver (2001), pp. 373–83.

88 Scott (1984), p. 147.

89 Senich (1982), p. 376.

90 Farago (1963), p. 28.

91 Jensen (2016), pp. 74–5.

92 *Kenosha Evening News*, April 16, 1946, p. 2.

93 Bellamy (2005), p. 171.

94 *arnhemjim.blogspot.com/2011/04/World War II-cutting-edge-night-vision-html*.

95 Gebhardt and Tamony (1942), pp. 56–8.

96 Norton and Stolinski (USMC NM M1903S).

97 Pavlichenko (2015), p. 102.

98 Patton (1947), p. 279.

99 Thomas (1978).

100 Lugs (1973), p. 191.

101 *sovietarmorer.wordpress.com/2014/11/01/BraMit-sound-suppressor/*.

102 Robert A. Steinler spoke with a German engineer for ammunition production. The Germans had a subsonic 7.92mm Mauser (aka 8mm Mauser) round that could be used in conjunction with their copy of the BraMit. See Truby (1972), p. 63.

Conclusion

1 Steiniger (2020), p. 154.

2 Chandler and Chandler, Vol. 5, p. 119.

One among many American propaganda posters promoting support for its allies. The subject of this particular of poster is a smiling Russian sniper armed with a top-mounted PE-scoped M91/30. He wears a Voroshilov Marksman badge and the prewar French Adrian helmet with a prominent Soviet red star emblazoned with the hammer and sickle. *Hennepin County Library*.

Glossary

2d/2nd, 3d/3rd—American 2d and 3d used throughout except for British and Commonwealth units which used 2nd/3rd etc.

ASTP—Army Specialized Training Program. U.S. Army program to send its brightest soldiers from basic training to college where they would be trained in engineering or other scientific fields thought useful to the army. Graduates would be commissioned. However, high casualties resulted in the termination of the program with the soldier students returning for advanced infantry training (or whatever branch they originated from).

APD—High speed transport (U.S. Navy designation).

BAR—Browning Automatic Rifle. American selective-fire, 20-round magazine-fed, hand-held, small arm used as a basis of maneuver by the U.S. Army infantry squad.

BR—British

Bren gun—30-round, magazine-fed LMG used by the British Army and Commonwealth nations as the infantry squad weapon.

Cartridge, caliber 30, ball, M2—U.S. Army designation for the .30-06 caliber rifle cartridge used in the M1903A4 Springfield, M1 Garand rifle, various machine guns, and BAR.

Comrades d'bataille—French system of pairing up soldiers to promote teamwork and for moral support. Battle buddy.

Co./Coy.—U.S./BR abbreviation for company.

CP—Command post.

Crocodile—Churchill tank adapted by addition of a flamethrower.

Desanti—Tank riders (Russian).

Druzhinniza—Field nurse (Russian).

Enfield—British arms company. Can be used in reference to the bolt-action .303in. caliber rifle or various .455in. or .38in. revolvers.

ETO—European Theater of Operations.

Fallschirmjäger—Paratrooper (German).

FG42—*Fallschirmjägergewehr* 42. Selective-fire rifle used by German paratroopers.

FM—Field manual (U.S. Army).

FOO—Forward observation officer (British).

Franc-tireur—Guerrillas, civilian combatants who harried the opposition. In the Soviet Union they were known as partisans.

Front—Soviet military formation roughly equivalent to an Allied army group (e.g. Karelian Front).

Frontovik—Experienced front-line soldier (Russian).

G&H—Griffin & Howe; American arms company.

Gebirgsjäger—Mountain soldier (German).

Gefreiter—German rank, equivalents: lance corporal (BR); acting corporal (US).

Ghillie—Servant in Gaelic. Ghillies were gamekeepers in Scotland. A ghillie suit is a camouflage suit (see p. 314).

IJN—Imperial Japanese Navy.

Jäger—Hunter (German). Applied militarily it usually meant light infantry.

Kampfgruppe—Battlegroup (German). It could vary in size depending on the resources and task at hand. It was generally named after its commanding officer.

Komsomol—Soviet communist youth organization. Membership was open to Soviet citizens from age 9 to 28.

LAC—Leading aircraftman (RAF).

Landser—Infantryman (German slang). Plural version is the same.

LCA—Landing craft, assault.

LCVP—Landing craft, vehicle, personnel.

LMG—Light machine gun.

M1 Carbine—Gas-operated, short-stroke-piston, magazine-fed .30in. caliber short-range shoulder arm intended to replace the handgun for officers or other qualified personnel.

M1 Garand—Gas-operated en-bloc clip-fed .30-06 caliber rifle used by the U.S. Army and USMC.

M1 Thompson—Simplified version of the M1928 Thompson SMG. It fired the .45 ACP bullet.

M1903A4—American 30-06 caliber manual bolt-action rifle. The "A4" was the sniper rifle version. M1903 is sometimes referred to by GIs as '03 or 1903.

Mauser K98k—Sometimes shortened to K98k or 98k, this was the standard German 8mm caliber bolt-action rifle used throughout World War II. It was licensed to be produced in other nations including Czechoslovakia, Poland, and Belgium.

MG42—German belt-fed machine gun capable of firing 1,200 rounds per minute. Firing at

almost twice the rate of fire of almost all other nations' machine guns, it was nicknamed "Hitler's buzzsaw" by the American GIs. It wasn't particularly accurate and the high rounds/minute meant regular barrel changes. It replaced the MG34 although both remained in service throughout the war.

Mustang—Marine commissioned from the enlisted ranks.

NKVD—People's Commissariat for Internal Affairs or Народный Комиссариат Внутренних Дел (*Narodnyy Komissariat Vnutrennikh Del*)—Soviet Secret Police.

NRA—National Rifle Association (in UK and United States).

Obergefreiter—German army rank equivalent to lance corporal.

Oberjäger—Luftwaffe paratrooper rank equivalent to lance corporal.

Osoaviakhim—Soviet paramilitary organization for promoting self-defense.

OSS—Office of Strategic Service.

OTC—Officer Training Candidates.

P08 Luger—*Pistole Modell 1908*. Toggle-operated semiautomatic 9mm pistol originally adopted in 1908 by Germany. Officially replaced in service in 1938 by the Walther P38.

P38 Walther—German 9mm double-action/single-action magazine-fed service pistol.

Panzerfaust—plural *Panzerfäuste*. Effective one-man-portable, hand-held German anti-tank weapon with a hollow-charge warhead. Versions effective from 30m to 150m.

PIAT—Projector, Infantry, Anti-Tank. One-man-portable, hand-held British anti-tank weapon with a hollow-charge warhead. Its major advantage was its lack of backblast, the projectile only igniting after it had left the projector.

PIB/PIR— Parachute infantry battalion/regiment.

PPSh-41—Tokarev 7.62mm caliber SMG designed for mass production and capable of being assembled by unskilled workers. Reliable, many were put into use by the Germans.

PzKpfw—*Panzerkampfwagen* (German abbreviation) —armored fighting vehicle or tank. Panzer is used today to mean a German tank.

Reichswehr—Armed forces of the Weimar Republic (1919–35), later expanded and renamed *Wehrmacht* during the Nazi era.

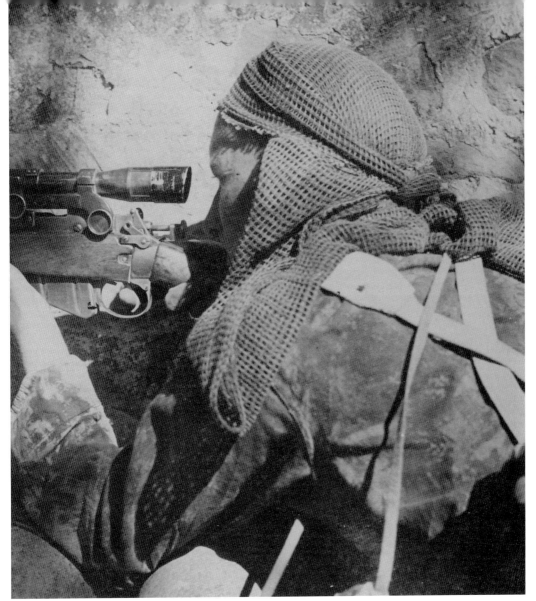

Pte. L. V. Hughes, Canadian 48th Highlanders, near the Foglio River in Italy. Note the rifle appears to be a 1931–33 Trials rifle converted to Mk. I sniper. Scope has an eyeshade. *NARA.*

RM—*Reichsmark* German currency 1924–48. At the start of WW2 2.50RM = $1US; at the end inflation had increased it to 10RM = $1US.

RM—Royal Marines

ROTC—Reserve Officer Training Corps. American military training offered to high school and college students.

RSAF—Royal Small Arms Factory.

Sambo—Russian martial arts system.

SA&MGS—Small Arms and Machine Gun Schools Corps (today, the Small Arms School Corps)

Scharfschütze and *Scharfschützen*—German for sharpshooter or sharpshooting and can be interpreted as sniper and sniping respectively.

Sergeant—Today the usual form of spelling. During the war, documents often use the older "serjeant." For consistency, this book uses sergeant.

Sherman—nickname for the American M4 medium tank.

SMG—Submachine gun.

SMLE—Short Magazine Lee-Enfield. British bolt-action rifle used during both world wars.

Starshina—Russian for sergeant major.

StG44—*Sturmgewehr 44* or assault rifle model 44. This stamped-steel construction selective-fire rifle fired a shorter mid-range rifle cartridge, the 7.92mm *kurz* (short) from a 30-round detachable box magazine.

Sturmgeschütz (StuG) III or IV—German SP gun on either the PzKpfw III or IV chassis.

T-34—Soviet tank featuring revolutionary sloped armor for greater protection, wide tracks for better mobility, and a powerful 76.2mm anti-tank gun (T-34/76). Later versions were upgraded with a larger 85mm gun (T-34/85).

Three Line—Russian nickname for the .30 caliber (7.92 x 54mm) Mosin-Nagant M91/30 rifle.

TOZ-8—Single-shot .22in. LR training rifle produced by the Tula Arsenal. A better finished sporting version was produced as the TOZ-9.

Unertl—Scope made by John Unertl and adopted by the U.S. Marine Corps.

UP—United Press.

Voroshilov—Marshal Kliment Voroshilov was People's Commissar for Defense of the Soviet Union who promoted military preparedness and marksmanship. A civilian marksmanship award and accompanying badge were named in his honor.

ZF—*das Zielfernrohr* = rifle scope (German).

Bibliography

Government Documents

Finland

Wartime Training Guide, No. 1, Sniper Training, Education Department, September 29, 1943.

Germany

Baum, John, trans. *Anleitung für die Ausbildung und den Einsatz von Scharfschützen,* Berlin, Oberkommado das Heeres, 1943.

Baum, John, trans. *Die Scharfschützen der Waffen-SS,* Berlin, SS Management Office, 1944.

Great Britain, War Office

51st Highland Division*, Intelligence from Alamein to Messina* (1943).

Army Training Instruction No. 9: The Organization, Training and Employement of Snipers. War Office, April 1944.

Army Training Memoranda: Nos. 29, 31, 37, 43.

Military Training Pamphlet No. 44 Notes on the Training of Snipers. War Office, 1940.

Small Arms Training, Vol. I, Pamphlet No. 1. Weapon Training, 1937. London: HMSO, 1939.

Union of Soviet Socialists Republics

Tamony, Paul M., trans. Central Artillery Directorate of the Red Army, *7.62 MM Sniper Rifle, Model 1891/1930r Description,* Military Press of the People's Commissariat of the Defence of the USSR, Moscow, 1945.

Gebhardt, James F. and Tamony, Paul, trans. Publishing House of the Central Committee of the Vsesoyuniy Leninski Kommunistichesky Sozyuz Molodyozhi (Young Communists Organization), *Sniper's Handbook,* 1942.

United States of America

Gebhardt, Maj. James F. *Leavenworth Papers No. 17 The Petsamo-Kirkenes Operation: Soviet Breakthrough and Pursuit in the Arctic, October 1944.* Combat Services Institute, 1989.

Training Memorandum Number 50 *Lessons from the Sicilian Campaign,* November 20, 1943.

War Department, *Combat Lessons,* No. 2, 1943, pp. 6–11, Walker, Lt. Col. F. L.: "Entering Towns."

War Department, *Combat Lessons,* No. 4, 1944, p. 50, Ross, Lt. Raymond H.: "Sniper Selection and Training."

War Department, *Combat Lessons,* No. 5, 1945, pp. 97–89, Jones, Maj. John: "Withdrawal Across a River Under Attack."

War Department, *FM7-5 Organization and Tactics of Infantry: The Rifle Battalion,* 1940.

War Department, *FM5-15 Engineer Field Manual: Field Fortifications,* 1940.

War Department, *FM5–20A Camouflage of Individuals and Infantry Weapons,* 1944.

War Department, *FM21-75 Infantry Scouting, Patrolling, and Sniping,* 1944.

War Department, *Intelligence Bulletin,* Vol. I, Nos. 2 and 4.

War Department, *Intelligence Bulletin,* Vol. II, Nos. 1, 2, 5, and 6.

War Department, *Intelligence Bulletin,* Vol. III, Nos. 1, 3, 5, 8, 10, and 11.

War Department, *Papuan Campaign.* Washington, DC: 1944.

War Department, *Tactical And Technical Trends,* Nos. 29 and 40.

War Department, *TM30-410: Handbook on the British Army.*

Williams, Lt. Col. Robert C. *Report on the Okinawa Operation.* Washington: HQ Army Ground Forces Army War College, May 1, 1945.

Letters, emails, & phone

Emails from Jacob Dent.

Email from Andreas Hartinger, 20 January 2020.

Email from Ben Hill, Feb. 2021.

Email from Nigel Greenway, 20 July, 2020.

Emails from Dr. Stephen Kong, 4 March, 2021.

Emails from Steve Norton, July 9, 2020.

Email from Philip Rosenkrantz, May 8, 2020.

Email from Herb Sheaner to author, 23 August 2019.

Emails from Natalia Smotrov, Nov. 21, 2021.

Email from RCMP Historian Mark Gaillard, CD & Chantal Renaud, RCMP Veterans' Association, Nov. 24, 2021.

Emails from Yulia Zhukova to author.

Email from Kai-Petri Hänninen to author, May 10, 2021.

Letter and email from Harry Furness to author, August 2020, September 2020. and December 2021.

Telephone conversation and text message with Jean Otto, 2 April, 2020.

Internet

Allen, Lee & Martin, Stephen T. "Herman Johann Friedrich Bottcher." Available at: *www. hermanbottcher.org.*

Arnhem Jim. "World War II British Special Forces Night Vision Technology—'Tabby' RG Receiver." available at: *arnhemjim.blogspot. com/2011/04/World War II-cutting-edge-night-vision-html.*

Anon. "'BraMit' sound suppressor." Available at: *sovietarmorer.wordpress.com/2014/11/01/ BraMit-sound-suppressor/.*

Anon. "Futuristic Prototype Of The First Soviet Night Vision Goggles." Available from: *designyoutrust.com/2017/09/futuristic-prototype-of-the-first-soviet-night-vision-goggles/.*

Anon. "Last Roll Call." Available at: *old.506infantry.org/Memorial/lastrollcall.htm.*

Anon. "Murrell Eugene 'Gene' Davis." 18 April, 2014. The New Orleans Advocate. Available at: *obits.nola.com/obituaries/nola/obituary. aspx?pid=170698460.*

Anon. "Rifles Part 7: Sniper Rifles." Available at: jaegerplatoon.net/RIFLES7.htm.

Anon. "John Wessel Spooner." Available at: honorstates.org/index.php?id=76284.

Blavatnik Archive Foundation. Bondarev, Isaiah. Interview available at: *blavatnikarchive. org/12301.*

Blavatnik Archive Foundation. Botnar, Irinia. Interview available at: *blavatnikarchive.org/ item/23418.*

Blavantik Archive Foundation. Epshtein, Mark. Interview available at: *blavatnikarchive.org/ item/5292.*

Blavantik Archive Foundation. Gak, Alexander. Interview available at: *blavatnikarchive.org/ item2422.*

Blavantik Archive Foundation. Liderman, Mikhail. Interview available at: *blavatnikarchive.org/ item/12271.*

Blavantik Archive Foundation. Solodar, Leonid Solodar. Interview available at: *blavanikarchive. org/item5504.*

Blavantik Archive Foundation. Zamarin, Mikhail. Interview available at: *blavatnikarchive.org/ item13547.*

Chambers, Pfc. Thomas R. "Three Enemies: German, Weather and Fear." Available at: *battleofbulgememories.be/stories26/us-army25/663-three-enemies-german-weather-and-fear.html.*

Chen, C. Peter. "New Guinea-Papua Campaign." Available at: ww2db.com/battle_spec.php?battle+id288.

Coomer, Sgt. Warren. "Memoirs of Major Sgt. Warren Kenneth Coomer." Available at: 80thdivision.com/oralhistories/WarrenCoomer.pdf.

Cottam, Kazimiera J. Soviet Women Soldiers in World War II. Hymel, Kevin M. "A Scout in Patton's Third Army." Available at: warfarehistorynetwork.com/2018/12/11/a-scout-in-pattons-third-army/.

iremember.ru/en/memoirs/snipers/alexandra-medvedeva-nazarkina/.

iremember/ru/en/memoirs/snipers/antonina-kotliarova/.

iremember.ru/en/memoirs/snipers/llavdia-kalugina/.

iremember.ru/enmemoirs/infantrymen/Vladimir-Zimakov/.

Isby, David C. "75 Years of U.S. Army Rangers: A Legend Begins." DefenseNetworkMedia, 1942.

Ivanov, Sergey. "Infrared rays are in service with the Red Army. The History of the creation of Soviet night vision technology." February, 2010. Available at: russianengineering.narod.ru/tank/russianfrarot.htm.

Kyodo, "Japan used chemical weapons during war against China and for the first time there's a military report to prove it." July 7, 2019. Available at: scmp.com/news/asia/east-asia/article/3017616/japan-used-chemical-weapons-while-war-china-and-first-time.

Kyodo, "Report Documenting how Japan used chemical weapons during Second Sino-Japanese War found for first time. July 8, 2019. Available at: japantimes.co.jp/news/2019/07/08/national/history/detailed-report-documents-japans-use-never-agents-second-sino-japanese-war/.

Lang, Russell E. "Kriege: Memoirs of Sgt. E. Russell Lang." Available at: 106thinfdivassn.org/stories/russell_lang_kriege.pdf.

Latimer, Jon (Warfare History Network). "The WWII Sniper: Caught in the Crosshairs of Famous Sharpshooters." November 17, 2018. Available at warfarehistorynetwork.com/2016/09/06/the-wwii-sniper-caught-in-the-crosshairs-of-famous-sharpshooters/.

Leefe, H. Col. John. "The West Nova Scout-Sniper Platoon. Available at: wnsr.ca/history/snipers.

National World War II Museum. "Disanza,William." Available at: ww2online.org/view/william-disanza#segment-9.

National World War II Museum. "Finkbeiner, Theodore." Available at: ww2online.org/view/theodore-finkbeiner#segment-3.

National World War II Museum. "Inouye Daniel." Available at: ww2online.org/view/daniel-inouye#segment2.

National World War II Museum. "Kanaya, Lt. Jimmie." Available at: ww2online.org/view/jimmie-kanaya#segment-8.

National World War II Museum. "Motil, Joseph." Available at: ww2online.org/view/joseph-motil#anecdotes-from-combat.

National World War II Museum. "Quigley Lt. Tom." Available at: ww2online.org/view/tom-quigley#hill-192-sniping-bar.

National World War II Museum. "Sakato, George." Available at: ww2.org/view/george-sakato/#fighting-in-the-hills-in-southern-france.

National World War II Museum. "Staymates, Arthur." Available at: ww2online.org/view/arthur-staymeates-O#bronze-star-and-purple-heart

New York State Military Museum. "Sebastian D Andriello, Technician 5th Grade, US Army, World War Two." dmna.nu.gov/historic/veterans/transcriptions/Andriello_Sebastian_D.pdf.

Norton, Steve & Stolinski, Andrew. "USMC M1903A5 Sniper Rifle." Available at: usmcweaponry.com/usmc-m1903-a5-sniper-rifle/.

Norton, Steve & Stolinski, Andrew. "USMC NM M1903S, M1903A1 Unertl Sniper Rifles & M1903A4 Sniper Rifles." Available at: usmcweaponry.com/usmc-national-match-m1903s-m1903a1-unertl-sniper-rifle/.

Pritzker Military Museum and Library. "Pritzker Military presents: Oral History of World War Veteran, U.S. Marine Corps Sergeant Lawrence Kirby." Available at: pritzermilitary.org/whats_on/holt-oral-history-program/lawrence-f-kirby-sergeant/#alt_podcast.

Schreckgengost, Gary. "Battle of the Bulge: U.S. Army 28th Infantry Division's 110th Regimental Combat Team Upset the German Timetable." January, 2001. Available at: Historynet.com/battle-of-the-bulge-us-army-28th-infantry-divisions-110-regimental-combat-team-upset-the-german-timetable.htm.

Spickelmier, Maj. Roger K. Training of The American Soldier during World War I and World War II. Master's thesis, University of Missouri, 1971. Available at apps.dtic.mil/dtic/tr/fulltext/u2/a185226.pdf.

Theise, SSG Jerome J., ed. History of the Three Hundred Twenty-Eighth Infantry Regiment.

328th Infantry Regiment, Verlagsdruckerei Wels, 1945. Available at ibiblio.org/mtivy/BAJ/328thpages/328page1.jpg.

Thomas, Vic. "Sniper Rifles of The Red Star." Available at: mosinnagant.net/sniper%20section/snipertext1.asp.

University of Utah. "Veterans Day Commemoration—Elbert L. Day." Available at: Veteransday.utah.edu/honorees/Elbert-l-day/.

USMC History Division. "First Lieutenant William Deane Hawkins, USMCR (Deceased)." Available at: usmc.edu/Marine-Corps-History-Division/Information-for-Units/Medal-of-Honor-Recipients-by-Unit/1stLt-William-Deane-Hawkins/.

USMC History Division. "War Dogs in the Marine Corps in World War II." Available at: usmc.edu/Research//Marine-Corps-History-Division/Information-for-Units/Shoulder-Patches-in-World-War-II/War-Dogs-in-the-Marine-Corps/.

Wikipedia. "Mariya Bayda." Available at: Wikipedia.og/wiki/Mariya_Bayda.

Wikipedia. "Vladimir Pchelintsev." Available at: ru.wikipedia.org/wiki/Пчелинцев,_Владимир_Николаевич.

Yuschenko, Alexander. "M91/30 Sniper Rifles" available at m9130.info/sniper-rifles.

Za Rodinu. "Anthony Chekhov—Teenage Soviet sniper at Stalingrad." Available at: flickr.com/photos/36919288%4ONO8/3548224139/ Sniper Chekhov 1942.

Findagrave

findagrave/memorial/27611823/elbert-lawson-day.

findagrave/memorial/184182936/frank-w_-rasonsky.

findagrave/memorial/129823154/lloyd-david-gunnels.

findagrave/memorial/110696220/melvin-w_-schulz.

findagrave.com/memorial/112710967/herman-theodore-vander_laan.

findagrave/memorial/56754519/hermann-johann_frederick-bottcher.

findagrave/memorial/74930411/millard-glen-gray.

findagrave.com/memorial/79634389/charles-theodore-zuke.

findagrave.com/memorial/14207015/horace-t-west.

findagrave.com/memorial/33795980/windom-guinn-craig.

findagrave.com/memorial/12938436/james-dyer-schloot.

findagrave.com/memorial/56655711/Gerald-j-gross.

findagrave.com/memorial/31205160/maynard-g-sullivan.

YouTube

Army University Press. "*France '44: The Red Ball Express.*" YouTube, September 3, 2020, *youtube. com/watch?v=T6WCFwUrKrA.*

Canada Strong. "Canadian Black Watch Snipers." YouTube, July12, 2017, *you.tube. com/9zmgjG3Wtn0.*

Docs&stuff. "German Sniper." YouTube, May 9, 2014, *youtube.com/watch?v=yNHeGrojUjg.*

glconceptsjw. "War Dogs—Canines in Combat." YouTube, March 15, 2017, *youtube.com/ watch?v=Vwv9CH.*

The Armchair Historian. "Life of a Soldier in Stalingrad: William Hoffman." YouTube, May 5, 2018. *youtube.watch?v=hrXGg4LRmbE.*

Michigan Military Technical & Historical Society. "106th Infantry Division in World War II." YouTube, December 6, 2016, *youtube.com/ watch?v=JtagCvGiJxy.*

Natick Veterans Oral History Project, Museum of World War II—Boston. "Larry Kirby World War II veteran U.S. Marine Corps." YouTube, January 28, 2015, *youtube.com/ watch?v=RvqPqqw0O3c.*

Natick Veterans Oral History Project, Museum of World War II—Boston. "(Sam) Berstein World War II veteran U.S. Marine Corps." YouTube, November 7, 2014, youtube.com/ watch?v=NZqLm_dvU_s.

Sputnikoff, Sergei. "Great books about Americans in Stalin's Soviet Russia." Youtube, May 24, 2019. Available at: youtube.com/ watch?v=YYZp8dhLqtM

Murrow, Edward R. "Person to Person: Basil Rathbone." Youtube. Formerly available at: *you. tube/g2F18zYO9u8.* Note: a partial transcription has been found at: *basilrathbone.net/biography/ ww1.htm.*

Formerly available at: *https://youtube.com/ watch?v=c5Sjs2gUDIE.*

Formerly available at: *https://www.youtube.com/ watch?v=v-ij45rESnl*

Newspaper articles

Anon. "35 in Group 31 Get Medals," in *Sikeston Standard*, May 30, 1944.

Anon. "45 Seconds Chock-Full of Action," in *The Lowell Sun*, November 8, 1943.

Anon. "A Bald Head Is An Enticing Target—Even to a Jap," in *Melbourne Argus,* November 16, 1944.

Anon. A. I F. Officer's Tribute to North Coast Soldiers," in *The Northern Star,* April 30, 1943.

Anon. Advertisement in (*Sydney) The Land*, May 29, 1936.

Anon. "Al Lust Back in Civilian Attire," in *Medicine Hat Daily News,* November 3, 1944.

Anon. "Albany Soldier Finds Nazi Woman Sniper," in *Troy Record*, December 1, 1944.

Anon. "Ambulance Plane Pilot Shoots Jap Sniper From Tree," in *Chicago South End Reporter*, March 28, 1945.

Anon. "America has its snipers, too!" in *Racine Journal Tines,* October 15, 1943.

Anon. "Army and Navy Camouflage Groups Observe Combat Demonstration," in *The Cornell Bulletin*, January 14, 1944.

Anon. "Army Develops new Camouflage Uniforms," in *Jefferson City Post Tribune*, October 23, 1940.

Anon. "Army Takes Wraps from Infra-Red Ray Weapons," in *Kenosha Evening News*, April 16, 1946.

Anon. "Army to Show Types of Guns Here Saturday," in *Cumberland Evening Times*, June 11, 1945.

Anon. "–And Pelelieu," in *Yank*, October 27, 1944.

Anon. "Artillery Studying 'Give-away' Sounds," in *Hope Star*, December 9, 1943.

Anon. "Australians Awake To Jungle Tricks," in *Singleton Argus*, November 6, 1942.

Anon. "Australians Halt Japs At Moresby," in *Brownsville Herald*, September 11, 1942.

Anon. "Berlin Warns British Against Civilian 'Snipers'" in *East Liverpool Review*, July 19, 1940.

Anon. "Best Shot Of War" Killed von Kleist," in *Newcastle Sun*, September 21, 1942.

Anon. "Big Game Hunter Uses His Skill in Killing Snipers," in *Alton Evening Telegraph*, January 15, 1943.

Anon. "Boot Display Is Drawing Interest," in *Hagerstown Daily Mail*, Aug 24, 1943.

Anon. "Brave Deeds Brings Honor," in *Winnipeg Free Press*, October 2, 1942.

Anon. "Brother, You'll Be Sorry," in *Rome Stars and Stripes*, October 4, 1944.

Anon. "Boy Scout Sniper Picking Off Japs In The Solomons," in *Northwest Arkansas Times*, January 27, 1943.

Anon. "Bravery of the A.I.F.," in *Adelaide News*, December 24, 1942.

Anon. "Calgary Heroine and 58 Service Men To Get Medals At Ottawa Investiture," in *The Lethbridge Herald*, December 1, 1942.

Anon. "Caught off Guard" in *Brisbane Courier Mail*, July 18, 1944.

Anon. "City Marine Back From North, Tropics," in *Bakersfield Californian*, June 5, 1943.

Anon. "City's 'Stay At Home' July 4 Program Draws Huge Audience," in *Evening Independent*, July 6, 1943.

Anon. "Colonel Hinds' School for Snipers," in *War Week,* March 20, 1945.

Anon. "Compassion In The Army," in *Sydney Smith's Weekly*, September 18, 1943.

Anon. "Condon, Portage, Bags Jap Sniper," in *Wisconsin State Journal*, November 9, 1944.

Anon. "Connie Mack to Be Honored At Local Dinner," in *Frederick News Post*, March 2, 1944.

Anon. "Cpl. Wehrli back from south Pacific action to aid in war production effort," *in Lincoln Sunday Journal and Star*, June 11, 1944.

Anon. "Crete Epic," in *The Auckland Star*, October 18, 1942.

Anon. "Daring Desert Dash By Free French Forces,' in *Launceston Examiner*, January 30, 1941.

Anon. "'Dead-Eye-Dick' Slays 216 Reds," in *The Charleston Gazette*, March 6, 1940.

Anon. "Dead Men's Tricks," in *Joplin Globe*. October 26, 1944.

Anon. "Deadly Sniper," in *Sydney Smith's Weekly,* February 20, 1943.

Anon. "Describes Capture of Woman Sniper," in *Brownsville Herald*, September 28, 1944.

Anon. "Dieppe Heroes Honored," in *Winnipeg Free Press*, October 2, 1942.

Anon. "Difficulty and Costly Getting News," in *Joplin Globe*, January 19, 1940.

Anon. "Dugger's Signals Annoy German Sniper," in *Newcastle Sun*, October 4, 1941.

Anon. "Earle Had Narrow Escape," in *East Liverpool Review*, December 17, 1942.

Anon. "East Texas Marine Sniper Loses One Eye In Driving Off Big Party of Japanese Troops To Protect Mates," in *Port Arthur News*, April 13, 1943.

Anon. "End of Sniper. Shot by Tank Officer," in *Perth West Australian*, January 8, 1943.

Anon. "Enemy Halted," in *Auckland Star*, October 9, 1942.

Anon. "European Conflict—More Canadians Arrive," in *Longreach Leader*, February 10, 1940.

Anon. "Eyewitness Account of Landing in Italy Given by Sergeant from Mexia," in *Mexia Weekly Herald*, December 10, 1943.

Anon. "Fast Man When it Comes to Thinking About Food," in *Lowell Sun*, March 8, 1944

Anon. "Feminine Sniper Tells Her Story," in *The Evening Sun*, August 29, 1942

Anon. "Fifty-Three of the 394th's Best Shots Attend Sniper School," in *Checkerboard*, June 21, 1944.

Anon. "Fighting in New Guinea," in *Manning River Times*, October 20, 1943.

Anon. "Fire Power!" in, *East Liverpool Review*, June 23, 1944.

Anon. "Five Jap Snipers Bagged by Ohioan," in *Washington Court House Record Herald*, December 30, 1943.

Anon. "Five Russian Snipers Kill 1,860 Germans," in *Tipton Daily Tribune*, October 5, 1942.

Anon. "Flame-Thrower Cuts Down Sniper's Tree," in *Oakland Tribune*, February 8, 1944.

Anon. "Forgotten Man… in Cig Shortage," in *Mason City Globe Gazette*, November 22, 1944.

Anon. "Former Millbank Clerk Shoots German Sniper," in *The Evening Huronite*, August 21, 1942.

Anon. "Frank Kviatek Is Given Decoration," in *The Lawton Constitution*, May 20, 1945.

Anon. "French to Kill 5 Hostages for Each Soldier Slain by Sniper," in *Alton Evening Telegraph*, November 29, 1944.

Anon. "Front-Line Headlines," in *Perth Truth*, January 3, 1943.

Anon. "Germans Admit Australians Superiority," in *Echuca Riverine Herald*, August 2, 1941.

Anon. "Georgia Flamethrower With 'Here's Your Infantry' Unit Coming to Albany Monday," in *The Lee County Journal*. June 1, 1945.

Anon. "German Sniper Tells of Shooting Five Americans," in *Galveston Daily News*, January 15, 1945.

Anon. "German Sniper Pays With His Life In Wounding Lewis Creddo, Local Soldier," in *Naugatuck Daily News*, July 21, 1945.

Anon. "Gilbert Victory Ranked As Marines' Bloodiest," in *North Africa Stars and Stripes*, December 4, 1943.

Anon. "Glass 'Ornaments' Saves Lives in War," in *Morgan County News*, August 3, 1945.

Anon. "Glen Gray Lauded For Marksmanship," in *Alton Evening Telegraph*, January 7, 1944.

Anon. "Groomalling V.D.C.," in *Toodyay Herald*, January 22, 1943.

Anon. "Great Britain Training An Army of Sharp-shooters," in *Brandon Daily Sun*, July 5, 1940.

Anon. "Greek Advance Slowed By Cold And Snow In The Mountain Areas," in *Chester Times*, December 17, 1942.

Anon. "Half of 4600 Prison Paroleees Now Helping Win the War," in *Oakland Tribune*, October 6, 1942.

Anon. "Have You Any Ideas for Secret Weapons?," in *Shannon Court Democrat*, September 21, 1944.

Anon. "Heads Sniper School," in *Brandon Daily Sun*, January 8, 1943.

Anon. "Hero of Crete," in *Auckland Star*, October 17, 1941.

Anon. "Hero of Okinawa Now Stanford Star," in *San Mateo Times*, October 12, 1946.

Anon. "Heroic Deeds Briefly Told In Citations," in *Winnipeg Tribune*, October 2, 1942.

Anon. "'Hey' Only A dog, Cited For Helping Allied Forces Dispose of Jap Sniper," in *Hagerstown Daily Mail*, April 27, 1943.

Anon. "Highest U.S. Decoration Won by Young Officer in Fight in Which He Died," in *Oil City Derrick*, January 20, 1942.

Anon. "Highly Trained 'Devil Dogs' Prove Value With Heroic Deeds in Marine Combat Engagements in South Pacific War Zone," in *Butte Montana Standard*, May 7, 1944.

Anon. "Hold Memorial Services For Marion Beebe," in *Jefferson Bee*, August 10, 1948.

Anon. "How the A.I.F. Out-Sniped The Jap," in *Sydney Smiths Weekly*, April 17, 1943.

Anon. "How Red Army Pools Its Ideas," in *Concord Enterprise*, May 7, 1942.

Anon. "In A Nutshell," in *The National Advocate* (Bathhurst), June 2, 1945.

Anon. "Ingenious," in *Sydney Truth*, June 18, 1944.

Anon. "Inside Story of Japanese Life On Attu and Kiska Told Masonic Club By Red Cross Writer At Luncheon," in *Palm Springs Sun*, December 3, 1943.

Anon. "Italian Partisans Who Helped Mop Up Germans," in *Reno Evening Gazette*, October 2, 1944.

Anon. "Invasion Flashes," in *The Stars and Stripes*, June 13, 1944.

Anon. "Jap Sniper's English Didn't Deceive U.S. Marine," in *Fremantle Mail*, January 1, 1944.

Anon. "Japanese Dog Captured on Guam Now Serving With Leathernecks," in *The Daily Messenger* (Canadaigua), March 26, 1945.

Anon. "Japanese Sniper Is Decapitated By Observation Plane," in *Sheboygan Press*, August 19, 1944.

Anon. "Jap. Sniper Out-Sniped," in *The Warwick Daily News*. October 12, 1942.

Anon. "Japs Got Own Pearl Harbor," in *Wisconsin State Journal*, August 15, 1943.

Anon. "Japs More Like Wild Animals Than Men," in *The Record*, December 19, 1942.

Anon. "Japs Out of Runing When Lowell Irishman and Italian Pal Team Up," in *Lowell Sun*, April 8, 1944.

Anon. "Japs Shed Shoe To Climb Trees," in *Abilene Reporter News*, November 16, 1943.

Anon. "Japs Then Shot Themselves," in *Hobart Courier*, October 5, 1942.

Anon. "Jungle Tricks," in *Lethbridge Herald*, October 13, 1942.

Anon. "Kenneth E. Gibbons Promoted to Corporal," in *Salamanca Republican Press*, January 8, 1943.

Anon. "King George Head Sniper," in (Sydney) *Daily Telegraph*, August 27, 1940.

Anon. "Kuban Struggle Goes On," in *Perth Daily News*, June 2, 1943.

Anon. "L/393 veteran seeks Purple Heart for wounds" in *Checkerboard*, 1st issue, 1998.

Anon. "Leave It to The Tankers to Think of One Like This," in *Middle East Stars and Stripes*. June 25, 1943.

Anon. "Liberal Man Home From The Pacific With Many Trinkets," in *The Hutchinson*, May 14, 1943.

Anon. "Life-Saving Hat," in *Madison Wisconsin State Journal*, November 22, 1943.

Anon. "Lone Nazi Sniper Picks Off Yanks From Church Top," in *Valparaiso Vidette Messenger*, February 14, 1945.

Anon. "Long Underwear Hides Yanks From German Sniper Bullets," in *Greenville Delta Democrat*, December 22, 1944.

Anon. "Look Out Below," in *Mason City Globe Gazette*, December 22, 1942.

Anon. "Man Gets Lady," in *Yank*, July 7, 1944.

Anon. "Marine Describes Solomons Battle 'Slaughter' Of Japs," in *El Paso Herald Post*, September 25, 1942.

Anon. "Marines Give Japs Surprise," in *Madison Wisconsin State Journal*, November 14, 1943.

Anon. "Marine's Luck News To Wife," in *Arizona Independent Republic*, December 25, 1943.

Anon. "Marines Need 60 Dogs - Doberman, German Shepard," in *Southern Economist*, September 20, 1944.

Anon. "Marine Tells How Jap Beat Him Into Unconsciousness," in *Dunkirk Evening Observer*, October 31, 1942.

Anon. "Marine War Dogs Prove Their Value in Action," in *Alatoona Mirror*, May 10, 1944.

Anon. "Milne Bay Ambush," in *Adelaide News*, September 9, 1942.

Anon. "Minnesota Ranger Shoots Nazi Sniper in Raid at Dieppe," in *The Evening Tribune*, August 21, 1942.

Anon. "Mortarman From Dauphin Acts As Sniper In Italy," in *Winnipeg Free Press*, January 15, 1945.

Anon. "Mounted Scout and Snipers Set Pace For Canadians," in *Brandon Daily Sun*, August 11, 1943.

Anon. "Nature's Aid In Army Camouflage," in *Sydney Sun*, September 1, 1941.

Anon. "Nazi Attack On King," in *The West Australian*, August 27, 1940.

Anon. "Nazi Diaper Sniper, Snared by Americans," in *The Stars and Stripes*, December 7, 1944.

Anon. "Nazi Army Faced With Grave Ordeal," in *Mansfield News Journal*, August 5, 1943.

Anon. "Nazis Use Wood Bullets on Yanks," in *Cedar Rapids Gazette*, June 11, 1944.

Anon. "Neat Strategy Bagged Sniper," in *Troy Record*, January 2, 1943.

Anon. "Nelson, WPB is Called Sniper," in *Escanaba Daily Press*, August 26, 1944.

Anon. "News Flash," in *San Mateo Times*, July 14, 1943.

Anon. "News of Boys," in *The Daily Banner, Green-Castle*, April 17, 1945.

Anon. "News Of Men And Women In The Service," in *Gasconade County Republican*, April 19, 1945.

Anon. "News of Our Men in Uniform," in *The Carbondale (ILL.) Free Press*, December 13, 1944.

Anon. "Norwegian Irregulars," in (Hanover, PA) *The Evening Sun*, April 12, 1940.

Anon. "Now You See Him—Now You Don't," in *Dungog Chronicle*, January 21, 1944.

Anon. "Officer Says 'God; Medics' Saved His Life," in *Fitchburg Sentinel*, March. 12, 1943.

Anon. "Ohioan Kills Five Japanese Snipers," in *Van Wert Times Bulletin*, December 30, 1042.

Anon. "One-Man Warfare: The Sniper's Craft," in *Perth West Australian*, November 5, 1940.

Anon. "One Shot By Yank Sniper Permits Town's Capture," in *Corona Daily Independence*, August 8, 1944.

Anon. "Only Two Shots Per Jap Sniper For Major Gen.," in *Cedar Rapids Gazette*, March 23, 1943.

Anon. "Pacific General Gets 'Call Down.' Uses Up 8 shots to Bag Jap Sniper," in *Rochester Catholic Courier*, April 1, 1943.

Anon. "Papuan M. M. Winner is Leading Sniper," in *Hobart Courier*, January 4, 1943.

Anon. "Patton Commends 90th Division," in *Rolfe Arrow*, January 4, 1945.

Anon. "Peasant Sniper Who Shot 219 Russians Given Holiday," in *Victoria Advocate*, February 29, 1940.

Anon. "Pet Dogs Are Doing Great Job in American War Effort," in *Burlington Daily Times News*, July 15, 1945.

Anon. "Pfc. Weldon Miller and Wife Visit in Madison," in *Moberly Monitor*, September 28, 1945.

Anon. "Platoon of Soviet Snipers Kills 2100 Germans in Month," in *Neosho Daily Democracy*, November 7, 1942.

Anon. "Pvt. George Burr Dies in Action in France," in *Brewster Standard*, August 10, 1944.

Anon. "Pvt. Martin Richie of Escanaba Describes Jap Cruelties in New Guinea," *in Escanaba Daily Press*, October 29, 1943.

Anon. "Red Cross Hears Blood Plasma Is Placed Above Surgery And Sulfa Drugs In Saving Lives," in (Annapolis) *Evening Capital*, December 11, 1943.

Anon. "Red Score General Advance," in *Ames Daily Tribune*, October 7, 1942.

Anon. "Reds Organize Contest for Scalps of Nazis," in *Helena Independent*, May 2, 1942.

Anon. "Reds Push Far Beyond Ceded Land," in *Hutchinson News*, June 29, 1940.

Anon. "Roland Blackburn Killed in Belgium," in *Jefferson Herald*, February 15, 1945.

Anon. "Rover And Fido Becomes Vets As Dogs Proved Worth In War," in *La Cross Tribune*, August 15, 1946.

Anon. "Russian Women At War," in *Adelaide Advertiser*, March 18, 1944.

Anon. "S. H. Patton, Jr. Given Citation," in *San Marino Tribune*, March 16, 1944.

Anon. "Saved By Dog Tag," in *Dubuque Telegraph Herald*, February 11, 1945.

Anon. "Service Men in the News: Murley Gets Jap Sniper," in *The Amarillo Globe*, January 20, 1944.

Anon. "She Got 309 Nazis," in *Yank*, September 23, 1942.

Anon. "Shooting Snipers On the Wing," in *Adelaide News*, December 9, 1942.

Anon. "Shot 100 Japs," in *Fairfield Daily Ledger*, April 24, 1943.

Anon. "Sniper," in *Manti Messenger*, July 19, 1940.

Anon. "Sniper," in *Sydney Daily Telegraph*, May 7, 1944.

Anon. "Sniper Dodges Bullets," in *Perth Daily News*, January 17, 1940.

Anon. "Sniper Duel Won By Queenslander," in *The Courier-Mail*, June 24, 1941.

Anon. "Snipers Harry Nippon Push Across Guinea," in *Abilene Reporter News*, March 21, 1942.

Anon. "Sniper is Where Wounded Soldier Thought He Was," in *Sheboygan Press*, June 9, 1945.

Anon. "Snipers in Training," in *Auckland Star*, January 27, 1941.

Anon. "Sniper Picks Plump Japs," in (Sydney) *Daily Telegraph*, February 12, 1942.

Anon. "Sniper Queen's Nephew," in *Auckland Star*, July 17, 1943.

Anon. "Snipers' Rifles Fired in South Australia for the First Time," in *Adelaide News*, July 17, 1941.

Anon. "Sniper Slays Bayonet Expert," in *The Berkeley Evening Eagle*, October 5, 1944.

Anon. "So They Say," in *Brownsville Herald*, September 21, 1942.

Anon. "Social Happenings: East Berlin," in *Gettysburg Time*, December 4, 1943.

Anon. "Soft Drink Stand Lear's Hideaway; Headers of General Artfully Camouflaged, Snipers Too," in *The Charleston Gazette*, September 13, 1941.

Anon. "Soldier Gets Jap War Bond," in *Racine Journal Times*, February 9, 1944.

Anon. "Soldiers See 'Spider Holes,'" in *La Crosse Tribune and Leader-Press*, March 26, 1943.

Anon. "Soviet Relief Column Pounds Along River," in *Sheboygan Press*, October 6, 1942.

Anon. "Soviet Russia's Moves Are Still In Doubt," in *Brandon Daily Sun*, June 29, 1940.

Anon. "Soviets Storm Orel, Important Defense Point; Ski Troops Threaten To Overrun Lines on Rzhev-Bryansk Sector," in *Albuquerque Journal*, January 1, 1942.

Anon. "Squirrel hunter Wounded after he Bags 22 Japs," in *Cumberland News*, December 22, 1942.

Anon. "Stars and Stripes," in *Laurens Sun*, July 13, 1944.

Anon. "Stephens Youth Killed In France," in *Camden News* (Arkansas), January 3, 1945.

Anon. "Story of Buna Told," in *Neosho Daily Democrat*, December 17, 1942.

Anon. "Strategic Yamil," in *Perth West Australian*, June 22, 1945.

Anon. "Surprise Drops From Sky into Anzac's Arms; Guess What/ A Nazi Parachute Trooper," in *Salt Lake Tribune*, November 16, 1941

Anon. "Talk of the Town," in *Fremantle Mail*, February 13, 1943.

Anon. "Tanks Surprised Japs: Shook Snipers Out Of Trees," in Newcastle *Morning Herald and Miners Advocate*, January 9, 1943.

Anon. "Tanks Took Japanese by Surprise," in *Mackay Daily Mercury*, January 1, 1943.

Anon. "Tells of Shooting a Woman Sniper," in *Marysville Daily Forum*. June 5, 1943.

Anon. "Tennessee Youth Is Sure Shot: Gets 47 Japs in Guadacanal," in *Tipton Daily News*, July 12, 1943.

Anon. "The Oxnarder," in *Oxnard Press Courier*, November 1, 1944.

Anon. "The Sniper: War's Most Dangerous Man," in *The Mackay Daily Mercury*, June 29, 1942.

Anon. "They Wouldn't Let Him Bring Back Jap Scalp," in *Amarillo Globe*, April 2, 1943.

Anon. "This Marine Finds Sniper Is a Woman," in *Suburbanite Economist*, July 11, 1943.

Anon. "Today's American Heroes," in *Victoria Advocate*, October 4, 1942.

Anon. "Top of Tree Shot Off Before Jap Is Killed," in *Edwardsville Intelligencer,* December 23, 1942.

Anon. "Troops Learn Jap Tricks," in *Sydney Daily Telegraph*, October 3, 1942.

Anon. "Two Women Snipers Caught by Invaders," in *Daily Telegraph,* June 15, 1945.

Anon. "Urge Second Front In '42," *Barnard Bulletin*, October 22, 1942.

Anon. "U.S. Air Awards Are Announced," *in La Cross Tribune and Leader Press*, February 4, 1943.

Anon. "U.S. Tank Tips Off Jap Sniper's Presence," in *La Crosse Tribune and Leader-Press*, March 4, 1944.

Anon. "Utility Lineman Climbs Tree and Picks Off Japs," in *Hammond Times*, December 27, 1942.

Anon. "Vernon Tompkins Tells of Fighting the Japanese," in *Humboldt Independent*, July 12, 1945.

Anon. "Veteran of Buna Tells Of Jap Fighters' Treachery," in *Manitowoc Herald-Times*, April 15, 1943.

Anon. "V. D. C. Activities," in *Mount Gambier Border Watch*, August 17, 1943.

Anon. "Westerner Head of Sniper School," in *Brandon Daily Sun*, September 16, 1944.

Anon. "What the War Costs You," in *Goomalling Weekly Gazette*, June 18, 1943.

Anon. "When Is A Woman a Soldier? Asks Nazi Army Heads As Russian Women Are Being Captured At The Front," in (Harlington) *Valley Sunday-Star Monitor.* July 25, 1942.

Anon. "Why Buy War Bonds? See Infantry School," in *Beatrice Daily News*, June, 22, 1945.

Anon. "Wilbur Grathwohl Real Fighting Marine," in *Hamilton Daily News*, March 10, 1943.

Anon. "With the Occupation Forces In Germany," in *Harper Herald*, July 6, 1945.

Anon. "Women Snipers Denied," in *Cedar Rapids Gazette*, July 4, 1944.

Anon. "Woman Sniper Terrorizes Nazis In East Prussia," in *Galveston Daily News*, September 24, 1944.

Anon. "Women Snipers Bother Canucks," in *Lethbridge Herald*, January 10, 1944.

Anon. "Would Use Poison Gas," in *Wagga Wagga Daily Advertiser*, July 28, 1942.

Anon. "Youthful 5th Marine Pulled Off Iwo Jima," in *Abilene Reporter News*, April 27, 1945.

Anon. (Danville) *The Bee*, December 19, 1944, p. 11.

Allen, Bill. "Lubbock Marines Eats First Chicken Dinner On Guam," in *Lubblock Avalanche Journal*, August 27, 1944.

Allen, Bill. "Modern Canadian Sniper Is 'The Invisible Man'" in Winnipege Tribune, February 5, 1941.

Allen, Ralph. "Stories of Snipers: Nine notches on Rifle Butt of Patient Cree," Newspaper unknown, June 16, 1944.

Alli, Staff Sgt. Joseph. "New 'Scout-Sniper' Revive Old Indian Fighters' Craft," in *Burlington Daily Times News.* November 11, 1943.

Anderson, James C. "Don Found Thrills He Wanted," in *Winnipeg Tribune*, January 3, 1942.

Annabel, Russell. "Yanks Polish off Jap Sniper of Stretchers," in *Burnet Bulletin.* June 10, 1943.

Armstrong, Richard, "American Soldiers Prove To Be Masters Of Art of Camouflaging Self In Jungle," in *Port Arthur News*, September 7, 1942.

Arn, Edward C. *Arn's War*. Akron: University of Ohio Press, 2006.

Arvad, Inga. "Being woman no fun in occupied countries of Hitler's Europe," in *Lincoln Nebraska State Journal*, June 27, 1943.

Ault, Phil. "Capture of Oran Took Prize in Excitement," in *Kannapolis Daily Independent*, November 15, 1942.

Aydelotte, Charles. "Camouflage Art Of U.S. Costing Japs Plenty Of Money," in *Dunkirk (NY) Evening Observer,* July 18, 1942.

A. L. B., "The Australian," in *Melbourne Australian*, August 3, 1940.

C. A. B., "The Art of the Sniper," in *Adelaide Advertiser*, 26 July, 1941.

Barclay, Foster. "Canadian-U.S. Force 'Best In 5th Army,'" in *Winnipeg Tribune*, January 19, 1944.

Barnabus, Pat. "The Passing Show," *in Murwillumbah Tweed Daily*, August 15, 1945.

Blitzstein, Madelin, "Experts of Death" in *Arizona Independent Republic*, October 1, 1944.

Bomar, Edward E. "Unofficial Military Rating Is Kicked Overboard Today," in *Burlington Daily Times News*, February 25, 1941.

Boni, William, "Montanans Draw Awards for the Deeds Done in New Guinea; Sniper Tells How

Battle Aainst the Japanese Went," in *The Helena Independent.* January 17, 1943.

Boyle, Harold. "Patton Touched As DSC Award Made," in *Morning Avalache.* September 3, 1943.

Brontman, L., "Sniper Must Be Patient, Expert Says," in *Nevada State Journal*, November 12, 1942.

Brunson, T/Sgt. Mason. "After Battle of Tarawa Order Was Restored In Short Time," in *The Daily News*, February 1, 1944.

Brunson, T/Sgt. Mason. "Texas Marine Credited With Longest Rifle Shot of War," in *Lubbock Morning Avalanche*, July 21, 1944.

Burkholdt, Bjorn, "All Snipers In Oslo Face Death Penalty," in *Albert lea Evening Tribune*, April 16, 1940

Benjamin, Burton. "Wermuth–Athlete, Soldier and All-Round Man," in *Charleston Daily Mail*, March 1, 1942.

Chodera, Paul J. "'You Learn to Pray, Shoot, Swear, Load Your Rifle In One Breath,' Writes Sniper," in *Medina County Gazette*, March 13, 1945.

Christopherson, Walter. "Cheering Pats Start Last Lap," in *Winnipeg Tribune,* October 2, 1945.

Caudill, Harry M., "My Experiences In the Army," in *The Mountain Eagle*, November 9, 1944.

Dixon, Kenneth L. "Crackle of Small Fires Means Hit The Dirt; Not So At Anzio," in *Kingsport News*, May 27, 1944.

Dixon, Kenneth L. "Even Heroes Have Their Troubles," in *The Era*, August 29, 1944.

Dixon, Kenneth L. "'It's Scratch One Kraut' As Colonel Turns Sniper," in *Oil City Derrick*, May 6, 1944.

Embso, Sgt. Charles. "Five Months of Tank Warfare," in *Freeburg Tribune*, September 10, 1943.

Erikson, Leif. "Col. Roosevelt in Makin Battle, Although Not a Combat Officer," in *Charleston Gazette*, November 29, 1944.

Finstein, Pfc. Gilbert, "Gen. Easley Was Symbol To The 96th," in *Middle Pacific Stars and Stripes*, June 21, 1945.

Folkard, F. C. "Jap Fortress At Sanananda Road Was Model," *Newcastle Sun*, January 19, 1943.

Folkard, F. C. "Left 'Fort in Hurry," in *Adelaide News*, January 20, 1943.

Fusk, Sgt. Louis. "Lake Sups Raise Sniping From Job to Position Class," in *The Maple Leaf*, May 21, 1945.

Fyre, William F. "Stop Gently, Strike Hard Says Jungle Veterans," in *Hattieburg (Miss.) American*, March 1, 1943.

Gaskill, Gordon. "Reporter In Africa," in *Panama City News Herald*, December 12, 1942.

Gillmore, Eddy. "Awards Given Russian Girls," in *The Decatur Daily*, March 21, 1943.

Gillmore, Eddy. "Sniper Girls Receive High Soviet Awards" in *The Lima News*, March 28, 1943

Geiger, Robert. "Texas General Is Killed By Bullet From Machinegun," in *The Brownsville Herald*, June 21, 1945.

Gonnell, Henry. "Nazis Stiffen Resistance On Entire Normandy Front," In *Middle East Stars and Stripes*, July 14, 1944.

Greaves, Corp. Joe. "Canadian Snipers are Glamor Boys of the Army" in *Brandon Daily Sun*, October 25, 1944.

Hague, Sgt. James E., "Decorah Marine Wire Trouble Man and Buddies Outsmart Jap Sniper," in *Waterloo Daily Courier*, December 16, 1943.

Hampson, Fred. "Date Line Pacific," in *The Paris News*, May 30, 1945.

Hampson, Fred. "Japs Abandon Field Without Finishing Game," in *Moberly Monitor Index*, January 30, 1945

Harriot, G. R. "A. I. F. Fighting to Difficult Country," in Adelaide Advertiser, July 4, 1941

Hewlett, Frank. "Americans in Philippines Going Strong," in *Montana Standard Butte*, Feb. 1, 1942.

Hewlett, Frank. "Captain (One Man Army) Wermuth Hasn't Killed a Jap Since Feb. 4, and He's Getting Fed Up With the Inactivity," in *The Amarillo Globe*, March 6, 1942.

Hewlett, Frank."Green-Painted Jap Sniper Nearly Kills U.S. Reporter," in *Oxnard Press Courier*. February *Times*, May 17, 1943.

Hewlett, Frank. "One-Man Army Kills 129 Nippons," in *Moorhead Daily News*, March 6, 1942.

Hewlett, Frank. "Tells About Hero of Buna Campaigning," in *Marshall Evening Chronicle*, December 17, 1942.

Hix, John. "Handkerchiefs For Soldiers," in *Brookfield Daily Argus*, June 24, 1942.

Hoge, Tom. "Snipers Harass GIs, Take Toll In Injured," in *European Stars and Stripes*, July 25, 1949.

Holt, Paul. "Moscow Schoolgirls," in (Hobart) *The Voice*, September 18, 1943.

Hovey, Graham. "Cassino Blow to Advocates of Airpower," in *Cedar Rapids Gazette*, April 23, 1944.

Jap Hater 1/c. "Jap Hater's Letter," in *Washington Citizen*, March 17, 1944.

Jarrell, John W. "Correspondent Tells of Heaviest Fighting Of American Campaign in North Africa," in *The Charleston Gazette*, November 16, 1942.

Johnathan, George. "Japanese At OIVI: Cunning And Camouflage," in *MacKay Daily Mercury*, November 20, 1942.

Johnson, SSG Earle W., "Arkansas Marine Tells Story About An Efficient Idahoan," in *Northwest Arkansas Times*, September 3, 1943.

Johnson, Edwin S. "Indian In England knows Location of Tecumseh's Grave," in *The Lethbridge Herald*, October 5, 1940.

Johnston, George H. "Allies' Triumph In Owen Stanley," in *Melbourne Argus*, November 10, 1942.

Johnston, George H. "Japanese at Oivi–Cunning and Camouflage," in *Mackay Daily Mercury*, November 20, 1942.

Joseph, Lucius. "Beaver Soldier Got Jap Sniper Who Tried to Get Him," in *The Raleigh Register*, January 15, 1945.

Kluckholm, Frank L. "Beating Tojo at his own Game," in *London Stars and Stripes*, February 10, 1944.

Kononenko, Elena. "Courage of the Russia Girl Shown in Front Line Gallantry," in *Winnipeg Free Press*, January 4, 1943.

Lait, George. "Wakde Battle Held Saga of Yank Heroism," in *Charleston Gazette*, May 23, 1944.

Lardner, John. "Bizzare Methods: Japanese In Warfare," in *Bay of Plenty Beacon*, September 9, 1942.

Lardner, John. "While Snipers Whine, Glasgow Sarge Leads Sing-Song in Bizerte Campaign," in *The Winnipeg Tribune*, May 12, 1943.

Lee, Clark. "57th Filipino Scouts Live Up To Traditions," *in Jefferson City Daily Capital News*, February 18, 1942.

Lee, Clark. "Americans Repel Japs on Bataan," in *Somerset Daily American*, January 26, 1942.

Lee, Clark. "Captured Jap Guns Are Source of Entertainment on Bataan," in *Butte Montana Standard*, February 16, 1942

Lee, Clark. "Dressed To Kill! Jap Sniper Carries Equipment Which Enables Him To Fight Independently For Two Weeks To A Month," in *East Liverpool Review*, February 2, 1942.

Lee, Clark. "Ex-S. D. Rancher Proves Himself To Be America's No. 1 One-Man Army," in *The Evening Huronite*, February 19, 1942.

Lee, Clark. "Japs took to the hills like rabbits when marines opened attack in Solomons," in (Lincoln) *Evening State Journal*, September 12, 1942.

Lee, Clark. "MacArthur's One-Man Army Kills 116 Known Japanese," in *Valley Morning Star*, February 15, 1942.

Leman, Albert N. "National Whirligig," in (Danville) *The Bee*, May 15, 1943.

Levitt, Sgt. Saul. "Airborne Action," in *Yank*, July 21, 1944.

Lovell, Edith. "Got His Man," in *Rapid City Reporter*, November 9, 1944.

Lyons, Leonard. "The Lyons Den," in *Endicott Daily Bulletin*, March 1, 1944.

McGurn, Sgt. Barrett, "Combat Virgins," in *Yank*, January 19, 1945.

McManus, Corp. Larry. "Random Notes on the Makin Operations, From a Reporter's Invasion Dairy," in *Yank*, January 27, 1944.

McMurtry, Charles. "Yanks on Island Startled by Nude Jap Woman Sniper," in *Arizona Republic*, March 13, 1943.

Malkin, Del. "Canadians March On Under Clear Skies," in *Winnipeg Free Press*, April 19, 1945.

Manning, Paul, "Canadians Fight Heroically on French Beaches," in *Ogden Standard Examiner*, June 16, 1944.

Marien, Bill. "Australian Commandos and Dutch Guerillas Pin Japanese Down in Timor," in *Proserpine Guardian,* January 29, 1943.

Marien, Bill. "'Worrying' The Japs: With the Commandos In Timor," in *Peterborough Times and Northern Advertiser,* February 5, 1942.

Miller, Lee G. "How Gen. Dalton Lost Life on Luzon," in *Port Arthur News*, June 1, 1945.

Miller, Sgt. Merle. "Makin Taken," in *Yank*. December 24, 1943.

Miller, Lt. George D. "Sniper Victim, Tells Experience From Army Hospital Bed," in *The Daily Iowan*, November 1, 1944.

Marker, "On The Range," in *The Australian*, September 28, 1940.

Morin, Relman. "Hungarian Trooper's Diary Found By Russians Tells Tragic Story," in *La Crosse Tribune and Leader Press*, February 28, 1943.

Morin, Relman. "Laughs, Tragedy Mingled On Road To Naples," in *Abilene Reporter News*, October 3, 1943.

Morris, James. "Snipers En Masse: Red Army Marksmen," in *Roma Western Star*, February 19, 1943.

Morriss, Sgt. Mack. "Rangers Come Home," in *Yank*, August 4, 1944.

Morozova, Vera. "Russian Sniper: 170 Germans Killed," in *Bay of Plenty Beacon,* July 20, 1943.

Murphy, Audie, "Youthful Texas Hero Tells of

Wounds in Hip and Praises Work of Nurses," in *Port Arthur News*, July 19, 1945.

Meyers, Laura Scott. "The Book Shelf: Torture In Hong Kong," in *El Paso Herald Post*, August 15, 1942.

Nichol, David M. "Two Moscow Girls Win Military Award," in *Winnipeg Free Press*, Feb. 19, 1943

Packard, Reynolds, "French 'Pistol Packin' Mama' Kills Two German Snipers, Hunts for Others," in *Harrisburg Daily Register*, August 28, 1944.

Pavlichenko, Lyudmila. "A Woman With A Rifle," in (Hobart) *Tribune*, February 17, 1943.

Peters, Sgt. Walter, "Sniper Killer" in *Yank*, August 18, 1944.

Pyle, Ernie. "Ravings," in *Butte Montana Standard*, November 9, 1944.

Pyle, Ernie. "Three-Star U.S. General Chases Off Axis Sniper," in *El Paso Herald Post*, August 21, 1943.

Rayburn, Wallace. "Fighting In Dieppe," in *Amarillo Globe*. August 31, 1942.

Remaly, Jack. "Marine Raiders Took No Jap Captives at Tulagi, Says Corporal," in *Endicott Daily Bulletin*. March 22, 1943.

Riley, Bernard. "Bluejacket Tells of Cold-Blooded Marine Raid On Solomons," in *Phoenix Arizona Republic*, September 8, 1942.

Roosevelt Eleanor, "My Day," in *Laredo Times*, October 8, 1942.

T. H. S. S., "Marines to Train At Sniper School," in *Melbourne Herald*, November 7, 1942.

Shanke, Edwin, "Nazis Prepare Defense Plans," in *Reno Evening Gazette*, September 1, 1944.

Shapiro, Henry. "Russian Winter Stalls Nazis," in *The Salt Lake Telegram*, November 12, 1942.

Slessor, Kenneth, "Artillery Breaks Up Attack By French Tanks," in *The Morning Bulletin, Rockhampton,* June 14, 1941.

Spencer, Murlin. "AP Reporter Spends 'Hot' Night in Marines' Trench," in *Beckley Sunday Register*, December 27, 1942.

Spencer, Murlin. "Captain Lauds Sniper Hunters," in *Reno Evening Gazette*, December 17, 1942.

Spencer, Murlin. "Mission Youth Kills Three Japs While 'Playing Dead' In fighting On New Guinea; Barnabee Injured in Fight," in *Valley Morning Star*, November 27, 1942.

Steele, A. T. "Leningrad Still Soviet's Big Problem," in *Syracuse Herald-Journal*, April 22, 1942.

Stinnet, Jack, "Washington in Wartime," in *Wilson Daily Times*, December 22, 1944.

Stone, John L. "Rio Roundup," in *Valley Morning Star*, January 7, 1943.

Terry, Tech Sgt. William K, "Freeporter Gets His Sniper As Japs Bites The Dust on Mankin," in *Freeport Facts*, March 2, 1944.

Treanor, Tom, "Forward Observer Is Eyes, Ears of Field Artillery; He Spots the Targets," in *Cedar Rapids Gazette,* January 3, 1944.

Treanor, Tom. "Life Half-Frozen Boys Out of Italian Trenches," in *Cedar Rapids Gazette*, December 15, 1943.

Tregaskis, Richard. "U.S. Marines Do 'Impossible' in Battle for Island," in *Salt Lake City Telegram*, August 29, 1942.

Tucker, George, "War Reporter's Notes: Snipers…." in *Ironwood Daily Globe*, 27 April, 1944

USMC Public Relations. "Former Yuman, Now Marine, Credited With An Important Role in the Conquest of Iwo Jima," in *Yuma Sun*, June 11, 1945.

Vanach, Yuli, "Latvian girl of 20 helps kill 12 Nazis as Sniper," in *Lincoln Evening State Journal*, November 11, 1942.

Vermillion, Robert. "Soldier who Shot 130 Germans isn't 'Too Proud of Killing,'" in *Racine Journal Times*, February 27, 1945.

Vernier. "Home Guard," in *Fremantle Mail*. June 19, 1943; June 26, 1943; July 3, 1943; July 31, 1943; August 7, 1943.

Vitale, A. M., "Parakeets Spot Jap Snipers," in *Menard News*, January 11, 1945.

Wagner, Elliot. "Sniper School gave 99th October Replacements," in *Checkerboard*, 2d Issue, 1999.

Waindel, Gerald A., It's All Quiet in the Jungles, At Least for Those Back Home," in *The Berkshire Evening Eagle*, May 26, 1944.

Wearly, John, "John Wearly Shares His Story" in *Checkerboard*, 3d Issue, 2012.

Weir, Pvt. Ralph. "La Ferian Bags 3 Japs During Iwo Jima Battle," in *Brownsville Herald*, 21 June 1945.

Weir, Pvt. Ralph. "Valley Youth Kills Sniper on Iwo Jima," in *El Paso Herald Post*, May 28, 1945.

Weller, George. "Jap Pillbox Lights Spy On Attackers," in *Winnipeg Free Press*, January 12, 1943.

Wemp, Major Bert S. "Last 12 Huns Glad to Quit to Deadly Canuck Sniper Knocking Off Their Pals," Newspaper unknown, December 21, 1943.

Weston, Joe. "How to Kill Foe With First Shot," in *War Week*, March 24, 1945.

Weston, Mervyn. "Mopping Up," in *The Daily Advertiser*, January 8, 1943.

Weston, Mervyn. "Was Killed By Sniper While Burying Dead," *in Hay Riverine Grazier*, January 19, 1943.

White, Charles W. "A Doughboy Recalls Epic Trek With a Paratrooper," in *London Stars and Stripes*, July 11, 1944.

White, William Smith. "Hire Woman Sniper Shot," in *Arizona Independent Republic*, June 15, 1944.

Whitehead, Don. "German Snipers; In All Kind of Garb, Shoot At Yankees," in *The Laredo Times*, June 11, 1944.

Whitehead, Don. "Yanks Prove Better Men Than Nazis In Sicily War," in *High Point Enterprise*, August 13, 1943.

Wilson, William A. "Allies Meet Stiff Resistance From German Howitzer Battery," in (Huntington) *The Daily News*, July 22, 1943.

Winchell. *Port Arthur News*. May 1, 1945.

Wolfert, Ira, "U.S. Troops Give Japs Lesson in Jungle Fighting," in *Pittsburg Evening gle*, July 22, 1943.

Worden, William. "Japs On Attu Lived in Caves and Tunnels," in *Hope Star*, June 2, 1943.

Worden, William L. "You Can't Figure the Japs— Ask the Marines on Guam," in *The News*, August 8, 1944.

Wright, Patty McKee, "Bring 'em Back Alive," in *The World News,* April 8, 1944.

Wright, Sgt. Richard T. "Survived Fire in Tank: 65 Japs Trap Crew of Yanks," in *Mason City Globe Gazette*. October 9, 1942.

Younger, Joan. "Sniping Miss Seeks Hubby; Wants Family," in *The Daily Independent*, September 24, 1942.

Zurlinden, T/Sgt. Pete. "Hanchette Recalls Best 'Jap-Erasing Mortars,'" in *Madison Wisconsin State Journal*, April 30, 1944.

Zurlinden, T/Sgt. Pete, "Texas Lieutenant and 35 Marines Wrote Heroic Chapter at Tarawa," in *The Port Arthur* News. December 19, 1943.

Hamilton Spectator, August 1, 1945.

Magazine/journal articles

Baumgardner. "The M-1 Garand and the German MK-4 Tank," *Tactical Shooter*, Vol. 3, No. 6, July 2000.

Bright, Maj. James B. "The Dime A Dozen Club," *American Rifleman*, January 1945.

Cotterill, Daniel. "A Grisly Business: Australia's Lee-Enfield Sniper Rifles," *American Rifleman*, August 2003.

Diamond, Lou. "Sniper!" *The American Rifleman Goes to War*, Washington, DC, NRA, 1992.

Emary, Dave. "Dad's World War II Luger Pistol," *Guns & Ammo*, March 2020.

Emary, Dave. "How to Get Into Vintage Sniper Rifle Matches," *Outdoor Life*, July 2019.

Flagg, Bob. "The '03: A Combat Infantryman's View," *American Rifleman*, June 1998.

Hope, Maj. N. K. P., RSigs. "Street Fighting in Germany 1945," *British Army Review*, Winter 2019.

Howell, C. H., Jr. "Sniping Rifles," in *American Rifleman*, April and May 1947.

Lister, C. B. "The Sniper," in *American Rifleman* September 1942, p 8.

McCallum, Walter. "Fire Less and Fire Better," in *American Rifleman* March 1943.

Norton, Steven. "The 1941 Marine Sniper Rifle with Unertl Scope," in *Garand Collectors' Association Journal,* Fall 2018.

Regamey, Amandine. "Soviet Women Snipers—Experience of fire." Paper presented and published *Sixièmes Journées Franco-Allemandes,* Berlin, January 29–30, 2015.

Rossino, Alexander B. "Nazi Anti-Jewish Policy during the Polish Campaign: The Case of Einsatzgruppe von Woyrsch," in *German Studies Review*, Vol. 24 No. 1, February 2001.

Shadel, William F. "Where are the Riflemen?" in *American Rifleman*, May 1945.

Sherrod, Robert. "Battle of The Pacific," in *Time*, December 5, 1942

Underhill, Garrett. "Under the Red Star," in *American Rifleman*, August 1941.

Venturino, Mike and Emary, Dave. "Myth Meets Fact: World War II Sniper Rifles-how good were they?" in *Guns Magazine*, February 2011.

Books

Abdulin, Mansor, and Drabkin, Artem [ed]. *Red Road From Stalingrad*. Barnsley: Pen & Sword, 2004.

Adkins, A. Z. and Adkins, A. Z., III. *You Can't Get Much Closer Than This*. Havertown: Casemate, 2005.

Alexievich, Sevetlana. *The Unwomanly Face of War: An Oral History of Women in World War II*. New York: Random House, 2017.

Allen, Robert S. *Lucky Forward: The History of Patton's Third U.S. Army*. New York: Vanguard Press, 1947.

Altner, Helmut. *Berlin Dance of Death*. Havertown: Casemate, 2002.

Anderson, Robert L. *Innocent Killer*. Baltimore, Publish America, 2003.

Angell, Stewart. *Secret Sussex Resistance: 1940-1944*. Midhurst: Middleton Press, 1996.

Anon. *The Tiger Triumphs*. London: HMSO, 1946.

Armstrong, Maj. Nevill A. D. *Fieldcraft, Sniping and Intelligence*. Aldershot: Gale & Polden, 1942.

Astor, Gerald. *June 6, 1944: The Voices of D-Day*. New York: St. Martin's Press, 1994.

Averbeck, Bernhard & Folkestad, William B. *Panzerjäger*. Shippensburg: White Mane Publishing, 2000.

Axell, Albert. *Russia's Heroes: 1941-45*. New York: Carroll & Graf, 2001.

Bartmann, Erwin. *Für Volk und Führer*. Solihull: Helion, 2013.

Bastable, Jonathan. *Voices from Stalingrad*. Newton Abbot: David & Charles, 2007.

Beetz, Günther Horst. *A Soldier Of The Reich*. England: Fonthill, 2018.

Beevor, Anthony, and Vinogradova, Luba, trans. *A Writer at War*. New York: Pantheon Books, 2005.

Beevor, Anthony. *Ardennes 1944*. New York: Viking, 2015.

Beevor, Anthony. *Stalingrad*. New York: Penguin, 1998.

Beevor, Anthony. *The Fall of Berlin, 1945*. New York: Viking, 2002.

Bellamy, Bill. *Troop Leader*. Thrupp: Sutton, 2005.

Berry, Henry. *Semper Fi, Mac*. New York: Berkley Book, 1982.

Bessonov, Evgeni. *Tank Rider*. London: Greenhill, 2003.

Bidermann, Gottlob Herbert. *In Deadly Combat*. Lawrence: University of Kansas, 2000.

Bilder, Michael. *A Footsoldier for Patton*. Philadelphia: Casemate, 2008.

Blackburn, Richard McCallion. *In The Company of Heroes*. Thorofare: Xlibris, 2013.

Blunt, Roscoe C., Jr. *Foot Soldier*. Cambridge: Da Capo Press, 2002.

Bogachev, Boris. *For the Motherland! For Stalin!* London: C. Hurst & Co., 2017

Bowlby, Alex. *The Recollections of Rifleman Bowlby*. London: Leo Cooper, 1969.

Bowser, Doug. *Rifles of the White Death*. McComb: Camelia City Military Publications, 1998.

Bradley, Omar and Blair, Clay. *A General's Life*. New York: Simon & Schuster, 1983.

Breuer, William E. *Drop Zone Sicily*. Novato: Presidio Press, 1983.

Brophy, William S. *The Springfield 1903 Rifles*. Stackpole Books, 1985.

Brotherton, Marcus. *Shifty's War*. Hudson: Berkley, 2011.

Brown, Al. *My Comrades and Me*. Thorofare: Xlibris, 2003.

Brutton, Philip. *Ensign in Italy*. London: Leo Cooper, 1992.

Burgett, Donald R. *Currahee! A Screaming Eagle at Normandy*. Novato: Presidio Press, 1967.

Burgett, Donald R. *The Road to Arnhem*. Novato: Presidio Press, 1999.

Burgin, R. V. with Marvel, Bill. *Islands of the Damned*. New York: Caliber, 2010.

Burns, Dwane T. *Jump*. Philadelphia, Casemate, 2006.

Burriss, T. Moffatt. *Strike And Hold*. Dulles: Virginia, 2000.

Canfield, Bruce N. *An Illustrated Guide to the '03 Springfield Service Rifle*. Lincoln: Mowbray, 2004.

Canfield, Bruce N. *The M1 Garand Rifle*. Lincoln: Mowbray, 2013.

Canfield, Bruce N. *U.S. Small Arms of World War II*. Lincoln: Mowbray, 2020.

Carrell, Paul. *Scorched Earth*. Atglen: Schiffer, 1994.

Carter, Ross S. *Those Devils in Baggy Pants*. Canton: Claymore, 1979.

Cawthon, Charles R. *Other Clay*. Niwot, Uiversity Press of Colorado, 1990.

Center of Military History. *The War Against Germany*. Washington: Brassey's, 1994.

Chandler, Roy and Chandler, Norman. *Death From Afar*. 5 vol. St Mary's City: Iron Brigade Armory, 1992–98.

Chandler, Roy. *One Shot Brotherhood*. Jacksonville, Iron Brigade Armory, 2001.

Cheall, Bill. *Fighting Through From Dunkirk To Hamburg*. Barnsley: Pen & Sword, 2011.

Chervinsky, Julie, ed. *Lives of the Great Patriotic War*. New York: Blavatnik Archive Foundation, 2011.

Chuikov, Vasili Ivanovich. *The Battle for Stalingrad*. New York: Holt, Rinehart and Winston, 1963.

Corti, Eugenio. *Few Returned: Twenty-eight Days on the Russian Front, Winter 1942–1943*. Columbia, University of Missouri Press, 1997.

Cosmas, Graham A. *The Medical Department: Medical Service in the European Theater of Operations*. Washington DC, Center of Military History, 1992.

Crossman, Edward C. *Book of the Springfield*. Prescott: Wolfe Publishing Company, 1989.

Cullen, James K. *Band of Strangers*. Coppell: Cullen, 2018.

De Giampietro, Sepp, *Blood And Soil*. Barnsley: Greenhill, 2019.

Daneman, Marty. *Do Well Or Die*. Brule, Cable Publishing, 2012.

Davis, Charles. *The Letters of a Combat Rifleman*. Pittsburg: Dorrance Publishing, 2001.

Davis, John. *Up Close: A Scout's Story*. Bennington: Merriam, 2012.

Deam, Donald L. *General Toothpick: The World War II Memoirs of 1st Sgt. Donald L. Deam*. Fort Campbell: 101 Airborne, 2008.

Degrelle, Léon. *The Eastern Front*. Newport Beach: Institute For Historical Review, 1985.

Drabkin, Artem & Kobylyanskiy, Isaak. *Red Army Infantrymen Remember the Great Patriotic War*. Las Vegas, Author House, 2009.

Dunlap, Roy F. *Ordnance Went Up Front*. Livonia: R&R Books, 1948.

Dunlop, Richard. *Behind Japanese Lines*. Chicago: Rand McNally, 1979.

Edwards, Denis. *The Devil's Own Luck*. London: Leo Cooper, 1999.

Egger, Bruce E. and Otts, Lee MacMillan. *G Company's War*. Tuscaloosa: University of Alabama Press, 1992.

Eisenhower, Dwight. *Crusade in Europe*. Garden City: Doubleday & Co., 1948.

Esfeld, Herman & Edna. *Brainwashed: Fighting For the Enemy*. North Charleston: CreateSpace, 2015.

Farago, Ladislas. *Patton: Ordeal and Triumph*. New York: Dell, 1963.

Farey, Pat and Spicer, Mark. *Sniping: An Illustrated History*. Minneapolis: Zenith Press, 2008.

Gardner, Ian & Day. Roger, *Tonight We Die As Men*. Oxford: Osprey, 2009.

Gavin, James M. *On To Berlin*. New York: Viking, 1978.

George, John. *Shots Fired in Anger*. Washington, D. C.: NRA, 1981.

Gendelman, Max. *A Tale of Two Soldiers: The Unexpected Friendship Between a World War II American Jewish Sniper and A German Military Pilot*. Minneapolis: Two Harbors Press, 2013.

Goodwin, Mark G., *US Infantry Weapons In Combat*. Export: Scott A. Duff Publications, 2005.

Gorbachevsky, Boris. *Through the Maelstrom*. Lawrence: University of Kansas Press, 2008.

Gregg, Victor. *Rifleman*. London: Bloomsbury, 2011.

Greiss, Thomas. *Atlas for the Second World War: Europe and the Mediterranean*. New York: Square One Press, 2002.

Guarnere, William and Heffron, Edward, with Post, Robyn. *Brothers in Battle, Best of Friends*. New York: Berkley, 2007.

Hartinger, Andreas. *Until The Eyes Shut*. Coppell: Hartinger, 2019.

Hastings, Max. *Overlord*. New York: Simon and Schuster, 1984.

Hesketh-Prichard, Maj. H. *Sniping in France*. London: Hutchinson & Co, 1920. Available at *openlibrary.org/works/OL7731796W/Sniping_in_France*.

Hilsman, Roger. *American Guerrilla*. Washington: Brassey, 1990.

Holl, Adelbert. *An Infantryman in Stalingrad*. Sydney, Leaping Horseman Books, 2005.

Horn, Lt. Col. Bernd, and Wyczynski, Michel. *Paras Versus the Reich Canada's Paratroopers at War, 1942–45*. Toronto: Pundurn Press, 2003.

Houghton, Steve. *The British Sniper: A Century of Evolution*. Eye: Swift & Bold, 2018.

Humphrey, Robert E. *Once Upon A Time In War*. Norman: University of Oklahoma Press, 2008.

Jensen, Karla R. *Nobody's Hero: The Story of a Marine Scout Sniper*. Beaver Dam: Little Dane Girl Press, 2016.

Johnston, Richard T. *Follow Me!* Nashville: Battery Press, 1987.

Jung, Helmut. *But Not For The Fuehrer*. Bloomington: First Books Library, 2003.

Karem, Bruce and Steves, Michael. *Karabiner 98K*. 3 vol. Ashland: Third Party Press, 2017.

Kaltenegger, Roland. *Eastern Front Sniper: The Life of Matthäus Hetzenauer*. London: Greenhill Books, 2017.

Kershaw, Alex. *The First Wave*. New York: Caliber, 2019.

Khoury, John M. *Love Company*. Chi Chi Press, Lovell, 2018.

King, Dan. *A Tomb Called Iwo Jima*. North Charleston: Create Space, 2014.

Kirby, Lawrence F. *Stories From the Pacific*. Coppell: 1st Books Library, 2004.

Kistemaker, Henk, *Wiking*. Holland: JustPublishers.NL, 2019.

Kobylyanskiy, Issak. *From Stalingrad to Pillau*. Lawrence, University of Kansas Press, 2008.

Kobylyanskiy, Isaak & Britton, Stuart. *Russian World War II Vocabulary*. Solilhull: Helion, 2013.

Koschorrek, Günter K., *Blood Red Snow*. London; Greenhill, 2002.

Koskimaki, George. *D-Day with the Screaming Eagles*. Havertown: Casemate, 2002.

Koskimaki, George. *Hell's Highway*. Havertown: Casemate, 2003 (in notes as 2003/1).

Koskimaki, George. *The Battered Bastards of Bastogne*. Havertown: Casemate, 2003 (in notes as 2003/2).

Kurowski, Franz. *Panzer Aces*. Toledo: Ballentine, 1992.

Lacey, Tom. *An Infantryman's Reflections on World War II*. Middletown: Lacey, 2019.

Ladd, James D. *By Sea, By Land The Authorised History of the The Royal Marines*. London: Collins, 1999.

Laidler, Peter. *An Armourer's Perspective: .303 No. 4(T) Sniper Rifle and the Holland & Holland Connection*. Margate: Skennerton, 1993.

Lapin, Terence W. *The Mosin-Nagant Rifle*, 6th ed. Tustin: North Cape Publications, 2013.

Lambert, Ray. *Every Man a Hero*. New York: Morrow, 2019.

Lauer, Walter E. *Battle Babies*. Nashville: Battery Press, 1986.

Lavender, Donald E. *Nudge Blue*. Bennington: Merriam Press, 1998.

Law, Clive M. *Without Warning*. Ottawa: Service Publications, 2004.

Law, Richard D. *Backbone of the Wehrmacht, Vol. II: Sniper Variations of the German K98k Rifle*. Toronto: Collectors' Grade Publication, 1st. ed. 1996; 2d. ed. 2002.

Lodieu, Didier. *Dying For Saint-Lô*. Paris: Histoire & Collections, 2007.

Lubbeck, William. *At Leningrad's Gates*. Drexel Hall: Casemate, 2006.

Lugs, Jaroslav. *Firearms Past and Present*. London: Grenville, 1973.

Lundhigh, *Show Me The Hero*. Bloomington: Author's House, 2009.

Lypka, Demetrius. *A Soldier Remembers*. Wheaton: Cantigny First Division Foundation, 2007.

McKenney, Tom C. *The Sniper Anthology*. Gretna: Pelican, 2012.

McManus, John C. *Fire and Fortitude*. New York: Caliber, 2019.

Mace, Sterling and Allen, Nick. *Battle Ground Pacific*. New York: St. Martin's Press, 2012.

Megallas, James. *All The Way To Berlin*. New York, Ballantine, 2003.

Magnan, Philip J. *Letters from the Pacific Front*. New York: Writers Advantage, 2003.

Makos, Adam. *Voices of the Pacific*. New York: Berkeley, 2013.

Malarky, Don with Welch, Bob. *Easy Company Soldier*. New York: St. Martins Press, 2008.

Manchester, William. *Goodbye, Darkness.* Boston: Little Brown and Company, 1979.

Martin, Frank Wayne. *Patton's Lucky Scout.* Milwaukee: Crickhollow, 2009

Mather, Carol. *When the Grass Stops Growing.* Barnsley: Pen & Sword. 1997.

Mayo, Lida. *Bloody Buna.* Garden City: Doubleday, 1974.

Meller, William F. *Bloody Roads to Germany.* New York: Berkeley Caliber, 2012.

Michaelis, Rolf. *The German Sniper Badge: 1944-44.* Atglen: Schiffer, 2012.

Mikhin, Petr. *Guns Against The Reich.* Barnsley: Pen and Sword, 2010.

Miller, Edward S. *War Plan Orange.* Annapolis: Naval Institute Press, 1991.

Mitchell, Lt. Robert J., et al. *The Capture of Attu.* Lincoln: The University of Nebraska Press, 2000.

Mogan, A. G. *Stalin's Sniper: The War Diary of Roza Shanina.* Coppell: Mogan, 2020.

Moniushko, Evgenni D. *From Leningrad to Hungary: Notes of a Red Army Soldier, 1941–1946.* London: Frank Cass, 2005.

Mowat, Farley. *And No Birds Sing.* Toronto: The Canadian Publishers, 1979.

Mowat, Farley. *The Regiment.* Belleville: Hastings and Prince Edwards Regimental Association, 2006.

Murphy, Audie. *To Hell And Back.* New York: MJF Books, 1977.

Nikolaev, Yevgeni. *Red Army Sniper: A Memoir of the Eastern Front in World War II.* London: Greenhill, 2017.

Nicholas, M. J. *Love and War, Book 2.* Mills Village, Wright, 2012.

NRA. *The American Rifleman Goes to War.* Fairfax: NRA, 1992.

Nunneley, John and Tamayama, Kazuo. *Tales By Japanese Soldiers.* London: Cassell, 1992.

O'Connell, Patrick. *Into the Rising Sun.* New York: Free Press, 2002.

O'Keefe, David. *Seven Days In Hell.* Toronto: Harper Collins, 2019.

Obraztsov, Ouri and Anders, Maud. *Soviet Women Snipers of the Second World War.* Paris: Historie & Collections, 2014.

Orwell, George. *Homage to Catalonia.* London: Secker & Warburg, 1938. Accessed online at *george-orwell.org/Homage_to_Catalonia/11.html.*

Parker, Danny S. *The Battle of the Bulge.* Conshohocken: Combined Books, 1991.

Patton, George S. *War As I Knew It.* Boston: Houghton Mifflin Company, 1947.

Pavlichenko, Lyudmila. *Lady Death: The Memoirs of Stalin's Sniper.* London: Greenhill Books, 2015.

Pechelintsev, Vladimir. *How I Became A Sniper.* Moscow: Military Publishing House of the People's Commissariat of Defense, 1943.

Pegler, Martin. *Out of Nowhere: A History of the Military Sniper.* Oxford: Osprey, 2004.

Pegler, Martin. *Sniping Rifles From the 19th to the 21st Century.* Oxford: Osprey, 2010.

Pegler, Martin. *Sniping Rifles on the Eastern Front: 1939–1945.* Oxford: Osprey, 2019.

Petrovskaya, Kyra. *Kyra.* Englewood Cliffs: Prentice Hall, 1959.

Pilyushin, Joseph. *Red Sniper on the Eastern Front: The Memoirs of Joseph Pilyushin.* Barnsley: Pen & Sword, 2010.

Plaster, John L. *The History of Sniping and Sharpshooting.* Boulder: Paladin Press, 2008.

Ponomarenko, Vladimir P. & Filachev, Anatoly M. *Infrared Techniques and Electro-Optics in Russia: A History 1946-2006.* Bellingham: Spie, 2007.

Pöppel, Martin. *Heaven and Hell.* Staplehurst: Spellmount, 1988.

Poschacher, Otto. *30 Years' Travel, Vol. II.* Coppell, 1st Library Books 2020

Poyer, Joe. *Collecting the American Sniper Rifle: 1900 to 1945.* Tustin: North Cape Publications, 2012.

Poyer, Joe. *Collecting the American Sniper Rifle: 1945 to 2000.* Tustin: North Cape Publications, 2014.

Putney, Capt. William W. *Always Faithful.* New York: Free Press, 2001.

Pyl'eyn, Alexander V. *Penalty Strike.* Solihull: Helion, 2006.

Pyle, Ernie. *Brave Men.* New York: Henry Holt & Company, 1943.

Pyle, Ernie. *Here Is Your War.* New York: World Publishing Company, 1945.

Ramage, C. Kenneth. *Lyman Centennial Journal: 1878-1978.* Middlefield: Lyman, 1978.

Rauch, Georg. *Unlikely Warrior.* New York, MacMillan, 2006.

Raus, Erhard. *Panzer Operations.* New York: Da Capo, 2003.

Reese, Willy Peter. *A Stranger to Myself.* New York: Farrar, Straus and Giroux, 2003.

Rehfeldt, Hans Heinz. *Mortar Gunner On The Eastern Front.* 2 vol. Barnsley: Greenhill, 2019.

Richardson, Stan. *Growing Up in A Foxhole.* Richardson: 2014.

Roberts, Joseph B., Jr., (ed). *The American Rifleman Goes to War.* Washington, DC, NRA, 1992.

Rochford, Caroline & Paddy. *In a Guardsman's Boots.* Barnsley: Pen & Sword, 2016.

Rosen, Richard Freiherr von. *Panzer Ace: The Memoirs of an Iron Cross Panzer Commander from Barbarossa to Normandy.* London: Greenhill, 2018.

Ross, Angus. *23 Battalion.* Part of *The Official History of New Zealand in the Second World War 1939–1945.* Wellington: Historical Publications Branch, 1959. (Available online at *nzetc.victoria.ac.nz/tm/scholarly/tei-WH2-23Ba-c5.html.*)

Rottman, Gordon L. *Soviet Rifleman 1941-45.* Oxford: Osprey, 2007.

Roush, John H. Jr. *World War II Reminiscences.* San Rafael: Reserve Officers' Association, 1995.

Russell, Bill. *The Shield of Mashona.* Dorset: New Guild, 1994.

Sajer, Guy. *The Forgotten Soldier.* Washington, D. C.: Potomac Books, 1971.

Sakaida, Henry. *Heroes of the Soviet Union.* Oxford: Osprey, 2004.

Sakakida, Richard. *A Spy In Their Midst.* Lanham: Madison Books, 1995.

Saarelainen, Tapio. *The Sniper Simo Häyhä.* Tampere: Apali Oy, 2008.

Sale, E. V. *Stepping Stones to the Solomons: the Unofficial History of the 29th Battalion with the Second New Zealand Expeditionary Force in the Pacific.* Wellington, NZ, Reed Publishing (NZ) Ltd, 1947.

Sandifer, John. *One Tough Ombre.* Bloomington: Xlibris, 2012.

Sandifer, Leon C. *Not in Vain: A Rifleman Remembers World War II.* Baton Rouge: Louisiana State University Press, 1992.

Sasser, Charles W. and Roberts, Craig. *One Shot—One Kill.* New York: Pocket Books, 1990.

Sauer, Arno. *In the Hell of the Eastern Front.* Yorkshire, Front Line Books, 2020.

Schaps, Ralph B. *500 Days of Front Line Combat.* New York: IUniverse, 2003.

Scheffel, Charles. *Crack! and Thump: With a Combat Infantry Officer in World War II.* Camroc Press, 2007.

Scheiderbauer, Armin. *Adventures in My Youth.* Solihull: BCA, 2003.

Schneider, George F. *Survivor: Memoirs of a World War II Vet.* Parker: Outskirts Press, 2017.

Schneider, Helmut, (ed). *Tiger Battalion 507.* Barnsley, Greenhill, 2020.

Scott, Hugh A. *The Blue and White Devils.* Nashville: The Battery Press, 1984.

Senich, Peter. *Limited War Sniping*. Boulder: Paladin Press, 1979.

Senich, Peter. *The Complete Book of U.S. Sniping*. Boulder: Paladin Press, 1988.

Senich, Peter. *The German Sniper: 1914-1945*. Boulder: Paladin Press, 1982.

Senich, Peter. *The One-Round War*. Boulder: Paladin Press, 1996.

Senich, Peter. *U.S. Marine Corps Scout-Snipers: World War II and Korea*. Boulder: Paladin, 1993.

Senich, Peter R. and Kyle, Howard. *The German Sniper: The Man—His Weapons*. Phoenix: Desert Publications, 1975.

Sheaner, Herb. *Prisoner's Odyssey*. Bloomington: Xlibris, 2009.

Shirley, John B. *I Remember*. Coppel: Shirley, 2017.

Shore, Clifford. *With British Snipers to the Reich*. Boulder: Paladin Press, 1988.

Siegert, Richard. *The Tiger From Poznan*. Barnsley, Pen And Sword, 2021.

Sisson, Frank. *I Marched With Patton*. New York: William Morrow, 2020.

Skennerton, Ian. *.303 Pattern 1914 Rifle and Sniping Variants*. Margate: Ian Skennerton, 1998.

Skennerton, Ian. *The British Sniper*. Margate: Ian Skennerton, 1993.

Slaughter, Bob. *Omaha Beach and Beyond*. St. Paul: Zenith Press, 2007.

Smith, W. H. B. & Ezell, Edward Clinton. *Small Arms of the World*. New York: Barnes & Noble, 1983.

Soskil, Murray. *From The Bronx To Berchtesgaden*. New York: Temurlone Press, 2012.

Spielauer, Robert. *Scharfschützen Zielfernrohre und Montagen 1914-1945*. Germany: Spielauer, 2007.

Stacey, Col. C. P. *The Canadian Army 1939-1945 An Official Historical Summary*. Ottawa: Department of National Defence, 1948.

Steiber, John. *Against The Odds*. Dublin: Poolbeg Press, 1995.

Steiniger, Erhard. *Radio Operator On The Eastern Front*. Barnsley, Greenhill, 2020.

Subbotin, Vassili. *We Stormed The Reichstag*. Barnsley, Pen & Sword, 2017.

Sutkus, Bruno. *Sniper Ace: From the Eastern Front to Sibera*. London: Frontline Books, 2009.

Tachovsky, Joseph and Kraack, Cynthia. *40 Thieves in Saipan*. Washington, DC: Regenery, 2020.

Taggert, Donald G., (ed). *History of the Third Infantry Division*. Nashville: Battery Press, 1987.

Tantum, William H., IV. *Sniper Rifles of the Two World Wars*. Ottawa: Museum Restoration Service, 1967.

Taylor, Thomas. *The Simple Sounds of Freedom*. New York: Random House, 2002.

Temkin, Gabiel. *My Just War*. Novato: Presidio Press, 1998.

Thomas, Donald G. *Silencer Patents, Vol II: European Patents*. Boulder: Paladin, 1978.

Truby, J. David. *Silencers, Snipers & Assassins*. Boulder: Paladin Press, 1972.

Vinogradova, Lyuba. *Avenging Angels: Young Women of the Soviet Union's World War II Sniper Corps*. New York: MacLehose Press, 2017.

Virski, Fred. *My Life In The Red Army*. New York: MacMillan, 1949.

Wacker, A. and de Vries, G. *German Sniper Rifles*. Netherlands: S. I. Publicaties BV, 2011.

Wacker, A. *Sniper on the Eastern Front: The Memoirs of Sepp Allerberger, Knight's Cross*. Barnsley: Pen and Sword, 2005.

Wagnon, Vaughn. *Foxhole Memoirs*. Wagnon, 2016.

Wahlert, Glenn and Linwood, Russell. *One Shot Kills: A History of Australian Army Sniping*. Canberra: Army History Unit, 2014.

Walter, John. *Snipers at War*. Barnsley: Greenhill, 2017.

Ward, Ray. *With The Argylls*. Edinburgh: Birlinn, 2014.

Way, Greg. *Fallschirmjäger!* Warwick: Helion, 2019.

Weaver, W. Darrin. *Hitler's Garand*. Ontario: Collectors' Grade Publications, 2001.

West, Hugh. *Recon Trooper*. Jefferson: McFarland, 2010.

Whelan, Townsend. *Telescopic Sights*. Plantersville: Small Arms Technical Publishing Co., 1944.

Williamson, Gordon. *Men at Arms 365 German Battle Insignia*. Oxford, Osprey Publishing, 2002.

Wilson, Charles. *If You Survive*. New York: Ivy, 1987.

Woolhouse, Andrew. *13—Lucky for Some. The History of the 13th (Lancashire) Parachute Battalion*. Self-published, 2013.

Wurst, Spencer F. and Gayle. *Descending from the Clouds*. Havertown: Casemate, 2004.

Wüster, Wigand. *An Artilleryman In Stalingrad*. Sydney: Leaping Horseman Books, 2007.

Wynne, Barry. *The Sniper*. London: MacDonald, 1968.

Yee, Gary. *Sharpshooters: Marksmen through the Ages*. Havertown: Casemate, 2017.

Yee, Gary. *Sharpshooters (1750–1900): The Men, Their Guns, Their Story*. Brisbane: Sharpshooter Press, 2009.

Zaitsev, Vassili. *Notes of a Sniper*. Los Angeles: 2826 Press, 2003.

Zhukova, Yulia. *Girl With a Sniper Rifle*. London: Greenhill, 2019.

German army *Schützenschnur* (marksman's lanyard)—see p. 29. The army version instituted in 1936 had four *Stufen* (grades)—plain and then with an extra acorn at grades 2–4. It was revised in 1938 to 12 *Stufen*, with various different shields, swords, and acorns. This one is grade 6 (silver; larger swords resting on oak leaves; a single acorn). *Stufen* 9–12 were gold rather than silver. *Richard Charlton Taylor.*

Index

References to images are in italics.